THE CULTURAL CONTEXT OF SEXUAL PLEASURE AND PROBLEMS

Using rich case material and research presented by distinguished authorities in the fields of sex, couple, family, and psychotherapy, this edited book contributes to our efforts to help individuals and couples increase their sexual satisfaction. The authors explore social and cultural backgrounds, the meaning of sexual problems in specific cultural contexts, and the way in which culture presents challenges to traditional psychotherapy. More importantly, they answer the question: should therapists accept any and all behaviors, values, and attitudes that are considered normal, *even if* they violate the therapist's own cultural standards? The case studies identify challenging cultural issues and provide clinicians with culturally sensitive treatment options. The book's sections also separate chapters based on the degree to which psychological treatments are recognized and utilized for dealing with sexual problems in different countries, making it an ideal reference for professionals and students. The concluding chapter looks at culture through the lens of the provider, rather than the patient, and ties together the major themes and questions posed.

Kathryn S. K. Hall, PhD, is a licensed psychologist with a private practice in Princeton, New Jersey, where she specializes in the treatment of sexual disorders.

Cynthia A. Graham, PhD, is a Senior Lecturer in the Department of Psychology at the University of Southampton, England, and a research fellow at The Kinsey Institute for Research in Sex, Gender, and Reproduction at Indiana University. She is also Editor-in-Chief of *The Journal of Sex Research*.

THE CULTURAL CONTEXT OF SEXUAL PLEASURE AND PROBLEMS

Psychotherapy with Diverse Clients

Edited by
*Kathryn S. K. Hall and
Cynthia A. Graham*

NEW YORK AND LONDON

First published 2013
by Routledge
711 Third Avenue, New York, NY 10017

Simultaneously published in the UK
by Routledge
27 Church Road, Hove, East Sussex BN3 2FA

Routledge is an imprint of the Taylor & Francis Group, an informa business

© 2013 Taylor & Francis

The right of the editors to be identified as the authors of the editorial material, and of the authors for their individual chapters, has been asserted in accordance with sections 77 and 78 of the Copyright, Designs and Patents Act 1988.

All rights reserved. No part of this book may be reprinted or reproduced or utilised in any form or by any electronic, mechanical, or other means, now known or hereafter invented, including photocopying and recording, or in any information storage or retrieval system, without permission in writing from the publishers.

Trademark notice: Product or corporate names may be trademarks or registered trademarks, and are used only for identification and explanation without intent to infringe.

Library of Congress Cataloging in Publication Data
The cultural context of sexual pleasure and problems : psychotherapy with diverse clients / edited by Cynthia A. Graham and Kathryn S.K. Hall.
   p. cm.
   Includes bibliographical references and index.
   1. Sex therapy. 2. Psychosexual disorders—Treatment. I. Graham, Cynthia A. II. Hall, Kathryn.
   RC557.C85 2012
   616.85'8306—dc23
   2012012588

ISBN: 978-0-415-99845-1 (hbk)
ISBN: 978-0-415-63494-6 (pbk)
ISBN: 978-0-203-09683-3 (ebk)

Typeset in Sabon
by EvS Communication Networx, Inc.

Printed and bound in the United States of America by Sheridan Books, Inc. (a Sheridan Group Company).

For my courageous mother, Eleanor Hall,
who crossed cultures long before it was popular.

KH

For John and his unwavering support.

CG

CONTENTS

Editor Biographies x
Contributor Biographies xi
Acknowledgements xiv

1 Introduction 1
  KATHRYN HALL AND CYNTHIA GRAHAM

SECTION I
Minorities: The Need for Cultural Sensitivity 21

2 Same-Sex Sexuality from a Global Perspective 22
  MARGARET NICHOLS

3 African American Couples and Sex 47
  SHALONDA KELLY AND JAMYE SHELTON

4 Understanding Latina Women's Sexuality in the United
  States: Analysis of an Innovative HIV Prevention Program 84
  RITA M. MELENDEZ, CARRIE DICKENSON, CATALINA SOL,
  LUZ AMPARO PINZON, BRIGIDA GUYOT, AND DILCIA MOLINA

SECTION II
Sex Therapy Is Not Practiced Here: Cultural Challenges 111

5 The Multicultural Complexity of Sexuality in Cameroon 112
  O. M. NJIKAM SAVAGE

6 Culturally based Sexual Problems in Traditional Areas of
  Kermanshah, Iran   135
  JAVAAD ZARGOOSHI, ELHAM RAHMANIAN, HIVA MOTAEE,
  MOZHGAAN KOHZADI, AND SAMAD NOURIZAD

7 Challenges Facing Sex Therapy in Korea   155
  GAHYUN YOUN

SECTION III
The Emerging Practice of Psychotherapy for Sexual Problems **171**

8 Sexuality in India: Ancient Beliefs, Present Day Problems,
  and Future Approaches to Management   172
  V. RAMANATHAN AND P. WEERAKOON

9 Sex, Sexual Problems, and Sexual Agency in Hong Kong
  Chinese Women   197
  ANNA NG HOI NGA AND PETULA HO SIK YING

10 Sex Therapy in Russia: Pleasure and Gender in a New
   Professional Field   220
   ANNA TEMKINA, ANNA ROTKIRCH, AND ELINA HAAVIO-MANNILA

SECTION IV
Cultural Adaptations of Psychotherapy Approaches to the Treatment of Sexual Problems **249**

11 Sexual Myths and Realities in Brazil   250
   JACQUELINE BRENDLER

12 Sexual Problems, Cultural Beliefs, and Psychosexual Therapy
   in Portugal   278
   CATARINA SOARES AND PEDRO NOBRE

13 The Role of Cultural Factors in the Course and Treatment
   of Sexual Problems: Failures, Pitfalls, and Successes in a
   Complicated Case from Turkey   307
   MEHMET SUNGUR

14 Israeli Sexuality at the Intersection of Tradition and
   Modernism 333
   R. ALONI, E. DE PAAUW, AND R. HERUTI

15 Sex, Pleasure, and Dyspareunia in Liberal Northern Europe:
   How Sexual Pleasure is Seen as the Most Important Goal
   of all Nonreproductive Sexual Activity in a Postmodern
   Northern European Society, but is Denied by Women
   and Scientists who are Still under the Influence of Male
   Dominated Sexual Scripts 355
   RIK H. W. VAN LUNSEN, MARIEKE BRAUER, AND ELLEN LAAN

SECTION V
The Other Side of the Couch: The Cultural Contribution of the Therapist 371

16 The Social and Professional Diversity of Sexology and Sex
   Therapy in Europe 372
   ALAIN GIAMI

   Index 394

EDITOR BIOGRAPHIES

Dr. Kathryn S. K. Hall received her PhD in clinical psychology from McGill University in 1986. She is a licensed psychologist with a private practice in Princeton NJ where she specializes in the treatment of sexual disorders. Dr. Hall has authored a popular book on women's sexual desire entitled *Reclaiming Your Sexual Self: How to Bring Desire Back Into Your Life*, which received the Consumer Book Award from the Society for Sex Therapy and Research. She is the co-editor of the fifth edition of the classic sex therapy text *Principles and Practices of Sex Therapy*. Dr. Hall is a member of numerous sex research and sex therapy organizations. She has written and lectured extensively on the subject of sexuality. Dr. Hall is the product of an interracial marriage, being of East Indian and British origin. She finds herself in the United States by way of Canada.

Dr. Cynthia A. Graham is a clinical psychologist who obtained her master's degree from the University of Glasgow, Scotland in 1982 and her PhD from McGill University in 1990. From 1996 to 2004 she was an Assistant Professor at Indiana University and Director of Graduate Education at the Kinsey Institute from 1999 to 2004. From 2004 to 2010 she was a Research Tutor on the Oxford Doctoral Course in Clinical Psychology and a Research Fellow at Harris Manchester College, University of Oxford, England. She is currently a Senior Lecturer in the Department of Psychology at the University of Southampton, England and is a research fellow at the Kinsey Institute for Research in Sex, Gender, and Reproduction and at the Rural Center for AIDS/STD Prevention at Indiana University. She is a current member of the DSM-5 Workgroup for Sexual and Gender Identity Disorders and is Editor-in-Chief of *The Journal of Sex Research*. Dr. Graham's research interests are in the area of sexual and reproductive health.

CONTRIBUTOR BIOGRAPHIES

Ronit Aloni, PhD
Private practice
Tel Aviv, Israel

Marieke Brauer, PhD
Faculty of Social and
 Behavioural Sciences,
 Utrecht University
Utrecht, the Netherlands

Jaqueline Brendler, MD
Brazilian Society of Studies in
 Human Sexuality (SBRASH)
Porto Alegre, Brazil

Esther de Paauw, MSW
Sexual Rehabilitation Clinic,
 Reuth Medical Center,
Tel-Aviv, Israel

Carrie Dickenson, MA
The Health Initiative of
 the Americas (HIA), UC
 Berkeley
Berkeley, CA

Alain Giami, PhD
French National Institute
 of Health and Medical
 Research (INSERM)
Paris, France

Brigida Guyot
Entre Amigas Team
La Clinica del Pueblo
Washington DC

**Elina Haavio-Mannila, Dr
 Social Sciences**
Department of Social Sciences,
 University of Helsinki
Helsinki, Finland

Rafi J. Heruti, MD
Sackler Faculty of Medicine,
 Tel-Aviv University,
Sexual Rehabilitation Clinic,
 Reuth Medical Center,
Tel-Aviv, Israel

Petula Ho Sik Ying, PhD
The University of Hong Kong
Hong Kong, China

Shalonda Kelly, PhD
Associate Professor
Graduate School of Applied &
 Professional Psychology
Rutgers, The State University
 of New Jersey
Piscataway, NJ

Mozhgaan Kohzadi, RM
The Rhazes Center for
 Research In Family Health
 and Sexual Medicine,
Kermanshah University of Medi-
cal Sciences
Kermanshah, Iran

Ellen Laan, PhD
Academic Medical Center,
 University of Amsterdam
Amsterdam, the Netherlands

Rita M. Melendez, PhD
Department of Sexuality
 Studies, San Francisco State
 University
San Francisco, CA

Dilcia Molina
Entre Amigas Team
La Clinica del Pueblo
Washington DC

Hiva Motaee, MD
The Rhazes Center for
 Research in Family Health
 and Sexual Medicine,
Kermanshah University of
 Medical Sciences
Kermanshah, Iran

Anna Ng Hoi Nga, PhD
Caritas Institute of Higher
 Education
Hong Kong, China

Pedro J. Nobre, PhD
Department of Education
University of Aveiro
Portugal

Margaret Nichols, PhD
Institute for Personal Growth
Highland Park, New Jersey

Samad Nourizad, MD
Department of Anesthesiology,
 Kermanshah University of
 Medical Sciences
Kermanshah, Iran

Luz Amparo Pinzon, PhD
University Research Co. LLC
Bethesda, MD

Elham Rahmanian, RN
The Rhazes Center for
 Research In Family Health
 and Sexual Medicine
Faculty of Nursing and
 Midwifery, Kermanshah
 University of Medical
 Sciences
Kermanshah, Iran

**Vijayasarathi Ramanathan,
 MBBS, PhD (candidate)**
The University of Sydney
 (Australia) /SSS Centre for
 Sexual Health (India)
Sydney, Australia

Anna Rotkirch
Population Research Institute,
 Väestöliitto—Finnish Family
 Federation
Helsinki, Finland

Olayinka M. Njikam Savage, PhD
Department of Anthropology,
University of Douala
Douala, Cameroon

Jamye Shelton, MEd, PsyM
Graduate School of Applied &
 Professional Psychology
Rutgers, The State University
 of New Jersey
Piscataway, NJ

Catarina Soares, PhD
Centro Hospitalar Psiquiatrico
 de Lisboa and
Instituto Superior de Ciencias
 da Saude Egas Moniz
Lisbon, Portugal

Catalina Sol
Entre Amigas Team
La Clinica del Pueblo
Washington DC

Mehmet Z. Sungur
Department of Psychiatry
Marmara University
Istanbul, Turkey

Anna Temkina, PhD
Novartis Chair in Sociology of Public Health and Gender
Department of Political Sciences and Sociology,
Gender Studies program
European University at St. Petersburg,
St. Petersburg, Russia

Rik H.W. van Lunsen, MD, PhD
Academic Medical Center, University of Amsterdam
Amsterdam, the Netherlands

Dr. Patricia Weerakoon, MBBS, MS
The University of Sydney (Australia)
Sydney, Australia

Gahyun Youn, PhD
Department of Psychology
Chonnam National University
Gwangju, KOREA

Javaad Zargooshi, MD
The Rhazes Center For Research In Family Health and Sexual Medicine,
Department of Urology,
Kermanshah University of Medical Sciences
Kermanshah, Iran

ACKNOWLEDGEMENTS

We are deeply indebted to those individuals around the world whose stories continue to inform the evolving treatment of sexual problems. We are especially grateful to those couples and individuals whose narratives are contained in the chapters of this book. To our authors, we express our heartfelt thanks and appreciation. Each and everyone of you worked tirelessly with us, often in a language not your own, to make clear the meaning of the sexual difficulties and their treatment in your country or culture. We are also indebted to the numerous colleagues who answered our calls for help finding authors in far away countries. Our professional associations were vital to this process and we expressly thank the International Academy of Sex Research, the Society for Sex Therapy and Research and the Society for the Scientific Study of Sexuality for getting out the word.

We value the foresight and encouragement we received from Dawn Moot, the editor who acquired this book for Routledge. To Marta Moldvai, the patient, always helpful and knowledgeable editor who shepherded this book through the long process, we are forever grateful. We also want to thank the production team at EvS Communications for taking the book from copyediting to indexing.

The editors met in graduate school at McGill University in Montreal Canada, and remain indebted to that institution for instilling the scholarly values that informed this book and for introducing us to each other. We also thank the clinical staff at the Sex and Couple Therapy Service/Service de Thérapie Sexuelle et de Couple at the McGill University Health Center for their comments during the process of editing this book. We thank John Bancroft for his critical feedback and support.

Finally, our deepest thanks go to Jim, Zach and Devin who were the North American support team and to John, Rosie and Jack who did the same in Britain.

INTRODUCTION

Kathryn Hall and Cynthia Graham

People worldwide engage in sex. While sexuality may be universal, the expression of sexuality is not. What might be considered creative and imaginative lovemaking in one culture may be viewed as immoral or sordid in another. Conversely, what is regarded as "problematic" sexual functioning may be normative in a different cultural context. For confirmation of this cultural variability we need look no further than to reactions to same-sex unions, requirements regarding premarital chastity, and variations in the importance placed on female sexual pleasure, marital fidelity, and attitudes toward recreational versus procreative sex.

Given that sexuality, in its various manifestations, is recognized as a fundamental aspect of being human "the right to pursue a satisfying, safe and pleasurable sexual life" (World Health Organization, 2006) is considered a basic human right (International Council of Human Rights Progress [ICHRP], 2009). A satisfying, safe, and pleasurable sexual life is also considered a mainstay of healthy emotional and psychological functioning and appropriate personality development. Whether it is a mental health issue, a human right, or a private matter, people around the world experience sexual difficulties that greatly impact the quality of their lives. We believe that efforts to help individuals and couples increase their sexual satisfaction will only be effective if informed by an understanding of their social and cultural background, and of the meaning of sexual problems in specific cultural contexts.

There is very little published literature on the specific ways in which culture and ethnicity define and shape sexuality, both "healthy" and problematic. There is even less clear guidance for clinicians on how to provide culturally sensitive treatment (Brotto, Chik, Ryder, Gorzalka, & Seal, 2005; Lewis, 2004). This gap was the impetus for this book. This collection of chapters from experts around the world offers a contextual understanding of the sexual issues that affect men and women across a wide range of cultures, and the ways in which culture presents challenges to traditional psychotherapy. Most of the chapters are illustrated with rich case material, which identifies challenging clinical issues and provides clinicians with culturally sensitive treatment options.

The questions raised by the contributors to this book make for compelling discussion. Is there a universal sexuality? How important is culture in defining our sexuality, our sexual behavior, and our sexual problems? Is cultural relativism the same as cultural competence? In other words, in order to work with people from cultures different from our own, should we accept as normal any and all behaviors, values, and attitudes that are considered normal in that culture? Should we consider acceptable, sexual behaviors considered normal in other cultures, even if they violate our own cultural standards? What do we do as practicing clinicians when our own notion of "healthy" is challenged in this way? Sex research and clinical case material can help to expand the borders and boundaries of our knowledge about human sexuality and the ways in which culture shapes it. This book is intended to widen our cultural perspective.

We have divided this book into five sections. The first section of the book is comprised of three chapters dealing with cultures within cultures. We start with a provocative chapter by Margaret Nichols on sexual minorities followed by chapters on African Americans and Latinas, two distinct cultural groups residing in the United States. We begin with these chapters for the important reason that they orient readers to the need for cultural sensitivity. From there we delve into cultures from other parts of the world. We have divided these chapters into three sections based upon the degree to which psychological treatments are recognized and utilized for dealing with sexual problems. In Korea, rural Iran, and Cameroon there are no well-established psychological treatments for sexual problems. In Hong Kong, India, and Russia, psychotherapy and sex therapy[1] are emerging as viable options for people with sexual problems. Finally, in Northern Europe, Portugal, Brazil, and Israel, psychotherapy and sex therapy are well established and much utilized. We end the book with the thought provoking chapter by Giami, in which he looks at culture through the lens of the provider of therapy rather than the lens of the patient or client.

The Importance of Culture

When we refer to culture we are referring to the way of life practiced by a distinct group of people. This is manifested by the shared beliefs, values, and behaviors that are passed along from one generation to the next; as Williams (1983) defined it, "the way of life for an entire society." While cultures vary in terms of how much diversity is tolerated, a shared group identity depends upon an expectation of similarity (Kelly, 1963). As will become apparent as you read through the chapters in this book, sexuality is culturally determined and defined. The meanings that are attached to sex and the value attached to sexual behavior or sexual abstinence vary across cultures.

INTRODUCTION

Religion overlaps with culture but it is not synonymous with it. The degree to which a culture embraces religious prohibitions and sexual proscriptions varies. While most religions tend to restrict sexuality in some way, the impact of various religions and the translation of religious practices into sexual behavior and attitudes fluctuate across cultural lines. The chapter on Russia provides an illustration of how the reintroduction of religion can influence sexual behavior. Temkina, Rotkirch, and Haavio-Mannila point out that the loosening of state restrictions that came with glasnost brought with it religious freedom, which, paradoxically, resulted in religious restrictions on sexual behavior. Interestingly, Aloni, Heruti, and DePaauw observed in their chapter on Israel that Russian immigrants to Israel often become more restrictive in their sexual behavior as they embrace Judaism. As chapters in this book demonstrate, religion is a factor of greater or lesser importance in understanding the sexual behavior, attitudes, and issues of a particular cultural group.

Race is also not the same as culture (Lewis, 2004). There are instances, however, where race may (partially) denote a specific cultural group within a larger cultural context. This is why we have included chapters on African Americans and Latinas in this volume, whereas elsewhere we define cultures by the boundaries of nations. We recognize that distinct cultural groups exist across and within a country's borders. The chapter on African Americans provides a good example of the difficulties facing a longstanding cultural group that is distinct from the mainstream culture of the United States, whereas the chapter by Melendez et al. on the large Latino culture that exists within the United States provides an illustration of the experience of more recent immigrants. Where possible, authors in this book have described the different cultural groups, but have focused primarily on the main or dominant culture in their country.

There are, perhaps, no other dimensions that so fully encompass an individual's identity as their sexuality and their cultural heritage. That these two facets of the self are interwoven there can be no doubt. Nowhere in the book is this as apparent as it is in the chapter on sexual minorities living in different cultures. In this chapter, Nichols aptly points out that the self-identified exclusively gay individual is an artifact of Western societies. She notes that in other cultures same-gender relations take various forms; for example, some homosexual relationships involve one partner assuming a "female" role, or more often one partner is considered a "third sex." She gives the examples of "two spirit" people in Native American culture, "ladyboys" in Thailand, and *travesti* in Brazil. While in Western culture it is the gender of one's partner that determines sexual orientation, in other cultures it is the particular sexual acts engaged in, and the role one plays that are important. Citing Jeffries

(2009), Nichols observes that in many Latin American cultures, the "insertor" in anal sex is not considered homosexual, only the "insertee." All of these examples point to the complexity of how notions of gender and sexual orientation interact with culture.

Culture is Dynamic

Cultures are dynamic, not static, and often change rapidly. Many of the authors in this volume highlight the fact that people of different age groups will have different experiences of their cultures. Zargooshi and his colleagues, for example, noted that Iran is a society in transition, and Temkina and her coauthors observed that in Soviet Russia, the men and women who came of age in previous generations differ distinctly in sexual values and behaviors from those coming of age now. In the chapter on South Korea, Youn chose to focus on the aging segment of the population that grew up in a time of rigid and gendered sexual mores. Consideration of this generation highlights some of the obstacles to sex therapy that are ingrained in Korean culture.

One of the most notable changes in many societies is the greater value now accorded to female sexual pleasure. According to Temkina et al., female orgasm is a matter of recent interest in Russia and Youn discusses how the rights of women to regulate their sexual activity (e.g., to say no to unwanted sex) is an idea gaining ground in South Korea. In Hong Kong and Brazil, women are recognizing sexual pleasure as a "right." In contrast, in some chapters, most notably those on India and Iran, women are conspicuously absent from the discussion on sexual pleasure.

The dynamic nature of culture is also due to the interaction between different societies. Cultural boundaries are porous. To quote Thomas Friedman (2005), "the world is flat." The globalization of world economies means that businesses developed in one area of the world are branching out to others, bringing with them merchandise, people, and culture. Travel and tourism are increasingly bringing people of different cultures in contact with each other. The Internet has made sexual content available to most (one notable exception is Iran, which continues to restrict the sexual content its citizens can access). At times, cultures clash. In India, young men can easily access pornography over the Internet, where sex is depicted in ways that may conflict with the values imparted by their parents. This makes the cultural prohibitions against masturbation extremely difficult to follow and is relevant to the culture bound syndrome known as *Dhat* syndrome. This syndrome is characterized by symptoms of anxiety, guilt, erectile dysfunction, fatigue, and depression related to the loss of semen through masturbation or nocturnal emissions (Ahmed & Bhugra, 2004). In those countries with limited sex education, the Internet may become a source of sexual knowledge and pleasure. However, some of the pornography available over the Internet may contribute to the sexual anxiety experienced by both men and women, especially those with little or no sexual education or experience.

The collision of cultural beliefs, when it arises quickly and represents different ends of a spectrum, may have unforeseen consequences. In her chapter, Savage attributes the unconventional sexual behavior now occurring in Cameroon to the overlap of modern and traditional values. In their quest to attain the outward trappings of modern success (e.g., wealth, cars, fashionable clothes), women, following the direction of their spiritual leaders, are having sex with "mad" men in Doula and other public places in Cameroon. Brazil has the second highest rate of cosmetic surgery worldwide (Domeles de Andrade, 2010), and Brendler notes that women in Brazil are having silicone breast implants in record numbers in order to more closely resemble the Western notion of a "sexy" woman. Reviewing the literature on gender differences in erotic plasticity, Baumeister (2000) argued that the female sex drive is fundamentally more malleable than the male's in response to sociocultural and situational factors. As Western notions of sexuality cross borders, we may see that female sexuality shows the most dramatic changes as a result.

Culturally Sensitive Psychotherapy for Sexual Problems

The U.S. Surgeon General and the American Psychological Association have issued statements regarding the importance of and need for culturally informed and sensitive treatment (American Psychological Association, 2003; U.S. Department of Health and Human Services, 2001). Although there is a dearth of research on sex therapy with ethnic minority clients, what little evidence there is suggests that the dropout rate from therapy for members of ethnic minorities is high (Christenson, 1988; Sue & Sue, 1999). Part of the problem is that despite the emphasis on evidence-based treatment, most psychotherapeutic interventions have been designed by Westerners and are evaluated with White, middle class, heterosexual clients. It is no wonder that these groups show the greatest treatment gains (Lewis, 2004).

While there is woefully little research examining effective psychotherapeutic interventions for improving sexual pleasure and performance among ethnic minority groups, there is in contrast a voluminous literature on problematic sexuality and its consequences, such as unplanned adolescent pregnancy and sexually transmitted infections in this population (Lewis, 2004). This emphasis on problematic sexuality may further contribute to stereotyped notions of ethnic minorities as sexually promiscuous and irresponsible. As greater numbers of ethnically diverse clients present for treatment, there will be an increased demand for culturally sensitive and effective therapeutic methods. Without adequate research or clinical evidence to challenge stereotypes and inform treatment, clinicians will be ill-equipped to deal with these clients.

The introduction to the section on sexual dysfunctions in the *Diagnostic and Statistical Manual of Mental Disorders* (DSM-IV-TR; American Psychiatric Association, 2000) includes the following statement: "Clinical judgments about the presence of a Sexual Dysfunction should take into account the individual's ethnic, cultural, religious and social background, which may influence sexual desire, expectations, and attitudes about performance" (p. 495). However, beyond this, there is no specific information about the role of cultural factors in influencing sexual problems (Brotto et al., 2005). In planning for the upcoming revision of the DSM (DSM-5), the recognition that cultural issues are of fundamental importance has been more explicitly acknowledged, with a special study group on culture and cross-cultural issues.

We join those who argue for a "culture-centered," or culturally competent, approach to psychotherapy (Hall, 2001). A "culture-centered" approach "recognizes culture as central and not marginal, fundamental and not exotic, for all appropriate counseling interventions" (Pederson, 2007, p. 5). Cultural competence "denotes the capacity to perform and obtain positive clinical outcomes in cross-cultural encounters ... generic cultural competence is the knowledge and skill set needed in any cross-cultural therapeutic encounter, and specific cultural competence enables clinicians to work effectively with a specific ethnocultural community. To provide culturally competent psychotherapy, both are essential" (Lo & Fung, 2003, p. 162). Successful treatment of sexual problems will require tailoring treatment to the unique cultural requirements of the individual or couple. In some cases traditional psychotherapy or sex therapy approaches can be modified (Ahmed & Bhugra, 2004; So & Cheung, 2004). Culture-specific modifications to the method of treatment may be most successful when the sexual problems are similar to those for which sex therapy was designed; for example, problems of sexual function, such as erectile dysfunction, ejaculatory problems, and orgasm difficulties. Sexual issues unique to a culture, such as *Dhat* syndrome, may require an entirely different approach.

Often culture is blamed for creating sexual problems, especially when the perception is that the culture espouses negative and erroneous beliefs about sex. As one example, many cultures value semen in a way that Western society does not. Culture bound syndromes relating to fear or guilt regarding semen loss may therefore be difficult for Western therapists to understand or treat. The value placed on female chastity may represent a similar clinical challenge, but because female virginity has historically been esteemed in Western society it is perhaps better understood. And yet, as Sungur suggests in his chapter, the degree to which a culture emphasizes the need to protect female virginity may be directly related to the prevalence of vaginismus within that culture. A culturally sensitive perspective goes beyond blaming a fault in the culture (e.g., the premium placed on semen or virginity) for sexual problems.

However, just because a belief or practice is culturally based does not mean that it should be condoned. Female genital cutting is a culturally entrenched practice, which is often abhorred by people from other cultures. The practice continues and is the subject of much debate about whether medical doctors should perform female circumcision to ensure sterile procedures and minimal genital damage or whether they should refuse to perform surgeries as a statement of their disapproval (Leonard, 2000; Wade, 2011).

Perhaps the greatest challenge for Western sex therapists and psychotherapists relates to the treatment of individuals and couples from cultures in which women are accorded a subordinate role, or in which women have little power or autonomy in their lives. We will examine this issue in greater depth later in this chapter.

Despite the obvious need, psychotherapy has yet to incorporate a culturally competent or, as we prefer to call it, a culturally sensitive approach to the treatment of sexual problems. The first steps in this process require us to view the assumptions we hold about sexuality as ethnocentric assumptions, and to challenge the universality of these assumptions by having a greater knowledge of cultural diversity. It is our hope that this book will contribute to this process.

A Universal Model of Sexuality?

Much of what is known about sexual problems and their treatment comes from Western societies (the United States, Canada, Britain, and Western Europe), where sex research was first established. Masters and Johnson (1966) are considered the pioneers of modern sex therapy. Their laboratory-based research gave us the human sexual response cycle and with it the assumption that men and women are fundamentally similar in their responses and in the sexual difficulties they experience (Tiefer, 1991). The DSM diagnostic categories of sexual dysfunction reflect this model, with separate disorders linked to different phases of the sexual response cycle. The existence of a universal, gender-neutral sexual response cycle is currently being challenged and with this challenge come questions regarding the universality of sexual dysfunctions (Tiefer, 2006). Just as there are cultural variations in how sexuality is expressed, a premise of this book is that there will be cultural variations in what is defined as a sexual problem. To date, the important question of what troubles people about their sexuality remains unanswered for much of the world's population.

Although a common statement in the clinical and research literature is that a high proportion of men and women worldwide experience sexual difficulties, it is difficult to estimate the true prevalence of sexual dysfunction from surveys (Graham & Bancroft, 2006; Mercer et al., 2003). Moreover, studies have demonstrated that transient, short-term sexual problems are very common, but more persistent problems much less so (Hayes, Dennerstein, Bennett, & Fairley, 2008; Mercer et al., 2003). Although the criterion of "distress" is required for a clinical diagnosis of any sexual disorder (American Psychiatric Association, 2000), most of the earlier epidemiological surveys carried out, including the widely cited National Health and Social Life survey (Laumann, Paik, & Rosen, 1999), did not assess distress about sexual functioning, but only the presence of symptoms. More recent surveys that have assessed distress (Bancroft, Loftus, & Long, 2003; Oberg, Fugl-Meyer, & Fugl-Meyer, 2004; Shifren, Monz, Russo, Segreti, & Johannes, 2008; Witting et al., 2008) show that prevalence estimates drop, usually by at least half, when distress about the sexual problem is assessed (Brotto et al., 2010; Hayes et al, 2008).

These same issues are present in the Global Study of Sexual Attitudes and Behavior (GSSAB) study, a Pfizer[2] funded survey of men and women (40–80 years) across 29 countries (Laumann et al., 2006). The results indicated that sexual difficulties were relatively common among men and women worldwide, but prevalence estimates showed great variation across cultures. Lack of interest in sex and inability to experience orgasm were the most frequently reported problems for women, while premature ejaculation was the most common complaint for men. Other sexual problems such as erectile dysfunction and vaginal dryness were also relatively common. However, the presence of sexual difficulties was assessed with one question ("During the last 12 months, have you ever experienced any of the following for a period of two months or more ..." [lacked interest in having sex, were unable to reach climax, etc.]. One wonders what the answers would have been had people been asked open-ended questions about their sexual experiences and difficulties. The GSSAB survey also did not ask about duration of the problems or whether individuals were distressed about their sexual functioning. The evidence to date suggests, however, that women are less distressed about their level of sexual function and more distressed about their relationship status or the quality of their relationship (Bancroft et al., 2003; Rosen et al., 2009); to our knowledge, there are no comparable data pertaining to men or to individuals from diverse cultures.

In our view, because of the dearth of research on sexual problems in non-Western cultures, it remains an open question as to what sexual issues are most important for people across different cultures. The types of treatments that can be offered and which are likely to be helpful will depend upon the answer to that question. In essence, we have tried to elucidate this by asking practitioners in different countries to tell us about the common sexual problems they see and treat.

Sex Therapy and Sexual Medicine

Whether the most important sex organ is between the ears or between the legs has been a matter of long-standing debate and has led particular professions to declare that understanding sexual dysfunction is within their purview and the treatment of sexual problems their area of expertise (Rowland, 2007). Masters and Johnson (1966) believed that the origin of most sexual dysfunctions was psychological in nature and proposed that performance anxiety and spectatoring (self-consciously evaluating one's performance) were at the root of many sexual problems. Relaxation, sensate focus, communication, and intimacy became the building blocks of "Western style" sex therapy. The practice of sex therapy has expanded greatly since Masters and Johnson's pioneering work, but the focus is still on understanding and addressing the psychological and relational factors that are believed to contribute to sexual distress and sexual inhibition (Bancroft & Janssen, 2000; Leiblum, 2001). However, as this book highlights, in many areas of the world, psychologically based approaches to treatment are not perceived as relevant. In some countries and cultures, there is no distinct discipline of psychology and no appreciation of the psychological origins of problems.

Sexual medicine, on the other hand, looks at the sexual problems experienced by men and women as being biologically based—problems with physical function that are amenable to medication or sometimes surgical intervention (Rowland, 2007). In some ways sexual medicine can be seen as an attempt to bypass the issue of culture by addressing only those problems that are organic rather than psychogenic in nature. While the shift toward the sexual medicine approach has been rapid in many countries (Rowland, 2007), it has not been universal; in Croatia, for example, medical professionals have been little involved in the treatment of sexual problems and psychologically based therapies for sexual difficulties are widely used (Stulhofer & Arbanas, 2009). In contrast, in the chapter on Iran, Zargooshi and colleagues argue that psychotherapy will be ineffective in addressing the immediate and pressing sexual problems of a distressed man or woman in rural Iran. They advocate for a sexual medicine approach to problems, even those psychogenic in origin. Their chapter raises the provocative issue of the applicability of Western-based medicine to treat culturally influenced sexual problems.

Unlike sex therapy, sexual medicine is ubiquitous. From the corner of Africa, to Russia and Brazil, Viagra and other PDE-5 inhibitors for the treatment of erectile dysfunction are widely available, often without the need for a formal prescription and through the Internet. We know that many initial prescriptions for Viagra are never refilled (Sato et al., 2007; Son, Park, Kim, & Paick, 2004). Although the reasons for this are still not well understood, it has become increasingly clear that PDE-5 inhibitor medication on its own is often ineffective. In the United States, the case is made that PDE-5 inhibitors should be integrated with psychologically based treatment (Rosen, 2007). Whether PDE-5 inhibitors would be more effective in other cultures if augmented by psychologically or spirituality based interventions, or by the ministrations of traditional healers, remains an open question.

In the chapter on Russia, the issue of love was raised by the authors. Several of the sex therapists surveyed by Temkina and her colleagues lamented that love was now absent from the discussion on sex. Tolstoy, they said, knew more about passion than can be found reading the insert on a Viagra prescription or a contraceptive pill.

Finally, we note that at present, sexual medicine has little to offer women in the way of treatment for sexual problems, as illustrated by some of the chapters in this volume that focused heavily on male sexual problems. The incursion of sexual medicine into some non-Western countries may address only the sexual needs of men and may heighten the imbalance between the perceived importance of the sexual needs of men and women. In exporting sexual medicine, we are also exporting Western notions about sexuality.

Spirituality and Traditional Healers

Our cultural beliefs help us to understand what is happening when we experience illness or misfortune. Whatever the perceived cause—performance anxiety, spirit possession, semen loss, or neurotransmitter depletion—our beliefs shape the course of illness and therefore its treatment (Watters, 2010). This is also the case for sexual problems, where what is labeled as a problem is not culturally invariant. For example, among Taoists practicing in many Asian countries, delayed ejaculation is not a problem but a desired outcome. In China, difficulty consummating a marriage is not a sexual problem but a fertility issue. In many areas of the world, sexual pleasure for women is not considered important, whereas in Northern Europe and Israel it has recently been regarded as a basic right. In Cameroon, sexual dreams and fantasies are often attributed to malevolent spiritual intervention. Conversely, in the West we perceive dreams and fantasies as a sign of healthy sexual interest and indeed may use fantasy in guided masturbation exercises or during partnered sex to improve arousal and orgasm. In Cameroon, as well as rural Turkey and other rural areas, sexual potency and the consummation of marriage indicate that one's ancestors have blessed the union. The converse also holds true; sexual dysfunction and infertility are sometimes seen as signs of ancestral or spiritual disapproval. In these contexts, medical or psychological interventions would likely be unwelcome without some way of gaining ancestral sanction.

In many cultures spirituality is an important factor in the understanding of sexuality and sexual dysfunction. Spiritual or traditional healers are often the ones turned to for help for sexual problems. Although there is certainly the opportunity for abuse by charlatans masquerading as spiritually based practitioners (discussed by Sungur in his chapter on Turkey), there is also an opportunity to learn from traditional healers and expand the practice of psychotherapy. Savage discusses the case of traditional healers in Cameroon working with medical clinics to effectively treat individuals with sexually transmitted infections. A similar model of collaboration may be possible for psychotherapists, sex therapists, and medical professionals in other cultures and with other sexual problems. The chapter on India presents a case of a young man suffering from masturbatory guilt. The treatment he is given is respectful of the patient's cultural beliefs, integrating medical testing and the provision of information to help alleviate his anxiety, rather than directly challenging his culturally held beliefs.

In his chapter on the training of sex therapists, Giami asks who is accorded the right or the privilege to access the sexual lives of people suffering from sexual dysfunction. As he noted, almost all sex therapists are first trained in another profession, such as nursing, medicine, or counseling and identify with that professional title. Traditional healers have so far been absent from this group. However, as Ahmed and Bhugra (2004) argued, and as many of our authors observed, the explanations traditional healers give regarding sexual dysfunction often match the patient's own understanding. They use a common language and their treatments are based on this mutual understanding, making for better treatment compliance. Perhaps even more importantly, in cultures in which there is no formal psychotherapy, traditional healers take the time to listen and this "therapeutic relationship" may be at the core of their effectiveness as healers. This would not be surprising, given the outcome data showing that the therapeutic relationship is one of the effective ingredients in psychotherapy (Lambert & Barley, 2001).

A View of Sex and Psychotherapy from the Western World

At least in the United States, Canada, the United Kingdom, and many parts of Europe, sex is regarded as important and as conducive to physical and psychological health. There are other assumptions about sexuality that are inherent in the practice of psychotherapy (including sex and marital therapy) that will be called into question as you read this book.

For example, therapists generally believe that sex should be mutually pleasurable, that sex in a relationship is improved by intimacy, and that communication about sex and sexual desires enhances sexual experiences. Fantasy, having a sexual imagination, and creativity are generally accepted and mostly approved of. Although the importance of biology is acknowledged, most therapists endorse the idea that psychological issues can cause/maintain sexual dysfunction and that psychological treatments ("talk therapies") can be effective remedies. Sex therapy and sexual medicine are both based on the premise that we can, and often should, change our sexual functioning.

The Russian belief in a sexual constitution challenges the American view that sexual desire is changeable. In Russia, a couple with a desire discrepancy may be told that is "just the way it is" and "you have to learn to live with it," as level of desire is assumed to be fixed in one's sexual constitution. In the United States, one member of the couple may receive a diagnosis of hypoactive sexual desire disorder and a prescription for some medication to help "boost" the libido. In a qualitative study of American women, Ellison (2000) found that many women perceived sexual problems as "that's the way life is" rather than "this is a problem." Other research has demonstrated that how professionals conceptualize sexual problems may be quite different from how people themselves perceive problems (King, Holt, & Nazareth, 2007).

The Importance of Sex and Sexual Pleasure

The importance of sex is certainly affirmed in many diverse areas of the world, but perhaps in ways not necessarily intuitive for Western sex therapists. In Iran and Cameroon, the one reason for which women can be granted a divorce is male sexual dysfunction, and in Iran it is the only way that a woman can receive monetary compensation in a divorce settlement. In the chapter on Israel, Aloni and her colleagues discuss how sexual rehabilitation, including the use of sexual surrogates, is offered by government agencies to soldiers and indeed all civilians because sexual functioning is considered a right for all people. In Turkey, the blood-stained handkerchief displayed on the wedding night is not just a symbol of the bride's chastity but also of the groom's virility. Among Latinos, Brazilians, and African Americans, sexual prowess and sexual conquest are historically synonymous with being male. In these cultures sex is important to masculine identity in the same way that sexual naïveté is important to femininity in male dominated cultures.

The idea that sex is important is not the same as the idea that sexual pleasure is important. According to the GSSAB Survey (Nicolosi et al., 2004), the belief that sex is or should be pleasurable for men was a universally held belief. In contrast, the idea that sex should be pleasurable for women was not universally endorsed. Indeed, the tremendous diversity in terms of the importance accorded to women's sexual pleasure and agency is evident in this book. For example, in traditional Korean, Iranian, and Chinese cultures, there is little emphasis on women's entitlement to sexual pleasure, whereas in other countries, such as Russia, attitudes toward women's sexual pleasure are undergoing rapid change. In Brazil and in African American cultures, stereotypes about highly sexual, skilled, and "hedonistic" women persist (Lewis, 2004), while among Latinos the discourse about female sexual pleasure has been largely absent because of greater concerns about safety and risks of intimate partner violence. At the other end of the spectrum, the authors from Northern Europe strongly asserted that female "sexual pleasure is not a 'bonus' that can also be discarded, but a necessary requirement for sexually rewarding and pain-free sexual interactions" (van Lunsen, Marieke Brauer, and Ellen Laan, this volume).

In keeping with the universal expectation that sex should be pleasurable for men is the related finding that men are more satisfied with their sex lives than are women and men tend to rate sex as more important than do women (Laumann et al., 2006). According to the results of the GSSAB survey, individuals reported the greatest level of emotional and physical satisfaction in Britain and Western European countries and in non-European English speaking countries such as Australia, Canada, New Zealand, the United States, and South Africa (Laumann et al, 2006). However, asking people to rate their emotional and physical satisfaction if they regard sex as a duty would be akin to asking Americans to rate their emotional satisfaction with vacuuming or doing the laundry. This may explain why in Asian countries such as Japan, Thailand, and the Philippines, sex was not rated as important by either men or women, and few reported emotional or physical satisfaction, despite adequate "sexual functioning." In countries where there is little equality for women and sex is for men's pleasure, the question of their own sexual satisfaction may simply be irrelevant to women.

Recent research has demonstrated that sexual pleasure is only one of many motivations of Westerners to have sex (Meston & Buss, 2007), but it is an important one and one that individuals often feel compelled to seek. Researchers have traditionally employed narrow definitions of sexual pleasure, often focused on heterosexual intercourse and prioritizing sexual pleasure for men (Dixon-Mueller, 1993). There is a need to conceptualize sexual pleasure more broadly (Graham, 2012; Higgins & Hirsch, 2007). In a qualitative study, American women and men identified several attributes of "pleasurable" sex; these included physical pleasure but also spontaneity and sexual "flow," closeness and intensity, pleasing one's partner, and lack of discomfort (Higgins & Hirsch,

2007). We know next to nothing about the meaning of sexual pleasure in non-Western societies.

In many parts of the world, it is fertility that is important. Sex, as a means to that end, becomes a significant factor when it is an obstacle to conception. The two couples described in the chapter on Hong Kong Chinese women illustrate this point. They functioned well as couples with little or no sexual activity and no intercourse until such time that children were desired. In one of these cases, after the couple had a baby they returned to their previous mode of sexual functioning and ceased having intercourse; both husband and wife were satisfied with this arrangement.

Sex as a Duty: The Status of Women and Sexual Agency

In many areas of the world sex is considered a duty and the pleasure of sex may therefore be the pleasure one experiences in fulfilling an obligation. In Korea, especially among the older population, sex is considered a marital duty to be performed by the wife (Youn, 2009). When Korean women refuse to have sex with their husbands, they may find themselves victims of domestic violence. In neighboring Hong Kong, however, Ng and Ho note that women are advocating for their sexual pleasure and their right to make sexual decisions. This is especially true of women who have achieved the status of motherhood and may not be the case for those women struggling with infertility (or those who choose childlessness). However, sexual decision making cannot be separated from women's ability or right to make other decisions or from her status within the larger community. In a study of women in sub-Saharan Africa, Hindin and Muntifering (2011) found that the degree of women's decision-making autonomy was related to the frequency of sexual activity with their spouses. As Melendez discusses in her chapter, many Latinas feel powerless to make sexual decisions regarding condom use because of their position within their community. Women who are sexually assertive are suspect in Latino culture. To try to improve the sexual assertiveness of women to ensure their partners wear condoms is therefore unlikely to be an effective strategy. Melendez and her coauthors describe an exciting and dynamic program for Latinas that focuses on strengthening their identity and capabilities as Latinas as part of a comprehensive program to help women advocate for the type of sex they want.

A striking aspect of many chapters from countries in which sex is considered a marital duty or obligation is the fact that men experience a great deal of anxiety about their ability to perform. The clinical case described in the chapter on India involves the case of a young man fearful that he had damaged himself by engaging in premarital masturbation. In the chapters on Turkey and Iran there are descriptions of the anxiety men experience due to their need to prove sexual potency on the wedding night, without the requisite knowledge of the basics of sex and sexual anatomy. In the chapter on Russia, we read that male anxiety may be related to the relatively new pressure to bring one's partner to orgasm, again without knowledge of anatomy or technique.

Culturally prescribed gender roles that carry the expectation of male sexual prowess and female chastity and naïveté may contribute to the development of sexual problems such as vaginismus, dyspareunia, erectile dysfunction, and premature ejaculation. As you will read in this book, treatment is often based upon what is considered culturally appropriate for men and women. Many authors in this volume discussed the treatment of vaginismus, and the varying treatment approaches seemed to reflect the status of women in the different countries. In Northern Europe, where there is the assumption of gender equality, treatment was focused on improving female pleasure so that a woman's vagina will accommodate a penis. In rural Iran, a traditionally male dominated culture, the focus was on creating a penis hard enough to withstand the reluctance of a bride and the timidity of her husband. In China, where the status of women is in transition, the treatment of vaginismus was oriented toward achieving pregnancy. With their newfound ability to make decisions, some Hong Kong Chinese women are deciding not to have intercourse, if it is not pleasurable and if they are not interested in conceiving.

Sexual Minorities

Mainstream sex therapy and research are very heterosexual-focused and, as Nichols emphasizes, homophobia/transphobia are still very much evident in many different cultures (Meyer, 2003). There are also still many prohibitions/legal sanctions in place against sexual minorities. The cultural issues one needs to consider in sex therapy are made much more complex when dealing with sexual minority clients. The conceptualizations of gender and sexual orientation are undergoing rapid change. As Nichols observes, the savvy therapist is aware of both the cultural and generational influences on sexual minorities. However, therapists also vary widely in their acceptance of diverse sexual lifestyles and sexual minority clients. One early survey by a task force of the American Psychological Association Committee on Lesbian and Gay Concerns (Garnets, Hancock, Conhran, Goodchilds, & Peplau, 1991) reported that therapists varied widely in their adherence to standards of unbiased practice with gay and lesbian clients.

The Need for Culturally Sensitive Treatment Approaches

The person or entities that we entrust our sexual stories to varies across cultures, and in his chapter, Giami reminds us that it is a "two-way street": patients and their problems may require treatment modifications, but the provider of the treatment brings his or her perspective to the problem, a perspective that is necessarily influenced by gender, training, and ethnicity. Most providers of sex therapy come to the profession from another professional background (physician, psychologist, social worker) and the degree of training they receive in providing sex therapy varies dramatically and influences treatment choices (Kontula, 2011). As you read through the chapters in this book, we encourage you to remember that the perspective you are getting is not only about the culture of the patient, but also of the provider, including his or her training and professional background.

Access to help for sexual problems is a matter of geography, economics, and cultural proscriptions. Help-seeking behavior for sexual problems varies across cultures (Moreira et al., 2005). The Western focus on individualism, pleasure, intimacy, and privacy inherent in the practice of psychotherapy is not necessarily applicable to other cultures. In countries where psychotherapy is not established, or is very difficult to access, traditional healers, such as the Ayurvedic in India or bride counselors in Israel, may be better placed to offer sexual counseling. In Britain, cognitive behavior therapy techniques (which are a major component of sex therapy) are being increasingly taught to nonprofessionals to deal with mental health problems such as phobias and anxiety (Clark et al., 2009). This model of service provision would likely work well for providing help to individuals with sexual problems in rural communities.

If psychotherapy is to be relevant to the treatment of sexual problems in an ever changing and varied cultural landscape, adaptation, innovation, and flexibility will be necessary. It is our hope that this book will inspire readers to devise and implement innovative and practical solutions to the sexual problems of people from diverse cultural backgrounds.

A Final Caveat

This book is by no means a complete, exhaustive, or even representative sample of cultures worldwide. It is but a sampling of the rich diversity of sexual beliefs, experiences, problems, and treatments that exist in the world. The selection of chapters was limited by several factors. The first was our ignorance of other professionals in some parts of the world—despite our memberships in several international professional sexology organizations. The second limiting factor was our criteria for authorship. We needed authors who had expertise treating sexual problems, who could write in English, and who would agree to contribute a chapter. We had several authors decline our invitation for reasons related to the political climate in their country. This brought the important reminder that it is not safe to talk openly about sexuality in every country or culture, and certainly not to talk about sexual pleasure (especially women's sexual pleasure). Finally, we were limited by the fact that sex therapy itself is limited in its international scope. There are many cultures where psychotherapy and especially sex therapy are nonexistent or marginalized. Nevertheless, we believe that we have put together an informative, thought provoking, and enlightening volume of work about the culturally sensitive treatment of sexual problems.

Notes

1. We use the term *sex therapy* to refer to a broad range of psychologically based treatment approaches directed at the resolution of sexual problems. We do not intend to refer to any specific set of techniques nor any specific theoretical orientation.
2. Pfizer Incorporated is a pharmaceutical company based in the United States which markets Viagra®.

References

Ahmed, K. & Bhugra, D. (2004). The role of culture in sexual dysfunction. *Psychiatry, 3*, 23–25.

American Psychiatric Association (2000). *Diagnostic and statistical manual of mental disorders* (4th ed., DSM-IV-TR). Washington, DC: Author.

American Psychological Association (2003). *Psychological treatment of ethnic minority populations*. Washington, DC: Author.

Bancroft, J., & Janssen, E. (2000). The dual control model of male sexual response: A theoretical approach to centrally mediated erectile dysfunction. *Neuroscience and Biobehavioral Reviews, 24*, 571–579.

Bancroft, J., Loftus, J., & Long, J. S. (2003). Distress about sex: A national survey of women in heterosexual relationships. *Archives of Sexual Behavior, 32*, 193–208.

Baumeister, R. F. (2000). Gender differences in erotic plasticity: The female sex drive as socially flexible and responsive. *Psychological Bulletin, 126*, 347–374.

Brotto, L. A., Chik, H. M., Ryder, A. G., Gorzalka, B. B., & Seal, B. N. (2005). Acculturation and sexual function in Asian women. *Archives of Sexual Behavior, 34*, 613–626.

Christenson, C. P. (1988). Issues in sex therapy with ethnic and racial minority women. *Women & Therapy, 7*, 187–205.

Clark, D. M., Layard, R., Smithies, R., Richard, D. A., Suckling, R., & Wright, B. (2009). Improving access to psychological therapy: Initial evaluation of two UK demonstration sites. *Behaviour Research and Therapy, 47*, 910–920.

Dixon-Mueller, R. (1993). The sexuality connection in reproductive health. *Studies in Family Planning, 24*, 269–282.

Domeles de Andrade, D. (2010). On norms and bodies: Findings from field research on cosmetic surgery in Rio de Janeiro, Brazil. *Reproductive Health Matters, 18*, 74–83.

Ellison C. (2000). *Women's sexualities*. Oakland, CA: New Harbinger.

Friedman, T. (2005). *The world is flat: A brief history of the twenty-first century*. New York: Farrar, Straus & Giroux.

Garnets, L. Hancock, K. A., Conhran, S. D., Goodchilds, J., & Peplau, L. A. (1991). Issues in psychotherapy with lesbian and gay men: A survey of psychologists. *American Psychologist, 46*, 964–972.

Graham, C. A. (2012). Condom use in the context of sex research. *Sexual Health, 9*, 103–108.

Graham, C. A., & Bancroft, J. (2006). Assessing the prevalence of female sexual dysfunction with surveys: What is feasible? In I. Goldstein, C. Meston, S. Davis, & A. Traish (Eds.), *Women's sexual function and dysfunction: Study, diagnosis and treatment* (pp. 52–60). London: Taylor & Francis.

Hall, G. C. N. (2001). Psychotherapy research with ethnic minorities: Empirical, ethical, and conceptual issues. *Journal of Consulting and Clinical Psychology, 3*, 502–510.

Hayes, R. D., Dennerstein, L., Bennett, C. M., & Fairley, C. K. (2008). What is the "true" prevalence of female sexual dysfunctions and does the way we assess these conditions have an impact? *Journal of Sexual Medicine, 5*, 777–787.

Higgins, J. A., & Hirsch, J. S. (2007). The pleasure deficit: Revisiting the "sexuality connection" in reproductive health. *Perspectives on Sexual and Reproductive Health, 39*, 240–247.

Hindin, M. J., & Muntifering, C. J. (2011). Women's autonomy and timing of most recent sexual intercourse in Sub-Saharan Africa: A multi-country analysis. *Journal of Sex Research, 48*, 511–519.

International Council on Human Rights Policy. (2009). *Sexuality and human rights* (Discussion paper). Geneva, Switzerland: Author.

Jeffries, W. L. (2009). A comparative analysis of homosexual behaviors, sex role preferences, and anal sex proclivities in Latino and non-Latino men. *Archives of Sexual Behavior, 38*, 765–778.

Kelly, G. A. (1963). *A theory of personality: The psychology of personal constructs*. New York: Norton.

King, M., Holt, V., & Nazareth, I. (2007). Women's views of their sexual difficulties: Agreement and disagreement with clinical diagnoses. *Archives of Sexual Behavior, 36*, 281–288.

Kontula, O. (2011). An essential component in promoting sexual health in Europe is training in sexology. *International Journal of Sexual Health, 23*, 168–180.

Lambert, M. J., & Barley, D. E. (2001). Research summary on the therapeutic relationship and psychotherapy outcome. *Psychotherapy: Theory, Research, Practice, Training, 8*, 357–361.

Laumann, E. O., Paik, A., Glasser, D. B., Kang, J. H., Wang, T., Levinson, B., ... Gingell, C. (2006). A cross-national study of subjective sexual well-being among older women and men: Findings from the Global Study of Sexual Attitudes and Behaviors. *Archives of Sexual Behavior, 35,* 145–161.

Laumann, E. O., Paik, A., & Rosen, R. C. (1999). Sexual dysfunctions in the United States: Prevalence and predictors. *Journal of the American Medical Association, 281,* 537–544.

Leiblum, S. R. (2001). Sex therapy today. In S. R. Leiblum (Ed.), *The principles and practices of sex therapy* (4th. ed., pp. 3–22). New York: Guilford.

Leonard, L. (2000). "We did it for pleasure only": Hearing alternative tales of female circumcision. *Qualitative Inquiry, 6,* 212–228.

Lewis, L. J. (2004). Examining sexual health discourses in a racial/ethnic context. *Archives of Sexual Behavior, 33,* 223–234.

Lo, H. T., & Fung, K. P. (2003). Culturally competent psychotherapy. *Canadian Journal of Psychiatry, 48,* 161–170.

Masters, W. H., & Johnson, V. E. (1966). *Human sexual response.* Boston, MA: Little, Brown.

Mercer, C. H., Fenton, K. A., Johnson, A. M., Wellings, K., Macdowall, W., McManus, S., ... Erens, B. (2003). Sexual function problems and help seeking behaviour in Britain: National probability sample survey. *British Medical Journal, 327,* 426–427.

Meston, C., & Buss, D. (2007). Why humans have sex. *Archives of Sexual Behavior, 36,* 477–507.

Meyer, I. H. (2003). Prejudice, social stress, and mental health in lesbian, gay, and bisexual populations: Conceptual issues and research evidence. *Psychological Bulletin, 129,* 674–697.

Moreira, E., Brock, G., Glasser, D., Nicolosi, A., Laumann, E., Paik, A., ... GSSAB Investigators Group. (2005). Help-seeking behaviour for sexual problems: The Global Study of Sexual Attitudes and Behaviors. *International Journal of Clinical Practice, 59,* 6–16.

Nicolosi, A., Laumann, E. O., Glasser, D. B., Moreira, E. D., Paik, A., & Gingell, C. (2004). Sexual behavior and sexual dysfunctions after age 40: The Global Study of Sexual Attitudes and Behaviors. *Urology, 64,* 991–997.

Oberg, K., Fugl-Meyer, A. R., & Fugl-Meyer, K. S. (2004). On categorization and quantification of women's sexual dysfunctions: An epidemiological approach. *International Journal of Impotence Research, 16,* 261–269.

Pederson, P. B. (2007). *Counseling across cultures* (6th ed.). London: Sage.

Rosen, R. C. (2007). Erectile dysfunction: Integration of medical and psychological approaches. In S. R. Leiblum (Ed.), *The principles and practices of sex therapy* (4th. ed., pp. 277–312). New York: Guilford.

Rosen, R. C., Shifren, J. L., Monz, B. U., Odom, D. M., Russo, P. A., & Johannes, C. B. (2009). Correlates of sexually related personal distress in women with low sexual desire. *The Journal of Sexual Medicine, 6,* 1549–1560.

Rowland, D. L. (2007). Will medical solutions to sexual problems make sexological care and science obsolete? *Journal of Sex & Marital Therapy, 33,* 385–397.

Sato, Y., Tanda, H., Kato, S., Onishi, S., Nitta, T. and Koroku, M. (2007). How long do patients with erectile dysfunction continue to use sildenafil citrate? Dropout rate from treatment course as outcome in real life. *International Journal of Urology, 14,* 339–342.

Shifren, J. L., Monz, B. U., Russo, P. A., Segreti, A., & Johannes, C. B. (2008). Sexual problems and distress in United States women. *Obstetrics and Gynecology, 112,* 970–978.

So, H., & Cheung, F. M. (2004). Review of Chinese sex attitudes and applicability for sex therapy for Chinese couples with sexual dysfunction. *Journal of Sex Research, 42,* 93–101.

Son, H., Park, K., Kim, S. W., & Paick, J. S. (2004). Reasons for discontinuation of sildenafil citrate after successful restoration of erectile function. *Asian Journal of Andrology, 6,* 117–120.

Stulhofer, A., & Arbanas, G. (2009). Sex therapy in a cultural context. *Archives of Sexual Behavior, 38,* 1044–1045.

Sue, D. W., & Sue, D. (1999). Counseling the culturally different: Theory and practice. New York: Wiley.

Tiefer, L. (1991). Historical, scientific, clinical and feminist criticisms of "The human sexual response cycle" model. *Annual Review of Sex Research, 2,* 1–23.

Tiefer, L. (2006). Female sexual dysfunction: A case study of disease mongering and activist resistance. *PLoS Medicine, 3,* e178.

U.S. Department of Health and Human Services. (2001). *Mental health: Culture, race, and ethnicity—A supplement to mental health: A report of the Surgeon General.* Rockville, MD: U.S. Department of Health and Human Services, Public Health Service, Office of the Surgeon General.

Wade, L. (2011). The politics of acculturation: Female genital cutting and the challenge of building multicultural democracies. *Social Problems, 58,* 518–537.

Watters, E. (2010). *Crazy like us: The globalization of the American psyche.* New York: Free Press.

Williams, C. (1983). *Culture and society, 1780–1950.* New York: Columbia University Press.

Witting, K., Santtila, P., Varjonen, M., Jern, P., Johansson, A., von der Pahlen, B., & Sandnabba, K. (2008). Female sexual dysfunction, sexual distress, and compatibility with partner. *Journal of Sexual Medicine, 5,* 2587–2599.

World Health Organization. (2006). *Defining sexual health: Report of a technical consultation on sexual health—28–31 January 2002, Geneva.* Geneva, Switzerland: Author.

Youn, G. (2009). Marital and sexual conflicts in elderly Korean people. *Journal of Sex & Marital Therapy, 35,* 230–238.

Section I

MINORITIES

The Need for Cultural Sensitivity

Editors Introduction to Chapter 2
Sexual Minorities

We begin our book with this chapter on sexual minorities by Margaret Nichols because it provides such a clear example of the limitations of an ethnocentric approach to the understanding and treatment of sexuality related problems.

Traditional notions of gender and sexuality are challenged in this provocative chapter. Surveying how other cultures understand same sex sexuality and gender, we are forced to confront the fact that the Western-style notion of a fixed lifetime sexual and gender identity is an artifact of culture. It is perhaps the way in which Western society makes homosexuality (and more recently, transgender issues) acceptable: homosexuality is not just a sexual orientation but an identity—the way someone is born, not a choice or a preference. Similarly, the idea that there are only two genders is not true worldwide, as many cultures allow for at least a third option. Trying to fit a client into a fixed identity is often counterproductive and countertherapeutic, as the clinical cases presented in this chapter clearly demonstrate. People who are both sexually and culturally in a dual minority class often face societal discrimination without the support of their family or cultural group, as well as discrimination and misunderstanding by health care professionals and therapists. This chapter illustrates a culturally sensitive approach to working with dual minority clients.

2

SAME-SEX SEXUALITY FROM A GLOBAL PERSPECTIVE

Margaret Nichols[1]

Introduction

While I am honored to contribute this chapter to Kathryn Hall and Cynthia Graham's book, I consider the circumstances revealing: I have been asked to cover lesbian, gay, bisexual, or transgender (LGBT) issues cross-culturally because none of the other authors did so in their individual chapters.

This situation speaks volumes about the status of people who love someone of the same gender or who are themselves gender variant. Even in the decade of the 2010s, throughout the world homophobia is still the biggest problem that LGBT people face. Only eight countries worldwide have no official heterosexist discrimination whatsoever[2] (Hopkins, 2008), and many dozens of countries still criminalize same-sex sexual acts, including most African countries and many Muslim countries (Human Rights Watch, 2010a). Male homosexual acts are punishable by death in Somaliland, United Arab Emirates, Iran, Pakistan, Yemen, and Somaliland, and as of this writing, in 2010 Uganda proposed a new law providing capital punishment for gays, despite worldwide protest (Tencer, 2010). In Senegal, there is increased police brutality against gays and reports of bodies of gay men dug up and desecrated (Ross, Rosser, & Smolenski, 2010). Violent antigay protestors in Serbia attacked demonstrators at a 2010 Gay Pride march. The attackers outnumbered the demonstrators by a nearly 10 to 1 margin, and gave Nazi salutes and shouted for the death of homosexuals (Radio Nederland Wereldomreop, 2010). Morocco and Mali were able to block, with the help of other Arab and African nations, a UN resolution on antigay violence in 2010 (Rod2.0:Beta, 2010). Even the relatively "tolerant" nation of Brazil was cited by Amnesty International for the frequency of its antigay hate crimes (Townsend, 2010). In 2010 the United States was rocked by a series of suicides of gay teens, most prominently Tyler Clementi, a young Rutgers student who jumped to his death after having a same-sex sexual encounter broadcast to the public via a hidden webcam (Friedman, 2010). Perhaps only in the Netherlands are gay and lesbian people the legal and cultural equals of heterosexuals, and they are relatively safe (Herdt, 1997).

So the silence of the contributors to this volume mirrors the stigma attached to homosexual behavior, especially male homosexual behavior, worldwide. Therefore, if this chapter has one take-home message, it is this: same-sex relationships encounter more social barriers than heterosexual relationships, and individuals who engage in same-sex sexuality suffer more societal discrimination than those who do not. Homophobia is a nearly universal worldwide problem and it does not simply take the form of overt oppression of gay people. More insidiously, it contributes to making homosexuality invisible; in cultures where same-sex relationships are stigmatized, even criminalized, there is tremendous pressure to repress or at least hide homosexual behavior. The countries with the harshest laws and practices often succeed in driving gay behavior so far into the shadows that the inhabitants of those countries may actually believe that their culture contains no homosexuals. In 2007, while speaking at Columbia University, Iranian President Mahmoud Ahmadinejad asserted "We don't have homosexuals, like in your country" (CNN, 2007). So the authors of the various chapters in this book may have also neglected to mention same-sex behavior from the mistaken belief that such activities are rare in their culture. As Herdt pointed out (1997), "in cultures that disapprove of homosexuality, people try to accommodate and blend in, to find what satisfaction they can through compromised relationships of marriage and friendship and extramarital same-gender relations" (p. 5).

There is no reason to believe that homosexual behavior is rare in *any* culture. Our 21st century beliefs about sexuality conform to the dominant paradigm, the Darwinian-based model that views procreation as the primary function of human sexual behavior. According to the dominant model, heterosexual intercourse is clearly the biological imperative, and other forms of sexual behavior, including same-sex behavior, require "explanations" in order to justify their continued existence. In fact, there is a virtual cottage industry of evolutionary psychological theories just to explain homosexuality, because according to a strict Darwinian model of sex, genes for homosexual behavior should have vanished from the gene pool eons ago. However, this model is being challenged more and more in biology (Baghemihl, 1999), evolutionary science (Roughgarden, 2004), and psychology (Ryan & Jetha, 2010). As Roughgarden asserted, the vast majority of sexual acts engaged in by mammals are nonprocreative in function. According to a more contemporary model, sexuality functions as an affiliative/interpersonal tool more often than as a mechanism of reproduction (Meston & Buss, 2007; Ryan and Jetha, 2010), and because it is "recognized as a way to build and maintain a network of mutually beneficial relationships, nonreproductive sex no longer requires special explanations" (Ryan & Jetha, p. 103).

This holds at the individual level as well as the species level. In other words, if one accepts, as I do, as a fundamental premise of this chapter, that sexual variety is a necessary, biologically "hard-wired" characteristic of the human species, then the reasons why one person is attracted to those of the same sex, another to the opposite sex, and another to both genders are not particularly relevant. In particular, from the clinician's point of view, same-sex behavior is just as "natural" as heterosexual behavior, and requires no psychodynamic explanation for its existence. While the form same-sex behavior takes varies from culture to culture and from one historical time period to another, its existence is "normal," even predictable. And while all sexuality can be used destructively as well as constructively, same-sex behavior is no more prone to be destructive than heterosexual activity.

From this perspective, same-gender sexuality and relationships are normal, predictable, and to varying degrees, stigmatized in most cultures. This means the therapist treating LGBT clients must have general familiarity with the stresses faced by all minorities who are discriminated against in the culture, as LGBT face those same stresses. LGBT clients have something else in common that cross-cuts ethnic, racial, and religious background, and it makes them different from many other ethnic, racial, or religious minorities: To the extent that the LGBT person's culture of origin rejects homosexuality, that person cannot depend on his or her family for support.

In this way LGBT clients are unique among minorities. Socially stigmatized subcultural groups can typically depend on their families of origin and immediate communities to buttress them from the assaults of the larger society. Immigrant minorities are often particularly dependent upon familial support, with children bridging the distance between the "old" world of their parents and the new culture into which they are trying to assimilate. But same-sex sexual attraction is generally recognized during adolescence or even earlier, a time when parental support and approval is still necessary. The LGBT youth who are also members of an ethnic or other minority face being ostracized by the culture at large, while also fearing rejection by the family that has sheltered them. While families can and often do eventually accept their LGBT children (LaSala, 2010), the process can be difficult and can leave the gay person extremely vulnerable. Sometimes clinicians forget that parents serve very basic purposes that we take for granted: the protection of their children from the outside world. This may not happen for LGBT youth. This makes it imperative that clinicians treating same-sex couples or individuals engaging in same-sex behavior be advocates as well as therapists, especially when working with children and young people.

Forms of Homosexual Behavior

While some form of same-sex sexual behavior exists in nearly all mammals (Baghemihl, 1999) and may be present in all cultures, the model of homosexuality held by most 21st century Westerners is far from universal. There is no Greek or Latin word that corresponds to the concept of homosexuality, and categorizing people as homosexual or heterosexual only began in the late 19th century in Europe with the concept of the "invert" (D'Emilio & Freedman, 1988). Moreover, although modern sexuality in Western cultures is generally preoccupied with the gender of the sexual partners, this has not always been the case nor is it always the case even now. As we shall see later in this chapter, for many cultures the particular sexual acts engaged in, and the role one plays, are more important than the gender of one's partner. In many Latin American cultures, for example, the "insertor" in anal sex is not considered homosexual, only the "insertee" (Jeffries, 2009).

Herdt (1997) outlined five widely agreed on forms of same-gender relations around the world, which are:

1. Age-structured relationships, usually between older and younger males;
2. Gender-transformed relationships, where one person takes the sex/gender role of the other gender;
3. Social roles that permit or demand same-gender relations as part of a niche in society;
4. Western homosexuality as a 19th century form of sexual identity; and
5. Late 20th century/21st century Western egalitarian relationships between persons of the same gender. Herdt included the provision that these persons self-identify as "essentially" gay, but more recent forms of these relationships may involve people who consider their identity more fluid (Diamond, 2008; Savin-Williams, 2005).

Age-structured relationships, which were the first type of same-sex relationships, are arguably the most common historically. The relationships between older men and young boys in Ancient Greece (and to a lesser extent, older women and girls, e.g., Sappho) are the best known of this form. In cultures where this exists, the homoerotic relationships are often viewed as an initiation into manhood/womanhood for the younger participant, who is eventually expected to marry and produce children, while graduating to the older role in another (usually) man–boy pairing.

Age-structured male homoerotic relationships have been recorded in Chinese, Korean, and Japanese cultures and both Northern and sub-Saharan African societies. Far from being stigmatized, cultures in which these kinds of homosexual relationships exist often lionize the role of the older male; samurai warriors in Japan, for example, mentored younger samurai males. In contemporary societies, most age-structured homoerotic relationships exist in cultures in the South Pacific.

Gender-transformed homoerotic relationships fit many of our stereotypes about homosexuality, and are most common in southeast Asia, parts of Africa, and both North and South America. Sometimes these relationships involve one partner assuming a "female" role, but more often one partner is considered a "third sex." Examples are "two spirit" people in Native American culture, "ladyboys" in Thailand, and *travesti* in Brazil (Nanda, 2000). While these relationships seem to exist more among men, there is historical evidence of women who have taken on male roles (D'Emilio & Freeman, 1988) and female partners, often without ever being detected.

In fact, anthropologists have speculated whether these gender-transformed systems have evolved in cultures as a way of accommodating individuals who do not fit into a binary gender system. Today, Western sexologists tend to make a bright-line distinction between gay and transgender people, and these "third-sex" people would be seen as transgender, not as gay. But in fact the prevalence of gender-transformed same-sex relationships throughout history and different cultures is testimony to the fact that gender and sexual orientation are more intimately intertwined than we currently believe. And in approaching LGBT clients from different cultures, it is particularly important to remember that many may have a gender-transformed model for relationships. For example, some urban lesbians of color in the United States identify as "AG," or "Aggressive," a synonym for "butch," or masculine in presentation, and protocol dictates that AGs pair with "femme" women, sometimes referred to as "wifey" by their partners (Hilliard, 2007). But AGs do not consider themselves transgender, making a distinction between the "stud" or AG style and women who want to take male hormones and undergo "top" surgery to remove their breasts.

Some cultures prescribe same-gender homoerotic relationships in order to fulfill a particular social role. Examples are castrati, eunuchs, and contemporary hijira of India (Herdt, 1993). Although this practice appears to resemble the creation of a third gender, like gender-transformed same-sex relationships, the difference is that only certain persons within the culture are permitted to take on these roles, and they are in fact mandated to perform their social roles. An interesting example of these practices from the last century is the "sworn virgin of the Balkans" (Gremaux, 1993; Young, 2000). In Albania, for example, up through the mid-20th century, an institutionalized form of gender crossing emerged in which some females were designated by their families to take on male roles and social identities. The "sworn virgins" vowed to abstain from matrimony and child-rearing. They became the heirs of the family in families that had no male children. One such "sworn virgin," named Tome, commanded an anticommunist fighter battalion in World War II (Nanda, 2000).

The last two forms of same-sex relations are the most common in contemporary American and Western European societies. Many cultural historians date the 19th century as a time when homosexuality changed from being viewed as a behavior to an identity. Before this, same-sex behavior was to an extent normalized. As Herdt (1997) noted, "According to the eighteenth century [European] worldview, all persons were capable of desiring both genders, at least on occasion" (p. 45). But gradually this view changed, and certain individuals were recognized as having a primary desire for the same gender. Typically, they were considered gender-variants, and in some areas of Europe it was believed that three genders existed: men and women (attracted to each other); sodomites (males attracted to other males); and sapphists (females attracted to other females). This was the beginning of the view that homosexuality, then considered a gender inversion, was an identity, an essential characteristic of the human being, as opposed to a behavior that might be indulged in at various times by most people. This view has persisted, although modern sexology attempts (and often fails) to make clear distinctions between people with same-sex attractions and those who are gender variant. This is the fourth form of same-gender sexuality.

The fifth form might be considered an elaboration of the fourth, and is perhaps the "ideal" of same-sex relations in the eyes of most Americans and Western Europeans. In this form of same-gender behavior, neither partner assumes a gender-variant role, both partners are presumed equal in power and are usually approximately equal in age, and both partners self-identify as gay or lesbian. While this is the "ideal," there are many variations, and there are indications in particular that the concept of a "gay identity" may be changing in younger, educated populations (Diamond, 2008; Nichols & Shernoff, 2007; Savin-Williams, 2005).

LGBT Lives in Different Cultures

Even a brief survey of how different cultures cope with same-sex relationships illustrates the variety of forms same-gender desires can take. The very terms we use, *gay, lesbian, LGBT,* reflect contemporary Western examples of homoeroticism (the fourth and fifth forms listed above). They describe individuals who see their sexual orientation as a fixed, lifetime identity and who see their orientation as separate and distinct from their gender identities or gender roles. In most cultures same-sex attraction is not viewed as having either of these attributes. In fact, asking the question, "Are you gay?" or "Are you homosexual?" is likely to evoke confusion and misunderstanding in many societies. This problem became so widespread in global research on HIV that researchers no longer use these terms, instead describing behavior; for example, men who have sex with men (MSM; Nichols & Shernoff, 2007).

Cultures vary greatly in their acceptance of homosexual behaviors or gender variant behaviors, and even when a society is accepting, it is usually tolerant only of a narrow range of homoeroticism or gender variance; typically, those behaviors specially sanctioned within that culture. For example, the Sambia of New Guinea practice universal male age-structured homoerotic relationships while a young boy is being initiated into manhood, but that boy is expected as a man to choose a wife and create a family (Herdt, 1993). In contemporary Iran, homosexual acts are punishable by death but transsexual operations are sanctioned by the theocratic state (Human Rights Watch, 2010b). Many cultures allow for "extramarital" relationships between men but do not consider the men themselves homosexual. To fully appreciate the multiple ways in which homoeroticism is expressed in different societies, with and without sanction, we must first rid ourselves of the egalitarian identity model that currently permeates the West as an ideal.

Moreover, the clinician trying to adapt information about how same-gender relations manifest in other cultures must keep in mind the difference between inhabitants of the "home" country and immigrants in the United States or other Western societies. For example, mainland China appears to be swiftly transforming into a gay-tolerant society: Some people have compared China's evolving culture of sexual tolerance to the United States in the 1960s and 1970s (Lau, 2010). And yet research has shown that Asian American gay youth are the least likely of any ethnic minority to "come out" to their parents (Grov, Bimbi, Nanin, & Parsons, 2006).

Indeed the experience of being an immigrant, or simply a person of color, often confers a "double stigma" upon a same-gender oriented person. As discussed earlier, a special aspect of the discrimination against same-sex attracted people is the lack of automatic family support. This is particularly devastating to someone who is already a member of an oppressed minority, because typically oppressed subgroups in society survive through collective, family, and community based effort. So, for example, rates of suicidality and mental disturbance are elevated in the United States among Asian, Black, or Latino same-sex oriented youth (LaSala, 2010). This is in part true because the "double stigma" makes these young people particularly vulnerable.

Two seemingly contradictory facts are true of cultures worldwide in how they regard same-sex behavior. Since the work of Clelland Ford and Frank Beach 60 years ago (Ford & Beach, 1951), it is widely accepted that about two thirds of world societies accept some form of same-sex behavior as part of the human life cycle. Western societies have been among the least accepting; as Herdt (1997) commented, "few societies have systematically forbidden and punished homosexuality as much as have historical western countries over the past century" (p. 14). And yet at the same time, it is Western societies that have developed this very modern and specialized variation of homoerotic behavior: the self-identified lifetime, full-time lifestyle, gay person. The last century, and especially the last half-century, has seen the emergence of a gay sexual life path that parallels the more conventional heterosexual pathway.

This is of tremendous historical significance, because most cultures throughout most of history have seen parenthood as synonymous with full personhood, and most modern societies see pair bonding as the necessary precursor to parenthood. Worldwide, many New World and Anglo-European countries sanction gay marriage or gay domestic partnership and allow gay adoption. Further, modern reproductive technology has made it possible for gay people to have biologically connected children through alternative mechanisms. One might say that many countries in the 21st century are evolving to accord same-sex oriented people the same full "personhood" granted to hetero-oriented persons.

Yet when examining other cultures it is important to remember that this Western egalitarian model of being gay not only does not exist in most places, it is not necessarily a better or more desirable model. In a conversation with a colleague about gender-role based homoerotic structures, he asked, "So, do you think we're just more evolved than those cultures?" Unconsciously, we may believe in our own superiority. We may see these forms as poor imitations of heterosexual roles or feeble attempts to maintain heteronormativity while allowing for same-sex expression. But gender-transformed homoeroticism, and the belief in a "third sex," are pervasive in human societies, and are found in animal communities as well (Roughgarden, 2004). Thus, it is likely that elements of gender-based same-sex roles will continue to exist, and we can learn from them, instead of condemning them as "unenlightened." In U.S. urban areas in the 21st century, many lesbians of color, Black, and Latina women, assume roles of "femme" or "AG" as part of their expression of lesbianism (Hilliard, 2007). This is a variation of the egalitarian form of being gay, not an inferior version of it.

It is also important to remember that within a given culture attitudes vary between individuals, subgroups, and families. Adherence to tradition and religiosity influence attitudes about same-gender orientation.

For example, although Christian religions generally embody more sex negativity than Judaism, a strictly traditional Orthodox Jewish family may sit shiva (ceremony for the dead) when a child is discovered to be gay, while an Italian Catholic family may simply look the other way. And, one must remember that even relatively tolerant societies are somewhat homophobic: the United States of the 21st century is increasingly accepting of homosexual identity and lifestyle, and yet antigay hate crimes are still relatively frequent. A growing body of research indicates that sexual minorities in the United States exhibit worse mental health than their heterosexual counterparts (Cochrane, Sullivan, & Mays, 2003; Reback & Larkins, 2010).

A rough sense of cross-cultural attitudes globally can be gleaned simply by perusing charts of LGBT laws worldwide (Wikipedia, 2010). As a continent, Africa has the harshest laws; male homosexuality, and sometimes female homosexuality, is illegal in all but a few African countries. By contrast, in the Americas, only Belize in Central America and some Caribbean nations have laws against same-sex sexual contact. No European countries outlaw homosexuality, although the Turkish government has been accused by Amnesty International of government harassment of gay groups (Amnesty International, 2010). Moreover, within the European Union acceptance of a homosexual lifestyle varies widely between countries. In a recent survey of homonegativity among European nations (Stulhofer & Rimac, 2009), respondents were asked a question about the desirability of having a homosexual as a neighbor. The percentage of people who would not want a homosexual as a neighbor varied from a low of 6% in the Netherlands and Sweden to a high of 65 to 67% in Lithuania, Romania, Ukraine, and Belarus. Asian cultures vary widely: Many Middle Eastern countries (e.g., Kuwait, Lebanon, Syria) still retain harsh penalties for male homosexual acts, including the death penalty in Saudi Arabia, United Arab Emirates, and Yemen. But Israel has among the most liberal LGBT laws in the world, permitting civil marriage, adoption, and the right to serve openly in the military. Many East Asian countries—China, Hong Kong, Japan, the Koreas—have decriminalized same-sex behaviors, as have countries like Indonesia, the Philippines, and Thailand. Both Hinduism and Buddhism incorporate more sex-positivity into their religious tenets than does Christianity, and the Hindu and Buddhist influence has to a degree mediated attitudes about homosexual behavior.

China, Korea, and Japan have historical traditions of tolerance for male same-sex relationships under certain conditions. Age-structured homoerotic relationships were common in Chinese culture going back to the Bronze Age (Herdt, 1997), and these types of relationships took their place alongside other familial and marital relationships. In the 20th century Maoist regime homosexuality came to be seen as a form of Western vice. Herdt noted that often homosexual practices are attributed to colonialism or other forms of outside cultural influence, even when the practices have been imbedded in the culture for centuries, as in certain African customs. Within the last 15, years the government of Mainland China has reversed the "colonial" view of homosexuality. In 1997 the government repealed the "hooligan act," the antigay law, and in 2001 the Chinese Psychiatric Association removed homosexuality from its list of mental disorders. Some observers have speculated that China has been able to move relatively rapidly to a new position on homosexuality (and here we *are* talking about Western style gay identity) for two reasons. First, as a secular society, there is no religious underpinning to antihomosexual bias. Second, as a society seriously concerned with population control, gay lifestyles fit the political agenda perfectly. In any case, it would be an exaggeration to say that gay life in China is free and liberated, but the culture does seem to be moving in that direction, and moving rather quickly (Lau, 2010).

Latin American countries by and large have legalized homosexual behavior, but nevertheless Latin American culture has clearly proscribed circumstances under which such behavior is and is not appropriate for men. We have seen that North American/European models of same-sex relationships are identity based and egalitarian. Latin American models derive from the sexual role one plays, regardless of whether one's partner is same or opposite sex. The anthropologist Joseph Carrier (1995) has studied male–male relationships in Mexican barrios and found them to be quite common. These relationships are quite gender-stereotyped, and the dominant partner, the "insertor" (the active partner in anal or oral sex) is not considered less masculine for his behavior. Only the passive male partner is considered feminine and thus homosexual. This theme is repeated everywhere in Latin American cultures; a certain latitude is permitted to dominant, insertive males, where it is acceptable for them to have relationships with both males and females without being considered gay or any less machismo. As described by Jeffries (2009), "Machismo ... does not preclude homosexual encounters as viable components to men's sexual experiences. Within this framework, to be a man necessitates that one is the insertive partner in sexual intercourse—regardless of the gender of one's sexual partners" (p. 765).

In general, then, the most "gay-affirmative" cultures are those of Western Europe, especially northern European countries, and Canada and the United States. The least gay affirmative are African, Middle Eastern, and some other Asian countries. Religion seems to play a role here, in two ways. In general, the more antisexual the religion is in general, the more antigay it will be and the more extreme the brand of religion is, the more it will be both antisexual in general and specifically antigay. Theocratic Muslim states are predictably the most virulently antigay, but Sufism, the mystical branch of Islam, has a long history of age-structured male homosexual relationships; American Sufis embrace a gay-affirmative form of the religion. And although European countries as a whole are relatively gay-accepting, the differences between them are to a degree associated with religion and secularity. Spain, which is 90% Catholic but which has, since the demise of Franco, become increasingly secular, is very gay-affirming (Donadio, 2009), while Austria, somewhat less Catholic but more traditionally religious, has less tolerance of homosexuality and a substantial rate of suicide attempts among LGBT youth and adults (Ploderl, Kralovec, & Fartacek, 2008). Additionally, the forms which same-sex behavior takes from culture to culture appears to be influenced by the openness of the society in general vis-à-vis gender roles and the access women have to power. Both gender and age structured forms of same-sex relations mirror dominant male/passive female social models. It is not surprising that Latin American machismo cultures have spawned forms of homosexuality that emphasize active/passive roles over biological gender. One would expect that as these countries evolve more toward gender parity, gender-structured homosexuality would become less prominent and be replaced by egalitarian forms; many observers of Latin American cultures believe this is already happening (Carrier, 1995; Herdt, 1997).

Finally, one can occasionally be fooled by apparent acceptance of same-sex behavior in virulently antigay cultures. An internationally traveled gay economist friend of mine related this story:

> Last year, I was in Istanbul with an Austrian friend. He observed Turkish men walking hand in hand and fumed that he could not do this in Austria. We talked about this and concluded that in repressive Turkey where "there are no gay men" is the official story, physical intimacy, even in public, is permissible because there is a complete denial that there is any affectionate/erotic aspect to it. On the other hand, in Austria where homosexuality is tolerated but not broadly accepted, any public display of intimacy is subject to disapproval. (E. White, personal correspondence, e-mail, January 1, 2011)

Moreover, members of a given culture are not necessarily the best reporters on sexual behavior in that culture. Ahmadinejad declared homosexuality a "Western phenomenon," but so have leaders of African nations, Caribbean islands, and mainland China. Behaviors repudiated by a culture tend to be ascribed to outsiders or colonizers. These assertions should be taken with a grain of salt because historical forms of homosexual behavior have been found in every country that currently denounces same-sex behavior as "Western" or "colonial" (Herdt, 1997, 1993).

Three Case Examples: Brazilian, African–American, and U.S. Urban Youth Cultures

A Brazilian Travesti

Brazilian sexuality of all kinds is marked by an openness and sensuality not common in North America, and by intense male/female dualism, rigid and polarized gender roles, and strong male dominance over women. Males are allowed sexual freedom; females are the possessions of men and need to be controlled (Herdt, 1997; Nanda, 2000; Phua, 2010). Young Brazilian boys commonly take part in sex games where they take turns inserting their penis into another boy's anus; the boys who prefer the receptive role come to be seen as effeminate/female in contrast to the insertors. As in other parts of Latin America, same-sex behavior is organized around masculine *actividade* and feminine *passividade* (Jeffries, 2009). The distinction is not so much between "male" and "female," however, as much as it is between "male" and "not-male." As Phua (2010) stated, "A man's sexuality and masculinity will not be challenged if he takes on what is considered a man's role in sexual acts, regardless of the sex of his partner. Some men would even boost their virility because they are desired and have willing sexual partners of both sexes catering to their needs" (p. 832).

On the other hand, the passive partners, while self-identifying as homosexual, also see themselves as "like women." Called *bichas* or *travestis*, these men occupy a psychic territory that bridges gender and sexual orientation. While *travestis* value their penises and have no desire to surgically remove them, they go to great trouble to be "like women": Nanda (2000) noted that "The sexually receptive partner is expected to enact other aspects of the feminine gender role: to behave and/or sound and/or dress in ways appropriate to women" (p. 46). This includes surgically modifying their bodies and taking cross-gender hormones, which can be obtained cheaply on the street in Brazil. But *travestis* do not consider themselves transgendered in the way North Americans might define transgender or transsexual. The *travesti* is feminine in response to her *marido*, the often hypermasculine boyfriend, and the epitome of her femininity is her passive sexual role. And the roles are "for life." Although the *travesti* often obtains money through prostitution, and her penis is valued in her prostitute activities, she considers her own active use of her penis a violation of her role and would not expect to perform these sex acts in her romantic relationship with the *marido*.

Joachim

Joachim was a 16-year-old Brazilian boy who had immigrated to New Jersey at the age of 13. He had grown up with an aunt in a poor, rural area in Brazil. His biological parents left for the United States when Joachim was quite young; they worked here and sent home money for his support until they were able to bring him to live with them permanently. While such disruptions in caretakers and lifestyle would be considered unusual and traumatic for a native U.S. citizen, these arrangements are quite common in immigrant communities. Because this lifestyle was normalized for him, Joachim showed no obvious negative consequences from these drastic changes in his life and the changes in caretakers. However, when Joachim arrived in the States his parents were disconcerted to find that he was quite feminine and clearly attracted to men. In fact, in Brazil his aunt had permitted him to dress in girls' clothes routinely, sensing from an early age that he was *travesti*, or inherently not-male. Joachim's parents had separated some years before his arrival in the States, and he had had little contact with his father. Joachim had hoped for some reunion with his father, but upon learning of his son's effeminacy, Joachim's father expressed shame about his orientation and avoided contact with him.

Joachim's mother tried to be supportive of him, but her cultural expectations of homosexuality had been influenced by many years of living in the United States (McGoldrick, Loonan, & Wohlsifer, 2007). Joachim's desire to look and act like a woman did not conform to his mother's Americanized vision of gay male behavior. While to me Joachim presented as "transgender," his mother, like the aunt, saw Joachim as a *travesti* and was horrified, since this represented everything she wanted her son to escape. At school Joachim suffered from the same lack of understanding. Although his high school had a Gay–Straight Alliance, Joachim did not match American models of a gay teen. His female persona and his insistence that he was not attracted to "gay" males, only to "straight" ones, set him apart even from other gay students. He did not identify with American gay men. In despair, Joachim sank into a depression and became suicidal. His high school guidance counselor began weekly sessions with him and introduced him to the concept of transsexualism. Joachim began to see himself as a transgender person and his suicidal desires decreased: there was an American cultural translation for his identity. After 6 months of meetings with this counselor, she left the high school for another job, and referred him to our agency, the Institute for Personal Growth, a multitherapist outpatient clinic known for work with the LGBT community in New Jersey. Joachim worked with me briefly and then with a male therapist when our schedules became discordant.

Upon intake, Joachim presented himself as a transgender person. However, from my Americanized model of sexual orientation and transgender variations, he did not fit the diagnosis of gender identity disorder, nor was he clearly a "gay male." While he had cross-dressed from an early age, Joachim did not report the Western transsexual narrative of "being a woman trapped in a man's body." When asked about his aspirations, he said he wanted to look like a Victoria's Secret model. He expressed intense interest in cross-gender hormones and various surgeries that might enhance his femininity, such as breast and hip enhancement, and cheek reconstruction, but was adamant about keeping his male genitals. He expressed no abhorrence or dislike of his penis. While he wanted to get rid of male secondary sex characteristics—body and facial hair, the slight Adam's apple, the deep voice—and wanted to develop breasts, he was baffled by my frequent questions about gender reassignment surgery.

Another way Joachim differed from American young gay males or transgender people is that he always had "boyfriends" whom he had met on transgender (TG) Internet dating sites. The boyfriends, usually other Latin American immigrants, were clearly seeking what we in the United States would call "chicks with dicks." In this way Joachim's self-image matched the image of what his boyfriends wanted. This is unusual in the United States. Boys who are gender-variant in childhood—like to wear dresses, prefer girls and girl activities—tend by adolescence to have separated themselves into two distinct groups (Green, 1987). Members of the first group self-identify as gay or bisexual males. They may also see themselves as "gender queer" or "gender benders"; that is, individuals who combine both male and female characteristics, often deliberately, but they are interested in other gay men as partners and affiliate with the gay community. Those in the second group identify as transgender. They do not see their attractions as "homosexual," and they yearn to be "real women," which they imagine will come after hormone treatment and gender reassignment surgery. They repudiate their genitals—indeed, the presence of male genitals is often seen as inhibiting their ability to have relationships—they are attracted to "straight" or "straight-appearing" males, and tend not to affiliate with the gay community or gay organizations.

Joachim did not fit neatly into either group. His presentation made no sense to me until the therapist to whom he was transferred, who had some familiarity with same-sex relationships in Brazil, pointed out the cultural aspects of his behavior. For the first few sessions I worked with Joachim, I struggled, with my American sensibilities, to figure out whether he was "really" gay or "really" transgender. In U.S. and Western conceptualizations of gender identity disorder, the defining criterion is the desire for surgery. As Bolin (1993) wrote, "Surgical conversion and hormonal reassignment have come to dominate the medical designation and psychological diagnosis of transsexualism.... In Benjamin's model (Harry Benjamin) fully developed transsexualism was diagnosed by the quest for surgery (p. 455). Once he was seen as a product of Brazilian culture, Joachim's behavior and identity became understandable. He felt out of place in the U.S. LGBT community because he *was* different. His aspirations—to take hormones but to keep his penis, and to seek out medical interventions that would make his body more female without considering himself a woman—made perfect sense in a Brazilian cultural context, but not from the framework of the American/European definition of gender identity disorder.

Joachim's transfer to a more culturally sensitive therapist, and our recognition that his worldview was Brazilian not North American, was the turning point in his therapy. We became advocates for him with his mother and with the medical establishment. Joachim's mother maintained that she could have accepted his being gay, but not transsexual. Viewed from a cultural context, her desires were that he be "American" and not lower-class Brazilian, as *travestis* usually are. She was persuaded that Joachim was a transgender person, but she was also educated about what this means in the United States, and she saw that he fit within an American subcultural community and was not doomed to a life of prostitution and poverty. She then gave her consent for Joachim to take cross-gender hormones. Our next task was to find an endocrinologist who would accept his desire to take lower or no doses of testosterone-inhibiting hormones but only estrogen. In the United States both are administered to transgender people, because one of the effects of testosterone inhibitors is often to eliminate erections, a desirable outcome for U.S.-style male to female transsexuals. But unlike most people suffering from gender identity disorder, Joachim was not interested in losing the functionality of his penis, only in adding feminine physical characteristics. Eventually we found such an endocrinologist, and Joachim was persuaded to take medically administered hormones instead of seeking them through the Internet as he had originally planned. Joachim began presenting more in female clothes and adopted a female persona using the name of a famous Brazilian supermodel. Now using female pronouns to define herself, she continued to have Latin American boyfriends she found online. Recently, she moved with her mother to a large urban area outside of New Jersey with a large Latino community, where she presumably will feel that she fits in with others like her.

Vi and Barb: The Double Stigma of being Gay and African American

Just as research has found LGBT adults and youth to have a higher incidence of mental illness, studies have reported that non-White minorities within the LGBT community have higher rates still (Cochrane et al., 2003; Grov et al., 2006; LaSala, 2010; McGoldrick et al., 2007). LaSala's study of how families responded to the coming out of a gay child found that non-White families always mentioned concern for the "double stigma" of being both an ethnic/racial minority and gay or lesbian. Gays of color perceive less support from their own communities of color than do European American LGBT people and many African American men who have sex with other men do so "'on the down low," that is, secretively, and so maintain a heterosexual self-identity (Greene, 2000; Reback & Larkins, 2010). The renowned strength of the Christian churches in the African American community backfires on gay people. Not only can they not depend on the church for support, but the evangelical nature of many of these churches tends to make them vocally and actively antigay; some of the support for Proposition 8, the California state amendment banning gay marriage, came from African American churches.

Vi and Barb, both African American self-defined lesbians in their late 30s, came for help with their relationship of 6 years. Like many lesbians of color, they presented physically and sexually as a butch–femme couple (Nestle, 1992), although they did not assume gender-based roles outside of the bedroom. Vi, the "butch," or AG lesbian, had a history of same-sex relationships since adolescence, and of estrangement from her family, who rejected her on religious grounds. Barbara, the more feminine partner, was in fact more bisexual in orientation. She married a man to whom she, at least originally, had been both romantically and sexually attracted. However, after having two children together, the marriage went sour for Barb as she discovered that her husband was perpetually immature and irresponsible; as she said, she felt like she had three children. As Barb's attraction to her husband waned, she became aware of attractions toward Vi, a neighbor and friend. As a child Barb had had some incidental crushes on girls but had not considered them serious. Now, she reevaluated and relabeled her identity in light of her relationship with Vi. She knew she had bisexual attractions, but referred to herself as lesbian because, as she pointed out, that's what she was in the eyes of the culture. Vi was Barb's first lesbian partner.

The women came for couples counseling and sex therapy because their sex life had dwindled to nothing and both felt distant in the relationship. Their main problems stemmed from the way that Barb's family related to the women as a couple. Barb's parents, her male sibling, and extended family, and her ex-husband all refused to believe that she was gay. Even though the two women had purchased a home together and lived in that home with Barb's two teenage children, Vi was regarded as an interloper in Barb's home. Despite the fact that Barb's ex-husband paid no child support and Vi in fact helped financially support Barb's children, the ex-husband was respected as a parent and Vi's right to supervise or act as an authority figure to the children was ignored, disrespected, and undermined. Since Barb's family and the ex-husband lived in the same community as the two women, they were able to interfere in the couple's lives with regularity. Barb, as a strong, nurturing African American woman and the eldest daughter, was expected to play a caretaking role in her extended family. When a nephew needed a place to live, Barb took him in; when a drug-addicted cousin needed help, she also opened her home to this relative. Vi was a nearly invisible, and completely ineffectual member of the family structure, as Barb's children quickly picked up the attitudes of their grandparents, aunts, and uncles.

To make matters worse, Barb ran a business from her home that relied on customers from the local church in which she had been a member since childhood. She could not be "out" to the church ladies, and so when these customers came to their home, Vi had to "disappear" or pretend to be merely a boarder in the home. It was no wonder that Vi felt distant from Barb; she felt marginalized in her own home, and yet having been raised in the same culture as Barb, Vi took for granted, on some level, Barb's family's right to treat the couple in this way. The last problem that plagued this couple was that Barb individually, and the couple, suffered from the lack of a supportive spiritual community. Vi had long ago withdrawn from religion, although a part of her still yearned for it. But Barb had been active in church not only during her childhood but during her entire adult life. Now she felt the hypocrite in her own church, could not introduce Vi as her loving partner into this religious community, and felt lost without this familiar and important component of spirituality her life.

It became quickly apparent to me that therapy involved family therapy and the creation of legitimate and legitimized boundaries around the couple and their family unit. Barb needed some individual sessions to help her see that she was caught in conflict between her family of origin and her partner. It was nearly impossible for her to contemplate giving up the role assigned to her by her family, until she realized that they placed her in that role because they saw her as a single woman, unencumbered by obligations to a partner. Once Barb recognized that her family valued her old marriage, in which she had been abused and neglected by her husband, over this new, much more loving and healthy relationship, she became angry. And ironically I, with my White middle class background, was easily able to validate the need and right for their new family to detach from the family of origin.

Barb was put in touch with a church headed by an openly lesbian African American minister, and this minister helped her reconcile her sexual orientation with her religion. Moreover, by attending the church together, the two women shared a strong spiritual connection, within a community that celebrated and honored their relationship openly.

All of these things gave Barb the resolve to support Vi with the children and with her own extended family. Family sessions were held in which Barb affirmed Vi's role as coparent to her two children, in front of the children, clearly and firmly. Surprisingly, both children responded well, perhaps because they recognized their father as a charming but completely unreliable figure in their lives, and perhaps because Vi coached local sports and both children had athletic interests themselves. In any case, they gave Vi no resistance and readily accepted, even welcomed, her authority once Barb clearly "gave" Vi authority to coparent. Barb's son developed an especially strong attachment to Vi, perhaps because Vi was an AG lesbian, making her a model for male characteristics even though she inhabited a female body.

Thus the two women became a solid unit as a pair, and the four of them had become a clear family unit. The relationship got better, and so did the sex. Over the last several years, the women have come back to me for "tune-ups" where they talk about how to handle "kid" issues and, most recently, how to carve out alone time in a busy household. They are a pleasure to have in the room, as even after the years and travails, the two women love, respect, and are happy with each other, and maintain a sexual attraction.

Colby: A Postmodern 21st Century American Young "Queer"

If one accepts the premise that both gender diversity and sexual orientation variations are intrinsic parts of being human, and are present in most if not all human societies, but that the forms they take are shaped by cultural and historical forces, then young teen, 20, and young 30-something "queer" people in the United States and some other European cultures represent the direction, or rather directions, of the future. The most exciting people writing about this today are Lisa Diamond (2008) and Ritch Savin-Williams (2005), although others (Bockting, Benner, & Coleman, 2009; Bolin, 1993) are also contributing new insights (ethnographies, if you will) on the emerging youth culture.

This is a special culture being described. As LaSala points out (2010), the youth being described come mostly from the culture of the educated middle and upper middle class. The "New Gay Youth," as Savin-Williams (2005) labeled them, are less commonly poor, uneducated, or people of color. Keeping in mind these caveats, the trends are still fascinating.

Briefly, Savin-Williams's sample consisted of individuals who were in their teens and 20s in the early to mid-2000s, people who were not entirely heterosexual behaviorally or in other ways. Instead of taking for granted the current paradigm, that of egalitarian identity-oriented homosexuality, Savin-Williams looked at how this younger generation of "queers," as many of them called themselves, viewed their lifestyles, behaviors, feelings, and identity. He found these young people often eschewed the concept of a permanent, stable, sexual, or even gender, identity. They were at the same time more comfortable with gay behavior, attractions, sexuality, and relationships, but baffled by the older generation of gay people's insistence on a permanent identity with only three possibilities: gay, heterosexual, (marginally) bisexual. And, many of these young nonheterosexual people were questioning other aspects of sexual, relationship, and gender mores as well. They were more likely to be polyamorous (multiple, concurrent romantic/sexual relationships), or familiar with BDSM (kink, fetishes, etc.) (Nichols & Shernoff, 2007).

Diamond's work followed women at Rutgers/Douglass College in the 1990s through the 2000s. These college women originally identified as lesbian or bisexual, and over time, Diamond found, they shifted between a variety of self-identifications without apparent discomfort and without a need to disavow previous identifications. In other words, these women did not see their sexual orientation as an essential, immutable part of their being, a perspective which is in direct opposition to Herdt's (1997) "Type 5" structure of same-sex relationships; that is, based on a stable lifelong identity.

The other striking trend, related to the one described above, is the way in which gender has become differentiated, especially since the trans community became a part (if still a marginalized part) of the lesbian, gay, and bisexual minority. Each "letter" added to the cultural trope represents a group that has had to struggle for acceptance even from other sexual minorities. The community started as "Gay," which came to be viewed by women as too male-oriented, and of course this was denied or defended by gay men for a while, until "Gay and Lesbian" or "Lesbian and Gay" began to replace "Gay" in designations of the community of people attracted to those of the same sex. Next, "Bisexuality" was added after the very concept had been mocked, denied, and vilified for years. The addition of transgender people was and still is more complex, because the community itself has redefined itself. In the 80s when I first learned sex therapy, transsexuals, who were overwhelmingly male-to-female, aspired to blend into the heterosexual community, not affiliate with the then-despised gay community. People, again primarily men, who cross-dressed were considered by the mental health field and by themselves to be a distinct type, completely different from transsexuals. Over the years the lines have blurred. Primarily through the Internet at first, transpeople started to come together and connect as activists and for mutual support. It became clear that one could not separate these people into neat groups. Variations started to emerge. Out of the lesbian community came more and more male to female transgender people, who called themselves "transmen," and challenged concepts of sexual orientation by, after "transitioning," becoming attracted to other transmen or to gay men, creating what Bockting et al. (2009) called a new sexual orientation: a transgender orientation. The concepts of "genderqueer" and "gender-fluid" began to be used, not just in queer studies programs but by young people on college campuses and in urban ghettos.

Colby is the poster child for nearly all the trends I have just described. I will use female pronouns to describe Colby, but Colby considers no pronoun really acceptable. Since the only thing consistent about Colby's gender and sexual orientation identities so far is her female body, the female pronouns also denote her female body, so far unchanged by hormones or surgery. Colby's name, however, represents her male identity; Colby's female name is Courtney, which she stopped using in her mid-20s. At around the same time she started therapy at IPG; she was a medical student at a nearby university back then, and, now in her residency, she continues in treatment nearly 7 years later. Colby sees her therapy as support for her sometimes difficult personal life transformations and explorations, not as evidence she is "sick," and she sees IPG as a place where she will never be ridiculed, denied, or pathologized, where her journey will be taken seriously, and where her therapists will be knowledgeable about her struggles. I saw Colby briefly until I was forced to take an extended leave from work. During this time Colby bonded with the therapist to whom she transferred, another "queer" woman, and has remained with this therapist since.

Colby completed her initial IPG paperwork with the name "Courtney (Colby) …", and indicated she preferred Colby right away. She also filled out the question about "gender," to which the choices were "F," "M," "Other" by writing "yes" and a smiley face after "Other." On another form when asked "Which of the following describe you", she checked off all the choices: "bisexual" "gay, "lesbian," "transgender," and "unsure." She reported a sexual history of "many" men and "6" female partners, but no biological male partners for several years. She considered herself sometimes polyamorous and kinky. At the time she entered treatment Colby had just ended a relationship with an FTM (female to male) transperson, Justin. Typical of many transmen, Justin had identified for a time as a "butch" lesbian, then as a transperson. He took testosterone and had had what is called "top" surgery: a double mastectomy and chest reconstruction. But few transmen get "bottom" surgery, in part because of the expense, in part because the final product is disappointing, and some because they maintain that their penis is not what defines them as men. What is most interesting is that transmen, who were often exclusively attracted to women when they identified as "butch" lesbians, are sometimes, after transitioning, attracted to other transmen, that is, Bockting's "new" orientation. This was true of Justin. Interestingly, it was true of Colby, as well, despite the fact that her male presentation was confined to her appearance and her name, or perhaps because Colby was bisexual. Colby and Justin had had a distinctive sexual relationship, as well: Justin was Colby's "Daddy," and Colby was the "boy," in a BDSM partnership. Colby's next relationship was with a vanilla lesbian and seemed solid in many ways, but unexciting to Colby sexually. Throughout the years, Colby has been consistent in her name, her dissatisfaction with *any* pronouns and with any gender definition, but also with her lack of interest in hormones or surgery. She had, until recently, seemed content with a female body and a male persona. She had primarily been polyamorous, and many of her relationships had been BDSM-oriented. She has had several female-bodied "Daddies" to which she has been "boy"; that is, lesbians who also have a male, dominant persona and are attracted to female-bodied submissives who have a young male persona. She had also had relationships in which she is "Daddy," and talks of these different sexual/gendered personas as different aspects of herself that are sometimes dominant and at other times disappear. She exhibited no signs of dissociative disorder or anything like it. In the sexual subculture in which Colby lived, these distinctions of personas or aspects of self were common, and commonly understood by others.

For several years Colby has been involved in a primary "girlfriend" relationship with Leslie. The couple is "open" and polyamorous. While they "play" with each other at BDSM events, they are not perfectly matched as sexual partners, and it may be possible that to maintain their relationship, which they both value, it is expedient to get some sexual needs met elsewhere.

Colby felt that no sexual orientation or gender labels fit. She called herself "gender fluid" and wished that the world recognized gender fluidity and gender complexity, as she felt it would make life easier for her. Most recently, Colby had expressed some dissatisfaction with her female body, but it is unclear whether this was because she was becoming gender dysphoric, or whether there was a more mundane reason. She had gained a substantial amount of weight, and may be primarily uncomfortable with her general body image, not the "femaleness" of her body.

Whatever happens with Colby, it is clear she cannot be put in a simple label or category. Her sexuality is defined as much by her BDSM proclivities and the roles she assumes with BDSM partners as it is by gender orientation. While she has been involved only with female-bodied partners in recent years, she has in the past also been sexual with transmen and biological males. While she presents primarily with a male persona, she has until recently seemed perfectly content with her female body.

Years ago, Pat Califia, an iconic "sexual outlaw" in the LGBT community since the 1980s (see http://www.queertheory.com/histories/c/califia_pat.htm) is famously rumored to have said, while self-identifying as lesbian, "if given the choice between a vanilla lesbian and gay male submissive, I'd take the gay boy anytime," thereby expressing her feeling that she was defined more by her BDSM sexuality, and particularly her persona as a dominant, than by her attraction to a particular gender. Califia, who ultimately transitioned to become a transman, Patrick Califia-Rice, involved with another transman, was prescient. Colby illustrates the fact that we have only begun to consider the many dimensions to sexuality; gender of partner is in some ways a simplistic view in the 21st century.

Summary

To reprise what was stated at the beginning of this chapter, the most important cross-cultural "facts" about homosexuality and transgenderism are: (a) that individuals who engage in same-sex sexuality suffer more societal discrimination than those who do not, as do gender variant people; (b) homophobia and transphobia are nearly universal worldwide problems. Given those truths, it is also true that different societies vary enormously in the extent of repression, the forms that same-sex attractions and gender variance manifest themselves, and the ways that cultures incorporate sexual and gender variations into the fabric of their societies. Just as importantly, cultures evolve and change in their tolerance for variant expression. A gay client who came of age in the United States before the 1960s will have had a very different life experience from one who matured post-Stonewall,[3] and even more different from the self-identified "gender-queer" young person of today. Therefore, the clinician who desires to be sensitive to LGBT issues must be familiar not only with cultural issues, but also with generational ones. Just as mainstream sexual mores change, so do subcultural sexual expressions, and a savvy therapist keeps abreast of those changes to understand the populations they serve.

Notes

1. My gratitude to my colleagues, licensed clinical social workers Michael LaSala, Susan Menahem, Jordan Hunt, Leora Perlman, and Michael Moran for the advice and experience they gave me in preparing this paper.
2. Argentine, Belgium, Iceland, Netherlands, Norway, Sweden, South Africa, and Spain.
3. The "Stonewall Revolution" in 1969, an event widely credited with beginning the Gay Liberation movement in the United States.

References

Amnesty International. (2010). Turkey urged to end discriminatory clampdown on gay rights groups. www-secure.amnesty.org

Baghemihl, B. (1999). *Biological exuberance*. New York: St. Martin's Press.
Bockting, W., Benner, A., & Coleman, E. (2009). Gay and bisexual identity development among female-to-male transsexuals in North America: Emergence of a transgender sexuality. *Archives of Sexual Behavior, 38*, 688–701.
Bolin, A. (1993). Transcending and transgendering: male to female transsexuals, dichotomy and diversity. In G. Herdt (Ed.), *Third sex, third gender* (pp. 447–485). New York: Zone Books.
Carrier, J. (1995). *De los otros: Intimacy and homosexuality among Mexican men*. New York: Columbia University Press.
CNN. (2007). Ahmadinejad speaks; Outrage and controversy follow. http://www.cnn.com/us
Cochrane, S. D., Sullivan, J. G., & Mays, V. M. (2003). Prevalence of mental disorders, psychological distress, and mental health services use among lesbian, gay and bisexual adults in the United States. *Journal of Consulting and Clinical Psychology, 71*, 53–61.
D'Emilio, J. D., & Freedman, E. B. (1988). *Intimate matters: A history of sexuality in America*. New York: Harper & Row.
Diamond, L. (2008). *Sexual fluidity: Understanding women's love and desire*. Cambridge, MA: Harvard University Press.
Donadio, R. (2009, January 5). Spain is a battleground for Church's future. http://www.nytimes.com
Friedman, E. (2010, September 29). Victim of secret dorm sex tape posts Facebook goodbye, jumps to his death. ABC News.
Ford, C., & Beach, F. (1951). *Patterns of sexual behavior*. New York: Harper & Brothers.
Green, R. (1987). *The sissy-boy syndrome and the development of homosexuality*. New Haven, CT: Yale University Press.
Greene, B. (2000). African American lesbian and bisexual women. *Journal of Social Issues: Women's Sexualities: Perspectives on Sexual Orientation and Gender, 56*, 239–249.
Gremaux, R. (1993). Woman becomes man in the Balkans. In G. Herdt (Ed.), *Third sex, third gender* (pp. 241–281). New York: Zone Books.
Grov, C., Bimbi, S., Nanin, J., & Parsons, J. (2006). Race, ethnicity, gender, and generational factors associated with the coming out process among gay, lesbian, and bisexual individuals. *Journal of Sex Research, 43*, 115–121
Herdt, G. (Ed.). (1993). *Third sex, third gender*. New York: Zone Books.
Herdt, G. (1997). *Same sex, different cultures*. Boulder, CO: Westview Press.
Hilliard, C. (2007, April 3). Girls to men: Young lesbians in Brooklyn find that a thug's life gets them more women. *Village Voice*. http://www.villagevoice.com
Hopkins, L. (2008, November 29). Top 10 gay friendly places to live: Countries where gays and lesbians have equal rights. http://www.*suite101.com*
Human Rights Watch. (2010a). Defending LGBT rights worldwide. http://www.hrw.org/en/news/2010/08/02/defending-lgbt-rights-worldwide
Human Rights Watch. (2010b, December 12). Iran: Discrimination and violence against sexual minorities. http://www.hrw.org
Jeffries, W., IV (2009). A comparative analysis of homosexual behaviors, sex role preferences, and anal sex proclivities in Latino and non-Latino men. *Archives of Sexual Behavior, 38*, 765–778.

LaSala, M. (2010, March 3). *Coming out, coming home.* New York: Columbia University Press.

Lau, S., (2010). Homosexuality in China. http://www.uschina.usc.edu

McGoldrick, M., Loonan, R., & Wohlsifer, D. (2007). Sexuality and culture, In S. Leiblum (Ed.), *Principles and practices of sex therapy* (4th ed., pp. 416–441). New York: Guilford.

Meston, C., & Buss, D. (2007). Why humans have sex. *Archives of Sexual Behavior, 36,* 477–507.

Nanda, S. (2000). *Gender diversity: Cross-cultural variations.* Long Grove, IL: Waveland Press.

Nestle, J. (1992). *The persistent desire: A femme-butch reader.* Boston, MA: Alyson Press.

Nichols, M., & Shernoff, M. (2007). Therapy with sexual minorities: Queering practice. In S. Leiblum (Ed.), *Principles and practices of sex therapy* (4th ed., pp. 379–415). New York: Guilford.

Phua, V. C. (2010). Negotiating sex and sexualities: the use of sexual tags in the Brazilian sex trade workplace. *Archives of Sexual Behavior, 39,* 831–841.

Ploderl, M., Kralovec, K., & Fartacek, R. (2008). The relation between sexual orientation and suicide attempts in Austria. *Archives of Sexual Behavior, 39,* 1403–1414.

Radio Nederland Wereldomreop (2010, October 10). Violence erupts at Serbia's Gay Pride parade. *Radio Netherlands Worldwide,* http: //www.mw.nl

Reback, C., & Larkins, S. (2010). Maintaining a heterosexual identity: Sexual meanings among a sample of heterosexually identified men who have sex with men. *Archives of Sexual Behavior, 39,* 766–773.

Rod2.0:Beta (2010, November 17). Arab, African nations block UN resolution on anti-gay violence. http://rodonline.typepad.com

Ross, M. Rosser, B., & Smolenski, D. (2010).The importance of measuring the internalized homophobia/homonegativity. *Archives of Sexual Behavior, 39,* 1207–1208.

Roughgarden, J. (2004). *Evolution's rainbow.* Berkeley: University of California Press.

Ryan, C., & Jetha, C. (2010). *Sex at dawn.* New York: Harper Collins.

Savin-Williams, R. C. (2005). *The new gay teenager.* Cambridge, MA: Harvard University Press.

Stulhofer, A., & Rimac, I. (2009). Determinants of homonegativity in Europe. *Journal of Sex Research, 46,* 24–32.

Tencer, D. (2010, October 28). Death penalty for gays will be law soon, Ugandan lawmaker says. http://www.rawstory.com

Townsend, M. (2010, October 28). Hey Brazil! Stop anti-gay hate crimes. http://www.gayrights.change.org .

Wikipedia. (2010). LGBT rights by country or territory. Retrieved from http://en.wikipedia.org/wiki/LGBT_rights_by_country_or_territory

Young, A. (2000). *Women who become men: Albanian sworn virgins.* Oxford, England: Burg.

Editors Introduction to Chapter 3
African Americans

African Americans are not only a distinct racial group, but are also a distinct cultural group inside the borders of the United States. Tracing their history in the United States from slavery to the present time, Kelly and Shelton observe that African Americans have been alienated from their traditional roots and are faced with a myriad of challenges to their sexuality and their relationships, not the least of which is the portrayal of African Americans in the media. African Americans differ from European Americans in many ways that are detailed in this chapter, including notions of beauty, fidelity, masculinity, family, and religion. The discrimination that many African Americans face is a vital difference in that it adds additional strain on families, relationships, and individual self-esteem.

Illustrated with the case of a couple dealing with infidelity, the authors describe how to tailor treatment to African Americans, drawing upon knowledge of the historical and current realities and myths about African American sexuality. The importance of communicating respect and affirming the positive in African American clients and couples is emphasized. Improving the couple's sexual relationship while addressing communication, trust, the need for excitement, and a revised masculine identity are all highlighted.

Therapists working in the United States will want to read this chapter to gain competence in working with African Americans. But the value of this chapter extends to therapists who want to understand the challenges of working with any strongly identified minority group, especially those that have a rather ambivalent relationship with the larger or more predominant culture.

3

AFRICAN AMERICAN COUPLES AND SEX

Shalonda Kelly and Jamye Shelton

Treatment of African American couples' sexual problems should include a contextualized understanding of their unique sexual and relationship profiles. African Americans engage in more premarital sex, have more frequent sex, and report more liberal attitudes about sex than their White counterparts (Cain et al., 2003; Mahay, Laumann, & Michaels, 2001; Weinberg & Williams, 1988). Despite some early evidence that African Americans fantasized more than their White counterparts, including fantasies of aggression, homosexual behavior, and oral and anal sex (Price & Miller, 1984), African Americans are less likely to engage in sexual activities outside of vaginal intercourse compared with Whites (Cain et al., 2003; Mahay et al., 2001). African American men also have more sexual partners than their White counterparts (Rao & Demaris, 1995). African American wives' sexual enjoyment is correlated with overall life satisfaction, whereas White wives' sexual enjoyment is correlated with feelings for their partners (Oggins, Veroff, & Leber, 1993). Because relationship quality and sexual functioning influence each other (Wiegel, Wincze, & Barlow, 2002), African Americans' higher never-married and divorce rates, lower remarriage rates, greater complaints of negative partner behavior, and lower relationship quality compared with their White counterparts is notable (Philips & Sweeney, 2005). The sexuality field has been criticized for failing to contextualize the foregoing descriptive findings. When taken out of the context of African Americans' unique experiences, the foregoing descriptive findings do not increase our understanding of African Americans, and may lead readers to pathologize them (McGruder, 2009; Wyatt, 1994).

This chapter serves three purposes. We first provide a context for understanding African American sexuality, which includes attention to historical, socialization, and oppression factors that they disproportionately experience, such as slavery, negative media images, socioeconomic issues, racism, stigma, and maladaptive methods used by some African Americans to cope with their context. We counterbalance negative contexts with a focus on the sexuality-related and general strengths of African Americans that can often go overlooked in the face of stigma and oppression. These include a favorable body image, liberal sexual attitudes and behavior, self-esteem and a positive identity, religiosity, and family and community ties. Second, we detail how knowledge of such contexts can be used to affirm African American couples and use their strengths to address sexual problems. This includes tailoring of assessments and instruments to overcome treatment reluctance, communicate respect, and obtain information unique to this group. We detail how treatment can reinstate lost strengths, counter negative myths and stressors with a positive identity, increase community support, and foster sexual communication and sexual variety. Third, this focus on strengths is demonstrated with a case example.

Historical and Socialization Factors Related to African American Sexuality

Slavery to Present Day Views of African Americans' Sexuality

When the ancestors of today's African Americans were brought to the Americas as slaves, family groups were separated, and their cultural norms were shattered (Hines & Boyd-Franklin, 2005; Staples, 1972). Traditional African families placed a priority on the extended family, which served as a link between each individual's present and past, and enabled all members to participate in the raising of children. Marriage was considered the linking of two families, and the core of the relationship was the reproduction of offspring (McDaniel, 1990). Conversely, slaves' marriage choices had no legal basis, and these unions were only acknowledged within their own communities. Moreover, husbands, wives, and children were separated without consideration for their chosen unions or their feelings. Men and women were forcibly paired and bred like livestock with the goal of producing offspring that were ideal for physical labor (Hines & Boyd-Franklin, 2005).

The traumas of slavery were accepted in part because African slaves were dehumanized through the perpetuation of overwhelmingly negative stereotypes about them. A deliberate attempt was made to invalidate and eradicate African slaves' culture and history of achievements (Black & Jackson, 2005). Simultaneously, Social Darwinist theories were applied negatively to slaves that portrayed them as inferior, amoral, and the lowest racial group in the hierarchy, deficient in areas of intelligence, health, civility, and basic reasoning (Goff, Eberhardt, Williams, & Jackson, 2008; Stephens & Philips, 2003). Such dehumanizing stereotypes of African slaves lowered their worth to three-fifths of the value of their White counterparts, and enabled cruel acts to be committed against them (Goff et al., 2008). A famous historical example of this dehumanization is the purportedly scientific examination of the deceased body of an African woman called the "Hottentot Venus," whose physical features were compared to those of orangutans. This perspective began a long history of oppression and invalidation based upon skin color and culture that continues into the present day (Stephens & Philips, 2003).

The dehumanization of slaves extended into the sexual arena. Widespread sexual abuse of African American women occurred during slavery, with the added benefit that the resulting children became property whose labor further contributed to the wealth of the slave masters (Stephens & Philips, 2003). Although slave women were made to satisfy their masters' sexual needs, negative sexual myths about their "animalistic" hypersexuality were perpetuated to legitimize these rapes. For example, the examination of the Hottentot Venus contributed to the belief that people of African descent were amoral, highly sexual, and promiscuous. African slave men were similarly portrayed as animalistic and hypersexual, as well as immoral, violent, and lazy (Blake & Darling, 1994). The additional portrayal of African American men as violent and predatory freed White men to harass and commit violence toward them for actual or imagined sexual interactions with White women (Donovan, 2007).

African Americans continue to be viewed negatively and stereotypically. Stephens and Phillips (2003) identified eight common stereotypes of African American women that build upon those begun in slavery, and present sex as a central feature of their identities. Three examples are the "freak," a sexually aggressive and wild woman who wants sex without an emotional attachment, the "matriarch," a controlling, emasculating woman who does not need a man for anything other than his seed, and the "gold digger," willing to provide sex for financial gain. The negative images of African American women perpetuate the views begun in slavery of African American men and women as animalistic and hypersexual, and they foster adversarial relationships between African American men and women (Hines & Boyd-Franklin, 2005; Stephens & Phillips 2003). They serve a second function of marginalizing African American men, because they also imply that African American men are not necessary for anything other than sex (Stephens & Phillips 2003). Indeed, a small qualitative study showed that African American boys and girls see African American males as both sexually driven and sexually knowledgeable (Stephens & Few, 2007). Such stereotypes perniciously perpetuate views that African American men are removed from active family life, and that they are uncaring, undependable, and unavailable to their families (Hines & Boyd-Franklin, 2005; Stephens

& Phillips, 2003). Socialization towards such stereotypes begins early, particularly with the media.

Media Socialization of Negative and Stereotypic Depictions of African Americans' Sexuality

Sexual images are broadcast widely to American youth, and are associated with negative effects (Ward, 2003; Ward, Hansbrough, & Walker, 2005). Mass media and television (TV) in particular are major sources of sexual knowledge, as the average American youth spends more time watching TV than interacting with his or her parents (Ward, 2003). Theories suggest that viewers adopt and mimic the portraits of reality presented in TV and other media, particularly if the images are accessible, deemed similar to the youth, are powerful, rewarded, fit with their experiences, and have functional value (Ward, 2003; Wingood et al., 2003). TV offers pervasive sexual content and numerous dynamic and appealing examples of being a man or a woman, but the roles are narrow, with women being depicted primarily as sexual objects, caregivers, or subordinates, and men as dominant and aggressive leaders (Ward, 2003; Ward et al., 2005). Also, 44 to 76% of music videos on TV contain sexual imagery, watched predominately by youth (Ward, 2003). Ward's (2003) review of 64 content analyses and 36 effects studies using predominately White samples consistently revealed that greater exposure to sexually oriented genres like music videos and magazines is associated with unhealthy sexual attitudes, expectations, and behaviors. Examples are greater acceptance of stereotypical and casual attitudes about sex, beliefs that sexual activity is common among youth, displeasure with virginity, attitudes that support sexual harassment, as well as more sexual partners and sexual experience, particularly for women (Peterson, Wingood, DiClemente, Harrington, & Davies, 2007; Ward, 2003; Ward et al., 2005).

Consistent with theories of media influence, African American adolescents may be at greater risk for developing negative sexual attitudes and behaviors (Ward et al., 2005). African American households watch 75 hours of TV per week, compared with 52 hours per week for the average American household (Tirodkar & Jain, 2003). Hip-hop and rap are the only genres that predominately contain images of African Americans, and they are popular among Black youth and more likely to be shown on channels marketed to African Americans (Ward et al., 2005). Prevalent themes in rap music videos include economic deprivation, racial injustice, social isolation, hopelessness, dysfunction, and disparaging images and treatment of women (Peterson et al., 2007). Rap and hip-hop also portray high sexual and negative content (Rouse-Arnett & Dilworth, 2006). For example, a content analysis examined rates of sex and violence across 203 randomly selected videos from the music genres of rap, hip-hop, rock, rhythm and blues, and country and western from Black Entertainment TV, MTV, VH-1, and TNN (Jones, 1997). Notably, hip-hop music presented significantly more fondling, simulated intercourse, simulated oral sex, sex talk, women wearing "hot" pants, and male and female sexual dancing than the other genres. Rap music presented significantly more images of simulated masturbation, as well as almost all forms of violence, profanity, and substance use as compared with the other genres.

Research suggests that some African American youth may embrace negative in-group stereotypes and incorrectly use them as norms by which to judge themselves and their peers. In a study of 152 male and female African American high school students, aged 14 to 18, youth reported watching an average of 3 hours per day of music videos (Ward et al., 2005). Factor analysis of a measure of gender role beliefs revealed a factor labeled "flash," containing items judging the importance of stereotypical traits such as being athletic, rich, attractive, and cool, and a factor labeled "substance," containing items judging the importance of being nice, intelligent, and having a good sense of humor. Watching music videos was associated with endorsing traditional gender role attitudes, such as beliefs that boys are better leaders than girls, and with assigning importance to flash for men and women. Moreover, youth in the condition of watching four sexually explicit videos endorsed more items reflecting flash as compared with those in the control group that watched music videos without sexual content. For these youth, high identification with the characters predicted endorsing flash as important (Ward et al., 2005).

Viewing of stereotypical images in music videos also predicts negative sexual behavior by African American youth. In one study of 522 adolescent African American females aged 14 to 18, over 95% had viewed rap videos, and the median hours of exposure to rap music was 14 hours per week (Wingood et al., 2003). Exposure to rap music was associated prospectively with increased odds of having multiple sexual partners, acquiring an STD, being arrested, committing violence, and using drugs and alcohol in the ensuing year (Wingood et al., 2003). Specifically, after controlling for amount of exposure and perceptions about what constitutes healthy relationships, perceptions that rap videos contained sexually stereotypical content (e.g., Black women are portrayed as sexual objects) was associated with greater odds of using alcohol and drugs, having multiple sex partners and a negative body image (Peterson et al., 2007). After controlling for depression, self-esteem, and body mass index, the female adolescents in the sample who had a negative body image were more likely to perceive themselves as having fewer options for sexual partners, having little control in their sexual relationships, fearing abandonment as a result of negotiating condom use, and reporting that they had not used condoms during sex in the past 30 days (Wingood, DiClemente, Harrington, & Davies, 2002).

Media stereotypes also reinforce negative views of African Americans for Whites who have little contact with them. A nationally representative study showed that the attitudes of Whites toward African Americans were more negative than their attitudes toward Whites and other ethnic minorities (Wilson, 1996). For example, one study exposed White male and female students to music sung by attractive African American females in the form of sexually explicit rap or romantic love songs, or to no music, and then asked them to rate African American and White women on a list of traits (Gan, Zillmann, & Mitrook, 1997). Beyond a main effect of White women being judged more positively than African American women for all ratings, exposure to sexually enticing rap music fostered perceptions of greater negative traits of African American women, and fewer positive traits, as compared with the control condition of no music. Notably, the negative perceptions of African American women that were fostered by the videos did not generalize to perceptions of White women (Gan et al., 1997). This may be due to the history of slavery and dehumanizing of those of African descent that prevents society from seeing African American women as pure and virginal (Stephens & Phillips, 2003). One study found that White male college undergraduates perceived Black female rape victims as more promiscuous than their White counterparts (Donovan, 2007). Moreover, 58% of the male participants and 63% of the female participants incorrectly rated Black males as most likely to rape a White woman (Donovan, 2007), further suggesting that the legacy of slavery persists.

While parental socialization is important for all youth, negative media images play a dominant role in relationship socialization for African American youth. The legacy of slavery and higher likelihood of being raised in a single-parent household (Hollar, 2001) results in fewer models of healthy intimate African American relationships to counter media effects (Kelly, 2003). African American parents socialize their children about sex, but the tendency for some to explain sex usually in the context of contraception and neglect discussion of STDs and relational concerns exacerbates their children's reliance on media images (Rouse-Arnett & Dilworth, 2006). Conversely, many African American couples model everyday examples of healthy intimacy, but some African American youth still prefer to embrace the desirable and exciting images in the media that receive greater public recognition and endorsement (Franklin, 2004).

Oppression Factors That Facilitate Negative Sexual Stereotypes and Behavior

Socioeconomic Status

Socioeconomic status (SES) is a general context indicative of structural advantage or disadvantage, and in the case of African Americans it is economic structural disadvantage that is disproportionately experienced by them. Poverty rates among African Americans are among the highest in America, and African Americans have significantly less education than their White counterparts (Dalaker, 2001). The family stress model, validated with African American and other couples, posits that limited socioeconomic resources lead to negative mood states that in turn lead to marital conflict, low levels of warmth in couple relationships, and problems in parent–child relationships (Conger & Donellan, 2007). Studies show too that employment problems, lower financial resources, financial strain, and lower levels of education are associated with marital conflict, less family and marital satisfaction, and divorce among African Americans (e.g., Brody, Stoneman, & Flor, 1995; Raur, Karney, Garvan, & Hou, 2008).

Low SES also is related to lower condom use, and casual sexual attitudes and behavior. Low SES groups are less likely to spend scarce financial resources on condoms (Wingood & DiClemente, 1998). They have higher rates of abusive relationships, and women in these relationships are also less likely to use condoms, so as to avoid physical harm (Wingood & DiClemente, 1997). Low SES groups tend to be more accepting of sexual activity and young women begin sexual relations earlier (Browning & Burrington, 2006). In fact, African Americans' higher endorsement of attitudes that are supportive of early sexual behavior are fully accounted for by individual/peer-, family-, and neighborhood-level factors, such as peer deviance, family attachment and support, and neighborhood poverty. In support of family and individual factors are findings that African American youth who are unemployed and have less parental monitoring have greater exposure to rap music, which in turn is associated with casual sexual attitudes and behavior (Wingood et al., 2003). Still, neighborhood poverty consistently and significantly accounts for over a quarter of the variance in the differences in racial attitudes even when family and individual variables are considered (Browning & Burrington, 2006).

Racism, Stigma, and Associated Ills

The pathology model that is commonly applied to African Americans proposes that they are deviant and inferior (Hines & Boyd-Franklin, 2005), such as with the aforementioned prevalent stereotypes. Thus, it is unsurprising that some African Americans accept and internalize negative images of their own group, which are associated with less individual well-being (Kelly, 2004), and poorer relationship quality (Kelly & Floyd, 2006). In fact, in Stephens and Few's (2007) small qualitative study of African American youth, both genders reported that boys preferred African American girls who were light skinned with long hair and whose features were commonly considered to be more characteristic of Whites than Blacks. Some African American women report significant concerns about societal preferences for White and light-skinned women (Kelly, Floyd, Bhagwat, Morgan, & Scott, 2010), and persons with phenotypic African features are judged more likely to have negative stereotypic traits ascribed to them (Blair, Judd, Sadler, & Jenkins, 2002). Moreover, in the National Survey of Black Americans, lighter skin tone of the women was significantly associated with greater attractiveness ratings (Hill, 2002). Conversely, White Americans are taught to fear African American men and treat them according to sexual and violent stereotypes, consistent with media showing them engaging in high rates of violence, drugs, and profanity (Jones, 1997). This renders invisible African American men's personal traits and accomplishments and marginalizes them (Franklin, 2004).

Likely due to their stigmatized status, African Americans receive differential treatment that adversely affects their individual and couple well-being. For example, they face discrimination in education, health care, employment, housing, and the media (Clark, Anderson, Clark, & Williams, 1999; Coleman, 2003; Coltraine & Messineo, 2000; Hollar, 2001; Ross & Turner, 2005). A review of 53 studies showed robust associations between self-reports of racism and personal distress (Williams, Neighbors, & Jackson, 2003). For African Americans, self-reports of racism are also associated with self-reports of poor relationship quality (Murry, Brown, Brody, Cutrona, & Simmons, 2001), and marital hostility (Murry, 2008).

Stigma and differential treatment of African Americans results in accumulated social ills that are not due to inherent pathology, but rather due to the aforementioned pernicious assaults. While all African Americans are affected by stigma in some way, there is evidence suggesting that the impact on African American men is greater. African American male youth have a 50% higher chance of dying before age 20 compared to White counterparts, primarily due to homicide, drug abuse, suicide, and accidents (Blake & Darling, 1994). Higher violence rates for African Americans can be largely explained by factors such as the neighborhood social context and family disruption (i.e. divorce and single parenthood; Sampson, Morenoff, & Raudenbush, 2005). Over 200,000 of the nearly 500,000 regular crack users are African American, the vast majority of whom are in the marriageable age range (Lawson & Thompson, 1994). Moreover, there is a one in four chance that an African American male will be incarcerated within his lifetime (Unnever, 2008). African American men are also at a higher risk to receive poor health care (Hollar, 2001), have prostate cancer, an earlier age of diagnosis, more advanced cancer at diagnosis, and increased mortality than men of other ethnicities (Jenkins et al., 2004).

Hypermasculinity as a Coping Response

Due to their extensive linkages with socioeconomic factors that are associated with masculine roles, the aforementioned social ills engender compensatory hypermasculine behaviors in some African American men. African American men perceive more racism than women (Clark, 2004), and their decreased economic opportunities coexist with a societal expectation that men are primary providers (Hines & Boyd-Franklin, 2005). Inability to meet provider roles is associated with reductions in family satisfaction and other quality of life indices (Bowman, 1992). Moreover, African American men's provider role difficulties and negative racial views sometimes elicit anxiety and distress that contribute to marital distress (Kelly & Floyd, 2001, 2006). Societal assaults on African American men can lead them to establish closer relationships with other African American men to buffer against such mistreatment and to provide reassurance about their masculinity and capacity to survive (Franklin, 2004; Majors & Billson, 1992). Due to fewer role models that are available, and the appealing nature of media images, African American adolescent males may begin to view media images as a false criterion for manhood, and encourage each other to enact those roles. Notably, these images present them in superficially appealing roles as athletes, criminals, cool and stylish, hypermasculine, and highly sexual, roles which are easy to enact in daily life (e.g. Franklin, 2004). A well-known example is the defiant, confident, highly sexual, and womanizing African American detective portrayed in the movie *Shaft* (Franklin, 2004).

Mahalik, Good, and Englar-Carlson (2003) reviewed studies showing that excessive beliefs in masculine ideals can hinder all men's mental health, and the quality of their intimate and sexual relationships. In the findings they reviewed, men who endorsed high levels of 11 masculine ideals reported greater personal distress. Some examples of masculine beliefs that are particularly pertinent to intimate relationships are the belief in the need to be the "strong and silent" partner, a "playboy," a "winner," or "independent." Men who feel a need to be "strong and silent" may be more likely to suppress emotions and fear intimacy in a relationship. Similarly, identification with being a "playboy" may lead to decreased emotional attachment and fear of intimacy, as well as the use of sex only to sate lust, and never as a means to increase emotional intimacy in a relationship. Moreover, because of the emphasis on multiple sexual partners, being a "playboy" can increase the risk of exposure to STDs. Those who believe that men are "winners" may view relationships in terms of winners and losers, and thus have a preponderance of adversarial relationships, including their romantic relationships. Also, those who hold that men should be "independent" may believe that they should not seek help, even from their mates, and thus be more stressed overall and aloof in their relationships (Mahalik et al., 2003). For African American men, beliefs in masculine ideals like these are associated with poor mental health (Mahalik, Pierre, & Wan, 2006), and nationally representative data show that they are less likely than other men to engage in sex because of love (Mahay et al., 2001).

The Sex Ratio Imbalance and Infidelity

The forgoing oppression factors and use of maladaptive coping responses contribute to a skewed sex ratio and infidelity. Skewed sex ratios refer to situations wherein many more African American women are available for relationships than there are African American men (Hines & Boyd-Franklin, 2005). While some African Americans maintain positive romantic relationships despite oppression, some cope maladaptively with the gender-ratio imbalance. For example, some African American women compete for men who refuse to commit because many women are available to them (Aborampah, 1989), which may lead both to believe that the women are rendered powerless to demand condom use during sex (Wingood & DiClemente, 1998). Alternatively, reluctant "man sharing" or infidelity may occur (Choi, Catania, & Dolcini, 1994; Wingood & DiClemente, 1998). SES can exacerbate sex ratio issues because African American men who cannot meet the societal expectations of the provider role may resort to infidelity as a maladaptive way to demonstrate their manhood (Kelly & Boyd-Franklin, 2009; Majors & Billson, 1992). Qualitative data suggest that struggles with competition and infidelity begin early for African American youth (Stephens & Few, 2007). Such situations promote adversarial relationships and reduced trust (Lawson & Thompson, 1994; Kelly, 2003).

Extramarital sexual relationships are more common among African American couples than White couples, and infidelity predicts marital instability. In one large nationally representative study, after controlling for education, not only did being a man increase the odds of infidelity by 79%, but being African American was associated with a 106% increase in the odds of infidelity (Treas & Giesen, 2000). Moreover, being African American remained a significant predictor of extramarital sex even after interest in sex, sexual values, opportunities for infidelity, and relationship quality were included in the model. Such findings should not be interpreted as inherently pathological, but as influenced by social ills (Kelly, 2003). Notably, the opportunities for infidelity that were measured in the study, such as having a job that requires touching, talking, or being alone with others, or having few shared family or friendship networks with the partner, all predicted odds of infidelity (Treas & Giesen, 2000). Yet the study did not measure potential opportunities for infidelity that may be specific to African Americans. For example, the imbalanced sex ratio may provide African American men with more opportunities for infidelity with unmarried African American women, which may contribute to the greater prevalence of extramarital affairs for this population (Choi, Catania, & Delcini, 1994; Treas & Giesen, 2000). Similarly, members of other societies use infidelity to cope with unbalanced sex ratios, because viable alternatives exist for the less available gender (Taylor, Chatters, & Jackson, 1997).

The sex ratio imbalance and infidelity are associated with other relationship problems, single-parenthood, and STDs that are disproportionately experienced by African Americans. For example, men with sexual problems are more likely to commit infidelity than their counterparts who do not have sexual problems, perhaps to validate themselves via sex with many women (Choi et al., 1994; Robinson, Scheltema, & Cherry, 2005). Also, a wide misconception is that partners' use of condoms is an indication of sexual disloyalty (Wingood & DiClemente, 1998). Consistent with this view, one study found that the majority of unfaithful men did not use condoms regularly (Choi et al., 1994). African Americans are significantly less likely than other groups to use condoms and other contraception (Gaydos, Neubert, Hogue, Kramer, & Yang, 2010), which can facilitate the greater rates of unplanned pregnancies and live births, and HIV/AIDS among African American women (Rao & Demaris, 1995; Salazar et al., 2005). Qualitative data provides context in suggesting that social ills and uncertainty faced by African American women may lead some to forego contraceptives and become single parents as an alternate route to stability and long term attachment (Burton & Tucker, 2009). Such complications likely make it harder to treat sexual problems.

Strengths that Enhance the Sexual Relationships of African Americans

Strengths in the Physical and Sexual Arenas

Despite the foregoing negative contexts, meta-analysis confirms more favorable body image evaluations for Blacks as compared with Whites, on both weight-focused and global body image measures (Roberts, Cash, Feingold, & Johnson, 2006). For example, African American women worry less about weight, dieting, or being thin, prefer being a little overweight versus a little underweight, and their weight loss attempts are more realistic and less extreme than White women's attempts (Molloy & Herzberger, 2002). They also report fewer negative thoughts about their bodies than their White counterparts (Miller, Gleaves, Hirsch, Green, Snow, & Corbett, 2000; Schooler, Ward, Merriwether, & Caruthers, 2004). Moreover, such differences in perceptions are present across each weight class (Siegel, 2002), and persist despite negative feedback about the impression that they make on others, unlike with their White counterparts (Henriques, Calhoun, & Cann, 1996). Theories about these differences range from African American women's greater emphasis on their ability as an indicator of self-worth, within-group comparisons that may be more favorable than out-group comparisons, fewer tendencies to perceive being overweight as unattractive, and greater focus on how to make the best of the bodies that they have (Siegel, 2002). Racial differences in body image are accounted for by African American women's more accurate beliefs that their men prefer larger women, as well as African American women's endorsement of more masculine self-descriptors as compared with their White counterparts (Demarest & Allen, 2000; Markey, Markey, & Birch, 2004; Molloy & Herzberger, 2002). These findings are consistent with data showing that women's endorsement of masculine and androgynous traits is associated with high self-esteem, positive body image, and satisfaction with their own sexuality (Lennon, Rudd, Sloan, & Kim, 1999; Molloy & Herzberger, 2002).

A positive body image has positive implications for the individual and the couple's sexual relationship, while a negative body image is associated with sexual difficulties. A positive body image is associated with higher self-esteem and decreased depression (Siegel, 2002). Satisfaction with body image also is associated with adolescents' perceptions of greater control in their sexual relationships (Wingood et al., 2002). Body image also includes perceptions of one's own sexual attractiveness, which are greater for African Americans than for their White counterparts (Miller et al., 2000; Schooler et al., 2004). In a sample of 320 predominately White college students, appearance concerns, aspects of an unfavorable body image, were associated with self-reported difficulties in achieving arousal and orgasm, and decreased sexual pleasure (Sanchez & Kiefer, 2007). Moreover, for both men and women, sexual self-consciousness during physical intimacy mediated the relationship between body shame and difficulties in achieving arousal, although the levels of these three variables were significantly higher and the relationship between them was stronger for women than for men (Sanchez & Kiefer, 2007). Thus, theory and data show that negative self-focused cognitions, including those about one's body image, impair sexual arousal and performance by interfering with concentration on sexual pleasure and erotic stimuli (Bach, Wincze, & Barlow, 2001; Sanchez & Kiefer, 2007).

African Americans' liberal sexual attitudes and behavior may be considered as an asset to their sexuality in the situations where they positively evaluate their sexual attitudes and behavior. African Americans rate sex as being more important and have more frequent sex than their White counterparts (Cain et al., 2003). Moreover, their sexual enjoyment is associated with greater life satisfaction, which is not the case for their White counterparts (Oggins et al., 1993). For example, using a national probability sample of African American and White women, Bancroft, Loftus, and Long (2003) found that women in relationships who had been sexually active in the past 4 weeks were more likely to think about sex with interest each day and feel more sexually attractive. Those who reported more frequent sex also reported less distress about their sexual relationship and greater mental health (Bancroft et al., 2003). Thus, perhaps African Americans' liberal attitudes and behavior may be more likely to result in a positive sexual relationship and good mental health than for their White counterparts. Such benefits may persist in the face of oppressive sexual stereotypes about African American women, as evidenced by findings that African American women who believed that they were *more* sexual than they ought to be ironically reported less dejection, less agitation, and fewer somatic complaints (Holmes, 2002). Yet it is important that African Americans positively evaluate their sexuality, as African American women who are bothered by the difference between their actual sexual selves and their sexual ideal are more likely to report dejection (Holmes, 2002).

General Strengths of African Americans that may be Applied to Their Sexual Relationships

Nationally representative data show that despite being more stigmatized than other groups (Wilson, 1996), African Americans tend to have higher self-esteem than both Whites and other persons of color (Gray-Little & Hafdahl, 2000; Twenge & Crocker, 2002). Self-esteem is positively associated with body esteem, body image, and body satisfaction (Molloy & Herzberger, 2002), as well as with sexual self-esteem (Zeanah & Schwarz, 1996). For African American female adolescents, self-esteem is positively associated with frequent communication with sex partners, and efficacious negotiation of condom usage (Salazar et al., 2005). Poor African American male youth report that they engage in sex and have more sexual partners as a means to increase their self-esteem and power (Robinson, Holmbeck, & Paikoff, 2007).

African Americans' positive racial or ethnic identity may provide some protection against racism and discrimination. Positive racial identity attitudes are associated with better well-being and less psychological distress (Franklin-Jackson & Carter, 2007; Kelly et al., 2010). Family preparation for the difficulties of overcoming racist barriers serves to buffer African Americans from the effects of racism on their own mental health (Fischer & Shaw, 1999). Also, discussing racial stress and discrimination with one's partner may elicit support and externalize the experience by placing it in a wider social context (Murry et al., 2001).

Research also has consistently shown positive associations between a positive ethnic or racial identity and self-esteem for African Americans

(Gray-Little & Hafdahl, 2000; Okech & Harrington, 2002). Conversely, endorsement of items indicating racial self-hatred is associated with poor self-esteem for African Americans (Vandiver, Cross, Worrell, & Fhagen-Smith, 2002). Moreover, studies show that ethnic identity is more salient for African Americans and more strongly associated with their self-esteem as compared with Whites (Gray-Little & Hafdahl, 2000). Meta-analytic findings show that African Americans' higher self-esteem relative to other groups began in the 60s, around the time of the civil rights era and Black pride movement, and that self-esteem is higher for African Americans residing in the South, where a higher proportion of African Americans reside. These and other patterns of findings suggest that African Americans' high self-esteem may be linked to the positivity and centrality of ethnic and racial identities (Gray-Little & Hafdahl, 2000; Twenge & Crocker, 2002).

A positive Black identity also may be beneficial for African Americans' sexual relationships, due to its links to a positive body image. For example, African American women's endorsement of internalization attitudes indicative of a positive Black racial identity is associated with more favorable evaluations of their physical appearance, level of fitness, and health orientation (Harris, 1995), and their endorsement of a positive ethnic identity is associated with fewer negative thoughts about their bodies (Schooler et al., 2004). In addition, degree of watching popular television shows with predominately Black casts (such as *Family Matters*, *Living Single*, and *Moesha*) for the two seasons considered in one study, is associated with more positive body images (Schooler et al., 2004). Conversely, endorsement of a racial identity that involves preference for White or mainstream culture is positively associated with a fear of fatness, drive for thinness, and restraining one's food intake among Black female college students (Abrams, Allen, & Gray, 1993). Fortunately, data also show that for African American women with low ethnic identities, watching Black television is associated with healthier body images as well (Schooler et al., 2004). Thus, a positive identity, self-esteem, and positive body image are potentially key factors in combating the societal emphasis on light skin tones and long straight hair as indicators of greater attractiveness (Hill, 2002).

Religiosity is a strength that contributes to African Americans' resilient adaptation to stress and discrimination as individuals and couples (Kelly, 2003). African Americans report higher levels of religiosity than other groups (Taylor, Mattis, & Chatters, 1999). The church is the most central, oldest, and influential institution within the African American community (Ward, 2005), and it provides status roles, such as deacons and pastors (Kelly, 2003). Churches have socially integrative functions; they provide doctrine regarding ideal marital roles and socialize couples in ways that positively impact their marital and family lives (Taylor et al., 1999). Moreover, many churches have marriage ministries designed to help couples to maintain their faith together, and to strengthen the marital relationship. Consistent with those doctrines and activities, married African Americans score significantly higher on religiosity variables than unmarried individuals (Taylor et al., 1999), likely due to their positive association with individual and family well-being for African Americans (Brody, Stoneman, & Flor, 1996). For example, high levels of religiosity are associated with warm, supportive interactions and low conflict between these spouses, which in turn leads to increased parent–child relationship quality (Brody, Stoneman, & Flor, 1995). Moreover, higher frequency of churchgoing in men is associated with lower levels of extramarital sexual activity (Choi et al., 1994).

African culture emphasizes family and community ties (Boyd-Franklin, 2003), and strong, familylike bonds can include anyone with whom individuals feel very close, including those unrelated by blood (Boyd-Franklin, 2003). Family and kinship bonds enable interdependence, such as turning to each other for help with marital and other problems, and sharing in decision making. African Americans' involvement in community organizations includes churches, fraternities, or sororities, and Black professional groups provide them with mentoring, resources, and services, and promote a self-help orientation (Kelly & Boyd-Franklin, 2009).

Treatment of African Americans' Sexual Problems in Context

Tailoring Assessment and Treatment to African Americans' Common Concerns

There is a community-wide reluctance for African Americans to participate in therapy for any problems, particularly among the poor (Kelly, 2003). This reluctance is due a lack of information about what therapy involves (Tucker, 1980), and healthy cultural paranoia in which Whites and service providers deemed as part of the establishment are not trusted (Boyd-Franklin, 2003). Empathic discussion of an individual's feelings about being in treatment that anticipates probable feelings of discomfort, normalizes those feelings as common, normal, healthy, and intelligent, and includes the therapist's discussion of honest positive feelings about the therapy, is crucial (Tucker, 1980). Sensitively and respectfully provided role-induction and joining can ensure that expectations are consistent across the therapist and the partner (Kelly, 2003). For example, in the first session, both African American and other couples should be made aware that no sexual behaviors are practiced within the session, but they will be asked to discuss their sexual desires, aversions, and experiences with arousal and orgasm, as well as their strengths, skills, and the most distressing aspect of their problem(s) (McCarthy & Thestrup, 2008). The therapist can note that any discomfort is likely to gradually reduce, and that the therapist will check in periodically to ensure that their concerns are treated with respect. It also can help for them to know that while the first session is devoted to exploring the sexual problem in the context of the relationship, during the one individual session with each that follows, they will be asked about their individual sexual histories and preferences, which implicitly conveys that sensitive or secret material doesn't have to be shared immediately in front of the partner (McCarthy & Thestrup, 2008). They also can be reassured that other individual sessions can occur on an as-needed basis, to discuss material that is hard to share in a conjoint format.

Therapists should know about African Americans' rates of sexual dysfunctions and common contributing factors. African American women have higher rates of disorders related to low sexual desire and low sexual pleasure than their White and Latina counterparts (Laumann, Paik, & Rosen, 1999). African American men have higher rates of erectile difficulties (Laumann, West, Glasser, Carson, Rosen, & Kang, 2007) and priapism, a sexual pain disorder characterized by a painful, prolonged erection that can occur as a complication of sickle cell disease (Bennett & Mulhall, 2008). Poor emotional well-being and a poor emotional relationship with the partner during sex predict women's distress about their sexual relationship and their own sexuality (Bancroft et al., 2003), while mental and physical health, less education and household income and more financial strain are risk factors for sexual dysfunctions in men and women (Laumann et al., 1999). Given that many of these factors are disproportionately experienced by African Americans, they need to be explored in relation to African Americans' sex lives.

Some African Americans are reluctant to share sensitive information with outsiders (Boyd-Franklin, 2003). Lack of discussion does not mean that there is no problem in the area that has not been discussed. Questionnaires regarding sexuality often can be less threatening and elicit information that is not offered verbally (Perry et al., 2002), which the therapist can use to facilitate discussions of taboo topics. Yet many sexuality-related measures do not have available norms (Wiegel et al., 2002), and typically only the ones assessing HIV/AIDs and risky sexual behaviors have specific norms for African Americans. Also, drop-out of African Americans seeking general couple therapy is positively associated with requests for them to complete a battery of questionnaires (Rogge et al., 2006), which may be even more likely with a sensitive topic like sexuality. Thus, therapists should not overwhelm African American couples with many questionnaires. Also, it helps to ask for elaboration on sensitive sexual topics at multiple points in treatment, because more information may be provided in later sessions after a rapport has been established and safety is assured. Within the individual sessions it is useful to ask each partner directly, gently, and empathically about their most negative, guilt inducing, or traumatic sexual experiences (McCarthy & Thestrup, 2008). Similarly, therapists should ask about the financial resources and status of the couple, which are vulnerable points for some African Americans that can affect their self-esteem, identity, or sexual performance (Kelly, 2003). Safety of disclosure can be increased by therapists' genuine notice of external contributors to problems, such as a tough economy and the foregoing structural factors that impact African Americans, and also by therapists' acceptance of racism frames as explanations.

Therapists also should ask African Americans about cultural identity and sources of self-esteem and pride as well as stigma, internalized negative stereotypes, and shame factors, which may be used in treatment (Hardy & Lazloffy 2002; Kelly & Boyd-Franklin, 2009). For example, therapists should ask couples to discuss important aspects of their identities, how it is for them as African Americans overall, and with others who are and are not African American, and about the ways that they do and do not identify with their racial and ethnic backgrounds. The goal is to convey that anything can be discussed, and to elicit both positive and negative in-group views, and views of the self as an African American (see Kelly & Boyd-Franklin, 2009 for more details). In addition, questionnaires can assess racial or ethnic identities and negative stereotypes (Kelly & Floyd, 2006; Phinney & Ong, 2007; Vandiver et al., 2002).

Therapists should be alert for and explore sexuality-specific experiences and perceived linkages between those experiences and being African American. These can include partners' perceptions about how African American sexuality is portrayed in the media, or any associations between sexuality and oppression. At times, experiences can lead some to belief in myths, such as that all African Americans are supposed to have sex frequently, having sex is central to how to be a man or a woman, or that African American men are automatically supposed to know what to do sexually. Therapists' responses to these experiences and beliefs should be to request elaboration, validate and empathize, corroborate (i.e. "others have said this too"), and ask about feelings related to such beliefs. For positive, prideful responses, therapists should acknowledge strengths or elicit additional information with positive conversation, and for negative in-group or shame-related responses, therapists should not take offense, but find ways to validate the person and empathize with negative feelings or views, such as with, "I think that experience would make any child feel isolated from their ethnic background." Indeed, participants who received such responses to disclosures about their ethnicity rated interviewers as more knowledgeable and respectful than interviewers who did not respond in that manner (Donohue et al., 2006).

Using African Americans' Strengths in Treatment

African Americans' strengths should be used in treatment to increase positive "vibes," a sound therapeutic alliance, and marshal previously unacknowledged resources (Kelly, 2003; Kelly & Boyd-Franklin, 2009). For African American men in particular, Tucker (1980) suggested interventions to boost African American men's egos in the face of oppression. These included being nondemanding, seeking and respecting their views, noting how sexual problems do not decrease their masculinity, and honestly praising positive attributes and behavior to boost their esteem. We perceive such an approach as a means of using strengths and communicating respect, and advocate its use with all African American partners (Kelly & Boyd-Franklin, 2009).

Sexual problems in relationships are associated with body image issues (Wiegel et al., 2002), and when that occurs with African Americans, it can be a sign that they have lost their strength of a positive racial identity that affirms their body shape, hair texture, and skin tone. Kelly and Boyd-Franklin (2005) have raised discussion of this issue with dark-skinned women who are more likely to be impacted by societal images, so that their experiences are normalized and linked to oppression, while African features are also highlighted as alternative standards of beauty. This approach is consistent with efficacious treatments of body image disorders, such as anorexia, wherein cognitive distortions supporting a super-thin ideal are restructured (Farrell, Shafran, & Lee, 2006). Moreover, providing positive statistics about African Americans' body image can emphasize their strengths, and can be used to engender useful discussion with community peers who may counter negative media messages.

Facilitating the development of a healthy racial and ethnic identity within African American couples does not mean focusing on superficially positive myths that may harm treatment. For example, many African Americans' apprehension about seeking treatment is partly due to the fact that treatment would contradict one superficially positive stereotype that African Americans are sexual experts (Tucker, 1980). One problem is that such stereotypes may result in overly high sexual expectations. Also, reliance on such stereotypes may be due to a lack of other means of excelling and fostering a positive identity (Tucker, 1980). For example, despite higher rates of some sexual problems within epidemiological studies (Laumann et al., 1999), African Americans reported fewer problems with sex in one study (Oggins et al., 1993). This may be due to greater sexual freedom experienced by some because of not having to meet virginal expectations, but also it may be due to fears of admitting that they are not sexual experts. Thus, therapists need to understand the power and joy many African Americans feel in performing well sexually, while also making them aware of how common sexual dissatisfactions and dysfunctions truly are for both African Americans and Whites (Tucker, 1980).

A second pernicious myth for African American men in particular is the masculine myth of being strong and not verbalizing vulnerable feelings. Endorsement of this myth denies the fact that enjoyable sex is dependent on communicating sexual likes and dislikes, and caring and complementary feelings, and can lead to defensiveness and low cooperation in treatment (Tucker, 1980). Mahalik, Talmadge, Locke, and Scott (2005) suggest specific methods of addressing hypermasculine ideas that may interfere with treatment. First, the therapist should elicit discussion of the benefits of conforming to the stereotype, so as to truly acknowledge how the masculine ideal works for the man. After acknowledgment of the positives, discussion of the costs of conforming to the ideal can occur, such as with eliciting discussion of the areas in the man's life where the stereotype does not work, with the goal of lowering the costs of rigid enactment of masculine ideals. We recommend this approach to address not only hypermasculine ideals, but also other racial myths that some African American couples may endorse.

Therapists who are "faith-friendly" can convey respect for many African American couples' religious and spiritual strength, which may reduce motivational barriers to treatment. Religious couples can be assisted in enacting changes that fit within the bounds of their faith, and helped to draw upon their faith as a resource to build agape love, or God's selfless love within the relationship (Beach, Fincham, Hurt, McNair, & Stanley, 2008a). While many African Americans do not pray for their partners, many are open to using or adapting sample prayers provided within couple treatment (Beach, Fincham, Hurt, McNair, & Stanley, 2008b). Religious and spiritual beliefs may be used to engender forgiveness, commitment, a long-term relationship perspective, and remind couples of their covenant before God (Beach et al., 2008a). Making these values salient can help with infidelity, or when one spouse considers divorce because of sexual difficulties. Yet pitfalls exist in "teaching" couples how to pray, or of prayers focusing on unhelpful goals of enduring the partner's transgressions or changing the partner and his or her shortcomings (Beach et al., 2008a), which may occur with infidelity and sexual dysfunction.

As with possible drawbacks to any treatment that does not address religion or spiritual beliefs of the couple, there may be drawbacks for couples who solely use religion to address sexual problems. First, some African American churches avoid discussing sexuality, partially so as not to confirm sexual stereotypes (Ward, 2005). Second, some African Americans hold myths that variety in sexual activity is a bad thing, such as with beliefs that oral sex is nasty, and that men are the only initiators in the sexual arena (Tucker, 1980). These beliefs may relate to religious modesty. For married couples in particular, therapists may address the areas that churches may be reluctant to discuss (McCarthy & Thestrup, 2008). Therapists should be careful not to embarrass African American couples, but can informally provide them with information conducive to attitude change, such as masturbation statistics, in a "matter of fact" manner (Tucker, 1980), that also can be conveyed via user-friendly handouts (McCarthy & Thestrup, 2008). Also, most religions are prosexuality when it occurs within marriage (McCarthy & Thestrup, 2008), and fidelity is encouraged. Thus, therapists can respect religious modesty outside of the bedroom and also draw upon African Americans' general strengths of fewer taboos about having sex, as well as their creativity and expressiveness (Kelly & Boyd-Franklin, 2009) to encourage varied sexual practices between married spouses (Tucker, 1980).

To overcome some African American couples' lack of experience with sexual communication, which can be due to factors such as religious modesty and myths of automatically having to be a sex expert, Tucker (1980) also advocated skills building, such as with a directive, step-by-step approach with couples. This includes lots of role play practice in couples communicating sexually and learning from each other and from educational materials, while stressing that they are not automatically supposed to know what is satisfying. Also, relationship enrichment activities should be included to awaken positive feelings, and build problem solving and conflict resolution skills (Tucker, 1980). These may be particularly important for African Americans, given their rates of relationship instability. Finally, all couples should be encouraged to develop a maintenance program to continue their gains beyond the first successful experience, as well as beyond treatment (McCarthy & Thestrup, 2008; Tucker, 1980).

African American partners' extended family and community ties, as well as others' views and communication about sexuality and gender roles may be assessed via genograms, otherwise known as family trees, which therapists construct while conversing with clients about their families (McGoldrick, Gerson, & Petry, 2008). Genograms can be a helpful resource in treating couple problems (Kelly & Boyd-Franklin, 2009), including sexual issues. The community can provide leadership and peer counseling roles to combat negative exposures to sexuality, such as in the media (Aronowitz, Rennells, & Todd, 2006). For example, therapists can help some African American couples to find trusted family and community members with whom they can discuss sexual matters, with a view towards decreasing belief in myths that they are the only one in the African American community with sexual problems, and increasing their support.

Case Example

The therapist saw Rob, aged 50 years, and Tina, aged 45 years, an African American working class couple from the South who had been married for 5 years. They had three children, 4-year-old Tiana, 3-year-old Rob Jr., and 6-month-old Tiffany. They sought treatment because of Rob's infidelity that occurred while Tina was pregnant with Tiffany, and complaints of an infrequent, restricted sexual repertoire. The first session revealed that Rob began feeling a loss of freedom and sexual satisfaction in the relationship once Rob Jr. was born. After surreptitious questions of his African American male friends revealed similar issues and some cheating, he began a 2-month sexual relationship with a former coworker that ended once Tina caught him cheating.

Both reported a solid, committed relationship, with some problems. Rob reported that he was happy with Tina and never intended to leave her. He stated that the conquest and variety that the single role yielded was not possible within marriage, and that fact and the "ball and chain" of marriage caused him to delay it for so long. Tina reported believing that their relationship was solid enough to withstand the infidelity if she could find a way to forgive him. They described their sexual relationship as initially good, but noted that the frequency of sex had declined when they became more serious, and reduced further (to once a month or less) after they began having children. Tina reported that when she tried to initiate sex or discuss how their sex life "died," he just changed the topic or made jokes. The couple reported additional conflicts with Rob being a "dreamer" and Tina being a "to-do list creator." The assessment revealed high relationship quality overall; the couple got along well, but displayed very low affection. Neither met criteria for any psychiatric disorder or sexual dysfunction, but both reported wanting more sex and attention to their sexual needs. Also, both desired more time for togetherness and leisure activities, and Tina wanted Rob to increase his household responsibilities. Also, both were highly stressed; Tina had subclinical but significant anxiety and depression symptoms, and Rob's endorsement of few symptoms at a high level suggested that he might be minimizing problems.

The interviews and genogram fleshed out issues regarding the infidelity and sexual problems. Rob reported feeling distant toward his family of origin, reporting that they were very secretive, and avoided discussing problems. He learned to "suck it up," be "hard like a rock," and not complain from his father, who was "not a family man." He also observed that his mother valued family highly, but was uncomfortable with sexuality in general, and she yelled and was controlling. They told him nothing about sex other than not to get a woman pregnant. Thus, he learned about sex from his friends and his own experiences, which taught him to be "cool" with women, and to separate the good girls from the "hos." He reported that he had many relationships prior to marrying Tina, with only one long term but nonmonogamous relationship. He reported satisfaction in his relationship with Tina, except that at times she told him what to do too much, and did not get out and have fun anymore. He reported a number of negative cognitions about sex and marriage, such as beliefs that marriage did not provide the benefits of escape, randomness, noncommittal, and outlandish repertoire that came with unmarried sex, which he especially began to realize with the accidental birth of their second child.

Tina's genogram revealed that she grew up in a close-knit family, but that she was a "late bloomer" who had had two serious relationships prior to Rob; one man failed to commit to monogamy, and the other left her for a woman who was light skinned (Tina was dark skinned). She related this to the infidelity, and wondered if Rob similarly had chosen her later in life as a "safe" or "default" partner to bear his children. She also reported feeling betrayed by the infidelity, and wondering if the foundation of their relationship was a lie. She admitted that she suspected Rob was engaging in extramarital sex much earlier in the marriage, but did little to address it because she "did not want to know." Like Rob, she noted a number of secrets and infidelities among her family and friends. She too reported negative expectancies in wondering about the possibility of fidelity in the marriage. She worried about "getting played" by Rob, referring to public embarrassment about womanizing or having others see a negative image of them as an African American couple.

The case revealed five issues formulated using an integrated cognitive-behavioral and family systems theoretical orientation. The couple's secrets led to an avoidance of communicating. Specifically, Tina's efforts to discuss sex and other problems like wanting more help in the household negatively reinforced Rob's escape behavior, positively reinforced her helpless and catastrophic thoughts, and negatively punished her initiation because of the loss of sex as a reinforcer. This was compounded by the second issue of little knowledge and skills to address the problems that they faced, due to few role models and lots of negative peer information, particularly for Rob. Third, their secondary distress behavior of withdrawing in response to problems, their stressful work life, having little children that they were unwilling to leave with others, and the crowded living conditions resulted in little positive time alone together. Fourth, these problems led to role imbalances in the family system, such that Tina became an overfunctioning spouse, and Rob became an underfunctioning and "bad" spouse, resulting in the triangle of infidelity with another woman.

The fifth issue pertained to their race/ethnicity and gender-related cognitive distortions, contextual factors, and values. Cognitive distortions included stereotypical beliefs that as African Americans, sex must be central to their identities, they must be sexual experts, and that cheating was normative or expected due to the sex ratio imbalance. Gendered distortions included Rob's view of women as good or bad, and his beliefs that he must be hypermasculine, enacted by controlling his emotions, idealizing the playboy role, and being self-reliant. Tina's gendered distortions included beliefs that she could not hold Rob to high standards, and that she had to work extra to keep Rob because of her dark skin and the imbalanced gender ratio within the African American community. They shared many of the aforementioned contextual factors common to many African Americans, such as family secrets and receiving little information about sex while growing up, the prominence of peers and the community, their crowded living environment, financial struggles and need to help out with their families of origin, and career stressors, including Tina's experiences of racism and sexism at work, and Rob's efforts to be his own boss and maintain his new landscaping business. Third, they shared values of family, community, religion, and role flexibility that are common to many African Americans.

All interventions were ideographically tailored to address how racial and ethnic factors were manifest within their relationship. For example, in the first session, Rob reported that although he is outgoing, he likes to keep private business to himself, and he only came to treatment because of how much he hurt Tina. Rather than convince him that treatment was best, he was thanked for his honesty and asked to talk more about things that he does not like, to ensure that treatment met his needs. Rob listed how he did not like to be told what to do or having things he says thrown back at him, that he likes to be in charge, and be selective about what he discusses and with whom. The therapist listed these as behaviors to avoid throughout treatment, and consistent with Tucker's (1980) recommendations, reassured him that he was in full control of what is discussed, and that the treatment would be confidential and tailored to reach his goals. He and Tina were asked always to give feedback about their wants and needs in treatment, and told that the therapist would always give multiple options and reasons for each option, from which they could decide what they wanted to do. Notably, Tina had no reservations about treatment. Role induction was accomplished by detailing the standard behavioral couple therapy model of the first four sessions (Epstein & Baucom, 2002), including: a joint session to obtain a sense of the problems in the relationship and the couple's history and strengths, and provide questionnaires to take home, two individual sessions to further discuss the relationship, their well-being, and prior romantic and family relationships, and a couple feedback session that provided a plan for treatment that Rob and Tina accepted.

The couple was given feedback that they had a strong, warm, and caring relationship, despite the infidelity. They were told that the relationship had developed normal problems that had been addressed maladaptively through an affair. Over time, individual and couple problems about which they could not communicate increased. Because neither was taught about sexual matters nor how to communicate about them, it was no wonder that sex had become a problem. They were told that part of the issue was their stressful life-cycle phase with young children, stressful jobs, and other pressures, which affected their thinking about their roles in marriage, such as with beliefs that real men don't complain, that sex and love are separate. In trying to address the problem, Rob had engaged in a secret affair, similar to some of their family and friends. This information was imparted in a conversational style, with the couple and the therapist collaborating in identifying examples of the formulation based upon their interviews, genogram, and questionnaire data.

Treatment addressed the infidelity, their sexual issues, and their general couple skills in an interrelated fashion. The couple was first asked to make time alone with each other, so that they could "date" and build a positive atmosphere to draw upon during tough discussions. Because they were so busy, considerable problem solving was done to achieve the solutions of Rob driving Tina to work for an hour, and the couple maintaining an extra "date" hour after each couple therapy session. Life issues were addressed, such that they transitioned their youngest child to sleep in her own room throughout the night to give them time alone and increased energy, and the normalizing theme of being in the life phase wherein they had "a lot going on" was regularly repeated to good effect. They were taught communication skills, such as assertiveness statements and validation skills (Epstein & Baucom, 2002). Some cognitive gains including having them check out their assumptions with each other. Thus, Tina learned that Rob saw her as his first choice, and still considered her to be his "princess."

Homework tasks were given to reduce avoidant behaviors by addressing some fears about each other, which the assessment revealed would be easily disconfirmed, as well as rekindle their skills and strengths. For homework, they were asked to look in the mirror together, view African American and mainstream beauty magazines, and look for the unique and beautiful features of African American women that society undervalued. This gave Rob a chance to remind Tina of how much he liked her body shape and "smooth chocolate skin," a phrase he often used back when he courted her, and which Tina reported had made her feel beautiful in Rob's eyes. Also, a homework task about sexual behaviors that they liked led Rob to discover that the church-going Tina was very willing to engage in "outlandish" sexual acts such as bondage, and the initial weeks after that disclosure led to more sex and fun than they had experienced in years. They built on these positive experiences with Rob's successful challenging of his own initial negative beliefs of the utility of treatment and of expressing emotions in the marital context, and Tina challenging her own catastrophic interpretations of any time he spent away from the home.

To counter their lack of information and show what lay ahead for the difficult issue of infidelity, the couple was provided with a one-page handout about the three stages of dealing with the aftermath distilled from Gordon, Baucom, and Snyder's (2005) work, including dealing with the impact, searching for meaning, and recovery or moving forward. They were told that treatment would involve gradual communication about the affair, and they would be helped to find acceptable ways to vent, like preventing a tea kettle from boiling over. Rob immediately raised concerns that Tina would re-live the pain, and that he would be punished and made to feel bad about himself, and that it is probably best if he opens up one-on-one with the therapist. The therapist said that while a one-on-one approach is fine, the session would remain a safe place to talk to each other about tough topics. She educated them that the way to prevent those fears would be to discuss the affair in a manageable way so that it could be laid to rest. She said that he did not have to take her word for it; she added those fears to the list of things that Rob did not want in treatment, promising to bring the list to each session and check in periodically so that these issues stayed nonexistent or minimal, and that the sessions stayed safe.

Infidelity treatment also involved dealing with flashbacks, normalizing, providing psychoeducation, and relapse prevention. The therapist provided the PTSD definition of flashbacks and described how they could be similar in the case of infidelity, as when Tina woke up angry with Rob due to infidelity-related dreams. The therapist broadened the concept to apply to many situations that carried any reminder of the infidelity. She taught the couple to ask each other if Tina's unexplainable or negative behavior might be due to a flashback, and taught them to engage in antecedent control for known situations, have a humorous code-word to check in with each other to see if a flashback was occurring, and to repair by processing it afterwards and noting what was similar to and different from the time of infidelity. For example, a common flashback for Tina involved noting any inattentiveness in front of her family, which she associated with "getting played" by him in public, and addressed through confrontation. Rob reported surprise that "flashbacks" were the cause of her publicly controlling behavior. The reframe of her negative behavior in a more positive light, as an expression of vulnerability, and of his withdrawal as a confusion reaction and way of reducing stress evoked the couple's strength of nurturing one another. For example, it motivated Rob to continue being Tina's "knight" by understanding and soothing her pain, without the drawbacks of feeling controlled, being weak, or evoking any of his other fears. This strength began the process of replacing the fighting that raised negative racial and gender stereotypes of the "controlling" African American woman and the "undependable" African American man, so that they saw each other as normally flawed and loveable. Moreover, normalizing the feelings of both increased their mutual empathy, and relapse prevention techniques helped them to control the situation so that they could recognize if infidelity became a risk again, and prevent it from getting that far.

Treatment revealed a core issue of Rob's underfunctioning and Tina's overfunctioning in the household. Rob admitted to liking lots of personal time, and escaping to a quiet room whenever Tina was not giving him a "to do" list. Tina again reported a view of Rob as undependable. Moreover, because she endorsed the myth that she had to go an extra mile to keep an African American man, she often assumed that Rob would not do "his share" and she took on extra child care and household burdens. The issue was addressed with communication that the dislike of feeling controlled was core for Rob, and that the need for help was core for Tina. In fact, she stated that his participation around the house made her feel more sexually attracted to him. A problem solving task was used to address the core issues, which led to a behavior exchange solution, in which Rob would do more child and home care during the mornings, in exchange for not receiving a "to do" list from Tina. An acceptance task was also used, eliciting Tina's admiration that Rob followed his dreams, though he did not address details much, and Rob's admiration of how Tina "makes things happen no matter what," though it sometimes led to a "to do" list. The gains in this area were finally consolidated when one more similar incident arose and the therapist challenged Tina's stereotypes that African American men were undependable and in need of coddling versus being held to clear, unwavering standards. Rob agreed that rather than lower standards, he needed to be told clearly what is expected of him. His underfunctioning was reframed as an issue of consistency. The therapist helped Rob to program tasks into his phone, and helped Tina to remind him in a positive way after any lapses, to maintain high marital standards.

After some sessions focused on the infidelity, the therapist found that the couple's sexual relationship declined again, consistent with Tucker's (1980) observation that African American couples' embarrassment can lead to sexual avoidance without tracking and encouragement. When asked about the decline, both complained of fatigue, being so busy that the marriage felt like a "business relationship," and not having space to focus on it. Given some finger pointing, each was asked to make time to independently initiate sex, just as they made time for the dates. The therapist provided psychoeducation that couples often feel pressure to have good sex, when happy couples actually have a mixture of good sex, bad/forgettable sex, scheduled sex, and spontaneous sex (McCarthy & Thestrup, 2008). She suggested that because the couple had not had sex in 2 months, scheduled bad sex would be fine to get them started. In the following session, Rob said he had initiated sex once, which Tina refused due to fatigue and upset at lack of household help, and neither asked the other again. Previously, Rob shared that the infidelity mainly had to do with his loss of the "player" role that led to conquests and feelings of being empowered and in control. Rob initially was resistant to labeling these beliefs as distortions. When the therapist and Tina suggested ways to include role-playing, bondage, and "outlandish" acts within their sexual relationship, he argued, "How can you have random and noncommittal sex with your wife?" Clearly, he valued a good/bad woman split and a hypermasculine gender stereotype held by some African American men (e.g., Mahalik et al., 2006).

Sex-specific treatment of the couple used a three-pronged approach to address Rob's hypermasculine gender stereotypes, racism, and sexual communication. First, Rob was asked about the benefits of being "a player" and making random conquests when he was single. He laughingly discussed how it made him feel attractive and in control, and that his "boys" were impressed. He discussed feeling less attractive as he got older, such as with his receding hairline and his lack of feeling in control with his business that led to ebbs and flows in their finances, and self-doubts. He was then asked about the cons of having been a player, such as hurting women, little intimacy, less time spent on productive pursuits, and not having Tina in his life. The therapist empathized with how important attractiveness, being in control, and feeling good about one's self were for him and for other African American men. Together they all explored if there were other areas in which he could address these important needs. The result was a plan for increasing his activity in the gym to "build my guns" (arm muscles) with weight-lifting, and "show the youngsters who is boss" in football. They identified other ways that he already was in control, such as having started his business, an accomplishment for which Tina's nephews looked up to him. This served to shift his comparisons from the wider world in which he was "one in a million" to the African American community, in which he had higher status and ability. Still, his acceptance of flexibly enacting his masculine "player" role via role play or other methods within his relationship with Tina was limited.

The therapist then noted how society exaggerated the images of African American men, and Rob and Tina enthusiastically noticed and debunked the stereotypes of the absent African American father, drug addicts, welfare women, and more negative images. They were asked, what about the positive images, such as all African American men are athletes that have sex every day? They laughed, and admitted that those were not always true, because Rob was terrible at basketball, and they had too much to do to have sex so often even when their sex life was thriving. Thus, the negative consequences of presumably positive stereotypes began to be explored. The therapist recounted Rob's reports of the negative consequences of the "player" role as well. She noted how some African American men had shared with her that marriage and commitment did in fact remove the player role of having sex just for the sake of fulfilling urges and being in control, but that many men reported that the vulnerability and shared intimacy of a mate made sex a passionate expression of their intimacy (Seal & Ehrhardt, 2003). She also read an excerpt from Franklin (2004) to him about how conquests prevent intimacy, so that he would receive another African American male's perspective, and it was well received. The therapist also wondered aloud if trying to live up to the "player" role was letting racism win by harming his family too.

At the next session, Rob reported that he had spoken about sex as an extension of intimacy with an older deacon at his church who really seemed to enjoy being married. He said that the deacon told him something similar, in that he found sex with his wife to be precious because he could trust her with all aspects of himself. The therapist suggested that Rob and Tina build upon their own trust by exploring more with each other their preferences in their sexual relationship, and learning to coach each other, using sensate focus. She opened the massage oil that she had brought to the session and instructed them to take turns using it to massage each other's hands, and coached them to say what they liked and what they did not like as much. She helped them to note which ways of communicating their likes and dislikes were useful and appreciated, and which ways were less useful. They reported having lots of fun with the task. It was given as homework, and over time they were instructed to progressively explore each other's bodies in stages and communicate likes and dislikes. The couple took to the treatment, with positive reports over time, such as with touching each other in new pleasurable ways, having sex, and using different mutually enjoyable positions.

Summary and Conclusions

African American couples face many challenges to developing healthy sexual identities, due to their history of oppression, sexualized socialization through the media, and social ills that adversely affect both their relationship quality and their sexual functioning and behavior. While many African Americans socialize their children towards healthy sexuality, and have healthy intimate relationships, some African Americans internalize racial stereotypes and societal conceptions of beauty, and cope maladaptively, such as with hypermasculine behavior, infidelity, and negative sexual behavior. While African American couples can benefit from core elements within standard treatments for sexual problems, therapists must counter common and reasonable reluctance of many within the African American community to be in treatment and to disclose to strangers. Moreover, they must be aware of and assess for prevalent historically based stereotypes that impact African Americans' sexual identities, expectations, experiences, and behaviors at all phases of development, and respond in positive ways that empathize with and acknowledge structural factors such as racism. Under-acknowledged strengths, such as a positive body image, a positive racial or ethnic identity, high self-esteem, religion, and family and community ties must be assessed and used to strengthen African Americans' couple and sexual relationships. As shown with the case of Rob and Tina, assessment, education, and intervention that contextualizes African Americans' sexual problems can help them to work together better to counteract the legacy of oppression, rather than succumb to it in the bedroom.

References

Aborampah, O. (1989). Black male-female relationships. *Journal of Black Studies, 19*, 320–342.

Abrams, K. K., Allen, L. R., & Gray, J. J. (1993). Disordered eating attitudes and behaviors, psychological adjustment, and ethnic identity: A comparison of black and white female college students. *International Journal of Eating Disorders, 14*, 49–57.

Aronowitz, T., Rennells, R. E. & Todd, E. (2006). Ecological influences of sexuality on early adolescent African American females. *Journal of Community Health Nursing, 23*, 113–122.

Bach, A. K., Wincze, J. P., & Barlow, D. H. (2001). Sexual dysfunction. In D. H. Barlow (Ed.), *Clinical handbook of psychological disorders* (3rd ed., pp. 562–608). New York: Guilford.

Bancroft, J., Loftus, J., & Long, J. S. (2003). Distress about sex: A national survey of women in heterosexual relationships. *Archives of Sexual Behavior, 32*, 193–208.

Beach, S. R. H., Fincham, F. D., Hurt, T. R., McNair, L. M., & Stanley, S. M. (2008a). Prayer and marital intervention: A conceptual framework. *Journal of Social and Clinical Psychology, 27*, 641–669.

Beach, S. R. H., Fincham, F. D., Hurt, T. R., McNair, L. M., & Stanley, S. M. (2008b). Prayer and marital intervention: Toward an open, empirically-grounded dialogue. *Journal of Social and Clinical Psychology, 27*, 693–710.

Bennett, N., & Mulhall, J. (2008). Sickle cell disease status and outcomes of African American men presenting with priapism. *Journal of Sexual Medicine, 5*, 1244–1250.

Black, L. & Jackson, V. (2005). Families of African origin: An overview. In M. McGoldrick, J. Giordano, & N. Garcia-Preto (Eds.), *Ethnicity & family therapy* (3rd ed., pp. 77–86). New York: Guilford.

Blair, I. V., Judd, C. M., Sadler, M. S., & Jenkins, C. (2002). The role of Afrocentric features in person perception: Judging by features and categories. *Journal of Personality and Social Psychology, 83,* 5–25.

Blake, W. M., & Darling, C. A. (1994). The dilemmas of the African American male. *Journal of Black Studies, 24,* 402–415.

Bowman, P. J. (1992). Coping with provider role strain: Adaptive cultural resources among Black husband-fathers. In A. K. H. Burlew, W. C. Banks, H. P. McAdoo, & D. A. Azibo (Eds.), *African American psychology: Theory, research, and practice* (pp. 135–151). Newbury Park, CA: Sage.

Boyd-Franklin, N. (2003). *Black families in therapy: Understanding the African American experience.* New York: Guilford.

Brody, G. H., Stoneman, Z., & Flor, D. (1995). Linking family processes and academic competence among rural African American youths. *Journal of Marriage & the Family, 57,* 567–579.

Brody, G. H., Stoneman, Z., & Flor, D. (1996). Parental religiosity, family processes, and youth competence in rural, two-parent African American families. *Developmental Psychology, 32,* 696–706.

Brody, G. H., Stoneman, Z., Flor, D., & McCrary, C. (1994). Religion's role in organizing family relationships: Family process in rural, two-parent African American families. *Journal of Marriage & the Family, 56,* 878–888.

Browning, C. R., & Burrington, L. A. (2006). Racial differences in sexual and fertility attitudes in an urban setting. *Journal of Marriage and Family, 68,* 236–251.

Burton, L. M., & Tucker, M. B. (2009). Romantic unions in an era of uncertainty: A post-Moynihan perspective on African American women and marriage. *The Annals of the American Academy of Political and Social Science, 621,* 132–148.

Cain V. S., Johannes, C. B., Avis, N. E., Mohr, B., Schocken, M., Skurnick, J., & Ory, M. (2003). Sexual functioning and practices in a multi-ethnic study of midlife women: Baseline results from SWAN. *Journal of Sex Research,, 40,* 266–276.

Choi, K. H., Catania, J. A., & Dolcini, M. M. (1994). Extramarital sex and HIV risk behavior among US adults: Results from the national AIDS behavioral survey. *American Journal of Public Health, 84,* 2003–2007.

Clark, R. (2004). Interethnic group and intraethnic group racism: Perception and coping in Black university students. *Journal of Black Psychology, 30,* 506–526.

Clark, R., Anderson, N. B., Clark, V. R., & Williams, D. R. (1999). Racism as a stressor for African Americans: A biopsychosocial model. *American Psychologist, 54,* 805–816.

Coleman, M. G. (2003). Job skill and Black male wage discrimination. *Social Science Quarterly, 84,* 892–905.

Coltraine, S., & Messineo, M. (2000). The perpetuation of subtle prejudice: Race and gender imagery in 1990s television advertising. *Sex Roles, 42,* 363–389.

Conger, R. D., & Donnellan, M. B. (2007). An interactionist perspective on the socioeconomic context of human development. *Annual Review of Psychology, 58,* 175–199.

Dalaker, J. (2001). *Poverty in the United States: 2000.* Washington, DC: U.S. Census Bureau.

Demarest, J., & Allen, R. (2000). Body image: Gender, ethnic, and age differences. *The Journal of Social Psychology, 140,* 465–472.

Donohue, B., Strada, M. J., Rosales, R., Taylor-Caldwell, A., Hise, D., Ahman, S., ... Laino, R. (2006). The semistructured interview for consideration of ethnic culture in therapy scale: Initial psychometric and outcome support. *Behavior Modification, 30,* 867–891.

Donovan, R. A. (2007). To blame or not to blame: Influences of target race and observer sex on rape blame attribution. *Journal of Interpersonal Violence, 22,* 722–736.

Epstein, N. B., & Baucom, D. H. (2002). *Enhanced cognitive-behavioral therapy for couples: A contextual approach.* Washington, DC: American Psychological Association.

Farrell, C., Shafran, R., & Lee, M. (2006). Empirically evaluated treatments for body image disturbance: A review. *European Eating Disorders Review, 14,* 289–300.

Fischer, A. R., & Shaw, C. M. (1999). African Americans' mental health and perceptions of racist discrimination: The moderating effects of racial socialization experiences and self-esteem. *Journal of Counseling Psychology, 46,* 395–407.

Franklin, A. J. (2004). *From brotherhood to manhood: How Black men rescue their relationships and dreams from the invisibility syndrome.* Hoboken, NJ: Wiley.

Franklin-Jackson, D., & Carter, R. T. (2007). The relationships between race-related stress, racial identity, and mental health for black Americans. *Journal of Black Psychology, 33,* 5–26.

Gan, S., Zillmann, D., & Mitrook, M. (1997). Stereotyping effect of black women's sexual rap on white audiences. *Basic and Applied Social Psychology, 19,* 381–399.

Gaydos, L. M, Neubert, B. D., Hogue, C. J. R., Kramer, M. R., & Yang, Z. (2010). Racial disparities in contraceptive use between student and nonstudent populations. *Journal of Women's Health, 19,* 589–595.

Goff, P. A., Eberhardt, J. L., Williams, M. J., & Jackson, M. C. (2008). Not yet human: Implicit knowledge, historical dehumanization, and contemporary consequences. *Journal of Personality and Social Psychology, 94,* 292–306.

Gordon, K. C., Baucom, D. H., & Snyder, D. K. (2005). Treating couples recovering from infidelity: An integrative approach. *Journal of Clinical Psychology, 61,* 1393–1405.

Gray-Little, B., & Hafdahl, A. R. (2000). Factors influencing racial comparisons of self-esteem: A quantitative review. *Psychological Bulletin, 126,* 26–54.

Hardy, K. V., & Laszloffy, T. A. (2002). Couple therapy using a multicultural perspective. In A. S. Gurman & N. S. Jacobson (Eds.), *Clinical handbook of couple therapy* (3rd ed., pp. 569–593). New York: Guilford.

Harris, S. M. (1995). Family, self, and sociocultural contributions to body-image attitudes of African-American women. *Psychology of Women Quarterly, 19,* 129–145.

Henriques, G. R., Calhoun, L. G., & Cann, A. (1996). Ethnic differences in women's body satisfaction: An experimental investigation. *The Journal of Social Psychology, 136*, 689–697.

Hill, M. E. (2002). Skin color and the perception of attractiveness among African Americans: Does gender make a difference? *Social Psychology Quarterly, 65*, 77–91.

Hines, P. M., & Boyd-Franklin, N. (2005). African American families. In M. McGoldrick, N. Garcia-Preto, & J. Giordano (Eds.), *Ethnicity and family therapy* (3rd ed., pp. 88–101). New York: Guilford.

Hollar, M. C. (2001). The impact of racism on the delivery of health care and mental health services. *Psychiatric Quarterly, 72*, 337–345.

Holmes, M. C. (2002). Mental health and sexual self-concept discrepancies in a sample of young black women. *Journal of Black Psychology, 28*, 347–370.

Jenkins, R., Schover, L. R., Fouladi, R. T., Warneke, C., Neese, L., Klein, E. A., ... Kupelian, P. (2004). Sexuality and health-related quality of life after prostate cancer in African-American and white men treated for localized disease. *Journal of Sex & Marital Therapy, 30*, 79–93.

Jones, K. (1997). Are rap videos more violent? Style differences and the prevalence of sex and violence in the age of MTV. *The Howard Journal of Communications, 8*, 343–356.

Kelly, S. (2003). African-American couples: Their importance to the stability of African-American families and their mental health issues. In J. S. Mio & G. Y. Iwamasa (Eds.), *Culturally diverse mental health: The challenges of research and resistance* (pp. 141–157). New York: Brunner-Routledge.

Kelly, S. (2004). Underlying components of scores assessing African Americans' racial perspectives. *Measurement and Evaluation in Counseling and Development, 37*, 28–40.

Kelly, S., & Boyd-Franklin, N. (2005). African American women in client, therapist, and supervisory relationships: The parallel processes of race, culture, and family. In M. Rastogi & E. Wieling (Eds.), *The voices of color: First person accounts of ethnic minority therapists* (pp. 67–89). Thousand Oaks, CA: Sage.

Kelly, S. & Boyd-Franklin, N. (2009) Joining, understanding, and supporting Black couples in treatment. In M. Rastogi & V. Thomas (Eds.), *Multicultural couple therapy* (pp. 235–254). Thousand Oaks, CA: Sage.

Kelly, S., & Floyd, F. J. (2001). The effects of negative racial stereotypes and Afrocentricity on Black couple relationships. *Journal of Family Psychology, 15*, 110–123.

Kelly, S., & Floyd, F. J. (2006). Impact of racial perspectives and contextual variables on marital trust and adjustment for African American couples. *Journal of Family Psychology, 20*, 79–87.

Kelly, S., Floyd, F. J., Bhagwat, R., Morgan, A., & Scott, A. (2010). *The interactive coping strategies used by Black couples to manage racial stressors*. Manuscript submitted for publication.

Laumann, E. O., Paik, A., & Rosen, R. C. (1999). Sexual dysfunction in the United States: Prevalence and predictors. *The Journal of the American Medical Association, 281*, 537–544.

Laumann, E. O., West, S., Glasser, D., Carson, C., Rosen, R., & Kang, J. (2007). Prevalence and correlates of erectile dysfunction by race and ethnicity among men aged 40 or older in the United States: From the Male Attitudes Regarding Sexual Health Survey. *Journal of Sexual Medicine, 4,* 57–65.

Lawson, E., & Thompson, A. (1994). The historical and social correlates of African American divorce: Review of the literature and implications for research. *Western Journal of Black Studies, 18,* 91–103.

Lennon, S. J., Rudd, N. A., Sloan, B., & Kim, J. S. (1999). Attitudes toward gender roles, self-esteem, and body image: Application of a model. *Clothing & Textiles Research Journal, 17,* 191–202.

Mahalik, J. R., Good, G. E., & Englar-Carson, M. (2003). Masculinity scripts, presenting concerns, and help seeking: Implications for practice and training. *Professional Psychology, Research and Practice, 34,* 123–131.

Mahalik, J. R., Pierre, M. R., & Wan, S. S. C. (2006). Examining racial identity and masculinity as correlates of self-esteem and psychological distress in black men. *Journal of Multicultural Counseling and Development, 34,* 94–104.

Mahalik, J. R., Talmadge, W. T., Locke, B. D., & Scott, R. P. J. (2005). Using the Conformity to Masculine Norms Inventory to work with men in a clinical setting. *Journal of Clinical Psychology, 61,* 661–674.

Mahay, J., Laumann, E. O., & Michaels, S. (2001). Race, gender, and class in sexual scripts. In E. O. Laumann & R. T. Michael (Eds.), *Sex, love, and health in America* (pp. 197–238). Chicago, IL: University of Chicago Press.

Majors, R., & Billson, J. M. (1992). *Cool pose: The dilemmas of Black manhood in America.* New York: Simon & Schuster.

Markey, C. N., Markey, P. M., & Birch, L. L. (2004). Understanding women's body satisfaction: The role of husbands. *Sex Roles, 51,* 209–216.

McCarthy, B. W., & Thestrup, M. (2008). Couple therapy and treatment of sexual dysfunction. In A. S. Gurman (Ed.), *Clinical handbook of couple therapy* (pp. 681–696). New York: Guilford.

McDaniel, A. (1990). The power of culture: A review of the ideas of Africa's influence of family structure in antebellum America. *Journal of Family History, 15,* 225–238.

McGoldrick, M., Gerson, R., & Petry, S. (2008). *Genograms: Assessment and intervention* (3rd ed.). New York: Norton.

McGruder, K. (2009). Black sexuality in the U.S.: Presentations as non-normative. *Journal of African American Studies, 13,* 251–262.

Miller, K. J., Gleaves, D. H., Hirsch, T. G., Green, B. A., Snow, A. C., & Corbett, C. C. (2000). Comparisons of body image dimensions by race/ethnicity and gender in a university population. *International Journal of Eating Disorders, 27,* 310–316.

Molloy, B. L., & Herzberger, S. D. (2002). Body image and self-esteem: A comparison of African-American and Caucasian women. In A. E. Hunter & C. Forden (Eds.), *Readings in the psychology of gender* (pp. 111–122). Needham Heights, MA: Allyn & Bacon.

Murry, V. M., Brown, P. A., Brody, G. H., Cutrona, C. E., & Simons, R. L. (2001). Racial discrimination as a moderator of the links among stress, maternal psychological functioning, and family relationships. *Journal of Marriage and Family, 63,* 915–926.

Murry, V. M. (2008). Long-term effects of stressors on relationship well-being and parenting among rural African American women. *Family Relations, 57,* 117–127.

Oggins, J., Veroff, J., & Leber, D. (1993). Race and gender differences in black and white newlyweds' perceptions of sexual and marital relations. *The Journal of Sex Research, 30,* 152–160.

Okech, A. P., & Harrington, R. (2002). The relationships among black consciousness, self-esteem, and academic self-efficacy in African American men. *The Journal of Psychology, 136,* 214–224.

Perry, L., Morgan, J., Reid, F., Brunton, J., O'Brien, A., Luck, A., & Lacey, H. (2002). Screening for symptoms of eating disorders: Reliability of the SCOFF screening tool with written compared to oral delivery. *International Journal of Eating Disorders, 32,* 466–472.

Peterson, S. H., Wingood, G. M., DiClemente, R. J., Harrington, K., & Davies, S. (2007). Images of sexual stereotypes in rap videos and the health of African American female adolescents. *Journal of Women's health, 16,* 1157–1164.

Phillips, J. A., & Sweeney, M. M. (2005). Premarital cohabitation and marital disruption among White, Black, and Mexican American women. *Journal of Marriage and Family, 67,* 296–314.

Phinney, J. S., & Ong, A. D. (2007). Conceptualization and measurement of ethnic identity: Current status and future directions. *Journal of Counseling Psychology, 54,* 271–281.

Price, J. H., & Miller, P. A. (1984). Sexual fantasies of black and of white college students. *Psychological Reports, 54,* 1007–1014.

Rao, K. V., & DeMaris, A. (1995). Coital frequency among married and cohabitating couples in the United States. *Journal of Biosocial Science, 27,* 135–150.

Rauer, A. J., Karney, B. R., Garvan, C. W., & Hou, W. (2008). Relationship risks in context: A cumulative risk approach to understanding relationship satisfaction. *Journal of Marriage and Family, 70,* 1122–1135.

Roberts, A., Cash, T. F., Feingold, A., & Johnson, B. T. (2006). Are black-white differences in females' body dissatisfaction decreasing? A meta-analytic review. *Journal of Consulting and Clinical Psychology, 74,* 1121–1131.

Robinson, B. E., Scheltema, K., & Cherry, T. (2005). Risky sexual behavior in low-income African American women: The impact of sexual health variables. *Journal of Sex Research, 42,* 224–237.

Robinson, M. L., Holmbeck, G. N., & Paikoff, R. (2007). Self-esteem enhancing reasons for having sex and the sexual behaviors of African American adolescents. *Journal of Youth and Adolescence, 36,* 453–464.

Rogge, R. D., Cobb, R. J., Story, L. B., Johnson, M. D., Lawrence, E. E., Rothman, A. D., & Bradbury, T. N. (2006). Recruitment and selection of couples for intervention research: Achieving developmental homogeneity at the cost of demographic diversity. *Journal of Consulting and Clinical Psychology, 74,* 777–784.

Ross, S. L., & Turner, M. A. (2005). Housing discrimination in metropolitan America: Explaining changes between 1989 and 2000. *Social Problems, 52,* 152–180.

Rouse-Arnett, M., & Dilworth, J.E.L. (2006). Early influences on African American women's sexuality. *Journal of Feminist Family Therapy, 18,* 39–61.

Salazar, L. F., Crosby, R. A., DiClemente, R. J., Wingood, G. M., Lescano, C. M., Brown, L. K., ... Davies, S. (2005). Self-esteem and theoretical mediators of safer sex among African American female adolescents: Implications for sexual risk reduction interventions. *Health Education & Behavior, 32,* 413–427.

Sampson, R. J., Morenoff, J. D., & Raudenbush, S. (2005). Social anatomy of racial and ethnic disparities in violence. *American Journal of Public Health, 95,* 224–232.

Sanchez, D. T., & Kiefer, A. K. (2007). Body concerns in and out of the bedroom: Implications for sexual pleasure and problems. *Archives of Sexual Behavior, 36,* 808–820.

Schooler, D., Ward, L. M., Merriwether, A., & Caruthers, A. (2004). Who's that girl: Television's role in the body image development of young white and black women. *Psychology of Women Quarterly, 28,* 38–47.

Seal, D. W., & Ehrhardt, A. A. (2003). Masculinity and urban men: Perceived scripts for courtship, romantic, and sexual interactions with women. *Culture, Health, & Sexuality, 5,* 295–319.

Siegel, J. M. (2002). Body image change and adolescent depressive symptoms. *Journal of Adolescent Research, 17,* 27–41.

Staples, R. (1972). Research on black sexuality: Its implication for family life, sex education, and public policy. *The Family Coordinator, 21,* 183–188.

Stephens, D. P., & Few, A. L. (2007). The effects of images of African American women in hip hop on early adolescents' attitudes toward physical attractiveness and interpersonal relationships. *Sex Roles, 56,* 251–264.

Stephens, D. P., & Phillips, L. D. (2003). Freaks, gold diggers, divas, and dykes: the sociohistorical development of adolescent African American women's sexual scripts. *Sexuality and Culture, 7,* 3–49.

Taylor, R. J., Chatters, L. M., & Jackson, J. S. (1997). Changes over time in support network involvement among Black Americans. In R. J. Taylor, J. S. Jackson, & L. M. Chatters (Eds.), *Family life in Black America* (pp. 293–316). Thousand Oaks, CA: Sage.

Taylor, R. J., Mattis, J., & Chatters, L. M. (1999). Subjective religiosity among African Americans: A synthesis of findings from five national samples. *Journal of Black Psychology, 25,* 524–543.

Tirodkar, M. A. & Jain, A. (2003). Food messages on African American television shows. *American Journal of Public Health, 93,* 439–441.

Treas, J., & Giesen, D. (2000). Sexual infidelity among married and cohabiting Americans. *Journal of Marriage and the Family, 62,* 48–60.

Tucker, C. M. (1980) Strategies for counseling blacks with sexual problems. *Journal of Non-White Concerns in Personnel and Guidance, 8,* 62–69.

Twenge, J. M., & Crocker, J. (2002). Race and self-esteem: Meta-analyses comparing Whites, Blacks, Hispanics, Asians, and American Indians and comment on Gray-Little and Hafdahl (2000). *Psychological Bulletin, 128,* 371–408.

Unnever, J. D. (2008). Two worlds far apart: Black-white differences in beliefs about why African-American men are disproportionately imprisoned. *Criminology, 46,* 511–538.

Vandiver, B. J., Cross, W. E., Worrell, F. C., & Fhagen-Smith, P. E. (2002). Validating the Cross Racial Identity Scale. *Journal of Counseling Psychology, 49,* 71–85.

Ward, L. M. (2003). Understanding the role of entertainment media in the sexual socialization of American youth: A review of empirical research. *Developmental Review, 23,* 347–388.

Ward, E. G. (2005). Homophobia, hypermasculinity and the US black church. *Culture, Health and Sexuality, 7,* 493–504.

Ward, L. M., Hansbrough, E., & Walker, E. (2005). Contributions of music video exposure to black adolescents' gender and sexual schemas. *Journal of Adolescent Research, 20,* 143–166.

Weinberg, M. S., & Williams, C. J. (1988). Black sexuality: A test of two theories. *The Journal of Sex Research, 25,* 197–218.

Wiegel, M., Wincze, J. P., & Barlow, D. H. (2002). Sexual dysfunction. In M. M. Antony, & D. H. Barlow (Eds.), *Handbook of assessment and treatment planning for psychological disorders* (pp. 481–522). New York: Guilford.

Williams, D. R., Neighbors, H. W., & Jackson, J. S. (2003). Racial/Ethnic discrimination and health: Findings from community studies. *American Journal of Public Health, 93,* 200–208.

Wilson, T. C. (1996). Cohort and prejudice: Whites' attitudes toward Blacks, Hispanics, Jews, and Asians. *Public Opinion Quarterly, 60,* 253–274.

Wingood, G. M., & DiClemente, R. J. (1997). The effects of an abusive primary partner on the condom use and sexual negotiation practices of African-American women. *American Journal of Public Health, 6,* 1016–1018.

Wingood, G. M., & DiClemente, R. J. (1998). Partner influences and gender-related factors associated with noncondom use among young adult African American women. *American Journal of Community Psychology, 26,* 29–51.

Wingood, G. M., DiClemente, R. J., Bernhardt, J. M., Harrington, K., Davies, S. L., Robillard, A., & Hook, E. W. (2003). A prospective study of exposure to rap music videos and African American female adolescents' health. *American Journal of Public Health, 93,* 437–439.

Wingood, G. M., DiClemente, R. J., Harrington, K., & Davies, S. L. (2002). Body image and African American females' sexual health. *Journal of Women's Health & Gender-Based Medicine, 11,* 433–439.

Wyatt, G. (1994). The sociocultural relevance of sex research: Challenges for the 1990s and beyond. *American Psychologist, 49,* 748–754.

Zeanah, P. D., & Schwarz, J. C. (1996). Reliability and validity of the Sexual Self-Esteem Inventory for women. *Assessment, 3,* 1–15.

Editors Introduction to Chapter 4
Latinos

We do not intend to add to stereotyped notions of ethnic minorities as sexually irresponsible by having a chapter on HIV prevention in the Latino population. It is a sad reality, however, that Latinos in the United States make up a large proportion of those who are living with HIV, and they are at increased risk for HIV infection compared to their White counterparts. There can be little discussion of sexual pleasure when sexual safety is not assured. Sexual safety is not an issue solely for ethnic minorities, but for men and women throughout the world. We encourage the reader to think beyond not only the target population, but also to expand the definition of sexual safety to include safety from all sexually transmitted infections, unwanted pregnancy, and sexual violence.

In this chapter, Melendez and her colleagues use the crisis of HIV to illustrate the sexual challenges facing Latinas and describe a unique and innovative approach to helping Latinas prevent HIV infection. According to the authors, taking an individual approach or encouraging women to insist on condom use will not and does not work in the Latino community. As you will read in this chapter, a sexually assertive or empowered woman is often considered suspect in Latino/Latina communities and she will lose ties and important connections to her friends, family, and community. Rather than alienating women, the program described in this chapter brings together a community of women so that they learn, not only about the dangers of sex, but about the pleasures; and that the way to have pleasure is to have safety, communication, and respect.

This is the only chapter in the book that deals with an immigrant population, raising the health paradox of acculturation: less acculturated Latinos have restricted access to health care and yet, once Latinos are more acculturated, they are found to suffer more from diseases (often those related to lifestyle choices such as smoking, drinking, and unprotected sex). Melendez and her coauthors illustrate how to navigate this paradox of acculturation by working with Latinas to maintain their ties to their community while also accessing the benefits of the larger society in which they live. Melendez and her colleagues provide an excellent example of how to work with immigrant and minority groups that will translate beyond the Latino population. Understanding the sexual, interpersonal, and larger community issues that impact sexuality will make for more effective interventions regarding sexual health and ultimately, sexual pleasure for men and women of diverse cultural backgrounds.

4

UNDERSTANDING LATINA WOMEN'S SEXUALITY IN THE UNITED STATES
Analysis of an Innovative HIV Prevention Program

Rita M. Melendez, Carrie Dickenson, Catalina Sol, Luz Amparo Pinzon, Brigida Guyot, and Dilcia Molina

Selena S is a 26-year-old Guatemalan woman living in Washington, DC. She married her high school boyfriend at the age of 19 but is currently single. She married him for a number of reasons: she loved him, was pregnant, did not want to feel "alone," wanted her family and friends to have respect for her as a married woman, and was asked by him. She came to live on the East Coast of the United States from Guatemala at age 11 and loves returning to visit her extended family. Selena never felt comfortable taking classes in English and so she only has a high school diploma. She speaks mainly Spanish with her family and friends. Selena is currently encountering a number of sexuality-related issues as she reemerges into the dating world and is sexually active.

For this chapter the story of Selena S will serve as a case study. She is a composite character taken from interviews and experiences with Latinas in an innovative HIV prevention program, and her experience brings forth issues of sexual pleasures and problems encountered by many Latinas in the United States.

Background

There are a number of social and cultural factors that form the context for Latino sexuality in the United States. Overall, Latinos comprise the largest "minority" group and the fastest growing ethnic group in the United States (U.S. Census Bureau, 2008). The term *Latino* generally refers to people who come or whose families have come from Latin American countries to live in the United States. It does not refer to any particular race or nationality. The term originally referred to those who originated in the Latin regions of Europe and who mainly spoke romance languages; however, it was adopted by the U.S. government in 1997 to refer to individuals in the United States coming from Latin America and it replaced the term *Hispanic*, which many saw as problematic (U.S. Census Bureau, 2008). There are a number of important differences among people who identify as Latino, including racial and ethnic differences, socioeconomic backgrounds, language, and culture. The diversity of Latinos makes dealing with topics such as sexuality and HIV particularly challenging and complex.

Studies indicate that Latinos in the United States make up a large portion of those living with HIV, accounting for 17% of new HIV infections in 2007 (Kaiser Family Foundation, 2006). Rates from the CDC surveillance report in 2007 indicated that Latinos were at an increased risk for HIV compared to their White counterparts (Centers for Disease Control [CDC], 2007a).[1] HIV prevention is therefore a health priority for this population.

The pathway to an effective HIV prevention program necessitates an examination of cultural and structural issues for the target population. Concerns over HIV often uncover preoccupations over contextual issues surrounding sexuality. HIV is often the "outcome" of both sexual pleasures and problems and thus pleasures and problems need to be investigated in the pursuit of HIV prevention. This chapter uses HIV as a springboard and the opportunity to discuss issues surrounding sexuality (pleasures and problems) relating to Latinas in the United States.

Gender Roles, Health Risks and Sexuality

Many understand gender to be the enactment of biological traits assigned at birth. Gender is expressed through emotions, thoughts, and behaviors that are ascribed to men and women by the dominant culture (Butler, 1993; Melendez & Tolman, 2006). Melendez and Tolman (2006) argued that "gender works together with larger social, cultural and economic structures to limit resources, ensuring that some individuals are more vulnerable to health risk than others" (p. 32). As West and Zimmerman (1987) explained, gender is a cultural construct and a feature of social structure, perpetuated because we continually "do gender." The manner in which women and men dress, talk, and interact with each other is representative of gender.

Gender roles refer to culturally prescribed norms or ways of being and acting that are particular to men and women (Gagnon & Parker, 1995). Gender roles found in cultural values and norms influence but do not define the behaviors of men and women (Amaro, Raj, Reed & Cranston, 2002). Traditional gender roles are most observable in heterosexual relationships where women's subordination and passive behavior to men is expected (Amaro, 1995; Ehrhardt & Exner, 2000; Wingood & DiClemente, 1995). Cultural norms often lead to gender roles where women are taught to be passive sexually (Amaro et al., 2002). Interpersonal sexual relationships are where gender roles are most evident, where women are expected to be passive and men active, women unknowledgeable and men knowledgeable, and women inexperienced compared to men's sexual experience. These roles often result in women's inability to demand safer sex practices from their male partners, to refuse sex when they are uncomfortable, and to continue in a relationship with an emotionally or physically abusive partner (Amaro et al., 2002). Such issues surrounding gender roles are especially relevant in the case of Latinos as much has been written about machismo and *marianismo*.

Machismo is the idea that a man is expected to be strong, sexually vigilant, and at the head of the household. Marianismo refers to the female virgin ideal, a woman who knows virtually nothing about sex (Burgos & Diaz-Perez, 1986). Marianismo characterizes women's roles in relation to men. It encourages women to be passive and naïve with regard to sex and to defer to their male partners. It refers to the ideal of women—to be like the Virgin Mary. Machismo and marianismo refer to an aspect of Latino culture which is not visible in all relationships and should not be applied to all Latinos/as carte blanche. Furthermore, these terms could easily be used to represent sexism and female status in a number of other cultures, including mainstream U.S. culture.

Another aspect of gender is that Latinas in the United States often feel put down and discriminated against. Many work long hours and have trouble finding support groups of other women to help them through their sometimes very challenging lives. When women have a partner, the partner often becomes their only source of support and comfort. Many women will not "rock the boat" by questioning their partner about sex outside the relationship or safer sex practices for fear of losing their partner and therefore their support. Women may feel validated in a relationship and they may feel that they must do everything to keep their partners happy: their own health and safety are not prioritized. These relationship dynamics oftentimes make it hard for women to advocate for their sexual pleasure or to protect themselves from HIV.

Many Latinas find it hard to talk to their partners about sex. The status of a woman vis-à-vis a man in a sexual relationship often does not allow for open and egalitarian communication regarding sexual matters and may lead to increased risk for HIV for Latinas (Amaro et al., 2002). Asking about a partner's current sexual health and practices is necessary and difficult. Women also have difficulty asking their partners to wear a condom as this brings up uncomfortable topics relating to multiple sexual partners. Some partners become angry and threatening.

Negotiating condom use can be particularly difficult in a long-term relationship, especially one in which there has been sex without a condom.

The experience of abuse and fear prevents women from protecting themselves. Typically, women give in to having sex under conditions that are unsafe. Many women experience physical, emotional, and sexual abuse when refusing sex with their partners or requesting that partners use a condom. Abuse among women often starts early in life. In a nationwide study of high school students, 15% of Latina high school students reported that they had been forced to have sex (Driscoll, Biggs, Brindis, & Yankah, 2001). Latinas who are forced to have sex are at risk for HIV through direct sexual contact with someone who may be HIV positive. Women who have experienced abuse in a relationship may find it especially hard to demand that their partner wear a condom to keep them safe from HIV.

Religion

Religion plays a large role in the sexual lives of many Latinas and several studies have demonstrated the effects of religious beliefs on the sexual beliefs and behaviors of women. Women are more likely to express interest in religion, have a stronger personal religious commitment, and attend church more frequently than men, regardless of religious affiliation or belief system (Batson, Schoenrade, & Ventis, 1993; Stark & Bainbridge, 1985). Moreover, women are more likely than men to pray and read the Bible (Davis & Smith, 1991). Women who score higher on femininity scales such as the Bem Sex Role Inventory (Bem, 1981) also score higher on religiosity measures such as spirituality and church attendance (Francis & Wilcox, 1996). Another study found that women who are religiously devout endorse more traditional attitudes toward gender roles than their less religiously committed counterparts (Morgan, 1987).

While many Latinas identify as Catholic, they represent a number of diverse religious backgrounds, including increasingly more popular forms of evangelical Christianity. How religion facilitates or prevents risky sexual behaviors relates to how the religious organizations discuss sexuality and gender roles. Women in many religious belief systems are seen as subservient to their male partners or husbands. In fact, they play secondary roles in religious services, for example, often assisting the male priest or male pastor. The roles women play in religious services are often replicated in the home between women and their male partners.

Acculturation and Health of Latinos in the United States

Immigrants cope with conflicting cultural and social norms and expectations while attempting to adjust to life in a new country (Rhodes,

Hergenrather, Zometa, Lindstrom, & Montano, 2008). Acculturation usually refers to the process by which immigrants learn a second culture—that of the predominant cultural group (Rogler, Malgady, Costantino, & Blumenthal, 1987), although there are many different interpretations of this term as well as methods of measurement. Acculturation, unlike assimilation where people lose their history, culture, and sense of self, refers to feeling comfortable and identifying with both cultures (Marin, 1992). With regard to Latino health, several studies have noted a "paradox." Studies have found a lower mortality rate among Latinos in the United States when compared to their White counterparts. The discrepancy is perplexing due to the lower rates of medical access of Latinos when compared to their White counterparts. More detailed investigations note that less acculturated Latinos have lower health risks such as smoking and alcohol use than higher acculturated Latinos (Abraído-Lanza, Chao, & Flórez, 2005). Therefore, some have noted that maintaining a connection to the culture and ways of life found in Latin America may be one explanation for the improved health outcome of Latinos.

Latinos with increased acculturation may face higher incidence of not only HIV, but also other illnesses such as diabetes, obesity, substance abuse, and heart disease—part of the "paradox" discussed earlier. Research by Harawa and colleagues found that most HIV positive Latino men become infected after their migration to the United States, suggesting that social and economic instability may increase susceptibility to HIV infections (Harawa, Bingham, Cochran, Greenland, & Cunningham, 2002). Although Latinos enter the country being HIV negative, they often seroconvert as they acculturate within the United States.

It is unclear how acculturation and adherence to gender roles work with respect to Latinas' HIV risk. Many Latinas may feel the need to identify and prove their cultural allegiance to their Latino roots and may enact the role of the traditional Latina—faithful to a husband or partner who may not be faithful to them. They may refuse to discuss issues relating to sexuality because their mothers and grandmothers taught them it was "improper" to talk about sex. They may also place the goal of a unified family over their own sexual needs and health.

Sexuality

Migration, hand in hand with acculturation, also has an impact on the sexual lives of Latinas. For Latinas, migration to the United States adds additional barriers for sexual health concerns. Couples where one person migrates to another country often experience long periods of separation. There is often an unspoken sentiment that the male partner (and sometimes the female partner) will have sex with other partners during the period of long separation. The lack of communication surrounding these plans can lead to increased tension in the relationship and may decrease sexual satisfaction among both men and women (Agger & Jensen, 1989). It has been noted that one of the main areas of risk for Latina women is their male partners' extradyadic relationships with both women and men (Gavey & McPhillips, 1997).

Women in particular may suffer from decreased sexual satisfaction due to increased stress relating to immigration. One study of Latina women (migrants in the United States) seeking gynecologic care compared their sexual pleasure with that of women who had migrated from Spain. The Latina women had lower scores on measures of sexual functioning than did the Spanish women. Although there are many possible confounding factors, it may be that Latinas have added pressures relating to migration to survive economically and socially and that in turn creates barriers to sexual satisfaction (Hullfish et al., 2009). There was also a higher incidence of anxiety and depression among the Latina women which correlated with decreased sexual pleasure. Despite reports of decreased pleasure, it appears that Latinas report similar or slightly higher rates of sexual activity when compared to U.S. White, Black, and Asian women (Huang et al., 2009). These data may indicate that Latinas feel a need to engage in sexual activity with their male partners despite lower sexual satisfaction. Gender role expectations for Latinas often include satisfying male partners but usually do not address issues of sexual satisfaction for women.

Many Latinas have left families behind in Latin America and are faced with minimal social networks, with the result that they are solely dependent on male partners for advice and survival. Dependence on a male partner may pressure women to stay in abusive relationships or to fear "rocking the boat" by confronting men about extradyadic relationships or practicing safer sex. Many migrant women face the burdens of childcare alone and find it difficult if not impossible to seek support outside of the home. Support from other women is difficult to find when you do not know anyone in the new country. Migration offers new challenges to the family and women feel the need to take care of those challenges for their families. This results in the reprioritization of women's concerns about their own issues below the health and well-being of her family.

HIV among Latinas

Rates of HIV infection are four times greater for Latinas than for White women (CDC, 2007a). Latinas comprise 21% of all AIDS diagnoses among Latinos, compared to 15% of White women and 36% of African American women, suggesting that Latinas may delay access to care after infection occurs. As a result, HIV positive Latinos/as, have lower CD4 counts and more opportunistic infections[2] than non-Hispanics Whites.

Nationally, the HIV/AIDS case rate among Latinos/as is 3.5 times higher than in Whites and is second only to that of African Americans (Kaiser Family Foundation, 2008).

The main source of infection for Latinas is heterosexual contact with men. The gender system espoused by many Latinos may also form critical barriers for both women and men in terms of HIV prevention and care. Latinas, like women all over the world, may find it difficult to negotiate safer sex practices with their male partners who may expect them to be passive and naive about sexuality and behaviors. There is little research comparing the sexual behaviors of Latino men to those of other ethnicities; however, many reports indicate that Latinos who engage in risky sexual behaviors may unknowingly place their female partners at risk for HIV. Risky behaviors include: sex with other female partners, sex with male partners, and intravenous drug use (see CDC, 2009). However, many Latinas do not see themselves at risk for sexually transmitted infections (STIs) or HIV since they have only one partner. Doctors may also reinforce this belief by not asking about HIV testing if married or in a monogamous relationship. Amongst Latinos, HIV is often considered a gay man's disease and not something they need to worry about. Additionally, a diagnosis of HIV is highly stigmatizing and women may fear losing their partners, children, and livelihood if they are found to be positive.

Access to Health Care

The increase in HIV risk among Latina immigrants is compounded by a widespread problem of access to health care. There are a number of factors that prevent Latinas from accessing adequate health care including: language, documentation issues, and perceptions of discrimination. Distrust of the health care system and of health service providers, limited clinic hours, lack of bilingual and bicultural resources, and insufficient public transportation also have been identified as significant barriers to accessing health care for this population (Rhodes et al., 2008).

Spanish-speaking Latinas may not seek care due to language barriers. Going to a health provider can be challenging for all individuals, but it is especially challenging if your provider does not understand what you are saying. Speaking the same language as a patient is one way health care providers can make Latinas feel welcome in their practice. Many Latinas will not have access to an interpreter who can translate for them. If they do have access to an interpreter, such as a child or friend, there are worries about confidentiality with regard to the information the medical professional provides. Women may be embarrassed about having their children or friends know about their sexual health issues such as HIV or other STIs. Since most routine annual check-ups for women also include a gynecological exam, this may cause embarrassment or concern about information that the translator will know (Rhodes et al., 2008).

In the recent past, the United States has experienced increased public concern and police activity surrounding illegal migration. For this reason, many documented and undocumented Latinas may fear visiting a health care provider. Documented Latinas (those with federal paperwork that verifies their legal residence in the United States) may not wish to be asked about their migration status and undocumented Latinas may fear that the health care provider will inform the authorities about their identity. Many Latinas in the United States will not seek health care services for fear they will be asked about their documentation status regardless of their actual status. Many fear being treated poorly by health care staff or not at all. These issues lead to the stigma Latinos/as may face when seeking HIV testing or services.

Many Latinas work in jobs with no health benefits and are not able to afford costly health services. These structural barriers mean that Latinas often go without routine medical care and may only discover illnesses otherwise caught by routine examinations, such as STIs, HIV, and breast or colon cancer. Due to the inability of many Latinas to pay for health care, they are often forced to navigate a system of free or low-cost health care which can be burdensome and bureaucratic. This may also lead to a sense that many barriers exist for health care, including uncertainty as to eligibility to receive free or low-cost health care.

A number of simple, logistic factors also deter Latinas from health care. Women grapple with often overbooked days juggling work, transportation to and from work, as well as care for children or other family members. Paying for transportation to and from health care sites may be a particular challenge, especially if home or work is located outside of city centers where many free and low-cost health services exist. Childcare is a major concern for women. Many Latinas may not want to bring their children to health care providers for fear of more stigma and discrimination and because they need privacy when seeking health care services.

Due to the barriers preventing health care access in the United States, many Latinas continue to seek care in their home countries or through self-medication. Many will return to medical professionals when returning home for visits, whereas others may seek more traditional medical practices and find home remedies (such as herbal teas or other medications) to help with symptoms of illnesses.

Approaches to Treatment: HIV Prevention Programs for Latinas

Information surrounding sexuality issues for Latinas is difficult to attain and a review of HIV prevention programs for Latinas highlights important issues and areas of concern for Latina sexuality. These programs often address many sexuality related issues that Latinas face in general in order to address HIV prevention. According to recent reports concerning HIV prevention (CDC, 2009; Diaz, Ayala, Bein, Henne, & Marin, 2001; Shedlin, Decena, & Oliver-Velez, 2005), there is an increasing need for the establishment of culturally sensitive intervention programs to address the needs of target populations. Many researchers have called for an increase in peer educators from target populations' communities to underscore the relevance of a program's content and the subsequent effectiveness (Bracero, 1998; Wingood & DiClemente, 1995; Flaskerud & Nyamathi, 1990; Mize, Robinson, Bockting, & Scheltema, 2002). Weeks, Schensul, Williams, and Grier (1995) suggested that culture-specific HIV prevention curriculum and education is more likely to lead to positive outcomes (Scott, Gilliam, & Braxton, 2005; Weeks et al., 1995).

In 1997, Flaskerud, Nyamathi, and Uman reviewed the literature on HIV interventions for Latina women and found that culturally competent programs typically emphasized four factors: (a) cultural values, customs, and traditions; (b) social networks and the use of the extended family; (c) peer counseling with an educator of the same ethnic and gender background; and (d) innovative communication strategies. Since the publication of this article, there has been a concerted effort among scholars to examine the relevance and effectiveness of culturally competent programs for Latinas. Mujeres Unidas y Activas (MUA), for instance, focuses on the empowerment of undocumented Latinas in San Francisco's Mission District. Specifically, the program seeks to provide women with the tools and information necessary to improve their economic, political, and social status as immigrants. Gomez, Hernandez, and Faigeles (1999) remarked that even though the primary focus at MUA is on the empowerment of Latina women, there are a number of specific HIV intervention strategies that have proven successful in this particular context. For instance, self-esteem support sessions and friendship circles provide Latinas with an important opportunity to discuss issues such as women's sexual rights, domestic violence, and HIV exposure and prevention, and the authors found that those who attended MUA showed significant changes in behaviors and perceptions after 6 months, including increased comfort while discussing sex, and a decrease in beliefs concerning traditional gender roles (Gomez, Hernandez, & Faigeles, 1999).

In 1997, Flaskerud et al. drew further attention to the need to expand and adapt HIV programs when they evaluated a Los Angeles low-income initiative that targeted Latinas. This particular program concentrated on HIV education, counseling, and antibody testing, and relied on a firm understanding of cultural values by making use of the role of the family and peer educators from similar ethnic, cultural, and linguistic backgrounds. A similar program focused on providing women with the vocabulary as well as a safe space to talk about sex was Salud, Educacion, Prevencion y Autocuidado (Project SEPA) in the Midwest. Project SEPA was designed as a pilot program for low-income Latinas in Chicago in order to evaluate the effectiveness of a culturally sensitive intervention program in reducing high-risk sexual behaviors. Latinas between the ages of 18 and 44 from low income Puerto Rican and Mexican communities, engaged in a series of activities like role-playing, skill determination homework, quizzes on condom use, HIV, and assertiveness. After 3 months, women's communication with their partners, their knowledge of HIV, and their condom use had increased, further demonstrating the importance of culture to HIV interventions (Peragallo et al., 2005). The Department of Public Health in Massachusetts also sought to promote communication surrounding sex and sexuality through the creation of two evidenced based HIV prevention programs for Latinas: the HIV-Intensive Prevention (HIV-IP) and the Women's Health Program. These two programs were completely Spanish-language based and culturally tailored to promote sexual risk reduction specifically for Latinas. In addition, the programs made use of bilingual community health educators who were respected in their communities and experienced in HIV education and curriculum. In terms of outcomes, participants in both groups responded positively to the culture-specific interventions. Overall, they felt safe and comfortable sharing their thoughts and feelings surrounding HIV during the sessions. Further, reviews also suggested that the women took pride in being a resource for their families on safe sex practices and HIV prevention (Raj et al., 2001).

Project Children's Health and Responsible Mothering (CHARM) in LA County devised an HIV education curriculum specifically for African American and Latina teen mothers. Among the topics discussed by the students were the impact of HIV on both the mother and the child, the prevention of HIV during pregnancy and postpartum, as well as any other special cultural concerns that came up for the teens during the course of the program. Between 1997 and 1999, the program was implemented in four local school districts. In terms of outcomes, CHARM received positive feedback from the participants largely because of its cultural focus and the fact that it was designed entirely for pregnant teens and young mothers. Based on this success, CHARM II was initiated specifically as a health promotion program and was administered to 150 girls during four 2-hour classes. Koniak-Griffen, Lesser, Uman, and Cumberland (2003) evaluated both programs and noted that the main benefits accrued by the young women were an increased knowledge of condom use and HIV. In terms of behavioral changes, the authors noted a decrease in the number of sex partners (Koniak-Griffen et al., 2003). Student Education Needed in Order to Reduce Infection and Transmission of AIDS/HIV and STDs (SENORITAS) was designed as a peer-based HIV education program for Latina and Caribbean students at Florida International University. The program was created in response to the increasing rates of HIV cases among female students in Miami and shown to reduce the incidence of HIV among college-age Latinas. In addition to implementing culturally competent programs, SENORITAS also made use of peer educators, who were responsible for designing the program's curriculum (Uno, Dos, Tres for the Latina students, Un, Deux, Trois for the Haitian students, and One, Two, Three for the Caribbean/West Indies students). Similar to other initiatives mentioned above that incorporate culture into their programs, SENORITAS resulted in positive outcomes; for example, the student peer educators' ability to teach the material increased considerably over the course of the semester, as did their knowledge of HIV transmission and comfort discussing prevention measures (Jones, Patsdaugher, Jorda, Hamilton, & Marlow, 2008).

In addition to developing programs specifically for Latinas, some efforts have been made to deal with young male Latinos in an attempt to address issues of gender equality and sexuality (see also Kegeles, Hays, & Coates, 1996). Program H, for instance, was developed in 1999 by four nongovernmental organizations (NGOs) in Latin America. The goal of Program H was to help young men in Latin America question traditional gender roles. A curriculum was designed that included several different types of material in order to promote attitude and behavior change among the participants and in the community. In addition, the program sought to reduce young men's barriers to clinic services. Results indicated that participation in the activities led to increased empathy on the part of the young men, which in turn led to a positive reflection on the treatment of their female partners (Barker, 2003). Peer-based health programs designed specifically for both sexes within the Latino community in the United States have also proven successful in HIV prevention. In North Carolina, for example, Protegiendo Nuestra Comunidad consisted of a 7-week, 21-hour culture-specific community based program conducted in Spanish to empower local health workers (McQuiston, Choi-Hevel, & Clawson, 2001; see also Land & Hudson, 2004). The idea behind the program was that once trained, these health workers would in turn help community members promote sexual health by disseminating information to friends, family, and coworkers. Preliminary results from an evaluation of the program indicated that participants viewed the training positively and were comfortable and able to actively discuss all topics covered. However, those sessions that covered sex roles and traditional values remained difficult for both men and women, especially when role-playing activities were involved, proving the need for more culture-specific training programs on sexuality and gender equality in HIV interventions (McQuiston et al., 2001).

The HIV prevention programs for Latinas emphasize several points relevant for Latina sexuality. First, there is a need to empower Latinas in their sexual relationships. Related to this point is the need to increase communication among Latinas, both with their male sex partners and also overall to gain more support and information concerning sex. Second, it is important to provide Spanish speaking and culturally relevant information. Latinas may be more comfortable and able to implement what they hear if it comes from women who feel familiar to them, especially with regard to language. Third, there is a great need to provide resources for Latinas to gain more access to services and basic information surrounding sexual health.

Case Study—"Entre Amigas"

The contextual issues of Latina sexuality result in a number of difficult sexual health outcomes for Latinas, including but not limited to HIV. Likewise, to adequately tackle HIV infection among Latinas, it is imperative that both the structural and cultural contextual issues be addressed. To this end, La Clínica del Pueblo, an NGO in Washington, DC, introduced an innovative HIV prevention program targeted to Latina immigrants—Entre Amigas. This program will be discussed as an example of issues relating to Latina sexuality that are commonplace in a number of communities in the United States.

La Clínica del Pueblo was founded in 1983 in Washington, DC to provide for the medical and mental health care needs of Salvadoran and other Central American immigrants. Many immigrants were unable to access health care due to the cultural and language barriers they found in the United States. Initially, La Clínica was a one-room clinic, operating one night per week, run by a volunteer doctor. Today, La Clínica has 85 staff members all of whom speak Spanish. Three quarters of the staff are from Central and South America and have characteristics similar to those of the patients. The clinic also has over 100 volunteers, several of them La Clínica patients and is now open 6 days a week; in 2007, it provided more than 55,000 services to over 7,500 individuals.

La Clínica is a pioneering organization that addresses many of the barriers discussed above for women by providing culturally competent care and services. By integrating a number of services under one roof, Latinos, both male and female, have a location they can count on that provides services in Spanish (from the front desk to the doctor's office), encourages comprehensive care, provides child care, is near public transportation, and occasionally takes its programs to suburban areas where Latinos reside. La Clínica offers primary care (with a focus on family medicine and including alternative medicine), mental health care, HIV/

AIDS prevention, social services, interpretation services, community health outreach and education, and advocacy.

Within La Clínica, Entre Amigas addresses HIV risk among Latinas. Entre Amigas is an educational program aimed at adult immigrant Latinas living in metropolitan DC. This educational HIV intervention addresses underlying sociocultural factors that place immigrant Latinas at risk for HIV. The most notable factors are a lack of access to culturally appropriate health care, information, and education about HIV in Spanish; a lack of awareness of how traditional gender roles in family relations, sexuality, sexual health, and gender violence, place them at risk of infection by HIV. The intervention consists of four workshops of 16 total hours plus a "graduation" delivered over 5 days. Each workshop lasts 4 hours and allows women to exchange ideas, feelings, and worries, as well as to reflect about these and to consider making healthy choices concerning their health and relationships including HIV prevention.

Entre Amigas and Selena S

Selena S was raised in a traditional, Guatemalan family. The family endured many changes upon migrating to the United States. Like other migrants, Selena felt isolated and spoke mainly with her family members and close friends. This meant she had few people to speak to about the problems she witnessed in her family, including alcoholism and abuse. While her father worked hard and provided for her family, he also drank a lot and would hit Selena's mother on occasion. Selena's mother found work only occasionally cleaning houses and she could not survive on her own. Selena grew up believing this happened in all families. In an effort to protect her children, her mother never spoke of the abuse. The mother also felt that having a partner who worked and could provide food and housing was better than living in poverty, so she put up with the abuse for the sake of her children.

When Selena met her future husband in high school, she felt that he too would be a good provider. She had never had a boyfriend. Although she was inexperienced, she enjoyed sex with her husband. The relationship with her husband began to change after the birth of her daughter. She did not know that her husband had begun to use drugs. His behavior seemed more and more erratic as time went on. She enjoyed sex less and finally not at all. One day he beat her up and she ended up in the emergency room. The hospital was the first place where she ever received any support or assistance for her domestic violence problems as she was visited by the staff social worker who spoke to her of her options if she decided to leave her husband. Her mother was unsupportive of her decision to leave her husband, saying that she should give him another chance and that she needed his help to survive.

After she left her husband, Selena dedicated herself to taking care of her daughter. For a time, she wanted nothing to do with men. But slowly she began to ease into dating and became less fearful that male partners would be like her former husband. She had no one to answer the many questions she had about dating. She did not know what men expected in terms of when they would expect to have sex, she did not know how her daughter would react to her having a boyfriend, and also Selena did not know anything about birth control. Selena's former husband had been her only boyfriend. She did not know what to expect from dating as an adult woman with a daughter.

Selena's cousin had gone through Entre Amigas and said that she should also go to this program. Sensing Selena's embarrassment about sexual topics, her aunt reassured her that the program was a way to learn about resources and to get to know women in the community. Because the program was in Spanish, provided women with child care, and was a way to meet others, Selena thought it would be fun to try.

The First Workshop. The first workshop centered on discussions and exercises about self-care aimed to create an integrative definition of health. By reflecting on Latinas' tendency to take care of others and to neglect themselves, participants uncovered their vulnerabilities with regard to health. One way this was accomplished was for the facilitators of the group to begin a discussion of what the most common daily activities were for each woman. As a group, participants noted that their activities centered on the maintenance and well-being of others, with little time for themselves. The activity was presented as an exercise where women retold their day-to-day activities, thus enabling them to see a pattern versus being told what the pattern was.

Selena noted that women struggled with putting themselves first before partners and family. Indeed, many women spoke about their family's needs and their role in making sure that they were taken care of. One women spoke about the guilt she felt for not helping her 23-year-old son to learn English. Another woman said, "We Latinas care more about our husbands and our children than ourselves." The feelings of self-sacrifice led to feelings of guilt for wanting to take care of themselves both physically as well as sexually. Women struggled with the notion of having a right to sexual pleasure. One participant said, "First we are mothers, and then we are women."

Selena immediately identified with the group. She noticed that while the other women had very different lives, all the women placed others' needs before their needs. Selena felt that she was consistently working to take care of her daughter; if her family needed help, she provided that help, but there was very little time left for Selena to do things that she cared for and that made her happy. Selena, like other women, had also put off going to the doctor because she had so little time.

The Second Workshop. The second workshop discussed the human body (giving names to female anatomy) and the expression of sexuality. One fun exercise Selena and the others engaged in was competing to see how many colloquial names they could come up with for "vagina" and "penis." This made the women laugh but also taught them how much they already have heard about sex. Selena learned how the increased surface area of the vagina makes women more vulnerable to HIV infection compared to men. They spoke about the sexual myths they had heard, such as that women do not have anal sex and that only gay men get HIV. The women also spoke about the difficulties women have negotiating safer sex with male partners. As a group the women fielded questions and supported each other in the challenge of getting more information about their sexual health and safety. It is important to understand that many of these women have difficulties understanding English and therefore names and information can become confused. In a group such as Entre Amigas, the diversity is a strength because some women may have the answers for other women, which may serve as a means of empowering all women.

Selena had never spoken so openly about her body and sex! She was surprised that women had many of the same questions she had. Even learning about her period was something new to her. Selena had never known that the clitoris existed and was happy to learn that clitoral stimulation resulted in orgasms. She felt empowered to know her body and to know what could bring her pleasure and felt that she knew she could ask this from her future male partners. While Selena was warming up to the group, she noticed that the women in the group were becoming friends and enjoying each other's company. She felt that the friendship and support she found in the group had been missing from her life.

In another exercise, women wrote down what they had heard about HIV with regard to transmission. The statements were reviewed as a group and discussed. Women were informed about the ways that HIV can be transmitted. They entered the program thinking that HIV can be transmitted by saliva, urine, hugging, and kissing and left knowing this was not correct. Selena thought that human papillomavirus (HPV) and HIV were the same thing. About one-third of the women (33%) thought that they could get HIV from hugging and kissing someone who is infected; this reduced to two women (10% of the participants) at the post workshop survey ($p = .087$). To address these issues, one exercise divided the room into three groups: "true," "false," and "don't know." Statements such as "HIV can be transmitted by blood" were read to the group and women moved around the room to note if they thought the statement was true or if they did not know. At first Selena waited until she saw where most of the women were moving and then she would go with the majority. However, it soon became obvious that the majority was not always right and Selena felt relaxed enough to make her own choices, to celebrate when she and the others were correct, and to laugh with her group when they found themselves in the wrong place.

Women who went through Entre Amigas also came to see themselves as at greater risk for HIV than they had previously thought. One woman said: "In my country, we don't talk about HIV. I used to believe that women cannot get infected because HIV was a disease of homosexuals." Many of the women suspected that their partners were having sex with other women, yet they still felt it was difficult to negotiate condom use with their partners for fear their partners would think they were being accused of "sleeping around." Selena had likewise felt uncomfortable sleeping with her ex-husband when she suspected he had slept around but felt too scared to bring it up with him. Condom negotiation remained difficult for women. Some women suggested telling their partner that the condom was to prevent pregnancy. Others said that the moment condoms are brought up with a partner trust has been broken ("It is accepting that infidelity exists"). Others said that negotiating condoms "makes infidelity a problem in the relationship." While many women felt that having a single partner made them safe with regard to infection, they were alerted by the information in the workshops as well as by the other women in the group that they too could be at risk for HIV through this single partner. Before the workshop 30% of the women knew that women are infected with HIV more easily than men; after the workshop, this had increased to 55% ($p = .022$).

Additionally, Selena and the women were uncomfortable handling condoms. They did not want to touch them and would make faces when they were passed around. The group at La Clínica met to discuss ways of making women more comfortable with male condoms with the hope that their comfort would translate to their sexual relationships. Each woman was given a male and female condom to play with during the session and they were also given these to take home. Their "homework" assignment was to use or to play with the condoms.

While no men attended the Entre Amigas program, there were a number of discussions surrounding male sexuality that came up in the groups. From the women's perspectives, men seemed to be burdened with their traditional gender role and unable to communicate effectively about their sexual desires with their long-term female partners. The women also felt that it was difficult to bring up their desires and needs with their male partners. For example, Selena was interested in and willing to have anal sex with a male partner. However, she felt guilty just admitting to herself that this is what she wanted and felt that she could never approach a man with this desire. However, the more she spent time in the program, the more she realized that all women had sexual desires that were unique to them and that they could be pursued much like men pursue their own sexual desires with women. For Selena, talking about sex, understanding that her sexual interests were normal and shared by other woman made her feel more relaxed about sex.

These experiences had multiple effects on the sexual lives of the Latinas in the group. Because it was difficult for the women to bring up their desires and needs with their male partners and because the male partners seemed reluctant to do the same, sex was not as pleasurable as it might otherwise have been. The majority of the women also feared that their male partners were having sex outside of the relationship. This fear led them to feel uncomfortable and uneasy in their relationships and specifically in their sexual activities with their partners.

The Third Workshop. The third workshop explored gender-based violence and the cycles of violence many women find themselves in, where women are brought up in a violent home and come to expect a life with violence from their male partner. The workshop endeavored to demonstrate how gender conditioning makes women more vulnerable to HIV infection, provoking a feminization of the HIV epidemic. In fact, 39% of participants said they did not know if their main partner was having sex with someone outside of the relationship. One example of an exercise for this session included asking the women to break into smaller groups and have them discuss and answer questions such as: "What is violence?" "What are the different forms of violence?" and "How does violence impact HIV?"

Relating to gender-based violence, the importance of discussing sexuality and pleasure was immediately apparent to the staff at La Clínica. Women were hindered in their discussion of sexual health because they were uncomfortable discussing and dealing with their sexuality. The workshops emphasized the need for safety within the context for pleasure. Part of sexual comfort for women is the knowledge and the ability to refuse sex when they feel unsafe. In the preworkshop survey, 45% of women said they felt comfortable refusing sex when asked by their male partner; this increased to 70% in the postworkshop survey ($p = .068$). Also important was the fact that about 10% more women said that they felt comfortable using condoms as part of sexual play after the workshops, compared with before the workshops started ($p = .05$).

Before the workshop, Selena had not identified different types of abuse in her marriage. However, she shared with others in the group that she had had sex with her husband on numerous occasions when she did not want to, in order to avoid a fight, prevent him from having sex with another woman, or to quell his jealousy that she might be interested in another man. Selena was able to share her story with the group because other women had similar stories. Recognizing that what she tried to do to save the relationship had taken the pleasure out of sex, Selena was rethinking this strategy. She was one of the women who felt that they would be able to refuse unwanted sex from their partner in the future. Selena thought she was doing the right thing, but now thought it is best to say "no" to sex when she doesn't want to have sex.

The Fourth Workshop. The fourth workshop discussed how immigration and acculturation processes impact self-esteem, feelings of isolation, and depression. It also provided information about resources available to Latinas and discussed the positive influence of support networks as a protective factor to prevent HIV infection. Women were asked to describe and write down some of the main concerns they had relating to stress in their lives. At the end of the discussion, resources were given to women to address these concerns; for example, women with unstable housing were referred to a partner organization that could help with public housing applications. In cases where there were no resources for women, plans were developed for ways to seek help or support.

Selena had a job that required long hours, no time off, and did not offer her health benefits. As a result, Selena had not had a pap smear in over 3 years. She was reminded that she could make an evening (after work) appointment with a physician at La Clínica for gynecologic care.

The Fifth Workshop. The fifth workshop was a collective celebration and a graduation ceremony emphasizing self-commitment and self-responsibility for the health and well-being of participants. Women received a certificate of completion and made plans about their future activities with regard not only to their sexual health, but their relationships, work, and their relationships with themselves. Selena used this time to make plans with the other women to continue seeing each other. Selena also found out about the resources offered at La Clínica and decided to come and find out about housing and employment workshops. She finished the program knowing that she had the tools to have a healthier relationship with a male partner in the future, one that did not involve abuse and would place her at decreased risk for HIV. More importantly, the relationship would bring her joy and pleasure in her life, rather than be a source of pain.

Summary

The program at Entre Amigas hit home on several issues for Selena and other Latinas. First of all, it talked about sex in a fun and interactive manner. Selena had only rudimentary knowledge of women's anatomy and had never learned about HIV in school. She had no idea about how her body functioned, how she was at risk for STIs, or even how to have an orgasm. As her primary language was Spanish, there was not enough time or motivation for her to pay close attention to the new words for the one or two times sex was discussed in her high school health class. She learned a lot in the Entre Amigas sessions because they were in Spanish and there was a lot of laughter surrounding all discussions that made women comfortable shouting out their answers to questions.

Selena, like her cousin, appreciated the opportunity she had at Entre Amigas to talk openly about sex. Although she considered herself to be Catholic, and went to church every week, over the years Selena recognized her inability to discuss or learn anything about sexuality in her church. She commented, "At Church, they only mention marriage, there is nothing outside the family. I could never even think of talking about my boyfriends with the priest or any of the people who I see in Church—they would look down on me." She went on to say, "the Church always likes putting the men on a higher level than women, like, women are supposed to do whatever the man says." Selena did not like being told that men should be in charge of her household, since she did not have a man in her life and because she felt that her ex-husband had not been a good husband to her. She also did not want a new boyfriend to take charge of her life in a way she felt the Church suggested. Selena had an increased sense of self-worth and felt that she needed to wait to have a husband who she liked. There was no longer an internal voice telling her she was not whole without a husband.

For Selena the information about condoms that Entre Amigas provided was invaluable. She had never asked a male partner to use a condom as she thought she would be insulting her partner by implying that he had a disease. She had, however, never associated her upbringing as a Latina with her inability to ask for a condom from a male partner. As she noted, "[a] lot of women grow up with the idea that their husband should be in control, especially when it comes to sexual situations, so it's hard for them to take control [to] sort of say, I need you to use a condom. That could also be really difficult if you've been having sex with your partner you know, for a long time without a condom and then you think … I want to stay safe and make sure everything is okay. That's really difficult." Selena's confidence negotiating with her male partners increased dramatically after Entre Amigas. She was able to talk openly about HIV with her partners. Because she was comfortable and confident, her partners rarely questioned her approach.

Although the program was dedicated to women and their sexuality, it had an interesting effect on the lives of the male partners. Because women knew more about sex, they were more comfortable having sex.

They also knew that it was OK to learn more about sex and to seek their own pleasure in their sex lives. This had the unexpected result of creating a more satisfying sex life for the male partners of the women who went through Entre Amigas. In fact, many male partners asked their partners to continue attending the classes because they enjoyed their partner's new found sexuality.

The tasks set out by La Clínica were challenging. Trying to incorporate a number of structural and cultural factors into one program to address the sexual health needs of Latinas was daunting even for this organization with long roots in the Latino communities in Washington. The trials and tribulations of the Entre Amigas program were presented here to offer some perspective as to what the challenges are now that the program has been running for some time and undergone a preliminary evaluation. Entre Amigas, we hope, will serve as an example for others interested in working with Latinas around issues of sexuality.

Lessons Learned

Taken together, the background information, experience with Entre Amigas and Selena's story point to a number of recommendations for providing assistance to Latinas surrounding sexual issues they encounter. This final section will touch on four key lessons: (a) issues to address with Latinos in sex therapy; (b) providing group level programs for women; (c) rechecking with the target population on content; (d) providing basic HIV information; and (e) getting support from a diverse group.

There are a number of factors that need to be addressed with regard to Latinos and sex therapy. First, it is imperative to recognize the vast diversity among Latinos and to know that all, some, or none of these issues may be pertinent to their lives. Immigration and the stress relating to being in a new culture or balancing two cultures is an important factor relating to sexuality for Latinos. The roles relating to family and gender may be important factors to consider in relation to how Latinos live out their sexual lives. Likewise, religion and family traditions can play a central role for Latinos with regard to their sexual relationships. While these topics are often difficult to approach, it is imperative that they be addressed as important factors contributing to sexual health and pleasure.

While many prefer to deal with sexual problems and issues on an individual level, a powerful case can be made that group level interventions offer a safe space for Latinas to discuss their sexuality and to learn important information. The group level program offered by Entre Amigas provided women from diverse areas of life the opportunity to learn from each other. Information was discussed in a social manner that led women to open up about their lives. The secondary effect of the program was for women to feel that they were not alone and that other women shared many of their concerns. There may be a lot of guilt surrounding the discussion of sexuality among Latinas. While individual discussions may help many Latinas with this, the group can help women open up about sexuality related topics and to learn from someone who they see as a peer.

There is an important need to "recheck" with the target population. Although researchers and NGOs have a good grasp of the needs of their target group, it is important to conduct basic research to ensure, validate, or change topics being addressed. The Latino population is a highly mobile and ever-changing group. The needs of one group may be different from another, and may also depend on age. The formative phase for Entre Amigas was crucial to ensure that the topics of the workshops were relevant for the group. The staff at Entre Amigas also made sure to integrate into existing groups new information or questions that had been raised in previous groups. It is important for NGOs to continually ensure that programs and workshops are up to date and relevant.

As with the women from Entre Amigas, the information that needs to be covered may be basic. While HIV information seems ubiquitous to many, for these women the basic knowledge they had was incorrect. Due to the fact that during the formative phase it was discovered that women were misunderstanding transmission routes for HIV, this was built into the program.

Finally, while many researchers limit the programs to a specific group or national background (such as 18- to 25-year-old women from Mexico), the diversity of Entre Amigas was a clear benefit to the program. Women from different backgrounds came together and discussed their experiences, which benefitted the group. Women who knew more about HIV provided the information they had to those who knew less. Women saw those who spoke about their sexual relationships or who knew about HIV or condoms and they had positive examples for emulating this kind of behavior. Women learned from each other and that strengthened them individually. The end result was a sense of empowerment for all women.

Acknowledgments

The authors would like to thank the participants of Entre Amigas. The National Aids Fund and the Johnson and Johnson Foundation supported Entre Amigas through the Generations II program. The first author would also like to thank the participants of the interviews conducted in 2009 and the HISTP program from Columbia School of Social Work for their support of this research.

Notes

1. The rate of HIV infection among Latinos in the United States is difficult to establish due to a number of factors, such as mobility within the United States, migration between the United States and the home country, lack of access to health insurance or care, lack of documentation and legal immigrant status, as well as cultural factors that prevent many Latinos from seeking HIV testing and care.
2. CD4 cells are white blood cells that fight infection. A CD4 count measures the strength of the immune system and indicates the stage of HIV disease. Opportunistic infections are infections and illnesses caused by the weakened immune system in people with HIV (CDC, 2007b).

References

Abraído-Lanza, A., F., Chao, M., T., & Flórez, K., R. (2005). Healthy behaviors decline with greater acculturation?: Implications for the Latino mortality paradox. *Social Science & Medicine, 61,* 1243–1255.

Agger, I., & Jensen, S. (1989). Couples in exile: Political consciousness as an element in the psychosexual dynamics of a Latin American refugee couple. *Sexual & Marital Therapy, 4,* 101–108.

Amaro, H. (1995). Love, sex and power: Considering women's realities in HIV prevention. *American Psychologist, 50,* 437–447.

Amaro, H., Raj, A., Reed, E., & Cranston, K. (2002). Implementation and long-term outcomes of two HIV intervention programs for Latinas. *Health Promotion Practice, 3,* 245–254.

Barker, G. (2003 October 21–24). *How do we know if men have changed? Promoting and measuring attitude change with young men.* Paper presented at the Lessons from Program H in Latin America. Expert Group Meeting on "The Role of Men and Boys in Achieving Gender Equality," Brasilia, Brazil.

Batson, C. D., Schoenrade, P., & Ventis, W. L. (1993). *Religion and the individual: A social-psychological perspective.* Oxford, England: Oxford University Press.

Bem, S. (1981). *Sex-role inventory: Professional manual.* Palo Alto, CA: Consulting Psychologists Press.

Bracero, W. (1998). Intimidades: Confianza, gender, and hierarchy in the construction of Latino-Latina therapeutic relationships. *Cultural Diversity and Dental Health, 4,* 264–277.

Burgos, N. M., & Diaz-Perez, N.M. (1986). An exploration of human sexuality in the Puerto Rican culture. *Journal of Social Work & Human Sexuality, 4,* 135–150.

Butler, J. (1993). *Bodies that matter: On the discursive limits of "sex."* New York: Routledge.

Centers for Disease Control and Prevention. (2007a). *A glance at the HIV/AIDS epidemic.* Atlanta, GA. Retrieved from http://www.cdc.gov/hiv/resources/factsheets/PDF/At-A-Glance.pdf.

Centers for Disease Control and Prevention. (2007b). *Living with HIV/AIDS*. Atlanta, GA. Retrieved from http://www.cdc.gov/hiv/resources/brochures/livingwithhiv.htm

Centers for Disease Control and Prevention. (2009). HIV/AIDS among Hispanics/Latinos. Retrieved from http://www.cdc.gov/hiv/hispanics/index.htm.

Davis, J. A., & Smith, T. W. (1991). *General social surveys, 1972–1991*. Chicago, IL: National Opinion Research Center.

Diaz, R., & Ayala, G. (2001). *National gay and lesbian task force report: Social discrimination and health, the case of Latino gay men and HIV risk*. Washington, DC: The Policy Institute of the National Gay and Lesbian Task Force.

Driscoll, A. K., Biggs, M. A., Brindis, C. D., & Yankah, E. (2001). Adolescent Latino reproductive health: A review of the literature. *Hispanic Journal of Behavioral Sciences, 23*, 255–326.

Ehrhardt, A. A., & Exner, T. M. (2000). Prevention of sexual risk behavior for HIV infection with women. *AIDS, 14*, S53–S57.

Flaskerud, J. H., & Nyamathi, A. M. (1990). Effects of an AIDS education program on the knowledge, attitudes and practices of low income black and Latina women. *Journal of Community Health, 15*, 343–355.

Flaskerud, J. H., Nyamathi, A. M., & Uman, G. C. (1997). Longitudinal effects of an HIV testing and counseling program for low-income Latina women. *Ethnicity & Health, 2*, 89–103.

Francis, L. J., & Wilcox, C. (1996). Religion and gender orientation. *Personality and Individual Differences, 20*, 119–120.

Gagnon, J. H., & Parker, R. G. (1995). Conceiving sexuality. In J. H. Gagnon & R. G. Parker (Eds.), *Conceiving sexuality: Approaches to sex research in a postmodern world*. New York: Routledge.

Gavey, N., & McPhillips, K. (1997). Women and the heterosexual transmission of HIV: Risks and prevention strategies. *Women & Health, 25*, 41–64.

Gomez, C. A., Hernandez, M., & Faigeles, B. (1999). Sex in the new world: An empowerment model for HIV prevention in Latina immigrant women. *Health Education & Behavior, 26*, 200–212.

Harawa N. T., Bingham T. A., Cochran S. D., Greenland, S., & Cunningham, W. E. (2002). HIV prevalence among foreign- and US-born clients of public STD clinics. *American Journal of Public Health, 92*, 1958–1963.

Huang, A., Subak, L., Thom, D., Van Den Eeden, S., Ragins, A., Kuppermann, M., ... Brown, J. S. (2009). Sexual function and aging in racially and ethnically diverse women. *Journal of the American Geriatrics Society, 57*, 1362–1368.

Hullfish, K. L., Pastore, L. M,, Mormon, A. J,, Wernecke, Y., Bovbjerg, V. E., & Clayton, A. H. (2009). Sexual functioning of Latino women seeking outpatient gynecologic care. *Journal of Sexual Medicine, 6*, 61–69.

Jones, S. G., Patsdaugher, C. A., Jorda, M. L., Hamilton, M., & Marlow, R. (2008). SENORITAS: An HIV/sexually transmitted infection prevention project for Latina college students at a Hispanic-serving university. *Journal of the Association of Nurses in AIDS Care, 19*, 311–319.

Kaiser Family Foundation. (2006). *HIV/AIDS policy fact sheet: Black Americans and HIV/AIDS*. Retrieved from http://www.kff.org/hivaids/3030.cfm.

Kaiser Family Foundation. (2008). *HIV/AIDS policy fact sheet*. Retrieved from http://www.kff.org/hivaids/3030.cfm.

Kegeles, S. M., Hays, R. B., & Coates, T. J. (1996). The Mpowerment project: A community-level HIV prevention intervention for young gay men. *American Journal of Public Health, 86,* 1129–1136.

Koniak-Griffen, D., Lesser, J., Uman, G., & Cumberland, W.G. (2003). Project CHARM: An HIV prevention program for adolescent mothers. *Family Community Health, 26,* 94–107.

Land, H., & Hudson, S. H. (2004). Stress, coping and depressive symptomatology in Latina and Anglo AIDS caregivers. *Psychology and Health, 19,* 643–665.

Marin, G. (1992). Issues in the measurement of acculturation among Hispanics. In F. Kurt (Ed.), *Psychological testing of Hispanics* (pp. 235–251). Washington, DC: American Psychological Association.

McQuiston, C., Choi-Hevel, S., & Clawson, M. (2001). Protegiendo nuestra comunidad: Empowerment participatory education for HIV prevention. *Journal of Transcultural Nursing, 12,* 275–283.

Melendez, R. M., & Tolman, D. L. (2006). Gender, vulnerability and young people. In Aggleton, P. Ball, A. & Mane, P. (Eds.), *Sex, drugs and young people: International perspectives*(pp. 29–48). New York: Routledge.

Mize, S. J. S., Robinson, B. E., Bockting, W. O., & Scheltema, K. E. (2002). Meta-analysis of the effectiveness of HIV prevention interventions for women. *AIDS Care, 14,* 163–180.

Morgan, M. Y. (1987). The impact of religion on gender-role attitudes. *Psychology of Women, 11,* 301–310.

Peragallo, N., DeForge, B., O'Campo, P., Mi Lee, S., Cianelli, R., & Ferrer, L. (2005). A randomized clinical trial of an HIV-risk- reduction intervention among low-income Latina women. *Nursing Research, 54,* 108–118.

Raj, A., Amaro, H., Cranston, K., Martin, B., Cabral, H., Navarro, A., & Conron, K. (2001). Is a general women's health promotion program as effective as an HIV-intensive prevention program in reducing HIV risk among Hispanic women? *Public Health Reports, 116,* 599–607.

Rhodes, S. D., Hergenrather, K. G., Zometa, C., Lindstrom, K., & Montano, J. (2008). Characteristics of immigrant Latino men who utilize formal healthcare services: Baseline findings from the HoMbreS Study. *Journal of the National Medical Association, 100,* 1177–1185.

Rogler, L. H., Malgady, R. G., Costantino, G., & Blumenthal, R. (1987). What do culturally sensitive mental health services mean? The case of Hispanics. *American Psychologist, 42,* 565–570.

Scott, K. D., Gilliam, A., & Braxton, K. (2005). Culturally competent HIV prevention strategies for women of color in the United States. *Health Care for Women International, 26,* 17–45.

Shedlin, M. G., Decena, C. U., & Oliver-Velez, D. (2005). Initial acculturation and HIV risk among new Hispanic immigrants. *Journal of the National Medical Association, 97,* 32S–37S.

Stark, R., & Bainbridge, W. (1985). *A future of religions*. Berkeley: University of California Press.

U.S. Census Bureau. (2008). *American community survey 1-year estimates.* Washington, DC: author.

U.S. Census Bureau. (n.d.). Hispanic or Latino Origin. Retrieved from http://factfinder.census.gov/servlet/DTTable?_bm=y&-geo_id=01000US&-ds_name=ACS_2008_1YR_G00_&-_lang=en&-mt_name=ACS_2008_1YR_G2000_B03001&-format=&-CONTEXT=dt.

Weeks, M. R., Schensul, J. J., Williams, M. S., & Grier, M. (1995). AIDS prevention for African-American and Latina women: Building a culturally and gender-appropriate intervention. *AIDS Education and Prevention, 7,* 251–263.

West, C., & Zimmerman, D. (1987). Doing gender. *Gender and Society, 1,* 125–151.

Wingood, G. M., & DiClemente, R. J. (1995). HIV sexual risk reduction interventions for women: A review. *American Journal of Preventative Medicine, 12,* 209–217.

Section II

SEX THERAPY IS NOT PRACTICED HERE

Cultural Challenges

Editors Introduction to Chapter 5
Cameroon

Cameroon is the sole representative of the African continent in this volume. Nevertheless, it is an apt one because the cultural diversity of Africa is apparent in this tiny country in the elbow of the continent's west coast.

In this chapter, Njikam Savage illustrates what happens when modern and traditional values intersect in a culturally diverse country. The traditional belief that luck is transferred through sexual contact makes prevention of sexually transmitted infections (STIs) challenging and has also resulted in seemingly bizarre sexual behavior (women engaging in sexual intercourse in public settings with mentally ill men). In a country where magical beliefs persist, traditional healers have teamed up with modern medical facilities to diagnose and treat STIs. Traditional healers are perhaps ideally situated to tend to the sexual problems of the people of Cameroon since sexual dysfunction is often attributed to mystical or spiritual forces and Western ideas regarding performance anxiety and problems of intimacy are regarded as irrelevant.

The strong message from this chapter is that it is more expedient to work within clients' existing belief structures to modify sexual behavior than to try to change or challenge that structure. A woman in Cameroon can therefore be persuaded to engage in seemingly deviant sexual behavior since it fits in with her belief that luck is transferred sexually. However, she is less likely to insist on condom use or complain about pain or lack of pleasure from sex.

Female sexual pleasure is only beginning to emerge as part of the conversation in Cameroon, brought about, at least partially, by older women challenging the custom of sexual retirement at menopause. This seemingly small step introduces the idea that women are interested in sex for pleasure, and that they can have a voice in asking for what they want sexually.

If the goal of sex therapy is to help people have better sex lives, then understanding the context in which sex occurs is vitally important. This chapter particularly challenges the reader to understand concepts that are very different from Western ideas regarding sexuality. It will be an interesting exercise for motivated readers to try to devise sex therapy interventions for some of the case examples given in the chapter.

5

THE MULTICULTURAL COMPLEXITY OF SEXUALITY IN CAMEROON[1]

O. M. Njikam Savage

Sexuality is complex within a multicultural society such as Cameroon. Sexuality pertains not only to sexual activity and by extension fertility, but also to the quest for sex, and the enhancement, control, management, and restoration of sex. The importance placed on sexuality across different cultures varies according to the place of its actors within the physical, social, reproductive, or developmental cycle. Thus, the importance placed on premarital chastity, fertility, and sexuality differs across cultures but is also mediated by a range of factors such as age, residence, status, kinship, mental health, and gender. Neither society nor culture exists in a vacuum, and the forces of urbanization, modernization, religion, and media also exert their own influence. However, these contemporary forces do not necessarily result in the abandonment of the traditional belief systems governing sexuality. Rather, traditional values and practices are maintained alongside more modern beliefs and behaviors. This coexistence is evident also in therapeutic systems of care, whereby modern medicine is accompanied by traditional and healing practices. This blending of the modern and the traditional is evident in Cameroon and offers a somewhat unique perspective on sexuality in a developing nation.

Sexual Norms and Values

Cameroon is often described as "Africa in miniature," with over 220 distinct ethnic groups and a variety of geographical zones. It has a population of over 12 million spread over 10 regions. Religious practices include Christianity, Islam, and indigenous systems, some of which are practiced jointly. Sexual behavior in Cameroon reflects a wide range of cultural norms and values. In some societies, such as the Beti in the Center and South Regions, demonstration of premarital fertility is a cultural norm (Meekers & Calves, 1997), whereas in others like the Hausa, Fulani of the Northern Regions, and Bamileke of the West Region, it is unacceptable. In northern Cameroon, honor killings as a result of premarital sex and subsequent pregnancy have been reported. Due to a range of factors such as Christianity, urbanization, education, mass media, and migration, traditional patterns of sexuality are increasingly being questioned and challenged (Feyisetan & Pebley, 1989; Nichols, Woods, Gates, & Sherman, 1987; Twa-Twa 1997; Zabin & Kiragu 1998).

Sex is still considered a cultural taboo in Cameroon. Even in contemporary society, discussions about sex are still met with a lot of reticence, awkwardness, and denial, especially within the context of what is culturally considered improper, such as parent–child sex education or discussion, unwanted teenage pregnancy or pregnancy in a woman considered to be past the child-bearing years (Hindin & Fatusi, 2009). Peer education is one of the strategies being adopted to address pressing issues such as appropriate sexuality and reproductive health education among youth (Kim, 2009; Organisation Mondiale de la Santé [OMS], 1997; Turner & Shepherd, 1999). Sexual intimacy is expected to take place behind closed doors. Consequently, discretion is expected as regards nonsanctioned sex such as pre- and extramarital relations.

Culturally, women are expected to be subservient, unknowledgeable, and passive so far as sex is concerned, while men are supposed to demonstrate sexual knowledge and prowess, but this attitude is changing rapidly. Attitudes have changed in terms of traditional attitudes to sex as a result of modernization, urbanization, education, access to media, and mobility, among other factors. Age at sexual debut has decreased and women as well as men expect to have sexually compatible partners. Intergenerational sex further complicates matters. Research shows that young girls often have sexual relations with older men in exchange for gifts, cash, and social status (Cockcroft et al., 2010; Masvawure, 2010).

According to a national demographic survey, the mean age of sexual debut for females and males was 15.8 years and 18 years, respectively (Cameroon Department of Health Services, 2004). Menarche constitutes an indicator of fertility as well as the commencement of sexual activity. In an environment where female social status is enhanced by fertility, motherhood is highly anticipated and valued (Hindin & Fatusi, 2009). Attempts are sometimes made by young girls to hasten menarche (Njikam Savage, 1998; Njikam Savage & Tchombe, 1994), by douching with kerosene. Douching with kerosene is believed to somehow artificially provoke menstruation. This is in sharp contrast with other cultural practices such as breast binding, which fall within the range of behaviors adopted to suppress or retard puberty or the development of physical female sexual features in the hope of safeguarding chastity (Renata, GTZ, Ministère de la Santé Publique, 2007).

Although marriage in this region is often polygynous, the original union is between a man and a woman, with other female partners being acquired over time. A recent survey of several civil status registries in Douala indicated that polygynous unions accounted for up to 30% or more of civil marriages in some urban councils (Njikam Savage, 2010b). Increasingly, however, the institution of polygyny is being challenged as being outdated in favor of monogamy. Nevertheless, the nostalgia for extramarital union remains strong. A study conducted among 130 disadvantaged male youths, aged between 18 years and 25 years, in Douala illustrated some of these complexities. Due to financial reasons the participants were all out of school, but were registered in informal educational institutions. The young men unanimously upheld the concept that one man was sufficient for a woman, the corollary that one woman was sufficient for one man, however, was not acceptable (Njikam Savage, 2001). An unexpected finding of this study was the declaration by 60 (46.1%) of the participants that they were virgins and desired to remain so until marriage.

Sex and Fertility

Closely associated with sex is the concept of fertility. Cameroon is largely pronatal as regards pregnancy and childbirth. Contraceptive use remains at a relatively low level despite the existence of family planning clinics (FPCs) at the primary, secondary, and tertiary levels of health care (Hindin & Fatusi, 2009). Traditionally, fertility regulation was a familial and communal affair. The creation of FPCs that made women the primary focus isolated women from the community and distorted this norm. It also created a multitude of problems for women by alienating men and making them publicly invisible, and thereby voiceless and powerless in the dynamics of fertility decision making. This unwittingly resulted in the creation of a huge gendered and power-based animosity within FPCs as well as in the domestic arena, making it difficult for women to have free access to fertility regulation, a culturally valued and highly endorsed practice. Female-centered methods of family planning appear to give women power and autonomy over fertility regulation and control, an issue that had always been vested in families, including extended family and community members (Njikam Savage, 1992, 1995).

Traditionally, the concept of the infertile male does not exist in Cameroon and infertility is still largely considered a "female" problem. Thus, male sexual dysfunction, especially if it interferes with conception, is perceived as a very serious issue but it is also not openly discussed (Dyer, 2007). A well-known and very wealthy ex-minister in the 1980s died shortly after an automobile accident that left him paralyzed. However, it was rumored that he had actually committed suicide, as he could not conceive of life as an impotent male, robbed of his manhood (Njikam

Savage, 1988, 1995). Cross-culturally, fertility remains highly valued and infertility is highly stigmatized in Cameroon as in many other developing countries (Cooper, Harries, Myer, Orner, Bracken, & Zweigenthal, 2007; Dodoo & Frost, 2008; Njikam Savage, 2010a).

Polygamy constitutes a cultural panacea for a plethora of fertility and sexual problems. The inability of a couple to produce a live birth is often solved by marrying a second or third spouse. In traditional society, male infertility is solved through the process of natural donor insemination (NDI). The donor is often close male kin, such as a brother, uncle, cousin, and sometimes older sons (especially in the case of older men with much younger wives), either by tacit or implicit agreement of the husband. In such circumstances, the blood line of the child is known and therefore its sociocultural and biological identity would not be a potential problem, as the child would be culturally and biologically of the same patrilineal group as its infertile parent. In some cases, the husband might choose one of his very close friends. By contrast, a donor from an unknown background might possess an unsavory character and could potentially transmit hereditary diseases or illnesses which, among other things, would indicate the fact that the child was from strange or "outside" stock (Njikam Savage, 1995). Nevertheless, in more recent times some couples have resorted to the use of artificial donor insemination (Njikam Savage, 1992).

Natural donor insemination may or may not be a closely guarded secret. The circle of those who are knowledgeable about the donor depends on the context within which NDI occurs. If it were with the consent of the husband, he and any other family members of his choice would know; if the conception plan was contrived and conducted solely by the wife, on the suspicion that her spouse is infertile, then the procedure would take place in the utmost secrecy to avoid sociocultural and legal sanctions, especially public ridicule and divorce. Some women in such circumstances feel they are between "a rock and a hard place." Failure to bear a child could lead to divorce and the stigma of infertility; exposure of a surreptitious recourse to natural donor insemination could also lead to stigma, ridicule, accusations of adultery, and divorce. To some extent, levirate and sororate marriages, whereby male and female relatives enter into already existing marriages as new partners, were also used as sociocultural alternatives to infertility. In such circumstances a levirate or sororate marriage transforms an existing monogamous union into a polygynous one, except in the case of widowhood where the deceased spouse is "replaced" by a living relative and the union maintains its monogamous structure.

Sex and Pregnancy

Despite high rates of maternal mortality in Cameroon and notwithstanding the occasional weeks or months of discomfort or actual ailments, pregnancy is not perceived as an illness. Pregnancy is expected to end in the happy event of a live birth and is locally called "good sick." Childbirth among the Bamileke is perceived as the ultimate proof of the consummation of a marriage as well as an ancestral blessing or approval of a physical union undertaken here on earth (Njikam Savage, 1996).

Sex during pregnancy is perceived as being essential for optimal fetal growth. The exchange of bodily fluids is thought to be particularly important for the conservation of the pregnancy. It is believed that the blood of the fetus is comprised of the combination of parental blood. Thus, female infidelity during pregnancy would lead to the intermingling of strange or "outside" blood and semen, which is perceived as incompatible with parental blood, resulting in miscarriage and fetal loss (Njikam Savage, 1996).

The crucial life events of marriage, birth, and burial are individualized, involving only one person at a time. As such, traditional marriages may not be conducted when a woman is pregnant. Cultural norms dictate that marriage must be conducted only in the single, nonpregnant state. Pregnancy in itself indicates a duality of personhood; thus, in the traditional context especially, the marriage process could only commence after delivery. Birth, even multiple births, is considered an individual event, as babies emerge singly. Similarly, burial, no matter the circumstances, is individualized. Thus, at the death of a pregnant woman, the fetus has to be extracted from her to ensure that each individual is buried separately. This is done for two reasons. First, each being represents a separate entity with a personalized place in the hereafter and second, ascent into the other world is also individualized; that is, one entity ascends at a time.

Sex and Menopause

Outside of pregnancy and procreation, sex is considered to be an important part of marriage, providing emotional stability and enhancing physical and psychological well-being. Indeed some middle-aged women report that they demand sex from their partners if it is less than regular (Njikam Savage & Tchombe, 1994). Nonetheless, culturally, there are social markers that herald the end of female sexual activity. On becoming grandmothers or at menopause women are expected to cease sexual activities. With the decrease in the age at menarche, low usage of fertility prevention methods, and subsequent untimely pregnancies, however, women are becoming grandparents in their mid-30s and 40s, earlier than their own mothers. Thus, grandparenthood no longer strictly corresponds with sexual retirement. In some Beti traditional societies such as the Akonolinga in the Center Region, herbal remedies (believed to be contraceptives) are given to women who wish to continue being sexually active. However, in an environment where the use of efficient fertility regulation methods is estimated to be low (13%; Cameroon DHS, 2004), pregnancy in older women does occur, although it is a breach of sociocultural norms (Njikam Savage, 1994). Despite the paucity in current knowledge as regards the role and value of sex in later life (Vincent, Riddell, & Shmueli, 2000), studies indicate that people can and do remain sexually active in later life (Matthias, Lubben, Atchison, & Schweitzer, 1997), sometimes adapting or reprioritizing as needed (Gott & Hinchliff, 2003; van der Geest, 2001).

Sexual Problems in Cameroon

Sexual problems reported by men and women are often complex and cut across social, cultural, economic status, and belief systems. Male sexual problems are perceived to be more serious than female problems because they are more likely to affect sexual performance (erection and penetration), and thus the ability to impregnate a woman. According to health professionals in Douala,[2] male complaints center on erectile problems and tend to be made more by older men than their younger counterparts. In comparison, premature ejaculation appears to be more problematic among younger men (Njikam Savage, 2010b).

In the Extreme North region, the families of the bride and groom are culturally expected to pay a visit to the newly married couple the morning after the wedding night. This visit is made first, to ascertain that the bride was a virgin and second, to verify the wife's satisfaction with the sexual prowess of her spouse. On the one hand, the declaration of lack or inadequate sexual satisfaction by the bride not only brings shame to her husband and his family, but also questions his manhood and is considered a legitimate reason for divorce. On the other hand, the display of a blood-stained bed sheet by the bride's family is proof of her virginity, honor, and value. Her husband is expected to present her with a gift in recognition and appreciation of this honor bestowed on him and his family. Fertility is often taken as an indication of sexual ability. Consequently, failure of the wife to conceive may also be interpreted as the inability of the husband to be a "man" in the bedroom. In addition to erectile dysfunction and premature ejaculation, low sperm count (oligospermia) or absence of sperm count (azoospermia) may be responsible for male infertility (Nasah, 1984).

A review of medicinal plants used by the Baka, an indigenous society in the East region (Betti, 2004) and in the Littoral, South West regions, and the Sudo-sahelian area in Cameroon (Jiofack, Fokunang, & Guedje, 2010) suggests that male and female sexual dysfunction are important ailments. The local names used for these dysfunctions include (male) sexual weakness, and female sterility. Baka men use local stimulants to enhance sexual performance. As an informant in Douala explained,

> the knowledge and utilization of such local plants was the secret behind the success of the marriage between much older men in their villages and young girls. When needed, they simply went to the backyard and plucked and chewed some leaves to ensure good performance and keep their wives happy.

According to physicians in Douala, there are growing numbers of male clients who complain of experiencing sexual dysfunction with their wives, but experience no sexual difficulties in sexual relationships outside of marriage (Njikam Savage, 2010). The following case is one that is typical of those seen in medical practice:

> Mr. P is a 55-year-old married male. He has been suffering from erectile dysfunction for the past 18 months. However, this "problem" only surfaces whenever he tries love making with his legally married wife at home. "Outside," he is quite active and does not need any stimulant either in the form of traditional therapies or Western medication. However, he has to use a series of medications, including Viagra (prescribed by a physician), to assist his performance in the domestic arena.

The incidence of "outside wives" in English-speaking Africa—called *"deuxième bureau"* in the French-speaking parts (translated as second office) or *nyumba ndogo* in Swahili (meaning, "little house")—is not uncommon in Cameroon. This refers to nonformalized marriage between men and women without the transfer of bride wealth. It may be seen as a compromise between formal polygyny and a noncontractual union with a married man or an informal form of polygyny. While it involves financial expenditure from the man, there are fewer constraints on sexual behavior between partners than in formal marriage. Despite the lack of statistics on this phenomenon, its occurrence is well documented in several parts of Africa (Baker & Bird, 1959; Little, 1973; Kalipeni, Craddock, Oppong, & Ghosh, 2004; Karanja, 1981; Southall, 1961), in West Africa (Aronson, 1978; Harrell-Bond, 1975; Karanja & Scott, 1982; Lacombe, 1983, 1987), Central, East, and Southern Africa (Carael, Ali & Cleland, 2001; Obbo, 1975, 1987; Zeitzen, 2008). The practice of having outside wives is controversial if it results in conferring a lower social status and economic insecurity upon the woman.

However, in Cameroon, both highly and poorly educated women become outside wives.

Mystical Beliefs and Sexuality

While this pattern of sexual problems with a wife, but not a mistress or outside wife, may be understood to stem from guilt or the fear of being discovered, or even to greater interest and arousal with the mistress, some sexually dysfunctional husbands attribute failing sexual prowess to mystical forces unleashed by jealous spouses. The following case illustrates this belief:

> Mr. B, is a 58-year-old married male. After discord with his wife, he severed sexual contact with her. He had a mistress outside who he saw regularly. He later found that he was unable to get an erection and therefore to have sex with her. Mr. B attributed his erectile dysfunction to the machinations of his legal wife who was out to disturb his happiness "outside." He felt that his wife might have ministered some potion in his meal or through other mystical means was endeavoring to make him "weak" and steal his manhood. He stopped eating food cooked by her in the house.

For many cultures in Cameroon, erotic dreams, especially those that involve sex, are seen as dangerous. Sexual dreams are considered to be mystical or malevolent spiritual attacks by spurned admirers or malicious persons (irrespective of the apparent identity of the person in the dream or his or her actual relationship in real life to the dreamer). This is because an enemy could easily be masked as a friend in order to gain confidence and thereby wreak maximum havoc. Thus, participation in an erotic dream with one's spouse or admirer is as dangerous as having sex with an enemy. Such a sexual encounter could result in male and female sexual dysfunction and other medical disorders, especially erectile dysfunction, premature ejaculation, infertility, frigidity, and menstrual disorders.

Magical thinking also extends to sexual thoughts and feelings that are not well understood or that are unwelcome and disturbing. The following case of a young man experiencing obsessive sexual thoughts and fantasies illustrates this point:

> Mr. A is a 35-year-old married male. He had been married for about 5 years when he became infatuated with a young woman. All his waking hours were spent fantasizing about having sex with her. Indeed, he spent hours devising ways of escaping from

work or any other engagement to spend time with her. She became an obsession. In the end the need to be with this other woman was so overwhelming that he began to neglect his wife and children and even risked his job. He started losing weight. At this point in time he called himself to order and wondered if indeed he had been charmed by her through the use of a love potion.

Female Sexual Dissatisfaction

During in-depth interviews[3] (Njikam Savage, 2010b), some women complained about a lack of awareness and sensitivity on the part of their spouses, which they attributed to the failure of their spouses to recognize the changing needs of their bodies. None of them attributed such shortcomings to mystical attacks either on them or their partners. Rather, women reported experiencing pressing familial or social problems, physical or emotional stress, the urgency of which they deemed more important than sex. As a result they were either sexually disinterested or distracted during sex. Women complained that their spouses expected immediate sexual responses and performance irrespective of domestic or other personal issues and with minimal foreplay (or none at all). The result was often painful or unsatisfactory sexual relations. Inability to discuss this with their spouses due to cultural norms compelled them to seek other options, which included avoiding the bedroom by delaying their own bedtime until their partners were safely asleep.

Female Genital Mutilation

Dry sex constitutes a technique used mostly by sex workers to satisfy clients. It involves the use of leaves, cloth, and a drying agent locally called "alum" to dry out the vagina. This is used to tighten the vagina and as such create an allusion of youthfulness to clients, thereby increasing sex workers' earning capacity (Njikam Savage, 1995). In addition to this harmful practice, other procedures are performed on girls and women in several regions of the world, including Africa, with implications for sexuality and reproductive well-being. These include *angurya* and *gishiri* cuts, usually termed female genital mutilation (FGM). In efforts to standardize its meaning, the World Health Organization (2010) defined FGM as all procedures which involve the partial or total removal of the external female genitalia or any other surgery to the female reproductive organs for nonmedical reasons. It is estimated that between 100 million to 140 million girls and women have undergone some type of FGM (Dorkenoo, 1995; Hosken, 1993). In Cameroon, FGM is performed among the Manyu and Ejagham in the South West region and the Shua

Arabs of the Extreme North regions, with a prevalence between 10% and 20% (Awuba & Macassa, 2007). *Angurya* and *gishiri* or *yankan* cuts are practiced by the Hausa in Nigeria, who also reside in northern Cameroon. While the former procedure involves the scraping of the tissue around the vaginal opening, the latter consists of making posterior cuts from the vagina into the perineum so as to increase the vaginal opening. These are performed on very young girls given the cultural practice of child brides (Awuba & Macassa, 2007). FGM is performed for a variety of reasons, but mainly to ensure female chastity, fidelity, and fertility. *Gishiri* cuts and other forms of FGM have been implicated in a range of complications, including infertility, obstructed labor, painful intercourse, vesico-vaginal and recto-vaginal fistula, and miscarriage (Edstrom, 1992; Hosken, 1993; Koso-Thomas, 1992; Mandara, 2004; Murphy, 1981; Tahzib, 1983, WHO, 1991). Some men in the South West region disclosed that it was easy for them to detect a woman who had undergone FGM, because it took longer for her to be sexually satisfied due to genital cutting (Njikam Savage, 2010b).

Another complication of FGM is the development of fistulas. Fistulas (vaginal or rectal) refer to conditions in which there is an abnormal opening between the bladder and vagina or between the rectum and vagina resulting in uncontrollable leakage of urine or feces through the vaginal walls. This results in the isolation, stigmatization, and ostracism of women with these conditions.

Surgical intervention is used to repair damage to female genitalia due to FGM and *gishiri* cuts. This surgery is mostly used to repair fistulas, but the procedure is not widely available nor is it affordable for the women who need it. While the success of surgical intervention is high, attempts to restore fertility are less successful, especially in terms of women's ability to have live births. There is an especially high rate of miscarriages and stillbirths (Mandara, 2004; Murphy, 1981).

Despite the above complications, attitudes to the cultural practice of FGM and *gishiri* cuts remain controversial. On one hand, there is increasing international and regional pressure for their eradication; on the other hand, there are calls for medicalization of these procedures to prevent both maternal and infant mortality and morbidity.

Approaches to Treatment: Traditional and Modern Therapies

Sex therapy as practiced in the Western world is not widely available or indeed practical for the majority of people living in Cameroon. Instead, people consult either physicians or traditional healers, depending upon factors such as wealth, geography, and education, as well as the perceived nature and cause of the sexual complaint. Due to their prolific advertising and claims to heal a multitude of ailments, traditional healers are well known. The successful treatment of sexual dysfunction is their most highly touted area of expertise. This extends from claims to cure sexual problems such as loss of libido, premature ejaculation, and frigidity, to sexually transmitted infections (STIs, HIV/AIDS) and infertility. Some merchants/healers are regularly found on long distance buses between large cities such as Douala, Yaoundé, and Bamenda, where they advertise their wares and promise reduced prices for prospective buyers. The more financially successful traditional healers advertise their prowess through the media and have offices in the large cities where they see their clients. Some of the most popular products sold include "African panacea" which sales agents/traditional healers promise can restore virility and cure a host of other ailments. Local remedies for sexual problems abound and include bitter kola, kola nut, aloe vera, and ginseng, which are also found in some pharmaceutical products. Their potency is reportedly enhanced when consumed with Guinness, a malt-based alcoholic drink. Local remedies have the advantage of being only a fraction of the cost of products sold in pharmacies.[4] Unlike medical doctors, traditional healers claim to have the flexibility of being able to tackle sexual problems emanating from spiritual or relational as well as physical sources.

At the 1994 International Conference on Population and Development in Cairo, sexual health was recognized as an integral part of reproductive health. The World Health Organization (WHO, 2010) and the United Nations Population Fund (UNFPA, 2004) similarly adopted this concept and its applicability has become more visible in family planning clinics in Cameroon. Increasingly, the right to a satisfying and safe sex life is being demanded by individuals. This in part reflects changing attitudes to sexual behavior and awareness of international trends (Correa, 2003; Shaw, 2006). Although the treatment of STIs is increasingly Western-oriented, traditional healers are still important sources of care for several reasons, of which gender and socioeconomic factors remain significant. First, access to treatment is easier, and consultation is cheaper and requires a shorter waiting time. Second, treatments administered and explained using familiar plants and concepts enhance treatment compliance. Increasingly, some modern traditional healers insist on having medical tests/investigations done by hospitals or clinics during consultations to maximize the efficacy of their treatments. Another option for the treatment of STIs is that of self-medication through the purchase of drugs either from a pharmacy or street vendor. This is often done without a formal prescription on the basis of symptoms such as pain during urination or discharge. Often, modern medical therapies are used as a last resort when all else has failed. Usually this means prolonged and more costly treatment, which then serves to reinforce previous beliefs about the expensive nature of doctors and hospitals. In addition, inappropriate or inefficient treatment has been associated with chronic and prolonged infection with the risks of secondary infertility and contamination of partners within the chain of the sexual network. In the case of polygynous unions, the favorite wife may be the only person treated, thereby increasing the vicious circle of reinfection and resistance (Nasah, 1984; Njikam Savage, 1991, 1995).

Western-style sex therapy with its emphasis on communication between partners is very slowly making an incursion in Cameroon as many of its cultures frown on talking about sex, especially outside the domestic or private arena. The belief in spiritual or magical intervention makes traditional healers more desirable as treatment providers for sexual problems. Sensate focus exercises and other sex therapy techniques, grounded in the idea of reducing anxiety and increasing intimacy, may not resonate well with men in Cameroon. Nonetheless, there is an indication of changing societal needs and subsequent changes in medical response to sexual issues. The creation of more family planning clinics and their increasing emphasis on couple orientation is indicative of these changes. Yet the stronghold of traditional beliefs and practices remains undeniable and is reflected in the continuing use of sex as a ritual within the context of posthumous cleansing and other contemporary emerging forms such as deviant sex, discussed below.

Posthumous Sexual Cleansing

In certain social and cultural settings in Cameroon, as in other parts of Africa, sexual activity is prescribed for cleansing or purification, for the transfer of ill-luck, for the acquisition of good luck, wealth, longevity, and youth. Within this context, physical satisfaction is trivial and unimportant. These sexual contacts are radically different from those based on conventional reasons of emotional attachment, commercial factors or even lust. Posthumous sexual cleansing is an example of sex prescribed for the transfer of ill luck and refers to the practice of surviving spouses engaging in sexual intercourse with unsuspecting partners.

In the "grass field" or "graffy" belt that covers the West and North West Regions, the belief in the individuality of death makes it culturally unacceptable for a person, female or male, to die with a swollen stomach, be it the result of pregnancy or illness. This situation, called *tchi* in Bamilike society, is perceived as bringing misfortune and bad luck through the surviving spouse to the extended family. Thus, in the case of a deceased pregnant woman, before the burial of mother and child, the husband/father is culturally required to undertake a sexual cleansing act. He must engage in sexual intercourse with an unknown person after which he must abandon all his clothes with her and then run away nude. An accomplice with a fresh set of clothes will be waiting for his exit. The ill-luck that resulted in the death of mother and child is thus physically severed from the genitor and subsequently from the family. The sexual cleansing serves as a preventive rite of avoidance for subsequent children the widower may have in the future. It also transfers this ill-fortune to the unwitting sexual partner. The widow of a sick man who died with a swollen stomach is culturally required to do the same. Medical staff in one of the reference hospitals in Douala recounted how male night staff had often been unwittingly seduced by desperate wives in a bid to perform the sexual cleansing rite immediately upon the death of their husbands and before leaving the hospital (Njikam Savage, 2010b).[5]

Posthumous sexual cleansing results in infertility in the unsuspecting victims engaged in the cleansing act. Those who become aware that they have been used in this way quickly rid themselves of this ill luck by performing the rite on another ignorant person. Traditional belief and practices belong to the realm of nonmaterial culture[6] and are extremely slow to change. They constitute the core of an individual. Irrespective of socioeconomic or educational status, familial pressures may compel individuals to act in conformity with cultural norms to avoid marginalization, negative consequences, or bad luck visited upon themselves or their children. This bad luck may include infertility, untimely death, and insanity; the fear of these possible consequences compels conformity on the part of practitioners. Christianity, and to some extent education, has reduced the frequency of this practice somewhat. However, cultural and religious syncretism is common. Thus, both Christian and traditional belief systems may operate side by side without any apparent conflict among practitioners.

Sexual purification in this context is an unusual procedure necessitated by circumstances and limited to certain cultural groups. Unlike sexual cleansing found in many other parts of Africa (Agot, 2005; Agot et al., 2010; Ambasa-Shisanya, 2007; Ayikukwei et al., 2007; Kalinda & Tembo, 2010; Lopman et al., 2009; Malungo, 2001; Okeyo & Allen, 1994), there is still little documented information on this practice in Cameroon. This may be because this practice is both stealthily undertaken and not widespread. In previous times, bodily fluids were exchanged and despite the advent of HIV/AIDS, this remains an important component of the rite. However, current efforts to control the spread of HIV have focused on providing culturally acceptable alternatives to the practice of widow or widower sexual cleansing. These alternatives include the use of herbs and roots, sliding over a naked person, being smeared with maize flour, and the substitution of a ritual whereby married couples privately have sex in the widow's home and thereafter present a beaded bracelet to be worn by the widow.

The Quest for Wealth: Sexual Requirements

The strong belief that luck, whether ill or good, is passed through sexual intercourse underlies the continuing practice of posthumous sexual cleansing and a newly observed behavior of women engaging in public sex with mentally ill men.

Contemporary society in Cameroon, as elsewhere, is characterized by a marked demand for wealth and riches, beauty and youth. There has been a corresponding rise in the number and popularity of religious sects that offer "short cuts," at a price, for immediate wealth, power, longevity, or youthfulness. Within the past 10 years, Douala, the economic capital of Cameroon, has seen an upsurge in the occurrence of nonconventional sexual activity believed to be prescribed by traditional healers, secret societies, and religious sects. In particular there have been reports of well-dressed women, following the dictates of their sect, having public sex with disheveled, unkempt, and apparently mentally ill men in an attempt to acquire wealth and good luck. The following case is one example:

> Lisette, an attractive woman in her mid-30s descended into one of the flower gardens around Bonanjo, a busy commercial district with an apparently "mad" man and subsequently commenced to have sex with him. As they were visible, the scene soon attracted a crowd, some bemused, and others irate. The story was immediately broadcast on the media. Soon traffic circulation was blocked and the police arrived on the scene. Lisette was escorted to the police station where she explained that her traditional healer had commanded her to do this as part of a cleansing exercise to ensure her well-being. She was subsequently released. Her mentally unfit partner, beyond his grin, was unable to articulate an explanation.

Sex, publicly enacted, between a woman and a visibly mentally impaired man (disheveled, dirty, foul and unkempt hair, tattered, dirty clothes, unwashed smelly body) is way beyond the cultural dictates of conventional sex and sexual partners. The fact that the women are well dressed and often drive their vehicles to the copulation venue suggests that they have at least a medium level of education or sufficient income to enable them to purchase cars and nice clothes. While such nonconventional sexual behavior is not exclusive to women, it has been increasingly observed among women in the public sphere and in broad daylight to the extent that it has become a conversational topic on public transport and is considered by some to be a mundane practice in places like the Central Market in Douala. About 15 such episodes were reported in Douala for 2009, whereas in previous years there were significantly fewer episodes (2 to 7 cases) (Tcheungna,, 2012).

Often, these sexual acts were undertaken in broad daylight and within the glare of the public eye. Marketplaces, crossroads, busy roads, and cemeteries appeared to be the most popular places for the audacious sexual displays between apparently "sane" and "insane" persons. Crossroads are often the venue of choice to dispel misfortune or cleanse and thereby rid a village of negative forces, "send it out" of the village. Public sacrifices for the well-being of society are often performed in marketplaces. Spirits are believed to go to markets just as human beings do. Thus, in traditional society, markets and crossroads are the choice venues for sacrifices or ritual practices (Idowu, 1963; Ikenga Metuh, 1987, 1991). According to the disclosure of study participants, the women involved in deviant sex acts were likely to have traveled from other towns in order to engage in public sex with less risk of recognition.[7]

Not all such sexual encounters are successful. Occasionally, the mentally impaired men turn down sexual advances. In Bessengue, a very busy commercial and residential district in Douala, a woman was unable to successfully cajole an apparently "insane" man to have sex. An unsuccessful sexual encounter of this kind was reported by Kemayou (2007) in Akwa, another busy district.

Women, Wealth, and the New Political Economy of Sex

Usually the aggressive quest for money is associated with men, in line with their traditional role as breadwinners and heads of family. Increasingly, these roles are being challenged by women, especially in urban area, as a result of the shrinking labor market, growth in the importance of the informal sector,[8] and the growing number of women who have a formal education, and subsequently are in paid employment. Urban women in particular are beginning to emerge in the public arena as financially independent agents acquiring their own property and wealth and making a name for themselves as local businesspeople, traders, and budding politicians. The hallmarks of their success include big cars, large houses, fashionable clothing with eye-catching jewelry, and trips abroad. The source of their success is not crucial nor does it diminish their stance in society. Rather, they are perceived as role models by other women to be at once envied and emulated. Some women are seemingly prepared to do everything and anything to acquire the outward trappings of success. Some women apparently join secret societies or sects either in a bid to acquire wealth and power or having already acquired them simply to maintain their status in society. In exchange for these goals, they are compelled to undertake sexually deviant actions publicly with the promise of a rapid, constant, and limitless supply of money and power as well as love, beauty, youth, and longevity.

The situation in Cameroon is somewhat similar to some of Hunter's (2007) findings in South Africa, where an increase in single headed households, rising levels of female migration, and social inequalities contributed to what he called the changing political economy of sex. Deviant sex contradicts and challenges the conventional and dominant norms of womanhood, which conjure a generous, all-giving female body that gives corporeal resources first to her partner, then to her offspring (Sutton, 2007). From this perspective, women are expected to dedicate their bodily energy to their families and communities regardless of their own needs and health. In Cameroon as in many other African countries, this translates into preadolescent and adolescent sexuality and fertility, and high levels of female mortality and morbidity from a range of medical conditions emanating from harmful traditional practices such as female genital mutilation, untimely pregnancies, and multiple childbirths. In the context of sane women having public sex with mentally ill men, it can be argued that the female body is being used by a small but growing number of women in the quest for personal power and wealth. Thus, this deviant sexual activity may be understood as a challenge to the status quo of male power and wealth.

Summary and Conclusions

The complexity of sexuality in Cameroon can only be understood by recognizing the diversity of its cultures and the central place accorded to sex and its associated rituals. The traditional practices of FGM and posthumous sexual cleansing are subjected to growing national and international criticism and calls for their abolition. Modernization and urbanization have also injected their own peculiarities into Cameroon's sexual arena. "Deviant" sexual practices, such as public sex with mentally impaired persons, may be seen as one end of this spectrum whereby all social and cultural sexual norms are breeched in favor of new options.

A blending of the traditional and the modern is also seen in the practice of having "outside wives" or *deuxième bureau* as well as in the use of modern therapies for STIs and couple-oriented FPC. Regarding treatment for sexual dysfunction, there remains a cultural lag between the attitudes and belief systems individuals adhere to and the actual choice and use of therapies. In some ways, traditional healers attempt to bridge this gap by modernizing their remedies (both in terms of their packaging and composition) and by utilizing medical tests/investigations performed by hospitals and medical clinics.

THE MULTICULTURAL COMPLEXITY OF SEXUALITY IN CAMEROON

In Cameroon, sexuality is intertwined with well-being in a number of ways and intersects with aspects of fertility, prosperity, and good fortune. While posthumous sexual cleansing and public sexual acts with mentally impaired persons challenge the boundaries of social norms, they also depict poorly explored and little understood effects of economic, social, spiritual, and political relations on the dynamics of sex. An exploration of traditional and "deviant" sexuality can provide meaningful insights into the complexity of sexuality in Cameroon.

Notes

1. Data presented here is the result of cross-cultural ethnographic research and in-depth interviews. Ethnographic research was undertaken in the Center, South, South West, Littoral, and West regions, as well as among the Bamileke of the West region on posthumous sexual cleansing. In addition, in-depth interviews were conducted among key informants from the West Region as well as health professionals residing in Douala.
2. In-depth interviews of health professionals (physicians, nurses) were conducted by the author.
3. In-depth interviews were conducted by the author in the Center, South, South West, Littoral, and West regions.
4. Based on an exchange rate of 532 cfa to $U.S.1.00, Viagra would cost over $50 and the generics about $13. This exchange rate was based on information from the U.S. Treasury Department website: www.fms.treas.gov/intn.html as of 2010.
5. Data on posthumous sexual cleansing was derived from research conducted among the Bamileke of the West region. In addition, in-depth interviews were conducted outside the region among Bamileke key informants and some health professionals residing in Douala. In many parts of Africa (including Central, Eastern and Southern areas) sexual cleansing may refer to different sexual acts, including forcing widows (and to a lesser extent widowers) to engage in intercourse with relatives of their deceased partners.
6. Sociologists distinguish between material and nonmaterial culture. Material culture is represented by physical objects, spaces, and resources. Nonmaterial culture refers to the ideational structure of a culture, the values and meanings by which the culture functions.
7. Information on sexual activity with the mentally disabled was based mostly on in-depth interviews conducted among observers of public sexual acts between sane and insane persons mostly in Douala (Littoral Region), Yaoundé (Center Region), and Bafoussam, and Dschang (West Region). A total of 500 in-depth interviews were conducted: 200 each in Douala and Yaoundé, the economic and political capital, respectively, of Cameroon and the largest concentrations of populations of mixed cultural diversity. Bafoussam and Dschang are much smaller cities in comparison and 50 in-depth interviews were conducted in each of them. These towns were chosen as a result of preliminary investigations which indicated that

public sexual activity between sane and insane persons was not only a known phenomenon there but was of increasing dimensions.

Attempts to conduct direct interviews with the mentally impaired or their sane partners after such public sexual acts proved futile. After accomplishing their missions the sane participants usually got dressed, climbed back into their cars, taxis, and onto their motor cycles, drove off or walked away. Others remained silent and taciturn; at best they just replied that they had been ordered by traditional healers to perform or conduct the act; or demanded to be left alone while their insane partners just grinned. Although information on sane men involved in sex with mentally impaired women and men was also collected, because the majority of those involved in deviant public sex were sane women, only the analysis of deviant female sex is presented here.

8. The term *informal economy* was adopted by the International Labour Organisation (ILO) in1972 and refers to economic exchanges that escape regulation, taxation, and enforcement. It operates in contexts where earning opportunities are scarce. It covers a diverse range of activities from legal to illegal, self-employed to owner of micro-enterprises. Increasingly, its importance as a significant source of revenue is being recognized, especially in developing but also developed countries. In Cameroon, as in many developing countries, there is a preponderance of women involved in the informal or shadow economy and they constitute the economic backbone of their families (ILO, 2002).

References

Agot, K. E. (2005). HIV/AIDS interventions and the politics of the African woman's body. In U. Nelson & J. Sieger, J. (Eds.), *A companion to feminist geography* (pp, 113–127). London: Macmillan.

Agot, K. E., Vander Stoep, A., Tracy, M., Obare, B. A., Bukusi, E. A., Ndinya-Achola, J. O., ... Weiss, N. S. (2010). Widowhood inheritance and HIV prevalence in Bondo District, Kenya: Baseline results from a prospective cohort study. *PLoS ONE, 5*(11), e14028. doi:10.1371/journal.pone.0014028

Ambasa-Shisanya, C. R. (2007). Widowhood in the era of HIV/AIDS: A case study of Slaya District, Kenya. *Sahara Journal, 2*, 606–615.

Aronson, D. (1978). *The city is our farm: Seven migrant Ijebu Yoruba families.* Boston, MA: G. K. Hall.

Awuba, J., & Macassa, G. (2007). HIV/AIDS in Cameroon: Rising gender issues in policy-making matters. *African Journal of Health Sciences 14,* 118–128.

Ayikukwei, R. M., Ngare, D., Sidle, J., Ayuku, D., Baliddawa, J., & Greene, J. (2007). Social and cultural significance of the sexual cleansing rituals and its impact on HIV prevention strategies in Western Kenya. *Sexuality and Culture, 11*(3), 32–50.

Ayikukwei, R. M., Ngare, D., Sidle, J. Ayuku, D., Baliddawa, J., & Greene, J. (2008). HIV/AIDS and cultural practices in Western Kenya: The impact of cleansing rituals on sexual behaviors. *Culture, Health and Sexuality, 6,* 587–599.

Baker, T., & Bird, M. (1959). Urbanization and the position of women. *Sociological Review. 7*, 115–116.
Betti, J. L. (2004). An ethnobotanical study of medicinal plants among the Baka Pygmies in the Dja biosphere reserve, Cameroon. *African Study Monographs, 1*, 1–27.
Carael, M., Ali, M., & Cleland, J. (2001). Nuptiality and risk behaviour in Lusaka and Kampala. *Africa Journal of Reproductive Health, 5*, 83–89.
Cockcroft, A., Kunda, J. L., Kgakole, L, Masisi, M., Laetsang, D., Ho-Foster, A., Marokoane, N., & Andersson, N. (2010). Community views of intergenerational sex: Findings from focus groups in Botswana, Namibia and Swaziland. *Psychology, Health and Medicine, 15*(5), 507–514.
Cooper, D., Harries, J., Myer, L., Orner, P., Bracken, H., & Zweigenthal, V. (2007). "Life is still going on": Reproductive intentions among HIV-positive women and men in South Africa. *Social Science and Medicine, 2*, 274–283.
Correa, S. (2003). From reproductive health to sexual rights achievements and future challenges. *Reproductive Health Matters, 10*, 107–116.
Dodoo, F., & Frost, A. (2008). Gender in African population research: The fertility/reproductive health example. *Annual Review of Sociology, 34*, 431–452.
Dorkenoo, E. (1995). *Female genital mutilation: The practice and its preventions.* London: Minority Rights Group.
Dyer, S. J. (2007). The value of children in African countries—Insights from studies on infertility. *Journal of Psychosomatic Obstetrics and Gynecology, 2*, 213–219.
Edstrom, J. (1992). Indicators for women's health in developing countries: What they reveal and conceal. *Institute of Developing Studies Bulletin, 1*, 38–49.
Feyisetan, B., & Pebley, A. (1989). Premarital sexuality in urban Nigeria. *Studies in Family Planning, 6*, 343–354.
Gott, M., & S. Hinchliff. (2003). How important is sex in later life? The views of older persons. *Social Science and Medicine, 56*, 1617–1628.
Harrell-Bond, B. E. (1975). *Modern marriage in Sierra Leone: A study of the professional group.* The Hague, Netherlands: Mouton.
Hindin, M., & Fatusi, A. (2009). Adolescent sexual and reproductive health in developing countries: An overview of trends and interventions. *International Perspectives on Family Planning, 2*, 58–62.
Hosken, F. (1993). *The Hosken report: Genital and sexual mutilation of females* (4th ed.). Lexington, MA: Women's International Network.
Hunter, M. (2007). The changing political economy of sex in South Africa: The significance of unemployment and inequalities to the scale of the AIDS pandemic. *Social Science and Medicine. 64*, 689–700.
Idowu, B. (1963). *Olodumare: God in Yoruba belief system.* London: Longmans.
Ikenga Metuh, E. (1987). *Comparative studies of African traditional religions.* IMICO.
Ikenga Metuh, E. (1991). *African religions in Western conceptual schemes: Essence and meanings of sacrifice.* IMICO.
INS (Institut National de la Statistique du Cameroun) and ORC Macro. (2004). *Executive Summary, Cameroon Demographic and Health Survey.* Calverton MD: INS and ORC Macro.

International Labour Organisation (ILO). (2002). *Men and women in the informal economy.* Geneva, Switzerland: Author.
Jiofack, T., Fokunang, C., & Guedje, N., (2010). Ethnobotanical uses of medicinal plants of two ethnoecological regions in Cameroon. *International Journal of Medicine and Medicinal Sciences, 3,* 60–79.
Kalinda, T., & Tembo, R. (2010). Sexual practices and levirate marriages in Mansa District of Zambia. *Journal of Human Sexuality, 13.* 1–12.
Kalipeni, E., Craddock, S., Oppong, J. R., & Ghosh, J. (2004). *HIV and AIDS in Africa: Beyond epidemiology.* Oxford, England: Blackwell.
Karanja, W. (1981). Women and work: A study of female and male attitudes in the modern sector of an African metropolis. In H. Ware (Ed.), *Women, education and modernization of the family in West Africa* (pp. 42–66). Canberra: The Australian National University Press.
Karanja, W., & Scott, J. (1982).Social structure, economic independence and the status of Nigerian women: The dialectics of power. In F. Adetowun Ogunsheye & F. Adetowun Ogunòshòeyòe (Eds.), *Nigerian women and development* (pp. 35–45). Ibadan, Nigeria: Ibadan University Press.
Kemayou, L-R. (2007). Dans la suite des femmes nues de la capital économique: ces pratiques font partie des conditionnalités posées dans certain sectes [Naked women in the economic capital: These practices are part of the rules of some sects]. *Le Messager, 2471,* 7.
Kim, C. (2009). Récents évaluations de l'approche d'éducation par les pairs à la santé sexuelle des adolescents: revue systématique [Recent evaluations of the effect of peer education on adolescents' sexual health: A systematic review [Special issue]. *Perspectives Internationales sur la Sante Sexuelle et Génésique,* 38–45.
Koso-Thomas, O. (1992). *The circumcision of women: A strategy for eradication.* New York: Zed Books.
Lacombe, B. (1983). *Le deuxième bureau: Secteur informel de la nuptialité en milieu urbain congolais* [The second office: Informal sector marriages in Congolese urban areas]. *Stateco, 35,* 58–78.
Lacombe, B. (1987). Informal unions in sub-Saharan Africa: The example of the Congolese «second office.» *Genus, 43*(1–2), 151–164.
Little, K. (1973). *African women in towns: An aspect of Africa's social revolution.* Cambridge, England: Cambridge University Press.
Lopman, B. A., Nyamukapa, C., Hallett, T. B., Mushati, P., Spark-du Preez, N., Kurwa, F., ... Gregson, S. (2009). Role of widows in the heterosexual transmission of HIV in Manicaland, Zimbabwe, 1998-2003. *Sexually Transmitted Infections, 85*(Suppl. 1), 141–148.
Malungo, J. R. (2001). Sexual cleansing (*Kusalazya*) and levirate marriage (*Kunjilila munganda*) in the era of AIDS: Changes in the perception and practices in Zambia. *Social Science and Medicine, 53,* 371–382.
Mandara, M. U. (2004). Female genital mutilation in Nigeria. *International Journal of Gynecology & Obstetrics, 3,* 291–298.
Masvawure, T. **(2010).** "I just need to be flashy on campus": Female students and transactional sex at a university in Zimbabwe. *Culture, Health, and Sexuality,* 12(8), 857–870.

Matthias, R., Lubben, J. E., Atchison, K. A., & Schweitzer, S. O. (1997). Sexual activity and satisfaction among very old adults: Results from a community-dwelling Medicare population survey. *The Gerontologist. 37*, 6–14.

Meekers, D., & Calves, A-E. (1997). Main-girlfriends, girlfriends, marriage and money. *Health Transition Review Supplement, 7,* 361–375.

Murphy, M. (1981). Social consequences of vesico-vaginal fistula in Northern Nigeria. *Journal of Biosocial Science, 13,*139–150.

Nasah, B. T. (1984). Infertility in reproductive health in Africa. In J. K. G. Mati, O. A. Ladipo, R. T. Burkman, R. H. Maganck, & D. Huber (Eds.), *Johns Hopkins program for international education in gynecology and obstetrics (JHPIEGO)* (p. 22). Baltimore, MD: Johns Hopkins University Press.

Nichols, D., Woods, E. T., Gates, D. S., & Sherman, J (1987). Sexual behavior, contraceptive practice, and reproductive health among Liberian adolescents. *Studies in Family Planning, 3,* 169–176.

Njikam Savage, O. M. (1988). Sociocultural aspects of infertility. Unpublished field notes.

Njikam Savage, O. M. (1991). *Some socio-cultural and behavioural aspects of sexually transmitted diseases (STD) and infertility in Cameroon* (University Annals of Medical Sciences). Yaoundé, Cameroon: Center for Medical and Health Sciences.

Njikam Savage, O. M. (1992). Artificial donor insemination in Yaoundé: Some socio-cultural considerations. *Social Science and Medicine. 7,* 907–913.

Njikam Savage, O. M., & Tchombe, T. (1994). Anthropological perspectives on sexual behaviour in Africa. *Annual Review of Sex Research. 5,* 50–72.

Njikam Savage, O. M. (1995). Continuing dialogue: Secrecy still the best policy: Donor insemination in Cameroon. *Politics and the Life Sciences, 1,* 87–88.

Njikam Savage, O. M. (1996). Children of the rope and other aspects of pregnancy loss in Cameroon. In R. Cecil (Ed.), *The anthropology of pregnancy loss* (Comparative Studies in Miscarriage, Stillbirth and Neonatal Death). Oxford, England: Berg.

Njikam Savage, O. M. (1998). Adolescents' beliefs and perceptions toward sexuality in urban Cameroon. In B. Kuate-Defo (Ed.), *Sexuality and reproductive health during adolescence in Africa* (pp. 77–90). Ottawa, Canada: University of Ottawa Press.

Njikam Savage, O. M. (2001). *Changing perspectives on sexuality, family and marriage among young male adults in Douala, Cameroon.* Presented at the Pan African Anthropologist Conference, Libreville, Gabon.

Njikam Savage, O. M. (2010a). Living with HIV/AIDS in Douala, Cameroon: Problems, challenges, aspirations and coping strategies. *MUTIBE, the Multidisciplinary & Biannual Review of the Faculty of Letters and Social Sciences of the University of Douala, 1*(4), 91–115.

Njikam Savage, O. M. (2010b). Types of marriages in Douala. Unpublished field reports.

Obbo, C. (1975). Women's careers in low income areas as indicators of country and town dynamics. In D. Parkin (Ed.), *Town and Country in Central and Eastern Africa* (pp. 288–293). Oxford, England: Oxford University Press.

Obbo, C. (1987). The old and the new in East Africa elite marriages. In D. Parkin & D. Nyamwaya (Eds.), *Transformations of African marriage.* (pp. 263–280). Manchester, England: Manchester University Press.

Okeyo, T. M., & Allen, A. K. (1994). Influence of widow inheritance on the epidemiology of AIDS in Africa. *Africa Journal of Medical Practice. 1*, 20–25.

Organisation Mondiale de la Santé (OMS), Fonds des Nations Unies pour la population et Fonds des Nations Unies pour l'enfance. (1997). *Action for adolescent health: Towards a common agenda.* Geneva, Switzerland: Author.

Renata, GTZ, Ministère de la Santé Publique. Les Associations de Tantines. (2007). Campagne contre le "repassage" des seins, un don de Dieu [Campaign against the "ironing" of breasts, a gift from God]. Retrieved from www.tantines.org/?page_id=95

Shaw, D. (2006). Sexual and reproductive health: rights and responsibilities. *Lancet, 9551*, 1941–1943.

Sutton, B. (2007). Poner el Cuerpo: Women's embodiment and political resistance in Argentina. *Latin America Politics and Society, 3*, 129–162.

Tahzib, F. (1983). Epidemiological determinants of vesico-vaginal fistulas. *British Journal of Obstetrics and Gynaecology, 90*, 387–391.

Tcheungna, R. (2012, January 19). Unusual sexual practices, the new trend for fame and fortune in Cameroon and the blackest side of black magic... *The Bridge Magazine.* Retrieved from: http://the-bridge-magazine.com/2012/02/unusual-sexual-practices-the-new-trend-for-fame-and-fortune-in-cameroon-and-the-blackest-side-of-black-magic/

Turner, G., & Shepherd, J. (1999). A method in search of a theory: Peer education and health promotion. *Health Education Research, 2*, 235–247.

Twa-Twa, J. (1997). The role of the environment in the sexual activity of school students in Tororo and Pallisa districts in Uganda. *Health Transition Review Supplements 7*, 67–81.

United Nations Population Fund (UNFPA). (2004). *State of the world population: The Cairo consensus at ten.* New York: Author.

Van der Geest, S. (2001). "No strength": Sex and old age in a rural town in Ghana. *Social Science and Medicine, 53*, 1383–1396.

Vincent, C., Riddell, J., & Shmueli, A. (2000). *Sexuality and the older woman: A literature review.* Oxford, England: Pennell

World Health Organization (WHO). (1991). Maternal mortality and morbidity: Obstetric fistulae. *Women's Global Network for Reproductive Rights. 37*, 8–9.

World Health Organization (WHO). (2010). Female genital mutilation fact sheet (No. 241). Geneva, Switzerland: Author.

Zabin, L. S., & Kiragu, K. (1998). The health consequences of adolescent sexual and fertility behaviour in sub-Saharan Africa. *Studies in Family Planning. 2*, 210–232.

Zeitzen, M. K. (2008). *Polygamy: A cross-cultural analysis.* Oxford, England: Berg.

Editors Introduction to Chapter 6
Iran

In this chapter we are taken into the workings of a busy clinic in rural Iran, a place where men (and occasionally women) come for help with sexual problems. The urgency for successful treatment to gain or restore sexual function is illustrated by the fact that marriages, reputations, and even lives hang in the balance. According to the authors, sex therapy, even were it available, is not a viable option in this part of the world where the need for immediate resolution of sexual dysfunction is intense. They advocate for a strictly sexual medicine approach to the treatment of sexual dysfunction. Somewhat controversially, they use intracavernosal injections for the treatment of unconsummated marriage without knowing whether there is a female dysfunction, specifically dyspareunia or vaginismus that might account for the problem. The authors observe that life for women in Iran will be dismal if they cannot have sex within their marriage. Such women are likely to be divorced, leaving them penniless and unmarriageable. Because of the cultural imperative, the discussion in this chapter centers on the importance of accomplishing penetrative sex. Pleasure and intimacy are absent from the discussion of treatment, especially for women. It will be important for the reader to decide whether this is a helpful treatment approach or not, but the issues raised in this chapter are certainly thought-provoking.

6

CULTURALLY BASED SEXUAL PROBLEMS IN TRADITIONAL AREAS OF KERMANSHAH, IRAN

Javaad Zargooshi, Elham Rahmanian, Hiva Motaee, Mozhgaan Kohzadi, and Samad Nourizad

Introduction

Culture affects all aspects of human life, and sexual life is no exception. In this chapter we discuss some unique sexual and genital problems that are prevalent in Kermanshah, Iran. The contents of this chapter are based on the extensive clinical experience of the first author (JZ).[1] In the Kermanshah province, with a population of 2 million, there is no dedicated sexual dysfunction clinic. Thus, during the past 15 years the first author's clinic has been the main provider of specialized sexual medicine health care and the sole destination for referrals in this province. The number of cases seen at the clinic for sexual complaints far exceeds the numbers typically seen in clinics in industrialized countries. For example, most urologists in the United States see less than one premature ejaculation (PE) patient per week (Shindel, Nelson, & Brandes, 2008), whereas at the Kermanshah clinic more than one patient each day complains of PE.

Between November 1996 and October 2011, 32,709 new patients were seen at the clinic. Of these cases, 5,412 were new, self-diagnosed PE patients, 6,279 patients presented with erectile dysfunction (ED), and 556 patients presented with unconsummated marriage (UCM). Thus, on average 1.2 new PE patients and 1.5 new ED patients were seen each day, with PE and ED comprising 16% and 19% of the cases, respectively.

There are several unique sexual problems in Kermanshah, Iran. In this chapter, after discussing sex in traditional sections of Iranian society, we focus on three topics: UCM, self-inflicted penile fracture, and culturally specific aspects of PE.

Sex in Traditional Societies in Iran

Iran has a rich cultural heritage, of which modern day Iranians are justifiably proud. The first historical evidence of human settlement and civilization in the Iranian plateau can be dated back well over 10,000 years ago. There are many cultural heritage sites all over Iran.

The fall of the Sassanid dynasty and conquest of Iran in 651 CE by Arab invaders was not able to destroy Persian culture. For 300 years, by banning native languages and customs, by burning large libraries, by destroying monumental sculptures and architecture, and by all other means, the Arab invaders sought to eradicate and annihilate Persian culture and language. Total destruction and extinction of the native cultures and languages of conquered territories was the standard practice of Arabs, and this differentiates them from other invaders of Iran, such as Alexander the Great and the Mongols. Wherever the Arab invaders went, the conquered people were forced to become Arabic speakers and change their identity. Thus, after a variable period, the people in occupied lands started considering themselves Arabs. The Arab conquest "Arabized" the Middle East and North Africa permanently (most notably Egypt, Syria, Jordan, Libya, Algeria, Tunisia, and Morocco). Although politically conquered, the Persians resisted assimilation into Arab culture and maintained a strong Persian identity. The success of this struggle is evident in the fact that present-day Iranians do not identify as Arab.

Sexual Medicine

Iran has more than 2,500 years of recorded history regarding the practice of medicine in which sexual medicine holds a central place. Over 1,100 years ago, the great Iranian physician Rhazes (865–925 CE),[2] wrote a scholarly monograph on impotence, and discussed the topic in other books, including his encyclopedic 70-volume *Liber Continens*. This tome covered the complete medical knowledge of the 10th century in addition to reporting Rhazes's own original observations and discoveries. Rhazes also wrote a monograph on men who have sex with men, the first detailed work of serious scholarship to deal with the subject. Various original therapies, including ointments, herbal remedies, and mixtures were administered to impotent men in ancient Persia and sexual matters were freely and explicitly taught and discussed in scientific circles. In medieval times, diet, physical, and mental health, as well as attraction to one's sexual partner were discussed as contributing to sexual health or problems (Ghadiri & Gorji, 2004). The past stands in sharp contrast to the present situation in Iran where sexual medicine has no place in universities and sex and sexual organs are excluded systematically from the study of medicine, thus leaving physicians unprepared to deal with a patient with sexual dysfunction. Also, the public has very limited access to scientific information about sex and sexual organs. We have previously reported on various consequences of this lack of information, the transmission of sexually transmitted infections (STIs) being a major concern. Many STIs are the result of unprotected sexual contact with sex workers and *sigheh*, or temporary wives[3] (Zargooshi, 2002a).

Sexually Transmitted Infections

Gonorrhea is the most common STI among nonincarcerated men in Iran. The first author followed 100 men who had positive Gram stains for gonorrhea between 1997 and 2000 (Zargoshi, 2002a). According to patient reports, the likely source of infection was girlfriends (4%), temporary (*sigheh*) wives (24%), and sex workers (64%). The remaining 8% of patients denied extramarital sex. In the cases of contact with sex workers, 89% of reported intercourse events were unprotected. Thirty-one out of 38 married men reported unprotected intercourse with their permanent wives in the presence of urethral discharge. Only 7 of the 100 patients accepted cotreatment for partners. There were several reasons given by patients for this low rate of cotreatment. In the case of refusing to allow treatment for a spouse, men were afraid of disclosing extramarital sex. When cotreatment was recommended for a sex worker, men refused, citing difficulty in locating the sex worker with whom sexual contact was made as well as a lack of commitment to her. Characteristics of patients and sex workers with gonorrhea in Kermanshah include: (a) failure of sex workers to present for treatment; (b) high rate of unprotected intercourse with sex workers and with permanent wives even when the patient had urethral discharge; (c) very high rate of persistent infection despite standard antibiotics; (d) high rate of presentation with false complaints (e.g., to get antibiotics, men often masked the true source or type of infection); (e) high rate of self-treatment; (f) resistance by patients to giving the prescribed drugs to wives; and (g) *sigheh* wives being an important source of infection (Zargooshi, 2002a).

Although there is no research on the prevalence of prostitution in Iran, there are unofficial estimates of 300,000 sex workers, including 45,000 in Tehran (Zargooshi, 2002a). Iranian sex workers seldom present for treatment of STIs. They often have erroneous information from pseudo-scientific propaganda about sex and often try to treat their symptoms with over-the-counter antibiotics. Fear of stigmatization and biased or prejudiced authorities have created an insecure environment for sex workers and they fear even the medical profession.

Marriage in Traditional Iran

Iran is currently ruled by Islamic sharia that permits polygyny. The number of legal permanent wives permitted is four per man; there is no limit to temporary (*sigheh*) wives. However, practicing polygyny is by no means popular. In fact the bigamist or polygamist is not viewed favorably by society. The practice of polygamy in Kermanshah, too, is very rare. Searching our electronic database of 33,052 patients (of which 26,778 [81%] were men), it become clear that only 46 men (0.1%) were bigamists and only one had three wives.

Over the past 150 years, Iran has made clear but uneven progress from a traditional to a modern society. Rural areas are being progressively urbanized and now 68% of Iran's population of 70 million lives in cities. However, traditional sections of the society still remain primarily in rural areas with their own social, cultural, and ethical mores intact. In these areas, girls must be virgins when they marry. The groom's family needs proof of the bride's virginity, and the proof is evidence of bleeding from the hymen onto a handkerchief during the first coitus. Brides must give the bloody handkerchief to the groom's relatives, most commonly the groom's mother, who will then show it to the whole family, as proof of the bride's virginity and honor and the groom's potency and ability. If the bride cannot produce this proof on her wedding night, her family and the groom's family are shamed.

Premarital and extramarital sex are acceptable for men but categorically unacceptable for women; thus, there exists a double standard for sexual behavior regarding women and men. This double standard extends to divorce. While men can divorce very easily and quickly from their wives, women can ask for a divorce only in very rare circumstances and with great difficulty, entailing a very long process, and then only by agreeing to receive no monetary compensation. Additionally, while a divorce has serious negative social consequences for women, even multiple divorces have no negative impact on men's reputation. The only exception to this involves cases in which a bride can prove that her husband is impotent (this includes all sexual dysfunctions such as ED and PE). In these cases a woman can secure a divorce and monetary reimbursement (*mahrie*) from her husband. There is shame and stigma attached to a man who is declared sexually dysfunctional. In fact, according to a popular online Iranian newspaper, a study of lawsuits in the Family Courts has shown that 50% of all divorces in Iran are due to sexual dysfunctions including PE (jamejamonline, n.d.).

Unconsummated Marriage

Unconsummated marriage (UCM) is a condition in which the first coitus in a marriage has not occurred in "due time" and thus the bride remains a virgin. In traditional sections of some societies, including Iran, this is considered shameful for the groom and a cause of great distress and conflict for the couple. Little research has been done regarding UCM and its accompanying male and female sexual dysfunctions.[4] In 2008, we reported on 417 patients with UCM (Zargooshi, 2008). Important causes of UCM in our patients, in decreasing order of prevalence were: handkerchief stress (anxiety related to the pressure to prove potency on the wedding night), PE, ED, vaginismus, performance anxiety, lack of knowledge about coital technique, and low sexual desire. Organic causes were less common, as reflected in the high response rate to intracavernosal injection (ICI) that is suggestive of the absence of neurogenic and vasculogenic ED.

In our patients, the age difference between grooms and brides was very striking. In the case of extreme age differences (where the husband is more than three times the age of the wife) and in loveless, obligatory marriages, it appeared that the bride's resistance to penetration was intentional rather than, or in addition to, vaginismus. Many of the cases of UCM seen at our clinic were legal cases in which the bride was seeking medical proof of her husband's impotence in order to secure a divorce and monetary reimbursement. Thus, in many cases, more important than the decision to divorce or not (many of the couples agreed to divorce) was the decision of whether or not to provide monetary reimbursement. We refused to give treatment to patients in legal cases and whenever there was a high probability of divorce, in obligatory, loveless marriages, in the presence of extreme age differences, and when major psychiatric disorders or significant learning difficulties were present. A large number of cases that did not respond to treatment or did not receive treatment ended in divorce. Divorce will very markedly decrease the chance of remarriage for woman in Iran, and those brides who lost their virginity before their divorce have almost no chance of remarriage. Therefore, to avoid inflicting permanent harm on the brides, we do not offer treatment to the grooms if we determined there was a high probability of divorce.

Some patients present to us with various premarital sexual concerns. Many of these patients had no prior coitus and this, coupled with body image problems related to penile size, made the first night of marriage a horrifying prospect for them. Some men obsessively worried that they had been damaged by their history of masturbation. Others had experienced ED or PE in their premarital encounters. There was a wide spectrum in the way couples coped with UCM; some were peacefully living together like "brother and sister," while others were intolerant of the problem and had constant conflict and legal problems. There were some self-reported psychological problems in husbands, but these were reported by a minority of men. Diagnostic yield of laboratory evaluation was low, and we now request laboratory tests very selectively. Also, considering safety, low cost, diagnostic utility, and high successes rate of ICI therapy, we do not recommend either nocturnal penile tumescence testing or dynamic penile color-duplex ultrasound, except in unusual cases of failure of treatment.

Fear of failure, PE, ED, and vaginismus were the main reasons for continued UCM. In longstanding UCM, relatives often interfered and their lack of knowledge worsened the matter. ICI is the first line treatment used in our clinic. Given our extensive experience with ICI in UCM we begin with a higher than usual dose (20 mg instead of 10 mg) of papaverine and lowered the maximum dose (40 mg instead of 120 mg). We offer ICI as the first-line treatment even for those having PE because our experience is that other treatments have proved to be of very limited value. ICI has also proved to be effective in many cases of apparent vaginismus. Although the husband may present with the complaint that his wife's vagina is too tight for penetration, in actuality the difficulty is due to his having only a semirigid erection. Without the recourse of divorce, a marriage with ongoing sexual dysfunction would have very negative consequences, particularly for women. We speculated that wives were perhaps unconsciously resisting penetration on those occasions when their husbands had at least a partial erection. By providing a rigid, sustained erection, ICI promised a better future to the wives and thus, the resistance to penetration lessened or disappeared.

We believe that ICI should be regarded as the first-line treatment of UCM even in industrialized countries. In contrast to multiple sessions of psychotherapy, ICI creates a very rapid response. ICI is much less expensive than psychotherapy. In many countries urologists performing ICI are more readily available than sex and marital therapists. In Iran there are few if any qualified sex and marital therapists. Deep, complex psychological problems are not a major cause of the vast majority of UCM cases and in our experience ICI has a curative effect in the majority, without the need for maintenance therapy. Using ICI does not interfere with psychotherapy and one can refer the ICI failures for psychotherapy. Being under heavy social pressure, UCM cases are unsuitable for a waiting-list.

The only problems with ICI are priapism and the invasiveness of the procedure (Zargooshi, 2000a). There were two main reasons for the high incidence of priapism in our patients: (a) relatively high doses were used as all injections were done by the first author and because most patients had come from remote rural areas, the injections had to be titrated so that the patients could reach home before detumescence; (b) Because of patients' low income and the unavailability of the prostaglandin E1, we used papaverine, which is known to have variable efficacy between doses, thus causing a higher incidence of priapism (using prostaglandin with papaverine will decrease the incidence of priapism). However, none of our patients who experienced ICI-induced priapism developed de novo ED. In some cases, despite our consistent advice to patients to return for detumescence if their erection persisted for more than 3 hours, patients did not return but neither did they experience observable sequelae related to the untreated ICI-induced priapism. In most cases, our patients' educational level was too low to safely allow them to administer the ICI, thus the first author performed all ICIs at the clinic. In industrialized countries urologists can teach patients to self-administer ICI, obviating the need for large doses and thus decreasing the incidence of priapism. Nodule formation (a small lump at the injection site) is irrelevant in UCM because only a few injections are needed. Regarding invasiveness, in our experience the patients are more than willing to tolerate the pain of a needle if they can reach a cure immediately. No patients, including those who experienced priapism, expressed regret for not undergoing alternative therapies.

Oral therapies are often considered the first-line treatment of ED. Despite proper use of sildenafil along with manual sexual stimulation, many of our patients failed to sustain an erection sufficient for vaginal penetration. The most common scenario was that sildenafil created an erection, but upon encountering vaginismus, or because of performance anxiety, the erection was lost and further attempts to regain an erection failed. Of course, cases of successful treatment with sildenafil by general physicians and others were not referred to us and almost all of our referral cases were sildenafil failures. However, in primary cases, too, our clinical experience prescribing PDE-5 inhibitors has been disappointing. Sildenafil is not expensive in Iran and a large number of our patients received it before presenting to us, in addition to those who received it by our own prescription. However, it is our experience that sildenafil is not an appropriate first-line treatment in UCM, not because of cost or availability, but because of lack of efficacy.[5]

We believe that the following factors are responsible for the failure of oral therapy in cases of UCM: UCM adds greatly to the complexity of ED and its repercussions; the dynamics of UCM marriages are different from 'straightforward' ED cases, and finally, an intact hymen is seen by many patients as a frightening obstacle to penetration. Compared to oral therapies, ICI-induced erections are far more rigid and sustained and thus much more resistant to detumescence when the groom encounters difficulties during the first coitus (Zargooshi, 2000b).

Other treatments for UCM include surgery, vacuum pumps and herbal remedies, none of which are effective in our experience. Hymenectomy was not helpful for the majority of women who underwent this procedure. Nonstandard vacuum constriction devices are sold in Tehran by con artists and swindlers to desperate patients. Those selling these devices make unsubstantiated claims that these provide "the only permanent, certified cure of ED" and that they are an "effective penile enlargement remedy." Of course, none of these claims are true, and these patients later presented to us after failing to respond to these devices. The lack of knowledge about sexual functioning in rural regions of Iran has resulted in many misconceptions. In rural areas a popular belief among some UCM couples is that the woman has become "locked" and need to be "opened"; thus, they had visited traditional healers before seeking medical help.

Given the increased mobility of populations, clinicians will likely see an increasing number of patients from a wide variety of cultural backgrounds. ICI should be considered the treatment of choice for UCM for couples with backgrounds similar to the couples presenting to our clinic. We offer two case studies, one that illustrates treatment success with ICI and the other, a legal case in which we refused to offer treatment.

Case Presentations[6]

Case 1: Effective Treatment of UCM due to ED in a Deeply Religious Man.

Maziar presented to our clinic with UCM of 4 days duration. A strictly religious man, he nonetheless had a history of furtive masturbation. In preparation for his wedding he read pseudoscientific books about sex that referenced the "grave irreparable complications" of masturbation. Thus Maziar anticipated sexual impotence as a result of masturbation. Maziar had no coitus or any other sexual experience. On his wedding night, family members were waiting impatiently behind the door to confirm and then celebrate coitus. They were anticipating the presentation of a blood-stained handkerchief which would be proof that the bride was a virgin and that Maziar was potent. The handkerchief was not presented that night, nor was it displayed to the family over the next three nights. Maziar was unable to get an erection firm enough for penetration. He presented to the clinic in a panicked and distressed state. He feared the shame that would be visited upon himself and his family if he did not succeed in having intercourse. On first meeting Maziar it was apparent that guilt feelings related to his premarital masturbation, the lack of dates or indeed any conversation with his future wife, his lack of any sexual experience before marriage, and "handkerchief stress" had all culminated in UCM. Maziar was assured that masturbation had not damaged his ability to be sexual. He was treated with ICI and easily consummated his marriage several hours later. A follow-up appointment several months later confirmed that Maziar was sexually functional without the need for injections or other treatment.

Case 2: A Legal Case that Was Refused Treatment

Darius was an engineer in his late 20s who was referred to us by the courts. He had a history of UCM of one month duration. His wife, Nazanin, also an engineer, asked for a divorce because of the UCM. Given the high probability that this marriage would end in divorce, they were not offered treatment. Nazanin and Darius were distantly related and so knew each other but had no sexual contact before marriage. Darius had no sexual desire and stated that he has no sexual affinity toward his wife because of the wife's hirsutism and small breasts. Though really very beautiful, Nazanin indeed had moderate hirsutism and small breasts. She was cultured, tender, and had many other very good qualities. Nazanin was clearly much superior to her husband in all key aspects of personality and beauty. Nevertheless, Darius felt no desire for Nazanin, to the point that he had never even undressed his wife. In sharp contrast, Nazanin had a very high level of sexual desire and need but her religious commitments prevented her from having any premarital or extramarital sex. Nazanin threatened divorce if Darius continued to abstain from sex. Ultimately the couple agreed to divorce but the only problem was the reimbursement fees. Nazanin asked the clinic to provide an "impotence document" and Darius, wanting to avoid payment, claimed in court that he was sexually functional (a confession of impotence would result in his obligation to pay full *mahrie* (money paid to wives after divorce if the husbands cannot perform sexually). After shared relatives interceded, Darius finally agreed to pay some amount of money (much less than full *mahrie*) to Nazanin. However, Nazanin felt cheated, and doubted the usefulness and rightness of her religious beliefs, according to which virtuous character and chastity are rewarded while those who behave immorally and are sexually promiscuous, will have misfortune befall them. As she commented, "neither my integrity and truthfulness, nor my prayers nor my sincere requests for good luck from God, helped me. Notorious wrongdoers did better in final term and have good luck."

Premature Ejaculation: Pleasure versus Control

Premature ejaculation (PE) is one of the most common complaints in the clinical practice of sexual medicine (Shindel et al., 2008). There are various definitions of PE. Most of these definitions are not evidence-based and some stress control of ejaculation, whereas others use latency to ejaculation as the critical measure. Even when the latter criterion is used there is variability in the definition of PE and ejaculation occurring within 1, 2, 3, or even 7 minutes of penetration have variously been considered as premature (Jannini & Lenzi, 2005).

The International Society for Sexual Medicine (ISSM) recently defined lifelong PE as a male sexual dysfunction characterized by (a) ejaculation which always or nearly always occurs before or within 1 minute of vaginal penetration; (b) the inability to delay ejaculation on all or nearly all occasions of vaginal penetrations, and (c) negative personal consequences, such as distress, bother, frustration and/or the avoidance of sexual intimacy (McMahon et al., 2008).

The proposed DSM-5 definition of PE (relabeled as "early ejaculation") is: "The following symptoms must have been present for at least 6 months and be experienced on most occasions of sexual activity: Persistent or recurrent pattern of ejaculation occurring during partnered sexual activity within approximately one minute of beginning of sexual activity and before the person wishes it." The problem must also cause distress and cannot be accounted for by any other psychiatric disorder or be due to the effects of medication or medical condition (American Psychiatric Association, 2011).

PE is the second most prevalent male sexual complaint seen at our clinic in Kermanshah, Iran (ED is the most prevalent). Here we discuss some aspects of PE that are culturally based. Having an Intravaginal Ejaculatory Latency Time (IELT) of less than 2 minutes and distress for the patient or his partner characterizes the majority of the patients who present to us with the chief complaint of PE. Although almost 80 percent of our patients presented with IELTs of less than 2 minutes, IELTs between 2 and 5 minutes collectively comprised 20% of all patients. A significant proportion of Iranian men who consider themselves to be premature ejaculators have IELTs of between 2 and 5 minutes. To treat or not to treat those with IELTs of longer than 1 to 2 minutes is a controversial issue. IELT in a nonclinical population has been studied only in a very small number of countries with small samples, and the resultant proposed normal limits and cutoffs have failed to gain widespread acceptance (Jannini & Lenzi, 2005). For example, while the ISSM has proposed the one minute cutoff point, recent studies have adopted a 2-minute cutoff (McMahon et al., 2008).

In our opinion, there is a need for the sexual medicine community to reach a consensus on the clinical diagnostic and therapeutic approach to those patients who consider themselves premature ejaculators and actively and insistently seek treatment, but have IELTs of more than 1 to 2 minutes (but less than 5 minutes). To be widely accepted and applicable worldwide, this consensus should be reached based on large studies by different researchers from diverse countries. In our clinic a significant minority of the single patients who have never attempted coitus presented with PE during noncoital sexual contacts, or masturbation, or other "noncontact" sexual situations (e.g., phone sex). PE in these circumstances was an important cause of premarital performance anxiety with resultant reluctance to marry. We think that in defining PE, these patients, too, should be considered.

Some patients presented to our clinic with what we term "second round" ED. These patients presented with difficulty getting an erection, but further questioning revealed that they had only PE. These men were fully potent in their first coitus. However, since they were unable to have an erection immediately after the first coitus (namely, during the refractory period), they came to us complaining of ED. This scenario was by no means rare; trying to have more than one intercourse in a single session was one of the most common strategies used by patients to bring their partner to orgasm. Whenever the patients were able to complete a "second round" of coitus, the negative impact of their PE on their partners was lessened. The therapeutic implication of this finding is clear; any patient who presents with ED should be interviewed carefully to determine whether he has true ED or ED only on his second attempt ("second round ED"). Failure to make this important differential diagnosis will result in giving ED treatment to patients who have PE only.

In contrast to the patients from industrialized countries, for whom the lack of control has been of utmost importance (Patrick, Rowland, & Rothman, 2007), in our patients the briefness of the latency time was the main concern (Zargooshi, 2009a). The lack of pleasure they experienced due to a brief IELT was a much more articulated concept than lack of control. In fact, complaining of no pleasure was another expression of having PE. PE was the most common reason for the lack of sexual satisfaction experienced, even by those men who reported no problems regarding sexual attraction to their partner, who had intimacy and good communication with their partner, and who had a satisfactory marital relationship. Thus, in cases that present with the complaint of no pleasure in sex, PE should always be ruled out. Many equated pleasure in sex with pleasure in life, typically saying "due to *sostie kamar* (PE), I live a pleasureless life." This was understandable considering the general lack of alternative sources of pleasure, especially in rural areas such as recreation and sports facilities. The systematic suppression of expressions of happiness such as dance and ceremonies left sexual intercourse as the only remaining source of pleasure for many. According to our patients, the very high unemployment rate, too, contributed to the increased importance of sexual pleasure. Unemployed men had many hours of being in the home with their wives and thus had ample time for sex. In our interviews, the common finding among our patients was that many of them allocated almost no time to foreplay and many had a lack of skills in foreplay. This limited their pleasurable time to the period of intravaginal penetration only, and that was naturally not too long.

The impact and implications of PE are very serious for Iranian men. As a consequence many patients reported using opium in order to delay ejaculation long enough to bring their partners to orgasm. One third of these users first used opium for PE but then become addicted to it. In fact, in our clinical experience, PE is one of the most important predisposing factors for opium addiction in Iran, and especially in Kermanshah. Opium addiction was more common than cigarette smoking among our PE patients. Some patients who stopped using opium presented to the clinic with the unrealistic expectation of being able to have intercourse last as long as it did when they were using opium. Some patients reported a decreased response to opium over time resulting in faster ejaculation times. Tramadol, an opiate agonist typically used to relieve pain, is sometimes prescribed for the treatment of PE. However, in our experience all patients who used Tramadol as a PE treatment became addicted to it. Thus we strongly oppose offering Tramadol as a PE treatment. Instead we use Clomipramine or Selective Serotonin Reuptake Inhibitors (SSRIs) because of their noted side effects of delaying ejaculation.

Case of Successful Treatment of PE in a Highly Distressed Couple

Babak was a 34-year-old teacher who presented to the clinic complaining of no pleasure from sex. Babak reported an IELT of less than 20 seconds. Over the course of his marriage Babak's interest in sex declined and he became increasingly anxious about his sexual ability. When he presented for treatment Babak was often unable to get an erection. Babak had been married for one year without producing a child. Sex was infrequent and marked by either a failure to get an erection or a very quick ejaculation. Sepideh, Babak's wife, was highly distressed about the sexual problems in their marriage. She criticized Babak and complained that his penis was too small. Sepideh wanted to file for a divorce, citing Babak's sexual dysfunction as the cause. Her family was not supportive of her desire for a divorce and so Sepideh attempted to kill herself by cutting her wrists. It was her suicide attempt (interrupted by Babak arriving home unexpectedly) that finally persuaded him to seek medical attention. Babak was anxious and despairing when he came to the clinic. He said: "Despite being 120 kilograms in weight and despite being a strong man, I felt misery and humiliation near my wife, because of sexual dysfunction." A physical examination was performed complete with blood work. Because Babak's prolactin level was high (although an MRI of the pituitary gland was unremarkable), he was prescribed bromocriptine, a dopamine receptor agonist used to treat symptoms of hyperprolactinemia. He was also given tadalafil, a PDE-5 inhibitor for his ED, and clomipramine, a tricyclic antidepressant commonly prescribed for symptoms of obsessive-compulsive disorder, for his PE. Babak was told to focus on pleasure rather than performance. He responded well to the medication and was satisfied with the results, reporting an IELT of almost 2 minutes. He also felt more pleasure in his sexual encounters because he was taking time to enjoy sex.

Taqaandan and Penile Fracture

Although not a sexual dysfunction per se, we see many cases of penile fracture which are attributable to a lack of sexual knowledge and thus avoidable. Sex therapists who encounter men coming from traditional sections of transitional societies such as Iran would do well to know about this issue and by providing information, may prevent penile injury. Penile "fracture," defined as a rupture of the tunica albuginea of the corpora cavernosa induced by blunt trauma to the erect penis, is an uncommon injury in industrialized countries. In contrast, it is unusually prevalent in Kermanshah. The reason is the widespread cultural practice of *taqaandan* or *qolenj shekestan* in this province (Zargooshi, 2000c, 2002b, 2004). Taqaandan is a self-inflicted injury, very similar to knuckle cracking, consisting of intentional forceful acute bending of part of the shaft of the erect penis in a downward, upward or lateral direction while holding the other part stationary. In 2009, we reported on 352 patients with penile fracture (Zargooshi, 2009b).

No single place in the world has more cases of penile fracture than Kermanshah, Iran, not only in terms of the total number of cases that have accumulated but also in terms of the new cases per week. This is unfortunate, because the widespread, dangerous practice of *taqaandan*, the main cause of penile fracture in this province, is preventable. *Taqaandan* is not a form of masturbation and does not culminate in ejaculation. It involves sudden application of force perpendicular to the long axis of the penis for a very short time. Whether performed routinely or only done occasionally, the motives given for this dangerous practice include: pleasure, to provide the penis with relaxation or relief, to release the pressure of libido, as recreation, to enlarge or straighten the penis, to produce detumescence, or because it is simply a habit. Other much less common causes include falls, manipulating or rolling over the penis during sleep and coital injury. In many cases, taqaandan was introduced to patients by their friends. Almost no patient knew beforehand that taqaandan could cause penile fracture. The great majority thought that the penis has cartilage. Patients' ignorance of the properties of penile tissue arises from the lack of access to scientific knowledge about the genitals. Systematically providing accurate information on genital anatomy could significantly reduce the abnormally high incidence of penile fracture in this poor community of largely uneducated and unemployed men. However, in Iran even search engines like Google and Yahoo are blocked from being searched for words like penile anatomy, safe sex, or sexual health. This is reminiscent of the prohibitions in sixteenth century France that were protested by the Renaissance scholar Michel de Montaigne in his Essays at 1580: "what has the act of generation, so natural, so necessary, and so just, done to men, to be a thing not to be spoken of without blushing, and to be excluded from all serious and moderate discourse? We boldly pronounce kill, rob, betray, and that we dare only to do betwixt the teeth" (quoted in Bakhtin, 1984, p. 320).

Taqaandan produced a sound in all cases and pain in none. Consistent signs and symptoms of penile fracture were "pop" or cracking sounds, ecchymosis, edema, curvature, and immediate detumescence. Most fractures were proximal in location. Midshaft tears were noted in a minority of cases.

Our time-tested approach to penile fracture is summarized as follows. We suggest a uniform surgical plan regardless of delay in presentation. Our findings show that in addition to embarrassment and fear, absence of pain, too, may be an important factor in not seeking immediate medical care. While there is no place for conservative management in penile fracture, there is no need to perform surgery immediately; rather surgery may be performed within 24 hours of presentation. In dealing with an uncomplicated case of penile fracture, apart from obtaining a history and performing a physical examination, there is no need to perform any diagnostic test, including cavernosography, ultrasonography, MRI or any other imaging. Prognostically, it is safe to inform the patients that after repair of penile fracture almost all patients will have a straight, painless penis with normal erectile function. In sharp contrast, without surgical intervention penile fracture results in chordee (downward bowing of the penis) and ED in most cases. The only legacy of surgery is a harmless, barely noticeable nodule that is not associated with any consequence in long-term follow-up.

Case: Successful Surgical Repair of Penile Fracture

Mazdak was a 30-year-old man who was employed as a bricklayer. He had been practicing taqaandan on a regular basis for the past several months. He had three friends who also practiced taqaandan and who introduced him to the practice. They told him that it would help to relax and refresh his penis. Mazdak also found that taqaandan provided some relief from his sexual urges as he was not yet married. His friends assured Mazdak that *taqaandan*, because it did not waste semen, would have none of the ill effects of masturbation. On the occasion when he injured his penis, Mazdak had a very firm erection and so he applied more force than usual to his penis. Mazdak heard a small popping sound and his erection immediately subsided. As he did not feel any pain he tried to believe that nothing serious was wrong. He believed that cartilage in the penis caused erections and so he was unaware that he had penile fracture. Swelling and a curvature in his penis, combined with the absence of erection over the next 24 hours frightened Mazdak. He presented to the clinic two days later in a state of high anxiety. A clinical interview and examination confirmed penile fracture, which was surgically repaired the following morning. Mazdak regained full potency following the surgery. At a 21-month follow-up, Mazdak continued to have good erectile capability.

Female Sexual Dysfunctions

There are few treatment options in Iran for women with sexual dysfunctions. There are no effective pharmacologic treatments and even in Tehran, there are no dedicated female sexual dysfunction clinics. There are also cultural barriers to seeking help for women with sexual complaints. The traditional sections of society would not condone such behavior. As is the case with men, the systematic blocking of the free flow of scientific sexual information prevents women from acquiring accurate knowledge about their sexual difficulties.

Despite the lack of treatment options, the few studies that have been done indicate that there is a high incidence of sexual dysfunction in Iranian women. In a community sample of 2,626 women aged 20 to 60 recruited from 28 provinces, 31.5% reported some sexual difficulties at interview: of these women, 37% reported orgasmic difficulty, 35% reported hypoactive sexual desire disorder, 30% reported arousal disorder, while dyspareunia was reported by 26.7% (Safarinejad, 2006). In a sample of urban women the prevalence of sexual dysfunction was also found to be high: 52% of 1,456 participants had experienced at least one type of sexual difficulty, including anorgasmia (21.3%) and lack of lubrication (11.9%) (Goshtasebi, Vahdaninia, & Rahimi Foroshani, 2006). Another community sample of 1,200 women found the prevalence of anorgasmia was 26.3% (Najafabady, Salmani, & Abedi, 2011). Not surprisingly, in this same study it was found that women with anorgasmia were less satisfied with their sexual relationship than were women who experienced orgasm. Women who were orgasmic were more likely to have received some sex education and were slightly older than their anorgasmic counterparts when they married (19 years versus 18 years). The majority of anorgasmic women reported that sex was a duty (58.5%), whereas only 20% thought that sex was a joy and 21%

thought that sex was both a duty and a joy. Of the orgasmic women, 44% believed that sex was a duty, 27% thought sex was a joy and 29% thought it was both a duty and a joy.

In a clinical sample of 300 married women presenting to family planning centers in Tehran, 38% reported at least one sexual dysfunction: inhibited desire (15%), inhibited orgasm (26%), lack of lubrication (15%), vaginismus (8%), and dyspareunia (10%). Common sexual complaints were "too little foreplay before intercourse" and "partner chooses inconvenient time" (8% each). Nevertheless, over one half of the women (51%) reported that their overall sexual relationship was satisfactory. In this sample of predominantly well-educated women, 74% had moderate knowledge about sexuality, and 53% had a conservative attitude toward sexuality. Better knowledge about sexuality was associated with more experiences of orgasm. There were also significant correlations between sexual attitudes and sexual function (orgasm, desire, lubrication); a conservative attitude was associated with more sexual dysfunction. Women who reported that their spouse had sexual dysfunction were more likely to report sexual dysfunction themselves (Shokrollahi, Mirmohamadi, Mehrabi, & Babael, 1999).

Our clinic is the main destination for women with sexual complaints in Kermanshah and the neighboring provinces. As of June, 2011, we had seen 33,080 patients, of which 6,114 (18%) were women. Of the women, 1,264 (21%) had sexual complaints. Of the women with sexual problems, 50% (635) had hypoactive sexual desire disorder, 26% (324) had anorgasmia (this included 35 women with delayed orgasm), 12% (158) had vaginal dryness, 7% (86) had dyspareunia and 5% (61) had vaginismus. Related concerns that were sometimes mentioned during clinic visits included: doubts over whether to marry a particular person, concerns about sexual orientation, body image problems, hirsutism, and a history of masturbation. While women can come to the clinic on their own, they are more commonly accompanied by a relative (e.g., husband, sister, brother, or mother). We can and do perform physical examinations of women without a family member in attendance. However, to protect ourselves from the very remote possibility of legal problems, whenever possible we ask chaperones (accompanied relatives) to be present during examination of young women.

The reason that the incidence of sexual dysfunction may be higher in urban as compared to rural areas of Iran is that urban centers are increasingly influenced by Western values with a corresponding emphasis on female sexual pleasure. Urban women who are not experiencing sexual pleasure feel entitled to say something about it. Urban men believe it is important to sexually satisfy their wives. The opposite is true for more traditional husbands dwelling in rural areas such as Kermanshah. Female sexual pleasure is not a concern and women who are assertive about their sexual needs are perceived as amoral and demanding. Women's complaining about a lack of sexual pleasure is culturally unacceptable in traditional areas of Iran.

In the absence of dedicated female sexual dysfunction clinics and psychologically oriented sex therapists, treatment options for Iranian women complaining of sexual difficulties are limited to educational approaches or pharmacotherapy with antidepressants. Both of these approaches have minimal efficacy in treating the wide array of female sexual problems.

Conclusions

Based on our clinical experience, Iranian patients with sexual dysfunction suffer greatly and often needlessly. The systematic blocking of the free flow of scientific sexual information leaves many Iranians, especially those in rural areas, ignorant of basic facts about their bodies and about sexual functioning. Many of them injure themselves from lack of information, or suffer and do not come for treatment. At present, sexual medicine addresses the needs of men suffering from sexual dysfunction much more than women. There is a need for a greater variety of treatment options for women. Sex therapy, which would include both husband and wife, is not available in the traditional Iranian community. The continued trend towards the modernization of Iran could eliminate many barriers to information and treatment and could help to eradicate many of the present sexual difficulties of Iranians.

Notes

1. Reports from this clinic have been published elsewhere (Zargooshi 2000a, 2000b, 2000c, 2002a, 2000b, 2004, 2008, 2009a, 2009b).
2. There is an erroneous belief that Rhazes was an "Arab." Rhazes was born in Iran, lived and died there, and never had any affinity or affiliation to anything Arab. However, during the Arab occupation period, many scholars like Rhazes had no option but to write in Arabic (the enforced, obligatory language of government and science), which led to the false assumption that he was an Arab.
3. *Sigheh* are women who enter into a legal contract with a man for a temporary marriage, lasting for however long the two agree. This can be for an hour, a day, a month or many years. The terms of the contract stipulate what each party is to receive—usually sex for men and some goods, often food, for the woman. Although a man may have as many temporary wives as he can afford, a woman cannot enter into a temporary marriage with more than one man at a time. It is clear that for many sigheh, the temporary marriage is for survival.

4. A PubMed search from 1954 to 2008 yielded 19 relevant articles. Of these, 2 were single case reports, while 6 had sample sizes ranging from 35 to 200 cases. The rest were either reviews or the number of cases was not presented.
5. To date, no independent researcher has compared the original Pfizer-made Viagra with the cheaper Iranian or Indian-made Sildenafil. However, many of our patients had used Pfizer's Viagra as well, with no benefit.
6. To observe privacy and confidentiality, all names are pseudonyms.

References

American Psychiatric Association (2011). Early ejaculation. Retrieved from http://www.dsm5.org/ProposedRevision/Pages/proposedrevision.aspx?rid=174

Bakhtin, M. M., (1984). Rabelais and his world (H. Iswolsky, Trans.). Bloomington: Indiana University Press.

Ghadiri, M. K., & Gorji, A. (2004). Natural remedies for impotence in medieval Persia. *International Journal of Impotence Research, 16,* 80–83.

Goshtasebi, A., Vahdaninia, M., & Rahimi Foroshani, A. (2009). Prevalence and potential risk factors of female sexual difficulties: an urban Iranian population-based study. *Journal of Sexual Medicine, 6,* 2988–2996.

Jamejamonline (n.d.). http://www.jamejamonline.ir/newstext.aspx?newsnum=100935174761 (in Persian)

Jannini, E. A., & Lenzi, A. (2005). Ejaculatory disorders: Epidemiology and current approaches to definition, classification and subtyping. *World Journal of Urology, 23,* 68–75.

McMahon, C. G., Althof, S. E., Waldinger, M. D., Porst, H., Dean, J., Sharlip, I. D., ... Segraves, R. (2008). An evidence-based definition of lifelong premature ejaculation: Report of the International Society for Sexual Medicine (ISSM) ad hoc committee for the definition of premature ejaculation. *Journal of Sexual Medicine, 5,* 1590–1606.

Najafabady, M. T., Salmani, Z., & Abedi, P. (2011). Prevalence and related factors for anorgasmia among reproductive aged women in Hesarak, Iran. *Clinics (Sao Paulo), 66,* 83–86.

Patrick, D. L., Rowland, D., & Rothman, M. (2007). Interrelationships among measures of premature ejaculation. The central role of perceived control. *Journal of Sexual Medicine, 4,* 780–788.

Safarinejad, M. R. (2006). Female sexual dysfunction in a population-based study in Iran: prevalence and associated risk factors. *International Journal of Impotence Research, 18,* 382–395.

Shindel, A., Nelson, C., & Brandes, S. Urologist practice patterns in the management of premature ejaculation: A nationwide survey. *Journal of Sexual Medicine, 5,* 199–205.

Shokrollahi, P., Mirmohamadi, M., Mehrabi, F., & Babaei, Gh. (1999). Prevalence of women seeking services at family planning centres in Tehran. *Journal of Sex & Marital Therapy, 25* (3), 211–215.

Zargooshi J. (2000a). Penile fracture in Kermanshah, Iran: Report of 172 cases *Journal of Urology, 164*, 364–366.

Zargooshi J. (2000b). Unconsummated marriage: Clarification of aetiology, treatment with intracorporeal injection. *British Journal of Urology International, 86*, 75–79.

Zargooshi J. (2000c). Priapism as a complication of high dose testosterone therapy in a man with hypogonadism. *Journal of Urology 163*, 907.

Zargooshi J. (2002a). Characteristics of gonorrhoea in Kermanshah, Iran. *Sexually Transmitted Infections, 78*, 460–461.

Zargooshi J. (2002b). Penile fracture in Kermanshah, Iran: the long-term results of surgical treatment. *British Journal of Urology International, 89*, 890–894.

Zargooshi J. (2004). Trauma as the cause of Peyronie's disease: penile fracture as a model of trauma. *Journal of Urology, 172*, 186–188.

Zargooshi J. (2008). Male sexual dysfunction in unconsummated marriage: long-term outcome in 417 patients. *Journal of Sexual Medicine, 5*, 2895–2903.

Zargooshi J. (2009a). Premature ejaculation: bother and intravaginal ejaculatory latency time in Iran. *Journal of Sexual Medicine, 6*, 3478–3489.

Zargooshi, J. (2009b). Sexual function and tunica albuginea wound healing following penile fracture: An 18-year follow-up study of 352 patients from Kermanshah, Iran. *Journal of Sexual Medicine, 6*, 1141–1150.

Editors Introduction to Chapter 7
Korea

In this chapter, Youn focuses on the sexual issues facing the elderly population. By doing so he has highlighted many of the entrenched values that impede the progress of sex therapy in this country and also the cultural values that underlie sexual relationships. In Korea, it is considered socially unacceptable to talk about sex and the concept of sexual pleasure is an extremely gendered one. Elderly people in Korea grew up with the idea that sexual pleasure was a privilege of being male and that women were to sexually satisfy their husbands. Domestic violence is a problem worldwide, but in this chapter Youn links it to the refusal of wives to have sex with husbands that they may not even like. Fast forward a generation and you will understand the family dynamics that many young Koreans face. Sexual violence and sexual harassment also appear to be issues that one must be sensitive to in the experience of Korean women of any age. Korean men, like the gentleman Youn describes in his case, are ill-equipped for relationships with assertive women and seem especially unprepared for sexual equality and the likely expectation of future generations of Korean women for sexual pleasure.

Although the population of Korea is aging, it is unlikely that the older generation will seek the help of a sex therapist. But it is possible that the younger generation will do so. The advent of sexual medicine, the sexual content available over the Internet and through other media sources, alongside the improving status of women, will challenge existing cultural standards regarding sexuality and may make sex therapy and other psychologically based treatment approaches more accessible to Koreans.

7
CHALLENGES FACING SEX THERAPY IN KOREA

Gahyun Youn

Introduction

South Korean society has undergone rapid change over the past 50 years. Until the 1960s, Korea was one of the poorest countries in the world, but it has now joined the ranks of the developed nations (Kuk, 2008). South Korea now represents the 15th largest economy in the world (U.S. Department of State, 2007). While profound changes are evident in the country's economic growth, the same cannot be said for Korean social and cultural values, and only recently has there been any public discussion of sexual rights. However, the introduction of sexual medicine, the changing demographic of the Korean population, and greater economic prosperity are creating a climate ripe for change. Korea is currently undergoing a transformation from a traditional male-dominated society to a more "gender-equal" society. However, the transition is less than complete and it is still not easy to discuss sexual topics or practice sex therapy in Korea.

The 48 million plus people who make up the population of South Korea[1] are an ethnically and linguistically homogenous group, being comprised mainly of ethnic Koreans with a small Chinese minority (about 20,000). Roughly half of the Korean population actively practice some form of religion. The major religions include Christianity, Buddhism, Shamanism, Confucianism, and Chondogyo or Heavenly Way.[2] Christianity and Buddhism are the major religions practiced by 29.2% and 22.8% of the Korean population, respectively (U.S. Department of State, 2007). During the Chosun Dynasty (also known as the Joseon or Yi Dynasty, 1392–1910), Confucianism was adopted as the official religion of Korea and many government policies and institutions were based on this ideology. So although less than 1% of South Koreans now identify themselves as Confucianists, Korean society remains highly imbued with Confucian values and beliefs.

Confucianism stresses the importance of a harmonious relationship between yin and yang, the basic elements of nature. Yang is male, positive, constructive, active, and strong. Yin is the negative counterpart to yang and is destructive, passive, and weak. Confucianism has been used to justify discrimination against women and a patriarchal system of male dominance. However, a strong feminist movement has challenged the status quo and is moving Korea toward gender equity (Palley, 1990).

Sexuality in Korea

Sexual values and attitudes in Korea are also strongly affected by Confucianism. The union of yin and yang is synonymous with sexual intercourse. This union reflects and maintains the balance and order of nature and so preserves the health and integrity of the family and society. It is not, per se, an act of pleasure, nor is it seen as an expression of intimacy. In Korea, sexual intercourse is a physiological event, a sort of tension release for the male (Choi, Ryu, Rha, Lee, & Yi, 2004). Female pleasure is not part of the discourse. The belief that women's sexuality, the yin, is weak, leads to the expectation that women do not have independent sexual desires and that their sexuality is only a reaction to a man's desire. In general, Koreans still expect men to take responsibility for initiating and ending sexual activity. Women are expected to be sexually passive. In response to the question, "How do you resolve sexual urges?" over 61% of young working women responded that they did not have sexual urges (J. H. Kim et al., 1998). Many Korean men, especially those 40 years of age and older, follow the traditional gender roles and treat their female partner as an instrument of sexual pleasure with no thought or regard for her needs or desires.

Integrity of the family line is of great importance in Korea. In order to ensure that the lineage remains pure, high value is placed not only on female virginity but also on fidelity. However, there exists a double standard in Korea; negative attitudes regarding premarital and extramarital sex are more stringent for women than for men. Homosexuality is considered socially unacceptable and dysfunctional (Choi et al., 2004)

Family Planning

Family planning has been an important objective of the South Korean government since the 1960s. The success of these efforts is evident in the fact that the birth rate has decreased from 6 births per fertile woman in 1960 to 1.7 in 2002 (Choi et al., 2004). The changing status of women in Korea has also had an impact on fertility. Women marry later now: In 1985 the average age for women at first marriage was 24.1 years, which rose to 28.1 years in 2007. The increased participation of women in the labor force and in higher education in Korea has also affected fertility. Less than a third of all women were enrolled in university in 1990, but by 2008, the rate of female enrollment in higher education had reached 83.8%. More women of childbearing age are working. In 1990 slightly more than 42% of women aged 25 to 29 years worked outside the home, whereas in 2007 68% were employed (Lee, 2009).

The low birth rate combined with high life expectancy has resulted in an aging population. In fact, aging adults comprise the fastest growing segment of the Korean population. It is estimated that almost 20% of all individuals residing in Korea will be 65 or older by the year 2025 (Korean National Statistical Office, 2007). Currently the Korean government is reversing its earlier policies and advocating policies designed to encourage fertility. These include tax incentives, family leave, and affordable childcare (S. Lee, 2009).

Sex Education

During the Chosun dynasty, sex education was limited to information regarding pregnancy. Newlyweds received advice as to the best times, positions, and practices for producing descendants of the highest quality. Brides were often given calendars with information about fertile times. The sex education that is now taught in schools is woefully inadequate. Sex education is hindered by the Confucian belief that ignorance of sex is a virtue. In school, girls are taught primarily about menstruation, pregnancy, and virginity. Boys are taught about sexually transmitted infections (Choi et al., 2004). Discussions of sexual topics are taboo. However, with easy access to the Internet, a large percentage of adolescent males (37.1%) now report that their main source of sexual knowledge is pornography and other adult materials (S. W. Kim, Shin, Song, & Park, 1996; Song & Kang, 2006).

Sexual Harassment and Violence

An unfortunate consequence of Internet availability has been the increase in online sexual harassment. The Ministry of Information and Communication sponsored a Report Center for Cyber Sexual Violence in 2000. They found that 58.9% of adolescents experienced some form of harassment, either in text transmissions, pornographic pictures, or movies being sent to them, or private videos being made public and broadcast over the Internet (as cited in Choi et al., 2004). Female high school students are subject to physical forms of sexual harassment as well. In one study over 45% of female students reported having been subjected to unwanted sexual touching on the breasts, hips, and genital areas by male classmates (S. W. Kim, Lee, Park, Kim, & Song, 1997).

While only a small percentage of female high school students (7.5%) acknowledged having had coital experience, over half of them reported that they were either verbally or emotionally coerced (38.7%) or physically assaulted (11.9%; S. W. Kim et al., 1997). While many assaults go unreported, it is clear that the incidence of sexual violence against women is rising in South Korea. In 2003, 10,365 reports of rape were made to the Prosecutor's office, over 3,000 more than were reported 10 years earlier (D. K. Lee, 2006). According to a recent government sponsored commercial, there were 1,081 reports of child sexual abuse made in 2007 (http://thegrandnarrative.com/2009/05/07/quick-statistics-on-child-sexual-abuse-in-korea/). Rape myths are still highly endorsed by Korean men. Byun, Won, and Chun, (2000, as cited by Choi et al., 2004) found that a majority of men agreed with the following statements: "Rape occurs because of men's uncontrollable sexual urge" (69.0%), "A sexy female's looks provoke rape" (93.9%), "The best prevention is women's caution" (66.2%), and "Rape cannot occur if women persistently refuse" (52.6%).

Sexual Dysfunction and Sex Therapy

There is a paucity of data regarding the incidence of sexual dysfunction in the Korean population. In a study of sexual behavior and problems in Koreans aged 40 to 80 years, over a third of the Korean men reported early ejaculation and erectile dysfunction (Moreira, Kim, Glasser, & Gingell, 2006). This is higher than the incidence of male sexual dysfunction reported in other Asian countries. The authors of the study speculated that the high percentage of male sexual dysfunction in Korea is due to the age, level of physical inactivity, smoking, and incidence of prostate disease in Korean men. In the same study, lack of sexual pleasure was reported by 37% of Korean women, and inability to reach orgasm was reported by 31%. Only 2% of Koreans experiencing sexual problems had consulted a medical doctor. Lack of awareness of treatment options, affordability, and a belief that the problem is not serious were reasons given for not seeking treatment.

There are several other studies on the incidence of erectile dysfunction in Korean men, placing the percentage of men suffering from ED between 32.2% (Cho et al., 2003) and 39.4% (Chew, Earle, Stuckey, Jamrozik, & Keough, 2000). Two Internet surveys estimated the incidence of premature ejaculation between 18.3% (Son et al., 2010) and 27.5% (H. J. Park et al., 2010). The sexual problems of Korean women are not much studied or understood. While the incidence of vaginismus is unknown, there has been one report of biofeedback combined with cognitive behavioral therapy being used to successfully treat 12 Korean women suffering from vaginismus (Seo, Choe, Lee, & Kim, 2005).

Despite the obvious need there are few trained sex therapists practicing in Korea. The Korean Association for Sexology has called for a system for licensing and credentialing sex therapists,[3] but it could be years before such a system can be established. To date there are only two established sex therapy clinics in South Korea: one at Yonsei Medical Center (established in 1986) and the second, the Seoul-Cornell Clinic for Human Sexuality, which opened in 1995.

In its first year of operation, the Yonsei sex therapy clinic saw 231 patients, the vast majority of whom were male (75.8%). The most common presenting complaints were erectile dysfunction (40.1%), premature ejaculation (20.3%), and inhibited female orgasm (10.6%). Less than 20% of the patients were seen in conjoint sex therapy, and when the presenting complaint was male sexual dysfunction, the percentage of couples in sex therapy fell to only 11.5%. These numbers are significantly lower than the number of couples opting for conjoint sex therapy in Western countries (Yoo et al., 1990). Ten years later, over 2,000 patients were seen at the same sex therapy clinic in an 18-month period. At that time the most common presenting complaint was erectile dysfunction and the most common treatment was medical intervention (64.7% of patients), with a 21.5% rate of successful penetration being reported at the end of treatment (Choi, 1998).

Public acceptance of sex therapy lags behind sexual medicine in Korea. In the past, Korean men depended on Chinese herbal products to enhance their stamina and sexual performance (Youn, 2001).[4] Nowadays, Korean men take Viagra which, along with intracavernosal injections and penile prosthetic implants, has been available in South Korea since 1999 and is available to any man over the age of 21 who has medical certification that he is free of cardiovascular disease. The monthly allotment of Viagra is eight tablets.

Many research articles report on medical treatments for erectile or ejaculatory problems (Kam & Lee, 2009; Kim & Moon, 2008), but very few focus on sexual psychotherapy. Men attempt to seek some medical assistance when they have sexual dysfunctions, whereas women typically do not consult anyone to resolve sexual satisfaction issues such as low sexual desire. Women who adhere to traditional Korean values consider any effort toward gaining sexual satisfaction as socially undesirable or inappropriate, even if their sexual problems are medical in nature. As a result, when Korean women reveal their sexual dissatisfaction, they mostly complain from the perspective of marital or relationship problems (e.g., marital conflicts related to the adulterous activities of their husbands; Youn, 2009). Women wishing to get help as a result of sexual violence or sexual infidelity sometimes access government-supported telephone help services which have been available since the early 1990s. In contrast, few women of any age visit counselors or therapists when they have sexual concerns. Similarly, the published literature contains only a few reports regarding the incidence and treatment of sexual problems related to gynecological disorders (Youn & Lee, 2001). Simply put, the level of gender equality in Korea falls far short of the standard in terms of promoting sexual rights.

Korean women are becoming more vocal about their dissatisfaction with their relationships and these issues may require marital and relationship therapy for resolution. The use of couple therapy with Korean couples, such as the Johnson et al. (2005) emotionally focused couple therapy (EFT), has been evaluated (S. Park & Lee, 2008). In this study it was found that relationship problems often caused or exacerbated sexual unhappiness. Among the many relationship problems or complaints that wives expressed, two issues were prominent: the husband had limited time for the family and there was one-sided decision-making by the husband. As a result of marital unhappiness, the wife typically then rejected her husband's sexual advances, and he responded to her sexual refusal with despair. Both husbands and wives who joined the EFT program showed a decrease in relationship dissatisfaction in general, but not in sexual dissatisfaction. Although couples who embarked on EFT after the husband's infidelity experienced less conflict in terms of emotional communication, the same observation may not be true for sexual satisfaction (S. Park & Lee, 2008). It seems as though once the issue of sexual refusal is resolved, the quality of the sexual relationship is still not a relevant topic for many Korean couples, nor is the quality of the sexual relationship adequately addressed by marital therapy alone.

Sexual Problems among Older Koreans

Many of the issues that Koreans face regarding sexuality are exacerbated in older Koreans. Korean women commonly marry men who are about 3 years older than they are; they also live longer than men do by almost 7 years (Korean National Statistical Office, 2008; Youn, 2004). As a result, older women spend their later years without a partner for an average of 10 years. Following Confucian tradition, a Korean woman should be devoted to one man in her lifetime, even if she loses her husband at a very young age. Thus, most widows do not remarry, irrespective of their age. In contrast, most widowers do remarry, particularly younger widowers. Elderly widows may become misandrists instead of finding new male partners. Some women have claimed that widowhood enabled them live in comfort because they no longer had to deal with troublesome husbands (Youn, 2004). In the past, widows would remain single because of sociocultural restrictions; however, many of today's widows choose to stay single because they disdain male partners (K. Lee & Youn, 2006). Korean culture, which values men over women likely contributes to the disdain women feel for their husbands and leads to their decision not to remarry.

More than half of middle-aged Koreans belong to the generation that had marriages that were arranged and mediated by matchmakers (Chung, 2008; Youn, 2009). For them, the motive of marriage was to establish a strong commitment between two families, and not to pursue love, intimacy, or passion. Korean couples who have marital problems typically do not divorce even when their relationships become sour. In the past, there were few opportunities for divorce. Interestingly, the divorce rate in Korea has increased rapidly since the late 1980s, and although it has somewhat decreased in recent years, the rate for older couples continues to rise. The number of cases wherein older husbands initiate divorce has increased from 245 in 1997 to 1,427 cases in 2007, while those initiated by wives have increased from 869 in 1997 to 3,622 cases in 2007 (Korean National Statistical Office, 2008). In Korea, people refer to divorce among older couples as "twilight divorce."[4] Most frequently, the decisive elements of divorce are related to cumulative relationship problems, the major igniters of which are infidelity and lack of an amicable resolution after infidelity (Youn, 2001). The rising rate of divorce predicts an increasing number of single men and women.

To date, relatively little attention has been focused on sexual problems and the concerns of this age group. Cultural attitudes that value reproduction and youthful good looks may contribute to the expectation that older people are, or should be, asexual (Deacon, Minichiello, & Plummer, 1995). With sex roles changing in recent years, as evidenced by increasing freedom of sexual expression since the late 1990s, the stereotypes or myths that older people are physically unattractive, uninterested in sex, and incapable of achieving sexual arousal have slowly disappeared (Youn, 2004). However, in this context, the elderly persons who actively seek their sexual rights are mostly men rather than women (K. Lee & Youn, 2006; Youn, 2004). Youn (2009) investigated the sexual interactions of older married couples. Since lack of privacy may be a problem when an older couple lives with their children, only elderly couples living independently were interviewed for this study. Even though very few of the older couples were sexually active, most participants regarded sex as an important part of their lives. However, their sexual interactions had not been harmonious, and thus their gender differences were pronounced (Youn, 2009). Most of the elderly women were sexually inactive and disinterested, which seemed directly related to unresolved marital conflicts, particularly male infidelity. The elderly men tended to think that they could have sex regardless of their partners' mood or state of health. Under these circumstances, many of the female respondents in this study envied single ladies who had lost or divorced their husbands, while the men were either despairing, angry, or sometimes violent (Youn, 2009).

According to traditional Korean culture, the role of women is to have sex when their husbands seek it. Until the late 1980s, women regarded complying with their husbands' requests for sex as a duty and would seldom refuse sex. However, present-day women are very different. As a result, men who are sexually frustrated by the refusal of their spouses may resort to violence (Youn, 2001, 2009). The use of physical violence by husbands frequently accompanies forceful sex, because men continue to attempt to have intercourse by whatever means are available (Youn, 2009). According to data issued by the National Police Agency of Korea, the number of male perpetrators of sexual violence aged 60 years and above has increased from 91 in 1996 to 598 in 2006 (Health Today, n.d.).

There are now corrective treatment programs for perpetrators of family violence in Korea (K. Kim & Kim, 2002). Although the perpetrators admit to using violence, they seem uninterested in ameliorating these acts, and instead complain about the refusal of their wives to accept their sexual advances. Perpetrators even appealed for support to legalize prostitution and advocated for public brothels (Youn, 2001). Some men view conjugal relations as a relation between master and servant from which emanates a communication style that is not based on mutual understanding, but on traditional sex roles. Thus, they regard wives following the orders of their husbands as a desirable form of communication.

There is a popular saying that frequent sex is injurious to one's health, but the adage "elderly men who do not have regular sex get old much quicker and die earlier" seems to be more popular (Youn, 2009). Men without the means to support a family and a girlfriend view prostitution as an option. In a recent study 10.6% of Korean men over the age of 60 acknowledged having sex with a prostitute in the previous year (Choe, Lee, Kin, & Cho, 2011). For elderly men, a new and affordable style of prostitution has recently emerged: Bacchus ladies. The *Bacchus lady* is a slang term for a woman who sells soft drinks, including "Bacchus," a popular brand of energy drink, and at the same time makes sexual overtures to elderly men idling in a public park. Most of the ladies are poor widows or divorcees in their early- or mid-50s. The phenomenon of the Bacchus ladies appeared around the early 1990s with the increase in the divorce rate, leaving many more women unable to support themselves financially. Prostitution is illegal, according to a special law that took effect in September 2004 (S. Kim, Kim, Youn, & Chae, 2008). However, sexual negotiations between elderly men and the Bacchus ladies take place in private and are rarely prosecuted.

A growing number of elderly patients are visiting public health centers to get treatment for sexually transmitted infections (STIs). The number of elderly men with STIs has increased from 6,557 in 2002 to 12,509 in 2006 (Health Today, 2009). Over half of sexually active elderly Koreans occasionally or never use condoms (Choe et al., 2011). Many of them did not have their STIs treated because either they had no money for a clinic visit or they wanted to avoid the prying eyes of other people (Ha et al., 2008).

Two Case Reports of Elderly Koreans Seeking Sexual Counseling

Sex therapy is still not widely accepted in Korea. It is not considered appropriate for women to complain about a lack of sexual desire or sexual problems. This is especially true for older widows. The following case illustrates the isolation and emotional confusion that older women with sexual problems may experience in Korea.

Mrs. P was a 67-year-old woman who had been widowed 28 years earlier at the age of 39. She had raised her two daughters on her own and did not date or associate with any men. When her daughters married and began their own families, Mrs. P was isolated and felt lonely. Her daughters and her in-laws expected her to stay single, as did Mrs. P herself. However, in a continuing education program for senior citizens, Mrs. P became friendly with a 73-year-old widower, Mr. S. She felt flattered by his attentions, but since she had had no dating experience she did not know how to interpret his sexual interest in her, nor did she know how to respond to his persistent sexual advances. Mrs. P was unaware of her own sexual feelings but she came to want a relationship and hoped perhaps for a marriage with Mr. S. After a month of secretly dating, Mrs. P had sex with Mr. S. The quality or quantity of sex was not an issue for Mrs. P. She wanted to have an emotionally fulfilling relationship with Mr. S so that she would not be alone for the rest of her life. However, after several months, it seemed to Mrs. P that her lover was less caring, less attentive, and less available to her. Finally, she learned that he was dating another widow from the same continuing education program. Mrs. P was devastated and this precipitated her consultation with me.

It is a sad commentary that Mrs. P felt such shame regarding her sexual relationship with Mr. S that she could not talk to her friends or family about it. Her consultation illustrates the isolation of many older Koreans. There is no one with whom they can comfortably discuss sexuality. If they are in a relationship, the assumption is that they will have sex according to the needs and desires of their male partner. If they are widowed or single, the assumption is that they are not sexual at all. Female sexuality is poorly understood and undervalued. As a result of these assumptions and the secrecy surrounding sexuality, women's emotional and psychological well-being may suffer as Mrs. P's did. Mrs. P's naiveté regarding the motivations and interests of her gentleman friend mimics that often seen in teenagers. The lack of sex education in Korea extends beyond a deficit in knowledge regarding anatomy, physiology, and function, to the emotional realm, leaving women like Mrs. P emotionally ill-equipped to negotiate relationships.

The single session that Mrs. P spent with me was very helpful to her. She was able to talk to someone about her feelings of hurt, sadness, and betrayal without feeling judged. Mrs. P felt a great deal of guilt for having sex with Mr. S because it violated traditional Korean values and the expectations of her family. She left the session with a better understanding of her own interest in having an intimate and sexual relationship with someone, although whether she will venture to do so again is questionable. Nevertheless, her guilt and sadness were lessened.

The second case is that of an older Korean man. This case illustrates the pressure that many older Korean men feel as a result of misunderstanding traditional sexual values. While it is clear that many Korean women have had sex that they did not want (but felt they had to have because of their husband's desire), the case of Mr. C. illustrates that cultural pressures also impact men's sexuality. Although Mr. C misinterprets Taoist doctrines regarding sex, his case is applicable to the many Korean men who misinterpret Confucian values to mean that they should have frequent sex with many women.

Mr. C's presenting complaint was related to his distress regarding the jealousy of his girlfriend and he wanted to be able to better deal with his relationship. Mr. C, a married man in his early 60s, had not had sex with his wife for over 10 years after she underwent brain surgery. Subsequent to her diagnosis and surgery for removal of a meningioma, Mrs. C consistently refused her husband's sexual overtures. After repressing his libido for several years, Mr. C began a secret sexual relationship with a younger woman (44 years of age). Mr. C reported that he had had sex with his girlfriend almost twice a week for the past 18 months. Shortly after their relationship began, Mr. C experienced difficulty maintaining his erection and so became an avid user of vardenafil (Levitra). His girlfriend did not know about this. Mr. C wanted to consult with me as a sexuality specialist, because of his trouble reading his girlfriend's jealous responses, which had begun several weeks ago. Although Mr. C mentioned talking highly of a good-looking woman, a friend of his girlfriend, and paying her a lot of attention, he did not see the connection between the two events. He sought help from me to advise him on the proper strategies to relate to his girlfriend, as he was fearful of losing her as a readily available sexual partner.

Mr. C and his girlfriend were heavy drinkers, and drinking was frequently part of their sexual routine. Mr. C boasted about his ability to engage in sex longer than 2 hours without having to ejaculate, although he needed the combination of alcohol and Levitra to accomplish this. Mr. C reported that he tried to remain at the plateau phase of intercourse for as long as possible to avoid orgasm and seminal emission. He described a lack of pleasure, and experienced only a sense of accomplishment for having a long lasting erection. While Mr. C had typically ejaculated once or twice during 10 occasions of intercourse, he now reported that he rarely ejaculated and never ejaculated intravaginally. When confronted with the possibility that he had a sexual dysfunction called delayed ejaculation, Mr. C instead insisted that he was a great man. He boasted that he practiced sex according to Taoist principles. Although Taoism as a religion was officially abolished in Korea during the Japanese invasion of 1592, Taoist literature continued to thrive. Taoists writings encourage Koreans to strive for immortality or rejuvenation. Most doctrines of Taoist sexual techniques are male-oriented, referring only to "gathering woman's yin to nourish man's yang." According to these doctrines, the yang essence (i.e., sexual vitality) of men is portrayed as limited; thus, men are encouraged to control ejaculation to preserve the yang essence. Taoists believe that a man may increase and nourish his own essence by bringing a woman to orgasm during intercourse and at the same time preventing his own ejaculation (Ruan, 1991). Regrettably, many Korean men, including Mr C, misinterpret the doctrines. Thus, they neglect the concept that sex should be pleasurable and focus instead only on the goal of achieving longevity (Ruan, 1991; Youn, 2008).

Mr C did not continue in therapy. He did not want to address his inappropriate behavior with regard to his girlfriend's jealousy, nor did he want to remedy his delayed ejaculation, but rather he wanted to be able to manipulate his girlfriend into staying in the sexual relationship with him. When he realized that sex therapy was not going to help him ensure access to a reliable sexual partner, he did not see any need for continuing therapy.

These two cases illustrate the difficulties of doing sex therapy in Korea. There is shame and secrecy surrounding discussions of sexual topics. Sexual pleasure for women is not part of the current discourse in Korea and many myths and misinterpretations exist regarding what is sexually healthy behavior for men.

Conclusion

Although there is a need for sex therapy in Korea, there are several challenges before it can be widely accepted by the general public. Korean people do not consider it appropriate to discuss sexual problems with anyone, let alone a stranger. Women do not have equal sexual rights and the right to sexual pleasure for women is still unrecognized in Korean culture. Sexual medicine is at present geared primarily toward the resolution of male sexual dysfunction. It is possible that as sexual medicine gains in popularity the need for sex therapy will be recognized. However, sex therapy will only be accepted when the gender imbalance in Korean culture has lessened.

Notes

1. Estimated at 48,754,657 as of July 2011 according to the U.S. Department of State website. Retrieved from www.state.gov/r/pa/ei/bgn/2800.htm#people)
2. An indigenous Korean religion that combines elements of Confucianism, Buddhism, Taoism, Shamanism, and Roman Catholicism.
3. The current author, as Vice-President of the Korean Association for Sexology, is still currently involved in initiating the system.
4. The products were made and sold by a Chinese or other Asian medical doctor, or a Korean herbal pharmacist who was running an Asian pharmacy that sells non-mainstream remedies.
5. The term *twilight divorce* began to gain acceptance in the press in the early 1990s. The term *jukunen rikon* in Japan is synonymous with twilight divorce in Korea.

References

Byun, W., Won, Y., & Chung, S. (2000). Study of sexual consciousness and violence against women [abstract in English]. Seoul, South Korea: Korean Women's Development Institute.

Chew, K. K., Earle, C. M., Stuckey, B. G. A., Jamrozik, K., & Keough, E. J. (2000). Erectile dysfunction in general medicine practice: Prevalence and clinical correlates. *International Journal of Impotence Research, 12,* 41–45.

Cho, B. L., Kim, Y. S., Choi, Y. S., Hong, M. H., Seo, H. G., Lee. S. Y., ... Kim, B. S. (2003). Prevalence and risk factors for erectile dysfunction in primary care: Results of a Korean study. *International Journal of Impotence Research, 15,* 323–328.

Choe, H. S., Lee, S. J., Kim, C. S., & Cho, Y. H. (2011). Prevalence of sexually transmitted infections and the sexual behavior of elderly people presenting to health examination centers in Korea. *Journal of Infections and Chemotherapy, 17,* 456–461.

Choi, H. K., Ryu, J. K., Rha, K. H., Lee, W. H., & Yi, H. (2004). South Korea. In R. T. Francoeur & R. J. Noonan (Eds.), *The continuum complete international encyclopedia of sexuality* (pp. 213–234). New York: Continuum.

Chung, O. (2008). *Psychology of adult years and aging.* Seoul, South Korea: Hakjisa.

Deacon, S., Minichiello, V., & Plummer, D. (1995). Sexuality and older people: Revisiting the assumptions. *Educational Gerontology, 21,* 497–513.

Ha, W., Sung, N., Kim, K., Lee, G., Park, J., Bae, J., & Nah, D. (2008). The ECG findings of patients aged 65 years and older performed by an outpatient department in hospital. *The DongGuk Journal of Medicine, 15,* 37–44.

Health Today. (n.d.). *Elderly sexuality*. Retrieved from http:// health.mdtoday.co.kr/life/index.html?gn=6&no=312

Johnson, S., Bradley, B., Furrow, J., Lee, A., Palmer, G., Tiley, D., & Wooley, S. (2005). *Becoming an emotionally focused couple therapist: The workbook*. New York: Routledge.

Kam, S., & Lee, S. (2009). New approach and treatment of premature ejaculation. *The Korean Journal of Andrology, 27*(3), 153–169.

Kim, J., & Moon, D. (2008). Past, present and future of PDE5 inhibitors. *The Korean Journal of Andrology, 26*(2), 49–60.

Kim, J. H., Lee, Y. J., Park, S. J., Song, E.I., Suh, J. A., & Oh, Y. J. (1998). A study of unmarried working adults' sexuality consciousness and sexual behaviors. Korea Research Institute for Culture and Sexuality Report [Seoul; abstract in English], 98–104.

Kim, K., & Kim, J. (2002). Analysis on the effectiveness of domestic violence offenders' intervention program: Focusing on wife abuse. *Journal of Family Relations, 7*, 137–158.

Kim, S., Kim, W., Youn, G., & Chae, K. (2008). *Human sexuality*. Seoul, South Korea: Koonja.

Kim, S. W., Lee, Y. J., Park, S. J., Kim, S. R., & Song, E. I. (1997). A study of high school girls' sexuality consciousness: Their sexual behaviors and problems of sexuality (Vol. 97, no. 102) [abstract in English]. Seoul, South Korea: The Korea Research Institute for Culture and Sexuality.

Kim, S. W., Shin, D. J., Song, I. S., & Park, S. J. (1996). A study of high school boys' sexuality consciousness. Seoul, South Korea: Korea Research Institute for Culture and Sexuality.

Korean National Statistical Office. (2007). *Population and its growth rate projected*. Seoul, South Korea: Author.

Korean National Statistical Office. (2008). *Dynamic statistics of population*. Seoul, South Korea: Author.

Kuk, M. (2008). Korean economic crisis and developmental state model. *Society and Theory, 13*(2), 213–249.

Lee, D. K. (2006). *Country report—Korea*. Paper presented at the 133rd International Training Course of the United Nations Asia and Far East Institute for the Prevention of Crime and Treatment of Offenders. Tokyo. Retrieved from www.unafei.or.jp/english/pdf/RS_No72/No72_15PA_Lee.pdf

Lee, K., & Youn, G. (2006). Sexuality for the elderly women who have been single. *Korean Journal of Research in Gerontology, 15*, 105–131.

Lee, S. (2009). Low fertility and policy responses in Korea. *The Japanese Journal of Population, 7*, 57–70.

Moreira, E. D., Kim, S.-C., Glasser, D., & Gingell, C. (2006). Sexual activity, prevalence of sexual problems, and associated help-seeking patterns in men and women aged 40–80 years in Korea: Data from the Global Study of Sexual Attitudes and Behaviors (GSSAB). *The Journal of Sexual Medicine, 3*, 201–211.

Palley, M. L. (1990). Women's status in South Korea: Tradition and change. *Asian Survey, 30*, 1136–1153. Retrieved from http://www.jstor.org/stable/2644990

Park, H. J., Park, J. K., Park, K., Lee, S. W., Kim, S. W., Yang, D. Y., ... Park, N. C. (2010). Prevalence of premature ejaculation in young and middle-aged men in Korea: A multicenter Internet-based survey from the Korean Andrological Society. *Asian Journal of Andrology, 12*(6), 880–889.

Park, S., & Lee, W. (2008). *The theory and practice of emotionally focused couple therapy.* Seoul, South Korea: Hakjisa.

Ruan, F. (1991). *Sex in China: Studies in sexology in Chinese culture.* New York: Plenum Press.

Seo, J. T., Choe, J. H., Less, W. S., & Kim, K. H. (2005). Efficacy of functional electrical stimulation-biofeedback with sexual cognitive-behavioral therapy as a treatment of vaginismus. *Urology, 66,* 77–81.

Son, H., Song, S. H., Kim, S. W., & Paick, J. S. (2010). Self-reported premature ejaculation prevalence and characteristics in Korean young males: Community based data from an internet survey. *Journal of Andrology, 6,* 540–546.

Song, Y. & Kang, N. M. (2006). Evaluation of sexuality information for Korean adolescents. *Studies in Health Technology and Informatics, 122,* 884.

U.S. Department of State, Bureau of East Asian and Pacific Affairs. (2007). Background note: South Korea. In *Diplomacy in action.* Retrieved from www.state.gov/r/pa/ei/bgn/2800.htm.

Yoo, K. J., Namkoong, K., Lee, H. Y., Lee, H. S., Oh, B. H., & Lee, B. Y. (1990). Clinical study of patients who visited a sex clinic. *Journal of Korean Society for Human Sexuality* [abstract in English], 2(1),77–91 .

Youn, G. (2001). *Sex and culture.* Seoul, South Korea: Hakminsa.

Youn, G. (2004). Elderly people and sexuality: Marriage and singlehood. *Korean Journal of Social Issues, 5,* 113–130.

Youn, G. (2008). A cultural perspective of erectile capacity and ejaculation. *Korean Journal of Andrology, 26*(4), 178–186.

Youn, G. (2009). Marital and sexual conflicts in elderly Korean people. *Journal of Sex and Marital Therapy, 35,* 230–238.

Youn, G., & Lee, E. (2001). Psychosexual adjustment in women with hysterectomy. *Korean Journal of Health Psychology, 6,* 107–125.

Section III

THE EMERGING PRACTICE OF PSYCHOTHERAPY FOR SEXUAL PROBLEMS

Editors Introduction to Chapter 8
India

The contradiction that is India is well illustrated in this chapter. Ramanathan and Weerakon note that although India is in various ways a modern society, it is also a sexually conservative society which values sexual purity over the erotic. While the Internet makes sexual content easy to access for young Indian men and women, this content is often at odds with the values and practices espoused by religious leaders, parents, and the larger community.

The effect of these contradictory and competing messages about sexuality is often confusion and anxiety. Ramanathan and Weerakoon observe that Western style sex therapy has not worked well on the Indian subcontinent, as demonstrated by the high dropout rate from treatment and the lack of significant treatment success. They attribute this failure to the Western emphasis on sexual pleasure inherent in therapy rather than on procreation, which is the primary concern of Indian couples. They also note that Asians do not commonly seek help for sexual disorders because they attribute the cause to their own "bad" behavior (often masturbation). Finally, the authors observe that challenging "irrational" beliefs, a mainstay of many psychotherapeutic approaches, is ineffective when the beliefs being challenged are culturally entrenched and currently reinforced by religion, family, and peers. Ramanathan and Weerakoon instead suggest a culturally sensitive approach to the treatment of male sexual dysfunction, which involves a psychological and medical collaboration. This approach is well illustrated in the detailed case presentation of the treatment of a young man with masturbatory guilt and sexual anxiety.

Sadly, the wealth of information contained in this chapter will not be as helpful in addressing the sexual concerns of Indian women. This does not reflect a bias on the authors' part, but rather the traditional culture of India. The authors remark that women in India have little control over their sexuality and over life decisions that impact it; they note, for example, that many Indian women have little or no choice in whom they marry or when, nor do they have a say in the timing or number of their children. Sexual "purity" or virginity is of the utmost importance for women prior to marriage, while after marriage the ability to give birth to a male child is paramount. While some women in India have achieved professional status and perhaps even financial independence, this autonomy often does not extend to sexuality. Indeed, as discussed in the chapter, sexual and domestic violence and sex trafficking are real problems facing many Indian girls and women. It appears that sexual pleasure for women in India will not be a priority until women in India are accorded equal status with men and have control over their lives and their sexuality.

After reading this chapter, it is not hard to see that there is an important role for a culturally sensitive approach to sex therapy in India. The blending of medical and psychological treatment the authors illustrated in their case presentation provides a workable model for how to successfully engage Indian men and treat their sexual dysfunctions and anxieties.

8

SEXUALITY IN INDIA

Ancient Beliefs, Present Day Problems, and Future Approaches to Management

V. Ramanathan and P. Weerakoon

Introduction

On the topic of sexuality, India is known to the Western world as the land of Kama Sutra and tantric sex. Popular texts like the Kama Sutra and the famous sculptures of Kajuraho[1] extol sexual pleasure and portray the liberal sexual attitudes of ancient India. But, it is debatable whether these laissez-faire attitudes were applicable to all social classes or only to the royal and wealthy classes. The beliefs, values, and practices that govern day-to-day life of many present day Indians, including sexuality, can be traced back to one of the four Vedas,[2] sacred works that are still considered to be a revelation from all-mighty God. According to Hinduism, which is the predominant religion of India, a prescribed rule (*smritis*) exists for all human behaviors from birth to death (Gupta, 1994). In this doctrine, sexual matters are not to be legislated but rather are left to the judgment of those involved, subject to community laws and customs (Cornog, 2003). Therefore, the sexual behaviors of Hindus are generally governed by the prescribed practices of the society.

Today, mainstream Indian society holds a conservative view toward sexuality, places high value on sexual purity, and disapproves of the erotic aspects of sexual life even within marriage. Influences that have lingered from the long years of British settlements in India (1612–1947) may provide a possible explanation for the shift to conservative sexual values from the earlier laissez-faire approach. The book *Empire and Sexuality* (Hyam, 1990) comprehensively discussed the shifts in values and attitudes among the British and its impact on India. The two significant events within the time period of British India were the launch of an antimasturbation campaign (1707–1717) and later the Purity campaign (1880; Hyam, 1990). Also of note is the fact that the native and holistic medical practice of Ayurveda[3] was slowly replaced by the Unani[4] brought in by the Mughals (1526–1858, during the period when Indo-Persian culture was established) and Western medicine brought in by the Europeans. These and other changes in what is considered healthy and normal have impacted Indians' sexual values and practices.

India is made up of multiethnic societies with numerous cultural identities, multiple classes, a complex caste system, varied religious practices, and diverse social customs. For this reason, it is difficult to generalize the beliefs, values, and attitudes toward sexuality to the whole of India. With this caveat in mind, this chapter will explore some of the basic tenets of Indian culture that influence sexual attitudes, values, and behavior. We will discuss different sexuality-related topics in the context of changing patterns and social norms due to rapid economic growth and modernization. An overview of commonly reported male sexual problems, sexual health services, and help-seeking behavior will be presented. A shorter section on female sexuality and sexual problems in the Indian context is provided. Various approaches to management of sexual problems in the Indian setting, the evidence behind such approaches, and gaps in research are also discussed. The sociocultural aspects of sexual problems and the cultural ambiguities are highlighted, using a detailed case study presentation of a young man experiencing some commonly reported, yet complex and challenging issues, including masturbatory guilt. The chapter concludes with a discussion on the management of the case, which places it in a rich cultural context.

Sexuality in Modern Day India

Attitudes toward sexuality have been changing rapidly in India over the past two decades along with economic liberalization and modernization. This is evident from various anecdotal observations, such as increased explicit eroticism in the mass media (Rao, 2007), and from social research involving young college students (Sachdev, 1998). The underlying conservative sexual attitudes coupled with diverse and conflicting influences of modern day India seems to create a certain cultural ambiguity regarding sexuality for the general public and especially for young adults and adolescents. Also, the youth of India are inundated with new ideas and knowledge regarding sexuality from the mass media and have better access to information through the Internet, all of which sources of knowledge compete with views passed on to them by their elders.

Marriage and Procreation

Marriage is still considered a sociocultural norm and is celebrated as an event to demonstrate the prestige and social status of the bride's and bridegroom's families. Procreation is perceived as a duty of every married couple and is regarded as a sacred part of life and celebrated by various ceremonies, mainly for women, from menarche, marriage, and through to childbirth. Marriage and procreation are rites of passage to the most important and wholesome stage of life, one by which the married couple can give birth to a son who will eventually release them from reincarnation. This strong belief about having a son underlies two major issues of public health concern: multiple pregnancies and female infanticides. The majority of marriages are still arranged by parents and significant family members.

Arranged Marriage

The positive aspect of arranged marriages is the support for the young married couple by the extended family. This of course works well when the couple has consented willingly to the union. On the other hand, the arranged marriage is likely to fail when the couple is forced into a union, bringing serious consequences to them and to their families' status. A study of marriages in India (Sandhya, 2009) highlighted that the early years of marriage were considered as the worst years by Indian couples, whereas couples from other parts of the world often call these the "honeymoon years."

Premarital Sex

In India, premarital sexual relationships are considered immoral and condemned by all religions, especially Hinduism and Islam, the two major religions in India. In *Atharvaveda* (chapter 14, hymn 1, verse 19), at her wedding the father gives permission to his daughter (to have sex):

> O bride, I free you from all the restrictions of the law and the life of celibacy with which you were bound. (Gupta, 1994)

Some of these traditional Indian norms and values around premarital and nonprocreative sex are being challenged and even rejected by both male and female youth of modern day urban India (Sachdev, 1998).

Sexual Pleasure and Its Expression

Ancient Indian texts like Kama Sutra highlighted the importance of sexual intimacy and pleasure within the context of marriage (Gupta, 1994). But in Indian society, there has traditionally been a general disapproval of the erotic aspect of sexual life, even within marriage, and this continues to inform contemporary attitudes toward sexuality (Nath

& Nayar, 2001). Expression of intimacy by a married couple in front of others (strangers, elder people, children) is seen as a sign of disrespect and unacceptable behavior. These aspects of shame, difficulties in expressing physical affection in front of family members, and lack of privacy are some of the factors that shape the expectations and values that couples bring to sex therapy. As part of sexual liberalization, themes about eroticism and sexual intimacy have been made explicit in recent Indian movies (Rao, 2007). The Indian movies produced during the postindependence era (1950–1990), when there was strict censorship, had themes of sexual pleasure but these were coded within the meanings of songs.

Sex during Menstrual Cycle

According to Hindu *smritis* (rules), a husband can only approach his wife on certain days of the menstrual cycle, excluding no moon and full moon days and other specific days that are devoted to certain Gods and Goddesses (Gupta, 1994).

Semen

Semen (*shukra*) is considered as the essence of all the characteristics of the human body and contains "soul," including the karmas from previous lives. According to *Sushruta Samhita*,[5] strong semen produces a male child. Since having a male child is important to Indians, having strong semen is considered essential. Semen is equated with strength and therefore considered precious. Ayurveda advises the need to conserve this precious fluid by limiting sexual intercourse to no more than two to three times a week in youth and one to two times a month in later life. This high cultural value placed on semen and conserving it explains why behaviors like masturbation and nocturnal emission were considered sinful acts and condemned. According to the Ayurvedic principles, loss of any of the *dhatu* (vital fluids of the human body system) in any form leads to draining of physical and mental energy and virility. A popular myth around the energy calculation of semen is that a drop of semen is equal to 40 drops of bone marrow, and each drop of bone marrow is of equal value to 40 drops of blood (Prakash, 2007). Even in modern day India, semen is regarded as a precious fluid and its loss is equated to a loss of vital energy. This is evident from the views held by young adult clients who access help for their perceived sexual problems related to loss of semen. However, there is a need for more research on this subject at a community level. Some of the other prevalent irrational beliefs about semen are: (a) semen loss leads to bodily weakness in the body, tremors in hands, inability to work, forgetfulness, anxiety, impotence, mental illness, thinning of semen, loss of male characteristics, and poor eyesight, and (b) masturbation leads to weakness in nerves and shrinkage of penis and testes (Manjula, Prasadarao, Kumaraiah, Mishra, & Raguram, 2003).

Masturbation

Seeking bodily pleasure through masturbation is condemned but only for those who have sworn to observe a life of chastity. All others were encouraged to make a light penance like having a bath, worshipping the sun, and offering prayers thrice after the act of masturbation (Bullough, 2003). There are no references in the religious texts of Hinduism to suggest that masturbation desecrates sexual purity (Cornog, 2003).

Migrants and Acculturation

Acculturation is defined as a process that entails contact between two cultural groups, which results in numerous cultural changes in both parties (Berry, 2001). Acculturation adds a new dimension to the cultural context of the human sexuality. Acculturation to Western culture, as well as maintaining an affiliation with one's traditional heritage, has been significantly and independently related to the sexual attitudes of Asian migrants (Brotto, Chik, Ryder, Gorzalka, & Seal, 2005). The cultural norm theory postulates that increasing contact with the mainstream or dominant culture introduces new values, which lead to changes in sexual attitudes and behaviors (Meston & Ahrold, 2010). There is a paucity of information about the possible effects of acculturation on sexuality and the sexual health of Indian migrants.

Homosexuality

Hinduism has never taken a strong position on the topic of homosexuality nor condemned it (Hinduism condemns only abortion and adultery). However, homosexuality remains a taboo topic that is rarely discussed openly in Indian society. By overruling a 148-year-old colonial law that describes a same-sex relationship as an "unnatural offence," on July 2, 2009 the High Court of New Delhi ruled that homosexual intercourse between consenting adults is not a criminal act.

Women's Sexuality

Through the depiction of a God named *Arthanatheswarar,* Hinduism conveys a strong message that men and women are equal.[6] In India, a woman's status in the society is equated with two parameters that are associated with sexuality, marriage and motherhood (Gupta & Jain, 2008). Virginity and chastity are often equated with purity and are integral to a woman's self-esteem and that of her family. One of the common perceptions about virginity among Indian women is that it is the most precious gift that a woman can offer to her husband. In some cultures within India, it is expected that a newlywed bride will prove her virginity to her mother-in-law by showing the blood spots on the bed sheet after the first night of sex. Many middle-class women still lack the power to make decisions about the choice of bridegroom or about the timing of the birth of their first child. Anecdotally, this contributes to marital dysfunction, relationship conflicts, sexual problems, general dissatisfaction, and overall poor quality of life. It is not uncommon for many women to stay in a married relationship for practical reasons, such as their children's future, social status and security, and financial dependence.

Sexual Violence and Commercial Sexual Exploitation

Lack of power and control over sexuality often make women the victims of domestic and sexual violence and in turn make them vulnerable to acquiring HIV/AIDS (Gupta, 2008). Commercial sexual exploitation of women and children is a fast growing concern in India, with a recent estimate of 2.8 million persons being trafficked in and out of India, the majority of whom are under 18 years of age and are forced into sex work due to poverty (Joffres et al., 2008). A very prevalent belief that having sex with a virgin girl will cure sexually transmitted infections and sexual dysfunctions was identified as one of the factors contributing to young girls' increased vulnerability to trafficking for sexual exploitation (Joffres et al., 2008).

Sexual Health Problems in India

The reported prevalence of sexual problems is: erectile dysfunction, 21 to 66%; premature ejaculation, 12 to 78%; *Dhat* syndrome,[7] 7 to 71% (Kulhara & Avasthi, 1995). The high prevalence of sexual problems needs careful interpretation as these data were drawn from the psychiatric clinics attached to teaching hospitals that were the prime sites for sexual health care and research. Most patients attributed semen loss as the main cause of their sexual problems and the vast majority of them practiced masturbation or had nocturnal emissions before developing sexual problems and had guilt about it (Kulhara & Avasthi, 1995).

The first community based study done in India found that the majority of men held a belief that semen loss is detrimental to health and semen should be preserved for good health (Kulhara & Avasthi, 1995). A review article (Jejeebhoy, 1998) reported that between 20 and 30%

of all Indian men and up to 10% of all women were sexually active during adolescence (before marriage), and had low levels of knowledge about sexuality. There was also a significant lack of information on reproductive and sexual health among adolescents. Two consecutive studies involving men from very low socioeconomic groups concluded that in addition to sexually transmitted infections, men were equally or more concerned about the quality and quantity of semen and about "impotence," the latter category encompassing erectile problems and premature ejaculation (Verma, Sharma, Singh, Rangaiyan, & Pelto, 2003; Verma, Singh, Sharma, & Pelto, 2001). Men in this study also considered wet dreams, masturbation, early ejaculation, sexual weakness, and other semen-related issues as serious sexual health problems. Suppression of sexual desire was one of the major causes perceived by men for wet dreams, whereas masturbation was seen as the major cause for perceived early ejaculation and distortion in the shape of the penis. A study involving heterosexual, low-income, unmarried, college-going youth (16–22 years of age) in an Indian metropolitan city identified three typologies of heterosexual peer networks: *bhai-behen* ("brother–sister like"), romantic "true love," and transitory and sexual "time pass" relationships (Abraham, 2002). The boundaries of these friendships are fluid and boys used this fluidity to their advantage as they engaged in multiple relationships, while girls mainly engaged in single, "true love" relationships. A study involving 149 Indian women found a very high proportion (two-thirds) of the sample of married women had some sexual dysfunction; the women were over 40 years of age and had little education (Singh, Tharyan, Kekre, Singh, & Gopalakrishnan, 2009). Another study using a purposive sampling of college girls (N = 530) reported on the frequency of masturbation and of demographic and sociocultural determinants of this behavior among young women (Sharma & Sharma, 1998). One third of these women did masturbate and felt that it was bad and caused weakness, disease, infertility, and marital disharmony. Interestingly, women who did masturbate were found to be significantly more knowledgeable about human sexuality and sexual behavior than nonmasturbators.

Help-Seeking Behavior of Indians

For Indian men, preparing themselves for marriage is the most important reason to seek help for sexual problems and the main sources of information about sexual health are friends and locally published (nonscientific) books and movies (Manjula, Prasadarao, Kumaraiah, Mishra, & Raguram, 2003). A study by Barua and Kurz (2001) explored the reproductive health seeking behavior of married adolescent girls in Maharashtra and reported that household work, protection of fertility, and silence arising from embarrassment related to sexual health problems, were the strongest factors that influenced care-seeking. Attribution of sexual disorders to nonmedical issues, such as bad behavior and guilt, was the most common reason for Indians not to seek medical professionals' help for their sexual problems (Kendurkar, Kaur, Agarwal, Singh, & Agarwal, 2008; Moreira et al., 2005). Access to specialist sexual health services in India (that are primarily in the metropolitan cities) and the cost of such services might be another possible reason why clients do not seek medical help. For these reasons, many clients/patients access local healers and self-proclaimed doctors who guarantee cure within a day, and the media promote these treatments (Rao & Avasthi, 2008). Although many Indians are hesitant to seek medical advice for sexual problems, Western medications are generally perceived as a quick and effective treatment option. Nutritional supplements, antibiotics, and analgesics were the most common drugs used as self-medication by the patients (Greenhalgh, 1987).

Approaches to Treatment for Sexual Problems

This section will attempt to integrate the evidence on various modalities of treatment for sexual problems in the context of the authors' personal experience of living and working in the Indian cultural context.

Psychotherapy

Several studies done in India, which were mainly based on psychiatric clinic samples, found masturbatory guilt was the most common male sexual problem and concluded that psychotherapy has limited success among Indians as it often challenges and confronts core cultural beliefs (Kendurkar, 2008; Kulhara & Avasthi, 1995; Manjula et al., 2003; Petrack & Keane, 1998; Schensul, Mekki-Berrada, Nastasi, Saggurti, & Verma, 2006). Western-based sexuality therapies have a primary focus on pleasure as an outcome for the management of sexual concerns that could conflict with Indian couples for whom the focus is on procreation rather than pleasure. Again, this could limit the benefits of psychotherapy in the Indian population. Even when attempts are made to modify the Western model to fit the Indian setting, there may be limited success due to a high dropout rate and sociocultural factors (Petrack & Keane, 1998).

The core process in psychotherapy is to challenge the maladaptive beliefs that clients hold and motivate them to overcome those beliefs and eventually solve the problem. This may not work for Indian clients for three reasons. First, Indians tend to keep strong hold of their cultural values and beliefs. Family and the wisdom of the elders are unquestionably accepted in the culture. Second, norms of behavior, especially in sex and sexuality, are an integral part of societal structure, constantly reinforced by religion, friends, and peers. Third, these same cultural and religious norms hamper comprehensive sex education at all ages.

Apart from their beliefs and values, there are a number of other reasons why Indians may be reluctant to seek psychotherapy for sexual problems. These include the sense of embarrassment and feelings of low self-esteem experienced by men at the prospect of disclosing a sexual problem to their partner or wife, financial factors (the high cost of repeated visits to a psychotherapist), and the lack of motivation to continue treatment that involves behavior rather than medication. Other factors such as living with extended family, with limited privacy, and restricted opportunity for sex, may contribute to performance difficulties and can impact on the application and outcome of certain sex therapies. Research also reports that Asians have a greater preference for physical treatments than do non-Asians (Petrack & Keane, 1998).

A review of the literature indicates that Western models of psychotherapy have been applied in the Indian setting with different levels of success and varied outcomes. Small sample size, high drop-out levels, and loss to follow-up in the reported studies make it very difficult to properly assess the application, outcome, and success of psychotherapy. In a 7-year longitudinal study of 66 men, four types of treatment were compared: Masters and Johnson's behavior therapy, psychotherapy of an eclectic nature, pharmacotherapy, and a combination of pharmacotherapy and psychotherapy (Kulhara & Avasthi, 1995). Twenty-five patients (38% of the sample) dropped out after the first consultation. Among those who reported improvement (n = 18), the combined therapy (psychotherapy + pharmacotherapy) was found to be effective. Interestingly, those men who reported improvement at one-year follow-up but who had dropped out after the first consultation had actually sought help elsewhere in the subsequent 6 years. When asked to state the perceived cause of their psychosexual dysfunction, many (over 40%) considered their problems mainly physical in nature; a common reason for discontinuing treatment was the belief that their problem was not psychological. The outcomes of this study need to be carefully interpreted because it was not scientifically rigorous, was mainly descriptive, and included no control group (Kulhara & Avasthi, 1995). A subsequent study by the same authors reported on a larger sample (N = 451) of men with sexual dysfunction who were managed with a package of sex education, relaxation exercises, marital therapy, psychotherapy, Masters and Johnson's treatment model, and psychotropic drugs (Kulhara & Avasthi,1995). The authors reported a 20% dropout rate after the first consultation, no change (42%), partial improvement (30%), and complete (28%) improvement. Attempts to develop an Indian version of the Masters and

Johnson approach failed, mainly due to dropouts that made interpretation of study results difficult. Some studies have highlighted the possible reason for high attrition from sex therapy as possible dissatisfaction of the patients with the explanation that "loss of semen was not harmful" (Kulhara & Avasthi, 1995). Factors that made sex therapy less acceptable to patients from different ethnic backgrounds were poor motivation, language difficulties, passivity of women, and seeking organic explanations for sexual dysfunction (Bhugra & Cordle, 1986). Also, direct contradiction of patients' attitudes, such as toward their view of the energy aspect of semen, could result in the therapeutic relationship being jeopardized (Petrack, 1998).

Indian Traditional Practice (Ayurveda and Unani)

Textbooks on traditional medicine describe the treatment of reproductive and sexual problems based on changes in lifestyle and sexual behavior, use of revitalizing and invigorating food, and natural (herbal) remedies (Schensul et al., 2006). In Ayurveda, sexual dysfunction in men can be primary (e.g., congenital conditions that damage or destroy semen-producing organs) or secondary (e.g., attributable to conditions like excessive indulgence in sex or masturbation that affects the quality of semen, making it impure). In Unani, the role of diet and masturbation are stressed in the management of sexual problems. Masturbation (causing semen loss) is said to be the single most important cause of the majority of sexual problems. Traditional (Ayurveda and Unani) practitioners seek to understand patients' physical complaints and conduct a detailed history of an individual's well-being, social problems, diet, rest, and activity patterns, including risky behavior that may have an impact on the patient's health. The traditional practitioners' cultural and medical knowledge about sexual problems is likely to be consistent with the clients' explanatory models and understanding of health and disease.

Traditional practitioners in modern day urban settings of India, however, tend to have shifted from this classical holism to a more fragmentary and expeditious symptomatic approach (Schensul et al., 2006). Cost was one of the significant factors in help seeking behavior, with traditional practitioners being much less expensive than modern medical doctors, therefore possibly making them more acceptable and accessible. Traditional practitioners vary in their view of the impact of nocturnal emissions and masturbation on sexual problems. With the intention of preventing further infections or sexual problems, these practitioners tend to proffer advice using statements such as "you could die" or "you will ruin your life and family," which eventually makes the client feel guilty, frightened, and anxious about their sexual behavior.

Folklore, Customs, and Remedies

Folklore customs and remedies are common practices in India not only for sexual problems but also for most ailments. This of course is not unusual for a country that has strong religious and cultural belief systems. While not scientific or evidence-based, they are acceptable to many clients and congruent with society's beliefs and values. A classic example would be simply wearing a sacred thread around the wrist or waist after prayers to keep away the evil spirits (assumed to be the cause of certain "bad" behaviors like masturbation).

Case Study

Initial Consultation

Rahul is a 26-year old-male working as a field supervisor at a local firm in India. He is a shy person and has never expressed any of his sexual feelings to anyone. At the age of 14, he first experienced nocturnal emission and started to masturbate regularly. Since then, he has masturbated once or twice daily. He considered masturbation as a dirty act and had tried to stop "now and then" but without success. He expressed guilt over his sinful masturbatory habit and linked it to both sexual and nonsexual problems that he currently experienced. Rahul's concerns included acne, weak eyesight, severe weakness of muscles, and a dark complexion. In the last 2 months, his ejaculations were quick (less than a minute). He considered premature ejaculation as a punishment for his many years practicing a bad habit (masturbation). A more recent complaint was a decrease in the amount of semen, which made him very anxious and stressed about his masculinity and fertility because his parents were keen to have him marry soon. In the past, Rahul had contacted some web-based services that offer advice for sexual problems. Some of the advice was to stop thinking about sex, drink plenty of water, and do physical exercises. One of the web-based services even recommended that he try sexual intercourse as an alternative measure to get over the masturbatory habit. Rahul found all of these recommendations to be unsatisfactory and ineffective. He also had a strong belief that premarital sex was bad and maintained that he would never engage in premarital intercourse, as this would exacerbate his existing guilt and remorse. Rahul's ultimate goal was to lead a satisfying and healthy life and prepare himself for future married life.

So to sum up Rahul's problems:

- Misconception: Acne is the result of the dirty act of masturbation.
- Hypochondriacal symptoms: weak eyesight, weakness of muscles, and a dark complexion.

- Presenting complaints: quick ejaculation, reduced quantity of semen, and stress and anxiety on anticipating marriage.
- Future concerns: Sexual potency, fertility, and maintaining a sexual relationship.
- Key values: Masturbation is a sinful act and premarital sexual intercourse is bad.
- Personality: Shy; not an outspoken person.
- Management history: Had only used information from websites in the past.

Case Management Plan

The case management plan below is discussed from the perspective of a medical professional with a specialty in sexology/sexual health. Certain aspects of the management like requests for blood work and a physical examination cannot be performed by sex therapists who are not physicians, depending on the country/jurisdiction in which they practice. In such situations, appropriate involvement and referral to physicians or general practitioners is recommended.

1. Case history elicitation: (a) sexual, (b) family and social, and (c) personal and medical
2. Validation of concerns and complaints
3. Physical examination
4. Education
5. Physical investigations
6. Referral
7. Advice and reassurance
8. Follow-up at 3 weeks and 7 weeks

Case History: Sexual

D Do you understand what masturbation is?
P Yes, we call it suya-inbam[8] in Tamil but more popularly as handjob.
D Describe the first experience of masturbation.
P I started passing kanji[9] in the night when I was about 14 years old. I remember sometimes I also had sexy dreams at that time. I used to sleep in the same room as my younger brother and I was frightened that he would see and tell my mother. Some boys in the school talked about how if you make the kanji come by rubbing the penis then the night dreams will stop. Now I can't stop myself from doing this and still have the night emissions also.
D Where or how did you learn about masturbation?

P   My cousin was visiting from the country and I told him what the boys in school told me. He took me into his room and started playing with my penis. I became hard and kanji came out. It was a pleasurable and intense experience. He then told me that I should continue doing it like that.
D   Where and when do you generally masturbate?
P   After that first time with my cousin, usually in the toilets or in the shower. I have to be quick, since I am afraid that someone would suspect. Now after a long day of work, I lock my door and do a handjob while watching porn movies on the Internet.
D   What triggers your desire to masturbate?
P   Before it was TV shows like fashion channels or glamorous scenes in films or magazines. Now I find that Internet porn is the best and quickest.
D   How do you masturbate? Use only hands or any other instruments?
P   (*Giggling*) My hand ... usually my left hand. Now, over the last 12 months I have to hold tighter and rub harder. The skin at the tip is feeling dry, so I bought some baby cream and use that also sometimes.
D   On average, how much time do you spend on masturbation?
P   While having a shower or in the toilet, I used to spend about 15 minutes. I can't spend more than that as someone in the family will knock on the door and scream at me. Nowadays, I spend much less time on this as the Internet pictures are very intense and I want to finish it quickly and go to bed.
D   Have you always masturbated by yourself?
P   Yes. Except for the first time when my cousin did it for me.
D   Are there any specific fantasies that accompany your masturbation?
P   I like to see completely naked images of women. (*Giggling*) I also like to see women in bikinis, short skirts, and tight dresses.
D   How do you feel and what do you do before and after masturbation?
P   Whenever I feel like and wanting to do handjob my strong liking to do it will tell me that it is OK to do it. While doing it, I actually feel sinful but the pleasure actually overrides the sinful thoughts. Once I ejaculate, I feel terribly bad and very guilty. I consider it as a failure because I could not control my thoughts and likings to do handjob. It is very confusing why I feel OK before doing it and then feel very bad later. Also, I feel very tired and don't want to do anything but simply sit and watch TV or sleep.
D   Where did you learn that masturbation is a sinful act?
P   (Silence) My dad, mum, uncles, and even some of my school friends have told me that handjob is very wrong and bad habit. Also, I heard a doctor on a TV show confirming that these sorts of habits are very wrong and should be stopped immediately by parents.

Case History: Family and Social

D   What sexual messages did you receive from your family?

P   I remember my father saying to me once that a boy must not have two bad habits, one is swapnadosh[10] and the other is hastadosh.[11] Also, my parents told me that they would punish me if I spent any time in thinking about sex and that it is all to be thought about and done after marriage. Once, my mum found the kanji on the blanket and scolded me for having swapnadosh. My father told me that semen is a very precious body fluid that has to be preserved with utmost care as each drop of it contains so much shakthi.[12]

D   Is there anyone in your family you can talk to about sexual matters?

P   No. There is no one in my family other than my cousin who initially taught me to do handjob.

D   What religious beliefs do you have around sexuality?

P   I am a Hindu and a Saivait.[13] I strongly believe in marriage and sex as a sacred union. I don't know why I think this way but it is what my parents and relatives told me. Also, many stories in Hinduism are about husband, wife, and children.

D   Did you get any form of sex education at school or elsewhere?

P   Yes but it is only about HIV/AIDS.

D   Have you spoken about your sexual concerns to anyone?

P   I wish to but could not talk to anyone about my problems. I have posted questions on websites for experts to answer but I had had no face-to-face consultation.

Case History: Personal and Medical

D   How do you feel about your current employment?

P   It is very physically demanding and very stressful in terms of achieving the day-to-day targets.

D   What makes you feel anxious and stressed about marriage?

P   I believe that a real man should be able to demonstrate his masculinity to society by means of sexual potency and fertility. Also, I want to perform well in sex in front of my wife, satisfy her, and be a good husband and lover. Otherwise, even my wife will not respect me and later will make fun of me. I have heard of some girls who left their husbands and ran away with a different man because the husband did not satisfy her. All these thoughts of marriage and sex are very challenging and make me very much worried and nervous. This is because I doubt and fear whether I won't have enough energy to have sex and produce babies, exactly as what my parents warned me of long time back.

D Do you exercise or play any sports/games?
P No. I used to play tennis and cricket but have not played it for few years now.
D Have you got any medical or surgical conditions?
P No.
D Do you drink alcohol or smoke?
P No. Not at all.
D Are you on any regular medication(s)?
P Yes. It is a herbal medicine called Deerghau,[14] one tablet twice a day before food as advised by one of the web service providers.

It was important to validate every single concern of the client and to listen to what he expressed and considered important. Concerns surrounding the sexual problem such as weak eyesight, tiredness, darkening of skin colour, acne, and psychological issues were assessed by means of physical investigations/examination and referral to appropriate health and allied health professionals in order to make sure that no complaint was overlooked and to make the client feel that all his concerns were given importance.

Case History: Physical Examination

The client's penis and scrotum were examined for any abnormalities. Importantly, the foreskin (in this case it was uncircumcised) and its tightness and retraction were examined by asking the client to roll back the foreskin as much as possible. The client was asked to show the therapist the sensitive zones of his penis (in this case it was the *coronal sulcus*, the region between the head and the shaft of the penis). A thick collection of smegma was seen under the foreskin. The physical examination was also used as an opportunity to educate the client about sexual anatomy and genital hygiene. This also provided an opportunity to observe the skin color of the client's body part that was least likely to be exposed to sunlight.

Case History: Patient Education

Using visual aids and charts, the internal anatomy of the genital system and the physiology of ejaculation were explained. Information on semen composition, production, and storage was provided. Advice on the maintenance of genital hygiene was given. Rahul was instructed to use only water to clean his penis by rolling the foreskin back. The chances of having a tight foreskin due to poor genital hygiene were explained.

Case History: Laboratory Work

Blood samples were taken for a full blood count, biochemistry, iron levels, and hormonal assays of testosterone and thyroid. A full semen analysis was carried out. The client was asked not to masturbate for 2 days before the sample for semen analysis was collected.

Case History: Referral

The client was referred to a dermatologist for review of his acne and possible causes of a dark complexion. To obtain a psychological profile, the client was referred to a clinical psychologist for assessment of guilt, anxiety, and stress. He was also referred to an optometrist for a vision examination.

Case History: Advice and Reassurance

Before the next consultation, the client was instructed to avoid known triggers and situations that would lead to a strong desire to masturbate. The next appointment was after a period of 3 weeks, allowing enough time for the results of the investigations and specialist opinions to be obtained. The client was reassured, using the clinician's experience and scientific knowledge as a reference, that masturbation would in no way hinder his capacity or performance as a husband. The different therapeutic choices available for his complaints and the situations in which these could be used were discussed. The risks of using commercially sold medications were highlighted.

Case History: Second Consultation (3-week Follow-Up)

Rahul kept his appointment and returned anxiously. He reported some improvement in the quantity of semen and control of his ejaculation. Also, he disclosed that he was able to control masturbation until the sample was collected for semen analysis. Thereafter, he could only resist masturbating for one day and perceived this as a failure.

Rahul's blood counts, hormonal levels, semen quantity, and sperm quality were all normal. It was noted that the quantity of semen was well within the normal range. The patient found the specialists' review to be a very informative and useful experience. He was very happy and relaxed when it was confirmed that his results were all well within the normal range.

Case History: Cognitive Restructuring/Behavioral Approach

The client's self-exploration for sexual pleasure (by means of masturbation), and his efforts to solve the perceived problems before marriage were framed in a positive manner. Explaining to him that his experience in sexual pleasure would enable him to be a good lover and caring husband did this. At the same time, the cultural/religious beliefs around sexuality as something that could be practiced only within marriage were acknowledged to be correct, but only in the context of ancient India when men got married at mid- or late adolescence. The disconnection between the stable nature of normal bodily (sexual) needs and the changing pattern of societal norms and expectations were explained using the following example: "Compare the age at which your grandparents and parents got married with that of yourself. If you do that, you will soon realize how much more stress, in terms of education and work, someone of your age has to go through even before considering marriage. What your father and uncles said to you about masturbation could be right because they were more likely to be married much earlier than you and were able to meet their needs by sexual intercourse." Masturbatory behavior was normalized in the context of Rahul being an unmarried male who has sexual urges and needs. Not only the act of masturbation but also the associated feeling of dirtiness and sinfulness were normalized in the South Asian cultural context. Importantly, the fact that he was not the only one who masturbates or has such concerns was strongly reinforced using statistics and anecdotal data from Indian culture.

The myth about the loss of blood cells in semen was replaced with scientific facts using the semen analysis report. It was also explained to Rahul that the feelings of guilt arising from his actions being in opposition to his cultural beliefs were the likely cause for all his concerns, rather than the actual act of masturbation. Without blatantly saying that masturbation is not a sinful act, the roots for the cultural belief and values around semen conservation and the context in which it was constructed were discussed in a nonthreatening manner. The traditional nature of beliefs and values around sexuality was discussed in the current context and the advances in scientific knowledge in the field of sexology were highlighted.

Avoidance of triggers and situations that could make it difficult for Rahul to resist masturbating was reinforced and his 3 weeks experience of resisting those triggers was discussed. The client's sense of failure to control masturbation, despite the advice given, was not judged as a failure, but rather, was reframed as an opportunity to learn about his semen quantity.

Case History: Exercise and Relaxation Techniques

The client was advised to do some basic exercises like walking or running for a set number of days, say twice a week, play any sports that he likes, or practice yoga or meditation. The techniques were kept open to allow for client choice.

Case Follow-up: Third Consultation—At 7 Weeks

Rahul returned 4 weeks after the second consultation. Generally, he appeared to be satisfied with the treatment outcome. Also, he was engaged to be married in 4 weeks and sounded very positive and happy about it. He was able to resist masturbation for 1 to 2 days and also reported improvement in his ejaculatory control. However, he stated that he was concerned about his sexual performance with his wife on the wedding night.

Case History: Advice and Reassurance

It was recommended that he access premarital counseling to explore more general issues in a new marital relationship. It was also suggested that he bring his future wife or ask her to attend a sex therapy clinic on her own (if acceptable to her) to get some information on what to expect and do on the first night. Printed information on female sexuality and intercourse was given to Rahul to pass on to his future wife.

Case Discussion

Rahul's case scenario is the most common presentation of sexual concerns or problems among young Indian men, especially those who are about to enter into an arranged marriage. The negative feelings and guilt from past sexual behavior and worries for the future are reflected in the present sexual complaints and concerns of the client. Rahul continued to practice masturbation despite the fact that he considered it to be an immoral act and a threat to his health. This suggested to us that he enjoyed the pleasure of self-stimulation to orgasm. There was a dissonance between his beliefs and his actions. Although he thought that masturbation was wrong, he was not prepared to give up his sexual enjoyment. Thus, for 12 years he continued to masturbate, but had feelings of guilt at the conflict between his sexual needs and pleasure, on the one hand, and his beliefs as to the moral view of his society, culture, and religion on self-stimulation and loss of semen, on the other. This sense of guilt at moral wrongdoing was the underlying cause for all his physical and physiological complaints and the hypochondriacal symptoms he experienced. These hypochondriacal symptoms are usually a consequence of lack of sex education and strong mythical beliefs propagated over centuries and constantly reinforced by elders, society, and media. Sex education, either one-to-one or population- based, is all that is needed for some clients and this could be offered through a single consultation or even through web-based services, coupled with some basic counseling and medications such as a placebo or anxiolytics if deemed necessary. However, for many clients, like Rahul, this basic approach is unavailable and leads them to "doctor-shop" in the quest for an instant cure. With repeated failures of nonsystematic approaches of treatment, the client's concerns tend to worsen and their anxiety and range of perceived symptoms increases. Irrespective of the nature of their sexual concerns, most men in this situation get married, compounding the situation and causing marital and relationship problems.

There are challenges involved in dealing with clients who have strong masturbatory guilt, with or without hypochondriacal symptoms, premarital anxiety, and stress. These challenges and the ways these were managed are discussed below.

Challenges Related to Masturbatory Guilt and Hypochondriacal Symptoms

A history of the client's belief that "masturbation is a sinful act" is insufficient information to effectively manage the sexual concerns and problems. Rather, the cognitions around that belief, such as why an individual considers masturbation a sinful act, and where and from whom he learned this is very important. Underlying this belief is often the knowledge, belief, and values that South Asians ascribe to the all-important body fluid (*dhatu*)—semen—and its conservation for strength, masculinity, potency, and fertility. Any thought or act that depletes this vital fluid is not permitted. A lack of knowledge about sexuality and sexual function coupled with a strong belief system around semen conservation, the myths and misconceptions on masturbation, nocturnal emission, and loss of semen in urine (*Dhat* syndrome) are propagated over generations. It is a challenge for a man to think outside what his family, society, and religion have taught and reinforced about the value of semen and effects of masturbation. Persons whom they respect and consider more important than a God pass on these strong beliefs and values to them. A famous quote in Hinduism sets a hierarchy for the four most important persons in each person's life: *Matha, Pitha, Guru, Theivam*, meaning mother, father, teacher, and God, respectively. The professional has to understand this in working with a client in order to replace his beliefs and values around semen and masturbation with scientific facts.

Psychotherapy is about challenging a client's core beliefs and making changes. This has to be cautiously applied to South Asians, especially clients with sexual concerns and problems. From past research, it is evident that the dropout rate from psychotherapy among South Asians is very high, especially after the first consultation.

For this reason, in the management of the case described in this chapter (Rahul), nothing challenging the client's core belief or values was discussed in the first consultation. More importantly, all his concerns and complaints were validated. Discussion around normalizing the cultural beliefs and values around semen and masturbation were reserved for later consultations. The test results, especially the semen analysis, were obtained before discussing any effects of masturbation on health. At the second consultation, discussion of the client's results related to semen quantity (which was well within the normal range) was used to demystify one of the client's concerns about reduced quantity of semen production due to the self-perceived bad habit of masturbation. The other physical parameters, from hemoglobin levels to hormone assays, were all used to demonstrate that his health was not adversely affected by the act of masturbation. The dermatologist's report was used not only to demonstrate that acne was not due to masturbation, but also to prove that other health professionals confirmed that masturbation was not harmful. By following this approach, trust and rapport with the client were efficiently built, which formed the basis for further management.

Challenges Related to Premarital Anxiety and Stress and Its Management

The context in which the client presented to the professional was to have his sexual problems overcome before his upcoming marriage. The pressure to reach a satisfactory resolution in a limited time frame could be a challenge for both the client and professional, but could also be used as an opportunity to educate the client, get the assessments done, and actively involve the client in the whole management process.

In India, the marriage night (popularly called the *first night*) is considered an important occasion for the bridegroom to prove that he is a man by demonstrating his strength, potency (penile erection), and love making ability. Culturally, masculinity is strongly linked to various aspects of sexuality, from performance to fertility. Even in modern India, it is a very common social expectation for the newly married man to make his wife pregnant within the first few months of marriage. All these sociocultural expectations of a man can make someone like Rahul very anxious and perceive marriage as more stressful than enjoyable. The anxiety that this client held toward marriage could be equated to that of an Indian student's anxiety about the prospect of a final year career-determining exam. These feelings were very pronounced for Rahul because for the first time in 12 years, his secret habit (masturbation) and the associated guilt were to be challenged in front of a woman. Thus, it was deemed important to guard against "honeymoon impotence" in this anxious client. Medication choices were discussed at the very first consultation rather than reserved for a later date because of the uncertainty as to whether he would return for a follow-up consultation. This helped establish the client's confidence in the health professional and paved the way for trust and rapport between the client and professional. This discussion of medical management was based on the assumption that the knowledge about available treatment options for anxiety would give the client more confidence and enable him to be more actively involved in the process of cognitive restructuring and behavior change.

Conclusions

Cultural beliefs, values, social norms, and gender roles that are reinforced by the family and the greater society, lack of formal sex education coupled with access to incorrect information, and living in a state of cultural ambiguity is the context in which many Indian clients present with sexual problems. The impact and importance of all of the above factors on the client's present complaints or future concerns should not be discounted. Rather, the complaints and concerns should be validated in this cultural context, irrespective of whether the client is seen in India or any other parts of the world. In addition, among migrant Indians, the process and impact of acculturation needs to be considered in the management plan. Physical examination and objective assessment of health is important, especially in the Indian context. It can be used to disprove some of the client's incorrect thoughts, challenge some long held beliefs, and it can act as a platform for sex education. Direct application of a Western model of psychotherapy may not be compatible with many Indian clients' treatment expectations, irrespective of where they live and access professionals for sexual health care. Systematic assessment and a multidisciplinary approach is the cornerstone of the management of sexual problems that are deeply rooted in cultural beliefs and values. Building trust and rapport with the clients through a nonchallenging, nonconfrontational, and nonjudgmental approach is important. This is especially so with clients who present with a long history of anxiety about sexual practices and behaviors. The overall management has to be focused on the individual client and his or her presenting complaints. However, it is equally important to place the client in his or her religiocultural context, consider issues that have led to the presenting complaints, and address potential future concerns.

Notes

1. Kajuraho was the capital of Chandellas, a Rajput dynasty and the sculptures (Devangana-mithuna) of Kajuraho were built between 950 and 1050 CE (Nath, 2004)
2. The Vedas are a large body of texts from ancient India, which form the oldest layer of Sanskrit literature, and are the oldest sacred texts of Hinduism.
3. Ayurveda is an Indian traditional medicine in which life is considered as the union of body, senses, mind, and soul.
4. Unani is a Greco-Arabic traditional system of medicine that is still widely practiced in the Indian subcontinent.
5. *Sushruta samhita* is the surgical treatise on Ayurvedic medicine written in the first millennium BCE.
6. Arthanatheswarar is the portrayal of one God with Shiva (male) and Shakthi (female) on right and left respectively to demonstrate that men and women are of equal importance and have an equal share and powers in life.
7. *Dhat* syndrome is characterized by vague somatic symptoms such as fatigue, listlessness, and loss of appetite, with or without psychosexual dysfunction. The complaints are attributed to loss of semen in urine as a direct result of masturbation or nocturnal emission.
8. In Tamil, *suya* means self, *inbam* means pleasure.
9. *Kanji* is a commonly used word for semen. In Tamil, *kanji* means rice porridge or the starch content of rice porridge.
10. *Swapna* means dream, *dosh* means bad.
11. *Hasta* means hand, *dosh* means bad.
12. The supreme power of creation according to the Hindu religion.
13. *Saivaits* are a group of people who follow the God Shiva and Goddess Shakthi.
14. Wheat grass is a nutritional supplement.

References

Abraham, L. (2002). Bhai-behen, true love, time pass: Friendships and sexual partnerships among youth in an Indian metropolis. *Culture, Health & Sexuality: An International Journal for Research, Intervention and Care, 4*(3), 337–353.

Barua, A., & Kurz, K. (2001). Reproductive health-seeking by married adolescent girls in Maharashtra, India. *Reproductive Health Matters, 9*(17), 53–62.

Berry, J. W. (2001). A psychology of immigration. *Journal of Social Issues, 57*(3), 615–631.

Bhugra, D., & Cordle, C. (1986). Sexual dysfunction in Asian couples. *British Medical Journal, 292*, 111–112.

Brotto, L. A., Chik, H. M., Ryder, A. G., Gorzalka, B. B., & Seal, B. N. (2005). Acculturation and sexual function in Asian women.. *Archives of Sexual Behavior, 34*(6), 613–626.

Bullough, V. L. (2003). Masturbation—A historical overview. *Journal of Psychology & Human Sexuality, 14*(2), 17–33.

Cornog, M. (2003). Religion: Spirituality and masturbation. In *The big book of masturbation* (pp. 181–182). San Francisco, CA: Down There Press.

Greenhalgh, T. (1987). Drug prescription and self-medication in India: An exploratory survey. *Social Science & Medicine, 25*(3), 307–318.

Gupta, M. (1994). Sexuality in the Indian subcontinent. *Journal of Sexual and Marital Therapy, 9*, 57–69.

Gupta N., & Jain, S (2008) Teenage pregnancy—Causes and concerns. *Journal of the Indian Medical Association, 106*, 516, 518–519.

Hyam, R. (1990). The British home base. In MacKenzie M. J. (Ed.), *Empire and sexuality* (pp 56– 87). Manchester, England: Manchester University Press.

Jejeebhoy, S. J. (1998). Adolescent sexual and reproductive behavior: A review of the evidence from India. *Social Science & Medicine, 46*(10), 1275–1290.

Joffres, C., Mills, E., Joffres, M., Khanna, T., Walia, H., & Grund, D. (2008). Sexual slavery without borders: Trafficking for commercial sexual exploitation in India. *International Journal for Equity in Health, 7*(1), 22.

Kendurkar, A., Kaur, B., Agarwal, A., Singh, H., & Agarwal, V. (2008). Profile of adult patients attending a marriage and sex clinic in India. *International Journal of Social Psychiatry, 54*(6), 486–493.

Kulhara, P., & Avasthi, A. (1995). Sexual dysfunction in the Indian subcontinent. *International Review of Psychiatry, 7*, 23 1–239.

Manjula, M., Prasadarao, P., Kumaraiah, V., Mishra, H., & Raguram, R. (2003). Sexual dysfunction in single males: A perspective from India. *Journal of Clinical Psychology, 59*(6), 701–713.

Meston, C. M., & Ahrold, T. (2010). Ethnic, gender, and acculturation influences on sexual behaviors. *Archives of Sexual Behavior, 39*(1), 179–189.

Moreira, E. D., Brock, G., Glasser, D. B., Nicolosi, A., Laumann, E. O., Paik, A., ... Gingell, C. (2005). Help-seeking behavior for sexual problems: the Global Study of Sexual Attitudes and Behaviors. *International Journal of Clinical Practice, 59*, 1, 6–16.

Nath, R. (2004). *Temples and erotic art of Kajuraho.* Noida, Uttar Pradesh, India: Gopsons.

Nath, J. K., & Nayar, V. R. (2001). India. In R. T. Francoeur (Ed.), *International encyclopedia of sexuality* (pp. 516–532). New York: Continuum.

Prakash, O. (2007). Lessons for postgraduate trainees about Dhat syndrome. *Indian Journal of Psychiatry, 49*, 208– 210.

Petrack, J., & Keane, F. (1998) Cultural beliefs and treatments of sexual dysfunction: An overview. *Journal of Sexual Dysfunction, 1*, 13–17.

Rao, S. (2007). The globalization of Bollywood: An ethnography of non-elite audiences in India. *The Communication Review, 10*(1), 57–76.

Rao, T. S., & Avasthi, A. (2008). Roadmap for sexual medicine: Agenda for Indian Psychiatry Society. *Indian Journal of Psychiatry, 50*(3), 153–154.

Sachdev, P. (1998). Sex on campus: A preliminary study of knowledge, attitudes and behavior of university students in Delhi, India. *Journal of Biosocial Sciences, 30*, 95–105.

Sandhya, S. (2009). The social context of marital happiness in urban Indian couples: Interplay of intimacy and conflict. *Journal of Marital and Family Therapy, 35*(1), 74–96.

Schensul, S. L., Mekki-Berrada, A., Nastasi, B., Saggurti, N., & Verma, R. K. (2006). Healing traditions and men's sexual health in Mumbai, India: The realities of medicine practiced in urban poor communities. *Social Science & Medicine, 62*(11), 2774–2785.

Sharma, V., & Sharma, A. (1998). The guilt and pleasure of masturbation: A study of college girls in Gujarat, India. *Sexual and Marital Therapy, 13*(1), 63–70.

Singh, J., Tharyan, P., Kekre, N., Singh, G., & Gopalakrishnan, G. (2009). Prevalence and risk factors for female sexual dysfunction in women attending a medical clinic in south India. *Journal of Postgraduate Medicine, 55*(2), 113–120.

Verma, R. K., Sharma, S., Singh, R., Rangaiyan, G., & Pelto, P. J. (2003). Beliefs concerning sexual health problems and treatment seeking among men in an Indian slum community. *Culture, Health & Sexuality: An International Journal for Research, Intervention and Care, 5*(3), 265–276.

Verma, R. K., Singh, R., Sharma, S., & Pelto, P. (2001). A study of male sexual health problems in a Mumbai slum population. *Culture, Health & Sexuality: An International Journal for Research, Intervention and Care, 3*(3), 339–352.

Editors Introduction to Chapter 9
Hong Kong Chinese

On July 1, 1997, China resumed sovereignty over Hong Kong, ending more than 150 years of British colonial rule. Hong Kong is therefore an interesting mix of Chinese and British influences. Ng and Ho provide an overview of some of the relevant sociocultural factors affecting sex, marriage, and procreation in China and in Hong Kong in particular. China's once rich and open approach to sexuality was changed by the influences of neo-Confucianism and Christianity. As a result, the valuing of sexual pleasure was supplanted by the importance placed on sexual restraint. The authors note the high incidence of sexual problems and dissatisfaction in the sexually conservative culture of Hong Kong. The emphasis on sexual purity or virginity for women has led to the idea that one's vagina can become "locked" leading to problems with painful intercourse.

While Hong Kong has been introduced to Western style sex therapy and sex therapy clinics have long waiting lists, it is unclear whether Western style sex therapy translates to the culture of Hong Kong or China. The cases presented here describe resolution of vaginismus, not by psychotherapy or sex therapy, but by a physician utilizing vaginal dilators. A didactic and directive approach is described in the two cases. As a result, successful treatment of vaginismus is not necessarily the same as the ability of the couple to have intercourse become part of their pleasurable sexual repertoire. The women described in the two cases wanted to have intercourse in order to have children.

The treatment option that is raised here is that it may be more expedient and more in keeping with cultural imperatives to separate intercourse from sexual pleasure in order to more quickly and efficiently achieve the goal of conception. Sexual pleasure for the women described in this chapter was reserved for nonpenetrative sex. The husbands of these women seemed agreeable to this strategy. It may not work well in some other cultures, but it may be a treatment option for those cultures in which women are able to exercise some control over their sexuality, once it is separated from their fertility.

9

SEX, SEXUAL PROBLEMS, AND SEXUAL AGENCY IN HONG KONG CHINESE WOMEN

Anna Ng Hoi Nga and Petula Ho Sik Ying

Clinicians and researchers believe that culture has important effects on women's sexual functioning and dysfunction and in particular, in relation to difficulty in having vaginal penetration (Hiller, 2000; Ng, 1999; Wood, Koch, & Mansfield, 2006). In Chinese traditional philosophy, there are different views toward sexual intercourse. Before the 13th century, in Chinese culture, sex was celebrated and freely talked about in people's daily lives. In a review article of sexuality in ancient China, Gulik (1961) concluded:

> Chinese people regard sexual intercourse as part of the natural order, thus it is the holy responsibility of every man and woman to do this behavior, sexual intercourse has never been connected with sin or feelings of moral rights or wrongs. Sexual intercourse is carried out at home privately, being controlled later by Confucianists' rules and regulations, not because sexual intercourse is shameful, so should be covered up, but because it is a holy thing, like other festival rituals (such as worshipping ancestors, doing prayers), should not be done in front of others, and should not [be] discuss[ed] with others. (pp. 50–51)

A similar idea was proposed by Pimpaneau (2003), who pointed out that in the United States, the erotic is sin par excellence. The expression of "living in sin" can mean "living together unmarried" and such an idea is greatly affected by Christian belief. Pimpaneau argued that in ancient China this link between sin and eroticism did not exist; as he stated, "eroticism was not marked with the stigma of sin, and was regarded as a natural pleasure as long as it presented no danger to the institutions of the family or State, and could even be incorporated by Taoism into its hygienic practices, almost like gymnastics." (Pimpaneau, 2003, p. 20)

Sexual Attitudes and Behaviors in Hong Kong

The sexual attitudes and behavior of Chinese people in Hong Kong today differ from those of ancient China and are affected by a variety of ethnic and religious factors, in particular by Chinese and British influences (Ng & Ma, 2004). As such, the concept of pleasure has been replaced by the value ascribed to sexual restraint. Two traditional Chinese belief systems are influential in current Hong Kong culture: the original Taoist-Confucian and the neo-Confucian systems. The Taoist-Confucian belief is that sex is an interaction of two cosmic forces, Yin and Yang. The philosophical concept of Yin-Yang expresses the interdependence of opposites. Yin is regarded as the female, the cold and negative aspect of nature while Yang is regarded as the male, the hot and the positive component (So & Cheung, 2005). The Yin–Yang interaction is thought to be universal and essential for the existence, change, and growth of all organisms; sex is just one mode of this interaction between living beings (Ng & Ma, 2004). This philosophical doctrine regards sex as important both for reproduction and for pleasure. However, the neo-Confucian teaching that developed following the Song Dynasty (960–1279 CE) denounced sexual intimacy, pleasure, and all types of physical enjoyment, which reduced the union of Yin and Yang to the reproductive aspect. It is this school of thought that has been very influential in shaping current Chinese perceptions of sexuality (Ng & Ma, 2004). Neo-Confucianism emphasized the harmfulness of sexual pleasure to physical health and to spiritual development. Female sexual chastity was especially valued and needed to be guarded at all costs, even at the expense of one's life. In addition, premarital sex, extramarital sex, and remarriage were seen as disgraceful subjects that should not be openly discussed (Ng & Ma, 2004).

As Hong Kong has been a British colony for more than 100 years, sexual attitudes have been affected not only by Chinese beliefs, but also by Christianity (Ng & Ma, 2004). Most of the elite schools in Hong Kong are Christian-affiliated and directed, and some instruction in Christian doctrine is standard and required for all students (Ng & Ma, 2004). In these schools, according to Ng and Ma, "fundamentalist Christian ideas of sex were sown, developed, and absorbed. These included the denunciation of sexual pleasure, the love-marriage-sex trilogy and the exclusively monogamous marital system" (p. 490). Both traditional Chinese and Christian value systems are characterized by patriarchy (Ho & Tsang, 2002; Ng & Ma, 2004; Tsang, 1987). Women's subordinate role in Hong Kong has affected their sexual attitudes, values, and practices (Chan & Wong, 2004; Leung, 1995). The inferior status accorded to Hong Kong Chinese women renders them less able to assert their sexual needs or advocate for their own sexual pleasure.

Sexual Values and Attitudes

Traditional patriarchal values in relation to sexuality are prevalent in Hong Kong among the Chinese population (Yan, Man-Sze Wu, Ho, & Pearson, 2011). In a qualitative study women reported that sexual intercourse was part of their duty in order to procreate and to fulfill their husband's sexual needs. Men considered sex a physical drive. Neither men nor women believed that sex was enjoyable for women or that women needed sex in the same way as men did.

Although premarital sex has become more prevalent in the last two decades (Kershaw & DeGolyer, 2006), most Hong Kong Chinese believe that sex is only acceptable in the context of a committed relationship. A survey by the Hong Kong Central Policy Unit (CPU, 2008) showed that 69% of 1,014 respondents (aged at least 18 years) agreed that premarital sex was acceptable if it involved two adults who planned to get married. About 50% thought premarital sex between two adults within a stable relationship was acceptable even if they had no plans to marry. However, only 14% of the sample agreed that sexual relationships between two adults who were not in a stable relationship were acceptable. The sexual behavior of young Hong Kong adults is consistent with their stated values regarding premarital sex. When surveyed, 90% of the young adults having premarital sex said they would consider marrying their current sexual partner and 70% of them felt confident they would stay with this partner for life (Kershaw & DeGolyer, 2006). This openness to premarital sex did not extend to extramarital activity, which was largely condemned. Approximately 90% of respondents stated that extramarital sex was always unacceptable, while 68% of the survey respondents even disapproved of intimate but platonic relationships between a married person and someone of the opposite sex. There were no age or socioeconomic status differences associated with the value placed on loyalty and commitment within marital relationships. However, a telephone survey of Chinese adults living in Hong Kong found evidence of extramarital activity despite the value placed on fidelity (Kim, Lau, & Cheuk, 2009). This study found that almost one third of married women 45 to 59 years of age reported having no sex (sexlessness) in the previous year. The substantially lower figure (17%) for married men of the same age group reporting sexlessness is suggestive of a high prevalence of extramarital relationships among Chinese men in Hong Kong.

Marriage, family, and children are highly valued in Hong Kong. The survey by the Hong Kong Central Policy Unit discussed previously

(CPU, 2008) reported that 70% of respondents regarded marriage as a necessary step in life. Sixty-six percent of respondents regarded childbearing as important in marriage.

While many Western values have permeated Hong Kong culture, choosing a marriage partner based on physical attraction is not one of them. A survey of women's sexuality (The Association for the Advancement of Feminism, 2005) reported that only 11.9% out of 250 female respondents would put a partner's appearance and physique as one of their top three criteria for choosing a sex partner, whilst more than 90% of women thought that understanding, caring, and respect were the most important qualities for a sexual partner. Even after marriage, some women valued tenderness and romance over sex in their daily life (Ho, 2007a).

Prevalence of Sexual Problems in Hong Kong

In general, the prevalence of sexual problems is high among both men and women in Hong Kong (J. T. F. Lau, Kim, & Tsui, 2005). Ng (1998), an influential sex therapy-trained physician, reported that approximately 20% of the clinical cases seen in his large general practice complained about sexual problems (Ng, 1998). Vaginismus, dyspareunia, and anorgasmia were the most frequent complaints for women, and erectile dysfunction and premature ejaculation were the most commonly reported male sexual problems (Ng, 1998). However, population based surveys have found even higher estimates of sexual dysfunction. A large scale survey of the prevalence of sexual problems in Hong Kong (J. T. F. Lau et al., 2005) reported that 50.9% of male and 54% of female respondents experienced sexual problems. The study analyzed data obtained from 1,516 men and 3,126 women. Approximately 50% of the respondents were dissatisfied with their sexual life. For men, the prevalence of sexual problems ranged from 3.4% (pain) to 29.7% (premature orgasm). For women, the prevalence of sexual problems ranged from 6.9% (anxiety) to 24.7% (lack of interest). The study also reported that the prevalence of erectile problems and lubrication problems was 9.6% and 23.6%, respectively. A more recent survey on female sexual function conducted by the Hong Kong Association of Sexuality Educators, Researchers and Therapists (2007) reported that 14.9% of Hong Kong women encountered difficulty in having vaginal penetration during intercourse.

In the study by J. T. F. Lau et al. (2005), more men (24%) than women (6%) regarded sex as being important to them. The gender difference regarding the perceived importance of sex may reflect that the traditional, male-dominant Chinese culture is repressive toward sexual pleasure-seeking in women but is less so regarding men (J. T. F. Lau et al., 2005). Though more men than women regarded sex as being important, the absolute percentage of men perceiving sex to be important was relatively small. Lau et al. (2005) concluded that the conservative social climate may not be conducive for discussion or promotion of sexual health in Hong Kong.

Approaches to Treatment

Chinese medical perspectives are affected by Taoism, which holds that humans should live in harmony with nature (Reid, 1989). Harmony is achieved by balancing the two opposing forces of Yin and Yang. Illness is the inevitable result when the forces of Yin and Yang are not balanced. From a Chinese herbalist perspective, sexual disorders are regarded as a form of weakness in kidney function (Y. L. Lau, 2005) and expressions like "Weakened Kidney" (腎虛 ShenShu) and "Withering of Yang" (陽痿 YangWei) are used to describe sexual dysfunction and low sexual interest. The kidney here does not just refer to the two real kidneys but more to the invisible energy or "chi" of the kidney (腎氣 ShenChi; Y. L. Lau, 2005). Thus, when there is sexual dysfunction, Chinese herbalists try to adjust the chi of the kidney (Y. L. Lau, 2005), since they believe that herbal medicine can enhance sexual desire or cure infertility.

Sex therapy is a newly developing and much needed profession in Hong Kong. A new sex counseling service was introduced by the Family Planning Association of Hong Kong (FPAHK) in 2003. By July 2004, appointments were already booked through to the end of the year, which meant that there was a 5-month waiting list (FPAHK, 2004). In 2004, the first Sex Therapy Certification Course, organized by the Hong Kong Association of Sexuality Educators, Researchers and Therapists, together with the Polytechnic University and the Florida Postgraduate Sex Therapy Training Institute, was held in Hong Kong. Two other similar courses were held in 2006 and 2008. Approximately 90 sex therapists have been trained through this certificate course[1] which focused on cognitive-behavioral therapies that were adapted from Masters and Johnson (1970), and Kaplan (1974).

So and Cheung (2005) published a comprehensive review on the applicability of sex therapy with Chinese couples. According to these authors, modifications need to be made to the core elements of the treatment process, namely education, stimulus control, cognitive restructuring, sensate focus, and communication training with special attention paid to the traditional Chinese Taoist concept of sex or folk beliefs, living environment, pace of work, and also the gender relationships inherent in the Chinese culture. Sexual myths and misconceptions based on folk beliefs can be effectively challenged by providing authoritative medical evidence. So and Cheung cited the example of reinterpreting the Taoist belief regarding conservation of semen by showing that ejaculation is actually essential for health. Stimulus control, which is the ability to have a pleasant and relaxing environment and state of mind for sex is problematic for the Chinese couple. In rural areas, privacy is difficult as it is in modern cities such as Hong Kong where space is at a premium. Many couples share the same room or even the same bed with children. Chinese women see sex as a duty to be performed, so sex is likely to be one more chore for them. A skilled therapist needs to be aware of these practical and emotional hurdles. Sensate focus exercises challenge the belief that sex is for procreation not pleasure and sex therapy exercises which require the active participation of both partners challenge the traditional gendered notion that men are active and women should be passive during sex. Since open communication about sex is rare in Chinese couples, communication exercises should focus on nonsexual topics first, and when there is more comfort and reciprocity, sexual topics can be broached. According to So and Cheung, with these modifications, cognitive therapy with behavioral assignments should be quite effective for treating Chinese clients because they expect the therapy process to be directive and authoritarian.

So and Cheung's (2005) review has provided a good resource for sex therapists when treating Chinese couples. Annon's permission, limited information, specific suggestions, and intensive therapy model (PLISSIT; 1976) can also be quite useful when applying Western sex therapy to Chinese couples. Some of the difficulties raised by So and Cheung (2005) can be resolved by adopting the PLISSIT model of sex counseling. For instance, by using this model, we can first educate our female clients that they have permission to be sexual and to enjoy sexual pleasure. Then, if we find that their sexual knowledge is very limited, we can share with them additional information about how to be sexual and how to attain sexual pleasure. We can then give them specific suggestions on how to tackle their sexual problems, followed by intensive therapy such as dilator exercises for women with vaginismus.

Extended Case Discussion

The two cases to be discussed in this chapter illustrate the effectiveness of cognitive-behavioral sex therapy for Chinese women experiencing difficulties with vaginal penetration. The two women, Ric, 39 years old, and Michelle, 40 years old, were research participants in the first author's doctoral research (H. N. Ng, 2010). A total of 21 women received treatment for sexual problems and were interviewed. The study was an exploration of how cultural elements interact with other factors, including familial and relationship dynamics as well as sexual attitudes, in causing sexual difficulties. The case descriptions are based on the women's recall of the treatment process.

Ric: Case background

Ric, 39 years old, was born in Hong Kong and worked as an accountant. She had been married for 10 years and during that time she and her husband had never consummated their marriage due to her fear of vaginal penetration. Her husband, Liu, 40 years old, was also an accountant and the couple worked together. Ric attributed her sexual difficulty to the beliefs about sex conveyed to her by her mother since childhood. She felt that her mother's constant reminders not to engage in sexual intercourse when she was a child had "locked" her vagina. Ric had come to believe that sex was something that was improper and indecent and when she married, this belief endured. Her mother's attitude, however, changed dramatically following Ric's marriage, as she then exhorted her daughter to have sex. To Ric, it felt as if her mother believed that the vagina was a switch that could be turned on or off.

Liu felt that his wife was outdated in her views toward sex and cruelly joked that her womb might be full of spider webs since it was a place that had never been visited. Ric believed that having sexual intercourse was a basic responsibility of a wife and she felt guilty about not being able to fulfill this responsibility within her marriage. She also thought that she would face the same issues if she started a relationship with another man or would have to face life alone after divorce.

Experience of the Sexual Difficulty. Ric revealed that she did not know how painful penetration would be, but she feared that it would be very painful and therefore she involuntarily withdrew her body when her husband tried to penetrate her. She said,

> Usually I can cooperate in the caressing process and my vagina wall also gets wet, but when he wanted to move further to enter, I would immediately wake up and the vagina wall dried up immediately. Then, you would just withdraw naturally.

The anticipation of pain was enough to make her scream during attempts at penetration. Ric remembered her mother's warnings before her marriage that sexual intercourse was very painful and that if she did it with someone who was not her husband, she would be an indecent and dirty woman and her face would "carry less light" (i.e., she would feel ashamed). During her dating days, if she stayed overnight at her boyfriend's house, her mother would call to warn her not to engage in sexual intercourse. When she was registered as married but was waiting for the Chinese wedding banquet to be held, her mother would still warn her not to have sexual intercourse before the ceremony. She therefore regarded herself as truly married only after the wedding banquet. She described her feelings after marriage:

> It's like there is a lock there [in the vagina]. She [Mother] did not understand. She [Mother] just thinks that it's like an on and off switch. Before marriage, it's off, once after marriage, it should be on, but it's not like that at all.

It seemed likely that her mother's sexual attitude had affected Ric's sexual response and explained at least in part why she was unable to adjust to the new sexual scripts for married women after having been sexually suppressed for so long. However, the persistence of her difficulty was also affected by her interaction with her husband Liu.

Ric's Interaction with Her Husband. Both Ric and Liu did not think about having a child at the beginning of their marriage as Liu was very busy with his work and always came home late at night. Ric said they were usually too tired to attempt sexual intercourse. However, though they did not have sexual intercourse, they did engage in other sexual activities, such as rubbing outside the vagina to attain mutual orgasm. However, after about 8 years into their marriage, when their financial status became more stable, Liu very much wanted to have children to secure their assets and continue the family line. He had repeatedly warned Ric that if they could not solve their sexual difficulty, they would need to divorce. The seriousness of this latest warning was the impetus for Ric to seek help.

Help Seeking and the Treatment Process. Liu had threatened divorce many times during the marriage when he felt frustrated by the lack of sexual intercourse. Ric tried to seek professional help in the third year of her marriage. She learned from a TV program that there were sex therapists in Hong Kong. She then searched on the Internet, but she was reluctant to contact any sex therapist as she did not know whether their services were intended for men or women. It was another 2 years before Ric read a newspaper article about a Christian nongovernmental organization (NGO), which mentioned treatment for female sexual dysfunction. Ric attended two sessions of sex counseling with this organization before dropping out because she felt that the counselor simply provided general sexual information that she already knew from newspapers and books. She later sought help from a psychiatrist who gave her medication, which was supposed to help her feel more relaxed during attempts at sexual intercourse. But she reported that after taking the medicine, she was hypervigilant and unable to have any sexual interaction with Liu. The medicine also made it hard for Ric to fall asleep at night. Another thing Ric tried was drinking wine to see if she could allow penetration if she was intoxicated. But after drinking an entire bottle of red wine, she felt sick and had chills, preventing any attempt to have sexual intercourse.

A year later, now 8 years into her marriage, and following pressure from her husband, Ric contacted a female author who had written many books related to love and sex. The author suggested that she contact a different NGO, which she did. Ric reported that the major progress she made in therapy at this NGO was that she was able to look at her husband's penis. Before the therapy, she said she never dared to look at it. She was also averse to seeing her own genitals and could not even look at illustrations of the anatomy of the female reproductive organs. Ric always turned the light off during sexual interactions with her husband. After five sessions of therapy, she was less sexually anxious and able to look at her husband's penis and watch erotic scenes in films.

The counselor at the NGO transferred Ric to a private physician (also a trained sex therapist) to have a physical examination and further sex therapy. The physician was able to insert a finger into Ric's vagina during a pelvic examination, which reassured her that the structure of her vagina was normal. The physician then showed Ric how to insert the smallest dilator inside her vagina and she was able to successfully do this in the first session. She was then asked to practice inserting the dilator five times each day at home; when she felt comfortable and confident with one size of dilator, she was told to proceed with the next bigger size. Over five sessions of treatment, spaced 2 weeks apart, Ric was able to insert three different sizes of dilator. In the final session, the physician asked Ric to invite her husband to attend, but Liu declined as he was too embarrassed. Typically, in this last session, the physician would instruct the husband how to hold his body in position above the wife's body. The wife would be the one to control the entrance and movement of the penis. The physician would teach the husband to follow the wife's instructions during attempts at sexual intercourse at home, with the purpose being to allow the wife to feel in control. She could guide her husband's penis into her vagina just as she had done with the dilators. Although Liu did not come to the final session, Ric and Liu successfully had sexual intercourse six to eight times in a 2-week period, resulting in Ric's pregnancy; their child is now 2 years old. However, since conceiving their child, Ric and Liu have not had sexual intercourse.

It is interesting to note that after Ric gave birth, she did not want to have coitus again as she had not found it enjoyable. She regarded coitus as a means to conceive and once she had a child, she no longer wanted to engage in intercourse. Despite finding intercourse pleasurable, Liu kept his promise to his wife that he would not request intercourse after they had a child. Despite the prevailing view of the subordinate Chinese wife, Ric was able to negotiate sex that was pleasurable to her. She and Liu continued to express their sexual desires through activities other than intercourse.

Michelle: Case background

Michelle, 38 years old, worked as a clerk and had been married for 9 years at the time of the interview. Her husband, Ray, was 43 years old and was employed as a sales manager. At the beginning of their marriage, Michelle did not think there was an urgent need to have sexual intercourse as she did not want to have a child. However, when she witnessed her mother-in-law become ill, she realized that it might be beneficial to have a child to take care of her when she got old. She then felt it was necessary to seek help in order to get pregnant. This was 7 years into her marriage. She and her husband had never had sexual intercourse during this first 7 years.

Michelle believed that it was very important for her to keep her virginity before marriage as she accepted that chastity was of crucial importance for women. Michelle said she was affected by the traditional Chinese beliefs that she had learned whilst living on the mainland of China before emigrating to Hong Kong at age 18. In discussing her belief in the importance of virginity before marriage, she stated:

> I learned about this idea since I was little, women should keep their chastity, we Chinese are very traditional, this is a traditional Chinese thoughts education, maybe I was more affected by the mainland teaching, since I only came to Hong Kong when I was nearing the end of secondary school, I heard about the three words *Shou Fu Dao* (守婦道; i.e., good conduct for a woman usually means maintaining virginity and loyalty in marriage) when I was on the mainland. Being a virgin before marriage means I am a woman of integrity and I have also followed the teaching of being *Shou Fu Dao* (守婦道).

Experience of the Sexual Difficulty. Michelle experienced pain when she tried to have sexual intercourse: "It's just as painful as putting a knife inside!" For so many years a gatekeeper to her vagina, it was understandable that she would withdraw her body and resist having sexual intercourse when she did not think of sexual intercourse as involving the expression of intimacy or pleasure. The couple used mutual masturbation to satisfy their sexual desires and felt that their sexual lives were quite satisfactory except for the lack of vaginal penetration.

Michelle's Interaction with Her Husband. When observing his wife's distress, Ray did not insist on having sexual intercourse. Michelle did not appreciate her husband's understanding, however, until she visited a gynecologist who told her that her husband had been kind to her, having accommodated her resistance to penetration for so many years. Interestingly, however, instead of gratitude, Michelle felt that Ray had contributed to the problem. She thought that if Ray had shown some anger or frustration about their difficulties, she would have been more motivated to solve their sexual problems. Because he was so accepting of the problem, she did not feel it was an issue requiring immediate action.

Help Seeking Treatment Process. Michelle only sought help when she felt it was time to have children. She was not motivated to have sexual intercourse for her own pleasure or that of her husband. Unlike Ric, she was not motivated to have intercourse because of a sense of marital duty, but because she wanted a child to look after her and her husband in their old age.

Michelle consulted a gynecologist in her hometown on the mainland, who suggested only that she relax during attempts at intercourse and also reminded her how many husbands might have already left the marriage after 7 years without intercourse. Later, while listening to a phone-in radio sex education program, Michelle heard about a family doctor who was trained in sex therapy. After 3 months in sex therapy, involving dilator insertion training exercises, she was able to have sexual intercourse. The couple have been engaging in intercourse on a frequent basis, but had yet to conceive at the time of the interview.

Discussion of the Two Cases

Effects of Cognitive-Behavioral Treatment

Both cases presented, Ric and Michelle, were seen by the same family doctor, who was trained in sex therapy, and who used a cognitive-behavioral approach, adapted from Masters and Johnson (1970) and Kaplan (1974). Ric reported that reframing her negative sexual attitudes toward sexual intercourse had enabled her to look at her husband's penis and to engage in sex with the lights on, but therapy had not reduced her fears about penetration. She claimed that it was only through the actual insertion of the dilator, following the doctor's instruction, that she realized her vagina could be penetrated without causing great pain. Thus, for Ric, cognitive reframing was important in overcoming her negative sexual attitudes, but the behavioral exercises were crucial to overcoming her fear of, and pain associated with, penetration.

The doctor assured Ric and Michelle that she would try her very best to help them to overcome their fear of penetration through dilator insertion exercises so that they might become pregnant. The doctor also told Ric and Michelle in the first session that they should be prepared to experience certain uncomfortable feelings and a certain degree of pain in the learning process. She referenced the saying "no pain, no gain," explaining that when participating in a race, people will experience great pain when they run very fast to the finishing line. She told Ric and Michelle that the pain would go away when their vaginal muscles got used to the penetration process. The doctor encouraged them to continue trying by telling the two women that through the continuous practice of sexual intercourse, it would be possible that they would someday enjoy an orgasm. However, for both these women, the promise of having a child was the incentive for treatment.

This coitus-oriented approach was very effective for Ric and Michelle in terms of enabling them to have sexual intercourse, but it did not help them to enjoy sex. Pleasure was not the outcome sought by these two women. The most powerful motivation for them was to preserve their marriage and to have children. Of course, sex therapy can also be used to help women become more open-minded in accepting different views regarding sexual practices and pleasure. The Chinese sexuality notion of sex for health and pleasure (evident before the Song Dynasty) is only one of the cultural resources for reference. Western research on how sexual interaction can benefit our health might also be useful in motivating men and women toward change (Jannini, Fisher, Bitzer, & McMahon, 2009).

Effects of Learned Sexual Attitudes

From Ric's and Michelle's reports, their husbands did make requests for sexual intercourse before marriage but these were rejected. They waited and expected that they would be able to have sexual intercourse once they were married. It seems that both women thought that their husbands had the right to ask them to have sexual intercourse in marriage and also perceived that intercourse was mainly for reproduction and fulfilling their husbands' sexual desire. However, Ric and Michelle had difficulty making the transition from being "good" and "chaste" to being sexual women. As such, it could be proposed that their sexual self-esteem was not well developed and they likely did not have a well-defined sense of their sexual selves. This is likely true of many Chinese women.

According to Zeanah and Schwartz (1996), components of sexual self-esteem include five dimensions: (a) skill/experience (i.e. evaluation of one's ability to please or be pleased by a sexual partner); (b) attractiveness (i.e. evaluation of one's sexual attractiveness); (c) control (i.e., evaluation of one's ability to control one's sexual thoughts, feelings, and behaviors); (d) moral judgment (i.e. evaluation of the congruence of one's sexual thoughts and feelings with one's moral standards); and (e) adaptiveness (i.e., evaluation of the compatibility of one's sexuality with other life goals) (Lemieux & Byers, 2008, p. 128). These dimensions can serve as a framework for us to examine how Ric and Michelle's sexual selves might have been affected by their learned sexual attitudes. It appears that control, moral judgment, and adaptiveness are the most relevant dimensions for Ric and Michelle, while experience and attractiveness are the dimensions that are lacking. This leaves Ric and Michelle with an incomplete sense of their own sexuality, although their sexual identity is compatible with their morality and with their need for control. Ric and Michelle grew up believing that they must control their sexual experiences. This control extended into their marriage. Neither woman was ready to have or interested in having intercourse after they were married. Pain or the anticipation of pain was the key factor in terms of delaying intercourse. Both of these women decided when, in the course of their marriage, they wanted to have intercourse (although Ric did experience some pressure from her husband).

The "adaptiveness" dimension was also very relevant in these cases. Prior to the decision to have children, sexual intercourse had no adaptive function for Michelle. Ric felt that having intercourse was the duty of a good wife and this explained her attempts to resolve her sexual difficulties earlier in her marriage. For both women, the wish to have a child gave sexual intercourse an adaptive function in their lives and a reason to seek help (sex therapy). Regarding sex as a means to conceive, rather than as an expression of intimacy or an experience of pleasure, may also have functioned as a way to achieve congruence between their sexual behavior and the moral standards with which they had been raised (and which were still influencing them). While they once had control over their sex lives (prior to marriage, and earlier in their marriages), Ric and Michelle had lost that control because when they wanted to have intercourse, they were unable to do so. Sex therapy helped them regain control. Indeed, Ric continued to exercise control after conceiving a child, refusing to have sexual intercourse because it was not pleasurable for her.

Importance of the Partner and the Marital Context

In Hong Kong the cultural contradictions toward sexual intercourse as being prohibited before marriage, yet encouraged in marriage to fulfill a husband's needs, have created conflicting expectations which can contribute to sexual difficulties. This was the case for Ric and Michelle, who were taught that they must be the gatekeepers of their virginity and were discouraged from exploring their sexuality. The radical change that is expected of women, from a girl who safeguards her virginity, to a wife who can readily engage in penetrative sex, partly accounts for their difficulty in adapting to marital sexual life.

These two women's lack of sexual feelings toward their husbands and their husbands' lack of sexual experience could also have contributed to their sexual difficulties. Ric and Michelle did not find their husbands sexually attractive when compared to the erotic or passionate experiences portrayed in films and romance novels. Neither Liu nor Ray had any sexual experience prior to marriage. It is therefore possible that their lack of sexual skill and sexual naïveté contributed to their inability to have penetrative sex. The duration of the sexual problems for both Ric and Michelle may also be in part related to their husbands' reactions (little pressure to have coitus) and to the fact that both couples could experience sexual pleasure without intercourse. Although neither of these clients' husbands participated in treatment, we would recommend that therapists pay attention to the role of sexual attraction and to the quality of the husbands' sexual skills.

Implications for Treatment

Various authors have argued that the treatment of vaginismus should not be coitus-oriented (Drenth, 1988; Kleinplatz, 1998; Shaw, 1994). These authors believe that the treatment goal should not be necessarily penetration and should depend on the client's choice. For Ric and Michelle, their goal was very clear: they wanted to have a baby as soon as possible. They claimed that the dilator insertion exercises effectively reduced their fear of, and the pain associated with, penetration. After only four or five dilator insertion sessions, both of these women were able to have coitus. Ric felt that the social workers' counseling helped her changed her negative sexual attitudes but did not help her to have sexual intercourse. She felt a bit impatient with the counseling, feeling that it mainly tried to reframe her negative sexual attitudes. It is unlikely that sex therapy that was not coitus focused would have been welcomed by either woman.

Both Ric and Michelle did not want to have penetrative sex for pleasure: intercourse for them was a means to an end. This is very much in keeping with traditional Chinese values, as there is an emphasis on reproduction and duty rather than pleasure for women. The dilation exercises prescribed for Ric and Michelle did not involve an exploration of the pleasurable aspects of intercourse, and so it is not surprising that increased pleasure was not an outcome of therapy. Ric and Michelle were very goal-oriented and the dilation exercises were appropriate for their goals. Neither woman expressed a desire to have more enjoyment from sex nor from sexual intercourse; focusing on pleasure would not have addressed these clients' needs. Their husbands were in agreement with their wives' goals and viewed intercourse as a means to have a child.

In summary, when treating Chinese women experiencing difficulty having vaginal sex, we need to know about their views regarding the role of sexual intercourse in their marriage, about the importance of pleasure, and about the goal(s) of treatment. However, if Chinese men and especially women present with a wish to have (more) sexual pleasure one can turn to ancient Chinese texts for support and inspiration.

Effects of Cultural Influence

Nonnative treatment providers should keep in mind the diversity of traditional Chinese culture in shaping an individual's sexuality. There are rich resources in traditional Chinese culture that can help clients to cultivate more open and positive sexual attitudes. For instance, the belief that sex is an interaction of two cosmic forces, Yin and Yang, can help promote the positive aspects of sexuality, thus mitigating an individual's sinful or "dirty" feelings toward sexual intercourse.

It should also be noted that there is a vigorous cultural exchange between Western countries and Chinese societies such as Hong Kong and these exchanges have complex effects on women's sexuality. There is a constant and dynamic exchange between individuals and their cultural and social contexts. It is in this interchange that self-image and sexuality are shaped. Neither culture, nor the people that inhabit them are static. The changing context of people's lives, and their past and present experiences subjectively determine and shape their interpretation and perception of this ongoing culture exchange (Yip, 2005). Significant others such as family members and peers also all have a crucial influence on men and women's internalization and manifestation of the cultural values. It is important that therapists are knowledgeable not only about Western sex therapy techniques, but also about traditional Chinese beliefs, as the therapy itself will become part of the dynamic interplay between cultures.

Redefining Vaginismus

Women like Ric and Michelle who experience difficulty and pain with vaginal penetration are usually diagnosed as having a sexual dysfunction known as vaginismus, which is not a concept that is found in traditional Chinese descriptions of sexual dysfunctions; the term translates as *pain in sexual intercourse* or *vaginal spasm*. In the *Diagnostic and Statistical Manual of Mental Disorders* (DSM-IV-TR; American Psychiatric Association, 2000) vaginismus is defined as "a recurrent or persistent involuntary spasm of the musculature of the outer third of the vagina that interferes with sexual intercourse, causing marked distress or interpersonal difficulty. The contraction may range from mild, inducing some tightness and discomfort, to severe, preventing penetration" (p. 22). Basson et al. (2003) suggested redefining vaginismus as "persistent difficulties to allow vaginal entry of a penis, a finger, and/or any object, despite the woman's expressed wish to do so. There is variable involuntary pelvic muscle contraction, (phobic) avoidance and anticipation/fear/ experience of pain. Structural or other physical abnormalities must be ruled out/addressed" (p. 226). The main difference between Basson et al.'s definition and the DSM-IV-TR version is that Basson did not include the criterion of vaginal spasm; the presence of the vaginal spasm has in fact never been documented (Reissing, Binik, & Khalife, 1999). According to Binik (2010), vaginal spasm has long been considered the defining diagnostic characteristic of vaginismus. This diagnostic characteristic has also been preserved in the DSM-IV-TR. Binik (2010) pointed out that empirical research does not support this definition. Binik proposed that vaginismus like dyspareunia should be regarded as genito-pelvic pain or penetration disorder (Bink, 2010).

Ng (1999, 2000) also suggested a redefinition of vaginismus, highlighting the fear and resistance of vaginal penetration which captures more about the psychological and social causes of the difficulty. The new term suggested by Ng (1999) is *Neurotic resistance to vaginal penetration* or *vaginopenetration resistance nervosa*. He also suggested a redefinition of vaginismus as "the recurrent or persistent fear and resistance to vaginal penetration or to its attempts, with or without pain or involuntary contraction of the perineal muscles" (p. 11). Ng highlighted fear and resistance as the core symptoms of vaginismus because these are usually the immediate cause of the difficulty in having vaginal penetration for many Chinese women. Ng (1999) also claimed that vaginismus can be regarded as a culture-bound syndrome. He suggested that female sexuality is suppressed in both Eastern and Western cultures that place high value on female virginity. Given that women may be influenced by their culture to keep their vagina closed against any penile or foreign body penetration, Ng speculated that vaginismus could be viewed as a culturally determined symptom.

In fact, neither Ric nor Michelle met the diagnostic criteria for vaginismus, as defined by the DSM-IV-TR (American Psychiatric Association, 2000) or by Basson et al. (2003). One might instead view Ric's and Michelle's avoidance of penetration as an expression of their preferences for sexual activity at particular times or at particular stages of their relationship. Getting married did not mean that they were ready for, or wanted to have, vaginal penetration.

A diagnosis of vaginismus may result in women feeling abnormal, or suspecting that their genitals have a different structure than those of other women. Though there may also be some positive effects from obtaining a diagnosis, redefining vaginismus in cultural and social terms can help take away the blame from women and "depathologize" the condition (Nicolson, 1993; Wood, Koch, & Mansfield, 2006). As Nicholson (1993) pointed out, the self-concept of women with sexual difficulties is affected by certain taken-for-granted sexual knowledge. Ric and Michelle felt abnormal because they accepted the "taken-for-granted" ease of having sexual intercourse right after marriage. We propose that in cultures where sex is viewed as dirty or sinful or necessarily painful, and where women are supposed to be the gatekeepers of their highly valued virginity, it would be normal for women to experience difficulty in having sexual intercourse after marriage.

The Meaning of Sexual Intercourse in Marriage and Respecting Women's Sexual Agency

As Ric's and Michelle's stories demonstrate, it is not necessarily problematic when a married couple does not have sexual intercourse. Instead of pathologizing women, we might instead understand that the timing of sexual intercourse is a choice.

Because they did not have penetrative sexual intercourse, both Ric and Michelle felt that they had not yet had "real sex" with their husbands even though they satisfied each other's sexual needs by engaging in other sexual activity. Instead of viewing sexual intercourse as synonymous with sex, it may be better understood as a negotiated action motivated by reasons such as the maintenance of marriage, reproductive needs, the reduction of husbands' anger, or the fulfillment of husbands' sexual needs. These female clients did not regard sexual intercourse as a way to fulfill their own sexual needs. Rather, the social construction of sexual intercourse as a "dirty" behavior has strongly controlled women's intention to involve themselves in sexual behaviors. As sexuality is conditioned by cultural and social contexts and women are raised in an environment where the exploration of sexuality is discouraged, sexual intercourse cannot be considered "natural" or "the ultimate expression of intimacy" (Friedman, 1971; Jackson, 2003). If we consider Ric's and Michelle's fear of penetration as an expression of sexual preference ("I do not want to have sexual intercourse"), then we might consider their marriages as a reflection of a new femininity (and masculinity), in which couples are free to determine their own sexual expression. Ho's work on Hong Kong Chinese women shows how they are enmeshed in, but manage to escape from, culture bound definitions of female identity and sexuality (Ding & Ho, 2008; Ho 2007a, b, c, 2008 a, b; Pei, Ho, & Ng, 2007; Wang & Ho, 2007). That means, on the one hand, that women may compromise in marriage and have intercourse because their husband desires it. On the other hand, when they encounter sexual difficulties, they might also be able to negotiate with their husbands such that they don't have to have sexual intercourse. Thus, in order to understand women with sexual difficulties, we should also attend to women's expressions, both those they can articulate, and those they find difficult to articulate but might express through behavior, such as refusal to engage in sexual intercourse. Women's refusal of sexual intercourse may not cause serious repercussions, such as divorce. This might be due to the fact that both Hong Kong men and women do not regard sex or sexual intercourse as important for their relationship (So & Cheung, 2005).

Recommendations Regarding the Provision of Sex Education and the Prevention of Sexual Problems

Sex educators and sex therapists should pay more attention to the interactive, dynamic, and contextual aspects of female sexuality. Our understanding of female sexuality should not be based solely on psychological and medical findings—historical and cultural issues should also be considered (Ussher & Baker, 1993). Social and emotional factors, such as the quality of people's relationships and lives, are important in sexual satisfaction (Ho, 2008a). Public education that promotes positive attitudes about sex, but which does not stigmatize those who do not follow cultural or societal norms, is needed.

Within the diverse cultures of Hong Kong there are many belief systems that highlight the positive aspects of sexuality. Sex educators and therapists can play a role in ensuring that people are exposed to these diverse views about sexuality and are aware of their sexual choices. For instance, the Taoist–Confucianism system promotes sexual interaction as being good for the existence, change, and growth of all living organisms (Ng & Ma, 2004). This is also in line with some Christian theorists who believe that sex needs to be learned and can represent something human and intelligent rather than bestial (Solomon, 2006). Sex education programs should also promote the idea that sexual expression is also self-expression, and that sex is not antithetical to the self except when we choose to make it so (Solomon, 2006).

What we can learn from individual cases like those of Ric and Michelle is that we should refrain from judging women by their virginity and basing women's value on the status of their vagina. It is also high time to "decentralize" the role of sexual intercourse in marriage and leave more freedom for women and men to exercise their sexual agency. Sexual intercourse is but one way to express intimacy, self-expression, and healthy sexual enjoyment. We should respect people's freedom of choice in expressing their sexual selves.

Liu's and Ray's accommodating attitudes toward their wives' resistance to penile–vaginal penetration reminds us that some husbands can afford to maintain their marital relationship without having sexual intercourse, although in the male-dominant culture it is taken for granted that wives should "allow" husbands to have sexual intercourse after marriage. There are likely many false gender assumptions in every culture. It would benefit both women and men if there were more sex or relationship counseling services that reflect "gender-based practice" (Chan, 2006, 2009). This model of services would expand our understanding of sexual problems beyond assuming individual inadequacies to include consideration of the unequal social structure and false gender assumptions within which sexual relationships exist. The ultimate goal is to create an equal society where both genders can prosper (Chan, 2009).

Note

1. The first author received training in this program in 2006.

References

American Psychiatric Association. (2000). *Diagnostic and statistical manual of mental disorders* (4th ed., text rev.) Washington, DC: Author.

Annon, J. S. (1976). *The behavioral treatment of sexual problems: Brief therapy*, New York: Harper & Row.

Association for the Advancement of Feminism (AAF). (2005). *Hong Kong Females' Sexual Life Survey*. Hong Kong: Sociology Department, University of Hong Kong & AAF.

Basson, R., Leiblum, S., Brotto, L., Derogatis, L., Fourcroy, J., Fugl-Meyer, K., & Schultz, W. W. (2003). Definitions of women's sexual dysfunction reconsidered: Advocating expansion and revision. *Journal of Psychosomatic Obstetrics and Gynecology, 24*, 221–229.

Binik, Y. M. (2010). The DSM diagnostic criteria for vaginisimus. *Archives of Sexual Behavior, 39*(2), 278–291.

Binik, Y. M, Meana, M., Berkley, K., & Khalife, S. (1999). The sexual pain disorders: Is the pain sexual or is the sex painful? *Annual Review of Sex Research, 10*, 210–235.

Central Policy Unit (CPU). (2008). *Trends in family attitudes and values in Hong Kong*. Hong Kong: Author.

Chan, K. H. (2006). Men and social work. In L. C. Leung & K. W. Chan (Eds.), *Gender and social work: Theory and practice* (pp. 53–66). Hong Kong: Chinese University Press. (in Chinese)

Chan, K. H. (2009). Self-help groups for men in Hong Kong: Experiences and prospects. *International Social Work, 52*, 343–356.

Chan, A. K. W., & Wong, W. L. (Eds.). (2004). *Gendering Hong Kong*. Hong Kong: Oxford University Press.

Ding, Y., & Ho, P. S. Y. (2008). Beyond sex work: An analysis of *xiaojies*' understandings of work in the Pearl River Delta Area, China. In S. Jackson, J. Liu, & J. Woo (Eds.), *East Asian sexualities: Modernity, gender and new sexual cultures* (pp. 123–138). London: Zed Books.

Drenth, J. J. (1988) Vaginismus and the desire for a child. *Psychosomatic Obstetrics and Gynecology, 9*(2), 125–137.

FPAHK. (2004). *Statistics from sex education website.* Retrieved December 12, 2004, from http://www.famplan.org.hk

Friedman, L. J. (1971). *Virgin wives: A study of unconsummated marriages.* London: Tavistock.

Gulik, R. H. (1961). *Sexual life in ancient China: A preliminary survey of Chinese sex and society from ca. 1500 B.C. till 1644 A.D.* Leiden, the Netherlands: E. J. Brill.

Ho, P. S. Y. (2007a). Eternal mothers or flexible housewives? Middle-aged Chinese married women in Hong Kong. *Sex Roles, 57,* 249–265.

Ho, P. S. Y. (2007b). Desperate housewives: The case of Chinese si-nais in Hong Kong. *Journal of Women and Social Work, 22,* 255–270.

Ho. P. S. Y. (2007c). "Money in the private chamber" – Hong Kong Chinese women's way of planning for their retirement. *Affilia: Journal of Women and Social Work, 22,* 84–98.

Ho, P. S. Y. (2008a). Not so great expectations: Sex and housewives in Hong Kong. *Journal of Sex Research, 45,* 338–349.

Ho, P. S. Y. (2008b). Squaring the "charmed" circle: Normality and happiness of married women in Hong Kong. *Asian Journal of Women Studies, 14,* 30–58

Ho, P. S. Y., & Tsang, A. K. T. (2002). The things girls shouldn't see: Relocating the penis in sex education in Hong Kong. *Sex Education, 2,* 61–73.

Hong Kong Association of Sexuality Educators, Researchers and Therapists (HKASERT). (2007). Hong Kong females' sexual function: Hong Kong: Author. Retrieved from http://www.hkasert.org.hk/events/survey_results.pdf

Hong Kong Education Department, Curriculum Development Committee. (1986). *Guidelines on sex education in secondary schools.* Hong Kong: Author.

Jackson, S. (2003). Heterosexuality, heteronormativity and gender hierarchy: Some reflections on recent debates. In J. Weeks, J. Holland, & M. Waites (Eds.), *Sexualities and society: A reader* (pp. 69–83). Malden, MA: Polity Press.

Jannini, E. A, Fisher, W. A., Bitzer, J., & McMahon, C. G. (2009). Is sex just fun? How sexual activity improves health. *Journal of Sexual Medicine, 6,* 2640–2648.

Kaplan, H. S. (1974). *The new sex therapy.* New York: Brunner/Mazel.

Kershaw, A., & DeGolyer, D. (2006). *The status of women and girls in Hong Kong.* Hong Kong: The Human Foundation.

Kim J. H., Lau, J. T. F., & Cheuk, K. K. (2009). Sexlessness among married Chinese adults in Hong Kong: Prevalence and associated factors. *Journal of Sexual Medicine, 6,* 2997–3007.

Kleinplatz, P. J. (1998). Sex therapy for vaginismus: A review, critique, and humanistic alternative. *Journal of Humanistic Psychology, 38,* 41–81.

Lau, J. T. F., Kim, J. H., & Tsui, H-Y. (2005). Prevalence of male and female sexual problems, perceptions related to sex and association with quality of life in a Chinese population: A population-based study. *International Journal of Impotence Research, 17,* 294–505. doi:10.1038/sj.ijir.3901342

Lau, Y. L. (2005). *Chum Sheung York Chi Fei Sheung Bian* (尋常藥治非常病) [Common herbals curing abnormal diseases]. Hong Kong: Cheuk Si. (in Chinese)

Lemieux, S. R., & Byers, E. S. (2008). The sexual well-being of women who have experienced child sexual abuse. *Psychology of Women Quarterly*, 32, 126–144.

Leung, B. K. P. (1995). Women and social change: the impact of industrialization on women in Hong Kong. In V. Pearson & B. K. P. Leung (Eds.), *Women in Hong Kong* (pp. 224–236). Hong Kong: Oxford University Press.

Masters, W. H., & Johnson, V. E. (1970). *Human sexual inadequacy*. Boston, MA: Little Brown.

Ng, H. N. (2010). *The meaning of sexual intercourse: Personal accounts of Hong Kong Chinese married women who have experienced difficulty in vaginal penetrative sex* (Doctoral dissertation). University of Hong Kong.

Ng, M. L. (1998). *Ru he ke fu xing ji neng zhang ai*. [How to overcome sexual dysfunction]. Hong Kong: MingPao.

Ng, M. L. (1999). Vaginismus—A disease, symptom or culture bound syndrome? *Sexual and Marital Therapy*, 14, 9–13.

Ng, M. L. (2000). Towards a bio-psychosocial model of vaginismus: A response to Janice Hiller. *Sexual and Relationship Therapy*, 15, 91–92.

Ng, M. L., & Ma, J. L. C. (2004). Hong Kong. In R. T. Francoeur & Noonan, R. J. (Eds.), *The international encyclopedia of sexuality* (Vol. 4, pp. 489–502). New York: Continuum.

Nicolson, P. (1993). Public values and private beliefs: Why do women refer themselves to sex therapy? In J. M. Ussher & C. D. Baker (Eds.), *Psychological perspectives on sexual problems: New directions in theory and practice*. (pp. 56–78). New York: Routledge.

Pei, Y., Ho, S. Y., & Ng, M. L. (2007). Studies on women's sexuality in China since 1980: A critical review. *Journal of Sex Research*, 44, 202–212.

Pimpaneau, J. (2003). Eroticism in ancient China. In F. M. Bertholet (Ed.), *Gardens of pleasure: Eroticism and art in China* (pp. 11–47). Munich, Germany: Prestel.

Reid, D. (1989). *The Tao of health, sex and longevity: A modern practical approach to the ancient way*. London: Simon & Schuster.

Reissing, E. D., Binik, Y., & Khalife, S. (1999). Does vaginismus exist? A critical review of the literature. *Journal of Nervous and Mental Disease*, 187, 261–274.

Shaw, J. (1994). Treatment of primary vaginismus: A new perspective. *Journal of Sex and Marital Therapy*, 20, 46–55.

So, H. W., & Cheung, F. M. (2005). Review of Chinese sex attitudes and applicability of sex therapy for Chinese couples with sexual dysfunction. *Journal of Sex Research*, 42, 93–101.

Solomon, R. C. (2006). *About Love: Reinventing romance for our times* (2nd. ed.). Cambridge, MA: Hackett.

Tsang, A. K. T. (1987). Sexuality: the Chinese and the Judeo-Christian traditions in Hong Kong. *Bulletin of the Hong Kong Psychological Society* (19), 19–28.

Ussher, J. M., & Baker, C. D. (Eds.). (1993). *Psychological perspectives on sexual problems: New directions in theory and practice*. New York: Routledge.

Wang, X. Y., & Ho, P. S. Y. (2007). My sassy girl: A qualitative study of women's aggression in dating relationships in Beijing. *Journal of Interpersonal Violence, 22,* 623–638.

Wijma, B., Engman, M., & Wijma, K. (2007). A model for critical review of literature with vaginismus as an example. *Journal of Psychosomatic Obstetrics & Gynecology, 28,* 21–36.

Wood, J. M., Koch, P. B., & Mansfield, P. K. (2006). Women's sexual desire: A feminist critique. *Journal of Sex Research, 43,* 236–244.

Yan, E., Man-Sze Wu, A., Ho, P., & Pearson, V. (2011). Older Chinese men and women's experiences and understanding of sexuality. *Culture, Health & Sexuality, 13,* 983–999.

Yip, K. S. (2005). A dynamic Asian response to globalization in cross-cultural social work. *International Social Work, 48,* 593–607

Zeanah, P. D., & Schwartz, J. C. (1996). Reliability and validity of the Sexual Self-esteem Inventory-Women. *Assessment, 3,* 1–15.

Editors Introduction to Chapter 10
Russia

It is not surprising that the land that gave us Tolstoy, Dostoyevsksy, and Chekhov, Tchaikovsky, and Rachmaninoff, as well as Pavlova, Nureyev, and Baryshnikov, would give us a romantic view of sexuality. It is in this chapter, and no other, that the idea of love is discussed in connection with sex. Fate also makes an appearance in the discussion of the existence of a hard-wired sexual constitution. According to some Russian sexologists, all men and women have a sexual constitution, which is a relatively fixed and stable level of sexual desire (strong, medium, or weak). If a person happens to marry someone with a different sexual constitution, therapy is geared toward helping that person, or the couple, understand that this is "just the way it is." This stands in stark contrast to the time and energy many American couples devote to trying to change or increase the level of sexual desire in the partner with less desire. While the notion of a sexual constitution may be foreign to many readers, challenging couples to find happiness together despite sexual differences is a treatment option that may be revisited upon reading this chapter.

Sexual dysfunctions in Russia are, however, often the focus of aggressive and multidisciplinary treatment including talk therapy, medication, and mechanical devices. The latter treatment is primarily geared toward resolving male sexual dysfunction, specifically erectile dysfunction. Awareness of the importance of helping women experience orgasm is a more recent phenomenon in Russian sex therapy and in Russian culture.

The authors of this chapter interviewed eight sex therapists (physicians and psychologists), reviewed the vast treatment literature, and present two case studies in order to show a view of Russian sexuality and sex therapy with the history, politics, culture, and religion of the country providing the contextual but ever changing backdrop.

10

SEXUAL THERAPY IN RUSSIA
Pleasure and Gender in a New Professional Field

Anna Temkina, Anna Rotkirch, and Elina Haavio-Mannila

Introduction

Sexual morality and behavior have changed radically in Russia during the last two decades. In the Soviet period, there was strict public control over sexual information and a great deal of ignorance and discrimination regarding sexual matters. Today, Russia is characterized by a myriad of often conflicting views on sex and sexual morality. The media are very outspoken on sexual matters and often promote a liberal and hedonistic view of sexuality. On the other hand, the Russian Orthodox Church opposes sex education, abortion, and the rights of sexual minorities. The threshold to seek professional advice for sexual problems is lower today, while the forms of therapy, treatment, and advice offered to clients vary widely.

In this chapter, we first give an overview of the changes that have occurred in Russian sexual culture since the fall of the Soviet Union. We then turn to Russian sexual therapy and discuss two clinical cases, the first an example of problems with female orgasm in a young couple, the second an example of male erection problems in a middle-aged couple. We are especially interested in how gender equality and sexual pleasure are perceived in Russian sex therapy. The overview relies on previous research, including autobiographies and in-depth interviews on sexual issues conducted between 1996 and 2004 and two representative surveys in St. Petersburg conducted in 1996 and 2004. Parts of the chapter are based on interviews with eight experts that were conducted in 2009 and 2010 with practicing sexologists in different parts of Russia.[1]

ANNA TEMKINA, ANNA ROTKIRCH, AND ELINA HAAVIO-MANNILA

Historical Aspects of Russian Sexual Culture

Sexual Behaviors

During most of the Soviet period there was an almost phobic avoidance of the topic of sex (Kon, 1995). After the October Revolution in 1917 and into the early 1920s, the Bolshevik rulers briefly challenged traditional marital and familial relationships when they experimented with free love and communal living. This era was short-lived and under the leadership of Josef Stalin (from the late 1920s to the early 1950s), Soviet ideology sanctioned heterosexual sex solely within the confines of marriage. The higher value of working for the common good was touted over the pursuit of individual pleasure, further supporting the constraints on sexual behavior and knowledge about sexuality. For instance, male homosexuality was criminalized because it was deemed antisocial. These values remained virtually unchanged during the period after Stalinism. Soviet Russia was insulated from the symbolic and ideological changes of the 1960s that in Western countries were known as the sexual revolution. Public discussion of sexuality and reproductive health, consumption of erotica and pornography, sex research, and sex education were allowed only in the late 1980s. This change arrived with glasnost, the policy of transparency that characterized the perestroika era which was initiated by Mikhail Gorbachev in 1985 and ended with the collapse of the Soviet Union in 1991 (Goldman, 1993; Kon, 1995; Stites, 1985).

Although governmental ideology restricting sex remained throughout the Soviet era, there were important shifts in sexual behavior. Soviet legislation promoted equality between the sexes in all spheres of life and made it easy to both marry and divorce. The state provided free or inexpensive education, housing, health care, and child care; abortion was legalized in 1920. This was a fatal blow to the traditional, patriarchal Russian family. Wars, famine, migration, and political repression further destabilized traditional ways of life from the 1920s to the 1940s. Russian women entered the labor force earlier than in most other European countries and increased their professional and economic independence. Women were able to control the numbers of children they had (typically by induced abortion), the birth rate fell dramatically, reaching an average of two children per woman in the 1960s and only one child in the 1990s (Lapidus, 1978; Rotkirch, 2000; Zakharov, 2008).

After the Second World War, premarital and extramarital sex, as well as divorce, became more common. Urbanization and industrialization went hand in hand with earlier onset of sexual activity, more sexual partners, and more liberal attitudes. Especially during the comparatively prosperous times of late socialism in the 1970s and 1980s, many Soviet citizens enjoyed recreational sex (Haavio-Mannila and Rotkirch 2010).

Sexual behavior in Russia in many ways resembles Western countries with a time lag of 10 to 20 years. For instance, Finns in the 1970s and Russians in the 1990s reported similar ages of first intercourse and the same amount of variability in positions used in intercourse (Rotkirch & Haavio-Mannila, 2000). Russian sexuality is also characterized by many partners, extramarital relations, and by double morality or different standards for men and women (Haavio-Mannila and Kontula 2003). In St. Petersburg in 1996, one in two men and more than one in four women living in a sexual relationship reported having other sexual relationships in addition to their main one. A majority of these relations were casual, but 9% of the men and 4% of the women reported permanent sexual relations in addition to those in their main relationship. Men were much more ready to accept the infidelity of a husband than that of a wife (Rotkirch & Haavio-Mannila, 2000).

Sexual culture in postcommunist Russia has undergone rapid changes. During the last two decades, access to sexual information and reliable contraceptives has greatly improved. Sexual behavior has become increasingly manifold, as manifested in the use of different sexual techniques and the numbers of lifetime partners. Homosexuality is no longer criminalized and homosexual subcultures proliferate in the big cities. However, hostility and discrimination toward homosexuals remains, especially in smaller urban centers and rural areas of Russia. Sexuality is also marked by geographic and socioeconomic divisions. The spread of poverty and social inequality have contributed to an increase in risky sexual behavior and sexually transmitted diseases (Regushevskaya, Dubikaytis, Nikula, Kuznetsova, & Hemminki, 2008). The growing affinity between the rulers of the Russian Federation and the Russian Orthodox Church has also affected sexual culture. The Orthodox Church supports a very strict sexual morality and condemns extramarital sex, abortion, and homosexuality.

Contraception

The lack of adequate contraception in Soviet Russia negatively affected women's health and sexual pleasure. Since the fall of the Soviet Union, Russian contraceptive culture has shifted from a high reliance on induced abortion to greater use of condoms. However, oral contraception is less popular than in many other European countries and unreliable methods are still widely used (Gerber & Berman, 2008; Kontula, 2004; Perelman & McKee, 2009; Regushevskaya, Dubikaytis, Nikula, Kuznetsova, & Hemminki, 2009). In 2004, three in four women in St. Petersburg had used some contraception. The most commonly used method was the male condom, but other popular methods were coitus interruptus, the rhythm method, and douching (Kesseli et al., 2005).

Although abortions have become less common, rates are still higher than in many other European countries. In 2004, 55% of women of reproductive age living in St. Petersburg reported having had at least one abortion, compared to 36% of Estonian women, despite the fact that Estonia and Russia share the same Soviet legacy. The number of abortions a woman in St. Petersburg reported was typically one or two, but 6% had had at least five abortions. Women who had married several times and had many children were most likely to have undergone several abortions (Haavio-Mannila, 2007).

Sex Education

Sexual issues are discussed more openly than was once the case, both in public and at home. In 1996 as many as 57% of women reported that they had not received any information about sexual matters when growing up, and only one in 10 women thought the amount of sexual information received from their parents had been sufficient. By 2004, correspondingly, 42% had received no information at all, and one in five said they had received sufficient sex information during childhood.

A similar improvement can be seen in school sex education. In 1996, about 70% of the respondents had not received any sex education at school but this had dropped to 50% in 2004. However, sex education within the school system remains woefully inadequate, with only 8% of respondents reporting a sufficient level of sex education. As a consequence, peer groups and haphazard information from diverse sources (e.g., television, religious groups, leaflets, books, Internet) shape the beliefs of young people, and the general level of sexual knowledge in Russia remains low (Kon, 2005; Snarskaya, 2009). As our first case description will illustrate, many young couples find it embarrassing to discuss sexuality and contraception with their partner (Meilakhs, 2008; Temkina, 2008).

The sex therapists we interviewed were critical of current approaches to sex education and family planning.[2] Some of the criticism centered on religious efforts that are in opposition to contraception and sex education. As one therapist expressed it:

> Yes there is, constantly, propaganda against family planning. They come and leave booklets called *Abortion Is Death* or *Diary of an Unborn Child*. There is a fight going on. The church is against contraceptives. I'm not against the ideal that sex belongs to marriage, but life is richer than that and can't be fit into one single Bible.

However, another sex therapist was critical of family planning programs, which he perceived to be representing Western commercial and amoral interests. The quotation below also illustrates the emphasis put on romantic and spiritual love that is still common in Russian culture, and apparently also among some providers of sex therapy.

> The family planning programs came to us from abroad and were related to the commercial activities of foundations. They include the exaggerated myth about AIDS and the myth about early sexual maturation. Children are taught not to love but to put on condoms. The best way to build a relationship is to know about moral and spiritual emotions, but in these programs there is not a single word about love. They talk about how to use contraceptives so as to not get infected by your partner. There are foreign brochures and booklets called *My friend the Condom* or *How to Avoid Infections*. They distribute condoms to prostitutes, which are then sold in drug stores. This whole business is without any interest for me. But it does much harm. Some make a living out of it, the teenagers are suffering, because they have been taught how to fuck but not how to love.

Other sexual therapists deplored the lack of deep emotions in public representations of sexuality. Thus, the attitudes varied substantially as to what kind of sexual education young people need.

Generational and Cultural Differences in Sexual Attitudes

There are marked generational differences in sexual attitudes and behaviors in present day Russia. Soviet people born in the 1920s and 1930s and growing up after the Second World War belong to a generation of forbidden and silenced sexual culture. The next generation, born in the 1940s and 1950s, experienced rapid behavioral changes and had fragmented access to sexual information. A minority of the Soviet population had consulted the so-called sexopathological services that were established during the 1970s (see below). The term *sexopathology* illustrates the way in which Soviet medicine equated sexual problems with pathological diseases (Kon, 1995; Rotkirch, 2000).

Women of the older Soviet generations were usually not satisfied with their sexual life. Many had never openly discussed their sexual experiences. During in-depth interviews middle class women used evasive terminology when referring to sexual acts. They described themselves as cold or frigid and deplored this state of affairs. Women were not supposed to make sexual advances and sex for many was a "shameful marital obligation," as a woman born in the 1930s described: "We were born in the Soviet times and thought that sex as such does not exist and it is shameful for a woman to …," she continued, not wanting to complete the sentence. Russian women also often interpret sexuality through the needs and desires of their male partners; according to one respondent, "The man is most important, I always adjust myself to him" (Temkina, 2008).

Soviet Russian men often told us how they suffered from lack of knowledge of the female body and of sexuality more generally. Men often feared the first intercourse as they did not always know what was supposed to happen. One couple had worried that their frequent intercourse as newlyweds was deviant and described their relief when 20 years later, during perestroika, the wife found a booklet about sex and realized that they had been "perfectly normal" (Rotkirch, 2003).

Sexual problems typical for the current Russian cultural context often arise in connection with infidelity, alcoholism, rape, and family violence. All of these are more frequent in Russia compared with most other European countries. Although alcoholism and family violence are now recognized as social problems, they are also often belittled or sidestepped. One sexologist we interviewed mentioned that several of his clients had suffered sexual violence in their youth. But another sexologist talked about marital violence only in passing, and seemed to imply that the woman was at least partly to blame for permitting violence: "Also women complain that their husband is fat and inattentive, that he may use violence. But if the woman's attitude to herself is such that one may be violent with her, then what kind of love is that?"

Changes in Russian sexuality are perhaps best typified by the transformation in attitudes toward female orgasm. In the older Soviet generations, there was little information about female orgasm and it was not typically seen as a prerequisite for satisfaction. As one woman stated through an in-depth interview, "It is more important for a woman how much attention the man gives her, his passion, caresses, and his degree of desire" (Temkina, 2008, p. 289). A woman's pleasure was seen to depend on her male partner. Women either thought they had been lucky and found a great lover, or they complained about men who were indifferent and selfish during intercourse. In younger generations, by contrast, it is more common to know about the female orgasm and how to achieve it. The previous romantic and male-centered view of sexuality has shifted toward an emphasis on pleasure and female activity. Russian women born after 1970 tend to see themselves as responsible for their sexual pleasure and orgasm and it has become accepted for women to take the initiative sexually (Temkina, 2008).

The availability of information and contraceptives is generally seen as a blessing. However, some people consider the new emphasis on pleasure and orgasm as a stressful obligation. The huge media focus on sexuality has also left many Russians longing for more emphasis on love and spirituality. Russian culture has always been proud of its philosophical and spiritual values and this applies to love and sexuality as well.

The national borders of Russian sexuality are blurred. Many emigrants from Russia now live in the United States, Israel, and the former Soviet republics, and many people from the former Soviet republics have moved to Russia. These migrants often have interesting reflections on Russian sexual culture. Western Europeans often perceive Russians as more traditional and conformist in their views on sexuality and gender (Chernetskaia, 2005; Watson, 1993). In contrast, in the southern post-Soviet republics, Russia is seen as a sexually liberal country with high gender equality. For instance, in Armenia premarital sexual relations for women were until very recently strongly condemned. Only today is female sexual activity, including female orgasm, recognized as existing, although it is linked to the woman's desire to satisfy her male partner. In another ex-Soviet republic, Tadzhikistan, premarital relations remain prohibited for women. Questions related to women's pleasure and orgasm are raised only in the context of marriage (Temkina, 2008). For this chapter we interviewed a sex therapist working in Kazan, the capital of the autonomous republic of Tatarstan in Russia. There, traditional patriarchal behaviors have recently grown in importance, including more instances of bride theft (the kidnapping of a woman which forces her to marry the abductor).

A wonderful illustration of the existing geographic disparity is provided by Colette Harris (2004) in her research on sexual and gender relations in Tajikistan. Harris tells about a Tajik man who after 3 years of marriage is finally told by Russian colleagues what to do to arouse his wife.

> One of the Russians explained what a man should do for his wife to enjoy sex.... [The husband] said that neither of them had known that a woman could enjoy sex.... This afternoon he came home and wanted to try out what he had learned. [The wife] became absolutely furious, accusing him of having taken a lover.... Then, a few days later she was talking with a Russian friend who explained that men discussed sex among themselves and that Russian men were much better informed than Tajiks. She realized that what her husband had told her was probably true and she went home and apologized for having misjudged him. Only then did she allow him to try what he had learnt and it was really great. (Harris, 2004, pp. 154–155)

Contemporary Sexual Discourse

Contemporary Russian public discourse is sensitive to questions of sexuality. It reflects a commercial and medical view of sexuality with pharmaceutical companies playing a prominent role. Sexual medical consultations have become more widespread and commercialized, and sexual experiences and problems are discussed on television talk shows. Famous sexologists such as Lev Shcheglov and the sociologist Igor Kon are asked for advice in the media and produce bestselling books (Kon, 1990, 1997a, 2002, 2005; Shcheglov, 1998, 2003). Various scientific, popular, and self-help books are translated from abroad and also written in Russia. The sex industry includes prostitution, striptease bars, gay clubs, pornographic products, Internet sites, and other sexual services. However, more neutral, pragmatic, and scientific approaches to sexuality remain scarce (Gessen 1995). There is also strong opposition to liberal views on sexuality, notably from the Orthodox Church and other religious groups, promoted through leaflets, actions, societies, and Internet sites.

Judging from popular medical discourse, male erection difficulties are the most common sexual problem. Women's orgasm problems are also often mentioned. There is a rapidly growing market for advice and help for sexual problems. Prescription drugs, special equipment, and specialist consultations are advertised in newspapers, radio, and TV and in drugstores. Take, for instance, this advertisement for Eli Lilly (manufacturers of the PDE5 drug Cialis) distributed in a Moscow drug store in 2009:

> Be confident, 95% of erection failure cases may be treated! Eli Lilly is ready to help. 40% of men over 40 years old suffer from erection problems. Return confidence in your power! Ask in the drugstore or turn to a doctor. Learn more at www.bud-uvere.ru. Or consult a specialist at ... 3636, the call is free.

On the Internet, you may find the following announcement. We quote it at length, because it is an interesting example of prevailing discourses on sex, health, and gender:

> There is currently an increase in the number of men in need of examination and treatment for sexual disorders such as erection failure, early (premature) ejaculation, and lack of libido or sexual desire. Until recently most sexual disorders were seen to have a psychological, functional origin. Sexual problems are almost always accompanied by neurosis, but in one case the neurosis may be the main cause of the disorder, in other cases its consequence. Views on the causes of the emergence of sexual dysfunctions have changed during recent years. About 80% of men's sexual problems have been shown to arise after illness in different organs and systems.

Therefore only a complex and individual approach makes it possible to diagnose and treat the different illnesses of men's sexual organs, as well as solve problems related to disturbances in sexual functioning.

It is really not easy to be a man in our times. You have to be the head of the family, that is, the breadwinner, in order to be respected and valued.... It is important not only to succeed socially, but also to maintain your health and an optimistic attitude to life.

Until they reach the age of 35, almost all men, notwithstanding their lifestyle, look rather attractive and do not experience health problems. After this age barrier has been crossed, many experience their first problems in intimate life. Here the advantage is on the side of those men who regularly undergo prophylactic examinations and carefully note even minor worrying changes in their well-being. (Andrological & Gynecological Clinic, Moscow, n.d.)[3]

The advertisement quoted above encourages men, especially those over 35 years old, to seek the new forms of sex therapy now available. Scientific authority ("80% of problems," "psychological, functional") is alluded to in a diffuse way and with no references. The advertisement promotes self-monitoring and early medical interventions. Interestingly, a man's sexual health is associated with psychological, medical, and social success. Having outlined the main changes in contemporary Russian sexual culture, let us now have a look at the field of sex therapy.

The Field of Professional Sexology

The roots of Russian sexology are found in Soviet sexopathology as established in the 1960s. Sexopathology views sexual problems as mainly a result of organic innate or acquired pathologies that require medical interventions. Medical education in sexology was under strong institutional and ideological control. One sexologist described the situation: "The Soviet Union was a repressive and totalitarian model which is why sexology appeared as sexopathology, it was allowed only within medicine."

The pioneering works in Russian medical sexology were published in the 1970s and include Svyadosh (1974), Vasilchenko (1977), and Isaev and Kagan (1979). However, access to these books and other sources on sexuality was restricted to specialists who consulted medical libraries. One sexual therapist remembered attending one of the very first lecture courses in sexology in Russia, held in Leningrad in 1977 at what is currently known as the Medical Academy of Postgraduate Studies and which established the first department of sexology in 1989. Igor Kon's pioneering *Introduction to Sexology* was also published in 1989, in a staggering edition of 250,000 copies, indicating the craving for reliable information during the perestroika era. Kon was also the author of a thorough overview (in English) of the first steps of Soviet sexology, which appeared in the *International Encyclopaedia of Sexuality* (Kon, 1997b, see also Kon, 2005).

After the fall of the Soviet Union in 1991, newly established non-governmental institutions were allowed to give lectures and organize seminars related to sexual therapy and education. The Russian Family Planning Association was founded in 1991 with support from the Russian Government and the International Planned Parenthood Federation. It began training medical professionals and founded three youth centers that provided sex education and psychological and sexual counseling (Kontula, 2004). These new organizations also incorporated psychology into Russian sexology. For instance, the Institute of Psychoanalysis opened in St. Petersburg and offered training, seminars, publications, and consultations (Temkina & Rotkirch, 1996). Neurolinguistic training, feminist therapy, and many other psychological therapies were introduced. New training programs and centers in sexual therapy also emerged within universities and high schools. Today, the most respected training institutes are the already mentioned Medical Academy of Postgraduate Studies in St Petersburg and the Federal Research Center for Medical Sexology in Moscow, which trains only medical doctors. Recently, formal sexological training has become available also to psychologists and teachers.[4]

The experts we interviewed illustrate this institutional and disciplinary diversity. They refer to their discipline as sex therapy but experts also included doctors-psychotherapists (5 respondents), a family psychotherapist (1), a medical psychologist (1), and a feminist psychologist (1). Two experts worked at a center affiliated with a university, one at a center for teenagers' sexual and reproductive health, two at hospital medical centers, one at a commercial medical center, one at a maternity hospital, and one at a feminist crisis center for women. As for theoretical influences, our respondents mentioned Sigmund Freud, C. G. Jung, Eric Fromm, Karen Horney, Alexander, F. Pearls, Frigga Haug, Masters and Johnson, T. D. Kemper, Eric Berne, and literary masters such as Leo Tolstoy. They also mentioned Russian colleagues and clinicians as crucial professional advisors. By contrast, the international community of sex therapists was mentioned as an important influence by only one expert. Several experts referred to specific Russian research concepts and tradition such as sexual maps or the theory of sexual constitution. The latter is a typology of sexual personalities based on the strength of the sexual drive and other physiological and developmental characteristics, developed by Vasilchenko and

Botneva. The theory is well-known among lay Russians but not among Western sex therapists (see "Assessment and Treatment" section).

The field of sex therapy in Russia is thus hard to define. There is a core of doctor-sexologists trained in Moscow or St. Petersburg and an array of sex therapists with other kinds of training, which is often less rigorous and may be somewhat at the level of psychological couple therapy. Solid professional associations, international contacts, agreed criteria for sexological clinical work, and evidence-based practices in this area are often lacking.

Typically, Russian sexologists work both with individuals and couples. With teenagers and young married couples, the work often involves parent–child relations. The price for visiting a sexologist varies. A medical sexologist may charge R15,000 to 18,000 (about €300 to 400) for one course of treatment, including ultrasound, hormonal tests, and the consultation. This price is considered average. In private clinics or in Moscow, the price may be more than twice as high. Most clients are middle- or upper-class men and women. Poor and other less affluent people usually lack the financial means to consult a sexologist. However, in some cities some groups such as young people, drug users, and battered women may have access to inexpensive treatment for sexual problems. For instance, at one youth center 9- to 17-year-old clients receive all treatments for free, while clients over 17 years may get substantial student reductions.

When starting their practice, our experts had been oriented toward either young people or middle-aged clients but were now also treating elderly clients. Several sexologists noted that their own views had changed regarding sexuality in older age, and they were now more aware of it as an issue and were more approving of it.

All of the experts we interviewed agreed that there were two main approaches to sexology in Russia: the predominantly medical and the predominantly psychodynamic. In the medical approach, the central problems relate to erection and orgasm, while the psychological approach deals more broadly with personality and interpersonal sexual relations. For instance, the following quotation illustrates a predominantly medical approach to sexual therapy:

> A sexologist is a doctor with a multidisciplinary specialty who works with the problems of sexual pathology, the disturbance of the copulative function in men and obviously in women also.... Sexology includes sexual pathology, criminal sexology, endocrinology, psychotherapy, and urology.

> Sexuality is biological by its very nature. Human beings are biosocial creatures, so probably doctors with medical training have the most

comprehensive view of sexuality. By contrast, the psychological approach has a different emphasis:

> I see myself as doing humanistic existential psychology. Sexology is the science of sexual relationships, not of the genital aspects but of the relationship between a man and a woman. The object of sexology is love.... All psychologists are sexologists. People may do it with the aid of a scalpel or the aid of chemicals. But there are authors who are experts on the sexual soul. The best book on sexology is *Father Sergey* by Lev Tolstoy! That's sexology for you. Or *The Kreutzer Sonata*. Sometimes it is more useful to read them than the contemporary advice booklets, "How to Get Married and What to Do with that Swine Afterwards."

Nevertheless, the divide between psychologists and medical doctors is a question of emphasis and most experts see sexual therapy as a multidisciplinary endeavor. Medically oriented sexologists also provide psychotherapy while psychologists may hold a medical degree and prescribe drug treatments.

Our eight experts espoused different attitudes toward homosexuality. For example, three disapproved of homosexuality (and one of these did not treat homosexual patients at all), one strongly approved of homosexuality, while four had neutral views. Several sexologists said homosexuality results from the childhood environment, especially because of an absent father, or due to hormonal influences or a single traumatic event. The current homosexual "fashion" in the media also provoked unease among some therapists. The following quotation by a politically liberal sex therapist blamed the way some single mothers bring up their children:

> Recently we have many similar cases. Homosexual or transsexual tendencies. They are terribly unhappy girls. Why? We have always had it, but we have noticed more girls with homosexual and transsexual orientations during the last years. Because of the sexual revolution. Before, these topics were taboo.... We see a tendency to behave like the other sex. The mother wanted a boy, but had a girl. There is a sex role identification lacking. This is especially in a single-mother family, where the mother is bringing the child up to "be what I want you to be like."

Assessment and Treatment of Sexual Problems

Most of the therapists we interviewed agreed that erection and orgasm problems constitute the main focus of their work. They also often mentioned combinations of marital and sexual problems, especially women who consult a therapist because their partner is having extramarital affairs or has left her for a younger woman. The comparatively high number of extramarital affairs in Russia is reflected in their clientele. Therapists also mentioned the special needs of different social groups, such as homosexual couples, transsexual people, elderly people, teenagers and teenage pregnancies, victims of violence, people who are HIV-positive, drug addicts, and sex workers.

What kind of diagnosis and treatment will couples with sexual problems receive in Russia? We provide an overview of assessment and treatment based on expert interviews and a review of the most influential scientific literature.

The leading sexologist Lev Shcheglov (2001) divides sexual disorders into two main types: (a) sexual dysfunctions in men (such as arousal, erection, and ejaculation problems) and in women (arousal and orgasm problems), and (b) sexual disharmony" (pp. 257–261). There are five categories of sexual disharmony: (a) social and psychological dysfunction/maladaptation; (b) lack of sexual and psychological adaptation in the couple; (c) lack of information and accurate knowledge; (d) sexual disharmony following sexual functional problems and typically leading to problems with erection and duration of intercourse in men; and (e) frigidity and anorgasmia in women. The experts we interviewed often provided information that was consistent with Shcheglov's classification. Additionally, they mentioned couples' communication problems.

Most sexologists saw their task as defining the problem and making a diagnosis, then treating the problem. A few regarded the definition of the problem as part of the treatment. Krishtal and Grigorian's (2005) textbook on sexology states that clinical sexology makes a diagnosis of the breach in sexual health, corrects it, and provides preventive measures Another recent textbook for medical students emphasizes four demands for sexological work: to take into account the large number of different specific etiological factors; to adopt a systemic approach; to compare sexual indicators with the corresponding age-specific norm; and to take into account individual traits in sexual constitution (Vasilchenko, 2005).

Diagnostic Tools

Among the various means used for making a diagnosis, Krishtal and Grigorian (2005) mention sexological studies and assessment of the spouses' psychological, social-psychological, and sexual-behavioral adaptation. Many therapists use sexological maps[5] that depict formal indicators of sexual problems and so direct the therapist to ask questions designed to elicit the relevant information. As one expert said: "Following that map I ask him questions relating to sex and his personality only.... But the discussion is more important. We can talk for an hour, an hour and a half, about what happens and when. This serves to enable a differentiated diagnosis to be made."

Other therapists mentioned discussion as a diagnostic tool and as a method of treatment —these two phases are not always easy to separate. They conducted discussions with each individual and then both members of the couple. Some traced the patient's life history since childhood, sometimes including the marital and sex life of his parents, while others focused on the here and now.

The therapist's perspective affects the definition of the problem. While medical doctors may focus on physical factors, a psychologist may emphasize other issues. One psychologist noted that "sexual problems are not problems of genital contact, but of relations and interaction." Most therapists, however, take into account both medical and psychological aspects, and their interaction.

The clear majority of experts used age, psychosexual types, and the type of sexual constitution as key references in diagnosis. Vasilchenko (2005) has claimed that both age and individual characteristics influence the intensity of human beings' sexual activity, which is also related to the individual's constitution. Lev Shcheglov also stressed individual differences in sexual constitution (2001). Individuals' sex drive may be divided into three groups: strong, medium, or weak. These groups are considered to relate to physiological, developmental, and behavioral factors. The male sexual constitution is considered to be related to age of sexual interest and first ejaculation, as well as degree of hairiness; women's sexual constitution is related to her age at the onset of menstruation and how easily she becomes pregnant and gives birth.[6]

This strong emphasis on personality and on psychophysiological sexual traits appears to be typical of contemporary Russian sexology. For instance, a medical doctor in Kazan mentioned that the main tool for preventing sexual problems would be to teach people how to find the right partner.

> You should look at the genetically based component, like the sexual constitution—if a man has a strong sexual constitution he may want it daily, maybe several times daily, until he is 80, and if he marries a woman with a weak sexual constitution, whose menstruation started after she turned 13 and who has not matured hormonally and maybe never will, it is clear that it will be pure violence to her.

Genetic and physiological factors may also contribute to constitutional sexual differences. In addition, sex therapists also referred to the impact of socialization. Single mothers were especially seen as detrimental to male and also often to female sexual development.

Assertive female sexuality may still be a problem in some Russian social circles, but this does not appear to be the case for sex therapists. On the contrary, one therapist was openly dismayed at how a male client reacted to his wife's sexual activity.

"Why did you come to see us? I ask. The client said, 'My wife has become more self-confident, more active and free. Somehow it's worrying.' When a woman becomes more active and confident men start worrying, that is a reason to go to psychotherapy!"

Sexologists may thus promote gender equality in sexual life and encourage men to be accepting of women's sexual demands. On the other hand, our interviews also featured examples of how sexologists reproduce gender inequalities. Men are often seen as more controlled by their biology and hormones than women, a view which assigns women the responsibility for changing and controlling the situation. As one expert put it, "We know that the man is biologically determined, he is active, hypersexual." We also detected a tendency to define male problems as more concrete (lack of erection), while more general problems are attributed to women (such as being either uninterested or too demanding). In a few cases, the therapist discussed his female clients in a derogatory way.

> Take the wife; she has such a puritanical attitude to everything. To put it bluntly, she can't even touch the male organ with her hands; it can only be put in with a fork.... There is a lack of sexual literacy, education, and information that leads to a lack of harmony between the two of them.

In the above quote, the sexologist was harsh in his comments about his female patient's reluctance to touch the penis, making a rude and aggressive comparison to a kitchen utensil. However, he did also stress a general lack of knowledge as contributing to the couple's misery.

The therapists noted that marital conflict can arise due to different levels of sexual desire and a lack of understanding. Crises in communication may be due to broader social issues, such as difficulties in combining work and family, and responsibilities toward other family members and kin. Several therapists mentioned work-related stress as a common source of Russian men's sexual problems. One of them talked about the "manager syndrome" in a way which reminded us of the advertisement for urological treatments quoted previously:

> My younger male patients often have problems with erection and ejaculation ... they have nervous crises over the situation at their workplace and lose interest in sex itself; there is that kind of manager syndrome. People work too much and don't wish to enter a relationship, they have no energy left: "I'd rather sleep a little or do something else, but absolutely no sex."

Treatments and Outcomes

Depending on the expertise of the sexologist, the patient is offered psychological help, medical treatment, or both.[5] If a sexologist provides mainly psychological counseling, she or he may consult with or refer the patient to a urologist, endocrinologist, or neuropathologist. Medication may include hormones in order to cure erectile problems. Although Viagra is much advertised and used in Russia, no prescription and therefore no medical appointment is needed. None of our experts mentioned Viagra as a treatment option. Physiological treatment may include massage and the use of mechanical devices. Treatment of anorgasmia predominantly includes education and information, taking into account individual characteristics, and therapeutic work with couple communication. Many therapists said that lack of knowledge was the principal reason behind women's orgasm problems. As one put it:

> Our young women are so little educated, it is tragicomic.... And not only the young. A woman came to me and cried here in my office, she was about 45 years old. Her first husband had died; she met another man 2 years ago. She said she had discovered orgasm. And she cried and cried that her life had been wasted. I said, but you should be happy, how many women live their whole lives without knowing anything at all.

The therapist may advise the client to acquire sex toys in order to have orgasm. One sexologist actually owned a sex shop and advised her clients to purchase items. Another therapist stressed that "You cannot work just on achieving orgasm, because there is no such point, no such pill, instead you must talk to your husband, restore family relations, solve problems on a purely psychological level." A medical psychologist described the need for communication within the relationship thus: "Women say, 'Where is that prelude? Where are the ways to arouse me? My husband doesn't know that I have a clitoral orgasm.' I ask them, so why don't you tell him about this! Not everybody knows these things." A third therapist mentioned that women may enter extramarital relations to express the desire and satisfaction they have lost in their marriage. "The husband comes to me and says she cannot reach orgasm. When you start sorting things out you learn that she has a third person on the horizon."

Fatigue and marital conflicts are also given as important reasons for lack of female orgasm, especially among older women. As one sexologist commented,

> Women often suffer anorgasmia. I have had cases with dysfunctional families, the husband started drinking, stopped earning

money, a conflict situation, much to do at the workplace, two children, it is clear that although everything was fine until now, and sexual life was enjoyable, for such a woman sexual relations have begun to feel like something forced on her. She has lost all desire for intimate relations.

All therapists said therapeutic discussions individually and with the couple were a main component of treatment. Some sexologists also used group discussion (either for women only or men only, or with several couples together). In the therapeutic discussions, the therapists distinguish between interpretations and recommendations. Interpretations are one way of suggesting to the patient what may be happening to him or her. Some sexologists stress reflection and "active listening" over practical advice: "I can recommend them to listen to themselves, not to lie to oneself…. I do not give them tasks, like read erotic literature, buy some tablets, or have sex three times a day." Other sexologists do give specific advice. Recommendations include books to read, films to watch, breathing exercises, or simply instructions to caress each other. Specific suggestions can also relate to the lifestyle as a whole, to physical activities and nutrition, and to self-reliance and self-esteem.

The type of recommendations often appears to vary by gender. For instance, the influential Shcheglov (2001) gave specific recommendations in the case of male erection problems due to marital disharmony. According to him, the woman should know the needs of her partner, she should affect his erogenous zones when they prepare to have sex, help him to become aroused, and take care of contraception. The main responsibility of restoring couple harmony is assigned to the woman.

We now provide two case descriptions in order to further illustrate the values, treatment, and techniques employed in Russian sex therapy.

Case 1: Lack of Female Orgasm in a Young Couple

Our first case describes a young married couple who sought sex therapy because the wife did not experience pleasure from intercourse. It illustrates the lack of basic physiological knowledge and couple communication skills that may still be found among young Russians. VB, a family psychologist, tells us:

> I had an incredible couple last week. She was 22 and he was 23 years old. Their joint sexual life began 7 years ago when they moved in together. They consulted me because of the wife's lack of sexual satisfaction. She had never experienced orgasm. She says she loves her husband, they are married, she feels pleasure thinking about him, feeling him, his scent, and his touch. But

still there is no satisfaction. They told me that during these 7 years nothing had changed in their sexual relations, they repeat the same habit. We found out that he knows very little about her. I asked him:
What does she like to read?
I don't know.
What food does she especially like?
I don't know.
Well, what do you think?
He mentions one kind of food, but she says she likes another. He doesn't know her tastes or interests. He doesn't know her body. I ask him:
What part of your wife's body is the most intensive erogenous zone?
He mentions one part, let's say the breast. She says, "No." He says, "Really?" The same can be said about her. For them, working with me meant exploring each other.

VB diagnosed the couple's lack of intimate communication and knowledge of each other as the basic problems. He further defined the problem as relating exclusively to their stereotypic relations with each other and the "lack of creativity, lack of self-assurance, the uncertainty, the lack of ability to accept the other and yourself." In this case, VB said that in a couple of sessions the couple solved their main problem (lack of female orgasm) after learning to discuss their erotic and sexual preferences.

Which traits typical of the Russian context can we detect from our first case? The early start of sexual relations is related to the liberalization of sexual norms that took place in the 1980s. Additionally, in Russia, a couple who had dated for so long would typically not be only cohabiting and married but also be the parents of at least one child (Zakharov, 2008). We also note the importance nowadays paid to female orgasm. The couple knew about its existence, although they could not achieve it. We also see how the psychologist does not blame one of the partners for the problems. He starts working with the husband but asks the same questions of the wife. He found that both were equally ignorant about the needs of each other. Female sexual pleasure is seen by both the therapist and the clients as a mutual concern for both spouses. Finally, the reader should not miss a very culturally specific trait in the first question: the therapist asks about reading habits, not pop stars or television sitcoms!

Case 2: Erection Problems in a Couple Relationship

This is how a doctor and sexologist, here called JJ, described his experience with a married heterosexual couple.

A couple saw me for a long time. They are married and have a big age difference: He is about 45 years old and she is 28. The relationship had deteriorated. He is a businessman, he works and is tired. He has a family from his first marriage. There is a conflict because he has to go and visit his children and provide them with money. His young wife criticizes him. They have started quarreling. She is an independent, beautiful woman. He has unpleasant feelings from sexual intercourse, he has lost sexual desire. Naturally, the wife does not understand that the reason for these problems is due to their conflicts. She has started accusing him of seeing his first wife or some other woman, and thus puts oil on the fire. They have a huge age difference. Her sexual type belongs to a category of strong personalities, she needs quite frequent and satisfying sex. When she married him she didn't think about this. After they had been married for some time, twice a week was enough for him, because he belongs to the middle type in terms of psychosexual development. He also has episodic relations with lovers. On the basis of these conflicts she has also begun to worry, she can't relax during intercourse. She has difficulties achieving orgasm although she previously reached orgasm almost every time. After their disputes she sleeps badly and is in an unstable mood. Sex has a bitter taste to him and he has lost his erection a couple of times. Such a bunch of complications: it's a classical case. Someone advised him to take a Viagra pill. He took it the wrong way[8] and it didn't work. He got even worse."

In this case, JJ followed a complex, multidisciplinary approach in his treatment of the couple. First, he interviewed the wife, then the husband, and defined their psychological and psychosexological traits. According to JJ, the husband was found to be "shy, emotional, and easily hurt. If he doesn't manage [to have an erection] he is on the verge of despair." Thus, he was considered to belong to the middle psychosexological type, who does not want sex more than twice a week after the age of 40. By contrast, the wife's "sexual type belongs to those with strong personalities. She needs quite frequent and quite good sex."

JJ described his work as paying attention to age and to the personalities and sexual needs of his clients. In the above case, he eventually defined the root of the couple's problem and predicted future developments based on the theory of sexual constitution. "The reasons for their problems became clear. I had to explain to her that when she married she chose a husband who was 17 years older than she was. After a couple of years he will need sex only once in two weeks, while she will need it every other day.

We note that neither the strong sexual appetite of the woman, nor the shyness of the man, was seen as problematic by the therapist. The couple's social situation (e.g., the man's relations to his children and ex-wife, the couple's economic decision making) was not mentioned except in passing. With another sexologist, these could be seen as the main problem. JJ worked two months with the couple and used all three main treatment methods: couple and individual psychotherapy, medication, and physiological treatment. In this case, the latter meant physiotherapy with an electrical device (the Iarilo) deemed by the therapist to have been quite effective in order to restore erection. This machine aims to improve erectile function of the penis by affecting the blood vessels by using air massage and laser treatment.[9] JJ reported that the machine is effective both in itself and as a placebo, as the mere sight of an erection can have a positive psychological impact. In this case the husband had restored confidence in himself and in his ability to get and maintain an erection.

This therapist also made specific suggestions to the wife and the husband regarding ways of reacting and acting towards each other: "So I also had to explain to him how to behave, what he needed to do, so as not to suffer so violently and to satisfy his woman. And to her I explained what she should feel, see, and say and how to manage her emotions. That is routine work."

Above, we noted that J J acknowledged the uneven levels of sexual desire of the spouses and did not judge the woman for having high sexual demands. However, he occasionally talked as if the couple's sexual incompatibility was something the woman should have taken into account to a larger extent than the man. Thus, he mentioned twice that the wife does not see the reason for their problems. By contrast, the wife's suspicion and concerns about her husband having an extramarital affair is not mentioned, although they turned out to be realistic.

Overall, JJ was positive about the outcome of this case and his method of combining different kinds of treatment. JJ said that in this case as in other cases, he rarely expects radical changes in couple behavior and aims at gradual improvement. He also pointed out that everything (the discussions, the medical treatment, and even the cashier) are located in the same place, so that the patient is not forced to "run from one doctor to the other" (which is not uncommon in Russian medicine; see Temkina & Zdravomyslova, 2008).

Preventive Advice and Morality

What kind of advice would Russian sexual therapists give to promote sexual health and well-being in the future? We asked our eight interviewees what prophylactic and preventive measures they recommended to enhance sexual well-being. Their approaches varied. We noted above that finding a partner with a compatible constitution and sexual appetite that matches your own was recommended by some therapists. One sexologist advocated regular sex, as well as a balanced diet, "in order to have enough testosterone in the blood," and an active way of life. Some recommended that after turning 40, a man should visit a urologist-andrologist and a sexpathologist once every year. Several sexual therapists emphasized the need for people to take care of their health (broadly defined) and to take into account age-specific influences in order to have realistic expectations about sexual functioning.

According to one medical psychologist, the crucial thing is to prevent young people from having intercourse at a young age: "I directly aim to prevent early sexual relations. That is clear. This correlates with a healthy lifestyle, with psychological and sexual health: abstinence, mainly, and reducing the popularity of early sex."

Another psychologist wanted to enhance marital harmony. Quite another approach was adopted by a doctor and psychotherapist, who said: "The best prophylactic model is to sleep with whomever you want to sleep with.... If it is your wife, perfect! If it is not—that is your problem. But it's not good if a person sleeps not with whom he wants to but with the one he is obliged to sleep with, because of his career, his family duty, or out of pity." For this therapist, normal sexual relations are exclusively built on love and attraction, and they do not always entail monogamy. When another therapist included among his recommendations to "take a second wife and do with her everything you wish to do," he seemed to accord men greater liberty and less responsibility. Again, although many sexologists wanted to restore the importance of love in sexual relations, at least some of them did not confine love to marriage.

Prolonged alcohol use is related to sexual dysfunction, including problems with arousal, erection, and vaginal lubrication (Peugh & Belenko, 2001). Nevertheless, not one of the experts we interviewed specifically discussed alcoholism in connection with sexual problems. They mentioned regular sex, love, special balanced diets, an active way of life, seeing a doctor in time, being careful about whom you sleep with, preventing marital conflicts, and enhancing harmony. Perhaps the problem with alcoholism is seen as too self-evident? Neither does the public and commercial sexual discourse in Russian society connect alcohol use with sexual health.

Therapists working with drug users or women who have been abused stress that the sexual life of their clients was very poor or nonexistent, and that these clients typically did not raise sexual topics. "Few of our clients report a satisfying sexual life. One group of clients says that they don't have any sexual relations at all; the other group says that 'I am forced to do it because everybody does it'."

One therapist emphasized that due to economic hardship, women's economic dependence, and family violence, poor men and women are in no position to concentrate on their sexual pleasure.

> The sexuality of Russian women is often secondary to questions of economic and social survival. Especially elderly women are often ready to stand discomfort related to male sexual problems.... There are more urgent things than women's sexual pleasure: economic and social factors, to have a husband and a father for your children.

Economic dependence fosters sexual corruption and "*blat*," a Russian expression for informal exchanges of services and access to goods. In some cases poor or disadvantaged women may offer sex in exchange for services or goods, but the reverse also happens. One case involved a client in her 50s who had boyfriend 20 years younger than herself. This partner beat her, had relations with other women, and took advantage of her having a good apartment. The woman was aware of being exploited, but stated that the sexual pleasure of having a young lover made her continue the relationship.

The prophylactic advice offered reflects the liberalization of sexual behavior and norms in Russia during the last several decades. Sex therapists acknowledge the increase in pre- and extramarital sex and both men's and women's quest for sexual pleasure. However, their moral attitude to this development differs. One deplored this development and wanted to partially restore the old traditions. For another, there was no going back to the old morality, but neither has the current form of liberating sexuality outweighed the social and economic difficulties:

> I have been working with women since the early 1990s. Although the word *sex* has suffered this incredible proliferation in various texts, pictures, discussions, and TV programs, I can't see that my clients have begun to respect themselves more as women.

How is treatment success evaluated? It is not easy to find evidence of this either in the scientific literature or on Internet sites nor from our interviews with experts. The continuation of a normal sexual life is often seen as the main general criterion, but more detailed evaluations are hard to make. One doctor simply said, "Either there is [clicks his tongue, imitates an erection with his hand] or there isn't." Others mentioned the difficulty of patients who have recurrent problems or who finish treatment too early. One sexologist saw the lack of ways to "tie the patient to the doctor" as her main professional challenge; the attitude of the spouse, such as lack of support or sexual interest, may also weaken treatment results. One sexologist described restoring a man's erection, but "the wife did not need that...so the work of the sexologist was in vain."

Several sexologists criticized those Russian men who are not ready to work with either their own issues or the relationship, but blame their female partners for all of the problems. One expert noted:

> It's worse when one of them wants to change the situation but the other couldn't care less. A husband who sees himself as a psychologist and sex pathologist tells his wife: "The problem is that you are so ugly, you need to lose weight. Go to fitness class, learn how to do a striptease, then you can come to me.... "

In sum, our cases represent typical types of marital conflict and sexological diagnosis in contemporary Russia. The first case described one psychological approach among many others, the second a medical approach combined with psychotherapy. In itself, these kinds of married couples would not have been unthinkable during the Soviet 1970s, but they would rarely have sought professional help and it would probably have been unusual for a woman to complain of lack of orgasm to the doctor in the presence of her husband. Neither would the kind of gender conflict evident in our second case, with the sexually demanding wife, have been described by the sexologist as "classical." The articulation and approval of female desire by both female clients and therapists is a novel phase in the development of sexology in Russia. This said, sexist attitudes may persist, where the woman is assigned more responsibility than the man for restoring the couple's harmony.

Many Russian sexologists stress that they are not moralists. However, in any society, sexologists' personal views on gender roles, normalcy, and illness may influence the diagnosis and recommended treatment. The contemporary morality of many Russian sexologists is tainted by liberal hedonism, stressing the right to individual sexual pleasure for all. Especially among the male doctors we interviewed, we heard little about partnership, mutual help and support, negotiations, and compromises. Not surprisingly, the only feminist psychologist we talked to presented a stark contrast to this picture.

Conclusions

This chapter has dealt with Russian sexual culture and encounters in the field of Russian sexology, its diverse practices, and socioeconomic context. In sharp contrast to the official secrecy and sexual puritanism of the Soviet era, sexual issues are expressed and discussed in manifold ways in contemporary Russia. Liberal, commercial, and medical approaches to sex are in competition with religious and traditional sexual morality.

The public and commercial discourse about sexual health focuses on erection and orgasm problems. Consulting a specialist for treatment of sexual problems has become an accepted and legitimate behavior. Treatment is typically not covered by national health insurance but has to be paid for by the patient or client, making it more accessible to the middle and upper classes. However, free or affordable treatment is often available to young or marginalized people.

Russian sexology was founded two decades ago and expanded throughout the 1990s. While the field is being institutionalized, there is little if any consensus about terminology, clinical practices, or ideological views. Sexologists use different methods and approaches and support different sexual moralities. Alongside the officially certified sexologist-physicians trained in St. Petersburg and Moscow, there exist a variety of psychologically trained therapists providing sexological services. Most sex therapists appear to combine both psychological and medical treatments. Treatment is multidisciplinary and not always evidence-based. Diagnosis often applies theories, diagnostic tools, such as sexual maps, and sometimes devices such as the Iarilo. The theory of sexual constitution, relating personality and the levels of sexual interest to physiological and developmental factors, is widespread among both sexologists and lay Russians.

We suggest that there are currently four important developments related to questions of pleasure and gender in Russian sexological encounters. First, Russian sexology has adopted a generally liberal and permissive view of sexual pleasure at all stages of the life cycle. Teenage sexuality and premarital sex is accepted, and also the sexual problems and pleasure of elderly people have recently received more attention and recognition. Second, there is a growing acceptance of sexual practices outside of heterosexual activities. Homosexuals and transsexuals are identified and recognized as a type of client, although there is also evidence that at least some sex therapists lack understanding of and discriminate against homosexuals. Third, women's sexual desire and sexual activity is broadly acknowledged. A recent development is the emphasis on female orgasm and sexual initiative. Male sexual problems are also being discussed, including work-related stress, allowing for a more vulnerable and health-oriented perception of Russian masculinity. This is not to say that Russian sex therapists always espouse gender equality. We also detected signs of double morality and of putting the responsibility for change in a heterosexual couple more on the woman than on the man. Finally, the scientific understanding of sexuality is strongly influenced by the theory of sexual constitution, which relates a person's level of sexual desire to genetic and developmental traits. This theory appears to be little known in Western countries but widely accepted in Russian-speaking communities.

Our analysis was based on two surveys and a small number of interviews that are not necessarily representative of the whole field of Russian sex therapy. Nevertheless, the diversity even among this small number of experts is apparent. One can detect varying and ambivalent attitudes to issues such as gender equality, sex education, and sexual orientation among Russian sexologists. Gender equality is present and encouraged, but not totally integrated, in Russian sexology. A person turning to professional help would have a hard time knowing what kind of approach to expect from his or her sex therapist.

Acknowledgments

The authors are especially grateful to Olga Tkach who conducted part of the expert interviews and provided valuable comments.

Notes

1. The interviews were conducted by trained sociologists between April 2009 and May 2010 in the cities of Moscow, St Petersburg, Samara, Archangelsk, and Kazan. We interviewed three women and five men who were 45 to 60 years old (three psychologists and five medical doctors). We refer to these respondents as "experts," "sexologists," or "sex therapists." The research is part of the project "Gender Arrangements in Private Life in Russian Regions" at the European University of St. Petersburg and has received financial support from the Ford Foundation and Novartis International AG.
2. Here and below all excerpts are from our research data unless otherwise indicated, see note 1.
3. http://www.lclinic.ru/content/view/1/2/
4. Information provided by Dr. Yuri Zharkov to Dr. Osmo Kontula by e-mail, May 2009, quoted with permission.
5. Sexological maps for studying men include questions about complaints made, libido, first ejaculation, orgasms, masturbation, dynamics of sex life, alcohol, living conditions, personality traits and the objective facts of treatment (Vasilchenko, 2005, pp. 277–279). Women's maps also include information on pregnancies and menstruation (Vasilchenko, 2005, pp. 402–407). The maps were developed at the sexopathological department of the Moscow Psychiatric Institute of the Ministry of Health of the Russian Federation. Krishtal and Grigorian (2005, pp. 384–386) add a map for sexological studies of the couple.
6. For an informative overview of the theory of sexual constitution, see http://big-archive.ru/med/sex/79.php. The theory is frequently mentioned in Russian language blogs (*polovaia konstitutsiia, seksual'naia konstitutsiia, seksual'naia sovmestimost'*) and "ask-the-doctor" Internet pages in Russia and abroad.

7. A textbook in sexology distinguishes between six types of corrections to problems with sexual health: psychotherapy, corrections of the psychological and social-psychological maladaptation between the spouses, medical treatment of sexual disorders, physiotherapy of sexual disorders, gymnastics, and different methods, including chirurgical operations, to treat impotence in men (Krishtal & Grigoryan, 2005.)
8. Often men do not understand that they need to take Viagra about an hour before they plan to have sex. Also, after eating a high-fat meal, it may take even longer for Viagra to take effect.
9. Iarilo was developed by the company Iarovit on the basis of research carried out in the department of biotechnical medical systems at the Moscow State Technical University and appears to be quite widely used in Russia and other CIS countries. The Internet site of Yarovit is http://www.yarovit-med.ru.

References

Chernetskaia, O. V. (2005). Mezhkulturnye razlichiia predstavlenii o seksualnosti russkih i finnov. Psychological dissertation [Crosscultural differences in Finns' and Russians' views of sexuality. Psychological dissertation], May 19, 2000. Moscow. Rossiiskaia gosudarstvennaia biblioteka, Otdel dissertatsii 61:06-19/659. http://www.lib.ua-ru.net/diss/cont/188929.html

Gessen, M. (1995). Sex in the media and the birth of the sex media in Russia. In E. Berry (Ed.), *Post-communism and the body politic* (pp. 197–228). New York University Press.

Goldman, W. Z. (1993) *Women, the state and revolution: Soviet family policy and social life, 1917–1936* (Russian, Soviet and Post-Soviet Studies, 90). Cambridge, England: Cambridge University Press.

Haavio-Mannila, E., & Kontula, O. (2003). *Sexual trends in the Baltic Sea area* (Population Research Institute, Series D41). Helsinki, Finland: Väestöliitto.

Haavio-Mannila, E., & A. Rotkirch (2010). Sexuality and family formation in Europe. In S. Immerfal & G. Therborn (Eds.), *Handbook of European societies: Social Transformations in the 21st century*. New York: Springer.

Harris, C. (2004) *Control and subversion: Gender relations in Tajikistan*. London: Sterling Virginia Pluto Press.

Isaev, D. V., & Kagan, V. Y. (1979) *Polovoe vospitanie i psykogigiena pola u detej* [Sexual education and psychological hygiene of children.] Leningrad: Meditsina.

Kesseli K., Regushevskaya, E., Doubikaytis,T., Kirichenko, S., Rotkirch, A., Haavio-Mannila, E., Kuznetsova, O.,Hemminki, E., and REFER group. (2005). Reproductive health and fertility in *St Petersburg: Report on a survey of 18–44 year old women in 2004* /Reproduktivnoe zdorov'e i fertil'nost' v Sankt-Peterburge (Bilingual English-Russian version). Working paper 60, Department of Sociology, University of Helsinki. http://www.stakes.fi/verkkojulkaisut/muut/WomenSurveyStP04_english.pdf

Katja Kesseli, Elena Regushevskaya, Tatyana Doubikaytis, Svetlana Kirichenko, Anna Rotkirch, Elina Haavio-Mannila, ... Elina Hemminki (2005): *Reproductive Health and Fertility in St. Petersburg 2004: Report on a survey of*

18-44 year old women in 2004 / Репродуктивное здоровье и фертилность в Санкт-Петербурге. (Bilingual English-Russian version) Working papers 60, Department of Sociology, University of Helsinki.

Kon, I. (1989). *Vvedenie v seksologiu* [Introduction to sexology]. Moscow, Russia: Meditsina.

Kon, I. (1995). *The sexual revolution in Russia: From the age of the Czars to today.* New York: Free Press.

Kon, I. (1997a). Seksual'naia kul'tura v Rossii. Klubnichka na berezke.[Sexual culture in Russia]. Moscow, Russia: O.G/I.

Kon, I. (1997b). Russia. In R. T. Francoeur and R. A. Noonan (Eds.), *The international encyclopaedia of sexuality* (Vol. 2, pp. 1045–1079. New York: Continuum. Retrieved from http://www2.hu-berlin.de/sexology/IES/russia.html

Kon, I. (2002). Chelovecheskie seksual'nosti na rubezhe XXI veka [Human sexualities on the threshold of the 21st century]. In E. Zdravomyslova & A.Temkina (Eds.), *V poiskah seksual'nosti. Sbornik statej* [In search of sexuality: An anthology] (pp. 24–46). St. Petersburg, Russia: Dm. Bulanin.

Kon, I. (2005) *Seksual'naia kul'tura v Rossii. Klubnichka na berezke. 2 izd. pererab. i dop* [Sexual culture in Russia] (2nd rev. ed.). Moscow, Russia: Airis-press.

Kontula, O. (2004) *Reproductive health behavior of young Europeans: Vol. 2. The role of education and information* (European Population Papers Series, 17). Strasbourg, France: The European Population Committee (CAHP), Council of Europe.

Krishtal, V., & Grigiryan, S. (2005). *Seksology* [Sexology]. Moscow, Russia: Per se.

Lapidus, G W. (1978). *Women in Soviet society: Equality, development, and social change.* Berkeley: University of California Press.

Meilakhs, N. (2008). Neslyshnye peregovory: vybor sposoba predokhraneniia i otnosheniia mezhdu partnerami [Silent negotiations: Choosing ways of contraception and type of couple relation]. In E. Zdravomyslova, A. Temkina, & A. Rotkirch (Eds.), *Novyj byt v sovremennoi Rossii: gendernye issledovaniia povsednevnosti* [New everyday life in contemporary Russia: a gendered approach] (pp. 356–372). St. Petersburg, Russia: European University of St. Petersburg Press.

Perelman, F., & McKee, M. N. (2009) Trends in family planning in Russia, 1994–2003. *Perspectives on Sexual and Reproductive Health, 41*(1), 40–50.

Peugh, M. A., & Belenko, S. (2001). Alcohol, drugs and sexual function: A review. *Journal of Psychoactive Drugs, 33*, 223–232.

Regushevskaya, E., Dubikaytis T., Nikula M., Kuznetsova, O., & Hemminki, E. (2008). The socioeconomic characteristics of risky sexual behavior among reproductive-age women in St. Petersburg. *Scandinavian Journal of Public Health, 36*, 143–152.

Regushevskaya, E., Dubikaytis, T., Nikula, M., Kuznetsova, O., & Hemminki, E. (2009). Contraceptive use and abortion among women of reproductive age in St. Petersburg, Russia. *Perspectives on Sexual and Reproductive Health, 41*(1), 51–58.

Rotkirch, A. (2000). *The man question: Loves and lives in late 20th century Russia* (Research Reports 1/2000). Helsinki, Finland: Department of Social Policy, University of Helsinki.

Rotkirch, A. (2003). "What kind of sex can you talk about?": Acquiring sexual knowledge in three Soviet generations. In D. Bertaux, P. Thompson, & A. Rotkirch (Eds.), *Living through Soviet Russia* (pp. 93–119). London: Routledge.

Rotkirch, A., & Haavio-Mannila, E. (2000). Gender polarisation and liberalisation: Comparing sexuality in St Petersburg, Finland and Sweden. *Idäntutkimus—Finnish Journal of Russian and Eastern European Studies, 3–4*, 4–26.

Shcheglov, L (1998) *Seksologiia i seksopatologiia. Vrachu i patsientu* [Sexology and sexopathology: For doctors and patients]. St. Petersburg, Russia: Sankt Petersburg Kult-Inform-Press.

Shcheglov, L (2001). *Seksologia* [Sexology]. St. Petersburg, Russia: Piter.

Shcheglov, L (2003). *Zapiski seksologa* [Notes of a sexologist]. Moscow, Russia: Amfora.

Snarskaya, O. (2009). Sexual'noe obrazovanie k sfera proizvodstva gendernyh razlichii i konstruirovania predstavlenii o "Nntsii" [Sexual education as the field of production of gender differences and construction of "nation"]. In A. Temkina & E. Zdravomyslova (Eds.), *Zdorov'e i doverie: Gendernyi podhod k reproduktivnoi meditsine* [Health and trust: a gender approach to reproductive medicine] (pp. 51–90). St. Petersburg, Russia: European University of St Petersburg Press.

Stites, R. (Ed.). (1985). *Bolshevik culture: Experiment and order in the Russian Revolution*. Bloomington: Indiana University Press.

Sviadosh, G. I. (1974). *Zhenskaia seksopatologiia* [Female sexopathology]. Moscow, Russia: Meditsina.

Temkina, A. (2008) *Seksual'naia zhizn' zhenshchiny: mezhdu podchineniem i svobodoi* [The sexual life of women: Between submission and freedom]. St. Petersburg, Russia: European University of St Petersburg Press.

Temkina, A., & Rotkirch, A. (1996). What does the (Russian) woman want? Women psychoanalysts talk. In E. Haavio-Mannila & A. Rotkirch (Eds.), *Women's voices in Russia today* (pp. 49–70). Aldershot: Dartmouth Publishing.

Temkina, A., & A. Rotkirch (2002): Sovetskie gendernye kontrakty i ih transformatsiia v sovremennoi Rossii [Soviet gender contracts and their changes in contemporary Russia]. *Sotsiologicheskie issledovaniia, 11*, 4–15.

Temkina, A., & Zdravomyslova, E. (2008). Patients in contemporary Russian reproductive health care institutions: Strategies of establishing trust. *Democratizatiya, 3*(3), 277–293.

Vasilchenko, G. S. (ed.) (2005). *Obshchaia seksopatologia: Rukovodstvo dlia vrachei* [General sexopathology, a guide for doctors] (2nd ed.). Moscow, Russia: Meditsina. (Original work published 1977)

Watson, P. (1993) Eastern Europe's silent revolution: Gender. *Sociology* 27(3), 471–487.

Zakharov, S (2008) Russian Federation: From the first to second demographic transition. *Demographic Research, 19*(24), 907–972.

Section IV

CULTURAL ADAPTATIONS OF PSYCHOTHERAPY APPROACHES TO THE TREATMENT OF SEXUAL PROBLEMS

Editors Introduction to Chapter 11
Brazil

When one thinks of Brazil images of scantily clad women dancing Samba during Carnival may arise. But away from the travel brochures and into the reality of Brazilian culture, one finds a traditional and sexually conservative society. Loss of sexual desire is commonly experienced by Brazilian women and according to Brendler, role strain is often at the root of the problem. Brazilian women are entering the professional workforce in record numbers but they are still adhering to their traditional values, which place prime importance on their roles as mothers, wives, and homemakers and minimize the importance of female sexuality. In this chapter Brendler demonstrates the value of helping women and men challenge culturally prescribed and restrictive roles in order to have a more fulfilling sexual relationship. One of the first steps in this approach to improving sexual desire is to alleviate the wife's burden of responsibility for housework and childcare. Then, using the described "sexual menu technique," Brazilian women "eroticize" their minds. With a wife more interested in sex, the therapist helps the husband understand the importance of seduction within marriage, rather than viewing sex as a male privilege in that relationship.

This chapter presents an excellent example of how to modify traditional sex therapy to be more culturally sensitive. It will serve as a template for culturally sensitive approaches to sexual problems across a variety of cultural contexts.

11

SEXUAL MYTHS AND REALITIES IN BRAZIL

Jacqueline Brendler

Sexuality in Brazil

It is a challenge to describe some of the values that influence the sexuality of men and women who live in a developing country with such continental dimensions as Brazil, the fifth largest country in the world behind Russia, China, Canada, and the United States. Brazil takes up most of the eastern part of South America and includes a very long coastline, much of the interior of the continent, as well as various islands. Brazil spans four time zones. The majority of the population lives in urban centers. The Amazon River is the second longest river in the world, with the largest drainage area, and there is extensive rain forest.

According to the latest national data from the Instituto Brasileiro de Geografia e Estatística, Brazil's population is 48.4% White, 43.8% mixed race, 6.8% Black, and 0.9% Asia or indigenous people (*Zero Hora*, 2009b).[1]

Until a few decades ago, Brazilian society, in its family organization and gender relations, maintained a system of male prestige and power that assumed men had the moral authority to dictate or control female sexual behavior (Fonseca et. al., 2000; Heilborn, 1991; Leal & Boff, 1996; Pitt-Rivers, 1966). This system has been called the "Mediterranean cultural complex," with marked representations of masculinity and femininity that are at odds with the reported and public liberal image of Brazil (Heilborn, Aquino, Bozon, & Knauth, 2006). Men and women who are now over 30 years of age had their emotional development embedded in this social and cultural context.

There are signs that the social structure in Brazil is changing, but many long-established values persist. It is still considered a sign of virility for men to have many sexual partners (Heilborn, 1992/2004). Conversely, a large number of sexual partners for women is considered evidence of sexual promiscuity and is linked to a questionable social status (Teixeira, Knauth, Fachel, & Leal, 2006). Statistics on the number of sexual partners for young men and women demonstrate conformity to social expectations. Among young women with four or more years of sexual experience, 41% reported having had three sexual partners, while 68.8% of the men with the same number of years of experience reported six or more partners (Heilborn et al., 2006). Thirty-five percent of women aged 18 to 24 years have had only one sexual partner (Teixeira, 2006). Interestingly, for young men, a higher number of sexual partners has been associated with greater use of condoms (Almeida, Aquino, Gaffikin, & Magnani, 2003; Teixeira et al., 2006), whereas for women under 24 years, the reverse relationship was found. For these women, a higher number of lifetime sexual partners was related to less condom use (Teixeira et. al., 2006). These women may have more difficulty not only in negotiating condom use with their partners, but also in other aspects of their relationship (e.g., transitioning from a casual to a long term and committed relationship) and this may be both a precursor and consequence of their lower social status.

The traditional view that women are responsible for dealing with male sexual advances in order to safeguard both their honor and the possibility of future relationships is still strongly evident (Azevedo, 1981; Fonseca et. al., 2000; Leal & Boff, 1996; Parker, Herdt, & Carballo 1991). In a recent large-scale survey of Brazilian sexual attitudes (Heilborn et al., 2006), 55% of Brazilian men expressed the belief that sexual desire was not something they could easily control, whereas 41% of (previously or currently cohabitating) women believed that they could "control" their sexual desire. These views are based on the belief that male sexuality is stronger than female sexuality, a view that is accepted among men of different educational backgrounds and the majority (58.5%) of women (Heilborn et al., 2006). Strong sexual desire is still considered a defining characteristic of men in Brazil.

In recent years, sexual attitudes and behaviors have been changing (at least among some Brazilians), as a result of education and exposure to Western values. For example, although the Heilborn et al. (2006) study showed a continuing belief in the strength of male sexual desire, there was also support for marital fidelity. The importance of a romantic or marital partner's fidelity was strongly endorsed by 80% of male participants and 90% of female participants. The option "only men can be unfaithful" in romantic relationships was endorsed by only 6% of men and 0.8% of women (Heilborn et al., 2006); thus, there is a weakening of the so-called sexual double standard, a cultural tradition so often associated with traditional Mediterranean societies (Saffioti & Almeida, 1995; Heilborn, 1991; Pitt-Rivers, 1966). However, an earlier survey carried out in 2002 showed a discrepancy between discourse and behavior, mainly in men, 37% of whom reported having multiple sexual relationships (Heilborn et al., 2006).

With regard to changes occurring in the last 10 years, there is evidence of growing support for sexual abstinence until marriage. This trend was found among men and women, of all education levels and religions, although support for abstinence was higher in women (63.9%) than in men (52.4%) (Paiva, Aranha, Bastos, & Grupo de Estudos em População, Sexualidade e Aids, 2008). Interestingly, among people with a higher level of education, support for sexual abstinence until marriage has more than doubled, from 17% in 1998 to 37.25% in 2005 (Paiva et al., 2008). On the other hand, there is also evidence that more Brazilian girls are having their first sexual intercourse early. Research involving a national sample of 15,000 Brazilian women between 15 and 49 years old (Ministério da Saúde, 2009a), pointed to a threefold increase in the percentage of girls who have had sexual intercourse by the age of 15 (33% in 2006 as compared to 11.5% in 1996; Ministério da Saúde, 2009b). Another population-based study looked at age at sexual initiation for women aged 16 to 19 years, who had only an elementary-level education (Barbosa, Koyama, & Grupo de Estudos em População, Sexualidade e Aids, 2008). This study found that the vast majority of these women had experienced sexual intercourse (90.7%) in 1998 and that by 2005 this pattern of earlier sexual initiation was nearly universal among this age group of women (97.4%).

Sexual initiation for most women in Brazil takes place within a romantic relationship, most often with a boyfriend (Borges, 2007; Borges & Schor, 2005; Brendler, 2004, 2009b; Knauth, Victoria, Leal, & Fachel, 2006; Teixeira et al., 2006). The importance of a relationship for sex was affirmed in a national study carried out in 2005 (Paiva et al., 2008). When asked "What does sex mean to you?" 39% of men and 47% of women endorsed the statement "sex is a proof of love for the partner," while only 20% of women and 18.9% of men responded that sex is "a source of pleasure and satisfaction."

The importance of relationships in defining female sexuality can also be seen in attitudes toward masturbation. In one study, masturbation was reported by 14.9% of women as occurring before their first partnered sexual experience, and after sexual initiation by 26% (Heilborn et al., 2006). Just over 75.9% of women reported masturbation in the presence of a male partner (Heilborn et al., 2006), which suggests that masturbation is more acceptable in a couple context, that is, as a relational practice (Bonzon, 2004; Heilborn, 1992/2004; Heilborn et al., 2006).

The gap between the stereotype of the sexually liberal and uninhibited Brazilian woman and the reality of most Brazilian women's sex lives is apparent also in the images of feminine beauty. Since the end of the 20th century, with the constant media attention on actresses and international top models in Brazilian society, there has been an emergence of an association between "body and prestige," as many women have become celebrities by virtue of their appearance (Goldenberg, 2002). This is the reason why many Brazilian women, starting in their teens, want to have a slender body (Bourdieu, 1999; Lipovetsky, 2000) and blond, straight hair, which is far different from what men desire (Goldenberg, 2004).

The women considered sexy by Brazilian men have plenty of salient curves (large breasts and buttocks). These two anatomic attributes are embedded in the idealization by both sexes of beauty (Goldenberg, 2002; Lipovetsky, 2000) and youth (Freyre, 1987; Lipovetsky, 2000). According to anthropologist Gilberto Freyre (1984), the preference of Brazilian men for women with large buttocks is a physical legacy from the African (16th century) and the Iberian (colonial) period. Another attractive feature is women's "whirling walking," ("as if dancing," to quote Havelock Ellis), which has erotic power. Freyre said that such preferences in Brazilian men, which are considered a "national passion," were inherited from ancestral Africans and from the aphrodisiac effect of women's prominent buttocks upon Europeans who came to settle in Brazil (in the 16th century); this feature reminded men of anal sex, a practice which they valued.

In the last decade, women's breasts have become fashionable in Brazil, a trend confirmed in 2002 by their gaining third place in male replies to the question, "What attracts you most sexually in a woman?" First and second preferences were buttocks and body, respectively (Goldenberg, 2002). Between September, 2007 and August, 2008, the silicone implant was the most common type of plastic surgery carried out, representing 33% of all aesthetic surgeries (Sociedade Brasileira de Cirurgia Plástica, 2009).

Within a couple's personal context, however, the role of a sexual woman or man (or a lover) does not depend on the presence of a body idealized as sexy. In my clinical experience, being a sexual person is related to the following several factors: having a positive view of sex/sexuality; viewing oneself as a sexual being (capable of having and giving pleasure); the perception of one's partner as a sexual (erotic) person; and having a satisfying sexual life.

In contrast to what promotes good sex, 2,564 women were asked to identify the situations that were most likely to negatively affect their sexual performance. Their responses were: tiredness (57.3%); daily activities (routine) (34.3%); being with a long-term partner (26.2%); anxiety (21.4%); and sex with "programming" (having sex in the same place, at the same time, on the same night; 20.7%) (Abdo, 2004).

Brazil is still a traditional society that considers household chores and child care to be women's work. It is no wonder then that once partnered and involved in raising children, stress and routine would negatively impact the sexual lives of many Brazilian women. A study of 800 Brazilian mothers, between the ages of 31 and 39 years, rated children as their highest priority, above husbands, themselves, and work (both paid and household chores) (Troiano, 2007). The Instituto Brasileiro de Geografia e Estatística revealed that in 2005, for women who worked outside the home the time spent weekly on home duties, which included taking care of children, outdid men's by 5 hours a week. Married or partnered women spent 29 hours a week on home tasks while single women who headed the family (i.e., had children but no partner) reported only 22 hours spent in home-related duties (*Zero Hora*, 2007).

While marriage and family are priorities, women in Brazil are increasingly being able to achieve their reproductive intentions, as evidenced by the fact that desired fecundity rates in 2006 (1.6 children) were very close to the actual birthrate (1.8 children) and represented a decrease from a birthrate of 2.5 children in 1996 (Ministério da Saúde, 2009c). Most Brazilian women have used some form of contraception; 66% of young women aged 15 to 19 years and 81% of those living with a steady partner had used some contraceptive method (Ministério da Saúde, 2009b). There still exists a discrepancy in Brazil among women with more and less education. Young women (15 to 19 years old) with little education account for 23% of the total fecundity rate in Brazil, with a birthrate of 4 children (Ministério da Saúde, 2009c).

Sexual Dysfunction in the Brazilian Population

In a national survey conducted in 2003, which included persons 18 years or older, 18.2% of men reported some sexual difficulty. In this study, 2.1% of the men complained of inhibition of sexual desire, 4.5% of pain during sexual intercourse, 5.1% of aversion to sex, 4.9% of difficulty reaching orgasm, 25.8 % of premature ejaculation, and 45.1% of erectile dysfunction—1.7% complete, 12.2% moderate, 31.2% mild (Abdo, 2004).

In the Brazilian Study of Sexual Behavior (BSSB; Abdo, Oliveira, Moreira, & Fittipaldi, 2004), involving 1,219 women, with an average age of 35.6 years, at least one sexual dysfunction was reported by 49% of women. The most common dysfunction, reported by 26.7% of the sample, was hypoactive sexual desire disorder (HSDD). Risk factors for this sexual dysfunction were being over 40 years old (regardless of race), and having had little education. In this study, HSDD was less common in women of mixed race compared to White women.

The Global Study of Sexual Attitudes and Behaviors (GSSAB; Laumann et al., 2005) collected data among women and men aged 40 to 80 years in 29 countries, across five continents, including Brazil. In all continents, lack of interest in sex and inability to reach orgasm were the most common sexual problems for women and early ejaculation was the most common complaint for men. Lack of interest in sex in women was associated with several factors: the belief that aging reduces sexual desire, thinking infrequently about sex, depression, low expectations for the future of one's relationship (in all regions except Southeast Asia), and infrequent sex (within all regions except East Asia). For men, lack of interest in sex was associated with older age, poor health, thinking about sex infrequently (in all regions except the Middle East), depression (in all regions except East Asia) and infrequent sex (in all regions except the Middle East).

The GSSAB identified the most common sexual difficulties in Brazilian women as problems with lubrication (23.4%) and lack of sexual interest (22.7%). Depression was significantly correlated with low sexual desire in women, though the study did not distinguish if this was a cause or consequence (Moreira, Glasser, Santos, & Gingell, 2005). Low sexual desire in women is the most common presenting problem in sex therapy clinics and was the most common diagnosis in my clinic samples over the last 8 years (Brendler, 2005a,b).

Low Sexual Desire and Brazilian Women

In Brazil the most accepted definition for HSDD is the one proposed by the Report of the International Consensus Conference (Basson et al., 2000): "the persistent or recurrent deficiency (or absence) of sexual fantasies/thoughts, and/or desire for or receptivity to sexual activity, which causes personal distress" (p. 890).

According to Kaplan, sexual desire is subject to bimodal control, influenced by sexual inciters and sexual suppressors (Kaplan, 1995). It is known that multiple factors may be involved in the etiology of HSDD, among them cultural, educational, and psychological factors, as well as physical and emotional illness, hormonal disturbance, and marital problems. In Brazil, a new etiological factor was proposed for HSDD; within a very traditional and sexually repressive culture, women may not identify with the role of a sexual woman, particularly in long-term relationships (Brendler, 2002).

Psycho-Socio-Cultural Factors in the Etiology of HSDD

Most Brazilian women have been educated in a repressive context regarding sexuality and perceive sex as something ugly, dirty, or sinful (Brendler, 2002). In Brazil, parents do not often speak to their children about sex or do so in an oblique way, mentioning only the negative consequences. Women repeatedly hear that sex leads to pregnancy and sexually transmitted diseases and some receive guidance on how to avoid these consequences (Brendler, 2002). All of these negative feelings and fears become associated with sexuality. Children seldom hear that sex is wonderful, that it brings satisfaction, increases self-esteem, and provides a stronger union between the couple (Brendler, 2002). Some women will overcome such negative socialization and will fully enjoy their sexuality. However, studies involving individuals with sexual problems in Brazil highlight the major influence of repressive sexual values on sexuality (Brendler, 1997; Brendler, 2000).

It is known that women play several roles: daughter, mother, professional, sexual woman, homemaker, and grandmother (Brendler, 2002). The family of origin and the culture in Brazil value motherhood, love, and professionalization as being "noble," and in contrast, sex and sexuality are seen as shameful and negative (Brendler, 2003b). Mainly for these reasons, since they were little girls, women often identify much more with the role of mother, which is valued more than the role of a "sexual woman" (Brendler, 2002).

Several authors have argued that passion elevates sexual appetite (Brendler, 2002; Brendler, 2005a, b; Fisher, 1992; Kaplan, 1995; Levine, 2003). In Brazil, Brendler (2002) proposed that it would be easier to maintain sexual desire beyond the initial passionate period of the relationship if the woman has internalized identification with the role of a sexual woman. The early passionate phase of a relationship may mask the lack of such an identification, which may become evident in a long-term relationship when sexual desire wanes (Brendler, 2002).

Sometimes, this type of problem becomes an important source of relationship conflict and personal suffering after the birth of the first child or of subsequent children (Brendler, 2003b). Motherhood requires time, dedication, and energy and women with HSDD often remain enraptured/captive in such a role, a role that they have dreamed of and for which they were trained (Brendler, 2003b).

The working role may be achieved through a job or a career, the latter demanding a continuous investment. In the case of a career, women will have to be able to manage their multiple roles. After motherhood, it becomes more important for working women to share their household chores with their husbands, in order to avoid significant stress. In 2008, women's share of participation in the work market was 51.4%, while that of men's was 66.9% (*Correio do Povo*, 2009b). The entry of women into the professional market has tripled their working hours. Moreover, according to the International Confederation of Free Trade Unions (ICFTU), Brazilian women have the largest discrepancy in income (relative to men's) in the world, earning 34% less than men (*Zero Hora*, 2009a). From 1993 to 2007, the number of Brazilian families headed by women increased tenfold, reaching 3.6 million in 2007 (*Correio do Povo*,

2009a). These statistics highlight the difficult balance between life and work for women. Most women in Brazil do not have equality, in either their family life or their working life outside the home. Many of them are unhappy about their partners' role in relation to the house and the children and women report that their tiredness and routine daily activities are the factors that most hamper their sexual functioning (Abdo, 2004).

Two factors emerge as especially relevant to the psycho-socio-cultural etiology of HSDD in Brazilian women: first, the lack of identification with the role of a sexual woman and second, a difficulty in managing traditional gender roles within a marriage embedded in the modern world.

Therapeutic Strategies in Cases of Low Sexual Desire

The Therapeutic Interview

Included in Kaplan's (1995) "sexual inciters," that is, the positive perceptions, thoughts, affects, and behaviors which can enhance sexual desire, are all of the following: partner's attractiveness; partner is congruent with sexual fantasy; partner is seductive; partner is responsive; conducive ambience; sexual fantasies; love; novelty; adequate physical stimulation; absence of negative emotions and thoughts; and a favorable situation. Sexual desire may be reduced in situations opposed to the ones above, and also if there are any of the following present: negative, repulsive, aversive, or frightening mental images, love for another person, inadequate physical stimulation, depression, anxiety, a threatening situation, and excessive familiarity with one's partner (Kaplan, 1995). All of these factors are considered by health professionals in Brazil when presented with a client with low sexual desire.

Most sex therapists in Brazil utilize a cognitive-behavioral approach. In the first session, after listening to the patient's or couple's account of their presenting problem, a therapeutic contract is negotiated, usually for one session a week. Individual psychotherapy will be indicated for the female partner only when she has no sexual dysfunction, when the man is seductive in such a way that could reasonably lead to sexual desire, when there are no unresolved gender issues between the couple, and when there are no major marital conflicts. If all of the above conditions are present, sex therapy will be indicated for the couple.

The psychotherapist must exclude medications, hormonal disorders, and physical and emotional disorders such as depression, that may cause HSDD. In order to rule out possible hormonal disorders, assessment of serum prolactin levels and thyroid hormones (Brendler, 2006) is recommended. Testosterone levels are not correlated with low sexual desire (Davis, Davidson, Donath, & Bell, 2005; Dennerstein, Randolph, Taffe,

Dudley, & Burger, 2002; North American Menopause Society, 2005) and the assessment of free serum testosterone levels is therefore controversial in the literature; nevertheless, it is often still carried out by doctors in Brazil in order to rule out any organic factor for HSDD. If abnormal prolactin and thyroid hormone levels are detected, these must be corrected. It is not uncommon that the HSDD complaint persists after hormonal treatment, necessitating a referral to a sex therapist; in some cases there is more than one etiology involved in the dysfunction (Brendler, 2006).

The second step in sex therapy, when the etiology is a psycho-sociocultural one (in all dysfunctions but particularly in relation to HSDD), is to perceive/visualize the woman in her general life context. How is her self-esteem? Does she feel valued as a person? How is her professional life? Besides the family life, is there a marital life? Does the couple exist beyond the social context, and can they be intimate? How does the erotic encounter take place? What are the feelings and perceptions about the couple's sexual life and self-eroticism? How much time is invested in herself, in the couple, and in the couple's sexuality? Is there energy for sex? Does sex take place when she is tired? Does she manage the home and the children on her own, or does a male partner play an important role? Although not all these questions will be addressed in the first interview, it is important that the therapist be cognizant of these over the first few sessions, as they will provide a "global map" of how the woman finds herself in relation to the exercise of her multiple roles.

Behavioral Assignments and Cognitive Techniques

Some of the approaches used for the treatment of HSDD and most other sexual problems are: (a) identifying and clarifying beliefs, values, and myths regarding sexuality; (b) support for the individual/couple; (c) cognitive restructuring (Ellis, 1991). Unlike other sexual problems, in the case of HSDD there is no consensus in the scientific literature about the optimal sequence for applying the various techniques. We discuss here the approach used most commonly in Brazil.

Kaplan (1995) suggested that in the treatment of HSDD, besides modifying or eliminating all countersexual behaviors, the sexual inciters must be found or reestablished. There must also be an emphasis on raising the patient's awareness of his or her tendency to engage in negative, antisexual (cognitive and perceptual) mental processes during sexual encounters that "turn off" sexual arousal, and cognitive restructuring to modify such processes. Most sexual therapists in Brazil first suggest "intercourse prohibition" (a ban on intercourse) for the couple as homework. This is a well-known intervention developed by Masters and Johnson (1970) and it is often used in Brazil for treating individuals with sexual problems. In some cases, during the "intercourse prohibition" phase, the man is free to have an orgasm on his own (i.e., during masturbation), mainly in the beginning of treatment. In this situation, there is less likelihood that the man will exert pressure for vaginal intercourse. Women with HSDD usually have little interest in engaging in any sexual behavior, including masturbation. The woman may also feel less guilty, as her partner will have orgasmic pleasure, while she will devote herself to sexual tasks aiming at rekindling her sexual desire.

The therapist also encourages better communication between the couple, suggesting that they discuss the homework, the feelings and sensations evoked, and that they bring such material to the next psychotherapy session. The woman's weekly agenda is discussed so that, besides her professional tasks, and those related to child care and household tasks, a space is created for her as a person, as a woman, and also for the homework. If during the stage of "intercourse prohibition," there has been an increase (even a slight one) in the woman's sexual desire, Sensate Focus I (SF-I), and later Sensate Focus II (SF-II), as described by Masters and Johnson (1970) may be introduced. In SF-I, the couple will be naked and one of them will gently caress the other's body, except for the genitals (and also the woman's breasts). One partner will be the touch "giver," and the other the "receiver." The receiver must focus on the sensations and feelings touching causes, without giving negative feedback (unless something feels uncomfortable). The person doing the touching may use different methods of contact, pressure, and texture. In SF-II, one starts by touching the body (as in SF-I) but there is also permission to touch the genitals and breasts. Oral sex is allowed. This will be particularly appropriate in cases in which the woman suffers from a mild reduction of her sexual desire or when the problem has existed for a short duration. Such clinical presentation is rare in Brazil, as most couples with sexual problems take many years to seek treatment (Brendler, 2001, 2003a).

Another technique that may be used in the early stage of treatment is the sexual menu (Brendler, 2005), which is based on "thinking about sexuality/sex or romance" through the creation of a "repertoire of erotic scenes," mainly comprised of films and books with some sensual, sexual, or romantic content, which will be part of the "homework." By thinking of the scenes in the sexual menu several times a day, a habit may be created of thinking positively about sexuality, which will facilitate the rekindling of sexual desire. This technique may be used for any type of sexual desire problem, in individual or couple therapy (Brendler, 2005b, 2007). For most of my patients, I prescribe the sexual menu technique before couples begin SF-I (Masters & Johnson, 1970), as women must first "eroticize" their minds before enjoying the benefits of the SF exercises.

In brief, the sexual menu technique has three steps (Brendler, 2005a,b). In Step 1, the woman is instructed to organize her day, so that she has a time slot when she is relaxed and on her own, to make use of the suggested material. If she is using a film, she is asked to rewatch the individual sensual/sexual or romantic scenes. If a book or short story has been chosen, she is asked to read the individual paragraphs with erotic or romantic content. She will note the scenes in films/books that she enjoyed and will then have a personal list of scenes that appealed most to her (her individual "sexual menu"). In Step 2, "scene memorization," it is suggested she rewatches/rereads the chosen scene, closes her eyes, and tries to imagine the scene. In Step 3, the woman is asked to think, many times during the day/night, about the sexuality/romance scenes chosen that comprise her sexual menu. As the introduction of new habits is a hard task, the therapist may suggest times for the woman to think of the sexual menu, which will help the development of the habit of "thinking about sexuality or romance." Initially, the woman is requested to make use of her repertoire of chosen scenes at three specified times a day. The times mentioned serve as a strategy to remind the patient of the firm commitment she has made to thinking about sexuality/sex/romance. The making of a list of appealing scenes will provide easy access to the chosen erotic scenes.

The woman is informed that it might be difficult to find scenes in books or films that she likes and finds erotic but the repetition of this technique with several films, books, or stories will provide suitable scenes. As the technique is to be used individually, the woman is free from the pressure of being observed by her partner and of attending to him or his sexual demands, which helps her to engage with her own feelings and sensations. Ideally, the sexual menu is used after the prescription of the intercourse prohibition technique as, free from the pressure of having sex with her partner and motivated by the habit of thinking and involving herself more with sexuality and romance in her daily life, her sexual desire will be stimulated. Subsequently, she will perceive the partner's sexual advances/approaches with more interest. This new, more sensual behavior will increase her self-esteem, leaving her more confident in her role of a sexual woman.

Films with two or three nonexplicit sex scenes are the early material often preferred by women who use the sexual menu. I suggest the use of specific films when the patient does not recall any material that she has found arousing in the past. Subsequently, short stories or books can be suggested. Regarding the use of romance in the sexual menu, some women, as a function of repressive social and cultural standards, have difficulty with more explicit sexuality. Therefore, a solution may be to use less explicit, more "romantic" stimuli. This "romantic sex" allows women to let themselves be sensually and erotically "taken," as love is perceived as something noble and respectable. Romance in films and books that have in their stories the familiar connection between affection and sexuality, which has been valued since their childhood, is often capable of reactivating sexual desire and arousal. There is also a much smaller group of women who, after the awakening of their sexual desire, migrate to more sexually explicit films.

In "Becoming Orgasmic," Heiman and LoPiccolo (1988) included a list of erotic books for women to read. The authors recommended that the reader combine genital self-stimulation with the erotic material, as part of the treatment of orgasmic dysfunction. Erotic films are the most commonly used material in laboratory research on sexual arousal in women (Meston & McCall, 2005). After the popularization of video and DVDs, films were also more broadly employed by sex therapists as homework in cases of orgasmic and arousal problems. The sexual menu is the first report of a technique using films/books for sexual desire problems in women, based on instruction to "frequently think" about sexuality/sex/romance scenes.

When, after using the sexual menu, a woman perceives any increase in her sexual desire, she may be asked if she could watch the film or read the book with her sexual partner (some women take this initiative without being directed to do so by the therapist). I do not prescribe sensate focus exercises I (SF-I) if, with the use of the sexual menu, a significant improvement in sexual desire occurs, because frequently in such cases, couples will start having sexual intercourse. When such an outcome occurs, besides the use of the sexual menu, it is due to the influence of the therapy sessions during the prior maintenance of the ban on intercourse. Other possible techniques are those of permission-giving, specific suggestions of the PLISSIT model (Annon, 1980), "fantasy training" (Kaplan, 1985, p. 154), and "fantasy sharing" (Kaplan, 1983, 1995; Masters & Johnson, 1988).

I use two questionnaires with patients: "What helps sexual arousal?" (Brendler, 2008, 2009a) and "What hampers sexual arousal?" (Brendler, 2010). These questionnaires,[2] which are completed at home and brought to therapy, are designed to help the individual/couple realize what their own "turn-ons" and "turn-offs" are. According to Basson (2000), responsive sexual desire comes after, or simultaneous with, sexual arousal, and it is most common in women in long-term relationships. In cases of HSDD, these questionnaires are given to patients after there has been some improvement in sexual desire. Often when they return with their questionnaires, I introduce permission for "fantasy sharing" because the individual/couple spontaneously mentions during the session some kind of special clothing or sexual practice in a specific situation as a factor that enhances arousal. I ask them to speak about their preferences after completing the "What helps sexual arousal?" questionnaire as one way of "fantasy sharing."

In cases of HSDD, it is also important that the therapist works on the following issues with the individual or couple: (a) investing in oneself (e.g., being in a continuous state of growth, not neglecting physical appearance); (b) investing in the relationship (e.g., trying to listen to the other, as well as initiating and maintaining dialogue, making time available for the relationship, protecting the couple's privacy); (c) investing in the other (e.g., being alert to the other's needs, desires, and interests, stimulating and validating the other's behavior (Brendler, 2005a,b); (d) investing in the negotiation of household chore sharing (e.g., encouraging the man to share domestic chores and child care (Brendler, 2007).

Marta and Carlos: A Case of Hypoactive Sexual Desire Disorder

Both Marta and Carlos[3] were 33 years old and White; she was a college professor; he was the owner of a store. He graduated as a veterinarian and she obtained a doctorate.

Reason for Consultation

The couple sought help because Marta didn't feel like having sex and this was a source of conflict between them. Carlos reported that the problem had been evident for 3 years, since their daughter's birth. When their daughter was 2 months old, they moved to the capital, when Marta became head of a college at the university. Marta said, "It was hard to deal with three new things at the same time: motherhood, the new job, and the unfamiliar city." For 2 years, "the house, the daughter, everything" was her responsibility, and Carlos was only in charge of the store. Before this time, she used to feel like having sex, and then "everything happened."

Marta had normal hormone levels (total and free testosterone and prolactin) and reported she had taken, upon her doctor's recommendation, Tribulus Terrestris (a herbal supplement that contains protodioscin, reputed to increase dehydroepiandrosterone (5-DHEA) and dehydrotestosterone (DHT), an off-label [unauthorized] prescription for low sexual desire). There had, however, been no improvement in her sexual drive. Marta also used oral contraception and had no physical health problems. Marta said her doctor had referred her to me and she had also visited my website (www.terapiadosexo.med.br) and was reassured by what she read there, particularly that she was not "the only one" with problems related to sexual desire. Marta also said "We initially sought a "magic pill" for my problem, but now sexual therapy is our last hope."

Carlos's and Marta's Families of Origin and Sexual Development

Marta was the youngest child, having one older brother. She lived in a town until she was 15; then, after her parents got divorced, she was forced to move to a farm. Her parents got divorced because the father had a "whore" girlfriend. She said her father was selfish, for he could support two families, but neglected his children. Until she was 15, she had only flirted a little. She didn't remember masturbating in childhood or adolescence, or engaging in any erotic play. Menarche occurred when she was 10 and her mother explained sex to her with the "little bee" book. Marta remembers her mother saying "but this is after your marriage" and "watch yourself, you are fertile now." Carlos had relationships with two girlfriends (each lasting less than 4 months) and first had sexual intercourse at 19 years old with a girlfriend. Carlos's father was a conservative person and spoke about fidelity in marriage, and traditional gender roles, but did not discuss sex or condoms. Five years ago Carlos's parents got divorced because his mother did not enjoy sex with his father.

Marta and Carlos were introduced through friends at university. Marta said she dated Carlos because: "he was unaffected and good-looking, was going to be faithful, transmitted trust." They had dated for 7 years before getting married. When she finished the doctorate and he finished college, they lived together for 3 months and then got married. Before meeting him, Marta did not trust men, for her father had been unfaithful after 25 years of marriage.

Carlos had had little sexual experience and Marta was a virgin when they met. Carlos was only her second boyfriend. Her first sexual experience was with Carlos, after they had dated for a year. She said that she was afraid to let her mother down, as she was a conservative and used to speak of "guarding yourself for marriage so as not to get a bad name." The first occasion the couple had sex, it was very good and Marta said she had had an orgasm.

The current situation was that the couple said that they loved each other, valued the family, and so wanted Marta's sexual drive to return. They had been married for almost 5 years, but had talked of separating because of the sexual problem. Carlos complained that Marta didn't want to be kissed. He felt rejected and said he knew that he was "edgy," but he thought it was normal to want sex every day. He couldn't understand Marta's reason for changing; when they had dated and early in their marriage, she had liked sex.

Carlos pressed Marta for sex every day. They had sex twice a week, and she complained: "this only makes everything worse, as it doesn't help emotionally." Marta spends weekdays at the university and commented that, "There is little time left for us at night" after cooking dinner and taking care of their daughter. Carlos spent the evening on the computer, talking with friends through social networking sites.

Marta said that both her mother and mother-in-law were homemakers and she had never imagined that balancing everything would be so hard. She says it was hard to accept the idea of having sex, but she did usually get aroused during intercourse; the "man-on-top" position was the easiest one for her to have an orgasm.

Summary of Therapy Sessions 1–4

In the first session, I commented that HSDD was the most common sexual problem among women, which Marta said made her feel better. When I asked about fantasies and sexual thoughts, Marta said she didn't have any fantasies. We discussed the fact that a true lack of sexual desire exists when a woman has an "inability to respond to cues and triggers that previously would have elicited sexual desire" (Basson, 2000 p.63). Marta did not have such an experience, as Carlos had not been seductive since they were married (e.g., he no longer wrote her erotic notes as he had during their dating period). We discussed the fact that if both of them made an effort, sexual therapy would be an opportunity for the couple to grow beyond the sexual issue. We made a therapy contract of one session per week and "intercourse prohibition" was introduced. I recommended that the couple not have sexual intercourse for a while, so as not to pressure Marta into having sexual desire. I asked how they felt about this. Carlos said: "I don't like it…but if it is for a while, I'll accept it." Marta liked the ban on intercourse and said she would remind Carlos of the ban if he insisted on having sex. As discussed earlier, Carlos was told that he could reach an orgasm on his own, but not during partnered sex. Emotional displays of affection between the couple were encouraged.

In the second session, Marta said she would like to kiss Carlos, but that he already had excess "fire." I reminded the couple that there was a ban on intercourse and reinforced again that showing affection verbally and also by kissing, hugging, and caressing was not prohibited.

In the third and fourth sessions, the couple reported that Marta felt more spontaneous about showing affection and had even accepted two French kisses. The couple recognized that this had reduced the affective and erotic detachment between them.

Session 5

We discussed the fact that for Marta there had been an internalization of values that linked her honor and the chance of getting married to her virginity. For her, due to her parents' divorce, sex had been a reason for emotional and economic suffering. During most of her life, sex was linked to threats and suffering, with the exception of the early passionate stage of the relationship with Carlos when she had enjoyed sex. I explained that such events had prevented her from identifying with the role of a "sexual woman" and that the reconnection with this role would be allowed and encouraged during treatment. Carlos felt relieved when we talked about Marta's history. Her negative view of sex predated their dating. Marta said she loved Carlos, but also perceived that her image of a man, after her father abandoned her, was negative. In regard to sexual roles, the couple agreed that since they both experienced their own mothers in the traditional role of homemaker, those roles were strongly internalized in them. Marta found it difficult to ask Carlo to share household chores and child care, and he found it difficult to take the initiative. We discussed the fact that values transmitted by the family and reinforced by the social group and the culture change very slowly. If Carlos shared house chores with Marta, she would have more free time and energy to take care of herself and perform the sex therapy homework. Carlos promised that, at night, he would cook dinner, clean up, and maybe give their daughter her bath, all before she arrived home from work. In regard to the homework, the "intercourse prohibition" was still maintained. I underlined the importance of the sexual menu homework.

Session 6

Carlos had cooked dinner and bathed their daughter. Marta had watched a film and liked the kissing and sex scenes. She commented that it was "a luxury, a gift" to watch the film by herself, and that she hadn't done this for 3 years.

Marta complained that she and Carlos always go out as a family and not as a couple. When I asked, Carlos responded by saying that if Marta were a new girlfriend he wouldn't spend so much time on the computer and they would go out as a couple.

Session 7

The couple disclosed that they called one another "daddy" and "mommy." I said that this was a reflection of their current life; they did not see themselves in the roles of a sexual man and woman. At home, Carlos had asked Marta: "How long will the coitus prohibition last? It is better to have an orgasm with you!" They argued, but he apologized because Marta had worked on her sexual menu and felt herself "getting enthusiastic" in one scene of the film. I gave her permission to masturbate if she felt sexual desire when watching the films. Carlos said he was keeping our agreement about home chores. We discussed the fact that they used to have sex last thing at night, when Marta was already very tired. They realized that this situation was antierotic, as were their arguments. For their homework, I suggested they begin SF-I. I advised the couple to first get naked. Marta would first initiate gently caresses of Carlos's body (front and back, except his penis). Then, it would be Carlos's turn to do the same (without touching Marta's breasts and genitals). The person receiving the touch should focus on the sensations and feelings caused by the touching. It was not necessary to comment on the touching, unless it was perceived as unpleasant. On a second occasion, touching could progress beyond light touching, in order to arouse different sexual dimensions (mild, firm, smooth, coarse, hot, cold); different textures may also be employed (silky, lacy, creamy). Besides providing a sense of well-being, touching would be an opportunity for the couple to first find out and learn what feels pleasant and what pleases the other. In the sexual menu technique, I suggested websites with erotic content.

Sessions 8 and 9

The couple reported that both had initiated one session of SF-I, Marta being the first to initiate touching. The technique reminded them of when they started dating (a good time). The couple commented that they were feeling closer. Marta had watched the erotic film and noticed that she "liked to hear what the man said during intercourse." She had also read erotic tales and thought about sex. We discussed other possible triggers for sexual drive, besides those already used (films, books, stories), as well as the sense organs and erotic play. I gave the couple the questionnaires on "what helps" and "what hampers" sexual arousal. Their responses to the questionnaire indicated that Carlos liked women to wear dresses and high-heeled boots and Marta discovered she liked to hear moaning in films and to be told that she was "hot." We discussed the factors that most affected their desire, arousal, and orgasm (positively and negatively). Regarding homework, I asked them to begin SF-II.

Session 10

Marta had watched three films, one of these with Carlos, as she had wanted "erotic play." She reported having often thought about sex and had suggested a SF-II session and had also worn sexy clothes. After this Marta had felt a lot of desire and had become very aroused and for the first time since the ban was introduced, the couple had engaged in intercourse, after 9 months of sex therapy. Marta marked the "erotic scene" in a story and asked Carlos to read it to her. I emphasized that Marta was more certain of her sexual drive and of her sexual potential.

Session 11

Carlos said that last week he had had "the best Valentine's Day in my life." Marta had bought sexual clothes and before leaving for work, she had scattered little notes around for him to "find his gift" (the sexy clothes she was going to wear). At night, Carlos gave her flowers and had hid the clothes again, to see her bending in search of them, so he could see her "from every angle". Marta had felt a lot of desire, and they had engaged in intercourse. She commented, "Sex is starting to be a part in my life."

Session 12

Marta had watched two movies. There was one day that she said, "I didn't stop thinking about sex." I commented that they both had to be congratulated but that to establish the new behaviors they needed to adhere to the ban on intercourse. Carlos responded, "I'd prefer to have it all allowed, but our team is winning!…so, and only so, I'll obey." We discussed the fact that it may not be easy for Carlos to be seductive for two reasons: first, he had received refusals from her and second, they had been socialized to believe that seduction belonged to the dating period and not to marriage. We talked about how one of the sexual challenges in marriage was to keep the seduction going.

Sessions 13 and 14

Carlos was again spending a great deal of time on the computer at night. I reminded him of his agreement to share the home chores and tell Marta "erotic stuff." Marta reported that she thought a lot about sex and the couple had engaged in erotic play on two occasions. Marta asked Carlos to record an erotic story on an MP3 player so that she could drive to work listening to the erotic story. Now Carlos is trying to "speak more during erotic play." Marta commented "We women are slaves of ancient and perfect dreams: of being a good mother, a good housewife, and now even a new dream, of being a good professional, but we never thought of the sexual woman, as if it were less important." As Marta had experienced sexual desire on many occasions, I lifted the ban on sexual intercourse.

Sessions 16 and 17

Marta and her daughter had stayed with her mother, apart from Carlos. The couple had missed each other, and upon reuniting, had intercourse. Carlos said he had spent more time with Marta and she thought that Carlos had been more talkative. Last week, Carlos asked for "something that would raise the dead, a female Viagra"; his view was that they had both progressed, but that he would like something more definitive and quick. Marta noted that her husband was "impatient." She had worn sexy clothes, watched a film, and thought about sex; there was a good atmosphere between them, and intercourse occurred. The couple was also planning to have another child.

Sessions 18 and 19

Marta had been away on two trips in 3 days. In the first trip with her students the topic on the bus was "sex all the time" and she had felt sexual desire. Carlos wanted to have sex on three occasions. She refused twice, being tired from the trips. Intercourse occurred once and it was great, as Carlos had called her "hot."

Sessions 20–22

Marta had bought a gift, "chocolate-flavored condoms" and had performed fellatio, with Carlos wearing a condom; they also had intercourse. Marta said she was thinking regularly about sex and romance. Two weeks ago they had gone to the beach, their first trip without their daughter. There they had intercourse on three occasions. After this trip, Marta said she had thought a lot about sex and they had intercourse on two occasions. The week before Marta had complained about Carlos's insistence on having intercourse without foreplay. They had watched three new films together, she had felt desire, and they had engaged in intercourse three times. Carlos acknowledged that he understood he had been raised with beliefs that did not encourage men to control their sex drive, but that it was possible to postpone intercourse. Through his initiative the couple had acquired a new habit, "dating" through a social network site during her breaks at university.

Sessions 23 and 24

Marta had said "no" to two professional invitations because staying home would give her more energy and make her feel less tired. Carlos gave her flowers again, they had a shower together, and there was erotic play and intercourse.

Sessions 25 and 29

Marta had been innovative: she had worn dental-floss panties and on another occasion she used flavored gel in her genitals. They had engaged in erotic play and intercourse. Carlos had written her a romantic card. Three weeks ago they had intercourse on three occasions, all of which were very good. He gave her flowers again. Two weeks ago they went to a dance party and 2 days later, as her desire was "accumulating and rising," they had intercourse. During the previous week Marta had been away to give a lecture and when she returned, Carlos gave her a love note. Marta noticed her self-esteem had improved.

Session 30

In this session we discussed the termination of sex therapy. Marta commented that "both of us used not to think of priorities: what is the time for each one, for courtship, for working, for the family?" She was committed to keep thinking about sexuality/sex and romance, and thought that this would be easy, as it was now a habit. ("Now, I can use the previous times" as "aphrodisiac scenes.") Marta said she wanted to have the experience of having a baby "with romance," that is, with both of them looking after the child, something Carlos had understood to be important.

Follow-Up Session

As previously agreed, approximately 2 months after termination, we met for a follow-up session. The couple was very confident about being able to maintain the new behaviors learned in sex therapy. They commented that "sexual desire made our sexuality spontaneous and our life happier."

Case Discussion

In therapy with Marta and Carlos, four techniques were instrumental: intercourse prohibition, cognitive restructuring, the sexual menu, and work on improving communication between the couple. Additional techniques used were fantasy sharing, permission-giving, specific suggestions, and therapeutic procedures common to other types of psychotherapy (e.g., empathy, support for the partner).

The ban on intercourse helped the couple express physical affection and nongenital touching and was also the basis for the sexual menu and SF-I and II techniques. Marta and Carlos were given guidance on how to improve their communication. An important part of improving communication involved the therapist inquiring into the etiology of the desire problems. Since the early sessions, we had discussed the fact that throughout her life Marta had internalized many of the traditional sexual standards; for example, in adolescence, her mother had emphasized that her virginity was highly valued. Marta felt she needed to control male advances on behalf of her honor and her marriage. She had felt pressured to remain a virgin, afraid to disappoint her mother by having sex before getting married. For Marta, sex was linked to emotional and financial suffering rather than pleasure. It was explained to the couple that Marta's early experiences had prevented her from identifying as a sexual woman, in contrast with the other roles with which she had identified (mother, professional, and homemaker). The sexual menu technique helped Marta develop and realize her own sexuality. The sexual menu initially conferred an unanticipated pleasure on Marta: having time to watch films by herself, something she hadn't been able to do for years. As with many other Brazilian women, Marta had had very little time for herself, as the priority in her life had been her daughter and her professional work.

Prior to therapy Marta had not been assertive about refusing intercourse. When approached by Carlos (daily), she gave in to his pressure and ended up having sex she didn't want twice a week. In the beginning of treatment, she already perceived that accepting sex created ambivalent feelings that "only made the situation worse." As her sexual desire and her self-esteem improved, she was able to feel less guilty about not having sexual desire all the time. Carlos's pressure to have sex only worked, before therapy, because of contributions from both of them; the "intercourse prohibition" technique was helpful in breaking this pattern of behavior. Carlos began to accept that his sexual desire was amenable to control.

Cognitive restructuring was used to challenge Carlos's belief that men do not need to seduce their wives. Another factor that helped Carlos create seduction strategies was the improvement in Marta's sexual desire, which resulted in her flirting and which reinforced Carlos's initial efforts at seduction. Discussion about factors that positively and negatively interfere with sexual desire was helpful (Kaplan, 1995). Finding novelty in the couple's erotic taste (using their responses to the "What helps sexual arousal?" questionnaires), improved sexual communication and allowed them to "share fantasies." Permission-giving was used in relation to the possibility of Marta's masturbation.

Cognitive restructuring was important in relation to gender roles. The couple came to understand the fact that since Marta had a career, Carlos needed to participate in the household chores. Confrontation was used effectively with Carlos, in relation to his "boycotting" both the chores and the treatment (e.g., his excessive time spent on the computer, and his reluctance to accept the intercourse prohibition).

Since values transmitted during social and cultural socialization change slowly, Marta and Carlos were having difficulty changing their behavior in their marriage. However, both partners were committed to maintaining the newly acquired flirting rituals: having lunch together, exchanging erotic ideas, going out as a couple. Carlos also committed himself to being seductive with Marta and Marta was committed to continue thinking about sexuality/sex/romance.

Summary and Conclusions

The image of the Brazilian woman publicized in pictures and movies, wearing loincloths and bikinis on Brazil's tropical beaches, as well as dancing samba wearing little clothing during carnival, is associated with liberal values that do not represent the profile of an ordinary woman, such as the one portrayed in this chapter.

Marta presented with the most common sexual problem affecting Brazilian women: low sexual desire (Abdo et al., 2004). Some of the etiological factors in this case were: lack of identification with the role of a sexual woman, a nonseductive partner, and difficulty dealing with gender roles. Marta, in common with many Brazilian women, had linked sexuality with affection during her emotional development. She had had her first sexual experience with her boyfriend, performed masturbation mostly in the couple context, and valued virginity and fidelity in affective bonds, which included the man's fidelity. Her expectations were not met after she and Carlos married. Carlos, like most Brazilian men, had internalized the stereotype of a virile man, one who has high levels of sexual desire that need to be satisfied. Seduction was important as a strategy for conquering new partners but not in a marriage. All of these internalizations were sources of sexual and marital conflict, and were very evident in this case. As the prevailing gender role socialization in Brazil still promulgates these traditional views of male and female sexuality, it is predictable that conflicts arise, particularly as nowadays most women work outside the home. In the case presented here, there was conflict in relation to those roles, which were successfully worked through in therapy. Marta, in common with most other Brazilian women, had learned to place a high value on motherhood/children and professional life. These values were passed on by her family of origin and reinforced by society and culture. Sex therapy helped Marta to identify with the role of a "sexual woman," in the context of a long-term relationship.

Health professionals in Brazil and other cultures should encourage sexual education for adults, so that they will perceive sexuality as something wonderful and essential to human happiness, and may pass on such positive images to their children. This type of education might permit more women to identify with the role of a sexual woman (Brendler, 2002).

Notes

1. Multiracial people with one Black parent and one White one are known as "mulatto" in Brazil.
2. English language versions of these questionnaires are available from the author.
3. "Marta" and "Carlos" are pseudonyms.

References

Abdo, C. H. N. (2004). *Estudo da Vida Sexual do Brasileiro* [Study of Brazilian sexual life]. São Paulo, Brazil: Editora Bregantini.

Abdo, C. H. N., Oliveira, W. M., Moreira, E. D., & Fittipaldi, J. A. S. (2004). Prevalence of sexual dysfunction and correlated conditions in a sample of Brazilian women—Results of Brazilian Study on Sexual Behavior (BSSB*). International Journal of Impotence Research, 16*, 160–166.

Almeida, M. C., Aquino, E. M., Gaffikin, L., & Magnani, R. J. (2003). Contraceptive use among adolescents at public schools in Brazil. *Revista de Saúde Pública, 37*, 566–575.

Annon, J. S. (1980). Tratamento Comportamental dos Problemas Sexuais [Behavioral treatment of sexual problems]. Maria A. Madail & Filipe da Cunha (trans). São Paulo, Brazil: Manole.

Azevedo, T. (1981). Namoro à antiga: tradição e mudança [Dating to the ancient, tradition and change]. In Velho, G. e Figueira, S. (orgs). *Família, psicologia e sociedade* [Family psychology and society] (pp. 219–276). Rio de Janeiro, Brazil: Campus.

Barbosa, R. M., Koyama, M. A. H., & Grupo de Estudos em População, Sexualidade e Aids (2008). Comportamento e práticas sexuais de homens e mulheres, Brasil 1998 e 2005 [Sexual behavior and practices of men and women, Brazil 1998 and 2005]. *Revista de Saúde Pública, 42*, 21–33.

Basson, R. (2000). The female sexual response: A different model. *Journal of Sex & Marital Therapy, 26*, 51–65.

Basson, R., Berman, J., Burnett, A., Derogatis, L., Fergunson, D., Fourcroy, J., ... Whipple, B. (2000). Report of international consensus development conference on female sexual dysfunction: Definitions and classifications. *The Journal of Urology, 163*, 888–893.

Bonzon, M. (2004). *Sociologia da Sexualidade* [Sociology and sexuality]. Rio de Janeiro, Brazil: Editora FGV.

Borges, A. L. V. (2007). Relações de gênero e iniciação sexual de mulheres adolescents [Gender relations and sexual initiation of adolescent women]. *Revista da Escola de Enfermagem da USP, 41,* 597–604.

Borges, A. L. V., & Schor, N. (2005). Início da vida sexual na adolescência e relações degênero: um estudo transversal em São Paulo, Brasil, 2002 [Onset of sexual relations in adolescence and gender: A cross-sectional study in São Paulo, Brazil, 2002]. *Caderno de Saúde Pública, 21*, 499–507.

Bourdieu, P. (1999). *A dominação masculine* [Male domination] M. H.Khuner (trans.). Rio de Janeiro, Brazil: Bertrand Brasil.

Brendler, J. (1997). Características de 55 casos de disfunções sexuais [Characteristics of 55 cases of sexual dysfunction]. *Revista Brasileirade Ginecologia e Obstetrícia* (Federação Brasileira das Sociedades de Ginecologia e Obstetrícia [Brazilian Federation of Societies of Gynecology and Obstetrics]), *19,* S, 159.

Brendler, J. (2000). Perfil de mulheres com algum tipo de anorgasmia [Profile of women with a type of anorgasmia]. *6° Congresso Brasileiro Obstetrícia e Ginecologia da Infância e Adolescência*, SOGIA [Proceedings of the 6th

Brazilian Congress of Obstetrics and Gynecology of Childhood and Adolescence, SOGIA], p. 46. http://www.sogia.com.br/

Brendler, J. (2001). A sexualidade de 35 mulheres com anorgasmia primária. *Anais do 8°* [The sexuality of 35 women with primary anorgasmia]. *Congresso Brasileiro de Sexualidade Humana*, SBRASH [Proceedings of the 8th Brazilian Congress of Human Sexuality, SBRASH], pp. 35–36. http://www.sbrash.org.br/

Brendler, J. (2002). A ausência de identificação feminina com a "mulher sexuada" apareceem relacionamentos de longa duração [The lack of identification with the female "sexual woman" appears in relationships of long duration]. *Revista Brasileira de Estudos em Sexualidade Humana*, 13, 15–19.

Brendler, J. (2003a). Incidence and profile of couples in which both partners have a sexual dysfunction. *Abstracts Book of 16th World Congress of Sexology*, WAS, p. 81.

Brendler, J. (2003b). A maternidade, o significado de ser mulher e o desejo sexual hipoativo [Motherhood, the meaning of being a woman and hypoactive sexual desire]. *Anais 6ª Jornada Gaúcha de sexualidade Humana—"Os Sentimentos,"* SBRASH [Proceedings of the 6th Day of Gaucho Human sexuality—" The Feelings," SBRASH], p. 11. http://www.sbrash.org.br/

Brendler, J. (2004). Características atuais do "ficar" entre mulheres e homens e a iniciação sexual. [Current characteristics of erotic behavior in men and women and sexual initiation]. *Revista da Associação Médica do RGS, Anais do 21ª Congresso da AMRIGS* [Journal of the Medical Association of the RGS, Proceedings of the 21st Congress of AMRIGS], p. 49.

Brendler, J. (2005a). "Sexual Menu": A new treatment based on "thinking about sex'" for women with hypoactive sexual desire disorder (HSDD). *Abstracts of the 17th World Congress of Sexology* (World Association for Sexual Health, abstract 311.9), p. 49.

Brendler, J. (2005b). "Cardápio Sexual": um novo tratamento baseado no "pensar emsexo" para mulheres com desejo sexual hipoativo (HSDD). ["Sexual Menu": A new treatment based on "thinking sex" for women with hypoactive sexual desire disorder (HSDD)]. *Revista Brasileira de Sexualidade Humana*, 16, 89–104.

Brendler, J. (2006). A sexualidade no climatério e o tratamento das disfunções sexuais noinício do século XXI [Sexuality during menopause and treatment of sexual dysfunctions in the 21st century]. *Revista Brasileira de Sexualidade Humana*, 17, 267–274.

Brendler, J. (2007). Reflexões sobre o papel da mulher em relação ao desejo sexual [Reflections on the role of women in relation to sexual desire]. *Revista Brasileira de Sexualidade Humana*, 18, 153–173.

Brendler, J. (2008). What helps sexual arousal of 726 Brazilian heterosexual women? *Sexologies: Abstracts of the 9th Congress of the European Federation of Sexology*, 17, S61.

Brendler, J. (2009a). What helps sexual arousal for 510 heterosexual men? *Abstract Book. The 19th World Congress for Sexual Health* (World Association for Sexual Health, abstract PO-1434), p. 206.

Brendler, J. (2009b). Choices, expectations, and attitudes in sex initiation of 700 Brazilian women. Abstract. *The 19th World Congress for Sexual Health* (World Association for Sexual Health, abstract PO-1435), p. 206.

Brendler, J. (2010). Questionnaire: what hampers heterosexual female sexual arousal? *Sexologies. Abstracts of the 10th Congress of the European Federation of Sexology* (Vol 19, Suppl. 1, S1-S150), p. S78 (T08.O.02).

Correio do Povo. (2009a, March 8). Chefes de família e donas do lar [Heads of families and home owners], p. 15.

Correio do Povo. (2009b, March 8). Elas procuram mais tempo por emprego [They seek more time for work], p. 15.

Davis, S. R., Davidson, S. L., Donath, S., & Bell, R. (2005). Relationships between circulating androgen levels and self-reported sexual function in women. *Journal of the American Medical Association, 294,* 91–96.

Dennerstein, L., Randolph, J., Taffe, J., Dudley, E., & Burger, H. (2002). Hormones, mood, sexuality, and the menopausal transition [Suppl.] *Fertility and Sterility, 77,* S42–S48.

Ellis, L. (1991). The revised ABC's of rational-emotive therapy (RET). *Journal of Rational-Emotive & Cognitive-Behavior Therapy, 9,* 139–172.

Fisher, H. (1992). *Anatomy of love: The mysteries of mating, marriage, and why we stray.* New York: Ballantine.

Fonseca, M. G., Bastos, F. I., Derrico, M., Tavares de Andrade, C. L., Travassos, C., & Landmann Szwarcwald, C. (2000). AIDS e grau de escolaridade no Brasil: evolução temporal de 1986 a 1996 [AIDS and level of education in Brazil: temporal evolution from 1986 to 1996]. *Cad. Saúde Pública, Rio de Janeiro, 16*(Sup. 1), 77–87.

Freyre, G. (1987). *Modos de homem, modas de mulher* [Men's modes, women's fashions]. Rio de Janeiro, Brazil: Record.

Goldenberg, M. (2002). *Nu & vestido* [Naked and dressed]. Rio de Janeiro, Brazil: Editora Record.

Goldenberg, M. (2004). *De perto ninguém é normal* [Close up no one is normal]. Rio de Janeiro, Brazil: Record.

Heilborn, M. L. (1991). Gênero e condição feminina: uma abordagem antropológica. In *IBAM (Instituto Brasileiro de Administração Municipal), Mulher e políticas públicas.* [Gender and status of women: An anthropological approach. In Brazilian Institute of Municipal Administration (IBAM), Women and public policy]. Rio de Janeiro, Brazil: IBAM/UNICEF.

Heilborn, M. L. (2004). *Dois é par: gênero e identidade sexual em contexto igualitário* [Gender and sexual identity in the context of equality] Rio de Janeiro, Brazil: Garamond. (Original work published 1992)

Heilborn, M. L., Aquino, E. M. L., Bozon, M., & Knauth, D. R. (2006). *O aprendizado da Sexualidade: reprodução e trajetórias sócias de jovens brasileiros* [The learning trajectories of young Brazilians in terms of sexuality, reproduction]. Rio de Janeiro, Brazil: Garamond.

Heilborn, M. L., & Cabral, C. S. (2006). Sexual practices in youth: Analysis of time, sexual trajectory, and last sexual intercourse. *Caderno de Saúde Pública, 22,* 1471–1481.

Heiman, J., LoPiccolo, L., & LoPiccolo, J. (1981). *Descobrindo o prazer: Uma proposta de crescimento sexual para a mulher* [Discovering pleasure. A pro-

posal for women's sexual growth]. Maria Helena Matarazzo, trans.). São Paulo, Brazil: Summus Editorial.
Kaplan, H. S. (1983). *O Desejo sexual e novos conceitos e técnicas da terapia do sexo: A nova terapia do sexo, Vol. 2*. [Sexual desire and new concepts and techniques of sex therapy: The new sex therapy, Vol. 2]. Aurea Weissenberg trans). Rio de Janeiro, Brazil: Editora Nova Fronteira.
Kaplan, H. S. (1985). *Comprehensive evaluation of disorders of sexual desire*. Arlington VA: American Psychiatric Press.
Kaplan, H. S. (1995). *The sexual desire disorders: Dysfunctional regulation of sexual motivation*. New York: Brunner/Mazel.
Knauth, D. R., Victoria, C. G., Leal, A. F., & Fachel, J. (2006). As trajetórias afetivo-sexuais: encontros, uniões e separação [The sexual-affective trajectories: Meetings, unions and separation]. In M. L. Heilborn, E. M. L. Aquino, M. Bozon, & D. R. Knauth (Eds.), *O aprendizado da Sexualidade: reprodução e trajetórias sócias de jovens brasileiros* [Learning about sexuality, reproduction and social trajectories of young Brazilians]. Rio de Janeiro, Brazil: Garamond.
Laumann, E. O., Nicolosi, A., Glasser, D. B., Paik, A., Gingell, C., Moreira, E., & Wang, T. (2005). Sexual problems among women and men aged 40–80y: Prevalence and correlates identified in the Global Study of Sexual Attitudes and Behaviors. *International Journal of Impotence Research, 17*, 39–57.
Leal, O. F., & Boff, A. M. (1996). Insultos, queixas, sedução e sexualidade: fragmentos deidentidade masculina em uma perspectiva relacional [Insults, complaints, seduction and sexuality: Fragments of masculine identity in a relational perspective]. In R. Parker & R. Barbosa (Eds.), *Sexualidades brasileiras* [Brazilian sexuality] (pp. 119–135). Rio de Janeiro, Brazil: Relume Dumará.
Levine, S. B. (2003). The nature of sexual desire: A clinician's perspective. *Archives of Sexual Behavior, 32*, 279–285.
Lipovetsky, G. (2000). *A terceira mulher:* permanência e revolução do feminine [The third woman: Permanence and feminine revolution]. (Maria Lucia Machado trans.). São Paulo: Companhia das Letras.
Masters, W. H., & Johnson, V. E. (1970). *Human sexual inadequacy*. Boston, MA: Little Brown.
Masters, W. H., Johnson, V. E. & Kolodny, R. (1988). Sexual fantasy. In. W. H. Masters, V. E. Johnson, & R. Kolodny (Eds.), *Masters and Johnson on Sex and Human Loving*. (pp. 263-281). Boston: Little Brown:
Meston, C. M., & McCall, K. M. (2005). Dopamine and norepinephrine responses to film-induced sexual arousal in sexually functional and sexually dysfunctional women. *Journal of Sex & Marital Therapy, 31*, 303–317.
Ministério da Saúde (2009a). A Pesquisa Nacional de Demografia e Saúde da Criança e da Mulher [National demographics and health of women and children]. http://bvsms.saude.gov.br/bvs/pnds/index.php
Ministério da saúde (2009b). Atividade Sexual e Anticoncepção [Sexual activity and contraception]. http://bvsms.saude.gov.br/bvs/pnds/atividade_sexual.php
Ministério da Saúde (2009c). Fecundidade e Intenções Reprodutivas das Mulheres [Fertility and reproductive intentions of women]. http://bvsms.saude.gov.br/bvs/pnds/fecundidade.php

Moreira, E. D. Jr., Glasser, D., Santos, B. D., & Gingell, C. (2005). Prevalence of sexual problems and related help-seeking behaviors among mature adults in Brazil: Data from the Global Study of Sexual Attitudes and Behaviors. *São Paulo Medical Journal, 123,* 23–41.

North American Menopause Society. (2005). The role of testosterone therapy in postmenopausal women: Position statement of The North American Menopause Society. *Menopause, 5,* 496–511, 649.

Paiva, V., Aranha, F., Bastos, F., & Grupo de Estudos em População, Sexualidade e Aids (2008). Opiniões e atitudes em relação a sexualidade: pesquisas âmbito nacional, Brasil 2005 [Opinions and attitudes toward sexuality: Research national survey, Brazil 2005]. [Suppl.] *Revista de Saúde Pública, 42,* S54–S64.

Parker, R. G., Herdt, G., & Carballo, M. (1991). Sexual culture, HIV transmission and AIDS research. *Journal of Sex Research, 28,* 77–98.

Pitt-Rivers, J. (1966). Honour and Social Status. In J. G. Peristiany (Ed.), *Honour and Shame* (pp. 19–77). London: Weidenfeld and Nicholson. Reprinted in J. Pitt-Rivers (1977). *The Fate of Shechem or the Politics of Sex: Essays in the Anthropology of the Mediterranean* (pp. 1–47). Cambridge, UK: Cambridge University Press, 1977.

Saffioti, H. I. B., & Almeida, S. S. (1995). *Violência de gênero: poder e impotência.* Rio de Janeiro: Revinter.

Sociedade Brasileira de Cirurgia Plástica. (2009). Plástica de mama ultrapassa lipo (Mammaplasty exceeds lipo]. http://www2.cirurgiaplastica.org.br/index.php?option=com_content&view=article&id=100:plastica-de-mama-ultrapassa-lipo&catid=42:saiu-na-midia&Itemid=87

Teixeira, A. M. F., Knauth, R. D., Fachel, J. M. G., & Leal, A. F (2006). Adolescentes e uso de preservativos: as escolhas dos jovens de três capitais brasileiras na iniciação e na ultima relação sexual [Adolescents and condom use: Choices by young people from three Brazilian state capitals in their first and last sexual intercourse]. *Caderno de Saúde Pública, 22,* 1385–1396.

Troiano, C. R. (2007). *Vida de equilibrista. Dores e delícias da mulher que trabalha* [The life of an acrobat: The pains and pleasures of a working woman]. São Paulo, Brasil: Cultrix.

Zero Hora. (2007, August 18). Brasileiro cada vez mais é dono de casa [Brazilians are increasingly home owners]. *Zero Hora,* p. 28.

Zero Hora. (2009a, March 8). Mulheres no comando: Vantagens e Desvantagens. Empregos & Oportunidades [Women in charge: The advantages and disadvantages. Jobs & Opportunities]. *Zero Hora,* p. 5.

Zero Hora. (2009b, October 10). Outros resultados da pesquisa do IBGE [Other search results IBGE]. Raça. Zero Hora, p. 31.

Editors Introduction to Chapter 12
Portugal

This chapter on Portugal presents an interesting example of what happens when sex therapy is imported from one culture to another. Soares and Nobre describe the "tidal wave of modernization" that swept across Portugal following the military coup in 1974. In the aftermath, the first psychology departments in Portuguese universities and in psychiatric hospitals were established, paving the way for the development of clinical sexology. The early pioneers of sex therapy and sex research in Portugal had strong ties to England, and in essence we see a British-inspired model of cognitive-behavioral sex therapy transplanted to the rich and diverse culture of Portugal. Several case examples illustrate the complexity of sexuality in Portugal, a country that is a blend of Arab, Jewish, Christian, and European influences. It is not hard to imagine that this scenario of importing and adapting sex therapy techniques to suit particular cultures will repeat itself in years to come as sex therapy makes inroads around the world.

12

SEXUAL PROBLEMS, CULTURAL BELIEFS, AND PSYCHOSEXUAL THERAPY IN PORTUGAL

Catarina Soares and Pedro Nobre

Historical Background

Whenever human sexuality is considered, it is inevitable to dwell upon its richness and complexity. It is the loom where all the strands that make us human are woven into a particular, idiosyncratic pattern. Those strands are emotions, physiology, psychological variables, social rules and norms, and, of course, the cultural traditions passed on through the generations from time immemorial. The further this complexity is unraveled, the clearer it becomes that to adequately understand it requires a truly psychosomatic approach (Bancroft, 2009).

To understand the demands on today's sex therapist it seems important to consider the cultural and social forces that have impacted both the shaping of present beliefs and behavior, and the creation of sexual therapy services.

Accordingly, let us briefly consider the following two aspects in relation to Portugal: the history of the study of sexuality, and how the current sexual therapy clinics were first developed in this country.

Portugal is of course universally known for its intrepid sailors, the so-called New World they discovered, and the long lasting empire therein established (the last Portuguese holding, Macao, was handed back to the Chinese in 1999). From its very foundation the country pulsed vitally with the three principal groups that made up its inhabitants. The conquered Arabs, many of whom remained and eventually blended in, left their distinct mark on the language, the names of many places, the architecture of the south of the country, the physical appearance of the people, and on many Portuguese customs and traditions. The traces of the Jews abound everywhere, be it in surnames, place names, recipes, and many traditions. Indeed, in faraway Istanbul, many families still keep the large front door key to the family home left behind in Portugal, when their forefathers were expelled from the country by order of the Inquisition. And lastly the Christians, who began their national existence in a climate of tolerance and acceptance of their neighbors, albeit post conquest, until the winds of religious intolerance were blown into a tornado by the Inquisition and much that was good was forever lost.

The discovery of the east trade routes meant the displacement of Venice, with Lisbon taking her place as the center of commercial enterprise and exchange. Making the sea its front door, the country prospered throughout the 16th century, and its capital became the hub of Europe and the melting pot of people of all colors, shapes, and sizes. More to the point, Lisbon became the meeting point for old and new ideas. Furthermore, as riches accumulated, there was more time and leisure for thinking and debating. Such a climate propitiated the old established schools while forging links with other European centers, and the country saw a flowering of learning.

The first prescriptions for sexual malaise, written in Portuguese, are to be found in the medical writings of two physicians of the 16th century. Garcia d'Horta was born in 1500, taught at Lisbon University, and spent his last years in Goa, where he died in 1568. In his discourses, writing about opium, he stated that the substance "does not incline them towards Venus, as some stupidly believe. Because opium not only does not stimulate Venus, but with its frigidity actually diminishes stimulation and contracts the spermatic vessels. And I know some lusitans (Portuguese) that through using it have become infertile and impotent." Thus, perhaps we could dispense similar advice to our drug addicted clients!

Amato Lusitano was born in 1511. He traveled widely and taught in many European universities, especially in Italy. In 1568 he died in Thessalonica, where he had taken refuge from the infamous Inquisition, and where he could at last publicly assume his Jewish faith. His prolific medical writings, known collectively as the *Centurias*, contained many references to sexual dysfunctions, both in the male and the female; both physical and psychological causes and possible remedies were discussed.

The Inquisition was established in Portugal by a papal bull of 1536, but it was slow to take root, whereupon, at the monarch's instance, it was confirmed by another papal bull in 1547, with the aim of "repressing Jewish, Lutheran or Islamic practices as well as witchcraft and magic" (Santinho Martins, 2007).[1] It proved disastrous to Portugal, eventually stunting commerce and culture and with long-term consequences, which some say are still to be felt.

The 20th century dawned on a country that the Catholic Church had put in a straitjacket, sandwiched between the Atlantic Ocean with Spain blocking its road to Europe, but nevertheless looking to France as cultural suzerain. After the fall of the monarchy in 1910 there was a brief flowering of democracy, both politically and culturally. This, however, was short lived, with government following upon government until the country descended into near anarchy. A coup ushered in a military dictatorship that led to the 1928 installation of the Salazar dictatorship. For the next 50 years Portugal was to live under the heavy yoke of a fascist dictatorship sanctioned by the church, ensuring an underdeveloped economy, massive emigration, education for just a few, repression of free speech, and an arid, stunted cultural climate.

At the time of the military coup in 1974, which ended dictatorship and brought in democracy, there were no psychology departments in the country's three universities. The regime would not allow them. The only exception was an Institute of Psychology, run by the Jesuits, in Lisbon. It is thus easily understood that in this sort of academic and cultural climate sexual matters, even if scientific, were not on the agenda. One notable exception must be mentioned. In 1901, Egas Moniz (a neurologist who would receive the Nobel Prize for medicine) published *Sexual Life*, a book that enjoyed tremendous success, with 23 editions! Alas, it was not written in the spirit of innovation of his 16th century peers, but rather in the spirit of Kraft-Ebbing. Egas Moniz, a man of his time, did not create or innovate in the said book; he just went on to perpetuate the wisdom of 19th century scientific discourse on the body and sexuality.

With the April 1974 coup d'état, Portugal began to change beyond recognition. Notwithstanding some expected and initial labor pains and the huge gaps to be filled in all walks of life, the country once again became a true part of Europe, both politically and culturally. A huge tidal wave of modernization swept the country, and the medical and clinical sciences were on the frontline.

As stated earlier, culturally Portugal traditionally looked to France. Thus, in psychiatry and what little clinical psychology there was, psychoanalysis was very much the dominant current influence. It seems thus most fitting that the pioneers of sex therapy were all in some professional capacity linked to England, especially to the Institute of Psychiatry in London and the University of Oxford, forging links that are still strong. Since its very beginnings, in this country, clinical sexology has always been very much a part of, or a by-product, of psychiatry (Gomes, Albuquerque, & Nunes, 1987). The first clinics, founded in Lisbon and Coimbra in the 1970s, were set up either in psychiatry departments of university hospitals (in the case of Lisbon and Coimbra), or in one case, in a psychiatric hospital (the Behavioral Therapy Department of Hospital Julio de Matos). All were started by psychiatrists, who went on to train psychiatrists and clinical psychologists. It was from the medical world that work in this field eventually spread to the universities (Albuquerque, 1997).

Additionally, there are a reasonable number of postgraduate courses, many at masters and master of philosophy level that are taught in the various universities. There are also some training courses, one provided by the professional and scientific association of clinical sexology (Portuguese Society of Clinical Sexology) and the other by a private institute, in partnership with an American university (Luso-American Institute of Sexology), providing training and accreditation.

Sexual Problems in Portugal

We will now briefly present the context of sexual problems in Portugal. We start with a review of the studies on prevalence, comorbidity, and demographic predictors of sexual difficulties. We then review the research on etiology and conceptual models of sexual problems, with a special emphasis on the work conducted in Portugal. Finally, we present the state of the art treatment approaches to sexual problems in Portugal.

Prevalence

Regarding prevalence of sexual problems in Portugal, there are four epidemiological studies that deserve mention. The Portuguese Society of Andrology published a study using 2,500 participants from the general Portuguese population (Vendeira, Pereira, Serrano, & Carvalheira, 2011; Vendeira, Pereira, Tomada, & LaFuente, 2011). Findings indicated that 56% of women who participated in the study presented with at least one sexual complaint. Among these women, 18.6% considered their sexual problems to be moderate to severe. Regarding men, findings indicated that 23.8% presented at least one sexual complaint, with 5.8% evaluating these as moderate to severe. Regarding specific sexual problems, 35% of women indicated low sexual desire, 32% arousal difficulties, 32% orgasmic problems, and 34% pain disorders. These relatively high prevalence rates may be related to the fact that distress was not assessed and mild complaints were also included. If we include only women with moderate to severe difficulties, the percentages decrease significantly: 12% desire problems, 9.3% arousal disorders, 11.1% orgasmic disorders, and 3.3% pain disorders.

Regarding men, 16% reported low sexual desire, 13% erectile dysfunction, and 11.6% complained of orgasmic problems (7% premature ejaculation and 9% retarded ejaculation). Again these percentages included mild to severe difficulties (if we consider only moderate to severe problems, the rates decrease to 6% for desire problems and 7% for erectile dysfunction) (see Table 12.1).

A second study was conducted in a community sample of 566 participants (303 men and 263 women) from the Portuguese general population

Table 12.1 Prevalence of Sexual Dysfunction in Portuguese Community Samples

Authors	Sample	Assessment	Prevalence					
			Desire disorder	Arousal disorder	Orgasmic disorder	Premature ejaculation	Dyspareunia	Vaginismus
Nobre (2003)	263 women from the community aged between 18–79	Questionnaire	15%*	5%*	15%*		5%*	4%*
	303 men from the community aged between 18–80		1.3%*	4.3%*	4.3%*	7.9%*		
Vendeira et al. (2005)	1,250 women from the community aged between 18–75	Interview + Questionnaire	35%**	32%**	32%**		34%**	
	1,250 men from the community aged between 18–75		16%	13%		8.7%		

* Percentages calculated taking into account the level and frequency of sexual difficulties from moderate to severe
** Percentages calculated taking into account the level and frequency of sexual difficulties from mild to severe

(Nobre, 2003). In women, the most common sexual dysfunction was hypoactive sexual desire disorder. Almost half of the women (47.8%) reported low sexual desire during at least half of their sexual interactions, with 15% indicating lack of sexual desire most of the time. Orgasmic disorders were also very common, with 15% of women presenting difficulties achieving orgasm in most of their sexual encounters. Sexual arousal difficulties were experienced by 5% of the women. Dyspareunia and vaginismus were experienced by 5 and 4%, respectively (Nobre, 2003).

In men, premature ejaculation was the most common dysfunction, with 7.9% indicating difficulties in most of their partnered sexual experiences. On the other hand, low desire was reported by only 1.3% of men. Erectile problems and orgasmic difficulties were both reported by 4.3% of men in more than half of occasions of sexual activity (Nobre, 2003; see Table 12.1).

A study on the prevalence of erectile disorders was conducted in a community sample of 3,548 men, aged between 40 and 69 years old and recruited in health care centers across Portugal (Teles et al., 2008). Findings indicated a prevalence rate of 48.1% for erectile problems, including 35% with minimal complaints, 9% with moderate difficulties, and 4% with severe levels of erectile difficulties, assessed using the International Index of Erectile Functioning (Rosen et al., 1997).

One of the present authors (CS) carried out a small prevalence study of sexual and psychiatric morbidity in a sample of female volunteers, recruited in a large firm in Lisbon (Soares & Félix da Costa, 1999). Of a working population of 345 women, 50 refused to participate, 90 were working away from Lisbon or on sick leave, and 205 completed the study. The assessment instruments included a structured interview, the 9th edition of the Present State Examination, and self-assessment questionnaires to evaluate body image, self-concept, and social and family life. The results yielded an overall rate of psychiatric morbidity of 25.7% and an overall rate of sexual morbidity in the sample of 25.5%. The most pertinent finding of this study was revealed when women with psychiatric morbidity were removed from the subgroup presenting with sexual morbidity. After excluding women with psychiatric pathology, the prevalence of sexual morbidity decreased from 25.5 to 15.7%. This finding highlights the need to control for the presence of psychiatric symptoms in population-based studies. Because many psychiatric illnesses have a deleterious effect on sexuality, either through direct or indirect effects (e.g., side effects of medication), this is a variable which will affect endpoints in studies of sexual morbidity. Therefore, it would seem that such studies, even when carried out in the general population, should control for psychiatric morbidity (Soares & Felix da Costa, 1999).

Regarding the prevalence and distribution of sexual complaints in Portuguese sex therapy clinics, results from two studies conducted in the same hospital with a 9-year interval indicate a very similar pattern. In a clinical sample of 33 women with sexual dysfunction, Gomes, Fonseca, and Gomes (1997) found that the major female clinical complaint was hypoactive sexual desire disorder (45%), followed by orgasmic disorders (33%), arousal disorders (12%), and vaginismus (9%). Nine years later in the same clinical setting with a sample of 47 women with sexual dysfunction, Nobre, Pinto-Gouveia, and Gomes (2006) reported the following primary diagnoses: 40.4% sexual desire problems, 21.3% orgasmic disorders, and 4.3% arousal disorders. Interestingly, the percentage of pain disorders was significantly higher (vaginismus, 21.3%, and dyspareunia, 6.4%) than in the earlier survey. This increase may be due to the fact that a specific treatment was being offered for vaginismus at the time of the Nobre et al. (2006) study (see Table 12.2).

In men, the above two studies reported almost identical findings. The most prevalent complaint was erectile disorder, with very high percentages in both studies (63% in Gomes et al., 1997 and 69% in Nobre et al., 2006), followed by premature ejaculation (21.2% and 22.4%, respectively). Orgasmic disorder (5.3% and 4.1%) and hypoactive sexual desire (11% and 2%, respectively) were less common primary diagnoses (see Table 12.2).

Demographic Predictors

Results on the demographic predictors of sexual functioning conducted in Portugal (Nobre, 2003, 2008) were similar to the Laumann, Paik, and Rosen (1999) epidemiological study conducted in the United States. In men, findings emphasized the effect of age on erectile dysfunction, with older men presenting more difficulties in this domain. Moreover, married men tended to show better erectile and orgasmic responses compared to single men. Higher educational levels also predicted higher levels of erectile and orgasmic functioning (Nobre, 2003, 2008). Regarding women, only age exerted significant effects on sexual functioning. The ability to lubricate showed a tendency to decrease with age, and dyspareunia was more common in younger women compared to women in their 40s (Nobre, 2003, 2008).

Psychological Factors Related to Sexual Dysfunction

Studies on the role of psychological factors on sexual dysfunction have resulted in a better understanding of their role in the last few decades. Among the variables that have received the most attention are dispositional variables such as personality, affect, and sexual inhibition

Table 12.2 Prevalence of Sexual Dysfunction in Sex Therapy Clinics

Authors	Sample	Assessment	Prevalence					
			Desire disorder	Arousal disorder	Orgasmic disorder	Premature ejaculation	Dyspareunia	Vaginismus
Gomes et al. (1997)	33 women with a mean age of 32 years old recruited from a sex therapy clinic	Clinical interview	45%	12%	33%		—	9%
	57 men with a mean age of 37 years old recruited from a sex therapy clinic		11%	63%	5%	21%		
Nobre et al. (2006)	47 women with a mean age of 29 years old recruited from a sex therapy clinic	Clinical interview	40%	4%	21%		6%	26%
	49 men with a mean age of 43 years old recruited from a sex therapy clinic		2%	69%	4%	22%		

(Bancroft & Janssen, 2000; Barlow, 2002), sexual beliefs (Nobre & Pinto-Gouveia, 2006a), cognitive schemas (Andersen & Cyranowski, 1994; Nobre & Pinto-Gouveia, 2009), automatic thoughts (Nobre & Pinto-Gouveia, 2008), and emotions (Mitchell, DiBartolo, Brown, & Barlow, 1998; Nobre & Pinto-Gouveia, 2006b; Nobre et al., 2004).

Personality and Trait-Affect

Barlow (2002) proposed a triple vulnerability model for emotional disorders (including sexual dysfunction), where he hypothesized that neuroticism and negative affect predict anxiety related disorders. Studies conducted in Portugal with men and women with and without sexual dysfunction have indicated that negative affect and neuroticism were significantly higher in clinical samples compared to controls (Oliveira & Nobre, 2008; Quinta-Gomes, & Nobre, 2011).

Bancroft and Janssen (2000) developed a theoretical model based on the dual control of sexual response (sexual inhibition/sexual excitation), postulating that individuals have a propensity for both mechanisms and that the balance between them predicts sexual response. Studies have partially corroborated this model, indicating that sexual inhibition is strongly correlated with impaired erectile response in men (Bancroft, Graham, Janssen, & Sanders, 2009)

Sexual Beliefs

Regarding the role of sexual beliefs and myths on sexual functioning, Zilbergeld (1999) stated that men with erectile disorders present a set of myths and erroneous beliefs about sexuality that serve as a vulnerability factor to the development of their difficulties. In Portugal, Nobre and Pinto-Gouveia (2006a) found that men and women with sexual dysfunction reported having higher scores on a scale of dysfunctional sexual beliefs (SDBQ; Nobre, Pinto-Gouveia, & Gomes, 2003) when compared to sexually healthy men and women (Nobre & Pinto-Gouveia, 2006a). Men with sexual dysfunction presented stronger beliefs in the "macho" myth, and beliefs related to women's sexual satisfaction in comparison to sexually healthy men. Women with sexual problems presented significantly more beliefs related to the role of age on sexual functioning and negative body image beliefs when compared to sexually healthy women.

Overall, women from this clinical sample endorsed the belief that the aging process is associated with decreased levels of sexual desire and pleasure (e.g., "after menopause women lose their sexual desire," "as women age, the pleasure they get from sex decreases," "after menopause women can't reach orgasm"). Moreover, the importance of body appearance as a central factor for sexual success and satisfaction was another distinctive characteristic of this clinical sample (e.g., "women who are not physically attractive can't be sexually satisfied"). Finally, although not statistically significant, women with sexual dysfunction also presented more sexually conservative beliefs and negative convictions regarding sex and pleasure as a sin (e.g., "masturbation is wrong and sinful, sex is dirty and sinful") than women without sexual problems (Nobre & Pinto-Gouveia, 2006a). These conservative and negative beliefs are still relatively common in older and less educated women and represent remnants of the strict Catholicism practiced in Portugal during the first three-quarters of the 20th century.

In men, although no statistically significant differences were found between clinical and nonclinical samples, individuals with sexual dysfunction reported higher scores on all dysfunctional belief dimensions, and in particular on beliefs about the macho stereotype and about women's sexual satisfaction. For example, men in the clinical sample were more likely to hold beliefs related to excessive sexual performance demands (e.g., "A real man has sexual intercourse very often," "in sex, getting to the climax is most important," "sex without orgasm can't be good"), and beliefs about women's sexual satisfaction and men's sexual functioning (e.g., "The quality of the erection is what most satisfies women," "a woman may have doubts about a man's virility when he fails to get an erection during sexual activity," "a man who doesn't sexually satisfy a woman is a failure"; Nobre & Pinto-Gouveia, 2006a). These sexual beliefs are very common in the Portuguese population and are not restricted to older or less educated men. The high standards regarding men's sexual performance that are transmitted through older generations, peers, and the media, and the absence of a tradition of formal sexual education in the schools may explain the persistence of these beliefs.

Conceptual Models of Sexual Dysfunction

In addition to sexual beliefs, Nobre and colleagues have also studied the role in sexual functioning of cognitive schemas (Nobre & Pinto-Gouveia, 2009), automatic thoughts (Nobre & Pinto-Gouveia, 2008), and emotions during sexual activity (Nobre & Pinto-Gouveia, 2006b). The authors have developed and tested conceptual models of sexual dysfunction in men and women, which they have based on the findings from these studies (Carvalho & Nobre, 2010a; Nobre, 2009, 2010, Vilarinho & Nobre, 2008). The conceptual framework for the models is cognitive theory. At a central level are the cognitive schemas (or core beliefs), composed of ideas we have about ourselves, others, and the future. These schemas are responsible for the meaning assigned to events (Beck, 1996). The model postulates that individuals with sexual dysfunction tend to activate more negative self-schemas when exposed to negative sexual situations (specifically, incompetence schemas).

Sexual beliefs constitute another central component of the model, consisting of ideas that individuals have about sexuality, based on earlier life experiences, culture, and learning processes. Sexual beliefs are conceptualized as conditional rules (Beck, 1996) presented in an "if... then" format. These conditional rules play a key role, since they stipulate the conditions necessary for the activation of the cognitive schemas. Whenever a sexual event fulfills the rules defined by the sexual belief, congruent cognitive schemas are activated. Therefore, sexual beliefs play a central role as vulnerability factors for the development of sexual dysfunction. Individuals who present with rigid, inflexible, and dysfunctional sexual beliefs are more prone to catastrophize negative sexual events and to activate negative self-schemas (mainly incompetence schemas; e.g., "I am incompetent, I am a failure").

In addition to sexual beliefs, the model postulates the existence of two more general vulnerability factors for sexual dysfunction: personality and trait-affect. Specifically, the model suggests that neuroticism, low positive trait-affect, and high negative trait-affect constitute risk factors for the development of sexual problems. These more general vulnerability factors, which were also found to be associated with anxiety and depressive disorders (Brown, Chorpita, & Barlow, 1998), are presumed to interact with dysfunctional sexual beliefs and moderate the process of meaning assignment to sexual situations, particularly the negative events.

Besides these central components, the model also includes cognitive and emotional responses resulting from the activation of cognitive schemas. For example, the activation of the cognitive schema "I'm a failure" would drive the development of automatic thoughts oriented to stimuli associated with failure and its possible negative consequences (e.g., failure anticipation and disengagement thoughts, lack of erotic thoughts), decrease the focus on erotic stimuli, and increase negative emotional responses (sadness, lack of pleasure and satisfaction). It is important to emphasize that these two components interact, each influencing the other and determining the sexual response. These automatic thoughts and negative emotions would also serve as maintaining factors for a sexual problem, since they prevent individuals from focusing attention on erotic cues and pleasurable sensations associated with sex.

In summary, sexual dysfunction would result from the integrated influence of the above mentioned psychological variables. However, it is also important to emphasize the fact that the model is not unidirectional. Sexual functioning also influences the activation of cognitive schemas in future sexually unsuccessful situations. The more problematic the individual's sexual functioning, the greater the probability of

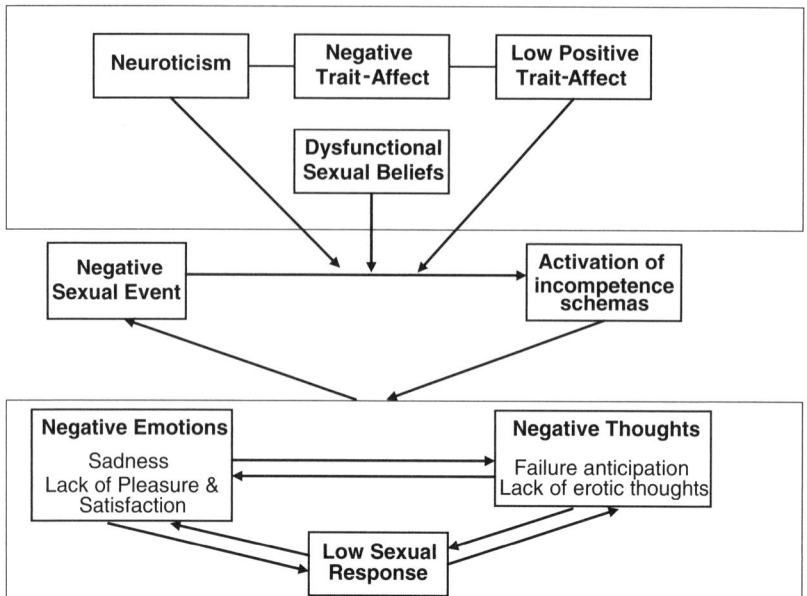

Figure 12.1 Nobre's Cognitive-Emotional Model

negative schema activation in future situations, which further maintains the cycle (see Figure 12.1).

This model was recently tested for male erectile disorder and female desire disorder using path analyses, with findings supporting the adequacy of the model fit to the data (Nobre, 2009, 2010). Moreover, recent studies further examined the impact of the main cognitive predictors of sexual functioning and satisfaction, in interaction with other major predictors of sexual response (e.g., medical factors, relationship factors, psychopathology). Findings supported the central role of the cognitive variables (e.g., automatic thoughts during sexual activity and sexual beliefs) as mediators and moderators of the relationship between the predictors mentioned above and sexual response in men and women (Carvalho & Nobre, 2010b, 2011; Vilarinho & Nobre, 2008).

Treatment Approaches to Sexual Problems

Despite the growing body of empirical data and conceptual models on psychological factors of sexual problems and specifically on the role of cognitive and affective variables, the application of this knowledge in terms of treatment approaches is still very limited. Notwithstanding the existence of some therapeutic protocols based on cognitive behavioral principles (Hawton, 1989; Rosen, Leiblum, & Spector, 1994; Wincze &

Carey, 2001), much sex therapy relies mainly on Masters and Johnson's sensate focus techniques. This is particularly the case in Portugal, where sex therapists most often use sensate focus techniques, systematic desensitization, or specific behavioral procedures (e.g., masturbation training, "squeeze," etc.). Training programs, although including some information on cognitive determinants and interventions, also focus mainly on traditional sex therapy techniques.

Finally, the lack of research on treatment outcome for sexual dysfunction is considerable. Empirically validated psychological treatments for sexual dysfunction are scarce and for the most part limited to Masters and Johnson's sensate focus approach or systematic desensitization procedures (Heiman, 2002; Heiman & Meston, 1998). To date no randomized controlled trials testing the efficacy of cognitive behavior interventions for sexual problems have been published. Results from two pilot studies indicated that a combination of oral medication (sildenafil) and CBT produced better treatment outcomes (sexual functioning and satisfaction) in men with ED compared to pharmacological treatment alone (Bach, Barlow, & Wincze, 2004; Banner & Anderson, 2007).

Taking these findings into consideration, and keeping in mind that CBT has proved to be the most efficacious treatment for a variety of psychological problems (Baker, McFall, & Shoham, 2009) and presents long-term effects superior to pharmacological treatments, we think that a systematic test of the treatment efficacy of CBT for sexual dysfunction, as well as research on the underlying mechanisms of change, may play an important role in developing better treatment options.

Approaches to Treatment: Examples from a Sex Therapy Clinic

The Sexual Therapy Clinic in Lisbon's Psychiatric Center, where one of the authors (CS) works, is typical of clinics in Portugal. It is run in a busy outpatient department of a national health psychiatric hospital, with a multidisciplinary team (clinical psychologists, psychologist trainees, psychiatrists, and an endocrinologist). The first intake interview is carried out by the senior psychologist together with the endocrinologist; basic diagnosis as well as primary psychological and physical factors involved are broadly assessed and if needed, laboratory or other auxiliary procedures requested. Specialist treatment is provided for the sexual dysfunctions, gender identity discordance (GID),[2] and the paraphilias. Approximately one fifth of the caseload comprises convicted sexual offenders sent by the courts (the large majority of these are child sexual abusers, with a small number of rapists and exhibitionists). Around a quarter are individuals with GID, at various stages of assessment, hormone therapy, and postsurgery follow-up or counseling. Individuals with sexual dysfunctions comprise the largest subgroup, with an approximate ratio of 10 men to 2 women. Our typical male patient is over 45 years of age, with concurrent physical morbidity, frequently taking one or more types of prescribed medication, presenting with erectile dysfunction. A smaller group of younger men (some as young as 18), roughly a quarter of the patients seen, seek help for premature ejaculation. Men with problems of low desire present infrequently and are sometimes cases of incorrect referral, where the primary problem is depression. Currently there are five men being seen in our clinic who presented with low sexual desire and were found to have abnormally low levels of testosterone. They are being treated with testosterone and couple sexual therapy.

The female patients are mainly in the 35- to 55-year age group, and by far the most frequent complaint is low, or absent, sexual desire. Orgasmic dysfunction appears occasionally (albeit sometimes as a "pseudo" dysfunction; these women are convinced they are suffering a dysfunction, as orgasm only occurs when there is direct stimulation of the clitoris and they think the normal thing would be to have "orgasm by penetration" (echoes of Freud …). Dyspaurenia and vaginismus appear rather infrequently in this hospital clinic setting.

It is worth mentioning that in private practice the population presenting with sexual problems differs in several important ways. Unsurprisingly, the most obvious difference is higher social class and higher education in the private practice patients. The age and presenting problems of the men tend to be similar to the hospital clinic patients. It is in the female group that the most striking differences are found. The women who seek help in private practice tend to be much younger, in the 18 to 30 age group, and the most frequent problem is vaginismus, for which a program with a very successful outcome is used. The diagnosis must be established by a gynecologist or a medical practitioner with specific training in the field. Individual interviewing of the woman is followed, when appropriate, by a couple interview where the problem is discussed and the treatment explained. As most of these women have no difficulties with desire or arousal, the couple are asked to maintain as much sexual interaction as they wish, but to abstain from attempted penetration. Individually, the woman is taught deep muscle relaxation. Through homework assignments, she is asked to thoroughly examine her genitals with the aid of a mirror, identify the various structures, and attempt to insert the tip of her well lubricated index finger. If she is successful, she is then given the first (well lubricated) vaginal dilator to try. When she can successfully introduce the dilators into the vagina during homework assignments, treatment proceeds along the lines of instructions in the office and homework assignments, which consist of vaginal penetration with the graded dilators, beginning with the smallest, which in the most difficult cases can be the equivalent diameter of a baby's little finger, and gradually proceeding to the last one, with the equivalent diameter of an average penis. In those cases where the woman is unable to insert the dilators by herself, these are carried out by the certified therapist, always after inducing relaxation, and using the same scheme of graded dilators. The dilator is then given to the woman for her to continue the procedure at home. Once the introduction of the middle sized dilator has been achieved, the woman is asked to experiment with tampons during menstruation and to introduce her finger, and then her partner's finger into the vagina, during sexual interaction. Upon achievement of vaginal penetration with the largest dilator, by which time most women report fantasising and desiring penile penetration, they are asked to attempt introduction of the tip of the penis into the vagina. Frequently at this stage the partner joins the therapy sessions. It must be said that in our clinical practice, the treatment of vaginismus has provided us with some of the most rewarding and satisfactory outcomes! The following is one example.

Ana is a very attractive 28-year-old, with a master's degree in marketing and international relations, and she works in the public sector. The presenting problem is that she cannot have sexual intercourse with her partner because of intense pain that leads her to "close up" and prevents vaginal penetration. She is the second child, having a brother 10 years older. Ana grew up a healthy, carefree, rather spoilt and overprotected, happy child showing exceptional brightness. Knowledge of sexual matters was casually picked up here and there, from her friends, female relatives, books, and television. She was always fairly relaxed about sex and does not remember any specific worries. Her parents never discussed sex openly with her and her mother only enlightened her regarding menstruation, about which she was already fully informed. Throughout her late teens she dated a couple of boys, but never developed serious relationships. Sexual contact with these boyfriends never went beyond heavy petting. Occasionally she would masturbate with no consequent feelings of guilt or discomfort.

She was 21 and still in university, when, at a friend's party she met the man who would change the placid course of her life. She fell deeply in love with this man, 2 years her senior, who came from a "good family" in the Portuguese former colony of Guinea, a man with very black skin. She began to date him assiduously, but carefully concealed the relationship from her parents, always telling them she was going out with her friends when she was seeing him. The relationship deepened, hardening her resolve to continue to see him. Still a virgin at 21, the couple initiated sexual contact very early (at the onset of the relationship), with all going well until penetration was attempted and found to be too painful. An intense sexual relationship began, with outings and meetings at his house. For 7 years the couple's sexual pattern was similar to what it was at the beginning: Desire, arousal, pleasure, and orgasm (for both partners) but no penetration. Ana admitted that she was always slightly tense when with her partner because she "may be caught and her parents discover her secret." She reported that she frequently had a sense of impending doom when she was with him, as it seemed inevitable that sooner or later "the cat will jump out of the bag."

At the beginning, Ana's partner took their sexual difficulties in a good spirit, thinking it was just a matter of time before the problem resolved. But as the years passed and no change came, the strain started to take its toll on the relationship, with both partners becoming angry and perplexed with the situation. Increasingly worried about her sexual problem and scared she might lose her boyfriend, although they had firm plans to marry, Ana confided in a friend, who, in turn, revealed to her that she had suffered from the same problem and had undergone successful treatment.

After the first interview assessment was carried out, Ana was referred to a gynecologist for a definite diagnosis. Vaginismus was confirmed, with remnants of the hymen still visible. Treatment, structured as outlined above, and needing only one session of vaginal dilation by the therapist, was carried out in 12 sessions (including the assessment and the final session). Except for the vaginal introduction of the first vaginal dilator, which was carried out by the therapist, all the other dilators were introduced by Ana during her homework assignments. Vaginal penetration with the penis began after the 10th therapy session and at the last session the couple were enjoying full sexual intercourse without any difficulty whatsoever. Ana felt confident and jubilant about her success and even more firmly resolved to marry her man. She considered that her father was the next task to tackle.

The above case raises some interesting points. As Binik (2005) cogently argued, the "sexual pain disorders" have been seriously under-researched. Indeed, it would seem that as far as psychological etiology of the sexual disorders is concerned, we have not progressed very far beyond "associated factors" rather than firmly established causes. Although not in a position to firmly attribute causes for Ana's difficulties, the most probable "cause" was the fear of being caught and the family fracas which would inevitably follow, which continued to be very much an issue. It seems undeniable that the strain placed upon her by keeping her relationship clandestine, together with the fear that her father would not accept her chosen partner, had dire consequences, which somehow, through unknown pathways, led to the contraction of her pelvic floor. In this case the pathognomonic factor was not avoidance, as she faced the obstacle often enough. More probably it was fear further reinforcing failure, which further increased fear and failure (similar to what occurs in performance anxiety). Even more intriguing is why the sexual difficulty was exclusively centered on penetration and during 7 years there was no generalization to her sexual response, allowing Ana to enjoy desire, pleasure, and orgasm. Therefore, the therapeutic effort had to be focused only on this one specific aspect of Ana's sexual response.

Low sexual desire complaints are usually seen in the context of marital breakdown or when an extramarital affair is taking place. And of course there is a small, but gradually increasing number of cases of marital conflict and sexual problems secondary to problems with cybersex.

Treatment procedures for sexual dysfunction largely follow the Masters and Johnson (1970) sensate focus model, with the corresponding cognitive restructuring. Nevertheless, most couple treatments also involve a great deal of training in nonsexual as well as sexual communication skills.

In the last few years our clinical practice has been much influenced by the dual control model (Bancroft & Janssen, 2000). Contrary to our previous approach where the sexual dysfunction would invariably be considered as "treatable" (except the most obvious nonstarters), in a growing number of cases "permission" to accept sexual difficulties is being encouraged. Consider the following case:

Sandra, 50 years old, unemployed, complained of long term inhibited sexual response. For years she had felt no desire for sex and when she did consent, she felt no arousal or pleasure, encouraging her husband to "hurry up" (although she could not verbalize this directly as he would get angry). After many years of her husband insisting she seek treatment, she finally did so because the accusations of adultery were increasing at an alarming rate.

The couple had been married for 20 years and initially the marriage was satisfactory, although from the beginning he became verbally abusive after occasional drinking bouts with his friends. They had two children, both at secondary school. Sandra was in full time employment until she was made redundant 5 years earlier and had not managed to find more than occasional house cleaning jobs since then. Her husband's drinking bouts became more frequent, occurring increasingly during the week as well as the weekend; concomitantly he became increasingly abusive. Occasionally the verbal abuse turned into physical abuse, especially if the children were out. Insidiously, Sandra became more and more distanced from him, only managing to endure sex by "escaping" into romantic fantasies of sex with other men. She stayed in the marriage because of economic dependence on her husband and "because of the children," who the father did not ill-treat. In Sandra's own words, love and affection "flew out of the window with his drunken brawls." Quite frequently, always when sober, he would demand sex; she felt no desire, no pleasure, and no love and increasingly refused sex, which led to violent accusations and threats. On occasion her husband would take her out, behave tenderly, and try to rekindle the flame between them, but she could not respond either sexually or with affection; "cold as a stone" was how she described her feelings. But his efforts left her guilt-ridden, and she felt even worse because of his disparaging comments and unfavorable comparisons with other women. Lately the accusations of her sexual coldness being due to her having "somebody else" had increased. Finally, she allowed herself to be persuaded and sought help at the clinic. She arrived on her own, although she had urged her husband to come with her, as she thought it was a couple's problem, having read about sexual therapy in a woman's magazine. Her husband had objected, arguing "there is nothing wrong with me, you are the one who is frigid." And so she attended and asked for help to "make her function."

Perhaps 20 years ago, Sandra might have been accepted as a clinical case, diagnosed with inhibited sexual desire, and a program of couple sexual therapy implemented. Or, if the partner refused, the program would have been implemented for her alone.

Our clinical approach was radically changed by the dual control model. Therapy now begins by informing Sandra that her response, or rather, the inhibition of her sexual responsiveness, is a well-adapted reaction to the destructive relationship she is in. The aim of any therapeutic approach would be the improvement of the marital relationship, and it would have to include a referral for the alcohol addiction. Should the couple therapy be refused by the husband, the alternative program offered would be individual psychotherapy to address her difficulties in asserting herself and her issues of low self-esteem.

The same guidelines, drawing heavily on the model of inhibition-proneness, are used in the cases, which present quite often, where the presenting partner (more often the woman) seeks help to reinstate the sexual desire she used to have for her husband/partner, because she wants to keep the marriage, but meanwhile has fallen in love with another man, with whom she has great sex. Guilt ridden because the husband/partner is such a "lovely person/ideal husband/great father and they have a good family life," this woman comes to the clinic almost desperately asking for the "magic potion" which will make her libidinous with the good husband for whom she no longer feels an iota of sexual desire, but does not want to hurt and leave. This type of case has become quite frequent, especially in private practice. The typical example is of a woman in her mid- to late 30s, university educated, and in a good professional or executive career. She will have fallen in love with someone from her professional universe, but is in turmoil because she cannot cut the ties with the original, longstanding partner, with whom she has built a home, a family, and a strong bond. The male counterpart of the female executive described above more frequently seeks help because he no longer has the sexual prowess to be in two sexual relationships, typically the wife and the mistress. He will be, on average, a decade older than the female presenter, and erectile failure looms up more and more often. He has occasionally resorted to the use of PDE-5 inhibitor medication to ensure perfect functioning, but thinks he is "too young for that sort of thing and it might harm his health anyway." His visit to the clinic was particularly prompted by serious worry as he had a nasty headache the last time he used medication.[3] In cases like these, involving two people very much embroiled in corporate efficiency (where ready-made solutions are much easier to come by), upon being told that there are no "magic potions," two types of outcome are possible. Either these individuals do not keep the second appointment, taking their quest for a quick solution elsewhere, or they accept that the problem is not sexual. Accordingly, individual therapy may be needed to address the issue of individual needs and lack of satisfaction, or in some cases marital therapy may be recommended, in order to address couple issues. In all our clinical practice, cognitive-behavioral treatment approaches are used.

Working with the couple in cases such as these, which we do not conceptualize as cases of sexual dysfunction, the aim of therapy is really to reduce, or eliminate, the inhibition of sexual responsiveness. Treatment is geared to establishing trust, comfort and well-being in physical intimacy, both sexual and nonsexual, to promote closeness, intimacy, and awareness of each other's needs and acceptance of one's own sexuality. As in all marital therapy, underlying issues, which may block achieving those objectives, have to be directly dealt with. These may be problems with how the other acts or reacts, which have to be faced and dealt with as a couple. Dysfunctional thoughts during sexual interaction may be a problem which has to be addressed in individual therapy. In conclusion, whenever embarking on a therapeutic process for sexual or relationship problems, an open mind has to be kept regarding the delivery format. Couple therapy may have to be interspersed with some sessions of individual therapy, or vice versa.

Extended Case Discussion

HH is a 35-year-old who was referred to the Sexual Therapy Clinic by his family doctor because of reported difficulty in maintaining an erection in the previous 12 months and lately, loss of interest in sexual activity.

The routine medical examination carried out at the clinic, revealed a reasonably good state of health, with the exception of HH being slightly overweight and cholesterol levels at the upper limit, for which dietary measures and an exercise plan were suggested. Testosterone levels were also found to be normal.

HH had been married for 6 years, and lived with his wife (IB) for 3 years before the marriage. The couple met when they were both at university, where both obtained master's degrees, he in computer sciences and she in economics. The relationship was considered a success by both partners, although much strain had been placed upon it since the beginning because his family, who much appreciated IB as HH's friend and colleague, thoroughly rejected her as his wife on religious grounds. The couple did not practice any form of religion, but HH's father, although himself married to a Catholic woman who adopted her husband's religion, was very orthodox in his Islamic faith and had neither accepted his daughter-in-law nor the two children she had borne his son.

HH and IB met in their second year at university and initially became friends. He was an introverted personality, never at ease in groups, and very shy with women, although good at maintaining long term relationships, but always with "few but good friends." IB was always very at ease socially and an assertive kind of person, nevertheless HH was her first "serious" boyfriend. There had been two previous, "very light" relationships, where physical contact had not gone beyond heavy petting. She was his first girlfriend, and his sexual behavior before meeting her had not gone beyond masturbation because of his excruciating shyness with the opposite sex.

The couple set up house together after leaving university and getting jobs, and married 3 years later when IB was pregnant with their first child, who was now 6 years old. The second child arrived 3 years later. From the start of their union the couple enjoyed a very happy and close relationship. Their sexual life was described by both as "blissful," both agreeing that they discovered sex with each other and "every time being a wonder" until the recent onset of their problems.

There were very few conflicts, even after both children arrived, both enjoying a very open, deep, and intimate relationship with each other. The only "dark issue" was his family; this was the only theme that would provoke disagreement and conflict, as IB was hurt and resented their discourteous treatment of herself and her children and felt that her husband "did not take her side sufficiently." Two years ago the couple's life changed radically, because of their elder child, who had an accident while playing, which left her brain damaged and meant she was in need of constant medical attention and specialized care. To enable them to spend more time with the child, HH changed his work schedule, working a short night shift and completing the rest of his professional tasks from home. Thus, the couple's life became more demanding and tiring with the added anxiety over the child's condition.

Over the last year HH noticed an insidious, but growing pattern of incapacity to maintain an erection. Initially erections were sufficient to maintain coitus, but gradually they became more and more difficult to maintain. When he asked for help, his erection only occasionally was sufficient for penetration. To each failure, which IB tried to minimize, attributing it to his tiredness and worrying, he responded with intense shame and refused to talk about it with his wife, thinking that she was just pretending to be nice, but in truth was hiding her feelings of contempt for him as a man. He increased his workload and avoided going to bed until she was asleep. All reminders of sex, such as provocative advertisements or film scenes made him feel ashamed to the point of blushing, even if alone. And his interest began to wane.

Petty arguments between the couple would develop into full blown storms, with the father-in-law issue looming larger and larger, with IB increasingly accusing him of cowardly behavior toward his father and not standing up for his wife and children.

Assessment of the couple revealed that HH felt desire for sex on average once or twice a month but tended to avoid it for fear of failing. Erotic dreams were quite frequent, as was nocturnal penile tumescence as well as morning erection. IB took the initiative for sex less and less, being very angry because of his frequent rejections, which took the form of somatic complaints, such as headache or indigestion. She was also exceedingly resentful because HH avoided all physical contact with her with the exception of the ritualized peck on the cheek. She maintained a considerable sense of humor and laughingly drove the spear home saying: "He has become a shy damsel. He thinks if he touches me I'll rape him."

Questionnaire assessment of HH revealed the following:
General Beliefs:
   High performance related beliefs
Sexual Beliefs:
   High scores on several erroneous, demanding, and catastrophic beliefs
   Penile erection is essential for a woman's sexual satisfaction
   Men who are not capable of penetrating women cannot satisfy them sexually
   The quality of erection is what most satisfies women
   A woman may have doubts about a man's virility when he fails to get an erection during sexual activity
   A woman may stop loving a man if he is not capable of satisfying her sexually
   A man who doesn't sexually satisfy a woman is a failure
   The consequences of sexual failure are catastrophic
Automatic Thoughts Questionnaire:
   Frequent negative automatic thoughts and emotions during sexual activity and lack of erotic thoughts and emotions
Cognitive Schemas:
   Activation of incompetence schemas (I'm incompetent, I'm a failure) whenever negative sexual events occur.

Therapeutic Intervention

Couple therapy was proposed and accepted, but frequency had to be negotiated. Weekly sessions were initially proposed and although both were anxious to start and go through the program, weekly attendance implied the need for an attendance certificate to justify the wife's absence from work. The attendance certificate had the name of the hospital where the clinic was situated, and it was a psychiatric hospital—old embedded stigmas are activated by the word *psychiatric*, so a way had to be found to circumvent the need for the attendance certificate and this implied fortnightly sessions.

Formulation of the problem excluded organic causal factors which provided great relief as both were imagining possible catastrophes! The plan outlined was basically three stranded:

1. Enhancing communication, which included increasing the time the couple spent together and consequently their intimacy.
2. Correcting misconceptions (cognitions regarding the self and the other).
3. Restructuring sexual and nonsexual contact. Because avoidance of almost all types of contact, unless it also involved the presence of the children, was becoming generalized it was agreed to tackle this problem initially. HH was confronted with his erroneous cognitions, namely that because he was "incapable in bed IB was contemptuous of him and did not want him near." As a couple they were challenged to define, for each other and for each one of them, the relative value of sexual togetherness and of physical tenderness. HH was actually startled into realization of how much his avoidance of physical tenderness added insult to injury and made IB feel so "angry and empty." As a homework assignment it was agreed that they abstain from any sexual approaches (which was accepted with much relief on both sides, his reasons being obvious and IB clearly stating "Good! No sex. We leave the monster with you!") and daily engaging in at least a half-hour of sitting closely together and gently caressing each other. They were also asked to refrain from discussing any topic other than daily matters.

The success of the homework assignment was quite obvious when at the next session, instead of drawing their chairs further apart from each other, they actually drew them closer together and sat close together and turned toward each other. From session 2 onwards the couple and therapist formed an isosceles rather than the equilateral triangle of the first session.

Communication skills were next on the agenda, wherein the importance of the following was outlined: speaking for oneself and not for the other; being reinforcing rather than punishing; stating issues clearly, not as a retaliation; not blaming the other for someone else's behavior. There were homework assignments to train these communication skills, one of the most important being the individual listing, in writing, what they liked in each other and what they liked least. This assignment proved invaluable in providing material to challenge the negative cognitions that HH had built of himself as a man. His wife's list was the living proof that his poor sexual performance had in no way diminished him as a man in her eyes. He confirmed that poor erections did not turn him into a failure and neither was the world about to fall on his head. At this point it was felt that the couple had become closer and less threatened by their sexual problems so that the time was right to face the sexual issues.

Basic information on sexual physiology and anatomy were provided, with much emphasis placed on how psychological mechanisms such as fear of failure and performance anxiety can actually disrupt normal sexual function. His medical check-up was again run through to emphasize these points. His negative cognitions were used as examples of psychological disruption and again challenged. An entire session was spent on identifying positive alternatives to his negative cognitions; for example, "Loss of erection is not loss of masculinity" or "She loves me even if I don't have an erection." The next homework assignments focused on sharing bedtime and cuddling before going to sleep. Sensate focus was implemented asking for abstinence from coitus. To challenge his conviction that no erection signified incapacity to satisfy women, sensate focus was to include him pleasuring her in any way they wished other than with his penis. The success of this phase in the treatment provided, in our opinion, the turning point to recovery. It was a moving experience to see this 35-year-old, capable and respected professional, father of two, show utter wonderment at his capacity, contrary to all he believed of himself, to give deep and satisfying sexual pleasure to the woman he loved, without using what he thought to be his indispensable penis! His wife was always attentive to his needs, challenging doubts and negative thoughts. Her obvious relish in her sexual pleasure and clear joy in their returned intimacy contributed immensely to rebuilding his self-confidence and clearly confronted his erroneous conceptions of his own male sexuality.

From this initial phase of sensate focus which lasted around a month (and two clinical sessions) HH and IB almost flew by themselves! He was already beginning to respond with partial erection when sensate focus with genital stimulation was implemented; despite their accomplishments there was still the hurdle of the niggling thought "erection is not enough. I may still lose it, like before." This was challenged and modified by maintaining in place the "coitus prohibition" enabling him to confront quite a few occasions of full erections, and changing his thoughts from "I'll lose it" to "I want to try; the world won't end if I lose it; I'll satisfy her anyway." Treatment was successfully completed in 11 sessions of couple therapy, over a 6-month period. At 6-month follow-up the couple remained well and satisfied with their relationship.

The 6-month follow-up session was essentially spent on recapitulating on the lessons learned by the couple. The onset of the problem was recalled to illustrate how dysfunctional thoughts are born of fear, avoidance, and replacing reality by speculative motive attribution and, furthermore, how irrational beliefs feed and grow on avoidance and lack of communication. Their process of change was also recalled to emphasize the need to challenge irrational beliefs with confronting reality, which they underwent by reestablishing communications and dropping avoidance strategies. Both agreed that the key to maintaining a satisfactory and fulfilling relationship was in always keeping open communication and facing fears and irrational thoughts together.

Case Discussion

This clinical case is a good example of how to use cognitive-behavior theory to conceptualize and plan a treatment intervention for sexual dysfunction. Taking into consideration the Nobre (2010) model presented in this chapter, one can understand how the typical macho beliefs presented by the male partner may have worked as vulnerability factors, predisposing HH to interpret negative sexual events as a sign of personal failure and incompetence. In fact, the occasional negative outcomes experienced at a very stressful period in this couple's life were interpreted by the male partner as a loss of masculinity. This negative interpretation led him to be increasingly worried about his sexual performance and to focus his attention (during sexual interaction) on his ability to have an erection. This attentional focus on performance rather than on erotic thoughts and emotions fueled the erectile difficulties, making the problem increasingly worse to the point of complete avoidance. The treatment approach was a good example of how to integrate classical sensate focus into cognitive restructuring. The sensate focus exercises were used as real life behavioral experiments, which played a significant role in questioning the patient's beliefs. A good example is described when the male was encouraged to pleasure his partner in any way they wished other than with his penis. The simple discovery that he was able to sexually satisfy his partner without using his penis was a crucial experience in challenging his misconceptions and constituted a turning point in therapy.

Summary and Conclusions

This small, and by no means expert glimpse into our history and cultural background, was given with the aim of providing a framework to understand our lackluster start in the "chose sexualle." The outburst of enthusiastic activity into which Portuguese therapists, mainly psychiatrists, plunged after the country shed its shackles in 1974, certainly developed deep roots. Today, there are public (national health) clinics, providing services in sexual therapy, in the country's three principal cities. And there is a busy, enthusiastic core of researchers, producing a great deal of work, some of which can be sampled in the present chapter. Most of the research effort is produced by colleagues based in the universities and linked to clinics. The best example of this integrated activity is the recently set up Laboratory for Sex Research (Sex Lab) at the University of Aveiro.

Of course the network is very restricted but we were late starters! Another important reason for the paucity in services are the recent state cutbacks in the provision of centralized hospitals which has led to an unsavory reduction in the already overstretched resources providing sexual therapy services. Also noteworthy is the caveat to be found in most of the clinics, namely that huge workloads and chronic understaffing must necessarily mean that research has to remain an unfulfilled goal. But perhaps the most serious caveat in the provision of sex therapy services in Portugal is the absence of organized inmate programs for sexual offenders serving sentences. Current services are stretched to the limit, very much impelled by individual heroic efforts on the part of the staff, but such goodwill is insufficient to provide the optimal services.

Nevertheless and, notwithstanding the many limitations, we hope to have been able to transmit an overall atmosphere of vital research and dedicated clinical service in Portugal, which in turn is infecting a whole younger generation, just as ours was infected by the bug of enthusiasm of those brave men and women who back in the 1970s built from nothing all we have been able to share with you, and to whom we gratefully dedicate this chapter.[4]

Notes

1. The authors thank Dr. Santinho Martins for permission to quote freely from his article "Amato Lusitano e a Sexologia" (2007).
2. We are indebted to Dr. John Bancroft for the term *gender identity discordance*, which he proposed in his book, *Human Sexuality and Its Problems* (2009), and which we find far more appropriate and fitting than the nomenclature in present use.
3. All examples used are drawn from clinical cases.

4. Drs. Afonso de Albuquerque, F. Allen Gomes, and J. Silveira Nunes initiated the first sexual therapy clinics in Portugal, and contributed to the training of most of the clinicians in the field.

References

Albuquerque, A. (1997). Subsídios para a historiografia da Sexologia em Portugal [Grants for the historiography of the Sexology in Portugal]. *Acta Portuguesa de Sexologia, 1*(2), 45–60.

Andersen, B., & Cyranowski, J. (1994). Women's sexual self-schema. *Journal of Personality and Social Psychology, 67,* 1079–1100.

Bach, A. K., Barlow, D. H., & Wincze, J. P. (2004). The enhancing effects of manualized treatment for erectile dysfunction among men using sildenafil: A preliminary investigation. *Behavior Therapy, 35*(1), 55–73.

Baker, T., McFall, R., & Shoham, V. (2009). Current status and future prospects of clinical psychology. *Psychological Science in the Public Interest, 9,* 67–103.

Bancroft, J. (2009). *Human sexuality and its problems* (3rd ed.). London: Churchill Livingstone: Elsevier.

Bancroft, J., Graham, C. A., Janssen, E., & Sanders, S. (2009). The dual control model: Current status and future directions. *Journal of Sex Research, 46,* 121–142.

Banner, L., & Anderson, R. (2007). Integrated sildenafil and cognitive-behavior sex therapy for psychogenic erectile dysfunction: A pilot study. *Journal of Sexual Medicine, 4,* 1117–1125.

Barlow, D. H. (2002). *Anxiety and its disorders: The nature and treatment of anxiety and panic.* New York: Guilford.

Beck, A. T. (1996). Beyond belief: A theory of modes, personality and psychopathology. In P. M. Salkovskis (Ed.), *Frontiers of cognitive therapy* (pp. 1–25). New York: Guilford.

Binik, Y. M. (2005). Should dyspareunia be retained as a sexual dysfunction in DSM-V? A painful classification decision. *Archives of Sexual Behavior, 34,* 11–21.

Brown, T. A., Chorpita, B. F., & Barlow, D. H. (1998). Structural relationships among dimensions of the DSM-IV anxiety and mood disorders and dimensions of negative affect, positive affect, and autonomic arousal. *Journal of Abnormal Psychology, 107,* 179–192.

Carvalho, J., Nobre, P. J. (2010a). Sexual desire in women: An integrative approach regarding psychological, medical, and relationship dimensions. *Journal of Sexual Medicine, 7,* 1807–1815

Carvalho, J., & Nobre, P. J. (2010b). Predictors of women's sexual desire: The role of psychopathology, cognitive-emotional determinants, relationship dimensions and medical factors. *Journal of Sexual Medicine, 7,* 928–937.

Carvalho, J., & Nobre, P. J. (2011). Predictors of men's sexual desire: The role of psychopathological, cognitive-emotional, relational, and medical factors. *Journal of Sex Research, 48,* 254–262.

Gomes, F. A., Fonseca, L., & Gomes, A. A. (1997). Comorbilidade psiquiátrica nas disfunções sexuais [Psychiatric comorbidity in sexual dysfunctions]. *Acta Portuguesa de Sexologia, 2,* 17–20.

Hawton, K. (1989). Sexual dysfunctions. In K. Hawton, P. M. Salkovskis, J. Kirk, & D. M. Clark (Eds.), *Cognitive behavior therapy for psychiatric problems: A practical guide.* Oxford, England: Oxford University Press.

Heiman, J. (2002). Psychological treatments for female sexual dysfunction: Are they effective and do we need them? *Archives of Sexual Behavior, 31,* 445–450.

Heiman, J. R., & Meston, C. M. (1998). Empirically validated treatments for sexual dysfunction. In Dobson & Craig (Eds.), *Empirically supported therapies: Best practice in professional psychology* (pp. 259–303). New York: Sage.

Laumann, E., Paik, A., & Rosen, R. (1999). Sexual dysfunction in the United States: Prevalence and predictors. *Journal of the American Medical Association, 281,* 537–544.

Masters, W. H., & Johnson, V. E. (1970). *Human sexual inadequacy.* Boston: Little, Brown.

Mitchell, W. B., DiBartolo, P. M., Brown, T. A., & Barlow, D. H. (1998). Effects of positive and negative mood on sexual arousal in sexually functional males. *Archives of Sexual Behavior, 27,* 197–207.

Nobre, P. J. (2003). *Disfunções sexuais: contributos para a construção de um modelo compreensivo baseado na teoria cognitiva* [Sexual dysfunction: Contributions for the development of a comprehensive model based on cognitive theory] (Unpublished doctoral dissertation). Universidade de Coimbra, Coimbra, Portugal.

Nobre, P. J. (2008). Patterns of association and overlapping among sexual dysfunction. *Sexologies, 17,* S 128.

Nobre, P. J. (2009). Determinants of sexual desire problems in women: Testing a cognitive-emotional model. *Journal of Sex & Marital Therapy, 35,* 360–377.

Nobre, P. J. (2010). Psychological determinants of erectile dysfunction: Testing a cognitive-emotional model. *Journal of Sexual Medicine, 7,* 1429–1437.

Nobre, P. J., & Pinto-Gouveia, J. (2006b). Emotions during sexual activity: Differences between sexually functional and dysfunctional men and women. *Archives of Sexual Behavior, 35,* 8–15.

Nobre, P. J., & Pinto-Gouveia, J. (2008). Differences in automatic thoughts presented during sexual activity between sexually functional and dysfunctional males and females. *Journal of Cognitive Therapy and Research, 32,* 37–49.

Nobre, P. J., & Pinto-Gouveia, J. (2009). Cognitive schemas associated with negative sexual events: A comparison of men and women with and without sexual dysfunction. *Archives of Sexual Behavior, 38,* 842–851.

Nobre, P. J., Pinto-Gouveia, J., & Gomes, F. A. (2006). Prevalence and comorbidity of sexual dysfunctions in a Portuguese clinical sample. *Journal of Sex & Marital Therapy, 32,* 173–182.

Nobre, P. J., Wiegel, M., Bach, A., Weisberg, R., Brown, T., Wincze, J., & Barlow, D. H. (2004). Determinants of sexual arousal and the accuracy of its self-estimation in sexually functional males. *Journal of Sex Research, 41,* 363–371.

Oliveira, C., & Nobre, P. J. (2008). Female sexual dysfunction: The role of schemas and affect. *Sexologies*, *17*, 128–129.

Quinta-Gomes, A., & Nobre, P. J. (2011). Personality traits and psychopathology on male sexual dysfunction: An Empirical Study. *Journal of Sexual Medicine*, *8*, 461–469.

Rosen, R. C., Leiblum, S. R., & Spector, I. (1994). Psychologically based treatment for male erectile disorder: A cognitive-interpersonal model. *Journal of Sex & Marital Therapy*, *20*, 67–85.

Rosen, R. C., Riley, A., Wagner, G., Osterloh, I. H., Kirkpatrick, J., & Mishra, A. (1997). The International Index of Erectile Function (IIEF): A multidimensional scale for assessment of erectile dysfunction. *Urology*, *49*, 822–830.

Santinho Martins, A. (2007, November). Amato Lusitano e a sexologia. Medicina Beira Interior—Da Pré-História ao Século XXI [Amato Lusitano and sexology: Internal medicine beira interior—From prehistory to the 21st century]. *Cadernos de Cultura*, No. 217.

Soares, C., & Félix da Costa, N. (1999). Morbilidade Psiquiátrica e morbilidade sexual numa população feminina não seleccionad [Psychiatric morbidity and sexual morbidity in a random female population]. *Psiquiatria Clínica*, *2* (3), 19--204

Teles, A., Carreira, M., Alarcão, V., Aragués, J., Lopes, L., Mascarenhas, M., & Costa, J. (2008). Prevalence, severity, and risk factors for erectile dysfunction in a representative sample of 3,548 Portuguese men aged 40 to 69 years attending primary healthcare centers: Results of the Portuguese Erectile Dysfunction Study. *Journal of Sexual Medicine*, *5*, 131–1324.

Vendeira, P. S., Pereira, N. M., Serrano, F., & Carvalheira, A. A (2011). Estudo Episex-PT/Feminino: prevalência das disfunções sexuais femininas em Portugal. [Episex-pt: Prevalence of female sexual dysfunction in Portugal]. *ISEX Cadernos de Sexologia Sex*, *4*, 7–14.

Vendeira, P. S., Pereira, N. M., Tomada, N., LaFuente, J. M. (2011). Estudo Episex-PT/Masculino: prevalência das disfunções sexuais masculinas em Portugal. [Episex-pt: Prevalence of male sexual dysfunction in Portugal]. *ISEX Cadernos de Sexologia*, *4*, 15–22.

Vilarinho S., & Nobre, P. J. (2008). Portuguese women's sexuality and biopsychosocial determinants. *Sexologies*, *17*, S 149.

Wiegel, M., Scepkowski, L., & Barlow, D. (2007). Cognitive-affective processes in sexual arousal and sexual dysfunction. In E. Janssen (Ed.). *The Psychophysiology of Sex* (pp. 143–165). Bloomington: Indiana University Press.

Wincze, J. P., & Carey, M. P. (2001). *Sexual dysfunction: A guide for assessment and treatment* (2nd ed.). New York: Guilford.

Zilbergeld, B. (1999). *The new male sexualiy* (rev. ed.). New York: Bantam.

Editors Introduction to Chapter 13
Turkey

In this chapter, Mehmet Sungur speculates that the value placed on virginity in Turkish culture may contribute to the high incidence of vaginismus observed in that country. Turkey, like many other countries, is transitioning from a rural agrarian economy to an urban one, and many Turkish people are themselves still in transition. The importance of extended family and notions of privacy thus differ from Western values. Respecting the priority of the extended family and working with privacy constraints, Sungur describes his treatment of a woman with long standing vaginismus, treatment that involved her in-laws. This chapter provides a wonderful template for providing culturally sensitive treatment in a larger family context—where sex is not a private matter between two consenting adults, but a matter for the wider family to be concerned about.

13

THE ROLE OF CULTURAL FACTORS IN THE COURSE AND TREATMENT OF SEXUAL PROBLEMS

Failures, Pitfalls, and Successes in a Complicated Case from Turkey

Mehmet Sungur

Societies with different cultural heritages differ about what behaviors will be accepted, tolerated, or rejected (Segall, Dasen, Berry & Poortinga, 1990) and, thus, problems and their management are not culture free (Bhugra & De Silva, 2007; De Silva & Rodrigo, 1995; De Silva, 1999; Sungur, 1994, 1999). Sexual behaviors are particularly open to cultural and social influences. Anthropologists and sociologists have shown how cultural and subcultural groups differ in the expression of sexuality (Kirmayer, 2007). Cultural factors determine what is permitted and what is prohibited regarding sexual attitudes, beliefs, and rituals related to sexual behavior and sexual relationships (De Silva, 1999). Cultural factors also influence the way sex therapy is offered and welcomed and therefore it is crucial to tailor and modify Western sex therapy programs to the needs and the value systems of individuals in specific cultures. Sex therapists, especially those practicing in multicultural societies, need to be flexible and adapt their therapies to the needs of individuals from different cultures and subcultures (Bhugra & De Silva 1993; D'Ardenne, 1991).

Increasing globalization, industrialization, cultural diffusion, and the spread of global media reduces the isolation of societies and cultures. Although this facilitates adaptation into a more "Western" lifestyle, these changes are not assimilated at the same rate in all parts of the society. Thus one can often observe a split between different parts of the same society, in terms of the degree to which they have incorporated Western values and behaviors. This is true of modern day Turkey.

Geographically, Turkey is located at an unusual intersection as it extends over two continents, with a smaller European and a larger Asian (Anatolian) part. The land literally creates a bridge between East and West, not only geographically but also politically, culturally, and with respect to religion. On the west side, Turkey shares borders with member states of the European Union and a long standing debate is still raging about Turkey's integration process into the European Union. On the east side, Turkey shares a border with Iran, a country that promotes a rather radical brand of Islam in contrast to the constitutionally secular state of Turkey. On the southeast, where a substantial Kurdish population lives, it shares borders with Iraq and Syria and on the northeast, Turkey borders Georgia and Armenia.

Turkey has an area of 780.580 km^2 with a population of 69 million. More than half of Turkey's population is under the age of 24 and the gender ratio is 1.02 male(s) to 1.0 female (State Institute of Statistics [SIS], 1995). Turkey's economy was traditionally based on agriculture but recently a radical transition toward industrial development has occurred. State possession and intervention in economic investments has gradually diminished since the 1980s and the current economy relies on free market rules.

Many ancient cultures, including the Mesopotamian, Sumerian, Hittite, Roman, Byzantine, and Ottoman cultures, constitute Turkey's cultural heritage. Islamic culture with Western elements is woven together into this rich cultural background. Most of Turkey's population is Muslim (predominantly Sunni). Although Muslim, Turkish people are unique in their interpretation of Islam as Turkey is constitutionally a secular state. It is therefore not governed by Şeriat (Islamic laws based on Koran) and the state and religion are separated from each other. Varieties of Islamic interpretation, such as the Alevi tradition (classified as a branch of Shi'a Islam in which worship takes place in assembly houses rather than mosques) and other religions exist side by side as part of the large cultural mosaic.

Turkey has experienced a huge population shift from the rural areas to big cities and especially to İstanbul. The urban/rural distribution is 71% to 29% (Central Intelligence Agency [CIA], 2002). This population shift facilitated changes in the family structure from a patriarchal to a nuclear model. But despite the overwhelming prevalence of nuclear families in urban areas, extended families and wider kinship ties remain important (Aydın & Gülçat, 2004). The typical lifecycle of the rural family involves several stages: First, the newly married couple lives with the husband's parents (the patriarchal extended family). This is both a valued pattern and an economic necessity. Next, the couple moves out on its own as its income improves and the couple gains autonomy (the nuclear family). Later, the aging parent(s) move into the couple's home for care and protection in old age (transient extended family). A combination of economic necessity, lack of institutional or other means of old age security, and the high value put on filial loyalty leads to this typical pattern. Even when members of the nuclear family live in separate houses, extended family members are called upon to provide support when needed, forming a "functional extended family" (Kağıtçıbaşı, 1982).

Family relations are still mostly patriarchal, with men having authority over their wives and children. As young brides in rural areas often live with their husband's family, there is the potential for interpersonal and role problems. This "extended family" sometimes holds three generations in the same household, with grandparents having the authority on child care and sometimes financial issues. The bride ascends to a higher status when she gives birth to a child.

Endogamous marriage, that is, marriage within one's own religious, ethnic, or kinship groups, is still prevalent in rural Turkey. People are tied in close kinship bonds, so individual acts such as divorce are limited. Arranged marriages, where the marriage decision is made by parents of both spouses, is part of endogamous marriage and is still practiced in rural areas. In the past proposed future spouses were not able to meet each other before the wedding. Rapid social and cultural changes did not totally eradicate arranged marriages but modified them in the sense that young people nowadays can meet each other before marriage as long as a certain physical distance is kept between them. By contrast, cohabitation is well accepted in big cities and many couples prefer to live together without getting married.

A rather conservative and reserved attitude is apparent regarding sexuality and discussions about sexual matters with children at home and in school. From a religious perspective, parents are expected to teach their children a ritual of Islamic attitude called *abdest* that involves bathing parts of the body in a predetermined order after any type of sexual activity, including wet dreams. Another culturally based attitude is the responsibility of elder family members to provide sexual information to the bride and the groom just before marriage. The *sağdıç* (best man) talks to the groom while the *yenge* (chaperone), an experienced female family member, informs the bride about sexual issues. For some young people in rural areas this is the only available source of sexual information before marriage (Aydın & Gülçat, 2004).

Although one main purpose of school education is to prepare young children for their future roles as a spouse or a parent, formal and comprehensive sexual education in schools is not yet available in Turkey.[1] One reason that Turkish parents avoid talking about sex is that they themselves lack basic knowledge about sex and do not know how and what kind of information or experience should be shared with their children. Thus, the main source of information about sex becomes peers.

One study revealed that for 15% of the adolescent sample, the source of sexual knowledge was the family, for 35% their peers, for 20% the media, for 8% the school, and for 12% "other" sources, such as popular publications and pornography (Ekşi, 1982). A more recent study conducted with a larger sample (N = 1,500), representative of the Turkish population, confirmed that the major source of information about sex across different age groups was peers and for married adult women, their husbands. The media and formal sources such as doctors and relevant books become sources of sex information only during adulthood, albeit still less popular than peers or spouses (Cinsel Eğitim Tedavi ve Araştırma Derneği, 2006; CETAD). In this same study, two thirds of the respondents favored sex education in schools and as the education level of participants increased, endorsement of sex education in schools increased. Efforts to incorporate sex education into academic curriculum at all levels is challenging and human sexuality, sexual functioning, and dysfunctions have only become part of the curriculum of some Turkish medical schools in the last two decades. The lack of formal sex education may explain why fear and anxiety are the main emotions associated with sex (Sungur, 1996). Many young boys and even adult men worry about the size of their penis or their sexual performance, whereas many young girls and women worry about their first sexual experience (Aydın & Gülçat, 2004).

Inadequate sex education may be an important predictor for the development of sexual myths which may then lead to sexual dysfunctions. Because the subject of sex is surrounded by ignorance, myths and dysfunctional beliefs abound. Some sexual "problems" simply reflect faulty expectations due to lack of accurate knowledge. Unrealistic expectations may lead to performance anxiety which may then lead to performance dissatisfaction (Sungur, 1998). A client who believed he suffered from premature ejaculation defined it as any ejaculation "before the partner's orgasm." He believed that partners must always have simultaneous orgasms; if this does not occur, the man must have premature ejaculation. A client considering himself "impotent" after having an erectile failure in his first experience at a brothel believed that "a real man must always be ready to offer sex regardless of the situation." A woman who suffered from orgasmic dysfunction resolved her problem just by learning that a genital area called the clitoris existed. It is therefore crucial to detect and correct dysfunctional beliefs and expectations held by patients, as this may sometimes resolve the problem without the need for further sex therapy (Sungur, 1998).

Masturbation is regarded as a sin by many Muslims, although there appears to be no definite rule in the Koran that prohibits masturbation. Nevertheless, a significant proportion of Turkish males do report masturbation. One study revealed that 11.5% of female, and 87.5% of male university students masturbated, while 21% of females and 26% of males regarded masturbation as "unhealthy," probably due to myths such as "masturbation is dirty, sinful and harmful" (Erkmen, Dilbaz, Seber, Kaptanoğlu, & Tekin, 1990). Another study revealed that male students considered masturbation as "distressing," particularly if their fathers were not well-educated (Ekşi, 1990). Clinical observation of patients with sexual dysfunction suggests that masturbation is more common and acceptable in men than in women. Another recent study conducted with 638 university students in southeast Turkey revealed that 53% of students had experience of masturbation; fewer women reported masturbation (9%) than men (83%) (Yasan, Eşsizoğlu & Yıldurum, 2009). Gender differences in masturbation rates are also consistently found in Western cultures as well (Petersen & Hyde, 2010).

In the same study, the rate of premarital sexual intercourse was 26%, with a significantly lower prevalence in female (3.5%), compared with male (41%), university students. More than half of the participants had engaged in masturbation, while only about one-fourth had experienced foreplay/sexual intercourse. These rates are lower than similar studies conducted in Western regions of Turkey such as İzmir (Aras, Orçin, Ozan, & Semin, 2007), İstanbul (Kaplan, 2000), and Antalya (Dönmez, 1999) and much lower than those in Western societies (Finer, 2007). The low rates of premarital sex amongst university students in the Yasan et al. (2009) study might be related to the location of the university, as southeast Anatolia is a place where traditional values about premarital sex and virginity are still very evident. The higher rate of premarital sexual experiences in western regions of Turkey might be explained by the rapid adoption of Western sex positive attitudes. Relatively higher rates of masturbation and sexual intercourse obtained in the Yasan et al. study (2009), when compared with research conducted in traditional Islamic countries (Lee, Chen, Lee, & Kaur, 2006; Simbar, Tehrani, & Hashemi, 2005), may reflect the dual effects of being a secular Muslim and, at least in the urban areas, being more "Westernized." The gender differences in terms of rates of sexual intercourse may reflect the ongoing sexual double standards in this area. Women who have premarital sex are sometimes not only blamed but are also exposed to severe family and social consequences. In contrast, Westernized parts of Turkey and Western societies report a narrowing of gender differences in premarital sexual experiences (Clements-Schreiber, Rempel, & Desmarais, 1998; Finer, 2007).

The large-scale CETAD study (2006) that investigated public knowledge, behavior, and attitudes toward sex showed that women reported lack of knowledge (e.g., responding "I have no idea" to items related to sexuality), whereas men's answers reflected incorrect or biased information about sex and a belief in many sexual myths. The most common myth endorsed by men was: "To achieve success is the most important issue in sex," followed by, "Any man ought to know how to give pleasure to any woman." The expectations created by such beliefs may impose great performance demands and anxiety on men. Other common myths were: "A man always wants and is always ready to have sex," and "Foreplay should always lead to intercourse." One myth shared by both men and women was, "Homosexuality is a psychiatric disorder that needs to be treated." This reflects the widespread homophobia present in Turkish society. Interestingly, issues of homosexuality and transsexuality are barely covered, even in sex education curricula for medical students, but are extensively discussed when the topic is related to HIV/AIDS, indicating another underlying myth that "AIDS is a disease of homosexuals."

Although epidemiological data are limited, there is enough clinical evidence to conclude that sexual dysfunction is present across all societies and cultures. The CETAD study (2006), discussed above, investigated the prevalence of sexual problems in Turkey. Overall, 53% of the respondents reported that they had never suffered from any sexual problem, while 25% indicated that they suffered from at least one specific sexual dysfunction. Sixty-five percent of this latter group never sought counseling or treatment for their problems. The majority of respondents reported that they had trouble talking about sexual difficulties and expected their health professional to initiate a discussion about sex and sexual problems.

Studies conducted with individuals who come forward to seek help from sexual dysfunction treatment centers located in different regions (east and west) of Turkey reflect a consistent pattern, indicating that vaginismus is the most common reason that women seek treatment (Doğan, 2009; Incesu & Yetkin, 2007; Özdemir, Şimşek, Incesu & Koç, 2006; Sungur, 1994; Tuğrul & Kabakçı, 1997; Yılmaz, 2007). Regarding men, most studies show that erectile dysfunction (ED) is the most common sexual problem that motivates help-seeking (Incesu & Yetkin, 2007; Kayır, Geyran & Tükel, 1990; Sungur, 1994).

Vaginismus is seen more frequently in Turkey compared to Western countries, where women more often present with orgasmic dysfunction (Basson et al., 2000; Sungur, 1994; Talakoub et al., 2002; Yasan & Akdeniz, 2009) and lack of sexual desire (Basson et al., 2000; Nobre, Gouveia, & Gomes, 2006). Vaginismus constitutes 52 to 73% of all female referrals made to sexual dysfunction treatment centers in Turkey (Kayır et al., 1990; Sungur, 1994; Tuğrul & Kabakçı, 1997). This is much higher than the 10 to 17% prevalence found in Western countries (Golombok, Rust, & Pickard, 1985; Hawton, 1985; Hirst, Baggaley, & Watson, 1996; Spector & Carey, 1990; Warner & Bancroft, 1987). The high frequency of vaginismus seen in outpatient treatment centers may not necessarily mean that vaginismus is the most common sexual disorder experienced by women in Turkey. Rather, these statistics may reflect the fact that vaginismus often poses a serious threat to the maintenance of marriage, and so a "crisis" situation may emerge. Moreover, Turkish women with impaired sexual desire or orgasmic dysfunction might have difficulty expressing their complaints about lack of pleasure. Studies conducted with nonclinical samples are needed to establish the prevalence of different sexual dysfunctions in Turkish women across urban areas and in more traditional Anatolian settings.

The large-scale CETAD study (2006) also revealed that 54% of female respondents tried to avoid their first sexual intercourse due to fears about experiencing pain. Fear and avoidance were more common in illiterate and less educated women. Interestingly, only 22% of these women's partners were aware of the problem. This may reflect either the reluctance of women to discuss their problems or the insensitivity of men toward understanding their partners' needs and their own unwillingness to talk about sexual matters.

One reason for the higher prevalence of vaginismus in Turkey may be the high premium placed on virginity. The extreme emphasis on protecting virginity until marriage may lead to fear of penetration, even when it is socially, culturally, and religiously sanctioned. The CETAD study (2006) investigated the meaning of virginity for Turkish men and women. The following four statements were provided and participants were asked how much they agreed with them: (a) virginity is an honor symbol for women; (b) virginity must be kept until marriage; (c) men should not marry women who are not virgins; and (d) virginity is the symbol of integrity for the husband candidate and for the father of the woman. Overall, the percentages of respondents who strongly agreed with the statements were 63%, 65%, 53%, and 57%, respectively. Agreement was found to be inversely proportional with education level and directly proportional to the ages of participants. Forty-four percent of the sample believed that considering the customs and traditions, crimes of adultery and honor could be understandable/acceptable. In the past, women were sentenced to imprisonment while men were not severely punished for adultery. New regulations in the civil code abolished this inequality and adultery is no longer a criminal act for either men or women. Virginity, however, is still highly valued for many women and especially those women living in partly Westernized Anatolian Turkey. Even some educated young people who engage in sexual activity reserve sexual intercourse until the wedding night. There are still cases where elder members of the family wait curiously outside the couple's room/house to see the blood stain on the bed sheet, which confirms the perforation of the hymen on the wedding night, although this is less common nowadays. The blood-stained sheet is expected to be displayed to family members and is taken as proof of chastity on the part of the woman, as well as being a badge of pride and honor for the man who has successfully performed the expected act. This so-called tradition becomes a major source of pressure for both men and women. The bride is expected to be a virgin and the groom is expected to perform sexually. Many cases of erectile failure or ejaculation problems can be attributed to these stress-provoking expectations and events taking place on the wedding night. Tragic consequences, including divorce, damaged reputations, and ruined family relations may follow if sexual intercourse does not happen. The bride's family may blame the groom for nonconsummation and thus, for being "impotent." On the other hand, in the absence of blood, some women are mistakenly accused of not being virgins, and the family of the groom may blame the bride and her family for not protecting the honored virginity. Some young couples adopt pragmatic solutions which involve cutting parts of their body and staining the sheet with blood to avoid the embarrassment and possibly tragic consequences of nonconsummation.

The characteristics of women with vaginismus and the characteristics of the culture may interact, resulting in the high prevalence of vaginismus in Turkey. Women with vaginismus have a fear of penetration due to apprehension of pain and the mistaken belief that the vagina is too small to accept the penis. The vulnerability of women to experience penetrative anxiety may be a universal phenomenon, whereas its frequency and expression may be determined by the culture, according to levels of sexual knowledge, sexual experience, bodily awareness, and the meaning attached to the act of penetration. Tuğrul and Kabakçı (1997) attributed the high prevalence of vaginismus in Turkey to the extreme importance given to virginity, along with avoidance of premarital sex and the taboo about talking about sex.

Many young women in underdeveloped parts of Turkey still believe that they can lose their virginity if they touch their genitals, masturbate, or even ride a bicycle, and many young people are unaware of the elasticity of vaginal walls. Parents also get overly concerned about even minor injuries to the female genital area. These factors, when compounded by expectations of unbearable pain and excessive bleeding during first sexual intercourse, may lead to the development of vaginismus.

The vulnerability of the penis to erectile difficulties can be likened to the vulnerability of the vagina to penetration anxiety. Many young men, especially those in arranged marriages, suffer from fears of erectile failure in the days after the wedding ceremony. Activation of performance anxiety leads to "spectatoring" and subsequently, to failure to obtain or maintain erections, which may then lead the young man to seek help. Sungur (1998) described a young man who presented at a sexual dysfunction treatment center for treatment of his erectile failure. This patient was due to have an arranged marriage in 15 days time. He stated that if he did not have "big enough" erections to consummate the marriage, he would commit suicide. He also threatened the therapist with murder if the problem was not solved. His main fear was being labeled as impotent by overinvolved family members if he was not able to have intercourse and show the blood-stained sheet.

A study conducted in the more traditional southeast part of Turkey showed that the primary motivation for treatment of sexual problems was a desire or pressure to have a child and to continue/maintain the marriage (Yasan & Gürgen, 2009), although this was not found in an earlier study conducted in a Westernized urban setting (İstanbul) (Özdemir et al., 2006). Özdemir et al. found that women were the ones to seek treatment even when the husbands' sexual problems were responsible for the nonconsummation of marriage. Another study, carried out with a clinical population in the city of Ankara (Sungur, 1994), found that the motivation of the male partner for couple and sex therapy was associated with treatment compliance and successful outcome. Taken together, these findings suggest that subcultural differences exist for treatment motivation; although it is generally women who motivate men to come forward to seek help, men determine adherence to, and success with, treatment. We must appreciate the efforts made by women to have a better marital and sexual life, especially in a slowly changing traditional culture. At the same time, there is also an apparent need to establish sex and couple therapy programs that will be more appealing for men.

Approaches to Treatment

One meaning of culture has to do with collective identity on the basis of history, language, religion, gender, and ethnicity (Kirmayer, 2007). Another aspect includes the manner of living in a certain society: its values, customs, beliefs, and practices that form a complex system (Kuper, 1999). All of these factors play a role in the presentation of sexual problems, help seeking behavior of individuals/couples, and the way help is offered via formal (medical, psychological) and informal (religious, spiritual, etc.) sources. Cultural factors influence all of the following: (a) the choice of the helping agencies the person/couple seeks help and advice from; (b) the timing of the demand for help; (c) attribution of the cause of the sexual difficulty or dysfunction; (d) expectations of what treatment will be given (individual or conjoint); (e) motivation for sex therapy or other means of treatments; (f) compliance with that treatment; and (g) resistance to some therapeutic strategies (Sungur, 1999).

In Turkey, many people suffering from sexual dysfunction come to sex therapists not as their first source of help, but often after having tried folk remedies. As the cause of the dysfunction is attributed to magical power, evil forces such as *büyü* (black magic), or magical processes initiated by those who are hostile or jealous of the couple, treatment is sought from traditional healers such as *hodgas*, psychics, fortune tellers, and from others believed to have the power to break the black magic. In some cases, the cause is attributed to *nazar* (evil eye) or to *jins* (genies), who are believed to reveal themselves to certain people. Those who believe in such notions seek treatment from religious healers. Although prohibited by law, these "healers" use prayers and rituals and thus exploit their clients, both time-wise and financially. Some younger couples or individuals living in the same subculture do not believe in supernatural phenomena but may not have access to medical treatments and may be pressured by older family members to seek solutions from traditional healers.

In the last 10 to 15 years, the establishment of sexual dysfunction treatment centers and the media coverage given to these services encouraged people to come forward to seek help. The demand for sex therapy is not yet met by the limited number of treatment centers that are primarily located in universities and national hospitals in large cities. One of the first two sexual treatment centers was established in a university setting by the author in Ankara 18 years ago. At that time the demand was so great that many professionals from different disciplines became enthusiastic about learning and applying sex therapy approaches. This enthusiasm in professionals as well as the intensive media coverage encouraged many "silent sufferers" to come forward to seek help. The majority of these cases were treatment successes. Unfortunately, this movement and its initial success also attracted some individuals who had little or no previous therapeutic experience. These people saw sex therapy as a means to make money. Some new but peculiar treatment approaches emerged such as one-session treatment of vaginismus, Botox treatment, and the *künde* technique (*künde* is a term used in wrestling). It has no place in the treatment of vaginismus but a few self-proclaimed "therapists" used the term to refer to a position recommended to women suffering from vaginismus in which there is no way they can avoid penetration during sexual activity. These approaches caused loss of time, loss of money, and loss of hope for many individuals and couples. Sadly, sex therapy lost some of the credibility it had earlier obtained. As the initial enthusiasm for sex therapy tempered through time, a more realistic attitude has emerged in which candidates for sex therapy training attend formal courses given by various associations established in the area of sexual health.[2]

Another major issue in clinical practice is to consider the timing of the demand for help. There is always a trigger that generates motivation in clients to seek help and the identification of this trigger may indicate where to commence the treatment. In Turkey, the author has seen many cases in which the trigger is a threat of separation made by the husband to his wife who suffers from vaginismus. One man gave his wife 2 weeks to sort out the problem and threatened her with divorce otherwise. The reason that many male patients seek help for primary PE many years after the onset of the problem is an extramarital affair during which their extramarital partner has criticized them for rapid ejaculation. In these cases it is better to start with the management of the crisis, the "trigger" that brings clients forward to seek treatment. This may be educating the threatened husband about vaginismus, which he may not be aware of. This may be educating the man with PE that although his wife may have never complained about it, he might still have rapid ejaculation that needs to be considered for better mutual satisfaction in future sexual relations (Sungur, 1998). It is therefore very important to educate the clients and tailor or modify treatment programs according to the unique formulation and conceptualization developed for each case.

In Turkey, male presenters are often unwilling to bring their spouses to participate in therapy. In some cases the female partner is unwilling to come and discuss private matters with a therapist. But most of the time, it is the men who are reluctant to bring their wives, despite being given information that a better outcome would be achieved if they are seen conjointly. Thus, a kind of "remote control" therapy is instituted where the instructions for joint homework are given to the male, who is expected to convey these instructions and explain details of the homework to his wife. Under these circumstances the clinician has no direct way of knowing whether the homework instructions are properly implemented or not.

Another difference in the practice of sex therapy in Turkey is clients' resistance to masturbation exercises. As religious norms have a powerful influence on what is seen as acceptable or forbidden, a minority of clients resist the idea of masturbation as they believe masturbation is prohibited in Islamic teaching. Masturbation is an important therapeutic element for those individuals who do not have a sexual partner and thus negative attitudes toward masturbation may block treatment.

Another major cultural difference is in the extent of involvement of extended family members in dealing with sexual problems. Despite the overwhelming prevalence of nuclear family households, extended families and wider kinship ties remain of great importance and therefore strict boundaries do not exist between the young couple and their first-degree relatives. This results in overinvolvement of family members, as they are called upon to provide support in times of crisis and confusion. In rural Turkey, the couple often tells their families about the sexual problem and tries to tackle the crisis within the family's own resources by taking advice from more experienced members and seeking solutions from traditional healers. When difficulties persist, partners and their families start blaming each other, and this threatens the survival of the marriage. It is at this point and often as a last resort, that the couple, along with the older members of the family, seeks a therapist. This sometimes creates a dilemma for therapists who have to make a decision between confidentiality and effectiveness. If the first- degree relatives are told that they cannot be involved in treatment, they feel rejected and often refuse to provide financial support for treatment or to bring the presenting couple to further sessions. Even if family members allow the couple to go to treatment alone, they often pressure the young couple, and especially the wife, to reveal what has transpired in the sessions and what has been suggested by the therapist. If the family members are allowed to attend treatment sessions, the couple feels uncomfortable about revealing information regarding their sexual problems and progress with homework instructions. The lack of boundaries becomes a major problem, especially for couples who live in the same household as the extended family.

Turkish couples who seek treatment may not necessarily be highly motivated for sex therapy. Some couples expect the therapist to magically cure the problem by a simple intervention, such as prescribing a medication, whereas others try to make the therapist a judge who will decide which partner is right and which is wrong. Some attend to prove to the other partner or the family members that even professional help will not be able to save the marriage, while others bring their "problematic partner" and expect her or him to be treated without having to get involved themselves (Sungur, 1998). As motivation is directly related to treatment outcome, it is crucial that both of the partners take responsibility for improving their general and sexual relationship.

Case Discussion

A 32-year-old woman, Rana, whose complaint was not being able to have sexual intercourse throughout her marriage, came to my office with her 34-year-old husband Tevfik.[3] They had been married for 12 years. Both partners had no sexual experience prior to their marriage.

Rana complained that she had never had intercourse with her husband due to very tense muscles and fears of pain and bleeding. The problem emerged on the first night of their marriage when her husband attempted but could not penetrate. Rana attributed this to minor fears related to her first sexual experience and thought that the problem would disappear with time. Rana and Tevfik decided to cut their arms and display the blood-soaked sheet to the curious relatives waiting outside, thus proving Rana's virginity and confirming their success in consummating the marriage. The couple was initially happy that they had avoided the rumors and complications of not succeeding at intercourse. They initially tried to have sexual intercourse as frequently as possible, but Rana was not even able to open her legs during attempts at penetration. At the end of 6 months, they realized that there was no point in attempting penetration and they became hopeless. Tevfik avoided intimacy as he was getting frustrated and perceived the situation as Rana rejecting him. Rana also avoided intimacy as she thought that if she permitted her husband to cuddle and hug her, he would ask for more and further attempts at penetration would end with the same disappointment. As a result, the couple not only faced sexual frustration, but also lacked intimacy, which then led to communication problems. Tevfik initially had no difficulty obtaining erections, but with ongoing marital and sexual difficulties, he started suffering from occasional erectile failure, both with masturbation and during attempts at vaginal penetration.

Given their poor communication and lack of intimacy, Rana and Tevfik were unable to deal with this problem on their own. They turned for help to the elder members of their family. Initially, both sets of parents were angry with the couple for hiding the problem from them and for the "white lies" they had told to sustain the illusion of a consummated marriage. Tevfik's parents blamed Rana, while her parents blamed Tevfik for not being experienced in sex and for not being competent. The anger and blaming reveals how private and intimate matters become a matter of pride within the larger family. An elderly family member who heard about the problem became a bridge between the two families and advised the couple to consult a traditional healer, a religious *hodga*, who was believed to have the power to solve the problem. The *hodga* defined the problem as being "tied up" by evil forces and applied prayers and rituals to break the black magic. As the problem persisted despite the efforts of the traditional healer, the couple was taken to a general practitioner (GP) in the belief that the problem must be physical in nature. The GP defined the problem as a transient reaction due to fears of penetration and prescribed anxiolytics. As the situation did not improve, the GP suggested that Rana drink alcohol to reduce her anxiety. Drinking was not acceptable in the culture of the family, so the couple hesitated initially but then decided to try this. Nothing changed, apart from Rana consuming larger amounts of alcohol each day. As she found it embarrassing to drink in the presence of her husband, Rana started to drink during the day, before Tevfik came home. Eventually Rana developed a problem with alcohol.

Since the family continued to believe in the physical nature of the problem, they thought that it was time to see a specialist, a gynecologist. After a difficult physical examination, the gynecologist diagnosed the problem as vaginismus. She recommended that a hymenectomy operation under anesthesia be performed. The rationale for the surgery was the belief that if the hymen was removed, there would not be any pain or bleeding during intercourse. The couple's marked feelings of helplessness made them agree to the surgery, notwithstanding their belief in the value of protecting virginity until intercourse with the husband. After the hymenectomy, nothing changed and the problem persisted. The couple and the extended family thought that the only way to save the marriage and avoid rumors among the neighbors was for Rana to become pregnant. The vaginismus problem was relabeled as a fertility problem. They saw another gynecologist and had two failed inseminations. Rana became depressed and Tevfik became more frustrated. An IVF procedure under anesthesia was finally successful and happily, Rana became pregnant. Through the later stages of pregnancy, Rana was preoccupied with fears regarding vaginal delivery and to avoid the anticipated pain, she asked for a cesarean section. Rana explained her fear by asking "How could a baby come out from such a small area where even a penis cannot penetrate?" Her request was not accepted by the doctor and the family members as they thought that if she delivered the baby vaginally, the vagina would expand and she would be able to have a normal sex life after the birth. Rana went through a long delivery process where she experienced a lot of pain, anxiety, and fear.

The couple now had a baby boy at the end of 5 years of marriage but their sex life had worsened. To avoid another painful birthing experience, Rana now refused any attempts at sexual intercourse. She felt guilty and she compensated by getting overoccupied in domestic activities such as cooking and cleaning to make her husband happy. Tevfik also felt guilty as he blamed himself for causing Rana extreme pain during the labor. Nevertheless, they had renewed hope for a resolution to their sexual problem when they heard about a psychiatrist who was promising a single session treatment of vaginismus. The treatment was expensive but they decided to pay to see this famous professional so that they could have a more satisfactory marital life. Like many other couples who have become victims of the same single session intervention, they did not think that logically, the doctor would need at least a second session to find out whether the single session treatment worked. In addition to making false promises, this psychiatrist also embarrassed Rana and Tevfik by seeing them in a group with seven other couples who suffered the same problem. This was done without informing them beforehand and without gaining their consent. Following the provision of simple advice, prescribing anesthetics, and sitting in a hot bath, the psychiatrist asked each couple to go into one of the rooms in his office and attempt intercourse. He also told them that he would come into their room accompanied by his wife in case the couple would need it or find it helpful. This shows the extent of abuse and exploitation practiced in the name of sex therapy. Not surprisingly, Rana and Tevfik were not able to have intercourse in the doctor's office. The couple lost a lot of money but more importantly, they lost their confidence in doctors. They suffered in silence for the next 4 years until they heard about the sexual dysfunction assessment and treatment center located in a university setting established by the author.

Treatment Program

When they first made contact with the clinic, Rana and Tevfik expressed their hopelessness and their lack of confidence in doctors. They told the author that they only came because they had heard of other couples who were treated successfully in the center. They also declared that they did not have the financial resources to cover the expenses of treatment. It is noteworthy that the couple came to the treatment center accompanied by both sets of parents.

After the couple and their parents gave a detailed account of their past experiences, the elder family members said they would contribute toward the financial costs of the treatment sessions only at the end of treatment and only if the couple had achieved their goal. This request was accepted. The author adopted a very flexible and nonjudgmental approach to the couple and the other family members throughout treatment to prevent a further loss of confidence in professionals and to establish a good therapeutic relationship. Rana and Tevfik were encouraged to come to treatment sessions conjointly and the other family members were asked to kindly give the couple space and not get too involved in the treatment. Unfortunately, the couple was living with the husband's family and keeping appropriate boundaries became an issue later in therapy. The treatment consisted of nine sessions with 15-day intervals during which time Rana and Tevfik did homework assignments. To reduce performance anxiety, attempts at intercourse were banned until the last session. Couple therapy was given in conjunction with sex education and sex therapy. Each session lasted 50 minutes.

During couple therapy the therapist's main goal was to improve communication and problem solving skills as well as reciprocal negotiation skills and encourage the setting of boundaries between the couple and the rest of the family. During the initial sessions, when the therapist used the downward arrow technique[4] to learn about Rana's perceptions of her vagina, hymen, and sexual intercourse, her automatic thoughts became apparent. Rana thought that as she was physically small her vagina must be smaller than other women's. She also thought that sexual intercourse would be painful and as she thought she was more vulnerable to pain than other women, she would not be able to cope with the pain. As a child, Rana was very much criticized by her father and this made her think that all men were insensitive and therefore her husband would also be insensitive to her pain. She worried that if she were sexually intimate with Tevfik he would try penetration without her consent and therefore cause unbearable pain. Rana also related that when she was growing up, talking about sex was forbidden at home and she was told that sex was both dirty and painful. Just before her marriage, she was told by older married women that sex may become pleasurable but she would have to initially experience a lot of bleeding and pain. With all this information, Rana was very anxious and fearful on the wedding night. She noted that as Tevfik was also not sexually experienced, he too was anxious and he did not know how to soothe and comfort her.

Rana's fears that she was very vulnerable to pain were confirmed when she confided in her parents about the situation; her mother responded by saying, "I knew you were too sensitive and would not be able to face the pain." As she focused her attention on possible pain, Rana did not feel any pleasure during sexual activity and she avoided intimacy.

During treatment Rana's irrational thoughts and beliefs were challenged. Her concern about her husband's insensitivity was challenged by considering the evidence "for" and "against" these thoughts. Her attitudes about her genitals were addressed with various sex therapy techniques, including self-exploration where she was encouraged to use a mirror at home to examine and touch her genitals in order to make her feel comfortable and familiar with them. Rana was taught about Kegel exercises so that she could gain more control over her vaginal muscle contractions. Later, she was encouraged to insert one finger in her vagina, simultaneously with the Kegel exercises, in order to feel her vaginal muscles tightening and relaxing. Rana was very surprised and happy when she managed to insert one finger inside her vagina without any pain. Nongenital sensate focus exercises were given to the couple to improve intimacy without the fear of penetration. As the marital relationship and communication improved, Tevfik was able to insert his finger inside his wife's vagina with her guidance and at her pace, so that Rana was in control of the whole process.

The couple's progress suddenly halted midtreatment when Rana stopped doing the homework assignments. This was surprising and when the author tried to identify the cause of the difficulty, Rana did not want to talk about it. The author asked Tevfik for permission to talk to his wife alone. When he left the room, Rana revealed that her husband's brother, who was living in another city, had come to visit the family and because of the lack of space at home, he was asked to sleep in the same room as the couple. Rana suspected that her brother-in-law had been sent by Tevfik's parents to check if they were doing the homework exercises given by the therapist. She noted that he went to bed before they did and pretended he was sleeping, but in fact he was awake and curious. This information was shared with Tevfik and with the couple's consent the author invited the parents to a session to talk about this issue. The author took a flexible and understanding attitude as he knew that if the parents became angry they would resist bringing the couple for further treatment sessions. The author told the family members that he would give them more information about the couple's progress and assured them that he would inform them if any treatment difficulties arose. Getting the extended family members more involved without breaking boundaries helped the couple improve without any further interference.

Subsequently, therapy progressed smoothly, including using tampons, until vaginal containment instructions were given in the "female superior position." This position was recommended so that Rana could be in control of vaginal penetration. However, when they attempted intercourse in this position, Tevfik was unable to sustain an erection. When this was discussed in therapy, it was clear that Tevfik held traditional views related to the dominance of the male partner during sexual activity. He said that he felt very passive when Rana was on top in the "female superior" position. This myth was challenged using a cognitive approach and fear of further erection failure was dealt with by suggesting that the couple use the "waxing and waning" exercise.[5]

Treatment of this couple presenting with a severe vaginismus problem with a duration of 12 years, compounded by lack of good practice by some medical professionals and dysfunctional cultural attitudes, was completed at the end of nine sessions. The couple now live in a separate flat from their parents and Rana has since given birth to a second baby by vaginal delivery without experiencing extreme anxiety and pain. The 2-year follow-up confirmed that they have a satisfactory sexual and marital life that includes vaginal intercourse.

Extended Case Discussion

The case illustrated above described one of the many women who suffers from primary vaginismus, complicated by ineffective treatment attempts carried out by traditional healers and also unfortunately by medical professionals. The events that occurred in this case after the emergence of the problem followed a typical pattern often seen in Turkey. The couple, who had never heard about a condition known as vaginismus, did not initially identify the severity of the problem and labeled it as a transient fear of the first sexual experience, which they believed would resolve on its own. This indicates the need for public sex education in Turkey regarding common sexual disorders. The fact that this couple simulated intercourse on the first night by cutting their arms and showing the blood-stained sheet to relatives demonstrates the extent of pressure and performance anxiety felt by this and other couples.

Following the crisis period, the couple was taken to a traditional healer because the elder members of the family defined the source of the problem as evil forces and black magic. This again shows the need for public education. After losing much time and money, the couple decided that there must be a physical cause of the problem and they first saw a GP and then a gynecologist and a psychiatrist. It is quite typical that people who suffer from sexual dysfunctions seek help from members of different disciplines such as psychologists, psychiatrists, urologists, gynecologists, and GPs, as treatment is not under the monopoly of one discipline. One would expect that this kind of enquiry to "safe hands" would be the end of this tragic story. Unfortunately, for this couple it was the beginning of further disappointments caused by lack of knowledge, lack of ethical and good practice, and exploitation of the couple. In a study carried out by the author, 50% of women with vaginismus had a history of hymenectomy operations (Sungur, 1998). Again, this shows the necessity for a closer liaison between health professionals and the development of minimal (preferably optimal) standards of care (Sungur, 1997).

Following these procedures, both of the partners became depressed and so frustrated that Tevfik had decreased sexual desire followed by erectile failure. The sexual problem persisting in one partner engendered sexual problems in the other partner. The couple finally gave up trying to find solutions to their sexual problem and decided to focus on the infertility caused by the problem.

Another gynecologist was successful in treating vaginismus solely as a fertility problem and helping the couple to conceive, but ignored the sexual, psychological, and relational aspects of the problem. Moreover, the gynecologist refused Rana's request to have a cesarean section, on the basis of her unvalidated belief that a vaginal birth would expand her vagina and loosen her contracting muscles. This attitude confirmed Rana's belief that her vagina was small and only resulted in a difficult and anxious experience of delivery.

Following the vaginal delivery, Rana was still unable to have intercourse and she also developed a fear of getting pregnant. Despite their futile efforts to solve the vaginismus problem, the couple was happy to have a baby and this strengthened the weakened bond in their relationship. This in turn increased their motivation to seek treatment and after 2 years they saw a psychiatrist, who exploited them financially when he promised that a single-session treatment would be effective

Many clients find it difficult and embarrassing to reveal their negative experiences with professionals during the long journey they have had to undergo in order to find a solution to their problems. But, as this couple sadly demonstrates, misguided and unethical treatment may exacerbate the problem. In order to effectively and sensitively help clients, it is important to ask about previous treatment and tailor therapy to take these issues into account. The treatment success achieved by the author entailed a very flexible, understanding, and nonjudgmental approach, both toward the couple and their extended family members. This helped to reestablish a good therapeutic alliance and therefore improved the couple's motivation for treatment and adherence to homework assignments. Modifying and tailoring the treatment program according to the needs of the couple and a cultural case conceptualization shared with the couple became significant components of treatment success for this couple who had previously undergone unnecessary and unsuccessful healing practices.

Summary and Conclusions

Cultural case formulations and conceptualizations provide therapists with tools for better understanding individual cases. By tailoring therapy to the needs of the individual/couple and the cultural environment that shapes their experience of sexual problems, treatment will be more successful and some treatment failures may be prevented. For therapists practicing in multicultural societies, it is certainly not enough to identify the ethnicity and cultural background of their clients, enlist an interpreter to overcome language barriers, identify that cultural issues exist, and refer the patient to a therapist from the same culture. Every patient should be offered equal opportunities for treatment. Referring the patient to a therapist from the same culture may not always be possible and when it is possible, she or he may not be able to offer the same treatment options, which means restricted access to available good practice that the native patient can receive.

Experienced sex therapists are aware that a direct transfer of Western-developed sex therapy programs can sometimes cause disappointment and refusal in patients coming from collectivist cultural backgrounds. As in the case discussed in this chapter, therapists may sometimes need to involve other family members when dealing with sexual problems of individuals or couples to increase collaboration and reduce dropouts. Techniques such as the "female superior" position during intercourse may be rejected or cause treatment resistance unless myths or dysfunctional beliefs are handled carefully. Use of explicit erotic material for enhancing sexual responsiveness or even for education purposes can also be problematic. Prescription of self-stimulation, including masturbation, may create difficulties for patients coming from religious backgrounds in which masturbation is either forbidden or unacceptable.

Another area of concern for the nonnative treatment provider relates to the embarrassment or misunderstandings caused by the terminology used during assessment and treatment. Patients coming from collectivist cultures may not be familiar with medical terms and may be embarrassed to say that they do not understand the therapist's language. It is therefore important to understand what terms are or are not understood and reach common ground over the vocabulary to be used in future sessions. Sometimes direct questions instead of open-ended ones can be helpful if a client becomes embarrassed. Direct questions may relieve some of the burden of using difficult vocabulary (Hawton, 1985). It is also important to check if the couple has understood the homework instructions provided. A therapist speaking to a patient from another culture may feel embarrassed or uncomfortable during sessions. Support from other experienced therapists and regular work with clients from diverse cultures may ease the problem and enhance self-confidence for the therapist.

As is highlighted in Rana's case, the diagnostic criteria offered by Western classification systems such as the *International Classification of Disorders* (ICD-10) (World Health Organization, 1992) and *Diagnostic and Statistical Manual of Mental Disorders* (American Psychiatric Association, 2000) for specific sexual disorders such as vaginismus are problematic cross-culturally. Both DSM and ICD definitions of vaginismus emphasize contractions of vaginal muscles and the penetrative aspect of sexual intercourse, a conceptualization based on traditional penile-vaginal penetration and interference with coitus. Focusing on vaginal spasms has spawned ineffective treatments such as local injections of botulinum toxin, local anesthesia, and muscle relaxants.

There is heterogeneity involved in different vaginismus cases such as those where fear and spasms occur only during attempts of sexual intercourse but not during vaginal examination, which makes one wonder whether vaginismus is a symptom or a disorder. Diagnosis and treatments based on muscle contractions and interference with penetration may result in misunderstanding the phenomenology and mechanism of the pathological process. It is very important to reduce the emphasis placed on contractions and thereby reduce the tendency to provide a "quick fix." Professionals should offer holistic treatment approaches based on formulations and conceptualizations of each individual case.

A model to explain the emergence and maintenance of vaginismus for many cases can be explained as follows: Every attempt at vaginal penetration provokes the automatic thought that penetration will be unpleasant and painful due to some dysfunctional beliefs such as "sex is painful and I am vulnerable." This automatic thought provoked by any attempt at penetration leads to increased fear of pain. Fear of pain leads to contraction of outer vaginal muscles, an avoidance behavior to escape from the aversive experience. Contractions therefore may not be the cause but rather the result of fear that penetration will be painful. Repeated attempts at penetration, despite contraction of muscles, cause pain even without any penetration and this leads to confirmation of the fear that the penetration will be painful. This results in further contraction of the vaginal muscles and the failure of penetrative efforts, which maintains the problem. Cultural values and attitudes may contribute to the development and/or the intensity of the fear of penetration while the focus of treatment (vaginal dilation) may confirm the belief that intercourse is extremely painful or that the woman has an unusually small or sensitive vaginal opening. Thus the focus of the treatment may also play a role in maintaining the problem and must share the responsibility for the treatment failures that may result.

Although vaginismus is described as a sexual disorder that responds well to treatment, there are still many questions left unanswered regarding its definition, classification, psychopathology, and thus treatment. Both DSM and ICD definitions emphasize the contractions of vaginal muscles and the penetrative aspect of sexual intercourse. Thus, according to these definitions it is not vaginismus if the muscles contract but penetration is possible! Surprisingly, anticipation of severe pain is not considered necessary or even mentioned for the diagnosis. Ward and Ogden (1994) demonstrated that most women with vaginismus attributed the cause of the problem to their fear of pain. Clinicians' observations in real life also confirm that treatment must lead to reduction of the fear of pain not the muscle contractions.

Some, but not all of these concerns have been addressed by the proposed revisions to the DSM (DSM-5; Binik, 2010). One recommendation is that the diagnoses of dyspareunia and vaginismus be combined into a single diagnosis called genito-pelvic pain/penetration disorder (GPPPD) which would have fear of penetration as a sufficient criterion for diagnosis. Unfortunately, the proposed diagnostic criteria for GPPPD suggest that one must suffer from persistent or recurrent difficulties for a minimum of 6 months in order to be diagnosed with GPPPD. Because of the increasing visibility of vaginismus in the media, many people now recognize the disorder at a very early stage and come forward to demand help soon after they experience the problem. Clinical experience shows that penetration attempts are more frequent following the initial experience of the problem and reduce over time due to frustration and hopelessness. It is difficult to understand why the diagnosis must be delayed for 6 months, when there may have been 20–30 attempts at intercourse made in the first few months following the initial exposure to the problem. Another concern with this diagnosis is the requirement of only one persistent or recurrent difficulty in order to diagnose GPPPD. Pain disorders are conceptualized as distinct from sexual dysfunction. The new proposed criteria fail to make the distinction between pain and fear of pain, and collapse them into a single diagnostic entity. Some diagnostic criteria, such as marked genito-pelvic pain during at least 50% of vaginal intercourse/penetration attempts, are associated with dyspareunia, whereas others such as marked fear of vaginal intercourse or of genito-pelvic pain are more associated with what was diagnosed as vaginismus in DSM-IV-TR. This may lead to confusion both for clients and clinicians who treat the condition.

Unfortunately, the focus of sex therapy has long been the treatment of the symptoms of sexual dysfunction rather than the sexual dysfunction itself. We, as sex therapists, fix the dysfunctional penis in front of the man but we forget the man behind the dysfunctional penis. We try to fix the vaginal spasms and dilate the vaginal opening, but we forget the woman who experiences fear of pain. In other words, we equate the symptom with the existing problem and then treat only the symptom. Thus we fail to distinguish symptoms of sexual difficulties from the person who suffers from those difficulties. Treatment success in attaining the limited goals of symptom recovery may then lead to further neglect of the meaning of presenting complaints. We treat without understanding just like we sometimes hear without listening. Cultural case formulations and conceptualizations are an important step in the development of holistic models for comprehensive understanding and treatment of sexual problems and the men and women who suffer from them.

Notes

1. During the past two decades, sex education has been a topic of debate and some efforts have been made by the Turkish Family Planning Association, Sexual Education, Treatment and Research Association and other organizations to promote sexual education. One major outcome was booklets prepared for teenage students, teachers, and parents titled "Changes During Adolescence and Youth," produced by a volunteer group working in the area of sex education under the sponsorship of the Health Chamber of the Ministry of Education (Öktem et al., 2000). The main aim of the authors of this booklet (which included the author) was to increase awareness of school children about sexual health and to train the teachers who would run the sex education courses in schools. This crucial effort did not entirely meet its goals due to the lack of consistent attitudes of teachers toward sex and sexual matters, responses of ministry staff who censored some important parts of the written material, and the conservative attitudes of professionals who were expected to take part in regular education programs.
2. There is still a need for more advanced training beyond the rote application of sex therapy techniques, including training in couple therapy. In addition, a closer liaison is needed between the different health professionals offering treatment for sexual dysfunction, including urologists, psychiatrists, gynecologists as well as family doctors and general practitioners.
3. Clients' names are pseudonyms.
4. Downward arrow technique is a powerful way to move from surface cognitions to deeper cognitive structures by asking questions such as, "If your thought were true, what would it say about you as a person?"
5. During the "waxing and waning" exercise, once the man has an erection, the partners are asked to cease caressing (genital or nongenital) for a few minutes to allow the erection to subside. They should then resume caressing with the female slowly stroking her partner's penis. This helps the male partner find that his erections return and dispels the fear that the erection

will not be regained. It is therefore a helpful technique to remove the pressure a man might feel to sustain his erection throughout lovemaking.

References

American Psychiatric Association. (2000). *Diagnostic and Statistical Manual of Mental Disorders* (4th ed., text rev.). Washington, DC: Author.
Aras, S., Orçin, E., Ozan, S., & Semin, S. (2007). Sexual behaviors and contraception among university students in Turkey. *Journal of Biosocial Science*, 39, 121–135.
Aydın, H., & Gülçat, Z. (2004). The Republic of Turkey. In R. T. Francoeur & R. J. Noonan (Eds.), *The Continuum complete international encyclopedia of sexuality* (pp. 1054–1071). New York: Continuum.
Basson, R., Berman, J., Burnett, A., Derogatis, L., Ferguson, D., Fourcroy, J., ... Whipple, B. (2000). Report of the International Consensus Development Conference on Female Sexual Dysfunction: Definitions and classification. *The Journal of Urology*, 163, 888–893.
Bhugra, D., & De Silva, P. (1993). Sexual dysfunction acrosss cultures. *International Review of Psychiatry*, 5, 243–252.
Bhugra, D. & De Silva, P. (2007). Sexual dysfunction acrosss cultures. In D. Bhugra & K. Bhui (Eds.), *Textbook of cultural psychiatry* (pp. 364–378). Cambridge, England: Cambridge University Press
Binik, Y. M. (2010). The DSM diagnostic criteria for dyspareunia. *Archives for Sexual Behavior*, 39, 292–303.
Cinsel Eğitim Tedavi ve Araştırma Derneği (CETAD). (2006). *Sexual and reproductive health research*. Istanbul, Turkey: Taylor Nelson Sofres/PIAR Research Counselling.
Central Intelligence Agency (CIA). (2002). *The world facebook 2002*. Washington, DC: Author. Retrieved from http//www.cia.gov/cia/publications/facebook/index.html.
Clements-Schreiber, M. E., Rempel, J. K., & Desmarais, S. (1998). Women's sexual pressure tactics and adherence to related attitudes: A step toward prediction. *Journal of Sex Research*, 35, 197–205.
D'Ardenne, P. (1991). Transcultural issues in couple therapy. In D. Hooper & W. Dryden (Eds.), *Couple therapy: A handbook* (pp. 179–195). Milton Keynes, England: Open University Press..
De Silva, P. (1999). Culture and sex therapy. *Sexual & Marital Therapy*, 14, 105–107.
De Silva, P., & Rodrigo, E. K. (1995). Sex therapy in Sri Lanka—Developments, problems and prospects. *International Review of Psychiatry*, 7, 241–247.
Doğan, S. (2009). Vaginismus and accompanying sexual dysfunctions in a Turkish clinical sample. *Journal of Sexual Medicine*, 6, 184–192.
Dönmez, L. (1999). Sexual attitudes and behaviors among students at Akdeniz University faculty of tourism and sports. *HIV/AIDS*, 2, 147–151.
Ekşi, A. (1982). *Gençlerimiz ve Sorunları* [Turkish teenagers and their problems]. İstanbul, Turkey: Bilgi.

Ekşi, A. (1990). *Çocuk, genç, anababalar* [Children, teenagers, parents]. İstanbul, Turkey: Bilgi.

Erkmen, H. N., Dilbaz, N., Seber, G., Kaptanoğlu, C., & Tekin, D. (1990). Sexual attitudes of Turkish university students. *Journal of Sex Education & Therapy, 16*, 251–261.

Finer, L. B. (2007). Trends in premarital sex in the United States, 1954–2003. *Public Health Reports, 122*, 102–112.

Golombok, S., Rust, J., & Pickard, C. (1984, December). Sexual problems encountered in general practice. *British Journal of Sexual Medicine*, 210–212.

Hawton, K. (1985). *Sex therapy: A practical guide.* Oxford, England: Oxford University Press.

Hirst, J. F., Baggaley, M. R. & Watson, J. P. (1996). A four year survey of an inner-city psychosexual problems clinic. *Sexual and Marital Therapy, 11*, 19–36.

Incesu, C., & Yetkin, N. (1997). *Assessment of 200 subjects referred to a sexual dysfunction outpatient clinic in Turkey.* Proceedings of the 13th World Congress of Sexology, Valencia.

Kağıtçıbaşı, C. (1982). Introduction. In C. Kağıtçıbaşı & D. Sunar (Eds.), *Sex roles, family and community in Turkey* (pp. 1–32). Bloomington: Indiana University Press.

Kaplan, P. (2000). *Cinselliği Bilmiyorlar* [They do not know sexuality]. Retrieved from http://www.radikal.com.tr/2000/01/12/turkiye/cin.html.

Kayır, A., Geyran, P., & Tukel, R. M. (1990). Cinsel sorunlarda başvuru özellikleri ve tedavi seçimi [Enquiry characteristics and treatment choices in sexual problems]. *Abstract book of 26th National Congress of Psychiatry, 2*, 451–458.

Kirmayer, L. J. (2007). Cultural psychiatry in historical perspective. In D. Bhugra & K. Bhui (Eds.), *Textbook of cultural psychiatry* (pp. 3–19). Cambridge, England: Cambridge University Press.

Kuper, A. (1999). *Culture: The anthropologists' account.* Cambridge, MA: Harvard University Press.

Lee, L. K., Chen, P. C., Lee, K. K., & Kaur, J. (2006). Premarital sexual intercourse among adolescents in Malaysia: A cross-sectional Malaysian school survey. *Singapore Medical Journal, 47*, 476–481.

Nobre, P. J., Gouveia, J. P., & Gomes, F. A. (2006). Prevalence and comorbidity of sexual dysfunctions in a Portuguese clinical sample. *Journal of Sex & Marital Therapy, 32*, 173–182.

Öktem, F., Kadayıfçı, O., Beyazova, U., Sungur, M. Z., Çipa, I., Şatıroğlu, H., ... Yılmazer, T. (2000). *Ergenlik döneminde değişim: Öğrenci kitabı* [Changes in adolescence: Handbook for students]. Ankara, Turkey: Ministry of Education, Chamber of Health.

Özdemir, Y. D., Şimşek, F., Incesu, C., & Koç, K. (2006). Socio-demographic and clinical characteristics of subjects referred to a multidisciplinary sexual dysfunction outpatient clinic. *European Journal of Sexual Health, 15*, 14–25.

Petersen, J. L., & Hyde, J. S. (2010). A meta-analytic review of research on gender differences in sexuality, 1993–2007. *Psychological Bulletin, 136*, 21–38.

Segall, M. H., Dasen, P. R., Berry, J. W., & Poortinga, Y. H. (1990). *Human behavior in global perspective.* New York: Pergamon.
Simbar, M., Tehrani, F. R., & Hashemi, Z. (2005). Reproductive health knowledge, attitudes and practices of Iranian college students. *Eastern Mediterranean Health Journal, 11,* 888–897.
Spector, I. P., & Carey, M. P. (1990). Incidence and prevalence of the sexual dysfunctions: A critical review of the empirical literature. *Archives of Sexual Behavior, 19,* 389–408.
State Institute of Statistics. (1995). Prime Ministry, Republic of Turkey, Divorce Statistics, Ankara.
Sungur, M. Z. (1994). Evaluation of couples referred to a sexual dysfunction unit and prognostic factors in sexual and marital therapy. *Sexual and Marital Therapy, 9,* 251–265.
Sungur, M. Z. (1996). *Hekimlik mesleği yönünden cinsel eğitim ve işbirliğinin önemi* [Significance of sexual education and interdisciplinary collaboration in medical profession]. *Psikiyatri Dünyası* [Psychiatry World], *2,* 37–38.
Sungur, M. Z. (1997). Sexual dysfunction and infertility. *Sexual and Marital Therapy, 12,* 181–182.
Sungur, M. Z. (1998). Difficulties encountered during the assessment and treatment of sexual dysfunction—A Turkish perspective. *Sexual and Marital Therapy, 13,* 71–81.
Sungur, M. Z. (1999). Cultural factors in sex therapy: The Turkish experience. *Sexual and Marital Therapy, 14,* 165–171.
Talakaub, L., Munarriz, R., Haag, L., Gioia, M., Flaherty, E., & Goldstein, I. (2002). Epidemiological characteristics of 250 women with sexual dysfunction who presented for initial evaluation. *Journal of Sex & Marital Therapy, 28,* 217–224.
Tuğrul, C. & Kabakçı, E. (1997). Vaginismus and its correlates. *Journal of Sex & Marital Therapy, 12,* 23–34.
Ward, E., & Ogden, J. (1994). Experiencing vaginismus: Sufferers' belief about causes and effects. *Sexual and Marital Therapy, 9,* 33–45.
Warner, P., & Bancroft, J. (1987). A regional clinical service for psychosexual problems: A three year study. *Sexual and Marital Therapy, 2,* 115–126.
World Health Organization. (1992). *The ICD-10 classification of mental and behavioral disorders: Diagnostic criteria for research.* Geneva, Switzerland: Author.
Yasan, A., & Akdeniz, N. (2009). Treatment of lifelong vaginismus in traditional Islamic couples: A prospective study. *Journal of Sexual Medicine, 6,* 1054–1061.
Yasan, A., Eşsizoğlu, A., & Yıldırım, E. A. (2009). Predictor factors associated with premarital sexual behaviors among university students in an Islamic culture. *International Journal of Sexual Health, 21,* 145–152.
Yasan, A., & Gürgen, F. (2009). Marital satisfaction, sexual problems and possible difficulties in sex therapy in traditional Islamic culture. *Journal of Sex & Marital Therapy, 35,* 68–75.
Yılmaz, F. (2007). *Cinsel Sorunlar ve Tutumlar üzerine bir epidemiyolojik araştırma* [An epidemiological study and sexual attitudes and problems]. Istanbul: First National Congress of Behavior Therapy Abstract Book.

Editors Introduction to Chapter 14
Israel

The family stands at the center of Israeli society so it follows that marriage and children are expected of most young people. However, many Israelis come of age during their mandatory military service, which shapes and defines their young adulthood in various ways. This chapter uses the case of a wounded Israeli soldier involved in sexual rehabilitation to illustrate the ways in which relational sexuality is integral to the Israeli experience. Because of the relational emphasis, sexual surrogates are used in Israel more often and more openly than elsewhere in the world. The fact that this chapter also highlights the treatment of someone with a disability makes this a chapter that in many ways deals with two cultures, that of Israel and that of the disabled.

14

ISRAELI SEXUALITY AT THE INTERSECTION OF TRADITION AND MODERNISM

R. Aloni, E. De Paauw, and R. Heruti

Introduction

Israel is a country of immigrants. Indeed only recently has Israel become the major country of origin for Israelis, with the Soviet Union in second place, and Morocco in third place (Israel Central Bureau of Statistics, 2009). Israel is also a country of minorities; although Jews make up the majority, it is a majority of people of different origins, traditions, and religious status. Likewise, the Arab population of Israel is also composed of small and distinct groups. Israelis view these differences as contributing to, rather than fragmenting society. As a result it is almost impossible to define "Israeli sexuality," as both Eastern and Western traditions, the past, modernism, and postmodernism all contribute to an understanding of Israeli people's sexuality.

Religion is a central feature of the country and plays a major role in shaping Israeli culture and lifestyle. Israel is the only country in the world in which the majority of its 7.7 million citizens are Jewish. According to the Israel Central Bureau of Statistics (2008), in 2008 the population of Israel was 75.4% Jewish, 20.6% Arab, and 4% other. Israel's Arab population of 1.3 million is made up of 82.7% Muslim, 8.4% Druze, and 8.3% Christian, Bedouin, and others such as the Adyghe. In Israel religious law and rituals (Judaic, Christian, Muslim) applies in all cases concerning marriage, divorce, inheritance, and other family matters.

Israel is a small and intimate society in which people often come into contact with each other. Many people have met each other at some point in their lives, and if they haven't met directly, then they most probably know a third person in common (Senor & Singer, 2009). As a result, men and women in Israel have strong, long lasting ties to their family and friends, so much so that they live and relate in an almost tribal fashion. These factors explain the strong social influences which affect the sexual attitudes, behavior, and lifestyles of Israelis, be they Jews, Muslims, or Druze.

In Israel the family stands at the center of society (Ekert-Jaffe & Stier, 2009); the family reflects the values of the long history of Judaism, provides security, and is the habitat that nurtures the country's most powerful resource: children (Shemer, 1992). The birth rate in Israel is 21.6 per 1,000 women and the average of three children per woman is the highest among the Organization for Economic Co-operation and Development (OECD) countries,[1] where the average is 1.7 children (Israel Central Bureau of Statistics, 2009). Israel has the highest ratio of in vitro fertilization (IVF) clinics in the world (1:230,000; Birenbaum-Carmeli, 2004). It is safe to say that Israel is a society that supports and encourages high fertility; indeed, the gay and lesbian community in Israel is now having a baby boom (New Family, n.d.; Creative Family Connections, n.d.). Israeli women, however, are employed in numbers similar to those of women in most European and North American countries (Ekert-Jaffe & Stier, 2009). Shemer, in a landmark study (1992), noted the various and overlapping roles that Israeli women identify with: 92% defined themselves as mothers, 84% as "women of valor" (an idiom taken from the Bible's book of Proverbs and meaning a powerful woman with practical sense, logic, and the capability to survive). Seventy-nine percent defined themselves as "Madonna" (meaning a peaceful woman, reasonable, reserved, a good listener for her partner, talks with a gentle voice and never teases her partner). Sixty percent defined themselves as a wife, and 52% as a lover. Seventy-five percent of Israeli women said they felt happiest when integrating these different roles. This image of an ideal woman, with her ability to multitask and synthesize opposing qualities at the same time, is a creation and reflection of societal norms and expectations and is the origin of frustration for women who cannot help but fail to meet them. The Israeli masculine model, at the onset of Jewish immigration to Israel, was the military macho figure (Almog, 2004). He was always part of a band that cherished, above all, friendship, loyalty, and heroic altruism (Talmon, 2001, pp. 3–6). The Hebrew language referred to his sex organs in a double meaning as "ammunition" with which he was expected to "tear, knock, conquer, and humiliate" (Nardi, 1992; Nardi & Nardi, 2011) and sensitivity was perceived as a threat to masculinity (Orian, 2008). Only in the last decades has the military man been held accountable in the "theater court" and is being blamed for arrogance and irresponsibility. Until the 90s men were the active characters in Israeli theater, but now they are often presented as annoying and stupid warmongers (Orian, 2008).

Marriage is idealized in Israel. Ynet (one of the most popular Internet sites in Israel) surveyed Israeli attitudes to marriage in 2004 and found that 69% of Israeli men and women who visited their site believed marriage to be the best and most acceptable way to live a happy life (Rudin, Almog, & Paz, 2009). In Shemer's study (1992), 85% of female respondents said that a long lasting relationship was the most important thing in their life, while 75% said they couldn't imagine their life without a partner. Sixty-five percent of single women reported being uncomfortable with their single status, with 56% planning to raise children alone if they did not marry by the age of 35 and 58% feeling social pressure to get married and have children.

Most Israelis leave their families and homes for the first time at the age of 18 to join the Israeli army, an experience that molds young Israelis in a unique way. Men and women in Israel are molded in such a way that their romantic associations, attitudes, vocabulary, and sometimes even their behavior are militarized. In Hebrew the same words are used to refer to both conquest of territory and romantic conquest. The words *love* and *devotion* also have a double meaning in Hebrew, referring to both a lover and to the country. The word *purity* can also be applied to both purity of sexual behavior and to the use of live ammunition in battle (Almog, 2004; Shtarkshall & Zemach, 1993).

Sexuality and Judaism: Sex According to *Halacha*

Judaism is not just a religion, but also a philosophy and way of life. It is therefore important to understand Judaism and its relation to sex and sexuality. Most Jewish Israelis feel that being Israeli (living among Jews, speaking Hebrew, and living in the Land of Israel) is in itself a sufficient expression of Judaism, without requiring any religious observance. An Israeli Central Bureau of Statistics (2010) report showed that in terms of religiosity, 8% of Israel's Jewish population defined itself as extremely observant, 12% as religious, 13% as traditional-religious, 25% as traditional, and 42% as secular. Most Israelis define themselves as nonobservant (Birenbaum-Carmeli, 2004).

In the last 20 years more than 100,000 Ethiopian Jews have immigrated to Israel, bringing with them traditional rural and religious attitudes regarding sexual behavior. For example, traditional Ethiopian Jews value premarital virginity, especially in women, and arrange marriages for their children (Nudelman, 2008). The effect of immigration to Israel and the influence of other Jewish denominations on their culture have led many Ethiopian Jews to adopt more liberal Israeli practices. The younger generation and those who enlist in the army tend to break from tradition, cohabitating before marriage, while parents turn a blind eye as long as their children intend to marry (Paz & Almog, 2009).

On the other hand, Jews who have emigrated from the former Soviet Union were almost completely disconnected from Jewish tradition and arrived with virtually no knowledge or observance of basic Jewish customs or practices. In their case, immigration has led them to adopt more traditional Jewish practices and customs. For example, when 1 million Soviet Jews immigrated to Israel during the 1980s and 1990s, circumcision was performed on adult males, at their own request, as part of their absorption into Israeli society.

There are many religious laws that directly or indirectly concern and affect sexuality. Marriages in Israel are only recognized if they occur between a man and a woman of the same religion and if the ceremony is performed by religious authority (whether it is Jewish Orthodox, Christian, Muslim, or Druze). Civil marriages are only officially sanctioned if performed abroad. As a result some Israelis choose to travel overseas in order to marry and many young couples cohabit so as to bypass the religious form of marriage (Israel Central Bureau of Statistics, 1990, 2009, 2010; Shtarkshall & Zemach, 1993).

Among Orthodox Jews sexual experimentation of any kind before marriage is unacceptable. During the wedding the husband signs a marriage contract (*ktuba*) which states that he will take care of his wife's economic needs, will make sure she will not suffer from hunger, and also that he will "provide her with cohabitation," meaning to please and satisfy her sexually. While menstruating and for the 7 days after menses, a married woman must abstain from sexual intercourse (*niddah*); in addition the husband is forbidden to touch his wife or share a bed with her. Repurification occurs through immersion in a ritual bath (*mikveh*) after 7 "clean days." The commandment (*mitzvah*) to be fruitful and multiply (*Pru u`rvu*) is one of the most important in Judaism.

One of the more difficult laws in Judaism to adhere to is the prohibition against "spilling seed in vain," which is in essence a complete prohibition on male masturbation and ejaculation outside of the vagina. According to this law, sperm should not be "wasted" and should be solely for fertility (Petok, 2001).

Sexual Issues in the Orthodox Community

In the ultra-Orthodox community children from a young age onwards grow up separated from the opposite sex. Any familiarity with the opposite sex occurs only within the family and not in the community at large. Even within the home modesty is strictly observed so that no body parts are revealed and no clear picture of the anatomy of the opposite sex develops. The first relationship a person has with his or her body is the need to conceal it with clothing, a fact that makes true mutual familiarity with a partner even more difficult.

It is not unusual for Orthodox men and women to use the services of a matchmaker. Until marriage physical contact and even eye contact with the opposite sex is forbidden. Individuals from the ultra-Orthodox community see the genitals of the opposite sex for the first time on their wedding night. For the most part there has been no sexual experimentation on either side. Browsing the Internet is considered immodest and is therefore prohibited. Because of this most couples' sexual knowledge is either limited or nonexistent and the first encounter is likely to be exceptionally frightening and threatening. After the wedding all these forbidden sexual behaviors become allowed and even obligatory. Not only is the husband required to make sexual contact with his wife but also to pleasure her. The "duty of intercourse" falls immediately upon young couples who marry under Jewish law. It is expected that they will have regular sexual relations beginning immediately after the wedding. This sharp shift from prohibition to obligation is neither easy nor simple and can cause considerable anxiety.

In order to cope with this difficult situation, prospective brides and grooms attend lessons with a same-sex marriage counselor (called the "bride/groom's counselor") in order to prepare themselves for married life. The training of these counselors is not uniform and is often quite limited. The role of the instructors is to help the bride and groom learn the different religious laws which deal with marital relations as well as the practical stages in having sexual intercourse. Judaism has clear rules regarding the conduct of "marital relations" (as it is called by the community). Straightforward words such as *sex* or *sexuality* are avoided, as are other words deemed unacceptable. For example, orgasm is referred to as *female pleasure*, and erection as *hardening*. In many cases the young couple has no understanding of what is expected from them during the first sexual encounter. Many couples who have not received sufficient or correct instruction come to a clinic for treatment simply because they don't know what to do during a sexual encounter. Nowadays there are more "certified" counselors who have learned how best to explain to young men and women what marital life is, practically speaking and in terms of Jewish law. Until recently, however, women's right to find pleasure through marital relations was rarely discussed, although the Talmud states that it is the husband's role to satisfy his wife. On the night of a woman's ritual bath (*mikveh*) the obligation is on her husband to "provide her with cohabitation," even if on that night he has no desire. This requirement can cause pressure and anxiety and can even lead to performance anxiety among men who must perform according to the exact timing of the menstrual cycle.

It is important for a therapist working with Orthodox clients to emphasize that it is difficult to improve intimacy and sexual functioning without being aware of one's body and its sensations. For the most part, after breaking the ice and the embarrassment, there is a willingness to hear, to know, and to continue therapy. We advocate a separation of the educational component of sex therapy from the psychotherapy component (in which the emotional difficulties which accompany the couple's relationship are discussed).

During the initial sessions it is often necessary to give the couple an overview of the physical aspects of sexuality; for example, to explain the anatomy and physiology of the sexual organs, the differences between men and women, and how sexual intercourse takes place. A basic explanation of the mechanisms of sexual arousal in men and women is also both important and helpful. For the therapist, provision of knowledge is often an essential first step in therapy with an Orthodox couple. It is also useful as a tool to build a connection and trust. Knowledge reduces anxiety, which in turn leads to better sex. A point of caution: the therapist should first ask the couple if they are interested in seeing a picture of the genitals (initially as a general diagram rather than a detailed picture) before presenting them with one. Not all clients are prepared for such graphic information at the beginning of therapy. Sometimes a number of sessions are needed before a couple opens up to this possibility.

Another stage in therapy that is liable to create problems for an ultra-Orthodox couple is the introduction of the sensate focus (SF) technique (Masters & Johnson, 1970). Sometimes the first stages of SF are held in darkness or under a blanket with underclothes on. SF also places the couple in situations that may be sexually stimulating. While the instruction is to avoid touching the genitals and causing ejaculation this may nevertheless occur. Ejaculation outside of the vagina is prohibited according to Jewish law. Thus, SF can create stress and feelings of shame, which may even lead to the cessation of therapy. It is important to emphasize to the couple that the therapy is a time-bound program and is designed to help couples achieve healthy sexual relations by the completion of therapy. It is therefore recommended that couples consult their Rabbi regarding the program before they begin. Many Rabbis categorize such a therapy as a part of fulfilling the commandment of sound relations and continued fertility. One Rabbi who was consulted on a sex therapy case ruled that if ejaculation did occur outside of the vagina, some of the fluid should be placed in the vagina with a finger, meaning that it would not be considered "wasted seed."

There needs to be considerable sensitivity and knowledge of the culture from which the couple comes and of the conditions for sexual activity that religion dictates. It is important that the therapist be attentive to cultural differences and has basic knowledge of the issues involved. For example, if therapists are using the SF program it is necessary for them to know that it can only be practiced on the days in which the couple is permitted physical contact.

Sexuality and Israeli Arabs

Amongst Israel's Arab population, the Arabic Forum for Sexuality of the Individual and the Family was established in 2007, having originally been part of the IPPF (International Planned Parenthood Foundation). The founders state that although today there is more tolerance of sex education, ignorance and prejudice still dominate in Muslim society (Almog, Awady, & Horenstein, 2010). Although Islam forbids sexual relationships before marriage for both men and women, in practice this law is only imposed on women.

Urban Arab society interacts with and is influenced by Jewish society to a greater degree than rural Arab society but even in the villages modernism prevails. In general, women are now better educated and the education of women is becoming more acceptable as their contribution to the economy is recognized. However, women are still expected to be devoted to their traditional roles. One of those roles is the upholding of family honor, meaning that the woman must be a virgin when she marries. This expectation holds true to a lesser degree for men. Young men and women in Arab society still consult with and are influenced by their parents so that a double standard between men and women may still be evident (Almog et al., 2010).

The Israeli Druze make up less than 100,000 people in Israel. They use the Arabic language and follow a social pattern very similar to the Arabs but are not Muslim and do not consider themselves to be Arabs. Israeli Druze do not allow intermarriage, although Druze men who serve in the army and Druze women who study at university are less inclined to accept interference from their families in their choice of a marriage partner; "blacklists" exist of those in the village who do not behave according to tradition (Almog & Horenstein, 2009).

Sexuality in the Israeli Population

In the last 20 years there has been increasing public discussion of sexual topics. Many newspapers and magazines include columns that provide professional answers to sexual questions and radio programs have been discussing intimate issues since the 1980s. Because of its visual element, television has struggled with the best way to address sexual matters. One source of public sexual knowledge unique to Israel is the Friday night talk shows which provide basic sexual information for couples in a humorous manner. The open discussion of sexual issues may well be a metaphor for a society that has lost its virginity. In such matters Israelis have gone from being naïve and traditional to the other side of the spectrum, where eroticism and pornography are publicly displayed (Almog, 2004).

The average age for onset of sexual relations is 16.74 years (Ben Natan, Danilov, & Evdokimovitz, 2010). However, the Internet site Ynet (2007) reported that boys become sexually active at age 14 and girls at 15. The commissioner of sex education at the Ministry of Education declared that only 30% of students are involved in sexual relationships; most of these are long term relationships, and the result of a thoughtful joint decision on the part of the two people (Almog, 2004).

Women born in Europe or America are considerably more likely than others to use modern contraceptives (e.g., the pill), whereas African and Asian-born women are more likely to use traditional contraceptive methods, especially withdrawal (Wilder, 2000). In a recent study, 71.7% of soldiers (women and men) used condoms the first time they had sexual relations (Ben Natan, 2010).

A special department in the Ministry of Education (n.d.) advises schools and teachers on sex education (educational psychology services), developing and updating programs for children from ages 4 to 18. Their aim is to inform and to normalize natural physical and emotional developmental processes, provide information, increase body awareness and responsibility, and discuss values, attitudes, and dilemmas that are raised within their peer groups. The sex education unit also publishes books such as *Intimacy without Violence*, *AIDS—A Question of Life*, *Children and Divorce*. They also publish books for target populations such as the vast immigrant population from the Soviet Union and for religious counselors.

Israel is an extremely modern society but one with strong links to tradition. This is true of both the Jewish majority and amongst the ethnic and religious minorities where these links are even stronger. As we will discuss in this chapter, modernism and tradition interact on numerous levels and predictably, also raise contradictions.

Sexual Dysfunction

In a sample of almost 6,000 men undergoing routine medical screening, 21.8% of men between the ages of 25 and 40 reported erectile dysfunction (ED; Heruti, Steinvil, & Shochat, 2008). This figure rises slightly (to 25%) when older men (25–55 years) are included in the sample (Heruti, Steinvil, & Shochat, 2008). In a similar study of men between the ages of 25 and 50 years, 26.9% reported ED on questionnaires but only 4.8% of these men sought help for their sexual problems (Heruti, Swartzon, & Shochat, 2007). Thirty-nine percent of men in this study were found to have premature ejaculation and 9.7% had other sexual dysfunctions or lack of sexual knowledge (Heruti, Ashkenazi, Shochat, Tekes-Manova, & Justo, 2005). There are as yet no epidemiological data regarding female sexual dysfunction in Israel.

Treatment of Sexual Problems

In Israel there are sex educators and sex therapists that are both professionally certified and organized. At the same time there are also traditional religious counselors who until recently were very poorly educated in matters of sexuality. Established in 1966, the IPPF's main focus is on educating the educators. It also provides information and counseling for teenagers through the Open Door project. The Open Door project is a network of centers providing information and advice on issues of sexual health, responsible behavior, love and relationships, dating, contraception, sexually transmitted diseases, AIDS, unwanted pregnancy, physical and sexual development, masturbation, sexual identity, sexual orientation, and sexual functioning. The target population is teenagers and young adults as well as parents and health professionals. According to their database, the Internet site registered over 1.2 million visits during 2009 alone. Teenagers can access information on the Internet site and apply for a free consultation by phone. One of these Open Door centers is the first in the world to be designed for youth with motor or sensual disabilities and is fully accessible. There are also a number of Open Door centers that serve Arab youth.

The Israeli Society of Sex Therapy (ISST) was established in 1983. It now has approximately 100 members and follows the code of ethics and membership procedures of the American Association of Sex Educators, Counselors and Therapists (AASECT). The ISST accepts for membership clinical social workers, clinical and rehabilitation psychologists, and medical doctors who have completed a program of sex therapy specialization.

Most sex therapy clinics in Israel are located in public hospitals or in specialist clinics under the auspices of the health care system. In public hospitals sex therapy is partially subsidized and available to all at a low cost. There are also specialized clinics for women and for people with disabilities. Private clinics are widespread throughout the country. The clients who are getting therapy at most of these clinics come from the modern Jewish population both secular and religiouse. Those who come from extremely religious communities, whether Jewish or Muslim, generally consult with their Rabbis or Kadis, who are often poorly educated in the modern field of sex therapy and who give advice according to the laws of the Bible or the Koran.

Amongst Israel's Arab population most people will turn to their parents for advice about sexual issues as opposed to consulting medical doctors. Only very few (the most educated) attend sex therapy clinics in public hospitals. Issues of privacy as well as difficulty in finding the right terminology to express their problems often interfere with Arab clients' ability to go for treatment.

To summarize, Israel offers sex education and therapy to the entire population at a low cost. All citizens have compulsory medical coverage that allows them to apply for help to government subsidized sex clinics. There are, however, traditional, religious, and cultural barriers amongst some sectors of the population that prevent individuals from taking advantage of these services.

As we stressed at the beginning of the chapter, Israel is a family oriented society (Birenbaum-Carmeli, 2004; Ekert-Jaffe & Stier, 2009) and sexuality is perceived as obligatory, necessary, and the glue that keeps the family together. Israeli society perceives the loss of one's ability to form a family and to procreate as one of the most significant and unfortunate losses. As a result, full sexual rehabilitation has become a recognized and accepted part of the rehabilitation process for injured soldiers and civilians in Israel. Because many disabled veterans are youth, significant numbers of them have not had the opportunity to develop committed relationships. This has led to the use of surrogates and the involvement of a surrogate partner has become almost mainstream in the field of sexual rehabilitation (Aloni, Keren, & Katz, 2007; Aloni & Heruti, 2009). Israel is a leader in sex therapy programs involving surrogates and sexual rehabilitation.

The following case study, involving a disabled veteran, demonstrates the value placed on partnered sexuality in Israel. Whereas treatment focused on self-stimulation and pleasuring may be considered acceptable in other societies, the use of a surrogate places sexuality in the context of a relationship. This is the form of sexuality which is valued in Israeli society.

Case Study

Rachel, a single, 36-year-old woman with a bachelor's degree in social science was born in Israel and had three older siblings, two brothers and a sister. An exceptionally intelligent woman, Rachel described herself as a sad, insecure girl who had never felt attractive and had shied away from looking at her body. During high school and during her army service she had few friends. However, one army friendship developed into a more intimate relationship and became her first sexual experience involving partial penetration. This relationship began 6 months before she had a serious car accident while In the army service, and continued until 6 months after the accident.

The accident occurred 17 years prior to beginning sex therapy, when Rachel was 19 years old and still a soldier. She sustained very serious injuries, dislocation of C4–5 and incomplete Tetraplegia below C–6, which left her wheelchair bound. Rachel had also developed osteoporosis, neurogenic bladder dysfunction, and neuropathic pains and thus also took a number of medications.

Rachel was very sensitive to any touch and experienced pain upon physical contact. Since her injury she had been in long-term psychotherapy. Her goals in therapy were to search for meaning in her life and recover her self-esteem. At the time of referral, she was still undergoing physiotherapy and hydrotherapy. She reported that while in water she could walk and perform other activities that she could not do elsewhere; in fact when in water she felt much less paralyzed.

Over the last few years Rachel had been extremely active in pursuing her studies and her career, which she combined with feminist activities. For example, she had been active in promoting accessibility to gynecological clinics for women who are wheelchair bound. All of these activities had contributed to her developing a better self-image as a woman and as a feminist.

Since the accident Rachel had avoided her sexuality and declared that she was not interested in having a relationship. Her disinterest seemed to be a reaction to her conviction that "no one will ever have any interest in me." However, shortly before she contacted rehabilitation services, Rachel experienced an intense sexual attraction to a male acquaintance, although no relationship developed. Since this experience she had been very aware of her natural sexual needs which she perceived as unfulfilled. She applied for sexual rehabilitation in order to fill this void in her life but also as a means of maintaining a connection with her body.

When I first met Rachel she was very fragile and cried a lot, especially when explaining the process of applying for sexual rehabilitation and her great need to actually experience her body rather than talk about it endlessly. Rachel applied for sexual rehabilitation combined with surrogate therapy. This is a level of therapy available only for severely injured soldiers and is paid for by the Ministry of Defense. Rachel seemed ambivalent about her decision to seek surrogate therapy in that she was both anxious and very excited at the same time. Her fears centered on concerns that her partner would be repulsed by her body, that she would be overwhelmed by her surrogate partner, that she would not have the energy to maintain another human relationship, that she would be abandoned, and that because she suffered pain when touched, she would not be able to enjoy any intimate contact.

The theme of disability was present in Rachel's sexual fantasies. In one scenario she met someone at work with whom a relationship gradually developed, becoming increasingly sexual. In this fantasy, Rachel was no longer confined to her wheelchair, her belly was not swollen, and her bones did not stick out. In another fantasy she was disabled but the man involved was one of her therapists. As a result he was familiar with her body and she was neither ashamed nor embarrassed in his presence.

In this fantasy her disability did not interfere with the relationship but rather became an advantage. In her fantasies Rachel felt wanted and admired and both she and the man involved were attractive. She was in a familiar place and could achieve what she desired in a spontaneous way, and felt confident, had privacy and control of the situation—the very three ingredients she lacked in her life. Bader (2002) suggested that people fantasize exactly about what they lack in their daily life.

Preparation for Surrogate Therapy

The initial stages of preparation for surrogate therapy include organizing the administrative aspects, such as financial coverage for the therapy from the Ministry of Defense and setting up sessions consistent with the three points of the therapy triangle: Therapist-Rachel, Therapist-Surrogate, and Rachel-Surrogate.

Like all other patients involved in surrogate therapy, Rachel had to sign a contract that outlined the relationship between herself and the surrogate. This contract stated that the relationship would be a temporary one, lasting only for the duration of therapy, and that she could only meet or have contact with the surrogate at the times and places specified by the clinic. Additionally, every session would have a predefined goal and this goal included the maximum limit of activity for that session. The contract also confirmed that the therapist received full details of what transpired during the sessions with the surrogate and that these would be discussed during the therapy sessions. The surrogates also signed a contract with the clinic that included similar terms. The clinic doctor monitored both the surrogate and Rachel and safe sex was always practiced during the sessions. Rachel understood that these boundaries were for her own benefit and was excited about starting therapy. In discussions leading up to her first meeting with the surrogate, she had difficulty defining the type of person she preferred. When a surrogate was selected she was excited to learn that he was the most experienced and gentle surrogate working at the clinic, that he was looking forward to the challenge of working with a woman with a disability, and that the process was transparent (meaning that she would be told about his experience with her and that everything that was expected would be clearly explained before a session commenced). Rachel also mentioned that the surrogate could look forward to a positive experience with her because of her good looks, because she put others at ease, and because she would care about him as well. She was very insistent on preventing her caregivers from meeting the surrogate, although she shared with them the fact that she was in therapy. As a result she had to function independently and receive help from the surrogate, directing him exactly how to help her.

Rachel's goals for the therapy were to get in touch with her body as a whole, experience her body to its fullest, and learn how to pleasure herself and her partner. She also wanted to learn how she could be sexually active in her wheelchair and other environments. Rachel wanted to learn to be helped by others rather than just by her caregivers so as to increase her levels of independence and trust. She wanted to experience how she felt next to a partner and learn about how he felt with her, to experience intimate touch and to learn how it affected her, as well as to improve her confidence, self-esteem and body image.

Sessions 1–3. During these meetings Yoav (the surrogate) and Rachel met in a café, at a park, and at the theater. They got to know each other and became more comfortable and confident with each other such that they were able to share their feelings. Rachel waited for his report of their meetings, at first with fear, and later curiosity to learn more about herself and Yoav. Up to this point only light body contact was allowed, but there was a growing feeling in her that she wanted much more.

Sessions 4–5. SF (Sensate Focus) in her wheelchair. These were the first meetings held at the clinic. Special rooms were used which were set up to resemble a standard room in a house. Since Rachel didn't want to stay in her wheelchair, she asked Yoav to transfer her to the sofa as she felt less disabled there. She was physically capable of helping with the transfer and could also achieve a standing position when aided, a position she very much wanted to be in with Yoav.

In these sessions Rachel started to experience pleasure and to identify specific areas and caresses that were pleasurable for her. She also practiced making her own touch gentler in order that it would be pleasurable for her partner. She was pleasantly surprised that she suffered no pain at all when Yoav touched her.

Sessions 6–9. These sessions took place in a sitting position on the sofa. When Yoav transferred her to the sofa, they both stood for a while hugging and kissing which allowed Rachel to feel able-bodied for a short time. She also felt connected to her femininity when in the presence of his masculinity. While they were practicing SF 2, which involves intimate touching with partial clothing (Masters & Johnson, 1970), Rachel discovered that watching Yoav's body excited her and that his arousal turned her on. Yoav also learned to position himself on her right side so that she could touch him more easily. Every time she exposed a new part of her body she felt reluctant and experienced feelings of disconnectedness. In fact during every "first time" she felt that "Rachel the disabled woman" was on trial. By the second time the exercises were performed she had progressed, becoming "Rachel the feminine woman." It was only during these second practice sessions that she felt comfortable with her body and was able to enjoy herself. Yoav also felt more and more at ease with her body and her touch. He reacted to and treated her body in a natural manner, which gave Rachel great comfort. He also challenged her, daring her to undress him, which she attempted after getting over her initial shock.

Rachel became more competent from week to week. Being active was of great importance to her and she considered solving "technical problems" such as positioning or undressing as a form of being active and taking responsibility for her life. Rachel had a hard time separating from Yoav at the end of each of their sessions and she was also projecting this difficulty onto the inevitable separation at the end of the therapy process. At this point she reframed the situation to allow herself to better deal with it. She achieved this by viewing her experiences with Yoav as analogous to "a property that belongs to her and which no one can take away."

Sessions 10–12. ("Getting friendly with the genitals"). Rachel was aware of the fact that there was a growing intimacy between her and Yoav. He taught her about his genitals in a humorous way which made her feel comfortable exploring him and learning new information. It was more difficult for her to expose her own genitals and reveal the fact that she didn't know what aroused her. When she followed his instructions on how to pleasure him, he told her that he had totally forgotten her disability. What struck her once again at this point was the fact that she only experienced pleasure at his touch and no pain at all.

Sessions 13–14. These sessions focused on getting to know the genitals in a more "sexy manner" so as to increase the levels of arousal and pleasure both partners experienced. Yoav reported to Rachel every movement he was performing when penetrating or exciting her with his finger. At the same time he was caressing and kissing her neck while she was trying to move her pelvis in response and using her upper body to pleasure him. Rachel wanted to increase her skills as a woman in order to pleasure men and felt that performing oral sex on Yoav was something she would now consider.

Rachel experienced deep intimacy with Yoav when they talked about daily events and the usual issues that couples share, such as repairing the car, etc. They also experienced their first misunderstanding that they had to overcome, improving their relationship and making it feel more natural in the process.

Sessions 15–16. These sessions focused on increasing Rachel's ability to become aroused as well as identifying a pain-free position for penetration.

Rachel suggested trying rear penetration during intercourse because in this position she felt less passive and because she found his touching her neck extremely arousing. As the end of therapy approached Rachel began to raise issues such as "Why did I ever try therapy? Now I have to deal with my yearnings and longings and what are my chances of finding a partner?" But she also voiced her belief that Yoav was attracted to her personality and "that had nothing to do with my body or my paralysis."

Sessions 17–19. Rachel experienced orgasm while she was guiding and directing Yoav how to pleasure her. She chose a very slow pace so that she could pay attention to each nuance and learn to be aroused by it. The fact that Rachel was in control allowed her to plan the session so that she could enjoy and make the most of the moments that were important for her. She could also prepare herself for the end of the meeting, arriving at it feeling fulfilled as opposed to feeling sexually frustrated. Although she was extremely satisfied by being in control she noticed that she missed being aware of Yoav's pleasure which led to her being worried about whether he had enjoyed himself with her.

Session 20. Farewell session. Rachel and Yoav decided that staying in the private room would be more intimate and suitable for them. They thanked each other, expressed their feelings for each other, and talked about the process they went through together. They wrote farewell letters for each other, and felt both sad and content at the same time. Following this last session with Yoav, therapy continued with the sex therapist focusing on translating and applying what Rachel learned with Yoav to her real life.

1-Year Follow-Up. It took Rachel a few months to overcome her anger and sorrow after the therapy with Yoav ended. Slowly she began to pay much more attention to her appearance and attracted compliments. She felt like an attractive woman and presented herself accordingly. Rachel no longer defined herself as a sad woman and initiated contact with men and reacted positively when men approached her, be it in rehabilitation clinics, conferences, and workshops she attended, or on Internet sites. Recently she was offered a paid job for the first time in her life. Rachel was always a woman with many positive qualities; however, she now valued them. Rachel was also much more positive about men in general and relationships in particular.

Discussion of the Case

When Rachel reached the age of 35 she, like many women in Israel, felt her biological clock ticking. Her younger sister had just given birth and this served to underscore her situation as an "older single woman." Although she advocated for her single status and said that she had no interest in a relationship or in being a mother, she could not totally resist cultural norms. As her therapy progressed Rachel explored her potential for having a relationship and for having children.

Rachel brought to therapy a poor body image and low self-esteem as a woman. Nonetheless, she was very open and willing to hear frank feedback from Yoav. Through surrogate therapy Rachel learned to modify her touch to become gentler, she was able to try different positions in order to better pleasure her partner, and she learned to compromise her urgent wish to kiss Yoav intensely with his desire to take things more slowly. Rachel was also extremely surprised to find out that even though she knew how she felt touching her body, Yoav's touch still felt so different. Having a severe disability, Rachel was used to having her body, including her genital area, touched by strangers (caregivers). In these intrusive situations Rachel disconnected from her body and described these experiences as physically painful for her. Yoav, however, touched her not because he was doing something for her as her caregiver but because he enjoyed touching her. This touch was a healing touch for Rachel.

Because people with a severe disability which keeps them wheelchair bound need round-the-clock support from a caregiver they feel a tremendous need for privacy and independence—a need that is incredibly important to their self-esteem as men or women. Accordingly, we try to work with them on achieving maximum independence and freedom from caregivers in order to enable them to enter into intimate relationships and activities. Rachel learned how to have intimate and sexual relations without penetration when in her wheelchair, something that is possible for many disabled individuals. This serves to free the disabled person from her or his caregivers and allows the privacy needed to create relationships. For Rachel, being able to meet Yoav without her caregivers being involved in any way (even without them having any knowledge of the fact that she was having surrogate therapy), was extremely important. It enabled her to feel that control over her privacy was an attainable goal. Even so, Rachel was reluctant to be passively treated. For her it was much more important to stand up next to Yoav, to hug him, and to be mobile rather than to sit on the sofa. Doing so meant that she felt her disability to a lesser degree. The combination that was applied of traditional sex therapy and a rehabilitation approach, emphasized Rachel's independence, and her ability to be active and take initiative and responsibility for her life, while receiving as little help as possible.

Many people with disabilities are shy about their disability and in their desire to hold on to their partners, are reluctant to discuss their limitations. Others start discussing medical issues early on as a means of being frank and sincere with their partners. In sexual rehabilitation, the disabled person has to address and rehearse how, when, and to what extent medical information should be shared with partners so that their role doesn't become one of a caregiver. Though Yoav indicated this to Rachel when she was flooding him with information he didn't need, Rachel sometimes mistakenly interpreted this reaction as rejection.

Intimacy, closeness, and falling in love with the surrogate all raise anxiety. In the past this anxiety caused Rachel to withdraw and abstain from developing intimate relationships, as well as serving to rationalize her choice of a single lifestyle. Whenever the degree of intimacy between her and Yoav increased, Rachel's anxiety increased and she would distance herself. This process repeated itself a number of times during the therapy process and became more frequent as the end of therapy drew nearer. At one point Rachel expressed her anxiety as anger toward the sexual rehabilitation therapist and the surrogate. For example, during sessions 17 and 18, Rachel's anger, frustration, complaints, and accusations had to be worked through. After two sessions she understood that such feelings might have arisen because she knew that therapy with Yoav was about to end. This raised feelings of anxiety about facing reality and about dating. Rachel still saw herself as having very little chance of finding a partner and her anticipation was that she would remain frustrated and emotionally unfulfilled. However, after working through this crisis and identifying her fear of abandonment it only took one more session for her to proudly state, "I can't wait to start dating."

From session 12, Rachel began sending the diary that she had been writing throughout the therapeutic process to her sex therapist. Keeping a diary had been introduced because Rachel felt uncomfortable talking about her sexual experiences. She had a much easier time acting on her immediate sexual needs with Yoav than talking about them. Rachel concluded that she couldn't have discovered and experienced her body without Yoav's support and confidence.

The one-year follow-up demonstrated that sex therapy with the use of a surrogate had changed Rachel life a great deal; it had influenced her work and social life, the way she perceived and presented herself, and had given her the tools to fulfill her wish to be in a relationship.

Sex therapy and rehabilitation with the help of surrogate partners was first introduced into Israel in 1989. At first it was solely available for people with disabilities but it has gradually become available for all. Initially it was part of the Rehabilitation Center of the Kibbutz Movement and obtained the approval of the Rabbinate representatives of the Kibbutz with the condition that the surrogates could not be married women (it was decided to make this ruling consistent for men as well). In 1992 the therapy program was presented at the World Association for Sexual Health conference in Amsterdam. The first group of surrogates included 12 candidates, of whom 33% had an academic degree, 25% had medical training (nurses), 25% were high school graduates, and 15% had other professional training. Most of the surrogates were employed in the helping services, and were either divorced or widowed (only two were single). Since the beginning of the program only surrogates who held a steady job were employed. Being a surrogate was an extra job for them, a measure taken to ensure that they did not take on the surrogate role solely in order to earn money. Surrogate training involves two weekends of intensive workshops, run according to the guidelines and the code of ethics of the International Professional Surrogate Association (IPSA). Participants pay for the training course themselves and there is no obligation to work as a surrogate at the end of the training. Most courses include surrogates for gay and lesbian clients, although there are very few referrals for them.

In 1996 the surrogate program was approved by the Ministry of Defense for individuals with severe spinal cord injuries and severe traumatic brain injuries. A few years later a young person with a severe injury as a result of a traffic accident demanded surrogate therapy as compensation and won, creating a legal precedent for surrogate therapy. These two steps positioned surrogate rehabilitation therapy almost in the mainstream of therapy in Israel.

Summary

Israeli society is, on the one hand, exceptionally traditional, and on the other hand, modern and open-minded to new and controversial ideas. It is also very sensitive to the human rights of those who are perceived as extremely unlucky (e.g., young wounded soldiers). The fact that surrogate therapy was initially introduced into Israeli society as part of sexual rehabilitation for wounded soldiers, gained it legitimacy and acceptance, which later expanded to apply to able-bodied applicants as well.

The Israeli administration approved and subsidized sexual rehabilitation with surrogates, which reflects the attitudes Israelis hold toward coupling and parenting. Israeli society understands the importance of family and children and strives to provide the means to fulfill these basic human rights, which are deeply rooted in able-bodied people, people with disabilities and within the gay and lesbian community, which, as noted above, is currently experiencing a baby boom. In Israel sex therapy combined with surrogate therapy focuses mainly on relationship skills and intimate skills rather than simply on overcoming sexual dysfunction. Because of this it is more easily accepted and embraced by all public domains, even the most traditional ones.

In this chapter we paid special attention to the unique community of ultra-Orthodox Jews and their corresponding needs; individuals from this culture can be found in communities all over the world and they may seek help for sexual problems. The importance of marriage and child bearing is not unique to ultra-Orthodox communities and is a traditional and religious norm that is fully embraced by mainstream secular society, including Israelis with disabilities.

Notes

1. The OECD countries are Italy, the United States, the United Kingdom, France, Finland, Sweden, Spain, and Canada as well as Israel.

References

Almog, O. (2004). *Preda mesrulik change values in the Israeli elite, From Puritanism to sexuality*. Israel: Zmora Beitan.

Almog, O., Awawdy, A., & Horenstein, S. (2010). Partnering in Muslim society in Israel— Features and trends. Retrieved from http://www.peopleil.org/details.aspx?itemID=7698&searchMode=0&index=1

Almog, O., & Hornstein, S. (2009, September). Dimensions of the Arab sector from a historical perspective. Retrieved from http://www.peopleil.org/details.aspx?itemID=7448&searchMode=0&index=45

Almog, O. Hornstein, S., Bisan, I., & Zeidan, A. (2009). Dating, engagement, marriage and divorce in the Druze community—Tradition and change. Retrieved from, http://www.peopleil.org/details.aspx?itemID=7740&searchMode=0&index=7

Aloni, R., & Heruti, R. (2009). Ethical issues in sex therapy with the help of a surrogate partner. *Harefua, 148,* 615–619.

Aloni, R. lKeren, O/ & Katz, S. (2007). Sex therapy surrogate partners for individuals with very limited functional ability following traumatic brain injury. *Sexuality and Disability, 25,* 153–190.

Bader, M. (2002). *Arousal, the secret logic of sexual fantasies*. New York: Thomas Dunne.

Ben Natan, M., Danilov, S., & Evdokimovitz, Y. (2010). Predictors of condom use among Israeli soldiers. *American Journal of Men's Health, 4,* 250–257.

Birenbaum-Carmeli, D. (2004). Cheaper than a newcomer: On the social production of IVF policy in Israel. *Sociology of Health & Illness, 26,* 897–924.

Creative Family Connections. (n.d.). https://www.creativefamilyconnections.com/articles/israel proud_parents.pdf

Ekert-Jaffe, O., & Stier, H. (2009). Normative or economic behavior: Fertility and women's employment in Israel. *Social Science Research, 38,* 644–655.

Guterman, M. A. (2008). Observance of the laws of family purity in modern-Orthodox Judaism. *Archives of Sexual Behavior, 37,* 340–345.

Haavio-Mannila, E., Laanpere, M., & Regushevskaya, E. (2007, October). *Two types of abortionists*. Paper presented at the 15th EUPHA (European Public Health Association) Conference, Helsinki.

Heruti, R., Ashkenazi, I., Shochat, T., Tekes-Manova, D., & Justo, D. (2005). Low scores in the Sexual Health Inventory for Men Questionnaire may indicate sexual disorders other than erectile dysfunction. *Journal of Sexual Medicine, 2,* 181–186.

Heruti, R., Steinvil, A., & Shochat, T. (2008). Screening for erectile dysfunction and associated cardiovascular risk factors in Israeli men. *Israeli Medical Association Journal (IMAJ), 10,* 686–690.

Heruti, R., Swartzon, M., & Shochat, T. (2007). The minority of young adult men with sexual disorders seek medical treatment, *Journal of Sexual Medicine, 4,* 1163–1166.

Heruti, R., Yossef, M., & Shochat, T. (2004). Screening for erectile dysfunction as part of periodic examination programs—Concept and implementation. *International Journal of Impotence Research, 16,* 341–345.

International Professional Surrogate Association (IPSA). http://www.surrogatetherapy.org/

Israel Central Bureau of Statistics. (2009). http://www.cbs.gov.il/reader

Israel Central Bureau of Statistics. (2010). http://www.cbs.gov.il/energy/shnatonhnew site.htm

Laumann, E. O., Paik, A., Glasser, D. B., & Kang, J. H. (2006). A cross-national study of subjective sexual well-being among older women and men: Findings from the Global Study of Sexual Attitudes and Behaviors. *Archives of Sexual Behavior, 35,* 145–161.

Masters, W. H., & Johnson, V. E. (1970). *Human sexual inadequacy.* New York: Bantam Books.

Ministry of Education. (n.d.). Educational psychology services. http://cms.education.gov.il/EducationCMS/Units/Shefi/pirusmim/catalog/Perek5.htmNET

Nardi, C. (1992). *Men in change.* Tel Aviv, Israel: Modan.

Nardi, R., & Nardi, C., (2011) *Couple discussion.* Tel Aviv, Israel: Hedim.

New Family. (n.d.). http://www.newfamily.org.il/en/1906/israel-a-paradise-for-gay-families-by-nathalie-hamou-in-israel/

Nudelman A. (2008). Adolescent sexuality among Ethiopian immigrants in Israel. Dissertation submitted to Eotvos Lorand University, Budapest, Hungary.

Open Door Program (IPPF). http://www.opendoor.org.il/aravit/About.aspx?did=277

Open Door Program (IPPF). http://www.opendoor.org.il/About.aspx?did=275. http://www.opendoor.org.il/SignIn.aspx?did=628).

Orian, D. (2008.) *Theatre in society.* Raanana, Israel: Open University.

Paz, D., & Almog, O. (2009). People, Israel; Director to the Israel society; traditional patterns of introduction and marriage among Ethiopian immigrants. Retrieved from http://www.peopleil.org/details.aspx?itemID=7680&index=30&searchMode=1

Petok, W. D. (2001). Religious observance and sex therapy with an orthodox Jewish couple. *Journal of Sex Education and Therapy, 26,* 22–27.

Rudin, S., Almog, O., & Paz, D. (2009). People, Israel; Director to the Israel society; Single parent family in Israel. Retrieved from http://www.peopleil.org/details.aspx?itemID=7544&index=25&searchMode=1

Senor, D., & Singer, S. (2009). *Start-up nation.* New York: Hachette Book Group.

Shemer, S. (1992). *An intimate report about women in Israel.* Ma'ariv Book Guild. Tel Aviv, Israel.

Shtarkshal, R., & Zemach, M. (1993). Israel. In *The international encyclopedia of sexuality.* retrieved from http://www2.hu-berlin.de/sexology/IES/israel.html

Talmon, M. (2001). *Bluz to the lost: Bands and nostalgia in the Israeli movie.* Raanana,Israel: Open University & Haifa University.

Wilder, E. (2000) .Contraceptive use at first intercourse among Jewish women ידרו (yvardi@rambam.health.gov.il in Israel, 1962–1988. *Population Research and Policy Review, 19,* 113–141.

Ynet. (2007). http://www.ynet.co.il/articles/0,7340,L-3355444,00.html

Websites

Israel annual statistics. (2007–2009). http://www.cbs.gov.il/reader/shnaton/shnatonh_new.htm?CYear=2009&Vol=60&CSubject=12

Editors Introduction to Chapter 15
Northern Europe

Northern Europe, as the title of this chapter suggests, is noted for its liberalism, including and perhaps most especially, the value placed on gender equality. While sexual pleasure is accepted for men worldwide, the same acceptance does not hold true for women. The authors of this chapter insist that pleasurable sex for women, as well as for men, must be the cornerstone of sex therapy. Using a case of a woman suffering from dyspareunia (painful intercourse), they describe an innovative treatment approach that focuses not on numbing medications or vaginal dilation, but on increasing sexual pleasure. The authors assert that the physiological changes that occur when women are sexually aroused are as indispensable for sexual intercourse as are erections for men.

This chapter stands in stark contrast to the treatment prescribed for women suffering from sexual pain in many other parts of the world, including that described in the chapters from Hong Kong, Turkey, and especially from Iran. In other cultures it appears that reproduction and performing a necessary marital duty take precedence over female pleasure. It will be left to the reader to determine whether the treatment described in this chapter might be appropriate for other cultures.

15

SEX, PLEASURE, AND DYSPAREUNIA IN LIBERAL NORTHERN EUROPE

How Sexual Pleasure is Seen as the Most Important Goal of all Nonreproductive Sexual Activity in a Postmodern Northern European Society, but is Denied by Women and Scientists who are Still under the Influence of Male Dominated Sexual Scripts

Rik H. W. van Lunsen, Marieke Brauer, and Ellen Laan

Introduction

The Netherlands, Denmark, Norway, and Sweden are countries where sexual and reproductive health issues are given high priority. Sexual health as defined by a working definition of the World Health Organization (Glasier, Gulmezoglu, Schmid, Garcia Moreno & van Look, 2006; WHO, 2002) is adopted as a primary goal of sexual and reproductive health (SRH) policies (Dutch Ministry of Health, Welfare and Sport, 2009; Ministry of Foreign Affairs of Denmark, 2006; Norwegian Directorate of Health, 2004; Swedish National Institute for Public Health, 2003). Sexual health is not only defined in the sense of the prevention of unwanted pregnancy, sexually transmitted infections (STIs), and sexual violence, coercion, and discrimination, but also in the sense of sexual rights "as a set of entitlements related to sexuality that emanate from the rights to freedom, equality, privacy, autonomy, integrity and dignity of all people" (International Planned Parenthood Federation, 2008, p. 16). In this vision sexual health is more than the prevention of possible harm by sexual activity and includes opportunities for pleasurable sexual experiences.

The typical Dutch and "Nordic" attitude toward sexual health is reflected by a fairly liberal attitude toward teenage sexual relationships

(Edgardh, 2002). For instance, while premarital sex is controversial and much debated in the United States, in most Northern European countries it is no longer an issue. In these countries, the term *premarital sex* has disappeared from the local vocabulary. Despite large cultural differences and different sexual morals, the median age of first sexual intercourse in all industrialized Western countries is around the age of 17 (van Lunsen, Laan, & van Dalen, 2006). Both an earlier sexual debut and the general tendency of women in Northern Europe to postpone childbearing has led to a prolonged period in which people engage in sexual activity without any procreational intentions. In these early stages of sexual careers the average sexual behavioral pattern in the Nordic countries is best characterized by "serial monogamy": most young men and women have several sexual partners before they start a family. Nevertheless, rates of teenage pregnancy, abortion, and STI among adolescents in these countries are among the lowest in the world, reflecting at least that young people in these countries succeed in rather effective preventive behavior.

Factors that have been identified that might explain these low rates of adverse SRH outcomes include (a) the degree of openness within society and in the media with regard to sexuality; (b) the availability of contraceptive methods and accessibility of SRH services; (c) the communication skills of male and female teenagers that enable them to negotiate and communicate about wishes, boundaries, and choices with regard to sexual behavior; (d) the quality of public prevention campaigns; and (e) the quality of sex education in the formal (school) and informal (family, social, environmental) educational curriculum (van Lunsen & van Dalen, 2007).

Sex education in Northern Europe has a long tradition. In Sweden Carl von Linné (Linnaeus, 1707–1778), who was well known for his "sexual system" of all flowering plants, also made pioneering efforts by lecturing on human sexuality in a very open manner. From the 18th century onwards, men and women were actively involved in public discussions about sexual health and gender equity. The Swedish Association for Sexual Education (RFSU) was founded in 1933. In 1942 a discussion about sex education in schools began and in 1962 sex education became a compulsory part of the Swedish school curriculum. In the Netherlands schools are required to provide sex education in primary and secondary schools. Teaching material is provided through nongovernmental organizations (NGOs), such as the Rutgers Nisso Group, founded in 1969, and the education is seen as a joint responsibility between the education system and the municipalities responsible for primary health care.

The primary objective of sex education programs in Sweden, Denmark, Norway, and the Netherlands is to provide "adults in the making" with the tools, skills, and attitudes they will need to be able to make their own mature and autonomous decisions about when, how, and with whom they want to start their sexual careers, guarding their own boundaries, and respecting those of others. The aim of sex education is to empower teenagers to make autonomous choices based on their emotional and sexual development and on their own ideas and wishes on how and when to start shaping their sexual relationships. There is convincing scientific evidence that this kind of sex education does not encourage youngsters to engage in sexual activity they are not ready for, does not lead to an earlier sexual debut, and reduces teenage pregnancy, abortion, and STI rates (Ingham, 2005; van Lunsen et al., 2006).

Pleasure as an Indicator of Sexual Health

Although the possibility of having pleasurable sexual experiences is an explicit component of current sexual health definitions (Glasier et al., 2006), the domination of public health outcomes as the indicator of the sexual health status of a population results in a lack of attention to pleasure as another main outcome of sexual health promotion. Health authorities are inclined to monitor the sexual health status of a population by means of statistics about contraceptive use, teenage pregnancies, abortions, condom use, STIs, and sexual violence.

Most research into young people's developing sexuality is concerned with risk avoidance and the reduction of negative outcomes (Kleinplatz, 2001). In many countries sex education programs focus more on the problematic aspects of sexuality than on its positive aspects. The role of pleasure in sexual development and relationships is usually not acknowledged in educational programs, although knowledge and communication of one's sexual wishes and limits and recognizing oneself as a sexual being have been stressed as important capacities in relation to sexual pleasure in general (Gold, Letourneau, & O'Donohue, 1995). Moreover, there are increasing indications that public sexual health outcomes may benefit from a greater acceptance of positive sexual experiences (Ingham, 2005). Satisfying sexual activity is strongly associated with positive experiences in sexual relationships and overall well-being (Laumann, Paik, & Rosen, 1999). Nevertheless, sex education interventions have traditionally focused on the dangers of sex: on prevention of STIs, unwanted pregnancies, and coercion. Sexual health is often defined in terms of the absence of these problems. To attain "healthy sexuality," however, as discussed earlier, more is required than prevention of adverse outcomes.

In the Netherlands NGOs that play a pivotal role in the development of sexual health education have recognized this error of problematizing sexuality without emphasis on the positive aspects of sexuality as a contributor of quality of life and relationships. As a result, relationship-oriented messages about sex and contraceptives have been incorporated in the national sex education curriculum "Long Live Love" (Wiefferink et al., 2005) A recent study analyzed the content of sex education materials in the Netherlands and found that they were characterized by consistent relationship-oriented messages, presenting sexual health topics in a positive light, and normalizing sexual feelings instead of inducing fear and shame (Ferguson, Vanwesenbeeck, & Knijn, 2008). Despite this focus on positive aspects of sexuality, interactional educational activities about the prerequisites for sexual pleasure have, until now, not been a visible part of sexual education (Ingham, 2005).

According to a recent nationwide investigation among 5,000 young people up to 25 years of age, girls and boys in contemporary Netherlands have access to a number of information sources on sexual and reproductive issues (Graaf, Meijer, Poelman, & Vanwesenbeeck, 2005). Most parents had discussed topics such as love, relationships, and birth control with their children, although more often with their daughters than with their sons. However, certain topics were less often discussed; for example, wishes and boundaries regarding sexuality. In the Graaf et al. study, sexual behavior, sexual health status, and sexual problems of the young were assessed, but sexual pleasure was not included as an endpoint. Nevertheless, the prevalence of sexual problems, particularly in girls, was high. For instance, for the majority of girls (57%) sexual intercourse was often or always painful. This lack of attention to sexual pleasure in the evaluation of sexual health, even in a study where an integrated approach to sexual health was promoted, is by no means an exception. Sexual pleasure is simply not acknowledged in most countries and, consequently, does not feature in SRH education programs or their evaluations (Ingham, 2005).

In the area of sexual function/dysfunction the concept of pleasure has also been largely ignored (Boul, Hallam-Jones, & Wylie, 2009), with a few exceptions. In a large representative U.S. sample, Meston and Buss investigated people's motives to engage in sexual intercourse (Meston & Buss, 2007). The most frequently endorsed reasons for having sex reflected what seems to motivate most people most of the time—attraction, pleasure, affection, love, romance, emotional closeness, arousal, the desire to please, adventure, excitement, experience, connection, celebration, curiosity, and opportunity. Factor analysis identified four main factors: physical reasons (e.g., stress reduction and pleasure), goal attainment (e.g., social status and revenge), emotional factors (e.g., love and commitment) and insecurity factors (e.g., duty/pressure and mate guarding). Most women reported having sex primarily for pleasure, love, and commitment. A French study found that regardless of gender, for the vast majority of individuals sexuality was synonymous with pleasure (44.0%) or love (42.1%) (Colson, Lemaire, Pinton, Hamidi, & Klein, 2006). As argued by Boul et al. (2009), sexual pleasure is not only physical and hedonic, but also "eudemonic"; that is, gaining sexual pleasure through the attainment of goals. In that sense, pleasure is the ultimate goal of sexuality. Sexual activities that are not experienced as pleasurable largely predict sexual dissatisfaction (Risen, 2003). According to the WHO working definition of sexual health, sexual health requires the possibility of having pleasurable sexual experiences (WHO, 2002). Sexual pleasure should therefore be regarded as a necessary requirement for sexual health. To date, studies that assess the importance of pleasure as an independent indicator of sexual health are lacking.

A wide spectrum of factors is associated with the etiology of sexual problems: biomedical, psychological, social, emotional, relational, and iatrogenic. Regardless of the nature and the cause of a sexual problem, we argue that lack of sexual pleasure is the most common cause of sexual problems, with sexual pain as the most poignant example.

Sexual Pleasure and Sexual Pain

Although compared to other societies sexual pleasure of women in the Netherlands and in the Nordic countries is valued as a relatively important aspect of their sexual health, the incidence and prevalence of sexual problems in these countries does not markedly differ from that of other Western societies. As a striking example, the general prevalence of dyspareunia in healthy young women in the Netherlands is between 14 and 34% (van Lankveld et al., 2010). In the majority of cases dyspareunia is not related to an identifiable medical condition. In a population-based study of Dutch women between 15 and 25 years, 57% of those with coital experience indicated that they experienced coital pain on most occasions of intercourse (de Graaf et al., 2005). In a Swedish study of 203 women aged 13 to 21 that consulted a youth sexual health center for reasons not related to sexual pain, 49% of those who reported having had sexual intercourse during the previous month had experienced coital pain or discomfort. Those experiences constituted a problem for just over half of these women (46 of 99; Elmerstig, Wijma, & Swahnberg, 2009). Remarkably, the other half of these young women did not consider this sexual pain to be a problem, either because they regarded painful sexual intercourse as being normal or perhaps because they obtained other, nonpleasure related rewards from coital activity.

The most common "cause" of pain with intercourse in these younger women is provoked vulvodynia (PVD; Pukall, Smith, & Chamberlain, 2007). Superficial dyspareunia and postcoital burning, the most typical complaints of PVD, are particularly prevalent in young women (Harlow, Wise & Stewart, 2001). Primary PVD means that the condition exists from the first sexual intercourse onwards. In secondary PVD women have experienced episodes of sexual intercourse without pain. We argue that secondary PVD is not simply a cause of dyspareunia but is, in the majority of cases, the result of a habit of accepting sexual penetration without sufficient sexual arousal. For many women, in contrast to men, sexual intercourse is not the most sexually stimulating sexual activity (Hite, 1976; Lloyd, 2005), particularly when it represents the sole source of sexual stimulation. Yet many women and men believe that women "can" (with some of them even believing that they "should") always have intercourse, whether they are sexually aroused or not. Their genital anatomy allows women to give precedence to sexual intercourse over sexual pleasure. Whereas men are protected by their anatomy in that sexual arousal (producing an erection) is needed for penetration, women have the capacity to "compromise their genitals" by allowing vaginal penetration without vaginal congestion (producing sexual lubrication) and "pouting" of the labia and introitus (producing an "airbag" that protects women's genitals from heavy thrusting). When we realize that these physiological changes in women are just as indispensable for sexual intercourse as are erections for men, then we understand that sexual pleasure should take priority over sexual intercourse.

Some Dutch and Swedish researchers have raised the obvious question: why do so many women in societies that claim to foster positive attitudes toward women's sexuality, continue to have sexual intercourse despite pain and lack of pleasure (de Jong, van Lunsen, Roberston, Stam, & Lammes, 1995; Elmerstig, Wijma, & Berterö, 2008)?

Women who continue to engage in painful intercourse ignore the primary function of pain as signaling damage to the body. Repetitive painful intercourse due to this ineffective pain behavior may then result in a further reduction of sexual arousal and vaginal lubrication. A reactive inability to sufficiently relax the pelvic floor muscles on subsequent intercourse occasions as a result of the anticipated pain aggravates the symptoms of pain and discomfort and may eventually lead to a situation in which intercourse becomes physically impossible (van Lunsen & Ramakers, 2002; Spano & Lamont, 1975). There is some preliminary evidence that women with dyspareunia and vaginismus and their partners differ in sexual behavior and in their response to the pain. In a very recent study, women with dyspareunia displayed less pleasure and more "duty" and mate guarding motives for sex than women with vaginismus and controls. Partners of women with dyspareunia responded more negatively to the sexual pain problem than partners of women with vaginismus (according to the men themselves), supporting "task-persistent" behavior on the part of the women with dyspareunia (Brauer, Lakeman, van Lunsen, & Laan, 2012). In addition, women with dyspareunia and vaginismus were less sexually autonomous than controls, suggesting that they have a smaller chance of attaining the sexual stimulation that is required in order to become aroused. As a further example of the central role given to intercourse rather than pleasure, 38% of the women with dyspareunia still had or attempted sexual intercourse at least once a week.

Approaches to Treatment

Dyspareunia is a multifaceted problem with medical, psychological, relational, and cultural sequelae. Treatment protocols should therefore include all physical, psychosexual, psychological, relational and contextual aspects of the problem. The first step in the treatment is to stop the habit of engaging in unaroused vaginal penetration. Subsequent treatment is aimed at sexual "rehabilitation" in which sexual pleasure is (re)discovered. In such a rehabilitation program there is encouragement to attend to the quality of sexual stimuli, context, and communication in a sexual repertoire that is less exclusively oriented at sexual intercourse. Education about differences (and similarities) in genital anatomy between men and women is an important ingredient in the program. Information about the relative inability of intercourse to lead to sexual arousal and orgasm in women may serve to remove any feelings of inferiority a female client may have and to prevent her from continuing sexual behavior that is insufficiently sexually arousing. Sometimes women themselves encourage their male partners to begin intercourse quickly. These women report that "foreplay" "does nothing" for them and even evokes an unpleasant "tickling" sensation; intercourse at least allows them to "feel something." An unpleasant tickling sensation during every occasion of physical intimacy in most cases is an indication of the woman being too tense physically. In this case, nongenital sensate focus exercises followed by well-timed genital sensate-focus exercises are indicated. These exercises may help to relax the woman and to refocus her attention: first to positive nongenital sensations, and later on to positive genital sensations. Important elements here are counteracting spectatoring, preventing goal-oriented behavior, and challenging any underlying inadequate cognitions and expectations by means of cognitive restructuring.

Case

April, aged 21, was referred to the outpatient sexual dysfunction clinic by her gynecologist, with the presenting problem of provoked vulvodynia. She had a history of chronic secondary superficial dyspareunia for over 2 years. Three years ago she began a sexual relationship with Marc. Before her complaints started, she and Marc had a period of several months of pleasurable, satisfying, and pain-free sexual experiences. The gynecologist was the first of many doctors she had consulted over the past few years who acknowledged the severity of her complaints. With careful and extensive inspection of the vulvar vestibule the gynecologist, by means of the "touch" or "cotton-swab" test, identified hyperesthetic foci in the vestibule at 5 and 7 hours, which is typical for PVD. Although April tended to contract her pelvic floor muscles when her vulva was touched, she succeeded in relaxing these muscles upon instruction and repeated reassurance that no speculum or fingers would be introduced during the examination. No abnormalities of the vulva and vaginal introitus were observed and direct microscopical examination of vaginal discharge, and the results of vaginal cultures, did not reveal underlying infectious causes. The gynecologist explained to April that she suffered from a painful condition, PVD, that the pain was not "in her head" (as another doctor previously said), and that she would like to refer her to the multidisciplinary team of the sexual dysfunction clinic. April was encouraged to visit this clinic together with her partner.

Because there was a well-documented diagnosis of the referring gynecologist, no further physical examination was conducted during the first visit. Instead, an extensive history that included all possible related physical, psychosexual, and relational aspects of the problem, was taken. For both April and Marc this relationship represented their first long-term sexual relationship. Both had had one or two previous sexual experiences with casual partners. At the age of 16 April had a boyfriend with whom she had, over the course of about 18 months, gradually discovered the pleasure of intimacy and sexual arousal in an age-specific stepwise manner. During this period she also discovered masturbation and experienced her first solo-orgasm before experiencing orgasm by mutual masturbation. At this time, she started oral contraceptive use in order to be able to decide when and how she would have her "first time." After about a year her boyfriend "talked her into" her first intercourse. She recollected agreeing with some hesitation related to doubts about the relationship, but insisted on doing it "safe." This first experience was reportedly "OK"; there was some pain upon vaginal entry, but overall, April regarded her sexual debut as a positive experience. Her first sexual experiences with Marc were very different; they were very much in love and had their first painless and pleasurable intercourse after a few weeks of dating, cuddling, and highly exciting mutual masturbation. During the first few months of this relationship they had satisfying sex, which did not always include intercourse, almost every time they saw each other, most of the times at his place where she experienced more privacy and could avoid the glances of her parents at the breakfast table. At that time they both were still in school and living with their parents.

They both graduated that year at age 18 and went to the same university, with April starting in law school and Marc in medical school. In the Netherlands, students generally do not live on a university campus. Marc found a room in a student house in town and April decided, mostly for financial reasons, to remain living with her parents. A few times a week she spent the night at Marc's place. Shortly after the start of their studies, April's pain complaints started. At first there was some pain on intromission that gradually disappeared during intercourse. Afterwards she then had a burning vulva, and a burning painful sensation (but no itching) in the vestibule, which gradually disappeared within a few hours. Because the pain did not last and she did not want to worry him, she never told Marc about the pain. "Besides," she argued in the first visit, "the pain wasn't that bad," so she just went on to grind her teeth in the expectation that the pain would soon disappear. April's confession was upsetting to Marc, as he recollected at a later stage in therapy, because the knowledge that she was having pain while he was enjoying intercourse made him feel like a "rapist." After a few months the pain got worse. The pain at intromission no longer subsided, making coital activity painful from beginning to end, with subsequent vulvar burning now lasting several days. Because she thought she might have a yeast infection, April went to her GP. He examined her, did not find any sign of a vulvo-vaginal mycosis, but prescribed an antimycotic "just to be sure." Following this appointment, her complaints subsided somewhat, but a few weeks later the same complaints recurred. In the subsequent months she had several other antimycotics prescribed, but the symptoms only got worse. After a year, intercourse became impossible. The couple still engaged in intercourse attempts regularly (and still did so at the time of the first visit), but these attempts were always painful. On several occasions Marc suggested that they abstain from trying, but April insisted on continuing their attempts even though at that time her sexual desire had completely disappeared.

In the year prior to the first visit to the sexual dysfunction clinic, April visited a gynecologist who told her that from a medical point of view, nothing was wrong and who referred her to a physical therapist because she had "to learn to relax her pelvic floor." Although in the past she had never had any urinary problems she began noticing increased frequency and experienced increased vulvar burning after micturition; by the time of the first visit the pain had become almost constant. After a few sessions the physical therapist concluded that she was perfectly able to relax her pelvic muscles and that there was nothing else she could do for her. Because April's complaints had not improved, she visited a second gynecologist, who told her she had "vulvar vestibulitis syndrome" (VVS), and that because she already had undergone pelvic floor physical therapy, surgery (in which a portion of the vestibular skin is removed) probably was the best option. April thought this to be rather radical and went on the Internet to look for information about VVS. She discovered that there were many conflicting opinions about this syndrome but that according to the website of the Dutch College of Obstetrics and Gynecology, a surgical intervention was only an option when all other more integrated treatment options have failed. That is how she finally visited the gynecologist who referred her to the outpatient sexual dysfunction clinic.

Over the course of this first joint interview and separate interviews with April and Marc, we found the following topics to be relevant:

1. Contextual and relational factors at the time of onset of the complaints;
2. Possible reasons for the inadequate pain behavior of the couple, such as April feeling guilty about her "lack" of desire and Marc unaware of the fact that April always had pain;
3. Current appraisal of sexuality and relationship;
4. Knowledge of both partners about prerequisites for pleasurable and pain-free intercourse.

It became clear that at the onset of the pain complaints April's level of sexual desire had started to decline. Her almost constant high levels of sexual desire during the first few months of being passionately in love had changed into a more responsive desire that was often triggered when they were spending time together and she felt intimate and close. In the first few months at university she often longed for the company of Marc, to share all the new experiences and impressions of this new phase of life, and to feel mentally and physically close. Sometimes their being together could result in sexual desire, but on other occasions it did not or she would simply feel too tired and just wanted to sleep in his arms. Because they saw each other only a few times a week and had developed the habit of having sex whenever they saw each other, sex always took place. Because she knew how much Marc valued having sex with her, April never let him know when she was not in the mood, and just followed Marc's script. She gradually developed the habit of engaging in intercourse even when she did not feel sexual desire and did not feel sexually aroused. Until a year ago, sexual arousal and desire would sometimes emerge during intercourse, but this had not happened since. Nevertheless, April continued urging Marc to start penetration after only a little foreplay. They had stopped engaging in noncoital sex leading to orgasm, and April became avoidant of physical intimacy altogether, fearing that it would result in painful sex. Of course, Marc noticed this. He often asked April if something was wrong, but never received an answer until the pain became so bad that she could no longer act as if nothing was wrong. Even at that point April did not want to disappoint Marc, so she told him that despite the pain, her sexual desire had not declined, as her being in love had evolved into deep affection and love.

The fact that April accepted and even solicited frequent unaroused penetration may be related to her personality traits. She was always taking care of others more than herself and was always inclined to see herself in the eyes of others. This external locus of control suggested that her self-image was primarily based on what she thought that others might think of her. Because she believed that intercourse was important for Marc, she was inclined to regard this as more important than her own wishes. She had recently been confronted with other nonsexual situations in which she failed to express her own wishes, expectations, and boundaries. For instance, with university group assignments she often found herself doing more than the other students, and she felt responsible for the group as a whole. In other words, she tried to be the ideal partner as well as the ideal student, just like she was the ideal daughter of parents who had always valued her for being very social and for keeping up with their high expectations.

Marc had quite a different personality: easy going, very fond of April, and never doing anything he didn't want to do. He enjoyed sex and intercourse and had always assumed that whatever he liked was pleasant for others as well. He had never imagined that April's wishes and expectations about their sexual relationship could be different than his. He was very much surprised, disappointed, and angry after discovering that April had frequently engaged in painful sexual intercourse without arousal and desire. He never would have intentionally hurt her and even though he did not communicate his feelings very easily, he knew one thing for sure. He loved April for what she was and did not want this problem to destroy their relationship. He never realized that women in fact have the same physical prerequisites for pleasurable sexual intercourse as men and remarked that, "It's rather crazy to start with it when you don't feel like it. Of course I wouldn't ever think of trying intercourse when I do not have an erection."

After extensive psychoeducation about the likely causes of PVD, therapy in this couple was straightforward. April was prescribed an inert ointment to be applied to the sensitive vestibular skin and was instructed on how to perform personal hygiene without using anything that might irritate the vulval skin. This personal hygiene routine involved daily irrigation of the vulval area with lukewarm water; careful patting dry of the area; further blow-drying with a cool chinook; and application of a very thin layer of the inert cream (which could be repeated, if necessary, prior to urination so as to protect the skin from urine). Also, she was instructed to drink more than her usual low fluid intake to avoid further irritation of the area by concentrated urine. In addition, April and Marc were encouraged to regain the pleasure in intimate physical contact they had experienced in the beginning of their relationship. Of course, all behaviors that could hurt the sensitive vestibule were banned, which meant that every attempt to penetrate, but also touching of the vestibule, was not allowed. They started with sensate focus type assignments, with emphasis on quality time together and communication about what kind of physical treatments they could give each other. Very soon this resulted in a reduction of tension for April. At one point April asked Marc to stimulate her genitally because she had experienced increasing sexual arousal and desire after a few weeks of this nongenital lovemaking. She explicitly explained to Marc how he could stimulate her without hurting her. This explanation was based on a recent experience she had had with masturbation. A few days earlier she had felt "horny" fantasizing about sex with Marc, with the memory of one of their very pleasant sexual encounters in the beginning of their relationship still very vivid. She discovered that she could experience orgasm by stimulating her glans clitoris, while avoiding touching her still very sensitive vestibule.

Several individual sessions with April focused on her lack of autonomy and her tendency to please others without sufficient attention to her own needs. In two individual sessions with Marc his inclination to assume that what was good for him must be good for others too was discussed. It became clear that he had always thought that he knew what April did and did not like sexually, and that he had based this belief on their enjoyable sexual debut. He learned to value that what is liked one day is not necessarily what is enjoyed another day and that partners always differ in their wishes, goals, and prerequisites for sexual desire, sexual arousal, and sexual satisfaction.

After 3 months of therapy, April tried to talk Marc into having intercourse again, but he refused until she was able to convince him that this was what she really wanted and that this time she did not want to have intercourse just to please him.

Discussion of the Case

The case of April and Marc is a prototypical example of secondary provoked vulvodynia in young women. The problem often begins with a few occasions of commencing intercourse without sexual desire, arousal, and a physical sexual response, but with a tensed pelvic floor. Following a number of such episodes, some women succeed in regaining pleasure, desire, and arousal by focusing on their own prerequisites for desire and arousal, and by communicating wishes, expectations, and boundaries to their partners. Others will abstain from painful experiences, end the relationship, or otherwise give expression to their lack of sexual desire and arousal. Some women, however, will continue to engage in unaroused sexual intercourse. These motives to continue painful intercourse seem to be driven by the wish to please and pleasure one's partner, to achieve the image of an "ideal" woman, by feelings of guilt, duty/pressure, and the fear of losing the partner (Ayling & Ussher, 2008; Brauer et al., 2012; Elmerstig et al., 2008).

Summary and Conclusions

Sexual health is more than the prevention of possible harm and adverse outcomes. It requires opportunities for (learning to acquire) pleasurable sexual experiences. There is convincing scientific evidence that sex education aimed at empowering young people to make autonomous sexual choices does not encourage them to engage in sexual activity they are not ready for, does not lead to an earlier sexual debut, and reduces teenage pregnancy, abortion, and STI rates (Lottes, 2002; van Lunsen & van Dalen, 2007). Despite the focus on positive aspects of sexuality and on communication skills to express wishes and boundaries, even in liberal Northern Europe, interactional educational activities about the prerequisites for sexual pleasure have not been a visible part of sexual education, whereas lack of sexual pleasure is the most common cause of sexual problems. In this chapter we have argued that for men and women alike, sexual pleasure is not a "bonus" that can also be discarded, but a necessary requirement for sexually rewarding and pain-free sexual interactions. We recommend that this "pleasure principle" be made an explicit part of sexual health education programs.

References

Ayling, K., & Ussher, J. M. (2008). "If sex hurts, am I still a woman?" The subjective experience of vulvodynia in heterosexual women. *Archives of Sexual Behavior, 37*, 294–304.

Boul, L., Hallam-Jones, R., & Wylie, K. R. (2009). Sexual pleasure and motivation. *Journal of Sex & Marital Therapy, 35*, 25–39.

Brauer, M., Lakeman, M., van Lunsen, R. H. W., & Laan, E. (2012). Inadequate pain behavior in women with sexual pain disorders. (manuscript submitted for publication)

Colson, M-H., Lemaire, A., Pinton, P., Hamidi, K., & Klein, P. (2006). Sexual behaviors and mental perception, satisfaction and expectations of sex life in men and women in France. *Journal of Sexual Medicine, 3*, 121–131.

Dutch Ministry of Health, Welfare and Sport (2009). Policy letter on sexual health. Retrieved from http://english.minvws.nl/en/kamerstukken/pg/2010/sexual-health.asp

Edgardh, K. (2002). Adolescent sexual health in Sweden. *Sexually Transmitted Infections, 78*, 352–356.

Elmerstig, E., Wijma, B., & Berterö, R. N. T. (2008). Why do young women continue to have sexual intercourse despite pain? *Journal of Adolescent Health, 43*, 357–363.

Elmerstig, E., Wijma, B., & Swahnberg K. (2009). Young Swedish women's experience of pain and discomfort during sexual intercourse. *Acta Obstetricia et Gynecologica, 88*, 98–103.

Ferguson, R., Vanwesenbeeck, I., & Knijn, T. (2008). A matter of facts ... and more: An exploratory analysis of the content of sexuality education in the Netherlands. *Sex Education, 8*, 93–106.

Glasier, A., Gulmezoglu, A. M., Schmid, G., Garcia Moreno, C., & van Look, P. F. A. (2006). Sexual and reproductive health: A matter of life and death. *Lancet, 368,* 1595–1607.

Gold, S. R., Letourneau, E. J., & O'Donohue, W. O. (1995). Sexual interaction skills. In W. O. O'Donohue & L. Krasner (Eds.), *Handbook of psychological skills training: Clinical techniques and applications* (pp. 229–246). Boston, MA: Allyn & Bacon.

Graaf, H. de, Meijer, S., Poelman, J., & Vanwesenbeeck, I. (2005). Seks onder je 25e, seksuele gezondheid van jongeren in Nederland [Sex under 25, sexual health of young people in the Netherlands]. Delft, the Netherlands: Eburon.

Harlow, B. L., Wise, L. A., & Stewart, E. G. (2001). Prevalence and predictors of chronic lower tract discomfort. *American Journal of Obstetrics and Gynecology, 185,* 545–550.

Hite, S. (1976). *The Hite report.* New York: Dell.

Ingham, R. (2005). "We didn't cover that at school": Education against pleasure or education for pleasure? *Sex Education, 5,* 377–390.

International Planned Parenthood Federation (2008). *Sexual rights: An IPPF declaration.* http://www.ippfwhr.org/en/node/658.

Jong, J. M. J. de, van Lunsen, R. H. W., Roberston, E. A., Stam, L. N. E., & Lammes, F. B. (1995). Focal vulvitis: A psychosexual problem for which surgery is not the answer. *Journal of Psychosomatic Obstetrics and Gynecology, 16,* 85–91.

Kleinplatz, P. J. (2001). A critique of the goals of sex therapy or the hazards of safer sex. In P. J. Kleinplatz (Ed.) *New directions in sex therapy: Innovations and alternatives* (pp. 109–131). Philadelphia, PA: Brunner-Routledge.

Lankveld, J. J. van, Granot, M., Weijmar Schultz, W. C., Binik, Y. M., Wesselmann, U., Pukall, C. F., ... Achtrari, C. (2010). Women's sexual pain disorders. *Journal of Sexual Medicine, 7,* 615–631.

Laumann, E. O., Paik, A., & Rosen, R. C. (1999). Sexual dysfunction in the United States: Prevalence and predictors. *Journal of the American Medical Association, 281,* 537–544.

Lloyd, E. A. (2005). *The case of the female orgasm: Bias in the science of evolution.* Cambridge, MA: Harvard University Press.

Lottes, I. L. (2002). Sexual health policies in other industrialized countries: Are there lessons for the United States? *Journal of Sex Research, 39,* 79–83.

Lunsen, R. H. W. van, van Dalen, L. (2007). Teenage pregnancy in the Netherlands, low rates, increases and decreases explained. In P. Baker, K. Guthrie, C. Hutchinson, R. Kane, & K. Wellings (Eds.), *Teenage pregnancy and reproductive health* (pp. 294–301). London: RCOG Press.

Lunsen, R. H. W. van, Laan, E., & van Dalen, L. (2006). Contraception and sexuality. In I. Milsom (Ed.), *Contraception and family planning* (pp. 5–18). Edinburgh, Scotland: Elsevier.

Lunsen, H. W. van, & Ramakers, M. (2002). The hyperactive pelvic floor syndrome (HPFS): Psychosomatic and psycho-sexual aspects of hyperactive pelvic floor disorders with comorbidity of urogynecological, gastrointestinal and sexual symptomatology. *Acta Endoscopia, 32,* 275–285.

Meston, C. M., & Buss, D. M. (2007). Why humans have sex. *Archives of Sexual Behavior, 36,* 477–507.

Ministry of Foreign Affairs of Denmark. (2006). *The promotion of sexual and reproductive health and rights.* Retrieved from http://www.netpublikationer.dk/um/6573/html/entire_publication.htm

Norwegian Directorate of Health. (2004). *Sex og samliv: Sexual and reproductive health and healthcare services.* Retrieved from http://www.helsedirektoratet.no/seksuellhelse/sex_og_samliv/reproductive_health_preventing_unwanted_pregnancies_5500

Pukall, C. F., Smith, K. B., & Chamberlain, S. M. (2007). Provoked vestibulodynia. *Women's Health, 3,* 583–592.

Risen, C. B. (2003). Listening to sexual stories. In S. B. Levine, C. B. Risen, & S. E. Althof (Eds.), *The handbook of clinical sexuality for mental health professionals* (pp. 1–20). New York: Brunner/Routledge.

Spano, L., & Lamont, J. A. (1975). Dyspareunia: A symptom of female sexual dysfunction. *The Canadian Nurse, 8,* 22–25.

Swedish National Institute for Public Health. (2003). *The national public health strategy in Sweden in brief.* Retrieved from http://www.fhi.se/en/Publications/All-publications-in-english/The-National-public-health-strategy-for-Sweden-in-brief/

Wiefferink, C. H., Poelman, J., Linthorst, M., Vanwesenbeeck, I., van Wijngaarden, J. C., & Paulussen, T. G. (2005). Outcomes of a systematically designed strategy for the implementation of sex education in Dutch secondary schools. *Health Education Research, 20,* 323–333.

World Health Organization. (2002). *Gender and reproductive rights.* Retrieved from http://www.who.int/reproductive-health/gender/glossary.htm

Section V

THE OTHER SIDE OF THE COUCH

The Cultural Contribution of the Therapist

Editors Introduction to Chapter 16
The Social and Professional Diversity of Sexology and Sex Therapy in Europe

We would be derelict if we failed to include in this book the perspective from the other side of the proverbial couch. We consider psychotherapy a dialogue between therapist and patient (of whatever culture) but there is also an ongoing discourse between the profession itself and the culture in which it is practiced. The professionals who choose to enter a particular field and the background of these individuals necessarily influence the profession, just as they are influenced by it. This is what this chapter by Alain Giami is about: the symbiotic relationship between sex therapy and the culture in which it is practiced.

As you will read, the treatment of sexual problems has evolved in different ways across different countries and cultures. Focusing on the European context, two interesting trends are noted. One is the feminization of the practice of sex therapy, with more women entering the field, and the second is the divergence in treatment approaches for sexual problems. Sexual medicine is gaining ground in many parts of the world, but in some countries, psychological treatments predominate. Understanding how the practice of sexology has evolved helps us to see how we have responded to people's need for treatment and how this need varies across cultures. It is important to contemplate that perhaps we have contributed to defining the needs of the patients we treat. Several authors in this book have noted that there is an increasing recognition of women's right to pleasurable sex. This may be influenced by the feminization of the profession of sexology and the response of the profession will reflect the increased presence of female sex therapists and researchers.

We close the book with the important observations about the practice of sex therapy that are contained in this chapter. We encourage readers to think about how the issues raised in this chapter may pertain to the profession of psychotherapy in general.

16

THE SOCIAL AND PROFESSIONAL DIVERSITY OF SEXOLOGY AND SEX THERAPY IN EUROPE

Alain Giami

Introduction

Sexology and sex therapy are not practiced in the same way in different cultures, even in different countries belonging to the same Western culture. A cultural approach to sexology must certainly take into account the "patient view" (Armstrong, 1984; Condrau, 2007), attending to their culturally "different" experiences, particularly when they are related to a non-Western culture, as is the case for the majority of the chapters published in this book. We know the extent to which culture shapes the sense of the self and subjectivities (Biehl, Good, & Kleinman, 2007; Wagner, 1981) as well as the healing practices of a particular group (Kleinman, 1980). Accounting for subjectivities and contexts should not be restricted to patients and those originating from non-Western cultures. Western individuals and professionals, in particular those who work in the field of sexuality, exert their own subjectivities that can be defined as countertransference (i.e., the subjective and somewhat unconscious emotional reactions of the clinician; Giami, 2001) or the "point of view of the professional." Given the diversified services offered to clients it is necessary to consider sexology and the practices of sexologists and sex therapists as an expression of the cultural and social milieu in which they occur. Sexology and sex therapy practices, as professional practices, present important variations across cultures, and also to a certain extent within the same culture. Such differences and variations, which are not accidental and include the national and cultural context, training, and social organization of health services and professional motivation, are identified and analyzed in this chapter.

What is Sexology?

The use of the word *sexology* is in itself problematic. Sexology as a specific field of knowledge, practice, and profession appeared in the second half of the 19th century (Ariès & Béjin, 1985; Bland & Doan, 1999; Hekma, 1994) and having developed first in Western Europe continued until the onset of Nazism, and then in the United States in the early 1960s (Bullough, 1994; Haeberle, 1981). But even more than a century after its emergence, sexology remains controversial; as Felski (1999) observed, "To speak of sexology is surely to invoke an obsolete science and a vanished world. The term brings to mind sepia-tinted images of earnest Victorian scholars labouring over lists of sexual perversions with the taxonomical zeal of an entomologist examining insects. Who would claim to be a sexologist nowadays?" (Felski, 1999, p. 1). This provocative question ignored the thousands of professionals around the world who identify themselves as sexologists, receive intensive training, practice their skills in the public and private sectors of health systems, belong to national and international organizations, adhere to strict codes of ethics, participate in international congresses, and who publish research in more than 60 journals around the world (Zucker, 2002). Many years ago, the American self-identified sexologist Leonore Tiefer published an editorial titled "Three Crises Facing Sexology," in which she observed that sexologists were losing control of their subject matter and therefore losing their professional legitimacy because they were confronted with new challenges regarding the situation of sexology in culture, in research, and in the academic world (Tiefer, 1994). Tiefer specifically noted the challenges to sexology arising from the medicalization of sexuality.

The term *sexology* as a unifying concept to identify the field of scientific knowledge and medical/psychological practice is becoming more and more controversial and heavily challenged as many professionals do not recognize themselves as sexologists. The terms *sexual medicine* and *specialist in sexual medicine*, have replaced *medical sexology* and *medical sexologist*, while in psychology and related fields "sexology" is challenged by the monikers of "sex therapists" or "sexual-relational therapists," the latter being especially popular in the United Kingdom (Wylie, de Colomby, & Giami, 2004). Continental Europe and Latin America remain bastions of sexology, where the term is still used to identify the practice and the practitioners in the clinical and educational field of sexuality. In francophone countries variants on the use of the word *sexology* include the terms *clinical sexology*, or *sexo-analysis* (used predominantly in Quebec). The future of *sexology* is unclear and the term might probably disappear since the field is currently being reorganized in four major directions: sexual health, sexual medicine, sexuality education, and sexual rights (Corrêa, Petchesky, & Parker, 2008). For the purposes of this chapter, sexology will be used to refer to an apparatus of scientific and technical knowledge about sexuality, a set of representations and ideas about sexuality and gender, a social organization of health professionals, and a set of practices.

This chapter explores the social and professional diversity of sexological practices across cultures and across history with a particular focus on intra-European diversity. The idea that "sexology," as a current and contemporary scientific discourse, is the expression of a universal, global, scientific, medical, and psychological knowledge is examined. This process of globalization of scientific discourse and medical technologies is not specific to sexology and has been described and analyzed with respect to other health conditions such as cancer. Regarding sexological medical scientific discourse, the process of globalization is in part initiated by international organizations such as the International Society for Sexual Medicine (ISSM), the World Association for Sexual Health (formerly the World Association for Sexology; WAS), and other satellites and regional affiliated organizations, which abandoned the term *sexology* in 2005. Currently, sexology as a multidisciplinary field is shepherded in the direction of sexual health and sexual medicine by these global organizations who edict professional rules, standards of practice, and codes of ethics (Giami, 2002). These global "umbrella organizations" are coordinating the integration of regional and national federations of sexual health and sexual medicine.

> National sexologies may be considered local variants of this international biomedical culture, which are powerfully influenced by societal and institutional contexts, traditional medical cultures, and the history of cosmopolitan medicine within those contexts. The distinctive aspects of biomedical culture are particularly evident when patterns of clinical discourse and relationships between physicians, patients and their families are examined. (Del Vecchio Good, Good, Schaffer, & Lind, 1990, p. 60)

This observation, constructed from the field of cancer, is certainly relevant to the understanding of the world of sexology. Sexology cannot be considered as a "hard science" to the same extent as oncology, so it is not only the clinical settings and the relationships between clinicians and patients that are influenced by the so-called local culture, but also the genuine production and the national translation of the global medical-scientific discourse on sexuality. In each country and culture the scientific discourse of sexology and the way it is constructed is influenced to a certain extent by the culture in which it is developed.

In this chapter it is argued that sexology and sexological interventions are located in local (national) history and culture and that "sexologists" across the world (including sex therapists and specialists in sexual medicine) do not share the same profile in terms of knowledge, disciplinary orientation, gender, initial profession, age, mode of practice, and even their professional designation. Consequently, sexological practices differ from one context to another. The case of Brazil provides an interesting example in this respect. Sexology developed in the mid-20th century in the two major regions of this country: Rio de Janeiro, the cultural and emblematic former capital of Brazil, and Sao Paulo, the economic and financial platform of the country. In Rio de Janeiro, sexology was developed by gynecologists and psychologists interested in the psychosexual approach, whereas in Sao Paulo it was developed by urologists (Cavalcanti, 1992; Russo, Rohden, Torres, & Faro, 2009; Russo et al., 2011). This quite unique situation was possible in a country characterized by a huge cultural diversity and reflects the influence of culture on the development of the field of sexology. It also reflects differential medical developments in two major cities. In most countries, the field is divided between the medical and the psychosexological approaches, which is reflected by the existence of concurrent professional and scientific organizations. In Europe, we see the coexistence of the European Federation of Sexology (EFS; affiliated with the WAS) alongside the more recent European Society for Sexual Medicine (ESSM) (affiliated with the ISSM). We can observe the same phenomena of duplication and coexistence of societies and federations in Latin America with, on the one hand, the Latin American Federation of Sexology and Sexuality Education (FLASSES), and on the other hand, the Latin American Society for Sexual Medicine (SLAMS). Each of these federations organizes its own specific conferences (and, in the case of the EFS, publishes its own journal: *Sexologies: European Journal of Sexology and Sexual Health*). But beyond these geographic and cultural differences, the scope and activities of the ESSM and SLAMS (both affiliated to the ISSM) present fewer differences than the activities placed under the aegis of WAS. Medical and pharmaceutical interventions appear more globalized than sexual health, sexuality education, and sexual rights issues, which are more grounded in the social context.

One major difference among sexologists and sex therapists across cultures is the gender of the professional. Being a male urologist and practicing sexology or sexual medicine in a major north-eastern city of the United States is quite different from being a female nurse or midwife practicing sexual education and counseling in a small town in Finland, a young Italian female psychologist practicing in Italy, or a male GP providing contraception and treatment for sexually transmitted infections (STI) among North African women, or treating male sexual disorders in a Paris suburb. As Fausto-Sterling (2000) wrote, "In my previous book ... I exhorted scholars to examine the personal and political components of their scholarly viewpoints. Individual scientists are inclined to believe one or another claim about biology based in part on scientific evidence and in part on whether the claim confirms some aspect of life that seems personally familiar" (Fausto-Sterling, 2000, p. ix). This statement can be applied not only to scientific activities but also to clinical activities and professional practices related to sexuality. It implies that sexology is conceived, represented, and practiced according to gender identity and stereotypes (Giami, 2007). In this regard this paper is written by a male social scientist and may be biased or limited but also may include appropriate points, because of the author's male gender. Moreover, the author comes from a French culture.

Historical Evolution of Sexology

Western sexology emerged in the mid-19th century. In a period first described as "protosexology" (Ariès & Béjin, 1985), the function of sexology was to treat "sexual perversions," regarded as social deviances that could be penalized under criminal law. Krafft-Ebing collected case studies of what were then considered sexual deviations and catalogued them in his classic work *Psychopathia sexualis*, which was published in the late 19th century. Homosexuality continued to be penalized in different European countries until the mid-1980s and, in some cases, reparative therapies are still implemented to treat unwanted sexual orientation (Zucker, 2003). While some sexologists provide treatment to perpetrators of crime and sexual offenses (Bradford & Greenberg, 1996), the different sexologies that were developed after the 1960s began to address the shortcomings of sexual function or sexual dissatisfaction; that is, "repairing the conjugal bed" (Irvine, 2005). The status of "sexual deviance" (Simon, 1994) is changing and now refers to sexual dissatisfaction and potential difficulties in performing a sexual role within a couple. From this dominant paradigm represented by sexological and sex therapy interventions, one can consider that sexological treatments aim at monitoring the performance of a standard sexual function from a perspective of good sexual health development, which is considered to be one of the most important components of well-being (Giami, 2002).

The Diversity of Sexologies around the World

Prior histories of sexology focusing on the European and U.S world analyzed medical and scientific knowledge, which constitutes the intellectual universe of sexologies (Bland & Doan, 1999; Irvine, 2005; McLaren, 2007; Weeks, 1985). Over the past few years, research has extended to other cultural and national areas, namely Japan (Fruhstuck, 2003), Brazil (Carrara & Russo, 2002; Rohden & Torres, 2006; Russo, et al.,

2009), France (Ariès & Béjin, 1982; Béjin & Giami, 2007; Bonierbale & Waynberg, 2007; Chaperon, 2007; Corbin, 2008; Giami, Chevret-Méasson, & Bonierbale, 2009) and Quebec (Dupras, 1989). These works revealed the various social and political objectives which were assigned to sexology in different contexts, including some aspects of eugenics in Western Europe and in Japan, the fight against venereal diseases, eradication of female prostitution, sexual education for the masses, prevention of birth out of wedlock, and sterilization of the "unfit. "

Sexology remains deeply anchored within the context of health professions and is subject to secondary or continuing education and training (Fruhstuck, 2003; Giami & de Colomby, 2003; Haeberle & Gindorf, 1993; Irvine, 2005). Moreover, it is interesting to observe that in some countries, the most influential and famous sexologists have started to write about the history of their discipline (Bancroft, 2005; Bonierbale & Waynberg, 2007; Cavalcanti, 1992; Lewis & Wagner, 2008), adopting the role of historians of their own discipline beyond their important scientific contribution to their field. This situation reflects a high level of multidisciplinarity and reflexivity among mainstream sexologists working in the clinical and scientific arena.

Since 1968, the University of Quebec in Montreal has had the only program worldwide which offers both a bachelor's and a master's degree in sexology. Students get academic and professional training in sexology as their primary discipline (Dupras, 1989). In European countries, sexology and now sexual medicine are taught in the context of continuing education in a related discipline; for example, subsequent to the acquisition of a first professional degree in medicine, psychology, or in another health care field such as nursing. Training programs and international rules governing the practice of sexology are currently being established (Kontula, 2011; Porto, 2006; Pryor, 2006). Nordic countries, including Denmark, Estonia, Finland, Iceland, Norway, and Sweden have developed their own consensus on sexology education and authorization of professionals (Almås et al., 2000). A new French Federation of Sexology and Sexual Health (created in 2010) is currently working on the certification of continuing education for health professionals. In summary, the practice of sexology is progressively being organized and legitimized in order to meet the standards required of all clinical disciplines, despite a shortage of resources and funding endemic to health systems in the current economic climate.

Cultural Differences in Sexology and Sexual Health

Among the cultural and social differences that we studied in the field of sexology and sex therapy, are a number of factors related to treatment providers, including gender, profession, and professional training, age, and of course cultural affiliation (which is of major importance in a world of increased migration, both temporary and permanent, of the professionals themselves). These factors are shaped by the cultural and social determinants of health care and the medical profession (Kleinman, 1980). In this respect, questions include: who is allowed (i.e., who has the social permission to access the sexual life and sexual problems of a population)? Who is officially allowed to deal with (and in some cases to observe, touch, intervene, modify, and comment on) the sexual organs of individuals? Regarding the possibility of touching and observing a patient's genital regions, gender has become a major issue. Health professionals are no longer entitled to perform clinical examinations of patients of the opposite sex or may do so only in the presence of a chaperone (Croft, Morrow, Randall, Webb, & Kishen, 1999), who will protect both the clinician and the patient from sexual abuse and unfounded complaints (Giuffre & Williams, 2000; Schneider & Philips, 1997).

Different Sexologies among European Countries

In order to illustrate the cultural diversity of sexologies and to demonstrate the importance of the influence of national sexual cultures on the social organization of sexology, the example of Western Europe will be highlighted. The "Euro-Sexo" study involved researchers from seven different countries (Giami, de Colomby, & Groupe-Euro-Sexo, 2006). The project began with a survey conducted in 1998–1999, which identified the major trends in the social organization of sexology, as well as the social and demographic characteristics of sexologists working in France. At the end of the 1990s, the majority (about 60%) of professional sexologists in France were men and approximately two-thirds were medical doctors (Giami & de Colomby, 2003). This was at first quite a surprising and counterintuitive finding, since we would have expected either that both genders would be equally represented in the profession or that women would be overrepresented, as is the case in the majority of health related professions. French sexology appeared to be a highly medicalized and male professional group (Giami, & de Colomby, 2002). In order to better understand this situation, it was decided to conduct an international comparative study on sexology in six other European countries, namely Denmark, Finland, Italy, Norway, the United Kingdom, and Sweden.

The questionnaire that had been developed and used for the French survey was translated into the languages of these six countries and revised to reflect national differences (e.g., regarding primary school, academic training and the social security systems). The protocol used for the identification and recruitment of the sexologists was developed through a partnership with the major associations for sexology. Our first task was to identify the scientific and professional organizations working in this field, then to locate the active individual members of these organizations, giving us access to directories and individuals to be surveyed. Individuals listed in the professional phone directory/yellow pages under "Sexologists" were also included in the survey. This was possible only in France and Sweden, which were the only European countries dedicating a section to "sexologists" in these directories. The presence of a "sexologist" category in the telephone directory of only two European countries is already anthropological information: it shows to what extent a practice is officially recognized in a country. The census designed for each country was then consolidated and the anonymous questionnaire was sent to the identified professionals. In each country, a team was responsible for the collection and the analysis of data. The detailed results of this project were published in a special issue of the journal "Sexologies: European Journal of Sexology and Sexual Health" (Giami, de Colomby, & Euro Sexo Group, 2006).

Estimated Numbers of Sexologists in Seven European Countries

The findings of the study provided an estimate of the number of sexologists working in the various European countries involved and from this data, the approximate number of sexologists per million inhabitants (Table 16.1). These estimates were based on the official population census carried out in each country and on the responses obtained through the questionnaire. The average frequency observed for the seven countries studied was 19 sexologists per million inhabitants, ranging from 13 (in France and in Italy), to over 100 sexologists per million inhabitants in Finland; that is, over 8 times higher than in southern Europe. One can observe that access to sexological services is not equally distributed across the countries of northern and southern Europe. We could conclude that there is greater access or higher public demand for sexology in northern versus southern European countries, or that the recourse to such health care services is more integrated in the cultural and health practices in Protestant as opposed to Catholic countries. But the interpretation of these differences is far more complex and reflects several issues. In the case of Finland, sex educators and sexual counselors were included in the sample, even when working in the sexual health arena was not their main professional activity. Conversely, in France, sex educators and sexual counselors are not professional specialties and those doing sex education are mostly recruited among secondary school teachers, who do not recognize themselves as sex educators and even less as sexologists. These sex educators were not included in the French survey. So the differences observed in the numbers of sexologists reflect not only the availability of sexological services but the variety of such services;

Table 16.1 Number of Sexologists, Frequency by Million Habitants and Response Rate by Country

Country	N of sexologists	Population in million habitants (2003)1	Incidence 1/1 Million habitants	Response rate to the survey (N and %)
Denmark	215	5.4	40	129 (60%)
Finland	567	5.2	109	366 (64.6%)
France (Metropolitan)	776	59.8	13	498 (63.1%)
Italy	800	57.2	14	201 (20%)
Norway	139	4.6	30	93 (67%)
United Kingdom	1110	59.2	19	814 (73.3%)
Sweden	196	9	22	157 (80%)
Overall	3803	200.2	19	2258 (59.4%)

1. Data on European Population. *Population et Sociétés*, No. 392, July–August 2003, Paris, INED.

that is, sex education and counseling being more accessible and widespread in Finland than in other countries, especially France.

Distribution of Sexologists by Gender and Primary Profession

The survey demonstrated that sexology is almost never a sexologists' initial profession. The vast majority of sexologists have undergone a primary professional training and obtained a degree in a health, medical, or nonmedical profession, and they have practiced for several years in this profession before beginning training and starting a practice in sexology. It is important to note that most of our respondents did not stop working in their initial profession and in fact many of them continued this activity as their major professional pursuit. In this perspective, a majority of "sexologists" did not work in the sexology field on a full-time basis and continued, to varying degrees, to work in their primary profession, in addition to their activity as sexologists.

As already mentioned, at the time the survey was carried out in France (1999), there was a clear predominance of medical doctors (62.7%) working in this field. This important predominance of physicians was not found in any of the other European countries surveyed (Table 16.2). In Finland, the United Kingdom, and Sweden, around 30% of medical doctors identified themselves as sexologists; comparative figures for

Norway, Italy, and Denmark were 31%, 42%, and 48%, respectively. In summary, in most European countries, medical doctors do not represent the principal profession, and sexology is mainly practiced by health professionals (nonphysicians).

Regarding the gender distribution in the seven European countries studied, we found a very strong association between being a medical doctor and being male, and a strong relation between being a nonphysician professional (psychologists, nurses, midwives, educators) and being female. This explains why, in countries where nurses and midwives are the most represented professions in the field of sexology, sexologists are much more often women than men. Countries could be classified into three groups, in terms of higher or lower frequency of women in the field. First, were the countries with high proportions (>60%) of female sexologists: Sweden, Finland, the UK, and Italy. Finland was the country that included the highest frequency of health care professionals (nurses and midwives made up nearly 45% of the total number). In Italy, the majority of nonphysician sexologists were psychologists (40% of the total) who were predominantly female. On the other hand, in Denmark and in Norway, the sexological workforce comprised nearly equal numbers of men and women. Finally, France showed the lowest rate as regards the "feminization" of sexology, with around one third of women among the MD sexologists and just over half in the nonphysician professions.

This particular gender ratio among sexologists in different European countries results from complex social processes involving the national and social organization of medical and other health care professions and from a gender-based division of labor, with a predominance of women among health care professionals (Tronto, 1993) and men in the medical profession. In each country sexology remains grounded in the existing system. This is well illustrated by the predominance of marital/relationship counselors in the UK (a profession which did not appear in other countries) and the importance of the nursing professions (nurses, midwives) in Finland, who represent about half of the sexologists in that country.

Changes Over Time: The "Feminization" of French Sexology

In 2009, a second survey was carried in France among French sexologists belonging to the major sexology organizations (Giami, Chevret-Méasson, & Bonierbale, 2009). The objective of this new study was to observe and evaluate changes, if any, in the sociodemographic distribution of sexologists by profession and gender, 10 years after the first study carried out. The results of this study confirmed that the professional distribution amongst sexologists in France remains very stable.

Table 16.2 Distribution of Sexologists According to Gender and Initial Profession, by Country (in %)

	Total	Men	Women	Not reported	Numbers
Denmark					
MD	48.1%	58.0%	38.7%	3.3%	62
Non-MD	51.9%	26.8%	73.1%	0.0%	67
Overall		41.8%	56.5%	1.7%	129
Finland					
MD	25.1%	58.7%	41.3%	0.0%	92
Non-MD	74.9%	12.8%	87.2%	0.0%	274
Overall		24.3%	75.7%	0.0%	366
France					
MD	62.7%	68.9%	29.8%	1.3%	312
Non-MD	37.3%	46.2%	51.1%	2.7%	186
Overall		60.4%	37.8%	1.8%	498
Italy					
MD	41.8%	59.5%	40.5%	0.0%	84
Non-MD	58.2%	20.5%	78.6%	0.9%	117
Overall		36.8%	62.7%	0.5%	201
Norway					
MD	31.2%	79.3%	20.7%	0.0%	29
Non-MD	68.8%	37.5%	62.5%	0.0%	64
Overall		50.5%	49.5%	0.0%	93
United Kingdom					
MD	34.3%	46.2%	49.5%	4.3%	279
Non-MD	65.7%	20.4%	76.8%	2.8%	535
Overall		29.2%	67.4%	3.3%	814
Sweden					
MD	23.7%	52.9%	47.1%	0.0%	34
Non-MD	76.2%	15.4%	84.6%	0.0%	109
Overall		22.0%	78.0%	0.0%	143

Nearly two-thirds of French sexologists were physicians and one third came from other health professions. These results corroborated the major trend observed in the 1999 survey: the strong medical and clinical anchorage of French sexology.

The most interesting result of the 2009 survey was the highly significant change in the distribution of sexologists according to gender. The proportion of female sexologists in France had significantly increased, rising from 39% in 1999 to 63% in 2009. This new distribution of gender among sexologists in France is now comparable to that observed in other European countries in 2006, where women represented the majority of sexologists (although these proportions varied from country to country). This observation reflected the existing proportion of males and females in health care professions in France. One might have thought that because there were more female sexologists, there would also be an increase in the proportion of nonphysicians (psychologists and paramedical professions) amongst sexologists. This is not the case: the feminization of sexology in France is the result of a process of global feminization of the medical profession in particular and of health care professionals more generally. The increase in the proportion of women in the profession of sexology who are physicians is part of a broader process of feminization of the medical profession in general. Current demographic data show that women constitute the majority among French physicians (especially among general practitioners; Bessière, 2005). These findings demonstrate that sexology is deeply embedded in the structure of health professions and health care and that its current distribution reflects more fundamental social processes. In this perspective, sexology cannot be considered as a unique field of practice but rather, a common and usual form of health and medical practice.

Training in Sexology

Professional training was assessed using multiple questions regarding factors such as the title of the course attended by professionals, the content and duration of the training, and also the kind of diploma/degree that was obtained at the end of the program. Overall, about 70% of the sexologists interviewed in these seven countries reported that they had attended at least one training course entitled "sexology" or "human sexuality." In Denmark, Finland, France, and Sweden, the proportion of respondents who were trained in sexology was approximately 90%. The situation was different in the United Kingdom and Norway, where only 69% and 46%, respectively, reported having attended at least one training course.[1] Meanwhile, nonphysician sexologists were more likely than medical doctors to have attended some training in sexology in Finland, France, Italy, and the United Kingdom (see Table 16.3).

Table 16.3 At Least One Training Course in Sexology and/or Human Sexuality according to Initial Profession (in %)

	MD	Non-MD	Total
Denmark	96.6%	90.8%	93.5%
Finland	64.2%	97.0%	88.0%
France	89.4%	92.5%	90.6%
Italy	75.0%	86.3%	81.6%
Norway	44.8%	46.9%	46.2%
United Kingdom	55.6%	75.3%	69.1%
Sweden	94.1%	94.3%	94.3%

These disparities suggest that the different professions involved in the field of sexology are subject to different professional requirements and forms of legitimatization, depending on the country. It is assumed that due to their primary training, medical doctors consider themselves much more legitimate in practicing sexology than other health care professionals involved in the field. This may explain why nonphysician sexologists are more likely to have attended a training program in sexology prior to becoming involved in this field. These data reinforce the idea of the domination of physicians in the field of sexology in France.

Proportion of Professional Activity Dedicated To Sexology

Most sexologists practicing in Europe reported that they dedicated less than 25% of their professional activity to sexology or to "human sexuality." Thus, for a majority of these professionals, sexology represented a minor part of their professional endeavors. This situation is quite far removed from the traditional depiction of great figures such as Kinsey or Masters and Johnson as pioneers dedicating their lives to sexology (Robinson, 1976). For a majority of professionals, sexology alone appears to be insufficient to occupy their entire professional activity, either due to insufficient demand, to their limited interest, or to the lack of opportunities offered by the institutions for which they work.

Overall, nonphysician sexologists were more likely than medical doctors to say that they dedicated over 75% of their professional time to sexology. Practicing sexology did not comprise a full-time job, but was, to a certain extent, an activity that fell within the practice of their primary profession as a diversification or an informal specialization.

Table 16.4 Percentage of Professional Activity Devoted to Sexology according to Initial Profession

	MD	Non-MD	Total
Denmark			
< 25%	76.3%	58.5%	66.9%
> 75 %	8.5%	12.3%	10.5%
Finland			
< 25%	89.1%	72.7%	76.8%
> 75 %	2.2%	10.8%	8.5%
France			
< 25%	59.6%	37.1%	51.2%
> 75 %	13.8%	30.1%	19.9%
Italy			
< 25%	42.9%	39.3%	40.8%
> 75 %	4.8%	9.4%	7.5%
Norway			
< 25%	89.7%	69.2%	76.3%
> 75 %	3.4%	10.8%	8.6%
United Kingdom			
< 25%	71.6%	43.7%	53.3%
> 75 %	8.2%	17.4%	14.3%
Sweden			
< 25%	61.8%	43.4%	47.4%
> 75 %	11.8%	29.5%	25.6%

The Professional Identity of Sexologists

Professional identity is a complex issue, especially when the profession is related to sexuality. Strong societal representations and prejudice still stigmatize those whose professional activity relates to sexuality. Prejudice based on a "sexy" image has also been reported about nurses involved in sex therapy (Kolodny, Masters, Johnson, & Biggs, 1979). Moreover, since sexology and sex therapy are not yet well established and recognized health care professional activities in Europe, the endorsement of a professional identity of sexologist remains problematic.

Sexologists practicing in Europe were identified through the directories published by their professional associations or the professional "yellow pages" in telephone directories. In both cases, the fact of being included in such a directory is based on a voluntary decision related to a professional ambition for visibility and public recognition, but this publicity does not always overlap with one's personal professional identity (Dubar & Tripier, 1998). We therefore asked these publicly "identified" sexologists whether they considered themselves primarily "sexologists," "sex therapists," both, or neither.

Overall, and for all the countries surveyed, a majority of respondents did not consider themselves as being primarily "sexologists" or "sex therapists." Their initial training, validated by a diploma or title such as MD, psychologist, or nurse, constituted the basis of their professional identity, even though they were listed in sex therapist and sexologist directories. Overall, less than one respondent out of two (irrespective of whether an MD or non-MD) identified him- or herself as a sexologist. Significant differences were observed across countries and across respondents' primary professions. Nonphysician professionals were more likely to identify themselves as sexologists or sex therapists than medical doctors in all countries except Finland (less than 5%) and Norway, where less than 50% identified themselves as one or the other. Self-identification as a sexologist or sex therapist was reported by over 77% of nonphysician professionals practicing in France, and up to 55% of nonphysician professionals in Italy, Denmark, and the United Kingdom. Conversely, less than 20% of medical doctors in the United Kingdom and less than 40% in Sweden and Italy identified themselves as sexologists. The most extreme discrepancies were observed in Finland (where 5% of nonphysician professionals and 60% of medical doctors identified themselves as sexologists or sex therapists) and in the UK (where 20% of medical doctors and 60% of nonmedical professionals identified themselves in this way).

The self-identification as a sexologist or sex therapist does not have the same meaning in these different countries. Identifying oneself as a sexologist appears to be more frequent either among GPs and medical specialists or among nonphysician professionals, depending on the country. Bearing in mind that the French survey demonstrated that medical specialists (such as gynecologists, psychiatrists, or urologists) were less willing to identify themselves as sexologists than general practitioners and nonphysician professionals, it appears that the title of sexologist does not provide the same benefits to health professionals belonging to different professions. One may observe, however, that in the Finnish survey, a large proportion of the respondents identified themselves as *sex counselors*, a term used to designate professionals working primarily in the area of sex education and prevention (which does not exist in France to the same extent as an identified and specific profession). Choosing to adopt a professional title has a strong symbolic importance and this choice must be considered as part of a professional and an identity strategy. As

Table 16.5 "Do You Identify Yourself Primarily as a Sexologist or a Sex-Therapist?" according to Initial Profession (in %)

	MD	Non-MD	Total
Denmark	50.8%	58.5%	54.8%
Finland	60.9%	4.7%	19.1%
France	65.7%	77.4%	70.1%
Italy	36.9%	55.6%	47.8%
Norway	53.6%	46.0%	48.4%
Sweden	35.3%	42.3%	40.8%
United Kingdom	19.7%	59.6%	45.9%

such, it seems that the various health professionals involved in the field of sexology do not derive the same benefits by identifying publicly as sexologists. A French GP or a psychologist will obtain more symbolic and economic gratification if he or she endorses the professional identity of sexologist than a medical specialist in urology or gynecology working in a major university hospital. Furthermore, the low proportion of professionals who declared themselves sexologists may also suggest that the term *sexologist* is becoming problematic and is no longer accorded the prestige that it was given during the 1930s in Europe (Bland & Doan, 1999). The recent renaming of the World Association for Sexology to the World Association for Sexual Health may reflect the progressive obsolescence of the term *sexology*. The presence of the term *human sexuality* in some current training programs may also give an indication of this potential obsolescence. Last but not least, the emergence of new concepts and practices included in "sexual health" and "sexual medicine" may also herald the end of "sexology as a discipline."

Conclusions

The historical material, sociological observations, and survey findings presented in this chapter can help us to understand the professional diversity and similarities that can be found in the practice of sexology in Europe. First of all, in the seven European countries surveyed (apart from France), sexology is practiced mostly by nonphysician health professionals and by women. This constitutes the first social and cultural difference between France and other European countries and can be explained by the strong influence of medicine on the health care system in France and the lesser space left to other health professionals. As an example, in France, nurses and midwives do not receive academic training that could lead to a PhD or an academic position in their specialty;

nursing is still confined to vocational schools, providing nurses with limited technical training curriculums. This gender distribution is changing in France where currently women represent the majority of sexologists (approximately 60%). The feminization of the French situation appears to align France with other European sexologists and other French health professionals, including physicians (Giami, Chevret-Méasson, & Bonierbale, 2009). But the feminization of French sexology did not contribute to the demedicalization of the professional group: French sexology is still and increasingly dominated by physicians.

Furthermore, nonphysician professionals who practice in France are more likely to identify themselves as sexologists or sex therapists than in the other countries surveyed. This situation may be related to the fact that nonphysician sex therapists practicing in France dedicate a larger part of their professional activity to sexology than they do in other countries, but also because the use of the title has no legal value (anyone is allowed to use the title of sexologist without permission or approval). Physicians in France tend to identify themselves as sexologists less than other health professionals, as the title is not a benefit for professionals who have a higher social status, or more particularly, a medical degree.

A majority, but not all, of respondents reported having received professional training in sexology or in human sexuality, although to varying degrees depending on the country. Medical doctors more frequently started practicing sexology without having received extensive training in this field and without identifying themselves primarily as sexologists. This situation is consistent with the fact that in France, a majority of medical sexologists believe that one has to be a medical doctor to practice sexology (Giami & de Colomby, 2003).

Nevertheless, procedures for accreditation, validation of training, and registration to practice have recently been implemented in France and in the Scandinavian countries (Kontula, 2011). Initial attempts to standardize training in sexual medicine are also underway at the European Academy for Sexual Medicine (EASM), and it is hoped in the near future that the European Commission will tackle this problem with a proposal to unify and standardize training curricula in sexology and licensing for practitioners. But standardization and licensing is likely to come upon a major stumbling block that characterizes sexology in Europe: the very fact that this profession is based on such broad professional diversity and even more importantly, the presence in the profession of physicians and nonphysicians. The profession of sexologist in Europe today is struggling to maintain an unstable balance resulting from its diversity. In the long term it is questionable whether this diversity can be preserved, or if the representatives of the different professions will prefer to reorganize the speciality into common structures for training and accreditation. In the long-term, there is the risk of an excessive globalization of sexology, which will sever sexological practices from their cultural roots.

European sexology presents an interesting example of productive contradictions between, on the one hand, attempts for globalization and unification of knowledge and rules, and on the other hand, a diversity of practical knowledge and practices. Sexological practices and professionals are anchored in their national culture, and especially in their health care system, which determines the type of therapist one should preferably consult for sexual disorders and difficulties. The same modern medical knowledge, "evidence based knowledge," is becoming the keystone for deciding the legitimacy of all therapeutic approaches, but sexuality, as it cannot be closeted in the medical field exclusively, still remains a domain open for local adaptation and creativity.

Note

1. At the time of the survey, organized training for sexology did not yet exist in Norway, which explains the low proportion of sexologists reporting they had not received training. Professional training courses for sex therapists was later organized and grouped under the aegis of the Nordic Association for Clinical Sexology, which federates sexology organizations in Scandinavian countries (Denmark, Finland, Iceland, Norway, Sweden and Estonia).

References

Almås, E., van Deurs, S., Johansen, B. D., Kristensen, E., Kaimola, K., & Kontula O. (2000). *Sexological education and authorization in the Nordic countries*. Berlin, Germany: European Federation of Sexology.

Ariès, P., & Béjin, A. (Eds.). (1985). *Western sexuality: Practice and precept in past and present times*. New York: Blackwell.

Ariès, P., Béjin, A. (Ed.). (1982). [Special issue].*Sexualités occidentales* [Western sexualities] *(numéro spécial)*. Paris, France.

Armstrong, D. (1984). The patient's view. *Social Science & Medicine, 18*(9), 737–744.

Bancroft, J. (2005). A history of sexual medicine in the United Kingdom. *Journal of Sexual Medicine, 2*, 569–574.

Béjin, A., & Giami, A. (Eds.). (2007). *Une histoire de la sexologie française* [A history of French sexology]. Sexologies, European Journal of Sexology and Sexual Health, 16(3), 169–170.

Bessière, S. (2005). La féminisation des professions de santé en France: données de cadrage [The feminization of the health professions in France]. *Revue Française des Affaires Sociales 1*, 19–33.

Biehl, J., Good, B., & Kleinman, A. (Eds.). (2007). *Subjectivity: Ethnographic investigations*. Berkeley: University of California Press.

Bland, L., & Doan, L. (Eds.). (1999). *Sexology in culture: Labelling bodies and desires*. Cambridge, England: Polity Press.

Bonierbale, M., & Waynberg, J. (2007). 70 ans de sexologie française [70 years of French sexology]. *Sexologies—Revue Européenne de Sexologie Médicale, 16*(3), 238–258.

Bradford, J. M. W., & Greenberg, D. M. (1996). Pharmacological treatment of deviant sexual behaviour. *Annual Review of Sex Research, 7*, 283–306.

Bullough, V. (1994). The development of sexology in the USA in the early twentieth century. In R. Porter & M. Teich (Eds.), *Sexual knowledge, sexual science: The history of attitudes to sexuality* (pp. 303–322). Cambridge, England: Cambridge University Press.

Carrara, S. L., & Russo, J. A. (2002). Psychoanalysis and sexology in Rio de Janeiro between the two world wars: Between science and self improvement. *História, Ciências, Saúde—Manguinhos, 9*(2), 273–290.

Cavalcanti, R. (1992). Alguns Aspectos da História da Sexologia no Brasil [Some aspects of the history of sexology in Brasil]. *Revista Brasileira de Sexualidade Humana, 3*(1), 56–65.

Chaperon, S. (2007). *Les origines de la sexologie 1850–1900* [The origins of sexology 1850–1900]. Paris: Audibert.

Condrau, F. (2007). The patient's view meets the clinical gaze. *Social History of Medicine, 20*(3), 525–540.

Corbin, A. (2008). *L'harmonie des plaisirs:Les manières de jouir du siècle des Lumières à l'avènement de la sexologie* [The harmony of pleasures: Ways to enjoy the Enlightenment to the advent of sexology]. Paris, France: Perrin.

Corrêa, S., Petchesky, R., & Parker, R. (Eds.). (2008). *Sexuality, health and human rights*. London: Routledge.

Croft, M., Morrow, J., Randall, S., Webb, A., & Kishen, M. (1999). Chaperones for genital examination. *British Medical Journal, 319*, 1266.

Del Vecchio Good, M.-J., Good, B., Schaffer, C., & Lind, S. (1990). American oncology and the discourse on hope. *Culture, Medicine and Psychiatry, 14*, 59–79.

Dubar, C., & Tripier, P. (1998). *Sociologie des professions* [Sociology of professions]. Paris: Armand-Colin.

Dupras, A. (Ed.). (1989). *La sexologie au Québec* [The sexology of Quebec]. Longueuil, Québec: Iris.

Fausto-Sterling, A. (2000). *Sexing the body: Gender politics and the construction of sexuality*. New York: Basic Books.

Felski, R. (1999). Introduction. In L. Bland & L. Doan (Eds.), *Sexology in culture: Labelling bodies and desires* (pp. 1–9). Cambridge, UK: Polity Press.

Fruhstuck, S. (2003). *Colonizing sex: Sexology and social control in modern Japan*. Berkeley: University of California Press.

Giami, A. (2001). *Countertransference in social and behavioral research: Beyond Georges Devereux* (Discussion Paper series). London: Department of Methodology, London School of Economics and Political Sciences.

Giami, A. (2002). Sexual health: The emergence, development and diversity of a concept. *Annual Review of Sex Research, 13*, 1–33.

Giami, A. (2007). Fonction sexuelle masculine et sexualité féminine: Permanence des représentations du genre en sexologie et en médecine sexuelle [The male sexual function and female sexuality: The permanence of gender representations in sexology and sexual medicine]. *Communications, 81*, 135–151.

Giami, A., Chevret-Méasson, M., & Bonierbale, M. (2009). Recent evolution to the profession of sexologist in France: First results of a 2009 survey in France. *Sexologies, European Journal of Sexology and Sexual Health, 18*(4), 238–242.

Giami, A., & de Colomby, P. (2002). La médicalisation de la sexologie en France [The medicalization of sexology in France]. *L'Evolution Psychiatrique,* 67(3), 558–570.

Giami, A., & de Colomby, P. (2003). Sexology as a profession in France. *Archives of Sexual Behavior, 32*(4), 371–379.

Giami, A., de Colomby, P., & Groupe-Euro-Sexo. (2006). La profession de sexologue en Europe: diversité et perspectives communes [The profession of sexologist in Europe: Diversity and shared perspectives]. *Sexologies. European Journal of Sexology and Sexual Health* (1), 7–13.

Giuffre, P., & Williams, C. (2000). Not just bodies. Strategies for desexualizing the physical examination of patients. *Gender & Society 14*(3), 457–482.

Haeberle, E., & Gindorf, R. (Eds.). (1993). *Sexology today: A brief introduction*. Berlin, Germany: DGSS.

Haeberle, E. J. (1981). Swastika, pink triangle, and yellow star: The destruction of sexology and the persecution of homosexuals in Nazi Germany. *Journal of Sex Research, 17*(3), 270–287.

Hekma, G. (1994). "A female soul in a male body": Sexual inversion as gender inversion in nineteenth-century sexology. In G. Herdt (Ed.), *Third sex, third gender:Beyond sexual dysmorphism in culture and history* (pp. 213–239). New York: Zone Books.

Irvine, M. J. (2005). *Disorders of desire: Sexuality in modern American sexology*. Philadelphia, PA: Temple University Press.

Kleinman, A. (1980). *Patients and healers in the context of culture: An exploration of the borderland between anthropology, medicine, and psychiatry.* Berkeley: University of California Press,.

Kolodny, R., Masters, W., Johnson, V., & Biggs, M. A. (1979). *Textbook of human sexuality for nurses.* Boston, MA: Little, Brown.

Kontula, O. (2011). An essential component in promoting sexual health in Europe is training in sexology. *International Journal of Sexual Health, 23*(3), 168–180.

Lewis, R., & Wagner, G. (2008). History of the International Society of Sexual Medicine (ISSM)—The beginnings. *Journal of Sexual Medicine, 5*, 740–745.

McLaren, A. (2007). *Impotence: A cultural history.* Chicago, IL: Chicago University Press.

Porto, R. (2006). Training in sexology in Europe: Past, present and future. *Sexual and Relationship Therapy, 21*(3), 281–287.

Pryor, J. (2006). The European Academy for Sexual Medicine (EASM): The challenge of developing European training standards in sexual medicine. *Sexual and Relationship Therapy, 21*(3), 281–287.

Robinson, P. (1976). *The modernization of sex.* New York: Harper & Row.

Rohden, F., & Torres, I. (2006). Le champ actuel de la sexologie au Brésil: Considérations initiales [The field of sexology in Brazil: Initial considerations]. *Sexologies, 15*, 64–71.

Russo, J., Rohden, F., Torres, I., & Faro, L. (2009). O campo da sexologia no Brasil : constituiçao e institutionalizaçao [The field of sexology in Brazil: Constitution and institutionalization]. *Physis Revista de Saude Coletiva, 19*(3), 617–636.

Russo, J., Rohden, F., Torrès, I., Faro, L., Fisher Nucci, M., & Giami, A. (Eds.). (2011). *Sexualidade, Ciencia e Profissao no Brasil* [Sexuality, science and profession]. Rio de Janeiro, Brazil: Centro Latino Americano em sexualidade e direitos humanos.

Schneider, M., & Philips, S. (1997). A qualitative study of sexual harassment of female doctors by patients. *Social Science & Medicine, 45*(5), 669–676.

Simon, W. (1994). Deviance as history: The future of perversion. *Archives of Sexual Behavior, 23*(1), 1–20.

Tiefer, L. (1994). Three crises facing sexology. *Archives of Sexual Behavior, 23*(4), 361–374.

Tronto, J. (1993). *Moral boundaries: A political argument for an ethic of care.* London: Routledge.

Wagner, R. (1981). *The invention of culture.* Chicago, IL: University of Chicago Press.

Weeks, J. (1985). *Sexuality and its discontents. meanings, myths and modern sexualities.* London: Routledge & Kegan Paul.

Wylie, K., de Colomby, P., & Giami, A. (2004). Sexology as a profession in the United Kingdom. *Internationl Journal of Clinical Practice, 58*(8), 764–768.

Zucker, K. (2002). From the editor's desk: Receiving the torch in the era of sexology renaissance. *Archives of Sexual Behavior, 31*(1), 1–6.

Zucker, K. (2003). Editorial: The politics and science of "reparative therapy." *Archives of Sexual Behavior, 32*(5), 399–402.

INDEX

Page locators in *italics* indicate figures and tables.

abortion in Russia, 222, 224
abuse, Latina women and HIV risk, 88
acculturation: and Indian sexuality, 177; Latina women's health, 88–89, 102
adolescents, African American, 50–52
African American couples and sexuality: overview, 3, 47, 48–49, 75–76; client strengths and sound therapeutic relationship, 65–67; contextual assessment and treatment, 62–65; and hypermasculinity, 56–57; media socialization of negative and stereotypic depictions of African American sexuality, 51–53; racism and stigmatization, 54–55; Rob and Tina case example, 68–75; self-esteem, positive ethnic identity, religiosity, 60–62; sex ratio imbalance and infidelity, 57–58; slavery and historical effects on present-day views of sexuality, 49–51; and socioeconomic status (SES), 53–54; strengths in physical and sexual arenas, 58–60; and women's sexual pleasure, 13
African American same-sex couples, Vi and Barb case example, 37–40
AG (Aggressive) urban lesbians, 27, 30, 38–40
age: age difference between grooms and brides in traditional Iran, 140; sexual debut age in Cameroon, 114; teenage sexual relationships in northern Europe, 356–58
age-structured relationships, same-gender relations, 26–27
Ahmadinejad, Mahmoud, 24
angyura female genital mutilation, 121–22

April and Marc case study, vulvodynia, 362–67
Arab Israeli sexuality, 340, 342
arranged marriage and Indian sexuality, 175
assessment. *See* treatment approaches
Ayurveda practices and Indian sexuality, 173–74, 176, 182

Bacchus ladies, 163
BDSM sexuality and queer youth, 41, 43
behavioral couple therapy, Rob and Tina case example, 70–71, 72
Bem Sex Role Inventory, 88
bisexuality. *See* lesbian, gay, bisexual, or transgender (LGBT) people
Black identity and African American sexuality, 61
body image: and African Americans, 58–59, 65; in Brazil, 253–54
Brazilian sexuality: overview, 4, 5, 250; Brazilian sexual dysfunction, 255–56; Brazilian sexuality, 251–55; Brazilian women and HSDD, 256; and etiology of HSDD, 256–58; HSDD treatment approaches, 258–63; Joachim *travesti* case example, 34–37; Marta and Carlos HSDD case study, 263–72; and women's sexual pleasure, 13

Califia-Rice, Patrick (Pat Califia), 43–44
Cameroon. *See* sexuality in Cameroon
casual sexual attitudes/behavior and socioeconomic status (SES), 54
CD4 cells and HIV positive Latinos/as, 90, 106*n*2
Centurias (Lusitano), 280
chastity, cultural valuation of, 6
Children's Health and Responsible Mothering (CHARM) project, 94

INDEX

China: and sexual tolerance, 29, 31–32. *See also* Hong Kong Chinese
Christianity and sexual attitudes/behavior in Hong Kong, 199–200
cleansing, posthumous sexual cleansing in Cameroon, 124–26
Clementi, Tyler, 23–24
client strengths and sound therapeutic relationship, 65–67
cognitive-behavioral therapy (CBT): and Brazilian sexuality, 258–63, 290–91; and Chinese sexuality, 208–9; Marta and Carlos HSDD case study, 263–72
cognitive theory and conceptual models of sexual dysfunction, 288–90, *290*
Colby, U.S. urban youth case example, 37–40
colonial views of homosexuality, 31–32
commercial sexual exploitation, Indian women and children, 178
communication: and Brazilian sexual therapy, 260, 262–63; health risks and Latina women, 87–88; migration and sexuality, 89–90; Rob and Tina infidelity case example, 69–72; and treatment approaches in Hong Kong, 203
conceptual models of sexual dysfunction, 288–90, *290*
condom use: in Brazil, 252; and communication difficulties, 87–88; and Entre Amigas program, 100, 103; in Russia, 223, 224–25
Confucianism: and Chinese views of sexual intercourse, 198–99; and sexuality in Korea, 157, 158, 161, 165
contextual assessment and treatment, 62–65
contraception: and family planning in Cameroon, 115; and family planning in Russia, 223–24, 230
control, lack of control and PE, 146–47
couples therapy in Korea, 161
culture: cultural influence and treatment effects, 212; culturally sensitive psychotherapy, 1–2, 5–7, 16; dynamic nature of, 4–5; Orthodox Jews and sexuality, 337–39; and Russian sexual attitudes, 225–27; and worldwide attitudes toward sexuality, 2–5. *See also* Turkish culture and sexual dysfunction

dehumanization and traumas of slavery, 49–50
delayed ejaculation, 165–66

Denmark. *See* Northern European sexuality
deuxième bureau, 119–20
Dhat syndrome, 4, 6, 191, 194*n*7
Diagnostic and Statistical Manual of Mental Disorders (DSM): recognition of cultural issues, 6; and vaginismus, 212–13, 327, 328; and Western views of sex and psychotherapy, 7
disabled individuals and surrogate therapy, Rachel case study, 343–51
distress as criterion for sexual disorder diagnosis, 8
divorce: in Iran, 139, 140, 144; Korean "twilight divorce", 162; and male sexual dysfunction, 12
double stigma: race or immigrant status and same-gender orientation, 29; Vi and Barb case example, 37–40
dreams, cultural views of erotic dreams, 120
dry sex, 121
dyspareunia: April and Marc case study, 362–67; cultural gender roles and development of sexual problems, 15; described, 360–62

education. *See* sex education
egalitarian same-gender relationships, 28
elderly Koreans and sexual dysfunction, 161–66
emotionally focused couple therapy (EFT), 161
Empire and Sexuality (Hyam), 173–74
empowerment, Latina women and Entre Amigas program, 99, 101, 102–4
Entre Amigas HIV prevention program, 96–105
erectile dysfunction (ED): cultural gender roles and development of sexual problems, 15; and effective use of PDE-5 inhibitors, 9–10; HH case study, 297–302; intracavernosal injection (ICI) treatment of, 140–42; Iranian patient case studies, 143–44; and Korean sexuality, 159; non-effective treatments for, 143; in Russia, 228–29, 236, 238–40; in Turkey, 315–16
Ethiopian Jews, 336
Europe. *See* Northern European sexuality
European sexology: overview, 372, 373, 388–90; cultural differences and sexual health, 378–79; definition of sexology, 374–77; European sexology diversity, 379–80; evolution of sexology, 377;

INDEX

European sexology (*continued*):
feminization of French sexologists, 382, 384; professional identity of sexologists, 386–88, *388*; professional sexologist demographics, 380–82, *381*, *383*; sexologist training, 384–85, *385*; sexology as percentage of professional activity, 385, *386*; and women's sexual pleasure, 13; worldwide sexology diversity, 377–78
extramarital sex: and African American, 57–58; in Cameroon, 115; in Hong Kong, 200; in Iran, 139; Rob and Tina case example, 68–75; in Russia, 222–23, 233

family planning: in Cameroon, 115; in Korea, 157–58; in Russia, 224–25, 230
family ties: and African American sexuality, 62; and Israeli society, 335
female genital mutilation (FGM), 7, 121–22
female orgasm: attitudes toward female orgasm in Russia, 226; Russian case study, 237–38; and sexual therapy for women, 236–37
female sexual dysfunction: in Cameroon, 121; in Iran, 150–52
female sexual pleasure: and African American sexuality, 13; in Cameroon, 112; and Korean sexuality, 13, 155, 157; Latina women, 13, 14, 90, 98; and Orthodox Jewish sexuality, 338–39
femininity: and Brazilian sexuality, 251–52; Brazilian *travesti* case example, 34–37; and Latina women, 87, 88
femme lesbians, 27, 30
fertility: and family planning in Korea, 157–58; and importance of sex, 12, 14; infertility in Cameroon, 115–16, 125; in Israel, 335; premarital fertility in Cameroon, 113–14; sex and fertility in Cameroon, 115–16; and sexual dysfunction in Cameroon, 118–19
fistulas, 122
flash, gender roles and African American youth, 52
flashbacks, Rob and Tina infidelity case example, 72–73

gay people. *See* lesbian, gay, bisexual, or transgender (LGBT) people
gender: Brazilian gender inequalities and HSDD, 257–58; culture and sexual orientation, 3–4; gender fluidity and queer youth, 40–44; and Russian sexuality, 234–35; third gender, 22; third-sex (transgender) people, 27
gender-based violence, 101–2
gender identity discordance (GID), 291
gender roles: African American youth, 52; and development of sexual problems, 15; elderly Koreans and sexual dysfunction, 162–63; and Latina women, 86–87; and sexuality in Cameroon, 114
gender-transformed relationships, 27
gender-variants, 28
generational differences in Russian sexual attitudes, 225–27
genito-pelvic pain/penetration disorder (GPPPD), 328
genograms, 67
gishiri female genital mutilation, 121–22
Global Study of Sexual Attitudes and Behavior (GSSAB) study, 8, 12–13, 255–56
globalization and sexual knowledge, 4

health and acculturation of Latina immigrants, 88–89
health care access, Latina women, 91–92
health risks, Latinas and HIV, 87–88
help-seeking behavior: and Chinese sexuality, 208; and Indian sexuality, 179–80
Hinduism and Indian sexuality, 173, 175, 176, 177
hip-hop music and negative stereotypes, 51–52
HIV infection rates: and Indian women, 178; Latina women, 90–91, 106n1; Latinos, 86; and posthumous sexual cleansing in Cameroon, 125–26
HIV-Intensive Prevention (HIV-IP), 94
HIV prevention, Selena S case study, 85, 96–105
HIV research and global views of same-sex attraction, 29
homoeroticism and age-structured relationships, 26–27
homosexuality: as 19th century identity, 28; criminalization of, 23–24, 31, 222, 223; and functions of sexual behavior, 24–25; and Indian sexuality, 177; myths regarding, 313; Russian therapists' attitudes toward, 232
Hong Kong Chinese: overview, 4, 197; cultural views of sexual intercourse, 198–99, 201, 203, 211, 214–15;

396

INDEX

Michelle case study, 207–14; Ric case study, 204–6, 208–14; sex education recommendations, 215–16; sexual attitudes and behaviors of, 199–200; sexual dysfunction prevalence, 201–2; sexual dysfunction treatment approaches, 202–3; sexual values and attitudes, 200–201; and women's sexual pleasure, 13, 14

Hottentot Venus, 50

human rights and sexuality, 1

hypermasculinity and African American sexuality, 56–57, 66, 74–75

hypoactive sexual desire disorder (HSDD): and Brazilian women, 256; described, 255; etiology of, 256–58; Marta and Carlos HSDD case study, 263–72; and Portuguese women, 292, 295–97; treatment approaches, 258–63

hypochondria and lack of sexual education, 190–92

identity, importance of cultural heritage and sexuality to, 3–4

ill-luck, posthumous sexual cleansing in Cameroon, 124–25

illness, pregnancy as "good sick", 117

immigrant acculturation and health, 88–89, 102

Indian sexuality: overview, 4, 172, 173–74, 193; folklore customs and remedies, 183; and help-seeking behavior, 179–80; and Hinduism, 173, 175, 176, 177; homosexuality, 177; marriage and procreation, 174–77; migrants and acculturation, 177; and psychotherapy, 180–82; Rahul case study, 183–93; and sexual health problems, 178–79; and spirituality, 11; traditional practices, 182; women's sexuality, 177–78

infertility in Cameroon, 115–16, 125

infidelity: and African Americans, 57–58; in Cameroon, 115; in Hong Kong, 200; in Iran, 139; Rob and Tina case example, 68–75; in Russia, 222–23, 233

Institute for Personal Growth (IPG), 35, 42

intercourse: Chinese cultural views of sexual intercourse, 198–99, 201, 211; and dyspareunia, 360–67; Orthodox Jewish view of, 338

International Classification of Disorders (World Health Organization), 327, 328

International Encyclopaedia of Sexuality (Kon), 230

International Professional Surrogate Association (IPSA), 351

International Society for Sexual Medicine (ISSM), 145

the Internet: and Orthodox Jewish sexuality, 337–38; and sex education in Korea, 158; and sexual information in Russia, 228–29; and sexual knowledge, 4–5, 149

intracavernosal injection (ICI), ED treatment, 140–42

Intravaginal Ejaculatory Latency Time (IELT), 145–46, 147–48

Introduction to Sexology (Kon), 230

Iran. *See* sexual dysfunction in Iran

Israeli sexuality: overview, 3, 333, 334–36; and Israeli Arabs, 340, 342; and Israeli society, 340–41; and Judaism, 336–37; Rachel (disabled veteran) case study, 343–51; and sexual dysfunction, 341; and sexual dysfunction treatment, 342–43; and ultra-Orthodox community, 337–39, 351–52

Israeli Society of Sex Therapy (ISST), 342

Joachim, Brazilian *travesti* case example, 34–37

Judaism and Israeli sexuality, 336–39, 351–52

Kama Sutra, 173, 175

kinship ties and African American sexuality, 62

Korean sexuality: overview, 4, 155, 156–57, 166–67; Confucianism and sexuality in Korea, 157, 158, 161, 165; family planning, 157–58; sex education, 158; sexual dysfunction among older Koreans, 161–66; sexual dysfunction and sexual therapy, 159–61; sexual harassment and violence, 158–59; and women's sexual pleasure, 13, 155, 163, 164–65; women's status and sex as a duty, 14, 155

La Clínica del Pueblo, 96–97

ladyboys, Thai culture, 27

Latin America: Brazilian *travesti* case example, 34–37; masculinity and same-sex behavior, 32

Latina women's sexuality in the United States, 84–106; overview, 3, 84, 85–86; communication and health risks, 87–88; and gender roles, 86–87; health and acculturation of immigrants, 88–89;

INDEX

Latina women's sexuality in the United States (*continued*): health care access, 91–92; HIV infection rates, 86, 90–91, 106n1; HIV prevention, 92–96; and religion, 88; Selena S case study, 85, 96–105; sexuality concerns, 89–90; and women's sexual pleasure, 13, 14, 90, 98

Latinos, and HIV, 86, 89, 90–91, 95

lesbian, gay, bisexual, or transgender (LGBT) people: Colby, U.S. urban youth case example, 37–40; and cross-cultural homophobia, 23; cultural variations in attitudes toward, 28–33; and gender-transformed relationships, 27; Joachim, Brazilian *travesti* case example, 34–37; and lack of family support, 25; and mental health, 31, 33, 37–38; Vi and Barb, African American lesbians case example, 37–40; worldwide laws affecting, 31. See also sexual minorities

libido: and differing views of sexual desire, 11. See also hypoactive sexual desire disorder (HSDD)

Linné, Carl von (Linnaeus), 357

Long Live Love curriculum, 358–59

low sexual desire. See hypoactive sexual desire disorder (HSDD)

luck: ill-luck and posthumous sexual cleansing in Cameroon, 124–26; wealth demands and sexual requirements in Cameroon, 126–27

machismo and Latino gender roles, 87

magical beliefs and sexual behavior in Cameroon, 112

mahrie, 139, 144

marianismo and Latino gender roles, 87

marriage: abstinence before marriage, 253; in Cameroon, 115; elderly Koreans and sexual dysfunction, 161–62; endogamous marriage in Turkey, 310; in Hong Kong, 200–201; and Indian sexuality, 174–75, 192–93; Israeli idealization of, 335–36; learned sexual attitudes and sexual self-esteem, 209–10; and Orthodox Jews, 337–38; Rob and Tina infidelity case example, 68–75; and sex as duty, 14–15; in traditional Iran, 139; and traumas of slavery, 49

Marta and Carlos HSDD case study, 263–72

masculinity: and Brazilian sexuality, 251–52; cultural gender roles and development of sexual problems, 15; and hypermasculinity, 56–57, 66, 74–75; and importance of sex, 12; and Israeli society, 335; and same-sex behavior, 32

masturbation: and Brazilian sexuality, 253, 260; cultural prohibitions against, 4; and ED treatment, 143–44; Indian anti-masturbation campaign, 173; Indian male (Rahul) case study, 183–93; and Indian sexuality, 177, 182–83; and Israeli sexuality, 337; *taqaandan* and penile fracture, 148–50; Turkish attitudes toward, 311–12, 315, 318

media socialization and African American sexuality, 51–53

medical approach to sexual therapy, 231–32

medicinal plants and sexual dysfunction in Cameroon, 118–19

Mediterranean cultural complex, 251

men: and infidelity, 57–58; marginalization of African American men, 50–51, 55

menopause, sex and menopause in Cameroon, 117–18

menstruation: and Indian sexuality, 176; and Israeli sexuality, 337

migration: and health care access, 91–92; and Latina sexuality, 89–90; migrants and Indian sexuality, 177; and Russian sexual culture, 227

Mujeres Unidas y Activas (MUA), 93

mystical beliefs and sexuality in Cameroon, 120–21

natural donor insemination (NDI), 116

neo-Confucianism, 199

the Netherlands. See Northern European sexuality

New Gay Youth, 40–41

New Guinea, homoerotic relationships, 29

nongovernmental organizations (NGOs): and HIV prevention, 95; and sex education in northern Europe, 357, 358–59

nonreproductive sex, 24–25

Northern European sexuality: overview, 355, 356–58, 368; April and Marc case study, 362–67; pleasure as sexual health indicator, 358–60; sexual pleasure and sexual pain, 360–62; treatment approaches, 362. See also European sexology

Norway. See Northern European sexuality

INDEX

nyumba ndogo, 119–20

Open Door project, 342
orgasm: attitudes toward female orgasm in Russia, 226; and Orthodox Jewish sexuality, 338; Russian case study, 237–38; and sexual therapy for women, 236–37. *See also* female sexual pleasure
Orthodox Jews and sexuality, 337–39, 351–52
"outside wives", 119–20

parenthood and personhood, 30
partnered sexuality, surrogate therapy, 343–51
PDE-5 inhibitors, 9–10, 142, 148, 228
penile fracture, *taqaandan* and sexual dysfunction in Iran, 148–50
permission, limited information, specific suggestions, and intensive therapy model (PLISSIT), 203, 262
political economy of sex in Cameroon, 127–28
polyamory, 41, 42, 43
polygamy, 116
polygyny, 119–20, 139
pornography and cultural dynamics, 4–5
Portuguese sexual dysfunction and therapy: overview, 278, 303; conceptual models of sexual dysfunction, 288–90, 290; and demographics, 285; HH case study, 297–302; history of Portuguese sexuality, 279–82; personality and trait-affect, 287; prevalence of sexual dysfunction, 282–85, 283, 286; psychological factors and sexual dysfunction, 285, 287; and sexual beliefs, 287–88; treatment approaches, 290–97
positive ethnic identity and African American sexuality, 60–61, 65–66
posthumous sexual cleansing, 124–26
pregnancy and sex, 117
premarital sex: in Cameroon, 114; in Hong Kong, 200; Indian male (Rahul) case study, 183–93; and Indian sexuality, 175; in Iran, 139; and Northern European sexuality, 356–57; in Russia, 222–23, 227; in Turkey, 312
premature ejaculation (PE): cultural gender roles and development of sexual problems, 15; differing cultural views of, 10; myths regarding, 311; and sexual dysfunction in traditional Kermanshah, Iran, 144–48

priapism, 63, 141–42
procreation: and functions of sexual behavior, 24–25; and Indian sexuality, 174–75
Program H, 95
Proposition 8, 38
Protogiendo Nuestra Comunidad, 95
provoked vulvodynia (PVD), 360–67
psychodynamic approach to sexual therapy, 231–32
psychotherapy. *See* treatment approaches
purification, posthumous sexual cleansing in Cameroon, 125–26
purity, Indian Purity campaign, 173

queer youth, Colby case example, 40–41

race: double stigma of race and same-gender orientation, 29; and sexuality, 3
Rachel (disabled veteran) case study, 343–51
racism: and hypermasculinity, 56; and infidelity, 69; Rob and Tina case example, 74–75; and stigmatization of African Americans, 54–55
Rahul case study, male Indian sexuality, 183–93
Rana and Tevfik vaginismus case study, 319–26
rap music and negative stereotypes, 51–52
rape, Korean myths regarding, 159
rapport and effective therapy, 63–64, 65, 191–92
religion: and attitudes toward same-gender orientation, 30–31, 32–33; and ED treatment, 143–44; evangelical churches and antigay stance, 38; and Israeli sexuality, 334, 336–39, 351–52; and Korean sexuality, 156–57; and Latina womens' sexuality, 88; and Portuguese sexuality, 280–81; religiosity and African American sexuality, 61–62, 66–67; and Russian sexuality, 221, 223, 228; and sex education in Turkey, 310; and sexual norms and values in Cameroon, 113; and sexuality, 3; and UCM treatment, 143–44; Vi and Barb case example, 38–40
risky behaviors and HIV infection, 91
Russian Family Planning Association, 230
Russian sexuality and sexual therapy: overview, 3, 4, 220, 221, 243–45; assessment of dysfunction, 232–35, 245n5; contemporary sexual discourse, 227–29; and contraception, 223–24;

399

INDEX

Russian sexuality and sexual therapy (*continued*): and discussions of love and sex, 10; and fixed sexual constitution theory, 12, 230–31, 234; generational and cultural differences in sexual attitudes, 225–27; historical sexual behaviors, 222–23; preventive advice and morality, 240–43; professional sexology in Russia, 229–32; and sex education, 224–25; treatment and outcomes, 235–40; and women's sexual pleasure, 13

Salud, Educacion, Prevencion y Autocuidado (Project SEPA), 94
same-gender relations: age-structured relationships, 26–27; criminalization of sexual acts, 23–24; egalitarian same-gender relationships, 28; gender-transformed relationships, 27; homosexuality as 19th century identity, 28; same-gender social roles, 27–28
same-gender social roles, 27–28
"second round" ED, 146
Selective Serotonin Reuptake Inhibitors (SSRIs) and PE treatment, 147
Selena S case study, HIV prevention, 85, 96–105
self-care and Entre Amigas program, 98–99
self-esteem and African American sexuality, 60–61
semen: cultural valuation of, 6; and Indian sexuality, 176–77, 178–79, 186, 191–92; and Israeli sexuality, 337; and sex during pregnancy, 117; Taoism and sexuality, 202–3
Sensate Focus (SF) exercises, 260, 262, 339, 346, 366–67
sex: and Chinese cultural views of sexual intercourse, 198–99, 201; and fertility, 115–16; importance of fertility vs. sexual pleasure, 12–14; and menopause, 117–18; and pregnancy, 117; Soviet-era attitudes toward, 225–27; in traditional Iranian societies, 137; Turkish attitudes toward, 312–13; women's status and sex as a duty, 14–15, 150–51
sex education: and Chinese sexuality, 210–11, 215–16; in Israel, 341; in Korea, 158, 165; in northern Europe, 357–58; in Russia, 224–25; sexual knowledge and the Internet, 4–5, 149; in Turkey, 310–11, 329*n*1
sex ratio imbalances, 57–58

sex therapy: described, 9–10; therapist training, 11; Western views of, 11–12. *See also* Korean sexuality; treatment approaches
sexology, European. *See* European sexology
sexology, Russian: described, 229–32; diagnoses, 233–35; preventive advice and morality, 240–43; treatment and outcomes, 236–40
sexopathology, 225
sexual and reproductive health (SRH), northern European sexuality, 356, 357
sexual beliefs and myths in Portugal, 287–88
sexual dysfunction: and African Americans, 63; assessment and treatment in Russia, 232–43; in Brazil, 255–56; in Cameroon, 118–20, 122–24; conceptual models of, 288–90, *290*; and culturally sensitive psychotherapy, 5–7; in Hong Kong, 201–3; in India, 178–79; in Israel, 341–43; and Korean sexuality, 159–61; in Portugal, 282–87, *283*, *286*; secondary provoked vulvodynia (PVD), 360–67; and universal model of sexuality, 7–9. *See also* sexual dysfunction in Iran; Turkish culture and sexual dysfunction
sexual dysfunction in Iran: overview, 4, 135, 136, 153; of females, 150–52; marriage in traditional Iran, 139; and premature ejaculation (PE), 144–48; sex in traditional Iranian societies, 137; sexual medicine, 137–38; and sexually transmitted infections (STIs), 138; *taqaandan* and penile fracture, 148–50; unconsummated marriage (UCM), 140–44; and women's sexual pleasure, 13
sexual functioning as basic right, 12
sexual harassment: abuse of Latina women and HIV risk, 88; Korean sexuality, 158–59. *See also* violence
sexual knowledge: and Chinese sexuality, 210–11, 215–16; and the Internet, 4–5, 149; and Israeli society, 340–41; and Orthodox Jews, 337–39; in Russia, 223, 224–25, 236. *See also* sex education
Sexual Life (Moniz), 281
sexual medicine: described, 9–10; and Korean sexuality, 160; and sexual dysfunction in Iran, 137–38
sexual menu therapeutic techniques, 260–62

400

INDEX

sexual minorities: overview, 3–4, 15, 22, 44; African American lesbians case example, 37–40; Brazilian *travesti* case example, 34–37; cross-cultural homophobia and stigmatization, 23–26; cultural variations in attitudes toward, 28–33; forms of homosexual behavior, 26–28; U.S. urban youth case example, 37–40

sexual naïveté, 12, 15

sexual orientation and gender, 3–4

sexual pleasure: and Chinese sexuality, 211–12, 214–15; Indian male (Rahul) case study, 183–93; and Indian sexuality, 175–76; as indicator of sexual health, 358–60; views of importance of, 12–14, 198–99, 201, 203. *See also* female sexual pleasure

sexual response cycle and universal model of sexuality, 7–9

sexual therapy. *See* Russian sexual therapy; treatment approaches

sexuality: African American attitudes toward, 59–60; Latina women and Entre Amigos program, 99–101, 102–3; learned sexual attitudes and sexual self-esteem, 209–10; and nonreproductive sex, 24–25; sexual norms and values in Cameroon, 113–15. *See also* Brazilian sexuality; Indian sexuality; Korean sexuality; northern European sexuality; Russian sexuality and sexual therapy; sexual dysfunction in Iran; sexuality in Cameroon; worldwide sexuality overview

sexuality in Cameroon: overview, 5, 112, 113, 128–29; female genital mutilation, 121–22; female sexual dissatisfaction, 121; mystical beliefs and sexuality, 120–21; posthumous sexual cleansing, 124–26; sex and fertility, 115–16; sex and menopause, 117–18; sex and pregnancy, 117; sexual norms and values, 113–15; sexual problems in Cameroon, 118–20; and spirituality, 10–11; treatment approaches, 122–24; wealth and political economy of sex, 127–28; wealth demands and sexual requirements, 126–27

sexually transmitted infections (STIs): in Cameroon, 112; elderly Koreans and sexual dysfunction, 163–64; and Latina women, 91–92; and Northern European sexuality, 356, 357–58; and reproductive health, 123–24;

and sexual dysfunction in traditional Kermanshah, Iran, 138

sigheh (temporary) wives, 139, 152n2

sildenafil and ED treatment, 142

slavery and African American sexuality, 49–51

Social Darwinism, 49–50

socioeconomic status (SES): and African American sexuality, 53–54; and sex ratio imbalances, 57

South Korea. *See* Korean sexuality

Soviet Russia: generational and cultural differences in sexual attitudes, 225–27; and professional sexology, 229–30; and sexual culture, 222–23

spirituality in Cameroon, 10–11

stereotypes and African American sexuality, 50–53

stigmatization: of African Americans, 54–55; and cross-cultural homophobia, 23–26

Student Education Needed in Order to Reduce Infection and Transmission of AIDS/HIV and STDs (SENORITAS), 94–95

substance, gender roles and African American youth, 52

Sufism, 33

surrogate therapy, Rachel (disabled veteran) case study, 343–51

Sweden. *See* Northern European sexuality

Swedish Association for Sexual Education (RFSU), 357

sworn virgins of the Balkans, 27–28

symptoms and sexual disorder diagnoses, 8

tantric sex, 173

Taoism and sexuality, 166, 199, 202–3

taqaandan and penile fracture in Iran, 148–50

teenage sexual relationships, northern European sexuality, 356–58

therapists: professional sexology in Russia, 229–32; therapist training in Hong Kong, 202

therapy. *See* treatment approaches

Tome (sworn virgin), 28

traditional healers: and ED treatment in Iran, 143; and Indian sexuality, 182–83; and Korean sexuality, 160; and sexual behavior in Cameroon, 112, 126–27; Taoism and sexuality in Hong Kong, 202; and treatment approaches in Cameroon, 122–24; and Turkish sexuality, 320, 324–25

401

transgenderism: gender fluidity and queer youth, 37–40; and Joachim *travesti* case example, 35–37. *See also* lesbian, gay, bisexual, or transgender (LGBT) people
travesti, 27, 35–37
treatment approaches: and African Americans, 65–67; in Cameroon, 122–24; hypoactive sexual desire disorder (HSDD), 258–63; and Korean sexuality, 160–61, 164–66; PE treatment, 147–48; in Portugal, 290–91; psychotherapy in India, 180–82; reluctance to participate in therapy, 62, 63–64; Rob and Tina infidelity case example, 68–75; in Russia, 236–43; surrogate therapy, 343–51; traditional Indian practices, 182; in Turkey, 316–19; for vaginismus, 201, 211–14
Turkish culture and sexual dysfunction: attitudes toward sex, 312–13; cultural overview, 307, 308–10; cultural sensitivity and Western sex therapy, 326–27; and erectile dysfunction, 315–16; and masturbation, 311–12, 315, 318; and premarital sex, 312; Rana and Tevfik vaginismus case study, 319–26; and sex education, 310–11; sexual dysfunction prevalence, 313; and spirituality, 10, 11; treatment approaches, 316–19; and vaginismus, 313–15
"twilight divorce", 162
two spirit people, Native American culture, 27
Type 5 structure of same-sex relationships, 41

Unani practices and Indian sexuality, 174, 182
unconsummated marriage (UCM), 140–44
universal model of sexuality, 7–9

vaginismus: Ana case study, 292–95; cultural gender roles and development of sexual problems, 15; and cultural valuation of female virginity, 6–7; diagnosis and treatment of, 327–29; and ED, 141; Michelle case study, 207–14; Rana and Tevfik vaginismus case study, 319–26; Ric case study, 204–6, 208–14; and sexual dysfunction in Hong Kong, 201, 211–14; in Turkey, 313–15
Vi and Barb, African American lesbians case example, 37–40
violence: and blaming women, 226; gender-based violence and Latina women, 101–2; sexual violence in India, 178; sexual violence in Korea, 158–59, 163
virginity: and Chinese sexuality, 207; cultural valuation of, 6–7; and Indian sexuality, 172, 178; proof of virgin brides, 139; and Turkish sexuality, 314–15
vulvar vestibulitis syndrome (VVS), 364
vulvodynia, April and Marc case study, 362–67

wealth and sexuality in Cameroon, 126–28
Western views of sex and psychotherapy: and culturally sensitive psychotherapy, 5–7; slowness to accept same-sex behavior, 30–31; worldwide sexuality overview, 11–12
women: and body image, 58–59; female sexual dysfunction in Iran, 150–52; Indian women's sexuality, 177–78; and lack of effective sexual medicine, 10; public sexual behavior in Cameroon, 126–27, 129–30*n*7; and quest for wealth in Cameroon, 127–28; Russian women's' sexuality, 241–42; stereotypes of African American women's' sexuality, 50. *See also* Brazilian sexuality; female sexual pleasure
Women's Health Program, 94
women's status and sex as a duty, worldwide sexuality overview, 14–15
worldwide sexuality overview: overview, 1–2, 16–17; and basic human rights, 1; and culturally sensitive psychotherapy, 1–2, 5–7, 16; culture and attitudes toward sexuality, 2–5; dynamic nature of culture, 4–5; importance of sex and sexual pleasure, 12–14; sex therapy and sexual medicine, 9–10; sexual minorities, 15; spirituality and traditional healers, 10–11; and universal model of sexuality, 7–9; Western views of sex and psychotherapy, 11–12; women's status and sex as a duty, 14–15